THE ALBANIAN BEKTASHI

THE ALBANIAN BEKTASHI

History and Culture of a Dervish Order in the Balkans

Robert Elsie

I.B. TAURIS
LONDON • NEW YORK • OXFORD • NEW DELHI • SYDNEY

I.B. TAURIS
Bloomsbury Publishing Plc
50 Bedford Square, London, WC1B 3DP, UK
1385 Broadway, New York, NY 10018, USA
29 Earlsfort Terrace, Dublin 2, Ireland

BLOOMSBURY, I.B. TAURIS and the I.B. Tauris logo are
trademarks of Bloomsbury Publishing Plc

First published in Great Britain 2019
Paperback edition first published 2021

Copyright © Robert Elsie, 2019

Robert Elsie has asserted his right under the Copyright,
Designs and Patents Act, 1988, to be identified as Author of this work.

For legal purposes the Acknowledgements on p. vii constitute
an extension of this copyright page.

Cover design: Adriana Brioso
Cover image © Author's personal collection

All rights reserved. No part of this publication may be reproduced or
transmitted in any form or by any means, electronic or mechanical,
including photocopying, recording, or any information storage or retrieval
system, without prior permission in writing from the publishers.

Bloomsbury Publishing Plc does not have any control over, or responsibility for,
any third-party websites referred to or in this book. All internet addresses given
in this book were correct at the time of going to press. The author and publisher
regret any inconvenience caused if addresses have changed or sites have
ceased to exist, but can accept no responsibility for any such changes.

A catalogue record for this book is available from the British Library.

A catalogue record for this book is available from the Library of Congress.

ISBN: HB: 978-1-7883-1569-2
PB: 978-0-7556-3646-4
ePDF: 978-1-7883-1570-8
eBook: 978-1-7883-1571-5

Typeset by Integra Software Services Pvt. Ltd.

To find out more about our authors and books visit
www.bloomsbury.com and sign up for our newsletters.

To the three Muses of Albanian Bektashi Studies: to the late Margaret Hasluck from Scotland who published her husband's seminal works on the subject and modestly added her own significant contribution to them; to Nathalie Clayer in Paris, whose many books and articles on the Albanian Bektashi and on the other dervish orders in the Balkans have been pioneering and are now standard works of reference; and to Frances Trix of Detroit, Michigan, whose writings, in particular on the late Baba Rexheb, have been inspiring and have opened so many doors for me. Without the three Muses, this book could not have been written.
— R.E.

Robert Elsie knew he would not live to see the release of this book. It was his wish that Francis Trix edit his manuscript and steer it through to publication. She has done so masterfully, with much energy and important contributions of her own. For this she deserves particular thanks.
— S.T.

Entryway to Bektashi Tekke at Fushë Kruja, Albania. Photo by Stephan Trierweiler.

Robert Elsie died in Germany on October 2, 2017. He was a beloved, prolific and highly respected scholar of Albanian studies. It was an honour and also his desire that he be buried in Albania. Since this book, *The Albanian Bektashi: History and Culture of a Dervish Order in the Balkans*, is his last book, it is only fitting that we include a photograph of one of the most beautiful places in Albania where he is buried.

Photograph of Theth, Albania, showing the village near where Robert Elsie was buried. Photo by Stephan Trierweiler.

CONTENTS

Preface   xvi

Chapter 1
THE HISTORY AND CULTURE OF THE ALBANIAN BEKTASHI   1
   Bektashi Beliefs and Hierarchy   1
   The Early History of the Bektashi   4
   The Spread of the Bektashi to the Balkans   6
   The Expansion of the Bektashi in Albania   7
   The Communist Dictatorship in Albania   12
   The Recovery of the Bektashi in Post-Communist Albania   13
   The Current Situation   14

Chapter 2
EARLY REPORTS AND SCHOLARLY ARTICLES ON THE ALBANIAN
BEKTASHI   17
   Evliya Çelebi – 'Notes on the Bektashi,' 1660–1670   17
   Johann Georg von Hahn: – 'The Fortress of Kanina,' 1854   19
   Monk Zosimas of Athos: – 'The Bektashi *Tekkes* of Thessaly,' 1888 20
   Andreas Karkavitsas: – 'Visions of Thessaly: the Bektashi *Tekke*,' 1892 22
   Antonio Baldacci: – 'Albanian Wanderings,' 1895   27
   Naim Frashëri: – 'The Bektashi Notebook,' 1896   30
   Alexandre Degrand: – 'The Legend of Sari Saltik,' 1901   36
   Sir Arthur Evans: – 'A Pillar Cult at the Shrine of Tekija near
      Skopje,' 1901   39
   Edith Durham: – 'A Visit to the Bektashi *Tekke* of Përmet,' 1904   41
   Theodor Ippen: – 'A Visit to Kruja,' 1907   43
   Ekrem bey Vlora: – 'The Bektashi on Mount Tomorr,' 1907   48
   Max Choublier: – 'The *Tekke* of Kalkandelen (Tetova),' 1909   50
   Gabriel Louis-Jaray: – 'A Visit to the *Tekke* of Baba Ibrahim Xhefai
      near Elbasan,' 1909   53
   Frederick Hasluck: – 'The Fourth Religion of Albania,' 1919   56
   Justin Godart: – 'The Place of the Bektashi among Albanian
      Religions,' 1921   58
   Margaret Hasluck: – 'The Nonconformist Moslems of Albania,' 1925   62
   Franz Babinger: – 'Among the Dervishes of Kruja,' 1929   69
   Dayrell Oakley-Hill: – 'Up to Mount Tomorr,' 1929   73
   Baba Ali Tomorri: – 'History of the Bektashi,' 1929   75
   Friedrich Markgraf: – 'A Botanist on Mount Tomorr,' 1930   82

Joseph Swire: – 'Thoughts on the Bektashi,' 1930	84
Richard Busch-Zantner: – 'The Bektashi Sect in Albania,' 1932	87
Richard Busch-Zantner: – 'The Town of the Forbidden Dervishes,' 1933	89
John Kingsley Birge: – 'Bektashiism in Albania,' 1937	93
Margaret Hasluck: – 'Baba Tomor,' 1939	95
Anon.: – 'The Mokattam *Tekke* of Cairo,' 1953	97
Osman Myderrizi: – 'The Beginnings of Bektashi Literature in Albania,' 1955	99
Kurt Seliger: – 'Meeting the Pope of the Bektashi,' 1957	108
Hans Joachim Kissling: – 'On the Origins of the Bektashi in Albania,' 1962	113
Dorothea Russell: – 'The Bektashi Monastery in Cairo,' 1962	117
Jules Leroy: – 'A Visit to the *Tekke* of the Bektashis in Cairo,' 1963	120
Georg Stadtmüller: – 'The Bektashi Dervish Order in Albania,' 1971	122
Frances Trix: – 'The Ashura Lament of Baba Rexheb,' 1995	126
Nathalie Clayer: – 'Bektashism and Albanian Nationalism,' 1995	138
Nathalie Clayer: – 'The Sacred Haunts of the Albanian Bektashi,' 1996	161
Machiel Kiel: – 'Durbali Sultan Resurrected?,' 2009	173

Chapter 3
THE *TEKKES* AND SHRINES OF THE ALBANIAN BEKTASHI — 177

***Tekkes* and Shrines in Albania**
Map of Albania (showing cities and towns with *tekkes*) — 177

Alipostivan (Përmet, Albania): the *tekke* of Baba Abdullah	178
Aranitas (Mallakastra, Albania): the *dervishia* of Aranitas	178
Backa (Skrapar, Albania): the *tekke* of Baba Fetah	178
Bënça (Tepelena, Albania): the *dervishia* of Bënça	179
Berat (Berat, Albania): the *tekke* of Baba Ali	179
Bllaca (Dibra, Albania): the *tekke* of Jusuf Baba	179
Borsh (Saranda, Albania): the *tekke* of Baba Xhafer	181
Brerima (Skrapar, Albania): the *tekke* of Baba Xhafer	181
Bubës i Parë (Përmet, Albania): the *tekke* of Baba Jemin	181
Bubës i Sipërm (Përmet, Albania): the *tekke* of Baba Ali	181
Bulqiza (Bulqiza, Albania): the *tekke* of Bulqiza	181
Cakran (Fier, Albania): the *tekke* of Cakran	182
Çerrica (Skrapar, Albania): the *tekke* of Çerrica	182
Çorrush (Mallakastra, Albania): the *dervishia* of Çorrush	182
Delvina (Delvina, Albania): the *dervishia* of Beqir Efendi	182
Drisht (Shkodra, Albania): the *tyrbe* of Baba Kamber	182
Drizar (Mallakastra, Albania): the *tekke* of Baba Xhelal	183
Dukaj (Tepelena, Albania): the *tekke* of Dukaj	183
Dushk (Gramsh, Albania): the *tekke* of Baba Ahmet	183
Elbasan (Elbasan, Albania): the *tekke* of Ibrahim Xhefai Baba	184

Elbasan (Elbasan, Albania): the *tekke* of Baba Ali Horasani 187
Elbasan (Elbasan, Albania): the *tekke* of Baba Hamit 188
Frashër (Përmet, Albania): the *tekke* of Baba Tahir Nasibi 189
Fratar (Mallakastra, Albania): the *dervishia* of Fratar 191
Fushë Kruja (Kruja, Albania): the *tekke* of Shemimi Baba 191
Gjirokastra (Gjirokastra, Albania): the Gravel *tekke* of Asim Baba 193
Gjirokastra (Gjirokastra, Albania): the Hajdërije *tekke* of Baba Sulejman 194
Gjirokastra (Gjirokastra, Albania): the *tekke* of Baba Zejnel 196
Gjonëm/Gjorm (Kurbin, Albania): the *tekke* of Hajdar Baba 197
Gjorm (Vlora, Albania): the *tekke* of Gjorm 197
Gllava (Tepelena, Albania): the *tekke* of Ismail Baba 198
Golimbas (Vlora, Albania): the *tekke* of Haxhi Baba Mehmet Aliu 198
Gorisht (Vlora, Albania): the *tekke* of Gorisht 199
Greshica (Mallakastra, Albania): the *tekke* of Baba Husejn 199
Gumen (Përmet, Albania): the *tekke* of Baba Husejn 199
Hekal (Mallakastra, Albania): the *tekke* of Hekal 199
Kanina (Vlora, Albania): the *tekke* of Sinan Pasha 200
Kapaj (Mallakastra, Albania): the *tekke* of Baba Ismail 202
Këlcyra (Përmet, Albania): the *tekke* of Hasan Dede 202
Kiçok (Tepelena, Albania): the *tekke* of Baba Kamber 202
Komar (Tepelena, Albania): the *tekke* of Baba Islam 203
Koshtan (Tepelena, Albania): the *tekke* of Baba Sadik 203
Kosina (Përmet, Albania): the *dervishia* of Kosina 204
Kostrec (Përmet, Albania): the *tekke* of Kostrec 204
Krahës (Tepelena, Albania): the *tekke* of Baba Husejn 204
Kremenar (Mallakastra, Albania): the *tekke* of Baba Hasan 205
Kreshova (Kolonja, Albania): the *tekke* of Baba Hasan 205
Kruja (Kruja, Albania): the *tekke* of Baba Hamza 206
Kruja (Kruja, Albania): the *tekke* of Haxhi Jahja Baba 207
Kruja (Kruja, Albania): the *tyrbe* of Mustafa Dollma 207
Kruja (Kruja, Albania): the *tyrbe* of Zemzi Baba 208
Kruja, Mount (Kruja, Albania): the *tyrbe* of Sari Saltik 208
Kuç (Devoll, Albania): the *tekke* of Baba Kasem 210
Kuç (Skrapar, Albania): the *tekke* of Kuç 211
Kuta (Mallakastra, Albania): the *tekke* of Baba Rifat 211
Lavdar (Skrapar, Albania): the *tekke* of Lavdar 211
Leskovik (Përmet, Albania): the *tekke* of Baba Abedin 211
Lushnja (Lushnja, Albania): the *tyrbe* of Baba Skënder 212
Luz i madh (Kavaja, Albania): the *tekke* of Baba Sako 212
Maricaj (Tepelena, Albania): the *tekke* of Baba Musa 212
Martanesh (Bulqiza, Albania): the *tekke* of Balim Sultan 213
Martanesh (Bulqiza, Albania): the *tekke* of Haxhi Hysen Baba 216
Matohasanaj (Tepelena, Albania): the *tekke* of Baba Salih 216
Mazreka (Korça, Albania): the *tekke* of Mazreka 216

Mbyet (Fier, Albania): the *tekke* of Baba Ali Horasani … 217
Melan (Gjirokastra, Albania): the *tekke* of Baba Ali … 217
Melçan (Korça, Albania): the *tekke* of Baba Hysen … 218
Memaliaj (Tepelena, Albania): the *tekke* of Memaliaj … 219
Ngrançija (Mallakastra, Albania): the *tekke* of Ngrançija … 220
Osmënzeza (Berat, Albania): the *tekke* of Baba Iljaz … 220
Pacomit (Përmet, Albania): the *tekke* of Pacomit … 220
Përmet (Përmet, Albania): the *tekke* of Baba Bektash … 220
Përmet (Përmet, Albania): the *tekke* of Baba Ali … 222
Përmet (Përmet, Albania): the *tekke* of Baba Zenel … 222
Petran (Përmet, Albania): the *tekke* of Petran … 222
Picar (Gjirokastra, Albania): the *dervishia* of Baba Hasan … 222
Plasa (Korça, Albania): the *tyrbe* of Plasa … 223
Plashnik (Berat, Albania): the *tekke* of Baba Muharrem … 223
Podgoran (Përmet, Albania): the *tekke* of Podgoran … 223
Polena (Korça, Albania): the *tekke* of Baba Ismail … 223
Prishta (Skrapar, Albania): the *tekke* of Baba Tahir … 224
Progonat (Tepelena, Albania): the *tekke* of Progonat … 225
Pulaha (Korça, Albania): the *tyrbe* of Pulaha … 225
Qatrom (Korça, Albania): the *tekke* of Beqir Efendi … 226
Qesaraka (Kolonja, Albania): the *tekke* of Haxhi Baba Horasani … 226
Qesarat (Tepelena, Albania): the *tyrbe* of Qesarat … 227
Rabija (Tepelena, Albania): the *tekke* of Baba Selman … 227
Rodenj (Përmet, Albania): the *tyrbe* of Rodenj … 228
Rozeç (Tepelena, Albania): the *dervishia* of Rozeç … 228
Sanjollas (Kolonja, Albania): the *tekke* of Baba Sulejman … 228
Saranda (Saranda, Albania): the *tekke* of Dede Reshat Bardhi … 229
Shëmbërdhenj (Gramsh, Albania): the *tekke* of Baba Mustafa … 229
Shkoza (Vlora, Albania): the *tekke* of Shkoza … 230
Shullaz (Kurbin, Albania): the *tekke* of Baba Isak … 230
Smokthina (Vlora, Albania): the *tekke* of Smokthina … 230
Starja (Kolonja, Albania): the *tekke* of Baba Husejn … 230
Straficka (Skrapar, Albania): the *tekke* of Baba Meleq … 231
Suka (Përmet, Albania): the *tekke* of Baba Tahir … 231
Tepelena (Tepelena, Albania): the *tekke* of Demir Han … 232
Therepel (Skrapar, Albania): the *tekke* of Baba Behlul … 232
Tirana (Tirana, Albania): the *Kryegjyshata* … 233
Tomorr, Mount (Berat, Albania): the *tekke* of Kulmak … 234
Turan (Korça, Albania): the *tekke* of Baba Salih Elbasani … 237
Turan (Tepelena, Albania): the *tekke* of Baba Ali … 239
Velabisht (Berat, Albania): the *tekke* of Baba Kamber … 239
Veliqot (Tepelena, Albania): the *tekke* of Baba Hysen … 240
Vloçisht (Korça, Albania): the *tekke* of Vloçisht … 240
Vlora (Vlora, Albania): the *tekke* of Kusum Baba … 240
Vokopola (Berat, Albania): the *tekke* of Baba Tahir … 241

Vrëpska (Korça, Albania): the *tekke* of Vrëpska 241
Zërqan (Bulqiza, Albania): the *tyrbe* of Baba Hysen 242
Zhepova (Përmet, Albania): the *tyrbe* of Zhepova 242

Tekkes and Shrines in Kosovo 243
Map of Kosovo

Gjakova (Gjakova, Kosovo): the *tekke* of Shemseddin Baba 243
Kaçanik (Kaçanik, Kosovo): the *tekke* of Kaçanik 244
Mitrovica (Mitrovica, Kosovo): the *tekke* of Mustafa Baba 244
Peja (Peja, Kosovo): the *tekke* of Peja 245
Prizren (Prizren, Kosovo): the *tekke* of Baba Adem 245

Tekkes and Shrines in the Republic of Macedonia 246
Map of Republic of Macedonia

Kanatlar (Prilep, Macedonia): the *tekke* of Dikmen Baba 246
Kërçova, (Kërçova, Macedonia): the *tekke* of Hidër Baba 247
Makedonski Brod (Makedonski Brod, Macedonia):
  tyrbe of Hidër Baba 248
Poroj (Tetova, Macedonia): the *tekke* of Jarar Baba 248
Saint Naum (Ohrid, Macedonia): the Monastery of Saint Naum 249
Shipkovica (Tetova, Macedonia): the *tekke* of Kojun Baba 249
Skopje (Skopje, Macedonia): the *tekkes* of Mustafa Baba,
  Sulejman Baba and Axhem Zade Hasan Efendi 249
Tekija (Ilinden, Macedonia): the *tekke* of Ahmet Karadja 250
Tetova (Tetova, Macedonia): the Harabati *tekke* 251
Veles (Veles, Macedonia): the *tekke* of Haxhi Baba 254
Vërtok (Gostivar, Macedonia): the *tekke* of Baba Xhafer 255

Tekkes and Shrines in Greece 256

Corfu (Epirus, Greece): the Church of Saint Spyridon 256
Didymóteichon (Eastern Macedonia and Thrace, Greece):
  the *tekke* of Seyyid Ali Sultan 257
Elassona (Thessaly, Greece): the *tekke* of Salih Baba 257
Farsala (Thessaly, Greece): the *tekke* of Durballi Sultan 257
Heraklion (Crete, Greece): the *tekke* of Ali Dede Horasani 260
Juma (West Macedonia, Greece): the *tekke* of Piri Baba 261
Kastoria (West Macedonia, Greece): the *tekke* of Kasem Baba 262
Katerini (Central Macedonia, Greece): the *tekke* of
  Abdullah Baba 263
Konitsa (Epirus, Greece): the *tekke* of Hysejn Baba 264
Odra (Western Macedonia, Greece): the *tekke* of Emine Baba 264
Vodhorina (Western Macedonia, Greece): the *tekke* of Emine Baba 264

***Tekkes* and Shrines in Other Countries**	266
Hacıbektaşköy (central Anatolia, Turkey): the *pir evi* of Hacı Bektaş Veli	266
Cairo (Egypt): the Mokattam *tekke*	267
Taylor (Detroit, Michigan, United States): the First Albanian Bektashi *tekke* in America	271

Chapter 4
NOTED HISTORICAL AND LEGENDARY FIGURES OF THE
ALBANIAN BEKTASHI 273

Abaz Hilmi, Dede Baba	273
Abbas Ali	274
Abdullah Baba of Melçan	275
Abedin Baba of Leskovik	275
Adem Baba of Prizren	275
Adem Vexh-hi Baba of Gjakova	276
Ahmet Baba of Prishta	277
Ahmet Baba of Turan	277
Ahmet Karadja	278
Ahmet Myftari, Dede Baba	278
Ahmet Sirri Baba of Mokattam	279
Ali Baba of Berat	281
Ali Baba of Tomorr	282
Ali Baba Horasani of Fushë Kruja	283
Ali Haqi Baba of Gjirokastra	284
Ali Riza of Elbasan, Dede Baba	285
Alush Baba of Frashër	285
Arshi Baba of Durballi Sultan	286
Arshi Baba of Gjirokastra	286
Asim Baba of Gjirokastra	287
Balim Sultan of Dimetoka, Dylgjer Hysejni of Elbasan	287
Edmond Brahimaj, Dede Baba	289
Faja Martaneshi Baba	289
Fetah Baba of Backa	290
Hajdar Hatemi Baba of Gjonëm	290
Hajdër Baba of Kardhiq	291
Haji Bektash	291
Hasan Dede of Përmet	292
Haxhi Baba Horasani of Përmet	292
Haxhi Baba of Fushë Kruja	292
Hidër Baba of Makedonski Brod	293
Hysen Baba of Melçan	293
Hysen Kukeli Baba of Fushë Kruja	294
Ibrahim Baba of Qesaraka	295

Ibrahim Xhefai Baba of Elbasan	295
Iljaz Vërzhezha, Dervish	296
Kamber Ali, Dede Baba	296
Kasem Baba of Kastoria	297
Kusum Baba of Vlora	298
Lutfi Baba of Mokattam	299
Mehmet Baba of Fushë Kruja	300
Meleq Shëmbërdhenji Baba	300
Muharrem Baba of Frashër	302
Muharrem Mahzuni Baba of Durballi Sultan	302
Myrteza Baba of Fushë Kruja	302
Qazim Baba of Elbasan	303
Qazim Baba of Gjakova	303
Qamil Baba of Gllava	304
Reshat Bardhi, Dede Baba	304
Rexheb Baba of Gjirokastra	304
Salih Baba of Matohasanaj	305
Salih Nijazi, Dede Baba	307
Sari Saltik	308
Seit Baba of Durballi Sultan	311
Selim Kaliçani Baba of Martanesh	311
Selim Ruhi Baba of Gjirokastra	312
Selman Xhemali Baba of Elbasan	313
Sersem Ali Baba of Tetova	314
Shemimi Baba of Fushë Kruja	314
Sulejman Baba of Gjirokastra	316
Tahir Nasibi Baba of Frashër	318
Tahir Baba of Prishta	318
Xhafer Sadiku, Dede Baba	319
Glossary of Terms	320
Notes	324
Bibliography	337
Index	355

PREFACE

This volume is devoted to the Bektashi dervish order in Albania and the role it played in Albanian history. It deals only peripherally with the Bektashi of Turkey and elsewhere, about whom much has already been written, though primarily in Turkish. The book is divided into four basic sections.

The first section is an overview of the history and culture of the Albanian Bektashi to serve as an introduction to the material, one which hopes to be general enough for the average reader, yet to contain sufficient detail to satisfy the demands of the 'non-average' reader.

This is followed by a longer section presenting a wide variety of writings on the Albanian Bektashi by early travellers and noted scholars. Included here are many seminal articles that approach Bektashi studies from various perspectives.

The third section offers an extensive catalogue of the major *tekkes* (convents) and *tyrbes* (shrines) of the Albanian Bektashi, given alphabetically according to place name, with historical information on their origin, development and significance, where available. The catalogue is by no means exhaustive as there are numerous smaller shrines and *tekkes* that have not been included here due to a lack of information about them. The reader will note that for some *tekkes* given in the catalogue the material is relatively comprehensive, whereas for many others there are gaps. Such is the state of Bektashi studies at the moment.

The fourth section of this book is a catalogue of the most notable historical and legendary figures of the Albanian Bektashi. Here again, the biographical information on some of these figures is sparse, but we have provided what could be garnered.

The main corpus of the book is rounded off with a glossary of terms and a bibliography to enable the interested reader to pursue further studies in the field if he or she should so wish.

At this juncture, a word of thanks. The author would like to express his gratitude to the *Kryegjyshata* (World Headquarters of the Bektashi) in Tirana for much assistance provided. Thanks go in particular to the ever-helpful *Kryegjysh*, Haxhi Dede Edmond Brahimaj (Baba Mondi), to the secretary general of the Bektashi Community, Nuri Çuni, and to the staff of the Bektashi archives. A word of thanks must also be said to the many simple Bektashi people in the mountains of southern Albania who showed me great hospitality during my travels. Many of them were able to provide much more information on local history and shrines than one would have thought possible.

Robert Elsie
Berlin, August 2017

1
THE HISTORY AND CULTURE OF THE ALBANIAN BEKTASHI

The Bektashi are a dervish order of Sufi Islamic inspiration, originally from Turkey. Although they were banned and suppressed in Turkey in 1925 during the modernisation of that country under Mustafa Kemal Atatürk (1881–1938), they flourished in Albania and quietly evolved into a major religious community there – Albania's fourth religion (after Sunni Islam, Eastern Orthodoxy and Roman Catholicism). It was a community that was to play a major role in Albanian history.

Bektashi beliefs and hierarchy

A few words must be said initially on the beliefs, rites and practices of the Bektashi. Bektashism has a long history and has absorbed many influences from various sources. Among the earliest components of Bektashi doctrines and beliefs in the Middle East were Turkmen heterodoxy, the ascetic Kalenderi (Qalandari) movement of the thirteenth–fourteenth centuries inspired by Persian and Indian mysticism, otherwordly Sufic Melametism, and later the gnostic and cabbalistic doctrines of Persian Hurufism. It also evolved in close contact with Shi'ite and Alevi Islam.

As to their core beliefs, about which the Bektashi were traditionally rather secretive, they believe in *Hakk* (the Truth), in Muhammed and in Imam Ali, to whom a special position is accorded. Indeed, Imam Ali, his wife Fatima and their two sons Hasan and Husein are central figures of the Bektashi and Shi'ite creed. Many Bektashi families have portraits of Ali in their homes, considering him to be a manifestation of God on earth. He is invoked on a variety of occasions by believers with a *'ya, Ali!'* or *'Muhammed-Ali!'* The concept of *Hakk*, Muhammed and Ali are central. The Bektashi, like other Shi'ites, also revere the Twelve Imams, particularly Imam Ali of course, and consider themselves descendants of the sixth imam, Jafer Sadik. Naturally, they also revere Haji Bektash as the founder of the order.

As in Sufism in general, the emphasis in Bektashism is on inner meaning rather than on the adherence to outer conventions. Instead of the main worship being public prayer on Friday, the Bektashi have a private ceremony in their *meydan*, their private prayer room, on Thursday evenings for initiated members with their clergy – dervishes and *babas*. The room, the *meydan*, is named after the *meydan*, the 'square' in Baghdad where the Sufi al-Hallaj was martyred in 922 by the authorities.

Unlike the Sunni Muslims who are encouraged to pray five times a day, the Bektashi pray twice a day, at sunrise and at sunset, and their prayers do not necessarily involve prostration. As with other Muslims, most Bektashi refuse to eat pork and they will especially avoid hares. Some Bektashis drink alcohol, although this varies from *tekke* to *tekke*.

Bektashi women participate on an equal footing with the men in ceremonies and gatherings. The Bektashi trace this to two sources: the importance of Kadıncık, a woman who helped Haji Bektash when he first came to central Anatolia in the thirteenth century, and to the more prominent place of women in Central Asia whence arrived the people who became Bektashi in Anatolia. What other Muslims do not understand about the equality of the *bacılar*, or sisters, as Bektashi women are called, is that when they are initiated, the men with whom they are initiated become their brothers and protect their honour the way any brother would. Thus women who participate in secret ceremonies are always in the company of their brothers. Most books of Bektashi poetry include sections of poems by the *bacılar*.

The main holiday of the Bektashi is *ashura*. The ten days of the month of Muharrem that precede it, known as *matem*, are a time during which the suffering and death of Imam Husein are commemorated. During the period of *matem*, Bektashi come to the *tekke* and listen to recitations of the suffering of Imam Husein. They also have a special fast at this time, drinking only a bitter yogurt drink and eating a lentil soup. After *matem* follows the feast of *ashura*, during which a dish is served that is made of cracked wheat, dried fruit, crushed nuts and cinnamon, all ceremoniously cooked together.

The other main Bektashi holiday is *Nevruz*. This is a solar holiday, the Persian New Year and the birthday of Imam Ali.

An important political perspective on late nineteenth-century Albanian Bektashi beliefs is the *Fletore e Bektashinjet* (Bektashi Notebook), written by one of the best known writers of Albanian literature, Naim bey Frashëri (1846–1900). Frashëri, who was the author of religious, nationalist and didactic works that had an exceptional impact on the Albanian national awakening of the late nineteenth century, had hoped that the liberal Bektashi beliefs to which he had been attached since his childhood in the village of Frashër would one day take hold as a new religion for all of Albania. Since they respected both Muslim and Christian figures, the Bektashi could promote unity among their religiously divided people. Naim Frashëri supported the confessional independence of the Albanian Bektashi movement from the central *pir evi* (master house or motherhouse) in the village of Hacıbektaşköy in central Anatolia and proposed an Albanian *baba* or *dede* as its leader, three decades before autonomy was achieved. He also promoted Albanian terms to replace the Turkish ones previously used by the Albanian Bektashi: Albanian *atë* 'father' for Turkish *baba*, and Albanian *gjysh* 'grandfather' for Turkish *dede*, to give his Bektashi religion a national character and to unite all Albanians.

The Bektashi Notebook contains an introductory profession of Bektashi faith and ten spiritual poems which provide a rare glimpse into the beliefs of the sect as Frashëri interpreted them. It begins as follows:

> The Bektashi believe in the great and true God, in Muhammed Ali, Hatije and Fatima, and in Hasan and Husein. The twelve Imams are Ali, Hasan, Husain, Zein-el-Abidin, Muhammed Bakir, Jafer Sadik, Musa Kiazim, Ali Riza, Muhammed Teki, Ali Neki, Hasan Askeri and Muhammed Mehdi. The father of all the Bektashi is Ali and their mother is Fatima. They believe in all the virtues of present and past. In particular, they believe in goodness and worship it. In addition to these, they also believe in Musa [Moses], Merjeme [Mary], Isa [Jesus] and their servants. Foremost among them is Jafer Sadik and their forefather is Haji Bektash Veli who is of the same family. All the above-mentioned have said: 'Do good and abstain from evil'. These words are the essence of the Bektashi faith. Truth, justice, wisdom and all virtues reign in this faith. The faith of the Bektashi is a broad path leading to enlightenment: wisdom, brotherhood, friendship, love, humanity and all virtues. This path is covered on the one hand by the flowers of wisdom and on the other hand by the flowers of truth. No one can be a genuine Bektashi without wisdom, truth and brotherhood. For the Bektashi, the universe is God himself. In this life, man is a representative of God.[1]

Despite such pantheism and universality, Naim Frashëri's Bektashi beliefs have a decidedly nationalist flavour:

> They are brothers and one in soul not only with other Bektashi, but with all mankind. They love other Muslims and Christians as they do their own souls, and they strive for good relations with all mankind. Yet above all, they love their country and their countrymen. This is the finest of all virtues ... May they strive day and night for that nation that calls them father and swears by them. May they work together with the notables and the elders for the salvation of Albania and the Albanians, for knowledge and culture for their people and their fatherland, for their language and for all progress and well-being.[2]

As a religious community, the Bektashi have a hierarchical structure, the main ranks of which are the following:

The *ashik*, Turkish *aşık*, literally 'lover,' is a Bektashi believer or faithful who has not been initiated. This is a person who has been drawn to a particular *baba* and has become devoted to him. The *muhib*, also meaning 'one who loves, sympathiser,' is a spiritual member of the Bektashi community, i.e. an individual who has received some initiation involving a ritual purification and a profession of faith during a ceremony held at a *tekke*.

After a trial period of 1001 days, a *muhib* may become a dervish. The dervish receives a white headdress called a *taj*, Albanian *taxh* from Turkish *tac*, as well as other special garments, and usually lives full-time at a *tekke*. He is in a sense the equivalent of a Christian monk.

The *myxher*, from Turkish *mücerred* 'person tried by experience, pure, unmarried,' is the member of a special category of dervishes, that of the celibate dervishes, who wear a ring in their right ear. There has been much controversy in the history of Bektashism about adherence to celibacy. In the Balkans, the celibate Bektashi dervishes and *babas* have been more revered.

The *baba*, also Albanian *atë* 'father,' is a spiritual master, equivalent to a sheikh in other dervish orders. Each *tekke* is normally headed by a *baba*.

The *gjysh*, literally 'grandfather,' equivalent to Turkish *dede*, is the superior of the *babas* and is responsible for all the *tekkes* of a certain region. The *gjysh* has passed through the final level of ceremony.

Finally, the *kryegjysh* 'head grandfather,' known in Turkish as *dede baba*, is the leader of the Bektashi Order as a whole, and is chosen from among all the *gjyshes*.

The early history of the Bektashi

Most of what we know of the beginnings of the Bektashi Order belong more to the realm of legendry than to documented history. The Bektashi claim their descent initially from a Turkoman holy man called Haji Bektash Veli (Albanian: *Haxhi Bektash Veli*, Turkish: *Hacı Bektaş Veli*) who came from the Khorasan region of northeastern Iran and settled around Kirshehir (Turkish: Kırşehir) in central Anatolia in the thirteenth century during a wave of Turkoman immigration from the east. The village where he settled is now named after him – Hacıbektaşköy (Haji Bektash Village). Haji Bektash is regarded as the founder and patron saint of the order. It was thus in the village of Hacıbektaşköy that the *pir evi* of the Bektashi Order arose and it was from here that the Bektashi movement spread.

Little else is known about this early period of the Bektashi. It was only in the early fifteenth century that the order took on a concrete form, under Balim Sultan (1457–1517), who is venerated as the second founder and *pir* of the order. Balim Sultan was raised at the shrine of Seyyid Ali Sultan near Dimetoka (Greek: Didymoteichon), 22 kilometres south of Edirne (Adrianople) in Thrace. He set off for the shrine of Haji Bektash in Anatolia and became head of the Bektashi in 1501. Balim Sultan centralized the authority of the Bektashi there and is said to have codified the hierarchical ranks, rites and practices of the movement. Here is an early historical reference to him:

> Upon a sign that came from Seyyid Ali Sultan in a dream, he [Balim Sultan] first went to the palace in Istanbul, where he was shown respect and reverence by the sultan [Bayezid II]. He headed for the convent of Hacı Bektaş with an imperial decree, and was the leader there until the year 922 AH [1516-1517 AD]. The rituals and rules of the Bektashi Order, which are in agreement with justice and true religion, were prescribed by him. [...] Also the revenues allocated for the dervishes and the *çelebis* (that is, the descendants of Hacı Bektaş) residing in the convent were donated by the sultan in the time of Balim Sultan.[3]

From this time on, we know somewhat more about the core beliefs of the Bektashi, with their emphasis on *Hakk*, Muhammed and Ali, and with stress on the Twelve Imams revered by the Shi'ites. Of particular significance was the sixth imam, Jafer Sadik (Albanian: Xhafer Sadiku; Turkish: Cafer Sadik), from whom they claimed to derive special authority.

The Bektashi Order rose to enjoy significant political power in Turkey in the second half of the fifteenth century due to its close ties to the Janissaries, the elite infantry units that formed the bodyguards and household troops of the Sultan. Indeed, the Janissaries were often known at the time as *Hacı Bektaş oğulları* (the sons of Haji Bektash).

According to John Norton,

> formal recognition came around 1591 when the head of the Bektashi Order was made an honorary colonel of the Janissaries and eight Bektashi dervishes were appointed to the 99th *orta* (battalion) to perform duties similar to those of an army chaplain. Thereafter, it was custom for each new head of the Bektashi Order to go to Istanbul to be 'crowned' by the commander of the Janissaries.[4]

With the expansion of the Ottoman Empire, the order spread from central Anatolia notably to the Balkans, Greece and Crete, where the Bektashi served as chaplains to the Janissaries and missionaries of Islam.

The power of the Janissaries grew to such an extent in Turkey that they could 'terrorize sultans and make and unmake grand viziers. From the time of Selim I in 1512 they demanded gifts from each sultan on his accession. When they upset their cauldrons, it was a sign of revolt and peace for the sultan could only be purchased by granting their demands.'[5]

Things could not last. The all-powerful Janissaries had become a State within the State, and Sultan Mahmud II (r. 1808–1839) resolved to act. On 15 June 1826, in an incident known in Turkish history as the 'Auspicious Event,' he

> sent in the morning the gunners and marines of the navy in one column and the bombardiers and sappers in another against the revolting Janissaries in their quarters on the Et Meydan. The great gate of the barracks was barricaded but fell under cannon fire. Fire was set to the barracks and before the night, the great Janissary Corps had been wiped out.[6]

It is said that about 4000 Janissaries were killed in the fighting and many more were later executed throughout the Empire.

The banning and violent end of the Janissary Corps could not be without major repercussions for the Bektashi Order that had been so closely associated with it. 'The leaders of other dervish orders, as well as the more orthodox *ulema* of the capital, proceeded immediately to bring in their reports of the heretical teachings of the Bektashi. On being faced with the evidence, the sultan ordered his representatives all over the country to search the Bektashi *tekkes* and to suppress the order.'⁷ On 10 July 1826, he issued a decree abolishing the Bektashi Order altogether. Many Bektashi leaders were put to death and others were sent into exile. Many went into hiding or 'refigured themselves as Nakshbandis to ride out the persecution'.⁸

The spread of the Bektashi to the Balkans

It is not known for certain when the Bektashi first made their appearance in Albania, but they no doubt arrived initially as part of the Janissary Corps that accompanied Ottoman forces in their conquest of the country. A good number of these Janissaries were in fact Albanians, men who had been taken from their homes at an early age and carried off to Turkey as blood tribute under the *devshirme* (child levy) system. Although they were initially enslaved, many of them were given a military education in the Janissary Corps or came to enjoy positions of power at the sultan's court. The Bektashi themselves associate their arrival in Albania with the legendary figure of Sari Saltik who was known in Kruja as early as 1567–1568. There is also mention of the founding of the *tekke* of Sersem Ali Baba in Tetova (Tetovo/Kalkandelen) in Macedonia in the mid-sixteenth century. If the legend is true, the *tekke* in Tetova would be the oldest one on Albanian-speaking territory.

The Turkish traveller Evliya Çelebi (1611–c. 1685), who visited the southern Balkan region in the second half of the seventeenth century, noted the presence of Bektashi *tekkes* in Mitrovica and Kaçanik in Kosovo in 1660. Ten years later, on a tour through southern Albania in the summer of 1670, he came across Bektashi *tekkes* in Kanina and Vlora.

In 1780 there followed the building of the Gravel *Tekke* (*Teqeja e Zallit*) in Gjirokastra under Asim Baba, who led it for sixteen years until his death in 1796. This *tekke* laid the foundations for the Bektashi movement in Albania itself and was of particular significance in the late nineteenth century.

Other early Bektashi foundations in Albania were the *tekke* of Shemimi Baba in Fushë Kruja (*c.* 1799), the *tekke* of Hajdar Baba in nearby Gjonëm (*c.* 1793), the *tekke* of Prishta in Skrapar, the *tekke* of Ibrahim Xhefai Baba in Elbasan (1803) and the *tekke* of Husejn Baba in Melçan near Korça, all of which probably stem originally from the last decade of the eighteenth century or the early years thereafter. It is in this period, *c.* 1790–1825, that we can speak of a firm presence of the Bektashi and their *tekkes* in Albania.

The rapid rise of the Bektashi in southern Albania is said to be linked particularly to Ali Pasha Tepelena (1744–1822), the awesome Lion of Janina, who is alleged to have been affiliated with the Bektashi and to have promoted the order. The English historian Frederick William Hasluck (1878–1920) suggests convincingly that Ali Pasha simply made use of the Bektashi to expand his realm and power against the will of the sultan in Istanbul.⁹ Hasluck's Scottish wife, the anthropologist Margaret Hasluck, née Hardie (1885–1948), notes that he used Bektashi dervishes as spies and diplomatic agents:

True, Ali Pasha of Tepelen and Yannina (1750-1822) had highly favoured and advanced the order for his own ends. As is well known from the writings of Colonel Leake and others, it was his ambition to carve himself out an independent satrapy from the Turkish empire, for which purpose, like the Janissaries before him, he found the Bektashis useful tools. One dervish, for instance, he used regularly as a diplomatic agent, another toured Albania, collecting contributions and doubtless information also for his master. In return Ali, who was possibly himself a lay member of the sect, built and endowed several Bektashi *tekkes*, but death ended his favours in 1822.[10]

Interestingly enough, it was precisely due to the influence of Ali Pasha that the Bektashi did not spread much in northern Albania, north of Kruja. Ali Pasha's northern Albanian rival, Mustafa Pasha Bushatlliu (1796-1860) of Shkodra, drove the Bektashi out of the region in the early nineteenth century, suspecting them of being supporters of his southern Albanian counterpart.

The 'Auspicious Event' of July 1826, when the Bektashi Order was banned by Sultan Mahmud II, had an immediate impact on the Bektashi of Albania. As in Turkey, many of the Bektashi establishments in Albania were burnt down or destroyed, including the *tekkes* of Melçan, Kuç and Qatrom in the Korça region, the *tekke* of Veliqot in the Tepelena region, the *tekke* of Baba Ali in Berat and perhaps many others. The *tekke* of Kanina was swiftly given over to the Halveti Order and may thus have been spared destruction. Most of the other sites were probably simply abandoned until the storm blew over.

The expansion of the Bektashi in Albania

By the second half of the nineteenth century, the Bektashi Order had recovered fully from the 'Auspicious Event' of 1826 and *tekkes* were being founded and built throughout the south of the country. Baba Ali Tomcri notes that before the refounding of the *tekke* of Prishta in 1860 by Baba Tahir of Crete, the number of Bektashi followers in the regions of Skrapar and Berat – later to become a Bektashi stronghold – could be counted on one's fingers.[11] Things changed quickly, in particular after 1878, when the Bektashi movement gained great popularity. It was in this period that most of the southern Albanian *tekkes* were founded. As Nathalie Clayer notes:

> In the early 1880s, after the Congress of Berlin, Bektashi propaganda in Albania took on a very nationalist colour. In these western reaches of the Ottoman Empire, Bektashism gradually crystallised as something eminently Albanian. A nationalist element had thus been added to the doctrine and the members of the order came to play a major role in the Albanian national awakening. Some of the *tekkes* served as clandestine schools where pupils were taught to read and write Albanian. They also served as bases for the distribution of Albanian spellers, periodicals and books. Since they were situated in the countryside, away from

urban centres, they could offer support for the bands of armed rebels that were beginning to gather forces from 1906. As such, the Albanian Bektashi enjoyed a period of great expansion, in particular among the Tosks in the south of the country, where nationalist sentiment arose earlier. In these regions, the number of Bektashi *tekkes* more than doubled from 1878 to 1912, going from about 20 to about 50. The rise in the number of *tekkes* was mirrored by an increase in the number of supporters and affiliates, among both the peasants and beys, who were drawn by the nationalist ideas propagated by the *babas* and dervishes, or who joined the order simply because they wanted to learn how to read and write in the *tekkes*.[12]

Since that time, patriotism has always been a strong component of Bektashi thinking. At the end of the nineteenth and in the early decades of the twentieth century leading up to Albanian independence in 1912, Bektashi leaders were ever in the vanguard of the struggle for national autonomy and Albanian self-determination. This is one reason why they enjoyed particular popularity among the Albanians, and still do today. Such was the level of conversion to the order that it grew into a religious community of its own and became the fourth religion of Albania.

The Albanians were especially receptive to certain features of Bektashism, namely its traditional tolerance and regard for other religions, and the related open-minded attitude to practices and beliefs. The Bektashi had a strong tendency to venerate saints and holy men at *tyrbes* (mausoleums) and, like all peoples in the Middle East, these included Christian saints and pre-Christian figures. Furthermore, they were receptive to local concerns and the local Albanian language in a simpler Latin script, in contrast to Sunni Islam, which was oriented primarily towards the Ottoman capital and promoted Arabic script.

It is estimated that at the beginning of the twentieth century, about 15 per cent of the population of Albania was Bektashi, equivalent to one-quarter of all Muslims in the country. Their *tekkes* served, in particular, for the underground propagation of Albanian-language books and education.

Despite this, the sect did not succeed in becoming the Albanian national religion, as many Bektashi intellectuals had hoped. One reason for this was their disproportionate concentration in the south of the country. About 70 per cent of all Bektashi *tekkes* were to be found south of Berat and only 3 per cent in the north.

The Bektashi renascence of the end of the nineteenth century came to an abrupt end in the period following Albanian independence, in November 1912. The *tekkes* of Albania suffered tremendous damage and destruction in the political instability, particularly during the Balkan Wars (1912–1913) and the first two years of the ensuing First World War (1914–1918).

The initial wave of destruction took place during a Sunni Muslim uprising in central Albania. The uprising began in mid-May 1914, but had its origins in 1913, when the newly independent government in Vlora founded the Albanian National Bank. Important concessions were made to Austrian and Italian financial interests, and the rebels, mostly illiterate peasants from the regions of Shijak, Kavaja and

Tirana, were afraid that their land would be bought up and taken away from them. In this context, the Muslim peasants were wary of Albanian independence, especially under a Christian prince, and called for continued rule by the sultan. On 23 May 1914, incited by Turkish agents agitating against the newly independent State, they attacked Durrës and on 3 June 1914, they made their demands known at a gathering in Kavaja. Among these were: a return to Ottoman rule or at least to rule by a Turkish prince instead of the German Protestant Prince Wilhelm zu Wied (1876–1945); the use of Ottoman Turkish as the national language or at least of Arabic script for writing Albanian; and use of the Ottoman flag only. The movement spread like wildfire throughout central Albania. Their slogan was *'Duam Babën'* (We want the Sultan), and they soon became known as Dumbabists. With the exception of the towns of Durrës, Vlora and Shkodra, most of the country came under their control. Long-simmering religious differences between the Sunni Muslim majority and the Shi'ite-oriented Bektashi minority broke out into violent conflict in which the fanaticized supporters of the uprising led by Haxhi Qamili (1876–1915) burnt down and destroyed many Bektashi *tekkes* from Martanesh in Bulqiza and as far south as Berat. The rebellion and conflict continued well into 1915.

Alas, this tragedy was superimposed by another – a far greater catastrophe that was to engulf southern Albania.

Albania had declared its independence in November 1912, but the country's southern border with Greece was long undefined. Fighting erupted between Greece and Albania, and between Orthodox Christians and Muslims, with Greek forces trying to get as much of the disputed territory as they could in order to annex it to Greece or at least to create an autonomous region of Northern Epirus in which the Orthodox population would have supremacy. An International Control Commission was set up to delineate the Albanian-Greek border, and Greek forces were subsequently forced to withdraw to the present border, but not before wreaking terrible destruction on southern Albania, in particular on everything Muslim and Bektashi. In his booklet *L'Affaire de l'Epire: le martyre d'un peuple* (The Epirus Question – the Martyrdom of a People), Sofia 1915, the Albanian political figure and publicist Mid'hat bey Frashëri (1880–1949), records the looting and destruction of no less than 145 southern Albanian villages. In the course of the carnage, Greek forces also burnt down or otherwise destroyed 48 *tekkes*.[13]

All in all, an estimated 80 per cent of the *tekkes* in Albania were severely damaged or completely destroyed in 1914–1915. It was an immeasurable loss from which this Islamic culture never really recovered. The *babas* and dervishes who survived fled to wherever they could find refuge – to central Albania outside of Greek control, to Italy, even to Egypt.

It was only after the First World War that a modicum of stability returned to Albania and to the surviving members of the Bektashi community. Many of the *tekkes* were rebuilt in the early 1920s.

The First World War was followed by the Greek-Turkish war of 1919–1922. One result of this equally bloody conflict was a major population exchange, though not involving Albania itself. According to the Convention on the Exchange of Greek and Turkish Population, signed in Lausanne in July 1923, Orthodox Christians in Turkey, over a million of them, were to be resettled/expelled to Greece, and Muslims living in Greece were to be resettled/expelled en masse to Turkey. Although the Cham Albanians living in Greece were largely exempt from the compulsory exchange, the mass expulsion of Muslims to Turkey resulted in the closure or abandonment of most of the old Bektashi *tekkes* in Epirus, Thessaly and elsewhere in what became Greek territory. In the heated atmosphere of the exchange, the *tekkes* in Greece, many of which had a strong Albanian character with mostly Albanian-speaking dervishes and *babas*, were attacked and destroyed, or simply given up. The Bektashi in southeastern Europe were thus increasingly concentrated in Albania and the contiguous Albanian-speaking regions.

In Albania itself, by 1920, the Bektashi had gained in certain recognition as a religious community in their own right. The High Regency Council (*Këshilli i Lartë i Regjencës*) governing Albania in the absence of Prince Wied consisted of four members, one for each of the four religious communities: Abdi bey Toptani (1864–1942) for the Muslims, Bishop Luigj Bumçi (1872–1945) for the Catholics, Michael Tourtoulis (1847–1935) for the Orthodox, and Aqif Pasha Biçaku of Elbasan (1861–1926) for the Bektashi. The Bektashi were thus now on par with the main religious communities.

At the First National Congress of the Bektashi, held at the *tekke* of Prishta in the Skrapar region on 14–17 January 1921, leaders adopted the name *Komuniteti Bektashian* (Bektashi community) and stressed that the Bektashi were the first religious community in Albania to be free of foreign domination. This marked the beginning of a break with the Bektashi in Turkey with whom the Albanians now had only sporadic contacts. The French parliamentarian Justin Godart (1871–1956) from Lyon, who was in Albania at the time, noted:

> Last January, a meeting of over 500 delegates freed Albanian Bektashism from its subordination to the supreme chief in Ankara. From then on, the sect became independent and national. It is run by an assembly of seven *babas* presided over by the *baba* of the *tekke* of Gjirokastra who has a higher rank in the hierarchy. At the moment he shares this task with the *baba* of Turan who is the oldest. It was also decided that they would not allow the foundation of any more *tekkes* so as to concentrate their resources and action.[14]

This congress, headed by Baba Ahmet Turani (1854–1928), was significantly attended by a representative of the new Albanian government under Sulejman bey Delvina (1884–1932) that had been created by the Congress of Lushnja.

At a Muslim conference held in Tirana in 1923, open discord then broke out between the Sunni Muslims and the Bektashi, with the Bektashi delegates leaving the meeting, declaring themselves autonomous and breaking relations with the Grand Mufti (*Şeyhülislam*) in Constantinople.[15]

In this period, the Albanian Bektashi community was administered by a council of seven *babas* presided over by Baba Sulejman of the Hajdërije *tekke* of Gjirokastra.

The Second National Congress of the Bektashi was held in Gjirokastra on 8–9 July 1924, again under the auspices of Baba Ahmet Turani. As a result of developments in Turkey, the Turkish Bektashi began thinking about transferring their world headquarters abroad, to Albania, and resolved that religious ceremonies could be conducted in Albanian as well as Turkish. At the same time, there was continued tension between the Bektashi and Sunni Muslim communities in Albania.

In the autumn of 1925 all the dervish orders were banned in Turkey. This measure was taken under Mustafa Kemal Atatürk, despite the fact that the Bektashi had supported many of the changes introduced by the Turkish Republic.

Salih Niyazi Dede, the head of all Bektashis from the *pir evi*, had gone to Mustafa Kemal to protest this new law, for he was his friend. Salih Dede reminded Mustafa Kemal of how the Bektashis had helped bring him to a position of high regard and of the assistance the Bektashis had afforded him and his forces. Salih Dede put it to him directly, 'And how is it now that you in your lifetime want to abolish us?' Atatürk responded, 'What can I do? I cannot make a special law for you. The entire Parliament resolved that the *tariqats* be abolished. For this reason, I can do nothing for you. It pains me, but I am unable to do anything'.[16] Thus they closed down all the *tekkes* in Turkey.

The Third National Congress of the Bektashi was held at the *tekke* of Turan near Korça on 23 September 1929 under Baba Zylfo of Melçan. This was the most important of the early Bektashi congresses, with new regulations and a new budget, because it was here that the Bektashi declared themselves to be a religious community of their own, i.e. autonomous from mainstream Islam. They also set up the institution of the *kryegjysh* (Turkish: *başdede*) and the *kryegjyshata* as their headquarters in Tirana. Up until 1937, the appointment of the *kryegjysh* had to be approved by King Zog.

In connection with the ban in Turkey and the closing of all the *tekkes* there, they resolved to invite the *başdede,* Salih Nijazi Dede (1876–1941), originally from the Kolonja region, to return to Albania. Salih Nijazi Dede thus moved back at the end of 1930, and re-established the headquarters of the Bektashi movement in Tirana the following year. The Bektashi community was then divided into six *gjyshatas* (administrative districts):

1. Kruja with its headquarters at the *tekke* of Fushë Kruja,
2. Elbasan with its headquarters at the *tekke* of Krasta,
3. Korça with its headquarters at the *tekke* of Melçan,
4. Gjirokastra with its headquarters at the *tekke* of Asim Baba,
5. Prishta representing Berat and part of Përmet, and
6. Vlora with its headquarters at the *tekke* of Frashër.

But how prevalent were the Bektashi at that time? The French journalist and writer Albert Mousset (1883–1975) noted around 1928 that there were 43 *tekkes* in Albania.[17] At about the same time, the Albanian publicist Teki Selenica

(1882–1962) recorded the presence in Albania of 65 *babas*, meaning theoretically that there must have been 65 *tekkes* in the country. According to the *Kalendari Enciklopedik* of 1933, there were 52 Bektashi *tekkes* in Albania.[18] There were also about a dozen Bektashi *tekkes* in Kosovo and several in the Albanian-speaking regions of Macedonia. By 1934, the Bektashi community was taking steps to open two seminaries for the training of clergy, one in Tirana and one in Korça,[19] but funds were lacking and nothing came of the venture.

Such was the situation until about 1947. By the mid-1940s there were an estimated 280 *babas* and dervishes in Albania,[20] and in the 1960s we know that there were still about fifty Bektashi *tekkes* in the country and about eighty dervishes, fifteen in Fushë Kruja alone.

The communist dictatorship in Albania

The situation of the Bektashi community became dire in the last years of the Second World War which were characterized by civil war and political chaos in the country. With the withdrawal of German forces from Albania at the end of November 1944, the communist partisans seized power in Tirana and a new Stalinist regime was set up which was eventually to ban the Bektashi community altogether.

A Fourth National Congress of the Bektashi was held in Tirana on 5 May 1945, during which new statutes were adopted and a new leadership was approved. Xhafer Sadiku Dede was made *kryegjysh* and the influential Baba Faja Martaneshi, a communist collaborator, was made secretary general. Xhafer Sadiku Dede died on 2 August 1945 and was replaced on 5 September 1945 by Abaz Hilmi Dede. Soon thereafter, however, on 19 March 1947, a spectacular conflict occurred. Abaz Hilmi Dede, the 'pope' of the Bektashi, shot and killed Baba Faja Martaneshi and Baba Fejzo Dervishi in what was described as a heated argument over religious matters, and then committed suicide.

With the ongoing Stalinist purges in the country, the communist authorities now had complete control over the Bektashi Order. In the ensuing atmosphere of political terror, most of the *babas* were frightened into submission or at least into silence. Many of its leaders soon met their deaths. Baba Qamil Gllava of Tepelena was executed in 1946 in Gjirokastra. Baba Ali Myrteza of Kruja (1912–1947) died after being tortured and thrown out of a prison window. The writer Baba Ali Tomorri (1900–1948) and Baba Shefket Koshtani of Tepelena were executed the following year. The American anthropologist Frances Trix has published a tentative list of Bektashi *babas* who suffered during the early years of communist rule.[21]

The *Kryegjyshata* was assumed on 8 June 1947 by Baba Ahmet Myftari (1916–1980), who had no choice but to be a puppet of the regime. In September 1953, for instance, he invited the Bektashi faithful to spend the Ashura feast in a spirit of 'hatred of the Anglo-American imperialists and of love for the people's power'.[22]

New statutes were once again promulgated at the Fifth National Congress of the Bektashi that was held in Tirana on 16 April 1950. In 1954, there were still some forty-three to sixty-eight *tekkes* in the country.²³

Dark times were, however, looming. The communist regime increasingly regarded all religious communities in Albania as rivals for power. Things came to a head in 1967 with a militant communist government campaign against religion. The new Albanian Constitution that year banned religion entirely. Article 37 stipulated: 'The State recognises no religion and supports and carries out atheistic propaganda in order to implant a scientific materialistic world outlook in people.' This ban was accompanied by a virulent political campaign to encourage young people throughout the country to attack mosques, churches and *tekkes* and to denounce members to the clergy to the authorities. Albania was in Cultural Revolution, following the example of Red China. The Bektashi community and all the other religious groups in Albania were forcefully disbanded. Not only that, most of the *tekkes* and *tyrbes* were razed to the ground, and their leaders, the *babas*, were sent into internal exile or were imprisoned. Of the fifty-three Bektashi *tekkes* that had existed, only six were left standing.²⁴ Equal destruction was wrought on churches and mosques.

The Bektashi community had been wiped out. All that remained were the memories of the faithful, old people who were too frightened to pass their knowledge on to the next generation.

Out of the reach of the Albanian communists, there were still two *tekkes* abroad that strove to carry on the tradition, but their impact on Albania was minimal. One was in Gjakova in Kosovo under the direction of Baba Qazim Bakalli (1895–1981), and the other in Taylor, near Detroit (Michigan, USA), founded in 1954 and long under the direction of the eminent Baba Rexheb (1901–1995). The beautiful *tekke* of Gjakova was later razed to the ground by Serbian forces in the spring of 1999 along with the whole of the old town.

The law against religion in Albania was finally rescinded in December 1990 when the unloved dictatorship gave a last groan and imploded. As of 1993, there were only five *babas* and one dervish left alive in Albania,²⁵ and only six *tekkes* remained standing in any recognizable state.

The recovery of the Bektashi in post-communist Albania

On 27 January 1991, after almost a quarter of a century of silence in Albania, a provisional committee for the revival of the Bektashi community was founded in Tirana. Since that time, the new community, initially under Baba Reshat Bardhi (1935–2011), has been active in reviving Bektashi traditions in Albania, no easy task after such immense destruction and after such a long interruption.

The *Kryegjyshata* in Tirana was reopened on 22 March 1991 in a moving ceremony on the occasion of *Nevruz* that was attended by Mother Teresa (1910–1997), and a Sixth National Congress of the Bektashi, one of joy and revival, was held on 19–20 July 1993. A Seventh National Congress of the Bektashi was held in Tirana on 23–24 September 2000; an Eighth National Congress took place in Tirana on 21 September 2005; and finally, a Ninth National Congress was held in Tirana on 6 July 2009, each gathering helping to reinforce a sense of cohesion among the Albanian Bektashi.

The current situation

Although there are no reliable statistics as to their numbers, it is possible that about 10 per cent of the population of Albania would consider themselves Bektashi.[26] For most of these people, this affiliation is one of cultural heritage rather than one of actual religious belief. Their numbers are said to be roughly equivalent to those of the Catholics in Albania.

As a Shi'ite-oriented community,[27] the Bektashi have much in common in their beliefs and customs with Alevi communities in Turkey and the Middle East, though they may not always adhere to these beliefs and customs with equal fervour. Contacts between the Albanian Bektashi and the many Alevi groupings in Turkey are now sporadic.

Relations between the main religious communities within Albania itself are generally very good, despite the occasional mutterings of displeasure by Sunni Muslims at the laissez-faire attitudes of the Bektashi to many of the tenets of Sunni Islam. In the past, these mutterings were the source of many discrete jokes among the Bektashi who saw the Sunni as focusing on the exterior. At any rate, the exemplary and much-lauded religious harmony that Albania enjoys is now an undeniable reality.

Since 1990 that saw the end of the communist dictatorship and of the ban on religion in Albania, the Bektashi community has managed to revive, but this revival has not been easy. When the dictatorship was over, much aid and assistance flowed in to the other religious communities in the country. The Catholics were given strong support by charitable organisations in Italy and Austria, such as Caritas, and by numerous religious orders, and the Vatican provided much direction for the training of Albanian clergy. The Muslim Community received massive financial and technical backing from Turkey, the Gulf States and Iran, such that every town and village in Albania soon had a brand new mosque and an imam to go with it. Orthodox Albanians, for their part, received much support from the Greek Orthodox Church in Athens and were able to re-establish their community relatively quickly. Churches and roadside shrines were rebuilt in the south of the country, and local clergy was trained for the priesthood, although this has sometimes involved infiltration by Greece and Greek priests.

For the Bektashi, things were more difficult because they did not have a foreign 'patron' to provide funding for the reconstruction of *tekkes* and *tyrbes* and for the training of local clergy, despite some modest gifts from Bektashi Albanians in America. With time and after some court litigation, the Bektashi community at least got much of its extensive one-time property back, and it is from this property, e.g. the leasing out of pastureland, that the community lives in good part.

The *Kryegjyshata* in Tirana, as the World Headquarters of the Bektashi, is now in a dignified state, with restoration work having been carried out on the existing buildings, and with reconstructed shrines, a new glass Odeon, a museum and archives as well as pleasant gardens. Functional administrative structures were also created, with the country being divided into six administrative districts (*gjyshatas*), based on the system set up in earlier years.

1. The *Gjyshata* of Gjirokastra with its seat at the *tekke* of Asim Baba, which oversees the regions of Gjirokastra, Saranda and Tepelena.
2. The *Gjyshata* of Korça with its seat at the *tekke* of Turan, which oversees the regions of Korça, Devoll, Pogradec and Kolonja, including Leskovik.
3. The *Gjyshata* of Kruja with its seat at the *tekke* of Fushë Kruja, which oversees the regions of Kruja, Kurbin, Bulqiza, Dibra, Mat, Shkodra and Durrës.
4. The *Gjyshata* of Elbasan with its seat at the *tekke* of Baba Xhefai, which oversees the regions of Elbasan, Gramsh, Peqin, Lushnja, Kavaja, and Librazhd, including Përrenjas.
5. The *Gjyshata* of Vlora with its seat at the *tekke* of Kusum Baba, which oversees the regions of Vlora, Mallakastra, Fier, including Patos and Roskovec.
6. The *Gjyshata* of Berat with its seat at the *tekke* of Prishta, which oversees the regions of Berat, Skrapar and Përmet.

Since the mid-1990s, most of the *tekkes* and *tyrbes* destroyed in the 'Cultural Revolution' of 1967 have been rebuilt, though usually in a simpler form. They now consist for the most part of a *tyrbe* and an adjacent one or two-room building for the custodian that also serves to welcome guests. Few of the centres are now active *tekkes* as they once were. In some cases, where funding was available, much more elaborate, some might say pompous, buildings have been constructed, such as those in Saranda, Alipostivan and Melçan. In Melçan, the beautiful old ruins that still stood on the hilltop in the early year of the twenty-first century were bulldozed to make way for a large new *tekke* that would be visible throughout the Plain of Korça, complete with driveways, parking lots and gardens. Alas, few of the new buildings have retained the style and atmosphere of the former *tekkes*.

One major problem being faced by the Bektashi community is the lack of clergy. Most of the surviving *babas* who carried on the traditions of Bektashism that they had learned before 1967 are now very elderly and there is little hope of finding younger ones to replace them. Nor are there many dervishes left in Albania. Currently (2017) there are nine *babas* and six dervishes active in the country, certainly not enough to keep up the many, recently restored *tekkes* in the countryside. The *Kryegjyshata* in Tirana claims to be the 'world headquarters' of the Bektashi and rightfully so, since the holy see was officially transferred from Hacıbektaşköy in Turkey to Albania in the late 1920s after the dervish orders were banned in Turkey in 1925. In reality, however, it is mostly only the Albanian Bektashi abroad who respect the authority of the *Kryegjyshata* in Tirana. The Bektashi in Turkey, of whom there are still many, tend to go their own way, although they maintain cordial relations with Tirana. Even some of the Albanian *tekkes*, in Macedonia for instance, waver in their allegiance.

It is difficult to predict what the future holds for the Bektashi community in Albania. The lack of clergy and funding and the paucity of fervent believers are certainly impediments. On the other hand, there is wide and enthusiastic support for the Bektashi in Albania from many people, some of significant political influence, who consider themselves Bektashi from a cultural perspective and who wish to uphold and promote Bektashi traditions. Volunteers from around the country, in particular in the Bektashi heartlands of Mallakastra, Tepelena and Skrapar, have been rebuilding *tekkes* and shrines and doing what they can to recreate and maintain viable structures. As the Bektashi enjoy respect and wide support in the Albanian population at large, i.e. among non-Bektashi, there is little chance that they will be 'edged out' by the other religious communities. Without the Bektashi, Albania would not be what it is today.

Robert Elsie

2

EARLY REPORTS AND SCHOLARLY ARTICLES ON THE ALBANIAN BEKTASHI

1660-1670
EVLIYA ÇELEBI
NOTES ON THE BEKTASHI

The famed Turkish traveller and writer Evliya Çelebi or Chelebi (1611–c.1685), from Constantinople, encountered Bektashi tekkes in Kosovo and in particular in the Vlora region of southern Albania during his early travels in the Balkans.

On Mitrovica in Kosovo – 1660

Because of that incident,[28] this lofty fortress of Mitrovica is called The Inauspicious Fortress. Situated at the extreme western point of the Kosovo plain, it is not dominated by any higher ground. It is oval-shaped and constructed of chiselled stonework. It is extremely solid and cannot be undermined with trenches or tunnels. There is a single gate. Inside, there are no memorable buildings. [...] At bowshot range from the fortress is the shrine of Mustafa Baba, with a *tekke* inhabited by Bektashi dervishes, where travellers can spend the night. Near this *tekke* is the town of Zveçan, at the utmost frontier.

On Kaçanik in Kosovo – 1660

The town contains one delightful congregational mosque, above the threshold of which is the following chronogram: ABy God, Da=i (?) has uttered its date: A fair temple and praiseworthy site, 1003 (1594 AD). There is one Bektashi *tekke*, one primary school, one great *han*, situated at the foot of the cliff and one small bathhouse. There is no sign of a bazaar, since Skopje is nearby.

On Kanina in southern Albania – 1670

Kanina is a lofty fortress rising to the heavens. It was constructed solidly on a mountain promontory of earth and pumice rock. [...] The roads in this fortress are all up and down. There are no bazaars, *hans*, bathhouses or public buildings inside the walls, but the open town (*varosh*) to the south of the fortress contains 300 stonework houses with tiled roofs and gardens and vineyards, all piled on top of one another. Here, too, there is no sign of a bazaar. There is only the spacious mosque of Sinan Pasha with its tall and elegant minaret. There is also a *tekke* of Hadji Bektash Veli here, which was also endowed by Sinan Pasha. This *tekke* is famous throughout Turkey, Arabia and Persia. Here one finds many devotees of the mystical sciences and the dervish life of poverty. Among them are lovely young boys. Visitors and pilgrims are fed copious meals from the kitchen and pantry of the *tekke* because all the surrounding mountains, vineyards and gardens belong to it. Near the *tekke*, the benefactor of the endowment, Ghazi Sinan Pasha, lies buried along with all his household and retainers in a mausoleum with a lofty dome – may God have mercy on their souls. In short, it is a rich and famous *tekke*, beyond my powers to describe.

On Vlora in southern Albania – 1670

To the east of the fortress and somewhat above it is a slope with olive trees. All the hills and fields in the area are covered in fruit trees, vineyards and olive orchards. On this high peak is situated the tomb of Kuzgun Baba Sultan with a few Bektashi dervishes.

There are three dervish convents, including the Halveti *tekke* of Yakub Efendi with hundreds of devout dervishes, barefooted and bareheaded, with patched woollen cloaks; and the above-mentioned *tekke* of Kusum (Kuzgun) Baba on a hillside overlooking the fortress, set amidst vineyards, like the fabled garden of Irem.

[Excerpts from: R. Dankoff and R. Elsie, *Evliya Çelebi in Albania and Adjacent Regions (Kosovo, Montenegro, Ohrid). The Relevant Sections of the Seyahatname.* Edited with Translation, Commentary and Introduction by Robert Dankoff and Robert Elsie (Leiden, New York, Cologne 2000), 167a-167b, pp. 10–13; 169a, pp. 24–25; 361a, pp. 130–133; 361b, pp. 136–141].

1854
JOHANN GEORG VON HAHN
THE FORTRESS OF KANINA

The German scholar and father of Albanian studies, Johann Georg von Hahn (1811–1869), travelled extensively in Albania in the mid-nineteenth century. His three-volume 'Albanesische Studien' (Albania Studies), Jena 1854, was the most influential work published on Albania for almost a century. In Kanina, he came across the tekke referred to two centuries before him by Evliya Çelebi.

Kanina – this name first appeared in the Middle Ages, replacing the ancient toponyms Byllis, Aulon and Oricum and is of particular interest for us Germans because the town appears as part of the dowry that King Manfred received when he married Helena, the daughter of Michael, the Despot of Epirus. Leake believes that the fortress was constructed on Greek foundations. When I examined the buildings, I discovered ancient hewn stones among the foundations, but they all seem to have been moved around. The fortress is now in ruins, but only seems to have been abandoned recently by its owners who spend the hot summer season here. These are the descendants of the first Turkish conqueror of the region, the famed Sinan Pasha of Konya, whose grave can be seen in a small *tekke* situated at the foot of the fortress. People come here from far and wide on pilgrimages because Sinan is considered holy by the Turks. According to legend, he conquered the fortress of Marco Kraal, the final prince of Kanina, whose last descendant is a poor old man whose only son was taken away from him two years ago to serve in the army.

[Excerpt from: Johann Georg von Hahn, *Albanesische Studien* (Jena 1854), p. 72. English version in: Johann Georg von Hahn, *The Discovery of Albania: Travel Writing and Anthropology in the Nineteenth-Century Balkans* (London 2015), p. 34. Translated and introduced by Robert Elsie.]

1888
MONK ZOSIMAS OF ATHOS
THE BEKTASHI TEKKES OF THESSALY

The Greek Orthodox monk Zosimas of Mount Athos provides a none-too-flattering description of the Bektashi tekkes of Thessaly and, in particular, the tekke of Durbalı Sultan with its 'illiterate and superstitious Albanians' that he visited in 1888.

South-east of this village (Irinì or Rinì in the deme of Skotousa), in a hilly and romantic situation among tall and shady trees (planes, dwarf-oaks, and cornels), stands the *tekke* of the Bektashi, an establishment famous throughout all Thessaly. In it, according to Government statistics, reside thirty-nine dervishes, but at the time of my visit (1888) I was told that there were, exclusive of servitors, fifty-four, all illiterate and superstitious Albanians. An intelligent dervish informed me that the *tekke* was formerly a monastery of the western church, and that the Turks took it over about 1630–40; there was a church of S. Demetrius, but the dervishes say it was dedicated to S. George, on account of the greater veneration they affect towards the latter.

For a time the *tekke* was occupied by Turkish dervishes from the great *tekke*, called Kulakli Baba, at Konia. But during the despotic reign of the famous Ali Pasha of Tepelen (according to the *Phonì toù Laoù*), who justified his contempt for religion by pretending to be a follower of the liberal Bektashi, it was given to the Albanians; at this time there were founded in Thessaly certain convents which were rather political rallying-points for the surrounding population than religious establishments.

There were four such convents, all situated at strategic points, commanding the more frequented highways. These were the *tekkes* of the Turbali Sultan near Rinì, on the road from Volo to Pharsala and Karditsa; of Balli Baba, near the village of Tatar, on the road between Lamia, Larissa, and Pharsala; of Shahin Baba, near the village of Kupekli; and Baba Tekke, in the celebrated Vale of Tempe, on the road from Larissa to Chaisi. These *tekkes* became the regular resorts of criminals, who plundered and spoiled the surrounding populations. So that, at the time of the destruction of the Janissaries by Sultan Mahmud, in 1826, an imperial order was issued for the destruction of the Bektashi, and the population, both Christian and Mohammedan, fell upon the *tekkes* and drove out their inmates. Two *tekkes*, those of the villages Tatar and Kupekli, were burnt; that of Rinì, either because its inmates put up a more determined resistance, or because it lay some distance from Pharsala, was spared.

From 1833 onwards all sorts of rascals, sometimes even brigands, began once more to congregate in it on the pretence of doing penance, and this state of things continued till the last years of Turkish rule under the direction of a former servant of the Muslim Aga, a certain Bairam Aga, who continues to preside over the *tekke*. Under him the system of rapine and pillage reached its height: the whole countryside was subjected by the raids of his armed brigands. A wily and far-sighted man, he legitimized his oppressive acts after the Union [of Thessaly with Greece in 1882] by forged documents, supplied him by the Turkish authorities, making the *tekke* his personal property. He had still two or three monks and a few servitors to back him.

There is a local tradition that the *tekke* was built on the site of an ancient Byzantine monastery of S. George, but it is impossible to confirm this by investigation as long as the Albanians remain in possession. The *tekke* has defences like a small fortress and entrance is forbidden.

At the time of the Union there were fifty monks or dervishes in the *tekke*: there are now only three and some paid servitors of Bairam Baba, all Albanians. The dervishes who formerly lived here were remarkable for the fact that they wore in their right ears a great iron earring, and hanging on their breasts an eight-sided stone; the novices wore white caps, and all shaved their heads once a week.

[From the journal *Prometheus*, Volos, 1893, no. 55, pp. 442 sq. Republished in: F. W. Hasluck, *Christianity and Islam under the Sultans*. Edited by Margaret M. Hasluck. 2 vols. (Oxford: Clarendon 1929), pp. 592–593 (766–768)].

1892
ANDREAS KARKAVITSAS
VISIONS OF THESSALY, THE BEKTASHI TEKKE

The Greek novelist Andreas Karkavitsas (1866–1922), from Elis in the Peloponnese, worked as an army doctor. Among his writings is a tale about his visit to the famed tekke of Durbalı Sultan in Thessaly (Greece) in the late nineteenth century, when the region was under Turkish rule.

I was travelling by train with an old friend of mine, the bey of Trikala, crossing the broad plains of Karditsa and Pharsala. When we arrived at Aivali, before getting out of the carriage, my travelling companion pointed to something up on a hill to the right, a grove of trees, and said with evident enthusiasm that there was a *tekke* there that we would be visiting.

It was July when the heat was at its worst in Thessaly. I took a look at the long road before us and the distant convent, with the haze spreading through the air as if from a limekiln, and gave a groan. I suggested to the bey that it would be nicer if we rolled out his carpets and asked the sheikh of Durballi to send us a carriage like the ones in my fantasies of the Orient. I hoped that the Bektashi dervishes would get right to it so that we could avoid the long journey on foot. But the bey thought otherwise, saying that since Allah had given his sons the sun and its rays, it would be inappropriate for us to turn our backs on them. Indeed, I have known many beys and aghas in Larisa whose minds were forever focused on the radiant gifts of Allah. They wear white sheets or towels around their heads. But Demis was a pious Muslim and he would even have opposed me if I had suggested that we take measures to protect ourselves from smallpox and cholera. I respected his faith so we set off courageously on our journey to the unknown.

The trail took us through a grove of harvested walnut trees to the village of Iriní that was inhabited by a few Greek families. The whole region and the *tekke* itself are named after this village. There the trail began to rise over the foothills of Narthakios, keeping to the left of a valley with heather and shady trees, and led us to the *tekke* in a crescent.

When we reached a large stone fountain in front of the garden, our ears were deafened by wild shouting and clanking. I was rather afraid at that moment that, instead of reaching a place of quiet meditation, as I knew the Bektashi, we had arrived among the followers of the Rufa'i sect who are forever shouting *Il Allah* in their noisy ceremonies. But this was not the case. The sage Bektashi dervishes were busy threshing grain and, instead of having the words of the Prophet on their lips, they were shouting and cursing in Albanian to get their dozens of loudly neighing horses to gallop around the threshing floor. Through a window, the *baba* with an old pipe in his mouth and prayer beads in his hands saw us coming and appeared to be delighted.

'*Selam-u aleyküm!*' he shouted joyfully.

'*Aleyküm selam!*' responded the bey while attempting to remove his shoes, and kissed the sheikh's hands with a radiant expression on his face. [...]

Durballi, the founder of the present *tekke*, was a heretical Albanian. It would seem that he had the same profession as his guards, i.e. he was a fighter. But when he reached old age, he put down his flail and cudgel, called for his prayer beads, and led a quiet life. He built the *tekke* and the believers came to call the sheikh *baba*.

The *tekke* is built on the edge of a hill overlooking the plain of Pharsala. It is surrounded by a high, thick wall with embrasures, towers, secret doorways and cellars, as well as passages to allow people to get down to the plain without being seen by anyone. The main gate has an alcove with embrasures and towers to the left and right to keep unwanted visitors away from the *tekkes* in times of tension. At one end of the flagstone yard are the kitchen and storage rooms, the corn crib and the barn. At the other end is a long two-storey building with an inner columned courtyard for the sheikh and the dervishes. A trellis, covered in healthy-looking woody vines rises from the main gate up to the second floor and there are two tall cypress trees in the middle of the courtyard, making it look like a place of worship for the clergy. [...]

The Bektashi have preserved this place in accord with the time-old ideas of their order, and still come here secretly to pay their respects and to keep the candles lit in honour of their patron, Haji Bektash Veli.

The present sheikh of the *tekke* is of average build, but is full of energy, courage and derring-do, like a good Albanian. He descends in direct lineage from Durballi and inherited the title and the fertile farmland of the *tekke*.

The *tekke* itself is rich, not only in dervishes, followers and notable adherents, but also in agricultural land, meadows and woods. Under Turkish rule, the name of this venerable *tekke* was known throughout Epirus and northern Thessaly and lower Greece. The grave of Durballi attracts many pilgrims every day who, in accordance with their customs, leave rich offerings. Aside from these assets, it owns two whole farming villages as *çifligs*, Iriní and Artuán, that pull in 1,000 to 2,000 Turkish lira a year from animal husbandry.

There are a total of ten dervishes at this *tekke*. They have no right to the ownership of agricultural land or to the many gifts given to this holy place by the believers. They feed and dress themselves and tend to the graves of Durballi Sultan and his successors, and they will bear knives against anyone who threatens their property.

The clothing of the dervishes and of the sheikh is very simple. They wear a white, twelve-sided *taxh* on their heads. It is the only distinctive sign of their order. The *taxh* is the symbol of the Bektashi and looks like the mitre of a Byzantine bishop. They wear long robes which are coloured and open at the front from the neck downwards to their bare feet. [...] They also have woollen or Kashmir cloaks, usually in brown. Only the sheikh wears green. Around their waists they have broad woven sashes, famed token and symbol of their withdrawal from earthly things.

The sash also serves to hold the sheaths of their knives and the other instruments and utensils they carry with them. Over their left shoulders they carry leather bags the size of a tobacco pouch, that can serve as a travelling bag. In earlier days, they carried leather sheaths for their guns, showing off the shining barrel or the jewel-studded butt. They all keep their hair short but grow long beards, and twirl their moustaches with pride like the early Janissaries did. [...]

After we had partaken of a good amount of *ouzo*, the sheikh led me into the *mysafir oda* (guest room), asking if I would like to have a rest. Instead of taking a nap, however, I wanted to have a good look around the room. The floor was covered in woollen carpets of local production. To the left and right there were six beds for any guests who might happen to come by. The walls were decked in portraits of holy men and imams, and beautifully written, coloured Koranic verse in excellent calligraphy. The order of the writing is very important to the Muslims. Some of the paintings were in Persian style. One of them showed a noble-looking head with eyes wide-open that seemed to want to take in everything around them, even the invisible, the secretive, and the hearts of the believers. Under its eyes was a black beard and a long moustache, all shining in black and adorning the bodiless head of Muhammed. Above the paintings were figures of birds and insects unknown to science, dragons and monsters, the products of Oriental fantasy. In another painting, there was a majestic lion, the one who was tamed by Haji Bektash. He led it through the streets of Konya and took it with him on his campaigns. In a leather pendant in the corner of the room there was a small axe embellished with sayings from the Koran, and several old wooden pipes said to have been smoked by Durballi himself. On the wall to the left there was his bow and a double-edged sword, a large axe with a long crescent-shaped blade – very sharp indeed. Farther along the wall hung a dusty *kudum* instrument, with a two-sided drum like the ones used in *tekkes* to call the dervishes. From the ceiling hung two bottle-shaped lights in which were reflected various landscapes on paper, with the Prophet and Koranic sayings. These were souvenirs that pilgrims had brought back from the holy sites – Mecca and Medina. All around the walls there were piles of cooking utensils, needed by the monks in their daily lives, and across from the entrance there was the ever-smoking hearth.

After inspecting the room, I went out to see the grave of Durballi. This truly venerable man lay buried in a special tomb. An elderly dervish, tall as a cypress tree and as silent as the grave, appeared. When he saw me, he came up and took me there, showing me the key, as if the well-respected sheikh had ordered him to do so. It was evident that nothing happened at the *tekke* without orders from the sheikh.

The graves of the Bektashi Order are not within the precinct as in Christian monasteries, but outside on the hillside. They are fenced in from the rest of the *tekke* with a large gate. Some of them were in the yard, large rectangular tombs with stakes at the head and feet with Turkish inscriptions on them that praised the virtues of the deceased. Other graves were simpler, with inscriptions only on the stake at the head. On the ground was the symbol of the *taxh* to show that they were clergymen. Other graves had curiously shaped vessels in the shape of flowerpots with copper coins in them, offerings from Turkish pilgrims. Above them all rose lofty cypress trees that waved mournfully whenever there was a bit of wind. All of these graves were of Bektashi dervishes who had served at the *tekke* over the last two hundred years. But there were also graves of other supporters of this order who had expressed the wish, while they were alive, to be buried near a dervish or a *baba* they had venerated.

The grave of Durballi was farther on, beyond the others, in a grove of green cypress trees. He lies in a domed mausoleum with a small door with arabesque ornamentation. The dervish opened the little door, left his shoes on the footstep and turned to me, pointing to me to follow him, which I did right away. I instinctively understood that he wanted me to walk behind him and imitated his gestures. The expression on his face was now, however, one of unusual displeasure and I realised that I had made some mistake or committed some sacrilege. I had thought it to be too much work for me to take off my shoes and entered the mausoleum as I was since I had no time to lose. I glanced around at everything there was to see in that mysterious chamber.

In fact, there was not much to see – only three graves flat on the ground in Turkish fashion. They were all covered in green cloth and at the end, the headstones were wrapped in various gold-embroidered turbans – green and black, some of which looked a bit rotten from the passing of time, as if the deceased had worn them during their lives. At their feet were stone vessels in the shape of flowerpots in which the faithful put presents and money: copper, silver and gold coins. On the southern side of the graves were some other things: embroidered silks, turbans, tufts, scarves and towels, all left behind as gifts from visiting pilgrims. At the heads of the graves were silver candlesticks and from the ceiling hung a copper candelabra. Of the graves, the middle one was higher than the others. I understood that this was the site where the holy Durballi slept the sleep of the dead. The other two graves, according to the dervish, were his father and his mother, but they may have been sheikhs who succeeded him.

In a corner stood the standards of the *baba*, wrapped with great care in a green cloth. One had a crescent at the end of it and the other had a lance. In the opposite corner, a mighty, long and rusty sabre hung from the wall together with a cudgel. In the middle of the wall was a glass frame with golden letters on a black background with various verses from the Koran.

Near the grave of Durballi there was another grave, but without a history, though it had an aura of holiness. As it was of someone very young, my dervish would certainly not know anything about it. The dervish assured me that when he left this world one day, he would be borne with his whole body would be and taken to the gardens of paradise.

When I returned from my visit to the graves, the sheikh and the bey were standing near the threshing floor, watching the grain being threshed. The sheikh told me with a smile that it was time for me to return if I wanted to catch the train and offered me his stallion to ride back down to the station. It was a fine animal, a proud beast of the sort that only the Ottomans knew how to ride. It had a Turkish saddle with visible crescent moons embroidered in silver threading in each corner of it and with gold tufts with all sorts of birds, animals and fish. The straps of the stirrups were woven with camel hair and embellished with full moons here and there. The reins were equally ornate, with red and green tufts. From the stallion's neck hung a boar tooth in crescent form and a triangular, red-leather sack with charms inside it to keep away the Evil Eye of other animals. I must admit that I was tempted not to accept the sheikh's offer out of fear that the cantankerous beast might throw me into a ditch. But I was a landowner and any offence to my person would have been a great insult to the Albanians so I decided to accept the offer and put myself in the hands of the God of the Christians.

I said farewell to the sheikh and the dervishes, and embraced the bey who intended to spend the night there, perhaps to pray at the grave of Durballi. I then mounted the stallion and set off with a young Albanian who accompanied me in order to take the horse back from the station. As I was riding down to the plain, the horse suddenly set off in a wild gallop, with its head raised high, its nostril flared and giving a sharp neigh. The wind whistled around me and my sword clang from my shoulder. I felt completely transformed. The turbans, the sabres, the axes, drums and cudgels, Haji Bektash and Muhammed, and Durballi with his standards and trophies! All awakened my fantasies. I found myself in another age when the passions of religious fanaticism raged over the two continents, toppling kings and generals and raising religion on high over the ruins. I looked back at the Albanian boy galloping behind me, saw his horse raging with pride and studied the plain with its sleepy villages in front of me. As we were hurtling down from the *tekke* where the sheikh had girded me with a scimitar and had blessed my banner, I thought for a moment that I was setting out to conquer new kingdoms.

[Andreas Karkavitsas, 'Thessalikai Eikones: O Tekke ton Bektasidon', *Hestia*, Athens, 15 March 1892, pp. 161–165. Translated by Robert Elsie.]

1895
ANTONIO BALDACCI
ALBANIAN WANDERINGS

The Italian scholar, botanist and geographer Antonio Baldacci (1867–1950) was born in Bologna. He first travelled to the Balkans in 1885 on an expedition to Montenegro and carried out serious field research in the southern Balkans from the end of the nineteenth century onwards. In addition to many articles on Albanian and Balkan flora, he is remembered for the monograph 'Itinerari albanesi, 1892–1902, con uno sguardo generale all' Albania e alle sue communicazioni stradali' (Albanian Wanderings, 1892–1902, with Special Attention to Albania and Its Road Network), Rome 1917, from which the following notes on the Bektashi are taken.

The soldiers that Turkey had set to guard the Zygos region were part of the military division deployed in Janina. This division had recently been reinforced by troops sent from the main army corps in Monastir (Bitola) and Salonica. Among these 'Anatolians' there were a lot of Albanian soldiers. I will never forget the reception I was given by these soldiers of the Crescent Moon. They insisted that I try the *pilaf* they had made for dinner. Then we had coffee, and in the end, the oldest of the soldiers brought an apple out of his box for me that he had been keeping like a treasure, as a treat for some infidel guest.

Among the Albanians there were some Bektashi. This Islamic religious order is not well known. It is veiled in an aura of mystery and is thus inaccessible both to Westerners and to Christians living in the Orient. In their regions of Berat, Tepelena and Gjirokastra, where I lived in the years around 1894, I was unable to penetrate the psychology of the Bektashi, although I was more attracted to and interested in them and their social structure than in the *çetas* (as the Turks call the *komitadji* and *antarti*). The Bektashi are striking in appearance. 'Anyone who has been to Albania,' says Enrico Insabato, 'can distinguish them immediately by the characteristic sugar bread headdress divided into segments like a melon, that is to say, into twelve segments that some say represent the imams who succeeded Muhammed and others say represent the Apostles of Issa (may Allah give them his blessing), i.e. of the prophet Jesus.'

In the doctrine of the Bektashi brotherhood one often comes upon undeniable Christian ideas and practices that make them look like heretics in the eyes of strict orthodox Muslims. They keep the dogma of the trinity (composed of Allah, Muhammed and Ali). In the weekly gatherings held in their *tekkes*, they eat ritual evening meals consisting of bread, cheese and wine, although the latter is forbidden in Islam.

They also practise confession and some of them practise celibacy, although Muhammed strictly forbade this religious practice.

The Bektashi make up almost all of the Muslim population in the Vilayet of Janina. They are to be encountered in good numbers and are visibly present in Berat, Tirana, Shkodra, Elbasan, Korça, Skopje (Uscub), Prizren and Gjakova, areas in which their major convents are to be found. Aside from this order, Insabato stated that Albania also has a Melami order which is a secretive grouping that spread through Albania half a century ago as a result of propaganda spread by an Arab sheikh. He was a well-educated, indeed saintly figure, with characteristics that enabled him to gather many followers around him. This sheikh preached fraternity among men, and explained to his closest disciples, when he was of the opinion that they were sufficiently initiated in the doctrine, that external rituals were only of use for the uneducated, that everything had one single origin, and that there was no need for a caliphate to give spiritual direction to the believers. This revolutionary doctrine, although preached to a very small number of initiates, soon became public and, on orders from the sultan, the sheikh was arrested and taken to Constantinople where he was subjected to an investigation by the *ulema*, i.e. an official religious commission.

However, his profound knowledge of theology saved him and he returned safe and sound to Albania to continue his mission. Of course, when he died, the persecution of the adepts of the Melami sect began again because there were many liberals, free thinkers and Albanian patriots among them.

By that time, all of them had adhered to the Bektashi because they were considered to be the most liberal and advanced of the orders. As a result, this faith was also subjected to the wrath and persecution of the Turkish government, but once the Melami were gone, the Bektashi were left in peace. The Turkish saying, *çikti Melamiler kurtuldu Bektaşiler* (When the Melami were gone, the Bektashi were left in peace), is very common in Albania.

Of course, such persecution forced the Melami to go into hiding and their order transformed itself into a truly secret society. When the Albanian nationalists, working hand in hand with the Young Turks, began preparing an uprising against Abdul Hamid, the Bektashi and Melami were among their most enthusiastical supporters. [...]

My Bektashi companion from Cukarela (as the Vlachs call Peristeri) was a gentle and easy-going fellow and I had confidence in him. He wanted me to be his friend even after death. I thanked him for his kind thoughts that were the expression of a pure mystic friendship. [...]

Aside from him, there was an Albanian Bektashi with us, and an Anatolian called Van who told me that in these regions he could only send letters back to his family once every five to six months. I noted the great difference between these two types of soldiers from the extreme opposite corners of the Empire. The Albanian showed a lively spirit and the intelligence of the Arian race, whereas the Semitic Asian was taciturn and mystical. They represented two opposite civilisations linked by one faith to which, in my candid view, the Albanian seemed to be less devoted than the Asian. [...]

The fruitful results of my 1895 expedition to southern Epirus, which at that time was under Turkish administration, and to the neighbouring regions of the northern district of the Tsumerca and the valleys of the upper Arta and Aspropotamo, enabled me to undertake another journey in the summer of 1896 to explore Janina, Përmet, Konitsa, Leskovik and Samarina, with particular interest in the mountain regions of Nemërçka, Vradeton and Pindus.

I arrived in Saranda from Brindisi on the Austrian Lloyd steamer, the Euterpe, at 10:30 on the morning of 6 June after a good crossing. The low-lying fog on the calm water prevented us from seeing the Acroceraunian region, except for the snow-covered peaks of Qora and Çika in lower Himara. The other travellers onboard were companions of Skrjabin, the Russian consul in Janina, and several notables from Delvina, a total of eight to ten people who disembarked at Saranda.

I was met at the wharf by Beqir, the Muslim kavass of the Italian consulate general in Janina, whom Commander Millelire, whose guest I was soon to be again, had sent to pick me up. I had known Beqir, a Tosk Epirot, since 1888, and had met him on my travels last year, too. He was a tall, good-looking fellow with long moustaches. He loved to wear the Albanian costume of Epirus, the most characteristic element of which was the white fustanella, perhaps a remnant of the dress of ancient Mycenae. In his sash he carried weapons with engraved silver handles, some in filigree, objects that have become very rare nowadays. In short, I met Beqir again, the very same good and hearty fellow, a year after our last meeting. [...]

On 3 July we set off to explore the springs of the Sarandoporos. We were up early, ready for the excursion before 5 AM. [...] This river, which marks the border between the *kazas* of Leskovik and Konitsa, carries much water throughout the year, even during the worst of the drought season. To its right, the population, made up of Christians and Muslims, has strong Albanian sentiments, the more so when you advance in a northern or northeasterly direction, whereas the more you go southwards, the Grecophile population predominates over the Albanian. Among the Muslims of this region there are many Bektashi who have numerous *tekkes* and much property here. The Muslims of this region make up one of the most active groups supporting Albanian nationalism. The same is true of the Albanian-speaking Christians who, despite their religion, provide considerable support for the Albanian national question. The Orthodox of Leskovik, Përmet, Kolonja and Korça keep to the beliefs of their elders, despite constant and futile attempts by Greek propaganda to denationalise them. [...]

These Albanians are working quietly for their autonomy and for Albanian independence, even though their activities are not recognised by the international community, the attention of which is usually restricted to momentary happenings. But they do not waver, and continue to work for their fatherland. The Albanians in this region have created important and prosperous colonies in America and Europe that hold and feed the torch of their ideals. [...]

I fondly remember the Albanians of Konitza, Filat [Filiates], Paramythia and Preveza who hold the national spirit high and detest the government in Istanbul. In their spirits are legends and in their hands they brandish their swords, calling for unity against the occupiers and against all the enemies of Albania. Albanian national spirit is perhaps strongest here in this magnificent region where the country is in contact with the neighbouring Vlachs. Here there is no sign of despair as there is in the other regions under Ottoman administration.

[Excerpt from Antonio Baldacci, *Itinerari albanesi (1892-1902) con uno sguardo generale all' Albania e alle sue communicazioni stradali* (Rome: Reale Società Geografica Italiana, 1917), pp. 215-217, 221-222, 238-240. Translated from the Italian by Robert Elsie.]

1896
NAIM FRASHËRI
THE BEKTASHI NOTEBOOK

Naim bey Frashëri (1846–1900) was a major protagonist of the Albanian national awakening at the end of the nineteenth century. He is also regarded by many as the Albanian national poet. Frashëri was a member and supporter of the Bektashi religious community. The following 'Bektashi Notebook,' published in 1896, is not only a profession of faith on his part, but a document of historical and cultural significance for the Bektashi community and for the Albanian national awakening.

The Bektashi believe in the great and true God, in Muhammed Ali, Hatije and Fatima, and in Hasan and Husein.

The twelve Imams are Ali, Hasan, Husain, Zein-el-Abidin, Muhammed Bakir, Jafer Sadik, Musa Kiazim, Ali Riza, Muhammed Teki, Ali Neki, Hasan Askeri and Muhammed Mehdi.

The father of all the Bektashi is Ali and their mother is Fatima. They believe in all the virtues of present and past. In particular, they believe in goodness and worship it. In addition to these, they also believe in Musa [Moses], Merjeme [Mary], Isa [Jesus] and their servants.

Foremost among them is Jafer Sadik and their forefather is Haji Bektash Veli who is of the same family. All the above-mentioned have said: 'Do good and abstain from evil.'

These words are the essence of the Bektashi faith.

Truth, justice, wisdom and all virtues reign in this faith. The faith of the Bektashi is a broad path leading to enlightenment: wisdom, brotherhood, friendship, love, humanity and all virtues. This path is covered on the one hand by the flowers of wisdom and on the other hand by the flowers of truth.

No one can be a genuine Bektashi without wisdom, truth and brotherhood. For the Bektashi, the universe is God himself. In this life, man is a representative of God. The good deeds of man reveal the True God, the angels, paradise and all virtues. Bad deeds reveal the devil, hell and all vices. Therefore he must love and devote himself to blessed virtues, and must despise and reject damned vices.

All things are in man, even the True God himself. When he wanted to reveal himself, God created man in his image.

The Bektashi believe that man does not die, but only changes and is made different, and he is always near to God, for the father is hidden in the son.

Those who do good, find good. Those who do evil, find evil. Those who depart from humanity, show themselves to be beasts.

The path of the Bektashi is open and straightforward. It is a path of wisdom and goodness for those who understand it.

Man is not bound, but is free in all things. He is responsible for all of his deeds.

He has a mind that reasons, knowledge to choose, a soul that understands, a heart that discerns, and a conscience that weighs all of his deeds. As such, he has everything that he requires and has no need to seek help elsewhere, since God has given him everything he needs.

Men and women are equal and do not divorce.

In a case of great misfortune, a man may divorce his wife, and in a case of great need, he may take a second wife.

The farther a woman is away from her family, the better it is for her to follow the path of the Bektashi so as not to give any motive for vice.

Women do not veil and cover themselves, except with the veil of modesty and honour. The path of the Bektashi is that of modesty and honour, humanity, wisdom and all virtues.

All evil deeds, all vices, follies, faithlessness and cunning are proscribed and accursed on this path. It is the path of God and of all good men.

As a testament of their faith, the Bektashi have the universe and especially mankind, because Lord Ali once said: 'Man is a testament that speaks. Faith is a word, but the ignorant have added hereto. Faith is in the breast, it is not a written charter.'

The Bektashi keep their hearts, their souls, their minds and their conscience clean and unblemished, as they do their bodies, their clothes, their homes, their honour and their esteem.

They are brothers and one in soul not only with other Bektashi, but with all mankind. They love other Muslims and Christians as they do their own souls, and they strive for good relations with all mankind.

Yet above all, they love their country and their countrymen. This is the finest of all virtues.

The Bektashi love mankind, they help the poor, they show pity and compassion in their hearts, and they are of good spirit, because this is the path. If it were not like this, it would not be the path.

To be well on the path, the Bektashi must be perfect in all things. All who are on the path are called Bektashi and need nothing more.

But those who wish to draw nearer, may be consecrated [may take the hand] and become initiates.

An initiate must be a particularly good person.

Those of the initiates who wish to take the habit and become 'poor dervishes' [*varfa*], as they are called, are consecrated [take the hand] once again.

Thereafter, they cannot take the habit off again. This is not allowed. A poor dervish must be a servant of mankind and must be very wise and gentle. He must be modest and submissive. Should he be cursed or struck by someone, he must not moan or say a word, but show patience.

If a poor dervish was married before taking the habit, he can stay at home with his family. If he vows that he will not marry, he is consecrated again. Once he has made this vow, he can never renege on it. Poor unmarried dervishes live in a house called a *tekke* [*teqe*] or *dergah*.

They have a chief, who is called a Father [*atë*] or Guide [*udhërrëfenjës*]. Every poor dervish has a job or carries out a service of his own.

The greatest among them is called a Leader [*shpënës*] because he leads to the Guide those who wish to take his hand. If there are many Fathers, they chose one from among them as their superior. He is called the Grandfather [*gjysh*].

Up to here is enough, and the topic of the path is now complete.

But it can happen that there are many Grandfathers, so they chose one from among them as their Great-grandfather [stërgjysh].

For someone to become an initiate or for an initiate to become a poor dervish, he must be consecrated [must take the hand]. For a poor dervish to take a vow of celibacy and become a Father [atë], he must be initiated by the Grandfather. Fathers, Grandfathers and Great-grandfathers, as these Guides are called, must be perfect in all things pertaining to the path.

Those who take the hand of the Guide join the ranks of the Virtuous for all virtues are hand in hand together. Accordingly, they enter the circle and the ranks of these great men.

As such, those who enter upon the path leave all vices behind them and keep only the virtues. With an impure heart, an evil soul and a bad conscience, they cannot sneak into the ranks of the Virtuous, who are closer to God.

For this, they must know themselves, since those who understand themselves, know what God is. They must be gentle as a lamb, not like a wild beast.

They must be reasonable, just, learned, benevolent and have all the virtues that are necessary for a man.

This path is the path of virtue, of friendship, of wisdom and of brotherhood.

It is a great sin to enter upon this path of beautiful, fragrant flowers, and to scatter thorns, thistles, stones and rubbish upon it, as the ignorant do.

For this path begins with virtue and ends in virtue.

The Guide who consecrates says: 'Today you have taken the hand of the Lord and have joined the virtuous. Therefore take up virtue, keep on their path and forget your sins. Do not take if you have not given. Honour great and small. Avoid malice, uncleanliness, evil and all vice, and enter into goodness and brotherhood, etc. etc.'

For a Bektashi, the wife of his neighbour is his sister, a wretched old woman is his mother, a poor man is his brother, and all men are his friends. He is a man of good character, his heart is full of compassion, he has a gentle spirit, and his path is virtue alone. Without these things, no Bektashi can exist.

The lights of this path are brotherhood, peace, love, compassion, nearness to God, friendship, good conscience and all virtues.

Above all else, love is nearness to God and prayer on this path. In addition to this, the Bektashi have a type of fasting and prayer.

The fasting is a reflexion of their mourning for the events of Kerbela, being the first ten days of the lunar month of Muharrem.

Some do not drink water during these days, but this is superfluous because it was only on the evening of the ninth day that the fighting came to an end and on the afternoon of the tenth, Imam Husain fell as a martyr with his men. It was only then that they were without water. For this reason, the period of mourning is kept for ten days, but abstention from water is practised only from the evening of the ninth day to the afternoon of the tenth day. But whoever wishes, may abstain from water during the period of mourning, too. This shows the love that the Bektashi have for all virtues.

They also have a prayer called *niyas* which the wise rarely perform, but the others perform a bit more often. This prayer may also be performed in a house of worship, called a mosque. Another prayer, called *namaz*, may also be performed there, since the Bektashi do not refuse to perform it, nor do they refuse to carry out the lunar monthly fast called Ramadan or any other religious duty since they are all necessary for mankind.

The servant of the house of worship carries out betrothals and marriages, buries the dead and performs all of his services and duties.

Before and after a meal, the Bektashi say: 'True God! Increase and multiply, for you nourish and protect the universe. All good things come from you. You gave life to man and all the beasts. May we never lack your goodness and mercy!'

'Great God! Muhammed Ali! The Twelve Imams! All good men! Haji Bektash Veli! To you we give thanks.'

At feasts and weddings, they say: 'Great and True God! Give and increase your favour to mankind. Do not send upon us sorrow, grief and misery. Grant us all good things!'

'Show us the path of righteousness and leave us not in darkness. Praised be your name now and for evermore. Lord Muhammed Ali! Hatije! Fatima! Hasan and Husein! Haji Bektash Veli! All you good ones, to you we give thanks!'

At betrothals they say: 'True God! At your command and in your name! Grant us unity and love. Give us your blessing and deliver us from evil. Grant us plenty and all good things!'

'In the name of Daut [David] and Sulejman [Solomon]! In the name of Harun [Aaron] and Musa [Moses]! In the name of Merjeme [Mary] and Husain! In the name of Haji Bektash Veli! In the name of all our Lords!'

'On the path of Muhammed Ali! In the teachings of Imam Jafer Sadik!'

At weddings, the following words are added: 'Unite these two as you united Adam and Eve, Muhammed and Hatije, Ali and Fatima! Grant them a long life, and good and obedient children. May their door be open forever, etc.'

At funerals they say: 'Great and True God! You turn day into night and night into day. You separate the living from the dead and the dead from the living. All things come from you and all things return to you again. Forgive the sins of mankind for your glory's sake. And lead us to the light, for you are the light of light. To you we give thanks evermore, etc.'

As such, the Bektashi need no foreign languages for matters of the path. The Bektashi mourn only with their tears, never with dirges and wailing.

They do not bury their dead immediately. They mourn in their hearts and speak well of the dead, saying: 'May his soul shine and may it be filled with joy!'

The path of the Bektashi holds all men, yes, all men, as friends and looks on them as one body and one soul.

These things are known by the educated Bektashi and by those who have reason.

The true Bektashi treat the religions of all men with respect and treat all men as their beloved brothers. They never look upon them as strangers.

They reject no religion, but respect them all, nor do they reject their holy books and the afterlife.

As feasts days, the Bektashi keep the first Bayram, which is the first day of the lunar month called Sheval, and the second Bayram which is on the tenth day of the lunar month called Dilhije. New Year's Day, called Novruz, is on the tenth day of March and the eleventh of the lunar month called Muharrem. During the ten days of mourning, they read the stories of the Imams.

Nonetheless, every day belongs to God and is good and excellent for the Bektashi.

The Guides, who worship the truth and goodness and reject deceit and evil, and who regard all of mankind as their beloved children on the path of Muhammed Ali, must be men of great intelligence and wisdom, with adequate learning, for the unlearned and the untrained are like unhewn wood. The unlettered is like a simpleton.

The Guides must be true men, without failings as we find nowadays, men of very high qualities, men who forsake greed, pride, anger and folly, who forsake intoxication and gluttony, and who reject lies, injustice and all evils that are outside the path of humanity.

May they strive day and night for that nation that calls them father and swears by them. May they work together with the notables and the elders for the salvation of Albania and the Albanians, for knowledge and culture for their people and their fatherland, for their language and for all progress and well-being, etc., etc.

May they bring peace to mankind and look after the poor. May they shun evil and folly. May they put on the proper path all that is needed for mankind and for religion, and bring about goodness, etc, etc.

Together with the elders and notables, may they encourage love, brotherhood, unity and friendship among all Albanians, that they not be divided among one another, that Christians and Muslims be together as one. May they make all things prosper so that the Albanian, who was once reputed throughout the world, be not despised today.

None of these things are difficult for those who use their brains and who think and work willingly and intelligently. They can be accomplished very easily.

When they accomplish these things, I will call them Fathers and Guides: but today I cannot call them so.

> Great and True God,
> And all you men of virtue,
> Do not leave us alone in misery,
> In flight and in the dark.
> Rather, grant Albania
> Fortune and freedom,
> Bliss instead of suffering,
> And all good things.
> Give Albania light,
> True God, that it may see

And understand goodness,
That it may know the truth.
Grant it unity and consolidation,
Courage and wisdom,
Dominion and salvation,
Faith and brotherhood.
May it be rid of its shackles,
So that it can live in honour, As a reigning lord,
Master of its own fate.

[From Naim Frashëri, *Fletore e Bektashinjet* (Bucharest 1896), pp. 3–17. Translated from the Albanian by Robert Elsie.]

1901
ALEXANDRE DEGRAND
THE LEGEND OF SARI SALTIK

Baron Jules Alexandre Degrand (1844–1911) was born in Paris and joined the French foreign service. From 1893 to 1899 he served as French consul in Shkodra. Degrand was especially interested in the history of the region, in particular its prehistory and antiquity, and visited fortresses, mediaeval churches and ruins, noting what he saw and what he was told by the people he spoke to. Two years after his departure from Albania, he published his 'Souvenirs de la Haute- Albanie' (Memories of High Albania), Paris 1901, a well-documented description of northern Albania of the period, that includes much material on the Bektashi and, in particular, a good account, given here, of the legend of Sari Saltik.

Of all the famed Bektashi dervishes that the inhabitants of Kruja are proud to have sheltered within their walls, none is better known than Sari Saltik, who was the protagonist of wondrous adventures.

In Kruja, there was once a Christian prince who had a charming daughter. He would have been the happiest father and prince, had it not been for a dragon, a terrible and immense monster which housed in a cave on the top of the mountain, where it spent the nights. In the daytime, the dragon took up residence in the ruins of a church that it seemed to guard. In order to protect the country from the attacks of the monster that they have failed to kill, the people were forced to offer it one inhabitant of the town per day, as food for the monster. The victims were chosen by lots.

One day, a venerable old man turned up in Kruja. He was dressed in the robes of a dervish and had a long white beard that drooped to his chest. The old man was girded with a wooden sword and bore the branch of a cypress tree in his hand. He entered a coffee shop and sat down all by himself. No one paid any attention to him as they were all upset at the fate of the prince's daughter who had been chosen for the next day. She was about to set off up the mountain, from which no one had ever returned.

The next morning, the old man set off on the path up the mountain, and met up with the young girl who was in tears. 'Why are you crying, my girl?' he asked. She told him the story of the dragon and the pledge her father had sworn that had made a victim of her. 'Do not weep,' replied the old man. 'We will go together. I will not leave you alone.' She followed him, moaning and groaning. After a while, they stopped for a rest and he said to her: 'Young girl, my hair is full of lice. I can't stand it any longer. Could you remove them for me?' She unwillingly assented. The old man sat down and placed his head in her lap and, although she did not like the job, she began removing the lice from his hair. The dervish fell asleep but was awakened by a tear that fell from her cheek. 'Don't cry,' he said. 'We will continue our journey.'

They soon reach the summit of the mountain. The fiery breath of the monster had singed and parched everything around them, and the air was burning hot. Such was the heat that the maiden began complaining of thirst. Thereupon, the old man plunged his staff into the cliff and out gushed a spring of water. After they had quenched their thirst, the old man advanced through the rubble that turned to mud in the heat and stuck to his feet. He told the girl to walk right behind him. Having caught sight of him, the monster tried to pull him out of the rocks, but the mud kept him put. The girl clung to him from behind.

'Now it is my turn,' he cried. Brandishing his wooden sword and extracting himself from the mud, he chased the dragon into the cave, lopped off its seven heads, and stuck the tips of its seven tongues into his pocket. Some say that when he slew the dragon, he seized it by the tail and hurled it northwards. The beast fell to earth at a place called Lesh (which means 'carrion' in Turkish) and is the Turkish word for Lezha.

With the exploit accomplished, they returned to town, each going his own way. Great was the joy of the people when they heard that the monster had been slain. The princess explained to her father how she had been saved. In his rapture, the father announced that he would give his daughter in marriage to the man who could prove that he had saved her. Many candidates came forth, each of whom stated that he had slain the monster. They brought parts of reptiles with them to prove it. But the girl just stood there in silence beside her father, with three apples in her hands.

The father then asked if perchance any strangers were in town and was told that people had seen an old man sitting by himself in the back of a coffee shop. He was brought to the palace and everyone made fun of him as he passed. As soon as she saw the old man, the princess gave him one of her apples. All the people shouted at him and told him that he had received his reward and should now go away. The princess then offered him a second apple. 'It cannot have been this old man,' cried the suitors. The princess then placed the third apple in his hands and said to her father: 'This is the man who saved me.'

The old man was satisfied that the truth had come out and showed the prince the tips of the seven tongues, saying: 'We dervishes do not marry women against their will. Keep your daughter and your treasures. Allow me only to live in the dragon's cave and have a bit of food brought up to me every day.'

'Agreed,' responded the prince, 'but on condition that you get rid of the monster's remains that are rotting and beginning to poison the land.'

The old man set off for the cave and, drawing his formidable wooden sword, struck a hole in the cliff that swallowed the remains of the dragon. There he lived for several years all by himself. Although he lived in peace and quiet, some people, in particular those in the prince's retinue, began to fear him. 'That old man,' they said, 'slew the dragon and made a hole in the cliff with this wooden sword. He could very easily kill us, too. He is a danger. We must get rid of him.'

One morning, the man in charge of bringing him his food arrived with a watermelon and wept, crying: 'Run away. They are coming to get you. They are going to kill you. They will be here any moment now.' Using his knife to carve up the watermelon, the dervish responded: 'I will leave them this in remembrance of me!' He then threw the watermelon into the air and it stuck to the roof of the cave. A mule then appeared. He mounted it and vanished right through the cliff.

When the dervish reached the top of the mountain, he got off the beast and, in four great strides, reached Corfu. The first step he took was in Kruja, the second was in Shijak, and the third was in Durrës. *Tekkes* were built in each of these places where the traces of his footsteps in the stone are objects of great veneration. He is said to have died in Corfu.

[Excerpt from: Alexandre Degrand, *Souvenirs de la Haute-Albanie* (Paris 1901), pp. 236–240. Translated from the French by Robert Elsie.]

1901
SIR ARTHUR EVANS
A PILLAR CULT AT THE SHRINE OF TEKIJA NEAR SKOPJE

Sir Arthur Evans (1851–1941) was a British archaeologist renowned for his discovery in 1900–1903 of the Minoan ruins of Knossos on the island of Crete. Less known is his passionate interest in the Balkans, as evinced not only by his publication 'Antiquarian Researches in Illyricum' (London 1885–1996), republished as 'Ancient Illyria: An Archaeological Exploration' (London 2006). In the late nineteenth century, he visited the Bektashi tekke of Tekija east of Skopje.

In the course of some archaeological investigations in upper Macedonia, I heard of a sacred stone at a Turkish village called Tekekiöi,[29] between Skopia and Istib, which was an object of veneration not only to the native Moslems, but to many Christians from the surrounding regions, who made it an object of pilgrimage on St. George's day. In company with my guide, a Mohammedan Albanian, I visited the spot and found that the stone was contained in a two-roomed shrine under the charge of a Dervish. There was here, in fact, a mosque, or *'mesgeda'* in the oldest sense of the word, as a shrine of pre-Islamic stone-worship, like that containing the pillar form of the God of Bostra.

For a better understanding of the ritual employed, I went through the whole ceremony myself. A roomy mud-floored ante-chamber, made for the convenience of the worshippers, communicated by an inner doorway with the shrine of the stone itself. The 'holy of holies' within was a plain square chamber, in the centre of which rose the sacred pillar. Like the bactylic stones of antiquity, it might be said to have 'fallen from heaven,' for, according to the local legend, it had flown here over a thousand years since from Khoressan.[30] The pillar consisted of an upright stone of square section with bevelled angles about 6½ feet high and 1¼ feet thick, supporting another smaller and somewhat irregular block. Both were black and greasy from secular anointing, recalling the time-honoured practice of pouring oil on sacred stones as Jacob did at Bethel.[31] On one side of this 'Niger Lapis' is a kind of sunken hearth-stone, upon which are set candlesticks of antique form for the nightly illumination of the stone – a distant reminiscence of the Phoenician candlestick altars and cressets, such as those seen on either side of the cone of Paphos upon some well-known coin-types. On the other side of the pillar is a small stone base, on which the votary stands for his prayers and ritual observances. The floor is strewn with the fleeces of sacrificed rams, and on the walls are suspended triangular plait-work offerings made of ears of corn, placed here by votaries who desire to draw forth from the Spirit of the stone a beneficent influence on their crops.

Taking his stand on the flat stone by the pillar, the suppliant utters a prayer for what he most wishes, and afterwards embraces the stone in such a way that the finger tips meet at its further side. A sick Albanian was walking round the pillar when I first saw it, kissing and embracing it at every turn. The worshipper who would conform to the full ritual now fills a keg of water from a spring that rises near the shrine – another primitive touch, and makes his way through a thorny grove up a neighbouring knoll, on which is a wooden enclosure surrounding a Mohammedan Saint's Grave or *Tekke*.[32] Over the headstone of this grows a thorn-tree hung with rags of diverse colours, attached to it – according to a wide-spread primitive rite – by sick persons who had made a pilgrimage to the tomb. The turbaned column itself represents in aniconic shape the visible presence of the departed Saint, and, conjointly with the thorn-bush, a material abode for the departed Spirit, so that we have here a curious illustration of the ancient connexion between Tree and Pillar worship.

In the centre of the grave was a hole, into which the water from the holy spring was poured, and mixed with the holy earth. Of this the votary drinks three times,[33] and he must thrice anoint his forehead with it. This draught is the true Arabian *solwān*, or 'draught of consolation.'[34]

It was now necessary to walk three times round the grave, each time kissing and touching with the forehead the stone at the head and foot of it. A handful of the grave dust was next given to me, to be made up into a triangular amulet and worn round the neck. An augury of pebbles, which were shuffled about under the Dervish's palms over a hollowed stone, having turned out propitious,[35] we now proceeded to the sacrifice. This took place outside the sepulchre enclosure, where the Priest of the Stone was presently ready with a young ram.[36] My Albanian guide cut its throat, and I was now instructed to dip my right hand little finger in the blood and to touch my forehead with it.

The sacrifice completed, we made our way down again to the shrine, while peals of thunder rolled through the glen from the Black Mountain above. It was now necessary to divest one's self of an article of clothing for the Dervish to wrap round the sacred pillar, where it remained all night. Due offerings of candles were made, which, as evening drew on, were lit on the sunken hearth beside the stone. We were given three barley corns to eat, and a share of the slaughtered ram, of which the rest was taken by the priest and was set apart for our supper in the adjoining antechamber. Here beneath the same roof with the stone, and within sight of it through the open doorway, we were bidden to pass the night, so that the occult influences due to its spiritual possession might shape our dreams as in the days of the patriarchs.

[Excerpt from Arthur J. Evans: 'Mycenaean Tree and Pillar Cult and Its Mediterranean Relations', *Journal of Hellenic Studies*, 21 (1901), pp. 201–204.]

1904
EDITH DURHAM
A VISIT TO THE BEKTASHI TEKKE OF PËRMET

On 30 March 1904, the British writer and traveller Mary Edith Durham (1863–1944) came across a Bektashi tekke in Përmet during her journey from inland Macedonia, where she had been doing relief work, to the Albanian coast, and invited herself in.

I sallied forth again, this time with a young Albanian officer, a cheery youth most anxious to show off his country.

We proceeded to explore things Moslem. In a little garden, hedged round by towering cypresses, lay the tomb of a holy Bektashite Dervish; here the good man had lived and died, and the spot is holy and works miracles. He was beheaded and died a martyr, but he picked up his head and carried it back to his garden. Of the respect in which he was held there was no doubt, for the grave was strewn with small coins, and a little wooden money-box was hung on the wall, and the spot was quite unprotected, save by the good man's spirit. Seeing that I was interested, the young officer, no doubt a Bektashite himself, at once offered, to my great surprise, to take me to a 'tekieh' (Bektashite monastery) that lay high on the hillside, above the town – a rich tekieh, so he said, owning wide lands and sunny vineyards.

It was a small, solid, stone building with a courtyard in front. At the entrance we waited while the officer went in to interview the 'Baba' (Father). My Christian guide doubted that we should be let in. We were, however, requested to go round to the back-door, and soon told the Baba was ready. In we went, to a bright little room with a low divan round it, and texts in Arabic on the walls, and big glass windows that commanded a grand view of all the valley.

The Baba entered almost at once, a very grave and reverend signor in a long white robe; under which he wore a shirt with narrow stripes of black, white, and yellow; on his head a high white felt cap, divided into segments like a melon, and bound round by a green turban; and round his waist a leathern thong fastened by a wondrous button of rock crystal, the size and shape of a large hen's egg, segmented like the cap and set at the big end with turquoises and a red stone. He was very dark, with piercing eyes, shaggy brows, gray hair, and a long beard.

Courteous and dignified, he thanked me for visiting a humble Dervish, and prayed that the Lord would protect me now and always, and teach me much upon my journey. He seemed to imagine I was on some sort of mysterious quest. I regretted deeply that I could not talk with him direct, as he sat there and expressed religious sentiments with impressive dignity.

'A man,' he said, 'must always do his duty, though he never lived to see the results. Those that come after him will benefit by his work. But we are all born either with a good or a bad nature. It is our fate. A man, though he work ever so hard, his work is vain if his nature be bad.'

He asked a good many questions about my journey, and seemed genuinely pleased to see me. After he had given us coffee he said that, as it was the first time I had ever visited a Bektashite tekieh, perhaps I should like to see all the building.

There were two other small dwelling-rooms. A priest and a pupil lived with him; their life, as I could see, was very simple, he said. They had many men to till the fields and make the bread. Giving bread to the needy was one of the duties of the monastery.

He led us to the kitchen, a fine room with a huge fire-place, arched over by a stone vault carried on four columns. Rows and rows of great loaves were laid out on benches, and more were being made.

Lastly, he showed the chapel. Of this I had but a passing glimpse from the doorway, for he did not invite me to enter. It had a divan round three sides of it, and an altar with candlesticks at one end, and was quite unlike a mosque.

When we left he showed us out at the front-door, shook my hand three times, said a long blessing over me, and hoped that I should be led that way again. I thanked him and he thanked me, and we parted. The young officer was greatly pleased with the success of the visit, and appeared to reverence the Baba greatly.

[Excerpt from: Edith Durham, *The Burden of the Balkans* (London 1905), pp. 270–273.]

1907
THEODOR IPPEN
A VISIT TO KRUJA

Theodor Ippen (1861–1935) was an Austrian scholar and diplomat who was born to a (baptized) Jewish family in Vienna. In 1884, he served at the Austro-Hungarian consulate in Shkodra, where, in 1887, he was appointed vice-consul. In 1895, he was made consul there. Ippen was the author of a number of German-language monographs on early northern Albanian history and ethnography, based on his travels in the region. In the early years of the twentieth century, he visited Kruja, a noted centre of the Bektashi.

We took a rough horse trail that sets off from the postal road on the plain near the sulphur baths of Ujbarz [Uji i bardhë] in the direction of Kroja [Kruja]. It led us through the beautiful and extensive high oak forest of Šperdet [Shpërdhet]. From the pass, the trail then snaked down into the gorge of the Droja River that was dashingly spanned by an old, one-arched Turkish bridge. Above the bridge, the river is so constricted by the long and narrow gorge of the Grüka Drojs [Droja Gorge] that there was only room for one narrow path along the precipitous cliffs of its left bank, which only the peasants of the nearby village of Škreta [Shkreta] lower down dare to use.

From the Droja, a steep trail winds up to Mount Krasna, on the upper slopes of which is Mali Krus [Mount Kruja] or Sarisaldik Kroja [Sari Saltik of Kruja] under the long cliffs of the limestone plateau that is visible from Skutari [Shkodra]. It is here that the old town of Kruja was founded in the folds of this natural fortress, with cliffs looming on all sides. We were captivated when we saw this unique settlement. Through the extensive growths of ancient olive trees, the light green hues of which were broken up effectively by copses of dark green cypress trees, emerged the vaulted domes of mausoleums, picturesque homes and the acropolis surrounded by high walls, with a massive clock tower and a slender minaret in striking contrast to one another.

The rows of little stone shops in the bazaar at the foot of the mountain had nothing of particular interest to offer. Much more pleasant was a walk in the park among the olive trees with its various views and lookouts, and the gravestones. The number of *tyrbes* [mausoleums] in Kruja is given as 366, most certainly an exaggeration on the part of local patriots. Not far from the bazaar is the mausoleum of Haji Hamsa Baba, surrounded by a little graveyard. The domed construction contains the wooden and silk-covered sarcophagus of the holy man who died in 940 AH. The building itself, dating from the end of the 18th century, was constructed by Kaplan Pasha Toptani in commemoration of his victory over the troops of the magnificent *serasker* and vizier of Shkodra, Kara Mahmud Pasha Bushati.

The *tyrbe* of Balim Sultan is of particular importance because solemn oaths are sworn here on the coffin of this holy man. The resting place of Shemsi Baba resembles a little house in a peaceful courtyard.

The largest burial sanctuary of the town, however, is up on the ledge of the plateau of Mount Kruja, in a crevasse in the cliffs, up through which leads a difficult, winding path over the scree. It is dedicated to Sarisaldik [Sari Saltik], the 'blond apostle.' A few steps lead down to a grating at which one is obliged to remove one's shoes. One proceeds through an antechamber containing the sarcophagi of the disciples of the saint and enters a well-tended chapel with the grave of the holy man himself. Our guide said a prayer and visitors place donations in an alms box.

All of these *tyrbes* make a vivid impression on the visitor. They transpire peace and tranquillity. The soul is filled with composure and contemplation until, with some difficulty, one comes to oneself. The appeal of the sacred surroundings is heightened all the more if a dervish or a *baba* is present to tend the grave. These men, who have withdrawn from the world, receive guests with extraordinary kindness and hospitality and offer philosophical thoughts free of any of the fanaticism that characterises and divides all of the Orient.

The *tyrbes* belong to the Muslim sect of the Bektashi. Originally, they were but a dervish order founded by Haji Veli Bektash at the beginning of the 14th century in the Anatolian province of Sivas. The establishment of the order occurred at the time of the rise of the Janissaries, and close ties grew between the two when Haji Veli Bektash gave his blessing to the first Janissaries. In remembrance of this is the hanging headdress of the warriors. It is to remind them of the broad sleeve of the blessing hand of Bektash that was laid upon their necks. The contacts between the two remained and were at the origin of the move of the order to Albania. The Janissaries originally arrived in the country to keep that unruly land in check. Gradually, they found in Albania a great reservoir of men to fill their ranks, and thus came to feel at home on the Adriatic coast. With them came the dervish order that spread its influence among increasingly large circles in the countryside and in the towns, among the notables and peasants. Despite the eradication of its armed supporters in 1826 and the bloody persecution that took place under Sultan Mahmud, wide regions still follow the Bektashi today, including the areas of Kruja, Çermenika, and the Bulčise [Bulqiza] and Okshtun valleys centred on Martanesh (not far from the source of the Mat River). In central Albania, the Bektashi have followers in the Mallakastra region, and in southern Albania in the areas of Korça, Kolonja, Leskovik, Premeti [Përmet] and Ginokastra [Gjirokastra]. In northeastern Albania, they have followers, though less in number, in Prizren, Üsküb [Skopje], Kalkandele [Tetova] and Krčovo [Kërçova/Kičevo]. The Bektashi were driven out of Shkodra at the start of the 19th century. The remnants of the Bektashi diaspora in Bosnia are cared for from Albania. Rejected by the local population, they have had no leadership and no *tekkes* (monasteries) since the death of Haji Mustafa Užičanin in Sarajevo in 1903.

The order has changed substantially over time. Founded as a strictly orthodox Muslim sect, it is now a fierce opponent and hater of official Islam, and is hated by Islam just as fiercely. Relations with the Christians, on the other hand, are peaceful. The peasants who follow the teachings of the order faithfully tend to the ruins of old churches. The orthodox Muslims spread all sorts of terrible tales about the Bektashi. Their teachings are described in the blackest of terms. They are said not to believe in redemption after death, not to be able to distinguish between good and evil, and their principal aim is to be the fulfilment of all their earthly wishes and desires.

It is impossible to verify these exaggerated and ugly accusations about Bektashi teachings, teachings that, in general, seem quite liberal, because they are kept secret and one can only draw conclusions from external appearances.

The Bektashi have no mosques. They do not observe the five daily prayers and do not carry out ritual ablutions. Prayers are carried out in silence at the graves of their holy men. Wherever there are Bektashi, one therefore finds well-kept mausoleums that can often be seen from a distance because of the cypress trees planted around them. The upkeep of the *tyrbes* is financed by donations. People travel from afar on pilgrimages to the graves of particularly honoured saints. Every Bektashi endeavours, at least once in his life, to visit the grave of Sari Saltik in Kruja. The cult of honouring the deceased leaders of their monasteries has given rise to religious veneration, and is reflected in the often amazing obedience that the Bektashi show to their living leaders.

The Bektashi do not observe Ramadan, the fasting month of the Muslims. However, they do observe the eleven days of penance in the Arabic month of Muharren, when they fast, withdraw from the world, and carry out all manner of mortification of the flesh. With this, like the Shiites, they commemorate the martyrs Hasan and Hussein, the sons of the Caliph Ali, who were killed in Kerbela near Baghdad at the orders of the Caliph Muavija.

A more detailed study of this sect that is so important for Albania remains to be carried out, but would require much more time that I have to devote to it. I will report here on my visit to a Bektashi monastery that I happened to come across.

Much of my time in Kruja was taken up visiting the fortress that is closely connected to the history of the native aristocratic Thopia family, of the struggles of Scanderbeg and of Venetian rule in Albania.

The cliffs upon which the fortress is built form a triangle rising from east to west. The walls and bastions are well preserved despite their having been partially razed in 1832. Particularly impressive are the fortifications of the gate on the northern side and the bastion to the west, on which the *tyrbe* of the Bektashi holy man, Baba Mustafa Dolma, is situated. Most of the interior of the fortress is covered in ruined and covered walls. Of older buildings, there are only the bell tower to the northeast that is now used as a clock tower and the house on the walls to the left of the gate. About twenty families live in abject poverty in the lower part of the fortress in uninteresting modern-type homes. A good example of traditional Albanian architecture is the building of the Turkish government administration that used to belong to the Toptani family and was bequeathed to the State. There is a broad loggia with columns in the middle section of the upper floor, flanked on the two sides by protruding corners. It is adorned with original, naïve frescos portraying an Oriental coastal town, no doubt Istanbul, with ships and huge fish abounding along the coastline. There is a reception room on the left side, a pleasant paneled chamber that is adorned with woodcarvings and painting. From this side, there is a wonderful view of the plains stretching down to Durazzo [Durrës] and the

Adriatic. The only thing that disturbs the tranquillity of the view is the prison in the courtyard, a large cage made of wooden beams with numerous prisoners in it, caught like animals in a menagerie.

All that I could find of antiquities were an ornamental star and two fragments of a rough relief with two animals, probably lions, lunging at one another, as well as two Turkish inscriptions, all on a fountain outside the walls when one climbs up towards the main gate. One of the inscriptions notes that the fountain was constructed in 850 AH by the Grand Vizier Gazi Evrenos. The second one concerns the restoration of the fountain in 1215.

There was a hole in one of the walls on the west side, out of which flows water from the Tasloja source. The town is named after this source, for *kru* means 'source' and *kruja* 'sources'. In Turkish, the town is known as Akçe Hisar meaning 'white fortress.'

The climb from Kruja down to the aforementioned Bektashi monastery takes one and a half hours. On the way, one passes by a little chapel called Gjurmë i shejntit meaning 'footprint of the saint,' i.e. of Baba Sari Saltik. The monastery of Tekke Fushë Kruja is situated not far from the postal road at the bottom of the hills, on the part of the plain belonging to Kruja, i.e. Fushë Kruja. Surrounded by lush green meadows, it offers an attractive though simple view. One would not guess what is to be found here, even when seeing the minaret. One has the impression of approaching the manor of some wealthy, landowning family. The monastery consists of a complex of simple, unadorned buildings with irregular, badly whitewashed facades and numerous windows of various sizes. The interior also resembles a house. We were invited up a wobbly wooden staircase to a reception room simply furnished with carpets and divans. On the walls were pictures with religious sayings in calligraphy, but also with human figures.

The dervishes, i.e. monks, were not all dressed the same. Each chooses for his garments the colours he prefers or that happen to be on sale in the bazaar. Only the headpieces were the same for all, a tall white felt cylinder without a brim. It is in the headdress that the various Muslim orders can be distinguished from one another. Each dervish wore a thick cord around his neck with a radiating star of carnelian attached to it. It is the *teslim tash* that they receive upon completion of their periods as novices. Some of them also have rows of olive-shaped, light grey opaque stones on their neck cords that come from Mesopotamia and are called *Durri Najaf*, the Pearl of Najaf, after the Shiite pilgrimage site near Baghdad.

Most of the dervishes present were young men. The older ones were away, some of them visiting other monasteries of the order, others on pilgrimages, the most popular of which was the journey to the graves of the Caliph Ali and his sons Hasan and Hussein in Mesopotamia. Others yet travelled to pay their respects to the graves of respected members and great teachers of the order. The head of a monastery holds the title *baba* 'father' although this title is also used by those who take care of mausoleums. As a sign of his rank and dignity, the *baba* wears a ring in his left ear in the form of a curious arabesque made of thick silver wire. Celibacy is required for those wishing to hold higher ranks in the order. In Fushë Kruja there were also some married dervishes who live outside the monastery.

After being offered refreshments, we were invited to have a look at the holy places of the monastery. Behind the buildings, on a meadow of blooming flowers, there was a very tall and picturesque cypress tree in the high grass and two whitewashed mausoleums – that of the founder of the monastery, Baba Ali, and that of Baba Hussein who died in 1890. The latter is also venerated as a holy man. Even during his lifetime his authority was far superior to that of the head of the *tekke* of Fushë Kruja, a highly respected man himself. All of the surrounding region beckoned to his call. Most of the room in the chapels is taken up by the sarcophaguses, five-sided in form, resting on the tiled floors. They are draped in cloth of silk and velvet, in which sayings and prayers have been embroidered and woven. Miracles can occur by touching the coffins. There is an alms box in every room. The dervishes who were with us told us that the huge cypress outside grew out of the boards with which Baba Ali had once made himself a cottage in the meadow. The legend arose as such from the particular shape of the branches of the tree. It is a *Cupressus horizontalis*. They are very large and so flat that they resemble boards and planks.

[Excerpt from: Theodor A. Ippen, *Skutari und die nordalbanische Küstenebene* (Sarajevo 1907), pp. 69-79. Translated from the German by Robert Elsie.]

1907
EKREM BEY VLORA
THE BEKTASHI ON MOUNT TOMORR

The Muslim Albanian writer and public figure Ekrem bey Vlora (1885–1964) was born in the town of Vlora as the son of one of the wealthiest landowning families of the south. His uncle, Ferid Pasha Vlora, was grand vizier during the Young Turk Revolution of 1908. He studied in Vienna and travelled extensively throughout the Ottoman Empire and Albania. Among his journeys was a visit to the Bektashi tekke on Mount Tomorr.

Some scholars who have written about Albania have attached great importance to a Muslim sect called the Bektashi, an importance that it does not merit. They have presented it as if the Bektashi were as significant as the non-Muslim population. I would like to add a few remarks about the Bektashi here so as to rectify this mistaken impression.

The Bektashi sect is one of the twelve *tarikat* of Islam. Their dogma is closer to that of the Shiites. They are different from the Sunnis in that they revere Ali more than the three other caliphs. The first imam of the Bektashi was Haji Bektash Veli who introduced the main tenets of the sect to Asia Minor around 1400. Their liberal and philosophical way of thinking allowed them to spread quickly among peoples who were not receptive to strict religious regulations, but with time, many bad habits found their way into Bektashi teachings and have given them a bad reputation. One often hears rumours in Albania of secret gathering involving orgies and the desecration of religion. I have seen no proof of this and believe, rather, that such ugly and unfounded rumours are spread by their enemies. I have, however, often noticed on my visits to their *tekkes* (monasteries) that their leaders, called *babas*, have an ability to consume *raki* that is quite unprecedented. This and other characteristics that reflect their free-thinking ways are probably the reasons why other people often do not particularly like them. I must add, however, that I have encountered very few Albanians, even among non-Bektashi, who would claim that they had never drunk *raki*.

Any negative aspect of their religion is more than adequately compensated for by their good, worldly characteristics. Their teachings encourage solidarity, which could be very important for a people like the Albanians. They call for mutual aid and in the places where they gather, their *tekkes*, they have laid the foundations for patriotic ideals and endeavours.

Each *tekke* is run by a *baba* to whom all of them offer virtually blind obedience. The *babas* are often wealthy and have much income at their disposal. Because there are less Bektashi adepts in the Sanjak of Berat than elsewhere, there is only one *tekke* in Berat and two in Skrapar, where the population is exclusively Bektashi, as it is in the southeast part of Mallakastra and in Tomorica. Among the Albanians of the *kazas* of Vlora and in Myzeqeja there are no Bektashi at all. This comes from the influence of the Vlora family that is a bulwark of the Mevlevi Order as they are said to stem from Konya. They generally dislike the Bektashi […]

We reached the peak of Mount Tomorr at 2,396 m in elevation, on which we came across a monument. This is a site of religious importance for the whole region, a place that we entered with mixed feelings. It was a circular construction of well-hewn stone blocks put together without mortar as a ring wall, and had a narrow entrance to the southeast. It is called a *mekam*, an Arabic word for a site, or more specifically a pilgrimage site. In its present form, the construction dates from the year 1880. Inside the walls there was nothing aside from a niche of rough stonework facing southwards, in which there were two candlesticks and tin plate. On the plate were a few coins donated as alms by the faithful. The *mekam* is a site that is holy both to Muslims and to Christians. Even the most unscrupulous of robbers not never dare to steal these coins. Mount Tomorr would no doubt strike them dead with a bolt of lightning.

On 15 August (old style), this desolate site comes to life for the feast of the Assumption of the Virgin Mary. It is mostly dervishes of the Bektashi Order who come here on pilgrimages to pray, sacrifice and collect alms. Among my travelling companions there were several Bektashi who only dared to penetrate the ring wall on their knees. In the battle between Imam Hussein, the son of the fourth Caliph Ali, and Yazid, according to their beliefs, the son of Muawiyah, the stepbrother of the former, called Abbas Ali (a son of Ali by another wife), managed to flee the carnage of Kerbela and after long wanderings reached the peak of Mount Tomorr which he chose as his place to die. Historically speaking, this figure is unknown.

The Christians pray here to Saint Mary, the holy virgin. Both religious communities use the oath '*për Baba Tomor!*' (by Father Tomorr!). They also believe that there was a temple here in ancient times. Our great poet, Naim bey Frashëri, mentioned it in one of his poems dealing with the history of the country:

(Herodotus said Than in ancient times The house of God Was on Tomorr.)
Thot Hérodoti, Qé nje hér moti Kish ne Tomor – Shtepi zoti.

[Excerpt from: Ekrem bey Vlora, *Aus Berat und vom Tomor. Tagebuchblätter* (Sarajevo 1911), pp. 34–35 and 106–107. Translated from the German by Robert Elsie.]

1909
MAX CHOUBLIER
THE *TEKKE* OF KALKANDELEN (TETOVA)

Max Choublier (1873-1933), from Saint Quentin in northern France, was the French vice-consul in Monastir (Bitola) in Macedonia from about 1901 to 1911. While in Macedonia he visited the tekke of Harabati Baba in Tetova on several occasions.

It was in 1909 that I got to know Ali, the *baba* as they called him, or grandfather of the *tekke* of Kalkandelen [Tetova]. He was suffering from neurasthenia at the time as the result of an overly sedentary lifestyle and an over-indulgence in coffee. With this ritual drink of the Sufis, he was endeavouring to overcome the effects of too many large doses of *raki*. For some reason, he had confidence in the medical advice I gave him, was grateful to me, and showed me kind attention. His gratitude expressed itself in particular in regular gifts of the monastery's famous apples that were as translucent as wax and were traditionally reserved for the sultan's table.

One of my visits to the *tekke* in the autumn of 1905 lasted for five days. I had never actually experienced a Bektashi monastery in a state of deprivation, and the one in Kalkandelen was quite affluent. What is rarer and virtually unique for Macedonia and northern Albania is that there was security.

Uskub [Skopje] is ten hours from Kalkandelen on horseback. After a long ride over the arid plain in the midday sun, on a dusty and desolate trail, the monastery, surrounded by withering yellow leaves, looked to me like the very abode of peace and tranquillity. It would not have been easy to enter it by force. The buildings and orchards were surrounded by high walls and over the only gateway was a balcony in the form of a terrace with parapets that gave onto a corridor between the two main buildings. The open door of the gatekeeper's room revealed five or six Martini-Henry rifles in a rack, in addition to a large old rampart gun no longer in use. Aside from this, there was nothing but peace and quiet, order and cleanliness.

To the left of the entrance, there was a pavilion over which rose a rectangular minaret. It served as a meeting place and was used for prayers. Straight ahead was a lawn and rose garden with ponds on both sides in which tamed herons stood unmoved. Around this central courtyard were the cells of the Bektashi fathers. In front of the largest of them, that of Ali Baba, there was a verandah above the ponds, and part of the wall below the verandah was covered in glazed, coloured tiles. In the evening to sunset, this was where the *baba* sat cross-legged on a white ritual lambskin.

From here he surveyed his little realm – some dervish fathers and just as many brothers with five or six initiates and about a dozen servants. The dervishes lived in separate cells, two or three of them in each, and seemed to spend most of their time in solitude in minor manual labour, this, I believe, being in conformity with the regulations of the Order.

I was given quarters in a pavilion not far from the hall where the *baba* received his guests. The main floor with the kitchen was taken up by my entourage. The upper floor consisted of a large room that served as my bedroom, sitting room and dining room because, in theory at least, I was to eat alone.

In the morning, the monks went out to work in the yard. Others drove the monastery's flocks out to the neighbouring fields. The foreheads of the cattle were dyed in henna and they wore necklaces of blue beads that preserved them from the Evil Eye. The Bektashi believe in local superstitions and the monastery's fields were protected from the Evil Eye, too, by the skulls of horses and cows stuck on poles and placed above the gateway.

Up to the gates of the *tekke* were walnut trees which the Albanians do not normally like to have near their homes because they believe such trees are inhabited by evil spirits. Anyone who falls asleep in the shade of such trees risks going blind or at least catching a fever because the two demons of Slavic origin, Samo Divi and Samo Vili, exert their nefarious influence there.

Near the last walnut trees at the foot of the mountain, at about three hundred metres from the *tekke*, there were several tombs that were assiduously kept and cared for. Among them were the tombs of venerated saints on which lamps of sacred oil were lit every night. The monastery was in general well maintained and extremely clean.

The dervishes were also impeccable in their cleanliness. Nothing in their day-to-day clothing distinguished them from other Muslims. They wore goatskin shoes that were stitched with the hide turned inwards, wide breeches buttoned up the legs, short vests hemmed in at the hips, baggy shirts, and felt caps wrapped in a length of white cloth to form a turban.

They ate normal Albanian food: cooked millet, poppy-seed bread, rice in milk or fat, fresh and dried fruits, dried fish, mutton and goat's meat, and yoghurt. To drink they had water, *boza* (millet beer) and coffee.

On feast days, they also partook of platters of sweets, creamed rice with strips of chicken meat in it, and various filled pastries. Their favourite dish was *ashureh*, a millet cream seasoned with dried fruit and served from a cauldron during the annual feast of Hajji Bektash. Invited to this feast were not only the members of the Order but the peasants of all the surrounding villages with whom they had contact. No distinction in religion was made.

The dervishes living at the *tekke* were celibate. There were a few other dervishes living in town who had married after taking their vows. They came around to the monastery for feast days and religious ceremonies. The Mevlevi dervishes of Salonica were the same, i.e. if they were married, they worked in town as handicraftsmen and merchants but attended the meetings of their order every week.

There were quite a few adepts in the surrounding villages, people who followed the faith without having sworn any special vows. Among them were Albanian peasants and small landowners not unlike French farmers with twenty to sixty hectares of land. Among the faithful were a few merchants and handicraftsmen in Kalkandelen, most of whom were rifle-makers.

The production and sale of these rifles was a curious business in which the monks were once involved. The Bektashi *tekke* itself was no doubt part and parcel of the business.

There is a street of shops under open awnings. The craftsmen who work there do so outside, but are thus protected from the elements. The iron rods that are hammered out in one shop are drilled in the second. The metalwork and woodwork continues to the last workshop where everything is assembled. In the end, customers can buy themselves Martini-Henry rifles that are quite capable of killing anyone.

Some of the beys of the surrounding region were said to be affiliated with the order and supported its ideas and interests, though they were apparently not particularly interested in the religious practices. Those of them that I met expressed the same wishes for the future of their country as Ali Baba. As the people are wont to say here, they commanded a hundred or two hundred rifles (i.e. armed men). The most powerful of them, Rustem Kabashi, commanded two thousand rifles.

The friends of the Bektashi met at the monastery. The monks themselves rarely left the compound, quite in contrast to their former pastimes. They used to visit towns and regions to beg for the monastery to the cry of Shehid Allah, and served as fortune-tellers and interpreters of dreams. They also healed the sick of all illnesses by making them drink water out of a copper cup incrusted with cabalistic signs, copper being a magic metal.

As I had not had any contact with the dervishes all that day at Kalkandelen, I went to visit the *baba* at sunset.

I found him all alone, sitting on his lambskin. We were brought coffee, cigarettes and jams. Visitors came in in silence, one after the other, including the fathers of the monastery. They greeted him and silently took their places in a fixed hierarchical order on the divan around the room. There they sat for two or three hours, but rarely took part in the conversation which, anyway, did not rise above the level of small talk until they left.

[Excerpt from: Max Choublier, 'Les Bektachis et la Roumélie', *Revue des études islamiques*, Paris, 1, 1927, pp. 428–432. Translated from the French by Robert Elsie.]

1909
GABRIEL LOUIS-JARAY
A VISIT TO THE *TEKKE* OF BABA IBRAHIM XHEFAI NEAR ELBASAN

The French travel writer Gabriel Louis-Jaray (1880-1964) visited Albania in the summer of 1909 and later in August 1919, and journeyed extensively in the country. He was present at the Albanian Congress of Elbasan in early September 1909 that was held to protest against Young Turk attitudes to Albanian-language schooling, and, while there, had occasion to visit the nearby tekke of Baba Ibrahim Xhefai.

At fifty metres from the river valley, on the southern slopes of the Krraba Mountains, is the Bektashi *tekke* of Elbasan. The buildings stretch among the lofty trees that provide the surrounding hills with verdure and shade.

Two roads come together at the foot of the Albanian monastery. One of them comes right from Elbasan, at a distance of less than three kilometres, the other one makes its way around Krasta, the little hill that rises verdant over the course of the Shkumbin River, forcing it to divert its course and serving as a spur between town and river. The valley, still narrow as it emerges from the mountains, opens up only enough to form an alluvial basin, from which Elbasan no doubt takes its name.

Those who build monasteries always seem to have a good sense of location and taste for favourable emplacements. Such is the case of this *tekke* situated at the entrance to this basin with the two roads that serve it. From the terraced slope one can see the valley of the Shkumbin to the east and the river itself to the south where it takes a sharp turn at the foot of the monastery. To the west, the river stretches on to the distant slopes bordering on fields of rice, maize and grain that dot the plain of Elbasan.

The Albanian Congress of Elbasan had just concluded. In the courtyard of the modest building in which it was held, the leaders unfurled a red flag with a crescent on it and asked me to photograph them in front of it. Then one of them, as if to thank me, said: 'I would like to show you the *tekke* nearby. You will see that it is quite charming. We would be delighted if you would visit the graves of our holy men who lie there.'

Qamil bey took me along with him. He called a friend and a servant and we left town together. We soon reached a verdant meadow behind which rose large leafy trees in the mellow sky. Behind us, the setting sun cast long fantastic shadows of us and turned the countless white gravestones to goldstones in rows like an army of tiny mausoleums. Between them walked farmers who were returning from the fields after a day of work with their donkeys, plodding ever so slowly in the evening sun. Qamil turned to me and said:

> You see, this is our cemetery. We have to cross it to get to the *tekke*. Look here at this white tombstone that was recently carved. The soil around it has not yet been tamped down because people go around it. It is the grave of a friend of mine who died last year. You can still distinguish his grave but, with time, it will be lost. There are always more and more dead coming, and more gravestones will be added to the old ones wherever there is room.

We passed among the stones of various shapes and sizes. Some had been cut by the pious, others were flat and thin like flagstones. Others still were small and left in a natural state. Some among them were carefully cut. Yet they all looked as if they have been cast at random sown by hand. Some were broken and fallen on the ground. Others were tilted in the tall grass that the cattle fed on in the graveyard.

A one-storey building appeared before us on the hillside. It was the monastery to which a tiny path led. We got there easily and Qamil presented me to the monks. There were not very many of them and the buildings at their disposal were more than sufficient. A *tekke* is a lodge of the Bektashi Order. Their religious headquarters are in Konya in Asia Minor, but their Albanian headquarters up to now have been in Kalkandelen [Tetova]. The Bektashi in Albania constitute a special order of Albanian Muslims. Their ranks are composed exclusively of Albanians and they have *tekkes* throughout the country: in Ipek [Peja], Diakovo [Gjakova], and Prizren in the north, and particularly and in greater numbers, in the south among the Tosks where they possess much land.

The genuine monks are dervishes but they are supported by Albanian beys as managers for the worldly administration of their land. The Congress of Elbasan was attended, for instance, by a bey from Kalkandelen who was the financial manager of the main *tekke* of the Bektashi there.

It is rather difficult to find out anything about the political activities of the Order. It would seem primarily to be in the service of the Albanian national cause. In former times, when the Albanians were omnipotent in Constantinople, the ministers close to the sultan used to be Bektashi. This custom disappeared in the mid-nineteenth century, in particular since the time of Sultan Mahmud, but under the reign of Abdul Hamid, the Bektashi were once again in favour with the padishah. Their rank as Muslim clerics protected them from the Young Turks, although the latter only unwillingly put up with the Albanian nationalism which the Order supported and promoted. They are invincible in Albania because the whole Muslim population – from the rich beys to the poor peasants – hold them in profound respect and unreserved veneration. In each *tekke*, the tomb of the saint serves as a venue of daily pilgrimage, and the faithful come with alms and gifts, large and small. Indeed the Order lives off the revenues from its land and the gifts of pious Muslims.

Despite the differences in religious doctrine, the form of organisation of the Muslim and Orthodox communities does not differ much. In addition to the secular clergy, i.e. the priests and hodjas who live among the faithful, participate in public life, marry and have families, both communities have a monastic element, i.e. monks who care for the shrines and tend graves that have been venerated for centuries. These monks live in convents under the direction of a leader and, with time, these convents have become focal points of nationalist fervour, centres reflecting the traditions and hopes of the people in these disputed regions of the Balkans. These convents support and encourage national sentiments.

It is the same among the Orthodox. Here, the monks, as opposed to the priests, do not marry but rather devote all their energy to nationalist propaganda and the defence of religious and national ideals.

The Bektashi, for their part, have their dervishes who, in solemn ceremonies, make vows and swear not to marry. They devote themselves to prayer and religious ceremonies, and to their work in the fields. It is their duty to care for the tombs which, in this case, was that of a great saint. His sepulchre was enclosed by a hexagonal stone construction a few metres above all the other buildings. The monks took me out to see it. On one side of the building there was a low open doorway and on the other sides there were narrow windows. I was invited into the interior where there was not really enough light to see. It contained a wooden grave in the ground covered in part by a green cloth. At the foot of the grave there were some pieces of embroidered linen and at the head there was a wooden stake planted obliquely around which a gauze veil was wrapped. That was all. There was nothing on the whitewashed walls, no inscriptions, not a word. The silence of the dead.

Leaving the *tekke*, I asked my guide if the monks came here to mediate. He responded simply: 'They don't need to because they live here.' It was difficult to pursue the conversation and I tried to imagine the state of mind of the dervishes who were accompanying me and to figure out how they differed from Western hermits. [...]

There is no element of torment or struggle in the life of Muslim monks, and the *tekke* is a place of refuge where the spirit is at rest. The sacred tomb does not cast its shadow over the existence of others, and the dervishes around me did not seem to know about anything but the beauty of the site chosen for them at the whims of the founder of the *tekke*.

The nearest one invited me to sit down under the trees looking out upon the valley where the shadows were growing longer. A table was set up and covered in grapes rinsed in fresh water and tiny cups of aromatic coffee. The day's heat had receded and the veil of night was extending up the valley dominated by the *tekke*. One of my companions, seized no doubt by memories of days gone by, broke into song, a proud and sad-sounding melody that the others took up – an Albanian song about Scanderbeg. [...]

When the melancholic song was finished, silence and tranquillity enveloped the *tekke* all the more. The wind died down and not a branch quivered. The acacia and laurel trees filled the air with their fragrance as the last rays of the sun turned the nearby vineyards to gold. Twilight is short-lived here and we had to get back to Elbasan before nightfall. But before leaving with my companions, I opened the door of the tomb and, as Albanian custom prescribes, left some alms – a few copper coins that I placed in a collection box on the wall, and several pieces of silver on the tomb itself.

The monks expressed their best wishes for a long and happy life for the 'Frank' come from overseas to visit his friends in Albania. For my part, I wished them a second Scanderbeg who would revive all the aspirations, sentiments and ideals I saw in them during the short time I spent at the Bektashi *tekke*.

[Excerpt from: Gabriel Jouis-Jaray, *Au jeune royaume d'Albanie* (Paris 1914), pp. 96–109. Translated from the French by Robert Elsie.]

1919
FREDERICK HASLUCK
THE FOURTH RELIGION OF ALBANIA

The English historian and archaeologist Frederick William Hasluck (1878–1920), born in Southgate, studied classics at King's College in Cambridge and did excavation work in Greece for the British School in Athens. He was particularly interested in the ties between Christianity and Islam in the Ottoman Empire and travelled extensively in Ottoman Greece and Albania. Of major importance to the study of the Bektashi is his two-volume Christianity and Islam under the Sultans *(Oxford 1929), published posthumously by his wife, Margaret Hasluck.*

Diversity of faith is notoriously one of the chief impediments to Albanian unity. As every student of Balkan affairs knows, the Albanians, though racially and linguistically homogeneous, are cleft by a threefold religious division. Roughly speaking, the population of the north is mixed Catholic and Mahommedan; of the south, mixed Orthodox and Mahommedan; and of the centre, predominantly Mahommedan. The extraordinary tenacity of Islam in other countries has led most people to regard the religious problem of Albania as insoluble, and the fanatical Albanian Moslem as a permanent stumbling-block in Balkan politics. It is much less generally known that there exists an important cleavage within the Mahommedan element itself. Islam the world over is divided into two irreconcilable camps, the Sunni and the Shia. The Mahommedans of southern (Tosk) Albania are to a very large extent open or secret adherents of the Bektashi sect, a mediaeval offshoot of the Shia heresy, while those of the (Gheg) centre and north hold, often fanatically, the rigid Sunni observance. It need hardly be said that the division here indicated is very rough. On the one hand, any large town may be regarded, owing to the organisation and influence of the official clergy, as a Sunni focus; on the other, Bektashism is far from unknown in the north, Croia, for example, the birthplace of Scanderbeg, being even a notable Bektashi centre.

Shia and Sunni, in Albania as elsewhere, are at daggers drawn, and the Bektashi hold, in fact, a somewhat equivocal position between the Sunni, who regard them as bad Moslems, and the Christians, who find them more open than the Sunni to ideas of tolerance. They have a further link with their Orthodox neighbours in the fact that most of them are very recent converts from Christianity, this being still remembered by both sides.

Bektashism, Anatolian in origin, seems to have been propagated in Albania, or at least to have taken considerable root there, not earlier than the second half of the eighteenth century, when several important beys, including the famous Ali Pasha of Yannina, were members of the sect. Their reasons for adherence were probably opportunist and political. Bektashism seems to have been widely organised as a society for mutual help and also for secret intelligence, the convents of the Bektashi dervishes, who form the hierarchy of the sect, being as it were the 'lodges' of the society. Of this political tendency we have fairly clear evidence in recorded history. The Pasha of Scutari when Ali reigned at Yannina refused to admit Bektashi dervishes to his province, considering them spies of Ali. The Topdan family of Croia, represented to-day by Essad Pasha of Tirana, first combined with the Bektashi, then fell out with the local sheikh, a *protégé* of Ali's, and eventually put him away; public opinion was so strongly in favour of the murdered dervish that the Topdan were driven to settle at Tirana. Croia is to-day, as we have said, a stronghold of Bektashism, while Essad Pasha Topdan is reputed a fanatical Sunni Mahommedan. It is curious to note that

"Ali's own capital, Yannina, has never possessed a Bektashi convent, the organised clergy being here, evidently, an efficient obstruction."

Among the Christian peasantry of the south, conversion to Bektashism seems to have been stimulated by persecution coincident with Russian pressure on the Porte. About the middle of the eighteenth century large mass-conversions to Islam were made in European Turkey, and in Albania particularly many converts seem to have adopted, then or later, the less rigid form of Islam offered by the sect. In point of dogma Bektashism is so lax that Christians may be admitted without renouncing their own faith; at the same time, a lax and nominal Mahommedanism was preferable from a material point of view to Christianity, and Bektashism found at this period, owing to its close connection with the Janissaries, influential backing at Constantinople.

It has thus come about that the Mahommedan element in southern Albania, largely composed of recent converts, is to be counted rather against than in favour of the cause of orthodox Islam, and in favourable circumstances might probably revert spontaneously to Christianity. Further, the laxity of Bektashi doctrine has the corresponding advantage of allowing it to adapt itself to the times. The national Albanian movement of 1880 was hatched at the Bektashi convent of Frasheri by a group of patriotic beys and dervishes, ostensibly to save to Turkey the threatened province of Yannina, but really aiming at an independent Albanian state. For the propaganda of the movement use was made of the Bektashi organisation, which thus eventually became suspect to Abdul Hamid. From this time onwards Bektashism and the national cause have been closely identified. A *rapprochement* with the young Turks at the time of the Constitution was disavowed as soon as the levelling and Ottomanising tendencies of the reformers became apparent. To-day Bektashism stands definitely for the integrity, unity and independence of Albania. It is recently reported from a good source that its propaganda has begun for these reasons to make considerable headway among the stiff-necked Sunni Ghegs; if this movement continues, Albania may be in a fair way to rid herself of one of the main moral obstacles to her national unity.

[Frederick William Hasluck, 'The Fourth Religion of Albania', *The New Europe*, 13, London, 6 November 1919, pp. 106–107.]

1921
JUSTIN GODART
THE PLACE OF THE BEKTASHI AMONG ALBANIAN RELIGIONS

Justin Godart (1871-1956) was a French parliamentarian from Lyon who served from 1906 to 1926 as the deputy for the Department of Rhone in the French National Assembly. He was a fervent supporter of Albania, in particular in the period 1920-1921, when the government and indeed the country were being reconstituted. Godart actively promoted Albania's admission to the League of Nations, in particular with his pamphlet 'Appel aux Grandes Puissances' (Appeal to the Great Powers). He visited Albania in the spring of 1921, a journey reflected in his 374-page book 'L'Albanie en 1921' (Albania in 1921), Paris 1922. On this journey he took a particular interest in the Bektashi and visited two of their tekkes: the Hajdërije tekke in Gjirokastra and the tekke of Ibrahim Xhefai Baba in Elbasan.

There is another element to the religious makeup of Albania which alleviates the sectarianism of the majority of Albanians who are Muslims and might be tempted to take advantage of their numbers, but have never done so. These are the Bektashi who are quite widespread in this country.

The Bektashi replace the personal idealism of the Muslims based on ritual practices with a collective idealism and solidarity devoid of external show, rather like the reformist church or the freemasons.

It is difficult to obtain information about the doctrine of the Bektashi sect because they are secretive and their adherents have sworn not to reveal it. I asked about it with great discretion and always sensed awkwardness and polite resistance to my questions. An Albanian officer told me that when he was young, he and his friends made a game of sending one of their number to join the sect and to tell them what he had learned. The fellow, a physician, agreed to do so and promised to reveal everything he learned. Despite his boastful intentions, however, once he was a member of the sect, he turned obstinately silent.

From what I was able to learn, Bektashism is rooted in pantheist free thinking. It is an extremely liberal sect in which God does not turn into a policeman to patrol and check up on the thoughts and deeds of others. The Bektashi do not go to the mosque and tend to look down a bit on hodjas and the ceremonies they carry out to fulfil their religious obligations. Every Bektashi is in himself a priest, a judge and a guide. He is careful to avoid anything that would put a stain on his conscience. It is quite conceivable, I think, that the Bektashi believe in the reincarnation of the soul. If the soul is degraded in this life, it suffers a decline in the next.

The head of the Bektashi is in Ankara. When his dervishes swear an oath of celibacy, which is optional, they live together in *tekkes* or convents headed by a superior. This superior is called a *baba* and is appointed by Ankara. There are 43 *tekkes* in Albania. For myself, I had occasion to visit the *tekkes* of Gjirokastra and Elbasan.

The *tekke* of Gjirokastra is situated not far from the town on a hill which it crowns with its walls, its tombs and its lofty dark cypress trees. We trudged up the terrible trail in the rain and were received under a canopy at the top of the steps by the dervishes in their white robes. Silently they led us in to see the *baba*.

Baba Sulejman was seated on a long-haired rug in the reception room. The floors were covered in carpets, some of which looked quite expensive. Over his white robe he was clad in a light green garment and wore the rigid cylindrical headpiece of the Bektashi. He received us warmly and had us seated on a small sofa. I had never felt as awkward as I did here on that ugly piece of modern furniture in the midst of such traditional surroundings, with our muddy boots set out on the Anatolian carpets rich in hues and design. A young dervish brought coffee in on a platter and every time he handed us a cup, his necklace of heavy cut glass banged against the metal tray. The conduct of the dervishes and of the *baba* was exemplary and left nothing to be desired.

We started up a conversation. The *baba* was absorbed by the national cause. The Turks had interned him for three years in Janina when they discovered Albanian books at the *tekke*. In 1914, the Greeks pillaged and burned the *tekke* down, at a time when it had just been reopened. There were twelve dervishes in all, but seven of them were still at the candidate level and were being tested to see if they were fit to put on the robes. Dervishes can marry but if they do, they have to leave the *tekke* and live like everyone else. However, they lose nothing of their power and authority. Baba Sulejman wore an earring in his right ear that distinguished him as a dervish who had committed himself to celibacy. It was a triangular piece of silver which was symbolic of something or other only revealed to the initiated.

What we learned from Baba Sulejman on the doctrine and role of the Bektashi can be summarized in the following few words: 'We strive for peace on earth and for the good of all mankind. We work to overcome fanaticism and are the friends of sincere believers of all religions.'

Baba Sulejman and his dervishes accompanied us down to the bottom of the hill. Dressed in white, they led us through the dark cypress trees to the tombs of former *babas*, on which lamps had already been lit for the night. The oldest of the dervishes, in a gesture of kind affection, handed us a little bouquet of wild geraniums and rock flowers with a simple country fragrance. We were quite moved as we departed, leaving these sage men behind us. They stood and watched us for a long time before they turned and returned to their tranquil asylum.

The *tekke* of Elbasan is situated on a hillside at the end of the gorge of the Shkumbin River. To get there from Elbasan, one crosses a large plain studded with tombstones. The *tekke* was burned down by Essadist rebels and was not rebuilt. The ruins standing on a number of terraces are slowly being overgrown in wild vines and fig trees. A long staircase led up to the tombs of the *babas*, encircled as they were by lofty cypress trees, the dark green of which made the surrounding olive trees look all the paler. The *baba* and his servants had found quarters in one of the farm buildings, for this *tekke* has quite a bit of farmland at its disposal. The tombs of the faithful lie under the olive trees on the hillside, and it is here that are buried the members of the family of Aqif Pasha Elbasani, one of the members of the High Regency Council.

The *tekkes* are not simply convents to which one comes for advice. They are centres of national resistance and patriotic propaganda. On many occasions it was from here that orders for an uprising against the invaders were issued. When Albania gained its independence, the Bektashi wanted to free themselves of all external authority, too. Last January, a meeting of over 500 delegates was held, in which the Albanian Bektashi put an end to their subordination to the supreme head of the sect in Ankara. The sect is now independent and national.

It is run by a council of seven *babas* presided over by the *baba* of the *tekke* of Gjirokastra, who is the highest man in the hierarchy. The appointment of *babas* will soon be entirely in his hands. At the moment, he shares this duty with the *baba* of Turan who is the oldest among them. It was also decided that no new *tekkes* should be created in order to concentrate resources and activities.

I have dealt at length with the Albanian Bektashi because it seems to me, in many ways, that they are the invisible, yet powerful guardian of the Albanian nation.

They have certainly had a profound influence on the liberality and tolerance of the Muslims and their friendly relations with the Christians. There is ample proof of this. Last March, in a Turcophile newspaper called *Shkreptima*, an Albanian in Korça wrote an injurious article about Christian women showing their faces in public. This attack greatly offended the Muslims who went and destroyed the journal's publishing office. The protesters tore the copies of the issue in question to pieces and cast them to the wind as a sign of their resolution to have anyone punished who acted to the detriment of Muslim–Christian relations.

There is another, more recent example of this. Last September, Professor Pittard of the University of Geneva set up the Albanian Red Cross in Tirana. The Albanian Muslims, far from demanding that it be called the Red Crescent, accepted the term Red Cross without any discussion.

In Albania, where the Muslims are in the majority, there is no Muslim preponderance. This is more than evident in a letter that Mid'hat Frashëri, the head of the Albanian delegation in France, wrote to me, in which he said:

> It is wrong to say that Albania is a Muslim country since the Albanian State has no official religion. Perfect equality and parity are sufficient guarantees for all religions.
>
> The non-Muslim character of Albania is illustrated in particular by the fact that it was a Catholic clergyman who long headed the Albanian delegation in Paris (Mons. Louis Bumçi, the Bishop of Lezha). Another bishop, Orthodox this time, Mons. Fan Noli, headed the Albanian delegation in Geneva where the mission was entirely composed of Christians and not a single Muslim.
>
> You can see for yourself that the prefects of Korça and Gjirokastra are Christians. The government is unconcerned at them being at the head of majority Muslim populations.
>
> You have also seen that Mr Pandeli Evangjeli, a Christian, was elected as speaker of parliament.

These are concrete examples that prove that it is rather the Muslim Albanians who suffer from the fanaticism and intolerance of our Christian neighbours. No Christian in Albania suffers because of his religion. We know what the Albanian Muslims have suffered at the hands of the Serbs in Kosovo. Burnt-out villages are still smoking in the mountains of Dibra. The heaped ashes of the 300 villages destroyed by the Greeks in 1914 are further eloquent proof.

We can conclude by stating with certitude that Albania has nothing to fear from religious division. Its national unity is the source of our strength, not beliefs. It is strong enough not to fear the diversity of our beliefs. [...]

[Excerpt from Justin Godart, *L'Albanie en 1921* (Paris: PUF 1922), pp. 162–168. Translated from the French by Robert Elsie.]

1925
MARGARET HASLUCK
THE NONCONFORMIST MOSLEMS OF ALBANIA

The Scottish anthropologist and scholar Margaret Masson Hasluck, née Hardie (1885-1948), also known as Peggy Hasluck, was born near Elgin in northern Scotland. In 1910, as the first woman ever, she won a scholarship to study at the British School of Archaeology in Athens and took part in archaeological excavations in Anatolia under Sir William Ramsay (1851-1939). It was at the British School that she met archaeologist and orientalist Frederick William Hasluck (1878-1920), whom she married in Scotland in September 1912. Her husband died in a Swiss sanatorium in 1920, and it was Margaret who edited and published his magnum opus entitled Christianity and Islam under the Sultans *(Oxford 1929). From 1923 onwards, Margaret Hasluck spent most of her years in Albania, spending much time in the back country where, in preparation for her husband's book, she did much research on the Bektashi. In 1935, she settled in Elbasan, where she bought land, built a house and lived until the Second World War.*

The most desultory student of Balkan politics is aware that three religions co-exist in Albania, viz., the Roman Catholic in the north, Mahomedan in the centre, and Greek Orthodox in the south. But not everyone seems aware that the Mahomedans are further sub-divided into orthodox Moslems *(Sunnis)*, who inhabit central Albania, and *Shia* sectarians of the Bektashi religious order, who live chiefly in the south. Otherwise certain writers could scarcely have stigmatised last summer's insurrection as a crusade of Christians against Moslems; in point of fact, it was a rebellion of the liberal, progressive Catholics, Orthodox, and Bektashis combined against the hide-bound, reactionary *Sunnis* of Ahmed Zogu's party. In these circumstances English readers may find some interest in an account of the Bektashis which will at least try to explain this union of Christian and Moslem against Moslem.

Albania is now the most important sphere of Bektashi activities; but the order is of Asia Minor origin, its reputed founder being Hadji Bektash, a fourteenth century saint who is traditionally said to have consecrated the first Janissaries raised by Sultan Orkhan. This consecration, says the legend, is commemorated in the Janissary headdress, where the flap behind is intended to recall the saint's sleeve, which slipped back as he raised his hand to bless the new recruits. The legend is picturesque, but probably not to be taken too seriously, especially as nothing is really known of the saint except that he lies buried in a convent *(tekke)* called by his name near Kirshehr in the depths of Asia Minor, and frequented by Bektashis as the centre of their order. It is not even certain how far he is responsible for present Bektashi beliefs, which have been much influenced by the Hurufi order. The latter was founded by a Persian mystic named Fadlullah, whom one of Timur the Tartar's sons martyred about fifty years after the alleged date of Hadji Bektash's death. Soon after, Fadlullah's disciples introduced the Hurufi doctrines, with their Persian tincture, to the inmates of Hadji Bektash's convent as the secret learning of Hadji Bektash himself. The simple dervishes accepted this and thenceforward, Hadji Bektash being still regarded as orthodox by the *Sunnis,* the Hurufi used his name as a stalking horse for the wider dissemination among the laity of their heretical beliefs. In this way the heresy was enabled to spread more or less unnoticed, until a considerable number of daughter convents had been established in Asia Minor, each with its dervish founder buried in it and worshipped as its chief saint.

Meantime the order had been gradually forming a connection with the Janissaries, no doubt for the purpose of their religious propaganda, while the soldiers, who had early begun to dabble in politics, found the dervishes useful in their political intrigues. Their connection remained unofficial until the end of the sixteenth century, by which time it was a matter of course that Bektashis should accompany the Janissaries everywhere, as the number of Bektashi tombs still extant in Turkish garrison centres testifies. By the opening years of the nineteenth century Bektashi doctrines held sway in almost every Turkish village in Asia and Europe, while the Janissaries had become as much of a political as a military force in the empire, even making and unmaking Sultans at their pleasure. The reforming Sultan, Mahmud II, therefore, considered them both a dangerous menace to the State and, to get rid of them, ordered a general massacre in 1826. He succeeded in permanently breaking the Janissaries but only crippled their dervish supporters, who lay low for a time and then emerged to grow stronger than ever. Albania, being remote and inadequately controlled by Turkey, was admirably adapted for both purposes.

This Bektashi need for shelter, by giving the dervishes opportunities to push their propaganda, probably changed the fortunes of Albania, which hitherto had not been much touched by the heresy. True, Ali Pasha of Tepelen and Yannina (1750–1822) had highly favoured and advanced the order for his own ends. As is well known from the writings of Colonel Leake and others, it was his ambition to carve himself out an independent satrapy from the Turkish empire, for which purpose, like the Janissaries before him, he found the Bektashis useful tools. One dervish, for instance, he used regularly as a diplomatic agent, another toured Albania, collecting contributions and doubtless information also for his master. In return Ali, who was possibly himself a lay member of the sect, built and endowed several Bektashi *tekkes,* but death ended his favours in 1822 when, in accordance with an early prophecy, he took his last journey to Constantinople 'with a red beard.' Afterwards, no doubt, his patronage did the Bektashis no good, while Sultan Mahmud's massacre, with all its consequences, followed immediately, as related above. The order nevertheless spread underground, until in the eighties of last century its members were again strong enough to take a prominent part in the agitation for Albanian independence, with which they have been closely and honourably associated ever since.

The protagonists of this early movement were the three Frasheri brothers, Sami, Abdul and Naim. If not themselves actually Bektashis, they came of Bektashi stock and dreamt of making their creed the State religion of an autonomous Albania. Politically, they made little headway; Bismarck cynically answered their pleadings for freedom by bidding them 'well water Albania with blood' first, while Abdul died a lingering death in a Turkish prison. On the other hand, their literary leanings, particularly Naim's, are 'still speaking' in Albania. The indigenous Albanian language was at that time without an alphabet and almost unwritten. Accordingly, whether the history of Greece and Serbia had taught him that the cultivation of his country's vernacular would afford a skilful means of undermining Turkish domination, or whether he merely wished to encourage education among his illiterate countrymen, Naim set himself to invent an alphabet and compose books, many of which are still widely read. Unfortunately, Turkey had become belatedly aware of the danger of allowing her *rayah* and non-Turkish subjects to read and write their own language, so she forbade the printing of books in Albanian within the Turkish empire and their importation from abroad. The Bektashis, however, came to the rescue. Many a foreign consulate's *cavass*, as a good Bektashi, had the forbidden books sent him from abroad under cover of the consulate's inviolability and distributed them to eager learners; many a dervish, too, acted as carrier of such books and, being caught, was imprisoned for the same. And so, in spite of Turkish obstruction, the educational movement slowly spread.

Then came the Young Turk Revolution with its promise of better things. The Albanian Bektashis took the professions of the Young Turks at their face value and voted solid for them, only to be disillusioned. Thereupon they reverted to the Frasheri ideal of Albanian independence, which brought them into conflict, not only with Turkey, but also with the Christian States that were waiting to step into her shoes. It is therefore not surprising that their nationalism cost them dear in the disorders which succeeded the Balkan wars, when Greek irregulars left scarcely a *tekke* standing in the south, while in the centre Serbian guerillas and Essad Pasha's *Sunni* partisans were equally thorough. They have now their reward, however, in the official position granted them in the young State of Albania, where, of the four Regents who head the administration, one must be Bektashi, as the others must be respectively Catholic, *Sunni,* and Greek Orthodox. In the security thus afforded them they are fast rebuilding their burnt sanctuaries, which now, to the number of nearly sixty, crowd south and central Albania as far north as Kruya and have even penetrated to fanatically *Sunni* Elbasan. The latest manifestation of their activity is the recent revolt, when, side by side, the Catholics of Scutari, the Orthodox of Koritza, and the Bektashis of Frasheri marched out to deliver their country from the tyranny of Ahmed Zogu's feudal *Sunni* partisans, and the threat to Albanian independence which Ahmed's exaggeratedly pro-Serbian sympathies were thought to imply.

Evidently, then, Bektashism is a powerful factor in Albanian history and politics, conciliating the Christians enough to make them forget their age-long antipathy to Islam, yet remaining itself a very living force within that religion. It is by no means uninteresting to seek the explanation of such a paradox. In its organisation there is nothing extraordinary. The rank and file are not outwardly distinguishable from other Moslems but recognise each other by a secret sign, consisting, it is said, in a certain, apparently casual, touching of the chin. Above them are dervishes, conspicuous by their tall, ridged hats of white felt, and celibate or married according to the branch they choose; a single earring denotes a celibate. As usual with Eastern priestly castes, they are bearded, the Serbs rousing more resentment by shaving the abbot of Martanesh than by burning his *tekke*. Laymen live at home, but dervishes must reside in a convent *(tekke)*, which the donations of the pious living and the legacies of the dead support; its essential feature is an oratory *(ibadet hane)* for common worship, and in it dervishes, as they die, are buried; a proper mosque is never attached. Dervishes are appointed by abbots *(babas),* who generally preside each over a *tekke* and are themselves, if of the celibate branch, appointed either by the superior abbots called *khalifehs,* of whom three exist in Albania alone, or by the Akhi Dede, supreme head of the celibates, who lives in the central *tekke* in Asia Minor. Should a vacancy occur in this office, it is filled by the dervishes of this *tekke* from among themselves, as Cardinals elect a new Pope from their own number. It is remarkable that the Akhi Dedes are generally Albanians, the intelligence of the race bringing them to the front in this as in other spheres. Latterly in Albania the tendency has been for the local *khalifehs* rather than the distant Akhi Dede to appoint abbots, an innovation due to the present Balkan rage for autocephalous Churches, which has so infected Albania that the Catholics of the north actually talk of disowning the supremacy of the Pope. Married abbots depend on the Akhi Dede's rival, the Tchelebi, who is himself married and claims to descend actually from Hadji Bektash, but the claim is not recognised by celibates, who keep him outside the central *tekke*.

In this Bektashi hierarchy there is nothing unusual to attract proselytes, but in their theology there is. They profess belief in God, Mahomed, his daughter Fatima, her husband Ali, and their sons Hassan and Hussein, Ali being obscurely identified with Mahomed, esteemed next to God, and considered to be represented on earth by any or every abbot, who is to be venerated accordingly. They believe further in the Twelve Imams, Moses, Mary, Jesus, and saints both ancient and modern. This worship of dead saints and of living abbots as saints on earth may be crude but has something tangible in it which appeals strongly to illiterate and superstitious minds. As to their form of worship, it is concealed from all but initiates and is therefore imperfectly known. Public prayers take place in the oratory of the parish *tekke* at sunrise and sundown only, not five times a day as in orthodox Islam. The abbot sits in his privileged corner, reciting prayers, some from the Koran, while the devotees squat in a semi-circle and bow to him, as Ali's representative, at intervals; twelve candles for the Twelve Imams burn on a three-tiered altar. No ritual ablutions precede the prayer, no genuflexions accompany it, as with *Sunnis*. Nor is it necessary to go to the *tekke* more than twice a year. It is said that Bektashi women, unlike their *Sunni* sisters, may join the men in prayer, but this seems doubtful, though there are certainly women members of the order. It is unknown whether Bektashis pray at home, as *Sunnis* do.

Vague as this information is, it makes it clear that less taxing prayers are enjoined on Bektashis than on their orthodox brethren. They are allowed more liberty also in such details of daily observance as the veiling of women and abstention from strong drink, while instead of Ramazan they keep the less rigorous Persian fast that commemorates the murdered sons of Ali. This greater freedom is attractive to Albanians, whose temperament dislikes discipline.

On the ethical side Bektashi doctrines have a considerable human appeal. Metempsychosis is preached. Death is but a change, souls merely pass on, men's to men, women's to women, animals' to animals, for women and animals in Bektashi, though not in *Sunni,* popular thought have souls. As a man does in this life, so will his soul's next reincarnation be, for better or for worse. Love is the mainspring of life; all men are brothers, women are men's equals, Bektashis should love their brothers, and their sisters, as themselves, but most of all should they love their country, because patriotism is the highest of human virtues – this last a point of much importance in Albanian eyes. Bektashis should also turn the cheek to the smiter, abstain from violence, injustice, and untruthfulness, honour great and small, and show charity and hospitality to all men. This Bektashi gospel, so different from the conventional 'fiery sword of Islam,' is actively preached; its emphasis on ethics differentiates it sharply from the other religions of the Near East which are only too often merely barren ritual, and therefore it is alive as they are stagnant.

Moreover, Bektashis generally practise what they preach, a feat they owe to careful selection of candidates in the first instance. Not everyone may become a Bektashi; neither heredity nor any other accident helps. Instead, a satisfactory sponsor must guarantee that the candidate believes in God and is of good moral character; he must also be come to years of discretion and understand the vows he takes. Lay members are made dervishes only after several years' probation in a *tekke* under the abbot's supervision and instruction; would-be abbots, for their further discipline and deeper initiation into Bektashi tenets, must serve under a *khalifeh* or at the Hadji Bektash *tekke* in Asia Minor. Then, with that curious mingling of the crude and the sublime which characterises them, they take certain precautions to prevent initiates from breaking their vows. Thus, at the banquet which precedes a layman's admission, there is much talk of the mystery to which he is about to be introduced, hobgoblin tales are told his simple mind of the evil fate which even in this life befell those who forswore their vows – one went mad, another broke his neck, a third lost a fortune. Strung up as he already is, a secretly administered dose of opium transports him to the seventh heaven of delight, in which ecstatic state he may fancy he beholds the Deity himself. It is a brave man who is wilfully false to the oaths he takes on such a night.

To preserve dervishes from worldly temptations, convents are normally built some distance from the neighbouring town or village; sometimes, as in one at Argirocastro, dervishes are cloistered altogether; if left freer, they must be within doors by sunset. Their mental and bodily functions are slowed down by opium judiciously given out each morning by the abbot and by copious draughts of native gin at night. The gentle, slightly bemused creature that results has little capacity for positive good or ill.

As a consequence of this careful selection and handling, the lives of Bektashi dervishes are so pure and selfless that no breath of scandal touches them, though *Sunni* Moslem *hodjas* and Orthodox Christian priests figure in half the irreverent tales of the Levant. As living embodiments of the Near East ideal of goodness, they exercise a power for good which is comparable only to that of our Western clergy, and half-unconsciously they thereby win numerous adherents for Bektashism. If we may judge from such indications as the greater respect paid the celibates and the esteem generally expressed for Catholic priests, the genuine celibacy of the Bektashi dervishes enormously enhances their influence. This is because in these latitudes there still prevails the curious ascetic doctrine that the marriage state is one of sin, so that the man or woman who lives and dies unmarried is by that fact alone raised above the vulgar – a doctrine once held by ourselves but now forgotten in the general decay of monasticism. Even the dervishes' undoubted ignorance scarcely detracts from presage again because this is the Orient, where knowledge is not popularly required of a 'man of God'; Christ's seeking His disciples among the humblest is a precedent quoted by Moslem and Christian alike. Albania, however, now takes the Western view, and talks of establishing a college where Bektashis must secure a diploma before turning dervish. Albania is also attacking the one failing which lowers dervishes in popular estimation, that is, the terrible weakness for drink which grows on most of them as a result of their nightly potations. At the great Bektashi Congress held in 1921, a resolution was passed to restrict them to one gill of spirits per night, an allowance which still seems ample, but is less than the quart they drank when left to themselves.

By its preached and practised gospel of love Bektashism therefore maintains its position among non-*Sunni* Moslems. *Sunnis,* however, abominate its adherents for their laxity about drink, veiling, daily prayer, etc., and their blasphemous equation of Ali to Mahomed. Said a *Sunni,* 'We may eat and drink with a Christian without harm, but we break the spoon with which a Bektashi has eaten, we refuse him water when he is thirsty, or, if he has already drunk, we break the pitcher and destroy the fountain from which he has drunk.' This is probably an extreme view, but recently in some *Sunni* villages in western Macedonia a Bektashi abbot was refused shelter for the night and stoned by children. As Christians, too, suffer from *Sunni* intolerance, Bektashis naturally feel drawn to them as fellow pariahs. Besides, it is explicitly taught Bektashis to make no distinction in their conduct between Mussulmans and non-Mussulmans. So, instead of opprobrious names, they call Christians 'brother,' and in picturesque Albanian phrase say that 'no more than the thickness of an onion-skin' divides them from each other. Theoretically, Christians may even be initiated as Bektashis without abandoning their own faith. If this remains a theory, as the evidence indicates, it is certain that Bektashi charity is extended to all without discrimination. Any traveller may verify this for himself, and notable historical examples are recorded. An unpublished case occurred in western Macedonia at the beginning of the Balkan wars, when certain Greek villages were preserved from destruction only by the personal intervention of the Bektashi abbot of Vodhorina.

Thus, on the social side, Bektashism makes definite attempts at bridging the gap between Christianity and Islam. On the religious side, its tolerance has resulted in Bektashis and Christians frequenting each other's shrines. The primary reason is the ordinary human desire for health of mind and body, fertility of crops, and the gift of children, which leads those to whom such blessings are denied to seek help from all possible quarters; even *Sunni* bigotry is not indefinitely proof against an aching tooth or heart and, when *Sunni* remedies have failed, will turn to Christian or Bektashi for relief. The latter go even further, and each claims as its own certain holy places which belong to the other. Thus, the very *tekke* of Hadji Bektash is visited by Christians as an ancient monastery of S. Charalambos, whom they make the hero of some of the best known legends of Mahomed himself. In Albania the Orthodox monastery of S. Naum, whose political fate was decided only the other day, is frequented by Bektashis as one of the seven shrines of their great missionary, Sari Saltik, as is also the Orthodox S. Spyridon of Corfu. S. Elias of Mount Tomor in central Albania has lately become Abbas Ali for Bektashis, with the consequence that during his great festival in August Christians jostle Bektashis in his precinct. To explain this strange phenomenon of common worship, Christians say the Bektashi shrines were formerly Christian; this seems true in some cases, not in others. Bektashis, being familiar with the doctrine of metempsychosis, find no difficulty in believing a saint to be at once Christian and Moslem. But whatever the cause or the explanation, the fact remains that Bektashis and Christians may pray according to their own mode in each others' sanctuaries without let or hindrance.

Bektashism, therefore, appeals to Albanians as human beings by its embodiment of the Near East ideal of goodness, its attractive gospel, the liberty it allows the individual, and the superstitious side which caters for mortal man's weaknesses. It attracts them as Albanians by its insistence on patriotism. Then Albania, with her face now turned towards the progressive West, feels that the conservative *Koran,* noble book though it be, hampers progress. Yet Islam, once embraced, is as difficult to abandon in favour of Christianity as Christianity is in favour of its Jewish predecessor. To Moslems who feel this difficulty, Bektashism offers an Islam that permits progress along Western lines. To Christians who wish to keep their religion, it extends the hand of fellowship without contempt or intolerance. But Albanian history shows that Albanians are peculiarly susceptible to the pressure of necessity or expediency, having been converted to Islam to a degree absolutely unparalleled in the other Christian countries conquered by the Turks in the Balkans. Consequently, as three-fourths of the population are Moslem, many Albanian Christians may find it best to adopt the predominant religion. To such, Bektashism offers an Islam without rigidity or vexatious exactions, no longer, since Turkey's departure, rendering its adherents suspect. In these circumstances this nonconformist Moslem sect can hardly fail to fulfil the prophecy that it will conquer Albania.

[Margaret Hasluck, 'The Nonconformist Moslems of Albania,' *Contemporary Review*, London, 127 (1925), pp. 599–606. Reprint in: *Moslem World* 15 (1925), pp. 388–398.]

1929
Franz Babinger
Among the Dervishes in Kruja

The German historian Franz Babinger (1891–1967) finished his habilitation in 1921 at the University of Berlin, where he was then professor, but he was forced to resign in 1934 out of differences with the Nazi regime in power and emigrated to Romania. In 1948, he was appointed to the new chair for the history and culture of the Middle East and Turkology at the University of Munich, where he remained until retirement in 1958. As a scholar, Babinger specialized in Ottoman history and culture and in the history of the early Renaissance. Of particular interest to Albanian studies is his book 'Das Ende der Arianiten' (The End of the Arianiti), Munich 1960. Babinger drowned accidentally during a stay in Albania, while at the beach in Durrës. His visit to the Bektashi tekke of Fushë Kruja and to the town of Kruja in 1929 is recorded in the following piece.

If you approach the Albanian capital, Tirana, from the north or the west, you will see up on the slope in the distance, high above the plains that descend gradually from Tirana in a northwardly direction, a curious eyrie, from which the Kruja mountain range takes its name. This is the town of Kruja with the famous fortress of Scanderbeg, known in Turkish as Akçe Hisar. You can easily visit it on a day's outing from Tirana for it is no more than 35 kilometres away. The main road that leads initially towards Durazzo [Durrës] is rutty and worn out from all the Italian trucks plying it, but it is otherwise in satisfactory condition when the weather is dry. From the junction where the road leads northwards to Alessio [Lezha] and Scutari [Shkodra], the tracks of the field railway laid by Austrian troops during the war are still intact. Overturned railway cars and large piles of scrap iron convey the impression that a mere few weeks have passed since the railway was in operation, instead of years.

We departed early in the morning and had left behind us the straight, broad street from the main square of Tirana and the inquisitive police checkpoint at the start of it. To our left stretched open fields and to our right rose hills, from some of which we caught glimpses of the estates of the landed gentry, the beys. The road was lined with little huts. Gone were the minarets and mosques of Tirana, and the farther we drove, the scarcer the huts became, until they disappeared altogether. To the northeast we could now see the white houses of Kruja. On the left side of the road there was a little coffee shop and the workshop of a blacksmith. Several trucks were stopped there in front of the wretched building that marked the turnoff of the road up into the Kruja mountains. We had another twelve kilometres to go.

Not far from the post road on low ground to the right, hidden in among the trees and surrounded by verdant meadows, lay the famed monastery of the Bektashi dervishes, Fushë Kruja. This was to be our first destination.

When you get close to the group of spaced-out, irregular, whitewashed buildings surrounded by a high wall, you would think you were entering the property of a wealthy landowner rather than a site of monastic contemplation. We entered the yard in which all sorts of animals were roaming about and came upon a modest, one-storey building with an open courtyard. There was not a person in sight. On the walls, in shiny green paint, we could read the name of Ali, the son-in-law of the Prophet who is idolized by the Bektashi. The trunks of the cypress trees were also painted in this colour. Our servant hastened off to inform the monks of our arrival who were busy building an addition behind a second wall. The main building of the monastery which, as we later learned, had burned down, was rebuilt and almost finished.

A dervish soon appeared, wearing the colourful turban of the Bektashi, a high, twelve-furrowed cylindrical headpiece of white felt, though he was otherwise dressed in normal clothes. He informed us that the Sheikh of the monastery would be with us shortly. We climbed a rickety wooden staircase to reach the veranda and were told to sit down. We were then given tobacco and coffee, the usual offerings made to visitors. Our conversation was conducted in Turkish, which, in addition to the national language, Albanian, is still used as a normal means of communication throughout the country. A few minutes later, the abbot himself arrived in slow and measured steps, dressed in a fine white robe and with a cylindrical felt headpiece wrapped in green cloth on his head. He was a venerable figure with his long flowing beard and a curious arabesque-shaped earring of thick silver wire in his left ear, a sign of his status. Hanging from a thick cord around his neck and around the necks of his brothers in faith, was a shiny carnelian star, the so-called *teslim tash*, that signified that he had finished his training as an initiate. As head of the monastery, he greeted us warmly and made us welcome. We soon got talking. It was evident from the start that Mehmet Baba was an intelligent man of liberal-minded judgment who had endeavoured to see and experience as much of the world as circumstances allowed. When I began talking about the creation of the Bektashi Order and its founder, Haji Bektash of Khorasan, he looked very surprised, but took up the subject with lively interest, though without any excessive religious zeal. When our conversation then turned to the greatest holy man of the Kruja region, Sari Saltik Dede, the legend and miracles of whom I had earlier studied, he became very talkative and went on and on in praise of the holy man.

After another round of refreshments, Mehmet Baba invited us to pay a visit to the holy tombs in his monastery. We walked through the central courtyard with its stables and new building and reached a tiny doorway leading to a large lawn, in the middle of which rose a huge, splendid cypress tree surrounded by a wooden fence. Around it on all sides were whitewashed *tyrbes*, the mausoleums of the holy men of the monastery that was said to have been founded by one Ali Baba in 1562 (970 AH). The looming cypress tree, allegedly stemming from the time of the founder, is said to have grown of its own accord out of the boarding he had used to make his hut. This legend stems no doubt from the curious form of the tree's branches, which were large and flat, like boards. In actual fact, the tree was probably much older.

Particularly venerated, in addition to the chapel of Ali Baba, was the chapel of Jelaladdin Ibrahim Shemimi Baba who finished his days as sheikh of the monastery in 1807 (1222 AH). He was a well-remembered and much-revered figure, not only as a sheikh but also as a poet. Through the opaque panes of the grated windows of the *tyrbe* we could see the sarcophagus of the saint, piled high with colourful towels as votive offerings. The third holy man to be venerated here was Haji Huseyn Baba who died in 1890. But the current head of the monastery was also held in great esteem.

Several hours passed and, since we also wanted to visit Kruja, we were forced to take leave of Mehmet Baba and his four dervishes. We took pictures of the dervish group and of the individual objects in the monastery and departed, together with the school principal of Kruja who had offered to accompany us. The road was initially straight but then continued in endless hairpins up the mountainside. Around us were beautiful groves of old olive trees. Soon we could see all of the plain stretching out below us, right to the Adriatic Sea shining in the distance. But our attention was diverted by the town of Kruja which was more attractive than anyone could possibly describe. The domes of the Bektashi sanctuaries and monasteries arose through the forest of splendid olive and dark cypress trees. Between them in picturesque groups were the houses of the town, crowned by the fortress girded by high walls. The only construction to have survived the years was a lonely clock tower rising from the ruins into the azure heavens. Behind the town were the steep, almost vertical cliffs of Mali i Krujës [Mount Kruja], on top of which lay the greatest sanctuary of Kruja, the grave of Sari Saltik Dede.

By now, our car had reached the entrance of the market, and we found a modest little restaurant that welcomed us. We were lucky to have brought food with us, because it had little to offer. Coffee, eggs, bread and yoghourt was all that the proprietor could give us on a Friday. Guided by our new acquaintance, we proceeded through the centre of the town, through what appeared to be a very old market street with wooden roofs. Most of the shops were, alas, closed because of the holiday so that we experienced nothing of the usual hustle and bustle that make market streets in the Orient so fascinating. Cats in great numbers skittered over the rotten boards and children nagged at us as beggars. Here and there, there were a few shopkeepers and handicraftsmen sitting on the stoops of their open shops. Otherwise there was not much life in Kruja, a once bustling and mighty town.

What was particularly noticeable was the rarity of mosques. I noticed two, only one of which was in use. According to the inscription on it, it was founded in 1533 (940 AH) and was renovated in 1837 (1253 AH) by Murad Bey. The other place of worship, built by Sultan Mehmed II the Conqueror with its splendid and colourfully stained windows was almost in ruins and the interior was in a sorry state. The lack of mosques can be explained by the fact that three-quarters of the people of the town (some 5,000 souls) are followers of the Bektashi, with the rest being Sunni Muslims. Since the Bektashi have no mosques there was no great need to have such places of worship. All the more impressive were the mausoleums, the domes of which rose here and there amidst the sombre cypress trees.

Kruja was one of the most important Turkish fortresses in the western part of the Empire. According to tradition, Christians were only allowed to enter the town in the daytime, in the company of Muslims. At night there were not permitted to be in town at all, under penalty of death. The once famed fortress on the rock made a sad impression on us. It was pulled down in 1832, but the walls and fortification towers survived to an extent. The interior of the fortress was full of ruins – remains of walls and big stone blocks. In several locations one could still see the remains of the old circular walls of the fortress which were probably very old. The view from the fortress was, however, overwhelming.

On our way from the fortress back down to the town, we came across a beautiful old administration building with curious frescos and carvings in a particular architectural style. Near it there was an ornate old but still functioning fountain in rough relief – two leaping lions and wheels. The inscription on it stated that it was donated in 1446 (850 AH) by Ghazi Evrenos, the famous Ottoman commander and nobleman. Another inscription stated that it had been renovated in 1834 (1250 AH). From this, it is clear that the fortress was in the temporary possession of the Turks before the final Ottoman occupation. We know that an Ottoman governor called Balaban Bey had his headquarters there in 1415.

Kruja has no lack of good water, indeed the word *kruja* in Albanian means 'spring, fountain'. Countless streams flow down Mount Kruja that are channelled into fountains throughout the town, providing cool, fresh water at all times. The Ghazi Evrenos Fountain comes right out of the rocks below the fortress, and the inscription on it is the only old inscription to be found. On the outer side of the fortress walls one could clearly see the site of an inscription plate, probably dating from the year of the conquest. It would have been of historical importance. The Turks are said to have removed it when they withdrew from Kruja fifteen years ago.

It was now late in the afternoon. We had something to drink at the little restaurant and then departed for Tirana, once again along the hairpin curves of the road. We stopped at a little chapel called *Gjurmë i Shejntit* (Footstep of the Saint) and had a last look up at Kruja. Soon thereafter, we passed the monastery of Fushë Kruja along the main road. The sky was now heavy with rainclouds and there were a few showers, but after a quarter of an hour, the setting sun came out with an impressive rainbow over the countryside to the east. It was a vision I do not remember ever having seen on my travels in the Orient. Before sinking into the sea, the golden ball of the sun cast its fiery red rays onto the slopes of the Kruja mountains that looked as if they were on fire. It was as if a huge forest fire were spreading from north to south and lighting up the whole countryside. Nature at its best, so beautiful that no pen can describe it and no paintbrush can reproduce it. A few minutes later, darkness spread over that mysterious land.

[Franz Babinger, *Bei den Derwischen von Kruja*, published in: *Münchner Neueste Nachrichten*, Munich, 7 January 1929, p. 3. Translated from the German by Robert Elsie.]

1929
DAYRELL OAKLEY-HILL
UP TO MOUNT TOMORR

The South African-born Dayrell Oakley-Hill (1898-1985) was a military figure among the British officers who were assigned the task of organizing the Albanian gendarmerie in the 1930s, under the direction of General Sir Jocelyn Percy. He was recruited for the Albanian mission in 1929 and served principally in Elbasan, where he learned Albanian and travelled extensively. His memoirs on his time in Albania, including this visit up to the tekke of Mount Tomorr, were published in the volume An Englishman in Albania: Memoirs of a British Officer, 1929-1955 *(London 2002).*

I had decided to go up Tomor, and to stay the night at a teqe (a monastery, or sometimes just a shrine) of the Bektashi Muslims, whose world headquarters is in Albania. This teqe was on a col just below the southern, lower peak of Tomor, on its eastern side. Opposite the village of Ujanik we turned up the slope, and were soon climbing through a forest of huge beeches. The climb was constant, and as we were flagging a little we met a local young man speeding down the slope. We asked him how far it was to the teqe and he said 'one hour'. Distances in the mountains were always reckoned in hours, and it is a habit of local men anywhere to encourage travellers by an underestimate. Certainly for them it is quicker, and they might sometimes think in terms of the downhill journey. We plodded on and I remember saying to myself 'Tomor, Tomor, Tomor, creeps on this petty pace from hour to hour'. After struggling upward for another 2½ hours we at last reached a level stretch and away on the left in a grove of trees stood a substantial building. This was the teqe. Unhappily the chief, or Baba, was away and the subordinate Dervish could not provide food. However, they gave us a room with beds, and some cheese and yogurt. They showed us their cheese dairy, where they made large quantities of cream cheese and harder cheeses and sold them far and wide. They even exported them to America, for the benefit of the Albanian community there.

Early in the morning, we scrambled up the final slope, mostly of scree, to the top of Tomor. The view was magnificent in every direction; mountain ridges everywhere, some clothed, some bare; the sea; and, seemingly close to the western foot, the town of Berat, with its low hills bordering the shiny strip of the Osum river. There was a small shrine on this peak, on a circular space of flat brown rock. In the rock was a clear imprint of a horse's foot. The legend was that some ancient saint had flown, Pegasus-wise, from Mount Dodona, near Janina in Greece, and landed here. Dodona was said to have been the home of Zeus and the other gods before Olympus; this I heard again when I visited Dodona many years later.

The ridge leading to the slightly higher northern point of Tomor was a knife edge, and I did not think I should care to walk along it. The climb from our peak down the southwest end of the mountain looked a little easier, largely over grassy lopes. However, I had to go back to the Tomorrëzë stream to make my way to Çerovodë, so we returned to the teqe, took our leave, and went back through the forest. [...]

We did not want to call at Çerovodë again so crossed the Osum at a point lower down. We rode eastward across undulating hills for hours and hours, with hardly a sign of life. If our guide had been anyone else I should have begun to think he was lost; but Esat cheerfully kept straight on. As the evening began to close in I asked him when we were going to reach his cousin's house, and where was it anyway? He said, 'It is just ahead, one hour. Don't worry!' However, he was only ½ hour out, and as darkness was closing around us we rode into a thicket of trees and there ahead was a substantial stone building. This was the Bektashi teqe, or monastery, of Prishte (also called Prilisht), and Esat's cousin was the Baba or head of it. The place was quite a distance to the south of Çerovodë. We were met by two or three dervishes (the name used by all the other priests or monks) who greeted us warmly and took over our animals and baggage. We had a very brief look round and noticed in a stone corridor several cats. They had a high stone table to eat on, so that the dogs could not worry them. The Bektashis were fond of animals. We were shown into a large bare room with two iron beds for us and were given water to wash in – we needed it. This was the longest day I had had since Mesopotamian times and I was quite tired. I don't know how Rosamond stuck it, but she was tough, and had been kept amused by Esat. The Bektashis seemed to have no objection to a woman guest.

We were then conducted to the reception room, large and square, with the Turkish-style padded wall benches to sit on. It was cosy and dim, lit by a few flickering candles and oil lamps. After we had sat for quite a time, the door opened and two dervishes brought in a table which they placed in front of us. This was like the Arabian Nights. The table was piled high with dishes of chicken and meat, bowls of fruit and bread, and glasses; there were melons, grapes, apples, pears, figs and nuts. It was unbelievable. The dervishes filled the little glasses with raki and passed them round. Then the Baba came in to welcome us; he was an oldish man with a large still dark beard, flowing robes, and the high, white turban-like head dress worn by all Bektashis. He bid us welcome very warmly and then said he would leave us to eat our meal. Seldom has a meal been more appreciated or seemed more sumptuous.

The next day Esat produced a guide to take us to Çepan, a Post at the southern end of his area, as he wanted to stay and talk to his friends at the teqe. He was a Bektashi himself. We managed to persuade the Baba and his dervishes to sit for a photograph, and then left the monastery after giving him our warmest thanks for that unforgettable welcome.

[Excerpt from: Dayrell R. Oakley-Hill, *An Englishman in Albania: Memoirs of a British Officer, 1929–1955* (London: Centre for Albanian Studies 2002), pp. 21–22 and 29–30.]

1929
BABA ALI TOMORRI
HISTORY OF THE BEKTASHI

Baba Ali Tomorri (1900–1948) stemmed from Shalës near Tepelena. He became a dervish at the tekke of Prishta in 1913. In 1922 he was made baba of the small tekke of Kulmak on Mount Tomorr that soon became an important centre of the Bektashi in central Albania. He was arrested by the communists in 1945 and executed in January 1948. Baba Ali Tomorri was the author of six books of Bektashi inspiration published in the 1920s and 1930s, including a short History of the Bektashi, *from which the following extract is taken.*

The Bektashi at the zenith of Albanian nationalism

In 1874 AD, the Çelebi dynasty approached the sultan and had Hadji Hasan Dede of Salonica removed from his position as spiritual master of the *tekke* of Hacıbektaş. He was a dignitary and a man of great courage.

In doing so, the Çelebi intended to take over the great *tekke*. They made other false accusations and reached their goal by having the sultan give them the title 'Sheh Nakshbandi,' i.e. official head of the seat of Hadji Bektash Veli.

The Bektashi all reacted bitterly to the removal of the *dede* from his position. Several thousand Bektashi women in Istanbul gathered before the Sublime Porte (Baba Ali) in a large demonstration against the steps taken by the sultan. The Sublime Porte, i.e. the Turkish government, was shaken by the high level of criticism expressed in educated circles in Istanbul and returned Hadji Hasan Dede to the position he had had, but Hadji Hasan Dede, who had thought the matter through, preferred exile and withdrew to Medina where he died in 1875 AD.

The severe and unjust steps taken by the sultan, as so often, depressed the Bektashi of Albania and made them very angry, and this at the very time when Baba Hysen of Kruja, Baba Alush of Frashër, Baba Adem of Melçan, Baba Ali of Gjirokastra, Baba Xhafer of Prishta, and Baba Muharrem of Koshtan were making great progress.

The learned and highly talented Baba Mehmed Ali of Merdivenköy in Istanbul and other well-known spiritual leaders were winning over the best and most noted statesmen of the country to Bektashism.

With the help of the *babas* of Albania, this Baba Mehmed Ali replaced Hadji Hasan Dede in Hacıbektaş as Hilmi Dede, doing so with the knowledge of the Turkish government and the aforementioned statesmen. But once again, the unrelenting Çelebi made accusations, bribed officials in the palace and, two year later, removed the great spiritual leader of Merdivenköy from his well-earned position.

The removal of the Bektashi *babas* from the *pir evi*, similar to when the pope of Rome was held captive in the city of Avignon at the time of King Philip IV, caused Baba Alush of Frashër to be very bitter. He was a well-respected *baba* in Albania.

As a sign of his frustration, he took to wearing black and withdrew to his *tekke*, never leaving it again until the moment he died. Yet at this critical time, when Baba Alush withdrew and mourned the loss of the *pir evi*, he did not abandon his activities entirely.

In 1877 AD, Sultan Abdul Hamid, worn down by the war with Russia, conceded important parts of Albanian territory to the other small countries – Greece, Serbia, Montenegro and Bulgaria.

A war cry and great commotion arose among the Albanians against these unjust actions. Abdyl bey [Frashëri] returned to his hometown of Frashër and held a national assembly under Baba Alush, the first such assembly since the death of Scanderbeg, and strove to save Albania from the perils with which it was surrounded.

Baba Alush and then all the Bektashi *babas* became the only figures to carry out the patriotic objectives of Abdyl bey. After the assembly in Frashër came the League of Prizren. When Abdyl bey and the other patriots were sent into exile by Turkey, the Bektashi *tekkes* were once again put under the sultan's thumb. He was only waiting for an excuse to wipe them off the face of the earth.

In this situation, Baba Hysen of Kruja, one of the most respected participants at the meeting in Frashër and one of the strongest supporters of the League of Prizren, was also sent into exile for several years.

Dervish Meleq Tahir Staravecka (who has been known more recently as Baba Meleq Shëmbërdhenji), for his part, spent thirty years travelling through Albania, from village to village, from Ulqin to Preveza, to distribute books on Albania's national awakening. All the *tekkes* were turned into Albanian schools and read the *Qerbela*, translated into lively verse by the immortal poet Naim bey Frashëri.

The activities of the Tekkes *after the Frashër meeting, and the catastrophe of 1914*

Hilmi Dede was succeeded at the *pir evi* by Hadji Mehmed Dede of Malatya. He, in turn, was succeeded by Fejzi Dede, an Albanian from Marican near Tepelena.

By the time Hilmi Dede was removed from his post at the *pir evi* in 1879 AD and replaced by Baba Mehmed Ali, he had accomplished much. He had won over many people to Bektashism by preaching at the *tekke* of Merdivenköy in Istanbul.

Strangely enough, in 1880 AD, pan-Albanian ideas were supported not only by the Bektashi of Albania, but by all the followers of Hadji Bektash on earth. Indeed, by 1885 AD, Bektashism had taken on a very Albanian colour, just as Orthodoxy had a Greek colour and Catholicism had a Latin, Italian colour.

Baba Alush passed away. When Baba Hysen died after him, Baba Abedin from Backa in the Skrapar region took over at the *tekke* of Frashër.

Baba Xhafer had also died in Prishta and was replaced by Baba Ahmet who was sent into exile by the Turks to Sinope where he was murdered by persons unknown because he supported the opponents of Turkish despotism.

It was also at this time that the head of the Hajdërie *tekke* in Gjirokastra, Baba Hajdër of Kardhiq, died. He had been an ardent collaborator of the nationalist figure Koto Hoxhi from Qesorat in Lunxhëria. Turkish government forces raided the *tekke* and discovered Albanian books, that were banned by the sultan, and sent the dervishes into exile to Janina. The *tekke* remained closed for quite some time.

But these terrible events did not persist for long. More and more educated Albanians began working for the nation. The simple people, who remembered the catastrophe suffered by the Bektashi eighty years earlier under Sultan Mahmud, had a folksong in Gjirokastra:

Moj Turqi e marrë!
Pse punon për lumë?
Prishe Bektashinë
Që nuk prishet kurr?

Oh, crazy Turkey,
Why do you swim against the tide,
Why've you raged against Bektashism,
That can never be destroyed!

A new generation of nationalist figures arose, such as Rexhep Pasha Mati, Shahin bey Kolonja, Mehmet Ali Pasha Vrioni, Ismail Qemal bey Vlora, Fadil Pasha Toptani and Bajo Topulli, who were supported by the Bektashi *tekkes*, represented by Baba Hysen of Melçan, Baba Abedin of Frashër, Baba Salih of Elbasan, Baba Ahmet of Koshtan, Baba Shaban of Prishta, and Baba Xhemal of Përmet.

The Ottoman Empire was in its last throes in 1907 AD. The people of Thrace and Macedonia rose in revolt for their freedom. In the ensuing confusion, even the Albanians, at the modest beginnings of their national movement, caused Turkey to shake in its boots and were noticed by all of Europe.

One of the main leaders of this movement who devoted himself to saving our homeland was Baba Hysen from Vërlen in the Devoll region. He was the *baba* of the *tekke* of Melçan near Korça. With Baba Hysen were Baba Abedin of Frashër and Baba Shaban of Prishta who spared no effort in the national cause as espoused by the armed band of the now deceased rebel leader Çerçiz Topulli.

In 1908–1909 AD, taking advantage of the promulgation of the Turkish Constitution and the freedoms proclaimed by the Young Turks, many Albanian intellectuals began teaching their people how to read and write in their mother tongue. Now that the Bektashi *tekkes* were free, they were transformed more or less into schools for Albanian-language teaching.

But soon thereafter, the Young Turks who had nobly proclaimed freedom began to abuse it. In their endeavour to denationalise the foreign peoples they had ruled over for centuries, they initiated a campaign to convince the Albanians to write in Turkish [Arabic] script instead of in the Latin script the Albanians wanted. However, they did not succeed. The Albanians were awake this time, no longer the drowsy peasants as they had been before.

The pan-Albanian idealists countered the anti-constitutional acts of the Young Turks by staunchly defending the alphabet they wanted for their language.

Baba Hysen of Melçan gave vital impetus and direction to a protest meeting that was held in Korça in 1909–1910 AD. Another meeting held in Përmet was headed by Baba Abedin of Frashëri. A further meeting in Berat was supported by the *babas* of Skrapar, Mallakastra and Tepelena, among whom were Baba Shaban of Prishta, Baba Behlul of Therepel and Baba Ismail of Gllava.

To win over the Albanian nationalists, the Young Turks sent a certain Mustafa Hexhri Baba from Ankara in 1910–1911 AD, who travelled from *tekke* to *tekke* in Albania, but he failed in his mission.

After the mission of Mustafa Hexhri Baba, one of the leaders of the Young Turks, Talaat bey (later to become Talaat Pasha) went to the Bektashi *tekke* of Salonica and became a Bektashi himself so as to convince the Bektashi of Albania to join the Young Turks, but this step was also in vain.

By this time, Albanian leaders began to realise that fighting with the pen was not enough. In 1910–1911 AD they took up the armed struggle and inspired the bloody uprisings in Kosovo – in Ferizaj, Kaçanik, Gjilan and Gjakova, proving that Albanian national sentiment was still alive five hundred years after Scanderbeg.

The uprising in Kosovo was followed by one in the highlands of Shkodra and in central Albania. In 1911 AD the rebels of Elbasan, Kruja and Korça took to the mountains under the motto 'Freedom or Death.' All of southern Albania was up in arms, as were the armed bands of Dervish Hima of Struga, Izet Zavalani, Namik Selimi of Delvina, Musa Demi, Muharrem Kocka, Bektash Cakrani and others. The success of their efforts was seen in a meeting at the *tekke* of Frashër in 1912 AD where an Albanian battalion was set up, made up of men who had deserted from the Turkish army. It was led by the immortal patriot Tajar bey of Tetova.

The meeting of the Albanian freedom-fighters that year at the *tekke* of Frashër, together with the open revolt of the Kosovars who entered Skopje triumphantly, turned into a general uprising. In this uprising, in which all the Bektashi *tekkes* played an active role, the elderly Baba Hysen of Melçan took to the hills and joined the rebels to give proof once more of the ardent desire in his heart for the freedom of his people.

As such, by the end of 1912, the victorious Albanians in their uprising had eked out a number of privileges from the Turkish regime that led to autonomy. This achievement caused panic in the other Balkan countries – Greece, Bulgaria, Serbia and Montenegro – that joined in an alliance and declared war to expel Turkey from Macedonia and to divide Albania up.

In this perilous situation, a meeting was held in Vlora on 28 November 1912 under Ismail Qemali. It was a national assembly of Albanian leaders that swiftly declared Albanian independence and put a stop to the country's downfall. The two major Albanian fortresses, Janina and Shkodra, had not yet fallen into the hands of the enemy and were being defended by local Albanian forces with the support of men sent by Baba Haxhi of Kruja in the north and by Baba Abedin of Frashër in the south.

Although the Albanians defended these two mighty fortresses with great ardour, the Turkish commanders took no heed of the borders of the new State declared in Vlora and decided to capitulate to the enemies [...]

In early 1913, shaken by the calamity the country was undergoing, Baba Abedin of Frashër died after a long illness. At the same time, the Greeks savagely murdered Baba Hafiz of the *tekke* of Kuç in Devoll, and the Serbs razed all the *tekkes* in Kosovo, and began building numerous churches and monasteries instead. [...]

In mid-1913, Skopje and Monastir were overrun by the Serbian army. Shkodra was occupied by the Montenegrin army and then taken over by international forces from Europe. Janina, Gjirokastra and Korça were conquered by Greek forces.

The interim government of free Albania, with its capital in Vlora, demanded the withdrawal of the Greeks and Serbs from its territory. Pressured by Austria, Serbia released the Albanian regions referred to at the Conference of London that year. However, Greece, with French and Russian support, refused to withdraw from the regions of Korça and Gjirokastra.

In this confusion, rival propaganda between the Greeks and Albanians spread in Europe, and, in particular, in Korça and Gjirokastra. The Greeks endeavoured to garner support in the Orthodox community, and the Albanians, who had no national church of their own, encouraged pan-Albanian nationalism in the Muslim community, in the spirit of the Bektashi *tekkes*. As they could not achieve their aims peacefully, the Greeks took to force, initially destroying the Gravel *Tekke* (*Teqeja e Zallit*) in Gjirokastra and attempted to assassinate the erudite leader of Albanian Bektashism, Baba Selim who, however, escaped and fled from the *tekke*. They then set up a network of spies around all the other *tekkes*.

In June 1914, the Greeks scorched and devastated all of southern Albania, with the exception of Vlora and Berat. Like a twentieth-century Nero, in their fury at the *tekkes* as centres of Albanian patriotism, they burned down the *tekkes* of Frashër, Prishta, Turan, Memaliaj and all the other smaller *tekkes* in the region.

The clergy of these sacred sites, ruined by human hand, took flight. About a hundred dervishes and *babas* from Kolonja, Leskovik, Përmet, Skrapar and Tepelena sought refuge in Vlora, but even there they found little comfort.

Even some of our brethren, incited by a certain Muslim cleric, sadly and shamefully whipped up turmoil in the country and attacked the national government. Just as the Greeks had done before them, they burned down the *tekke* of Elbasan, captured and imprisoned dervishes and *muhips*, burned down the *tekke* of Kruja, and destroyed the *tekkes* of Berat and Mallakastra. As if this were not enough, their rebel leaders, who took over Vlora, imprisoned all the *babas* and dervishes who had fled there from southern Albania, from their beloved and scorched land.

Baba Salih of Elbasan, imprisoned by the rebels of Durrës, died in 1915. Baba Sulejman of Barmash in the Kolonja region was caught in Berat in 1914 and martyred after endless tribulation. Among those imprisoned in Vlora were: Baba Shemja of Frashër (the deputy of the unforgotten Baba Abedin), Baba Ahmet of Turan and about 100 dervishes.

Baba Myheddin of Gllava, the deputy of the venerable Baba Ismail, put up heroic resistance with the men of the immortal Tafil Buza, before his *tekke* was burned down by the rebels. To escape from their merciless hands, he sought refuge in Bari, in Italy.

Like this patriotic and undaunted cleric, Baba Kamber of Berat fled to the *tekke* of Gjirokastra. Baba Shaban of Prishta, Baba Ahmet of Koshtan and Baba Zejnel of Kruja, for their part, fled to the *tekke* of Kaygusuz Sultan in Egypt where Baba Shaban of Prishta died in longing for the homeland he had been obliged to abandon.

In short, in 1914 the Greeks and the [Sunni] rebels devastated Bektashism in Albania, doing more to destroy it than Sultan Mahmud had done a hundred years before them, because the Bektashi were Albanian patriots and men of liberal convictions.

The highlanders of Martanesh and part of the mountains of Dibra were luckier. The *tekkes* of Martanesh and Bllaca were spared and not burned down. The men of these rugged mountains had sworn to oppose the rebels who were thus not able to penetrate their region, so these two *tekkes* were saved from the catastrophe that struck all the rest.

In all, eighty *tekkes* were burned and razed to the ground by the rebels and the Greeks. This catastrophe that struck the Bektashi in 1914 will remain a painful and unforgotten memory in history.

The reconstruction of the Tekkes, the patriotic activities of the Bektashi after the World War, and religious reforms

At the end of 1914, the Italian army occupied Vlora as a military measure against Austria.

When Italian troops landed in Vlora, the rebels withdrew and the Bektashi clergy were released from prison.

In the spring of 1915, Essad Pasha Toptani, who had inspired the rebel uprising, formed another Albanian government. In this little Albania, stretching from Berat to Mirdita, Albanian nationalists lived in relative freedom. The Bektashi clergy also profited from this freedom and were able to return to their homes, i.e. the ruins of their burnt-out *tekkes*.

The poor Bektashi, as if having survived the flood in Noah's Ark, spent the years from 1917 to 1919 in dire straits and many were on the verge of starvation. Nonetheless, they laid the foundations for new buildings and worked hard towards their unwavering objective of a better life in a free Albania.

In addition to the re-established *tekkes*, a new *tekke* was built in 1916, one of great significance, on Mount Tomorr. It was founded by Iljaz Vërzhezha, an admirable dervish who had earlier built roads, dug wells and fountains in the mountains, and collected money from the rich to feed the poor and to enable orphaned girls to get married.

In 1600 AD, Hadji Baba from the *tekke* of Hacıbektaş arrived at the top of Mount Tomorr and on that peak venerated by the Albanians since ancient times, he set a sign and told the people that the site would thereafter be visited in the name of Abbas Ali, the brother of Imam Husein and standard-bearer of Kerbela. After leaving this sign on Tomorr, Hadji Baba went to Përmet where he died. From there, his body was taken to Qesaraka in the Kolonja region where a *tekke* and a *tyrbe* were built in his honour that still exist in all their glory to the present day. For three hundred years, Baba Tomorr, a mountain of the pagans for two thousand years, has been a centre of veneration for the great martyr of Kerbela and a true site of pilgrimage, being visited by all the Bektashi of Albania every year on 12 August [old style].

Since its establishment by Dervish Iljaz in 1916 near the holy shrine, Tomorr has become a site of great national and religious significance, not only for the Bektashi but for all Albanians.

In 1919 AD, when the world was again at peace, the efforts of all Albanians were once more called for to defend the country's independence. Active among them were the Bektashi, devoted as always to this goal.

In 1920 AD, Baba Ramadan of Qatrom near Korça, Baba Ahmet of Turan, Baba Mustafa of Frashër, Baba Xhemal of Përmet, Baba Hysen of Skrapar, and Baba Sulejman and Baba Selim of Gjirokastra all strove to get the population behind a national congress that was held in Lushnja and proved to be sacred to the memory of the Albanians. There, the Albanians proved for the first time since the death of Scanderbeg that they were a resilient nation and saved Albania for a second time since the congress of Vlora that had declared Albanian independence in 1912. […]

[Excerpt from: Ali Tomorri, *Historija e Bektashinjvet* (Tirana 1929), pp. 82–94. Translated from the Albanian by Robert Elsie.]

1930
FRIEDRICH MARKGRAF
A BOTANIST ON MOUNT TOMORR

The German botanist Friedrich Markgraf (1897-1987), who worked for the Botanical Gardens in Berlin, travelled much in Albania in the 1920s to study and collect plants for his postdoctoral thesis on the 'Plant Geography of Central Albania'. His journey to the top of Mount Tomorr took him to the Bektashi tekke and the shrine of Abbas Ali.

At five o'clock we saw something green in a crease just before we got to the pass. It was a small alpine hut called Kulmak, with a good source of spring water. We allowed the pack animal to drink in silence for a few minutes. I then called over a shepherd because we wanted to set up our tent there. He was a Vlach and replied sullenly: 'Why don't you go to the convent? It's just over the pass.' This time, the information I was given proved to be right. As we continued, we could see what seemed to be a large building in the distance. It reminded me of a solitary monastery in the highlands of Tibet. Behind it was the mountain ridge. We met the abbot at the gate and were immediately invited in with great hospitality.

The Muslim convent was small and was inhabited by two abbots and five monks, as well as by a family that did the farming and provided other services. Our stay here had the additional advantage that we could give our pack animals adequate shelter in a stable. We spent most of our time sitting on the portico that extended down the whole side of the building. The rest of the time, we were with the monks in the refectory, a large room in traditional Albanian style. Here we were able to warm up and cook our food. The mountain tea that we had brought with us was prepared in style by one of the monks. When we offered them a cup, they refused because they were fasting. It was thus all the more admirable that they prepared meals for us.

They belonged to the liberal Bektashi Order that is widespread in Albania. They wore white robes, with dark coats when they were outside. The abbots wore green coats, the colour of the standard of the Prophet. On their heads they wore tall white felt cylinders, of course without a tassel but with nice vertical folds. Around the cylinders they wove a green cloth. Part of the dervish costume was the full beard that struck us in particular because beards are otherwise rare in Albania. Like the Muslims in the towns, they carried a string of amber beads that they fingered constantly. In the picture I took, one can see a metal star with a gem in it worn by the second person from the left in the second row. It is the *teslim tash*, the symbol of his vows. The abbot is distinguished from the others by the large earring of polished glass that dangles over his shoulder from his left ear lobe. He had the title *baba*, i.e. 'father' and bore the name Ali in whose memory the convent was built. At that time, there were two Ali Babas, but only one of them wore the glass earring (the one in the picture on the left with a cane in his hand). He spoke good French as he had spent much time in Egypt. The person after whom the convent was named is Abbas Ali who is said to be buried up on Tomorr. A lantern is kept burning day and night in the stone foundations in front of the convent, and at his grave on the southern peak of the mountain there is a small shrine. Although the site was sacred, the *baba* gave us room to sleep in the chapel which was the cleanest and nicest part in the building. This was very obliging of him and is a good reflection of the free-thinking spirit of his order. The chapel, devoid of any religious icons or pictures, had a wonderful wooden ceiling that they had made themselves. It had dark blue boards crossing the ceiling at an oblique angle and a square standing on end with a colourful star from which a light hung. The gaps between the boards were filled with gold-coloured wooden mouldings with crescents on them from one end to the other. The four corners of the ceiling had scarlet triangles with black double-headed eagles on them, the arms of the Albanian State.

We were well looked after. Our host took pleasure in talking to us and taught us the names of the various plants, etc. We had found some calcite that we showed to him. He called it *gur delesh*, i.e. sheep stone, and said that they used it instead of rennin to make cheese.

On 20 June we began our climb up to the southern peak called *Varri i Abaz Aliut* (The Grave of Abbas Ali). It was a fantastic sunny morning. Our servant, another fellow called Ibrahim, asked us if he could come to the shrine with us. Since the pack animals were well looked after, we agreed and began to climb in a northwesterly direction, mostly over limestone gravel. The lower part was covered in an open forest of Bosnian pine (*pinus leucodermis*), a grove that had been badly damaged in a forest fire. There was no sign of beeches or firs. We collected interesting plants along the way, and many were in bloom. We slowly made our way up the mountain until we reached the pilgrims' trail. [...]

We then began the climb up the gravel cone leading to the peak. Rain and hail beat down upon us but the strong wind fortunately drove the precipitation away just as fast as it had brought it. Right under the peak, pilgrims had built themselves protective walls and holes. The many goat horns were proof of the sacrifices made there. At the top was the *mekam*, a circular stone wall with a small stone altar in the middle. All around the inner side of the wall were niches with lanterns for the festivities. We got some protection from the elements here. [...]

[On our return,] we quickly said farewell and were very much surprised that the abbot decidedly refused to accept our gift of money although he had given us some of his valuable bread at our request. The monks here make cornbread that they bake on both sides. I never had such a good meal!

[Excerpt from Friedrich Markgraf, *In Albaniens Bergen* (Stuttgart: Strecker & Schröder 1930), pp. 101–105. Translated from the German by Robert Elsie.]

1930
JOSEPH SWIRE
THOUGHTS ON THE BEKTASHI

The British journalist and author Joseph Swire (1903–1978), from Yorkshire, was early to be attracted to the Balkans. He visited Albania for the first time as a student in 1924 and was in the Balkans again at the end of the decade where he gathered material for his first book: Albania: The Rise of a Kingdom *(London 1929). His second book on the Balkan country,* King Zog's Albania *(London 1937), was written in 1932. He travelled much in the back country and was exceptionally well informed.*

We camped outside Leskovik and returned next day to Permeti. Then, leaving Këlcyra on our left we went to the Bektash *tekké* of Suka in a narrow cultivated valley. The *tekké*, strongly built of stone by dervishes in 1920, is rectangular and somewhat like a Yorkshire dales farmhouse; it stands on a hillside, owning about fifty acres which are tilled by its ten dervishes. Passages and rooms were very clean but sparsely furnished. *Baba-i-madh* (grandfather or bishop) Kamber Ali who happened to be there, a portly jovial old man in flowing white robe and very ecclesiastical manner, has his seat at the *tekké* of Tahir Baba at Prishtë. He had been to America and spoke English. A dervish brought coffee and cigarettes and *lokoum,* and a rose each – for the rose is an emblem of Bektashism; but the *Baba-i-madh* would not let me photograph him because he had drunk no water for twelve days (a self-disciplinary practice) – though what that had to do with it he did not explain.

Bektashism was founded by one Haxhi Bektash Veli, a Persian, who died in 1338 (though some say the doctrine is really that of a sect called Houroufi, founded by a mystic named Fadlullah who was murdered in 1394). It is a philosophy rather than a religion, having a common base with Buddhism and Zoroastrianism, and was propagated in the Islamic world beneath the religious cloak of Mahometanism – though it has little in common with that religion. Indeed the Bektashis are only partly guided by the Prophet and ignore many of his injunctions (notably in regard to abstention from strong drink, the veiling of women, and regular prayer). Though they have found it discreet to do so, they need not observe the Moslem feasts and fasts (which hamper evolution), they dislike Moslem fanaticism, pray only at sunrise and sunset, and do not turn towards Mecca when they pray. Nor are prayers obligatory – and their prayers are not for thanksgiving or supplication to some external power but rather a meditation or self-analysis. There is little outward ceremony; and the Bektashis have no ideas of penance, though abstinence at appointed times from drinking pure water or killing animals for food is practised for self-discipline. They have no mosques but pray anywhere, the dervishes of a *tekke* generally in the *Baba's* private room. They have secret signs whereby members of the sect may know each other in times of persecution or political danger.

The mysteries of Bektashism, closely guarded secrets, are revealed to adherents of the sect by stages as their knowledge evolves away from the dogmatic observances, prohibitions, and superstitions of popular religions and towards the enlightened philosophy which inspires the highest orders; but there are certain fundamental mysteries which remain unrevealed, and revelation will come only at the psychological moment in the social and political evolution of the world.

Though there is practically no literature upon the Bektashis, the main principles of their teaching are known. They hold that God is the Divine Spirit of Goodness, the life and soul of all, which manifests itself from time to time through different beings according to circumstances – for man is the highest expression of Divine power, with innate knowledge of good and evil. So Christ, Mahomet, and other prophets, saints and leaders too are all revered by the Bektashis as manifestations of that Spirit. Man does not die but is transformed; and there is no heaven nor hell but those man creates for himself by his deeds. The Bektashis are almost pantheistic; they find God in nature, on the mountain tops, in the smiling valleys, in animals, in human kindness and understanding. They live their philosophy from day to day with allowances for human frailties, teaching simplicity and brotherly love and gentleness towards all living creatures. Their beliefs are certainly confused with pagan superstitions and legends – many of these deliberately invented to identify (for gaining a hold over ignorant masses) some local saint or shrine or tribal deity with their own. St. Naoum, for one, they identify with Sari Sallteku, so the saint's tomb at the monastery of Shën Naoum is their place of pilgrimage. But tolerance is the essence of their views, for they see good in all creeds, perfection in none. Christians, Moslems, and others may join the order and share its secrets without being called upon to forswear their original faith; and Bektashis will marry those of other creeds without seeking to force a change of their partners' privy beliefs. They respect women who may visit their *tekkés*, they ignore social inequalities, and they hold work a duty whereby man earns his right to food. They teach that it is wrong to be full while others are hungry, evil to boast one's own righteousness while denying good in others.

Bektashism was introduced into Albania by dervish Sari Sallteku, who came from Corfu where Bektashism had taken root in the second half of the thirteenth century. Sallteku founded seven *tekkés,* among them that of Sari Saltik upon the crags above Kruja – where he slew a dragon. According to Ali Tyrabiu of Tomori, Skenderbeg became a Bektash while in the Turkish service but reverted to Roman Catholicism (probably as a matter of policy).

In Albania the sect grew steadily in strength and *tekkés* were established early at Tepeleni, Gjinokastra, Konica, Mecovo and Janina. The Bektashis began to spread too in North Albania, but Kara Mahmoud Bushati dislodged them from Shkodër, Kruja and Tirana, destroying their *tekkés;* and at the beginning of the nineteenth century the Sultan attempted to suppress a sect which threatened his omnipotence within the Empire, massacring the Bektash Janissaries. The refugees from North Albania found a friend in Ali Pasha because their support was valuable to him against the Moslem Turks who persecuted them. Ali was himself secretly converted to Bektashism by Baba Shëmin of Kruja, and with his support Shëmin re-established the sect at Kruja and founded the *tekké* of Melçani at Korça. During his wanderings Shëmim spent a night with the Zogus in Mati and blessed the family.

The Bektashis led Albanian nationalism, their tolerance of all creeds making easy their co-operation with northern Catholics and southern Orthodox alike where Christian fanaticism did not supervene (as among some of the Orthodox during the struggle with Greece in 1913–14); and their principal adversaries were, and are, the fanatical Moslems of the plains. These fanatics did their best to wreck the Albanian national cause, rebelling (in alliance with Serbs and Greeks) in 1914 against Prince Wilhelm and persecuting the Bektashis, though the latter and the Christian nationalists kept them out of the mountains. Now that Turkey has 'gone modern' the fanatics are no longer pro-Turkish, but they still hold a central position, geographically and politically, in Albania, and only time and education can shake their power. A Bektash leader told me the central Albanian Moslems remain the most retrograde and unenlightened of all Albanians, men debased and corrupted, who have neither loyalty nor honour.

In January, 1922, an assembly of 500 Bektash delegates resolved to break away from the tutelage of Ankara, hitherto the seat of the Supreme Bektash (an Albanian) who transferred himself to Tirana, which became the headquarters of the sect when in September, 1925, the Turkish Republican government suppressed religious orders of dervishes in Turkey and closed the Bektash *tekkés*. But Bektash relations with the Moslems of Albania remained anomalous until 1929, when the organisation of the Moslem religious community came up for consideration by the government. Supported by the Orthodox Prime Minister Kotta, the Bektashis demanded complete religious independence; but the Moslems were too strong for them and they gained only spiritual and executive autonomy within the Moslem community, a compromise which ill satisfied them, for they dislike such identification with the fanatics.

Their statutes were drawn up at Korça, in 1929. The sect has clergy, confirmed members and laity; and their clergy consist, in Albania, of one 'arch-grandfather,' five 'grandfathers,' fathers and priests. There are said to be 7,370,000 Bektashis of whom 200,000 are Albanians, most of these in southern Albania. They are gaining ground among both Moslems and Orthodox Christians, their nationalism, the mystery of their philosophy and the absence of ritual making a strong appeal to the younger people, and their simplicity, hospitality and courtesy giving them much prestige. There is no doubt of their influence for good, for it is almost tangible in the districts where it prevails.

[Excerpt from: Joseph Swire, *King Zog's Albania* (London: Robert Hale 1937), pp. 240–244.]

1932
RICHARD BUSCH-ZANTNER
THE BEKTASHI SECT IN ALBANIA

The German scholar and social geographer Richard Busch-Zantner (1911-1942) was born in Munich. From 1925 to 1929, he and his mother went on annual holidays to the Balkans and many of the trips took them to Albania. He seems to have been in Albania on at least four occasions. He joined the Nazi Party in 1933 and was later the author of 'Albanien: Neues Land im Imperium' (Albania: A New Country in the Empire), Leipzig 1939, a work of somewhat Fascist inspiration. He died as a soldier on the Russian front in 1942.

In early 1932, King Zog I recognised the teachings of the dervish sect of the Bektashi as a religion of its own in Albania. This has added a fourth religion to the three traditional religions in the country. It is substantially different from Sunni Islam, which was constituted as an official independent religious community in 1923. With its c. 100,000 adepts, it now comes in third place between the Orthodox Christians (170,000) and the Roman Catholics (95,000). Leading the list is still Sunni Islam, even though it has now lost 100,000 followers.

The sect was originally a simple dervish order from Asia Minor but then, probably as a result of its close ties to the Janissaries, whose military chaplains were Bektashi, it spread to Europe. Its legendary founder Bektash is said to be buried in the Beshiktash suburb of Constantinople. Records show that the order was present in Albania as early as 1530. It spread among the Albanians under Ali Pasha of Janina in particular. In 1826, Sultan Mahmud II banned and bloodily suppressed the order due to the influential political relations of the Bektashi and its ever increasing distance from official Islam. But he did not manage to get rid of the order entirely. It survived not only in Asia Minor (Lycia) and the region of Constantinople, but also in Egypt. The main area into which it spread, however, was Albania, centred on Kruja, where records show that it was present in the 16th century. In the course of the 19th century, it spread from there, and has recently been the object of more scholarly attention, even though the modern evolution in its dogma has not been well understood. The teachings of the Bektashi, which developed early from an order to a full religious sect, are closer to, though not entirely the same as the teachings of the Shi'ites.

The reasons behind the recent independence of the sect in 1928, much discussed by the Albanian public since then, are not to be found so much in politics (the waning influence of the Orthodox and fanatical Sunni clergy) as in the fact that the royal family and their relatives, including the feudal dynasty of the Toptani family, the age-old rulers of Kruja and Tirana, have been adepts of the Bektashi sect for generations. A preference for the teachings of the Bektashi can also be seen in some of the king's other regulations on religion, for instance the ban on veils. Connected to all of this, at any rate, is the fact that, in accordance with the teachings of the Bektashi who attribute little importance to ritual prayers in mosques, many mosques have been torn down even in entirely Muslim towns. The increasing attention paid to this sect has thus also had a substantial influence on the cultural landscape.

The Bektashi are presently distributed in northern coastal Albania, with the exception of Shkodra where the sect was driven out in the 18th or 19th century, and in the regions of Mat, Mallakastra, Dropull, Kolonja and Korça. But there are Bektashi adepts everywhere. The most important monasteries that have now gained in significance (with the names of the abbots as leaders of the new movement) are those of Fushë Kruja (under Mehmed Baba) and Gjirokastra (under Selman Baba), but there are also other less influential monasteries in Tirana, in Elbasan and in the region of Gjirokastra.

[Richard Busch-Zantner, 'Die Sekte der Bektashi in Albanien', *Petermanns Geographische Mitteilungen*, Gotha, 78 (1932), p. 245. Translated from the German by Robert Elsie.]

1933
RICHARD BUSCH-ZANTNER
THE TOWN OF THE FORBIDDEN DERVISHES

In about 1933, the young German scholar and social geographer Richard Busch-Zantner (1911-1942) had occasion to visit the town of Kruja, known for its large Bektashi community.

If you travel down the main coastal road from Shkodra southwards to Tirana, your driver will not fail to point out the fascinating little town of Kruja in among the limestone mountains to the left. There it perches – steep, bold and open to the world. This little town is rich in historical venues.

The first and most important site to be seen in Kruja is the mausoleum (*tyrbe*) of the 'Five Pilgrims to Mecca' (Haji Hamsa). Here lie all five of the venerable old members of the Bektashi dervish order, who have had their seat in Kruja for a long time. One sees a simple domed building (domed constructions are otherwise rare in Albanian Islam), painted on the inside and probably stemming from the eighteenth century. Tradition has it otherwise, i.e. that the mausoleum of the Five Hajis was built in the year 1562. This seems unlikely although the dome could well stem from that period. What is, however, certain is that it is a foundation of great significance for the Bektashi dervish order. This order rejects religious services in mosques and prefers to hold them in the mausoleums of their holy men. It is for this reason that the sacred emblems of the Bektashi Order are to be seen here in the Mausoleum of Haji Hamsa: a battle-axe and the standard, the latter being a white, or in this case faded yellow cloth with red symbols attached to it. One can make out a hand, a star, a crescent and a sword. No one knows exactly what their significance is. Christians are not allowed to learn the mysteries of this sect, and not even all Muslims understand them. There are five sarcophagi in the room, the largest being directly under the vaulted dome and the others situated on the two long sides. Fine, smooth silk of white and green (the latter being covered in Arabic script) covers the catafalques under which the holy men are buried.

There are still at least fifty mausoleums in Kruja, the domes of which rise amidst a confusion of tiled roofs, often graced by slender and mysteriously dark cypresses. In 1900 there were still 350 such *tyrbes*, and in the nineteenth century there were about 500. To name but a few, there is the *tyrbe* of Sultan Baba and the *tyrbe* of Shenusi Baba.

There is one mausoleum that is particularly impressive – the *tyrbe* of Sari Saltik Baba. It is situated in a cave up in the limestone cliffs of Kruja, carved as it were into live stone. Stairs and goat trails take one up to the top of the mountain, and then there are a few steps down into the cave. One first enters a sort of antechamber, on the left and right of which are the sarcophagi of the favourite disciples of the master, each covered once again in silken cloth on which little coins have been cast as an oblation. Oil lanterns clinging to knotted and broken ropes that hang from the roof of the cave flicker in the dark, and there is an old hunch-backed dervish with the obligatory white fez who tends to the graves. The chamber in which the somewhat elevated grave of Sari Saltik is situation is closed off by a wonderful and finely fashioned grille, the work of a Muslim gypsy. It is surrounded by playful cats, holy animals in Islam. The pale light from the oil lamps casts the shadow of the grille onto the wall, creating grotesque and fantastic forms, and the cold air from the interior of the mountain can be felt through the crack in the door. The rays of the southern sun hardly make it into the cave at all.

It is an astounding world, an experience rarely to be had in Europe. Suddenly I became aware that the great order of the Bektashi dervishes had its centre right here in this mountain cave. The order was once spread over Asia and Africa and is intrinsically linked to the history of the Janissaries. It is somewhat of a surprise to find such mysterious Oriental religiosity in Europe and to see the graves of so many holy men in a little town like this.

In 1357 Haji Veli Bektash from Khorasan founded the order on the Kizilirmak River in Sivas. It was also Haji Veli Bektash who gave his blessing to the Janissary order, thus establishing the link between the two. The Bektashi Order was intimately connected to the Janissaries. The Janissaries ruled the Ottoman state and the Bektashi ruled the Turkish people, that is, until Sultan Mahmud II wiped the Janissaries out and banned the Bektashi Order in 1826. Since that time, the Bektashi have played no noticeable role in history or in scholarly research. Despite everything, the sect lives on here in Europe, in the eyrie of Kruja, the same Bektashi sect that was alleged to be 'under control' a hundred years ago.

A difficult, stony path leads to the fortress of Kruja, once ruled by Scanderbeg, the unforgotten national hero of the Albanians. First of all, the traveller will stop and visit the manor of the Toptani family, the great patrons of the Bektashi. It is a marvellously comfortable eighteenth-century Turkish villa. It has breezy balconies in the middle, protruding wings on each side, and in the interior there is one great hall with wonderful wood carvings and with paintings and frescoes on the walls revealing quiet stylised landscapes and urban settings. It is all baroque in the Oriental manner. From the windows there is a fantastic panoramic view of the coastal plain right to the blue horizon where the sky meets the Adriatic Sea.

Also exceptional is the view of the fortress itself, to which the path leads. It is the very antithesis of the manor. Behind the steep cliffs of the fortress rise vertical walls of limestone which impede the view beyond them. However, the immediate surroundings are impressive enough, with the lowlands stretching miles and miles around us as on a map.

There are traces of the Bektashi in the fortress, too. The mausoleum of Baba Mustafa Dollma was built in a bastion protruding to the west, and the one-time fortress church of the Turk-hating Scanderberg was transformed into a mosque. Akhisar, which means White Castle, is what the Turks called Kruja, yet the Turks never really regarded this grandiose eyrie as the fortress, at least not after the fifteenth century. Otherwise they would not have transformed the keep into a civilian clock tower. If Akhisar had actually been a fortified armoury, it would hardly have contained a monastery. Christians were not allowed to visit the town unless they were accompanied by a Muslim. In fact they were subject to death if they entered the fortress at night. This regulation was still in force in 1832 when the walls of the fortress were pulled down. As it was never rescinded, it is probably still valid today, although it is no longer enforced.

Who are the Bektashi?

It is difficult to give an answer to this in a few words. What is for sure is that the Bektashi no longer exist officially and, although Theodor Ippen noted their presence in Kruja in no uncertain terms, no one took any more interest in them as a phenomenon of importance for the history of Islam. It is known that, like other dervishes, they lived in lodges or monasteries (*tekkes*) and that only the higher ranks were celibate. The head of a *tekke* is called a *baba*, whose symbol is a large golden, or occasionally silver ring in his left ear. Some of these rings have an unusual style of their own. Otherwise the *babas* are dressed in a large white garment with the usual Bektashi headpiece of white felt. This headpiece is cylindrical in form with twelve pleats and is wrapped in a green cloth making it look like a turban. The other members of the order wear this headpiece too, although without the green wrap. Their symbol is a cord around their necks from which hangs a carved, star-shaped carnelian called a *teslim tash*. They receive this as a token when they finish their training.

What is interesting is that the Bektashi Order became so influential in Albania that it was able to attempt a transformation of Islam in a way it could never have done elsewhere in the Turkish Empire. This was an important step in the history of Islam, the practical effects of which can be seen in a few details. Originally, the Bektashi were proponents of official Islam – strict to the extreme in their beliefs. This was reflected in their mystical ties to the Janissaries. The very opposite is true today. The Bektashi are foes of official Islam, which they despise, and they have created their own dogma, independent of their surroundings. Perhaps it was this, among other things, that caused them to be banned in 1826. In Kruja, one sees many things that are reminiscence of Shia Islam, which is diametrically opposed to the precepts of the Sunni beliefs that were so firmly anchored in Ottoman culture. The Bektashi are nowadays friendly and hospitable to Christians. They do not use mosques except on special occasions. Their most sacred sites are their *tyrbes* (mausoleums). This explains the endless number of mausoleums in Kruja, a town with only one mosque. They do not keep the five ritual prayers a day, nor ablution, nor Ramadan. They do celebrate the latter to an extent, but it is less important than the eleven days of penance and fasting in the month of Muharrem. This reveals their connection to the Shia, as does their particular reverence for Husayn and Hasan, the martyrs of Kerbela.

It is difficult to say why the Bektashi gravitated towards Europe and, in particular to Kruja. Perhaps it was the Janissaries who were centred in Constantinople, with the help of whom they spread to all the conquered territories. Be this as it may, they first appeared in Kruja in 1530, at a time when the fortress was no longer of strategic interest. It is possible that they arrived there with the troops, but this is simply speculation. As to their distribution today, one must distinguish between an upper class and a lower class. The teachings of the Bektashi were known not only to the dervishes but also became very influential in the population at large. Among the areas in which the Bektashi are present are the northern coastal plain (with the exception of Shkodra from which they were expelled in the eighteenth or nineteenth century), Tirana and its surroundings, Mallakastra, and the inland valley regions of Dropull, Kolonja, Korça and Mat. They do not seem to be present beyond territories of Albanian settlement [...] although they do have a few and now increasing number of followers in Bosnia, where a Bektashi community was founded in Sarajevo in 1903 by the late dervish Mustafa Usicanovic.

Closely attached to the Bektashi are the noted feudal Toptani family, the rulers of Tirana, and the reigning monarch of Albania who is from Mat and is closely related to the Toptani.

Let us recapitulate the religious characteristics of the order: they are open-minded to people of other faiths, they have mausoleums instead of mosques, they reject ablution and they ignore the five daily prayers. These four characteristics have had an influence in Muslim religious life in modern-day Albania. They explain why a fanatically religious town such as Tirana has torn down almost all of its mosques. Indeed there are very few mosques throughout this Muslim region of Europe (Sarajevo used to have 300!). It is apparent why the mosques were torn down whereas the mausoleums were not only preserved but are still attended. It also explains why so few people in Albania attend the five daily prayers and why there are so few fountains for ritual ablution, which are missing in no town or village in Bosnia and Herzegovina.

The influence of the Bektashi has become more visible than ever, now that Islam has become the major religious community in Albania. The Bektashi have gone their own way, separate from the official Islam promoted by the Sunni Sublime Porte, and so, too, has Albanian culture, influenced by the ideology of a sect that, since 1826, is said to be banned and non-existent.

[Richard Busch-Zantner, 'Die Stadt der verbotenen Derwische', *Moslemische Revue*, Berlin, January 1934, pp. 1–6. Translated from the German by Robert Elsie.]

1937
JOHN KINGSLEY BIRGE
BEKTASHIISM IN ALBANIA

John Kingsley Birge (1888-1952) was an American Protestant missionary who was active in Turkey, mainly in Izmir, from 1914 onwards. He was born in Bristol, Connecticut, studied at Yale University and trained at Hartford Seminary. While in Turkey, Birge took a great interest in the Bektashi Order and was subsequently the author of the classic Bektashi Order of Dervishes *(London 1937), the first work of substance in English on the Bektashi. Birge visited Albania in 1933 and devoted a chapter of his book to the early history of the Bektashi in that country.*

Since in our own day the Bektashi Order has found its most congenial home in Albania, let us turn for the moment our attention to that land and consider the spread of the Bektashi doctrines there. Any satisfactory investigation is made difficult, if not impossible, by the absence of definite historical data. We know that the invasion of Albania by Turkish troops under Murat II began at least as early as 1431 when Yannina was captured. Evliya Çelebi who reports that the famous Evrenos Gazi, with whose name we are already familiar in connection with the founding of the Janissaries, advanced as far as Lake Ochrida.[37] Since Evrenos is known to have died in 1417,[38] and is supposed to have been over 100 years old at the time, it is probable that his advance campaign must have taken place in the reign of Beyazit I who was campaigning on the borders of Albania when attracted away by the invasion of Timurlane in 1402. With his soldiers, and even more probably with those of Murat II, must have gone some of the Bektashi companions of the Janissaries who would not have failed to leave their influence both on those who settled there and on the local inhabitants who now found it wise to come into the Moslem faith. So far as the writer has been able to discover there is, however, no direct mention of Bektashis by Evliya Çelebi, even in connection with his travels in the seventeenth century. That the doctrines of the Bektashis are clearly there, and probably the Bektashis themselves, is shown, nevertheless, by many a reference. In one place he met people who were doing all they could to spread abroad a hatred of the Umayyad Caliphs, Muaviye and Yezit.[39] They refused to wear blue because Muaviye wore that colour. They would not drink *boza*[40] because Muaviye made and consumed the beverage. This attitude, common to all Shiis, is very characteristic of the Bektashis with their emphasis on Teberrâ, or hatred of those who do not love the family of the Prophet. At Ergeri he met people who on occasions failed to observe the canonical prohibition against strong drink, and who observed in their religious practices New Year's Day and the festival of Sari Saltik, the Bektashi saint.[41] At Elbasan he found a *tekke* of dervishes who followed the Way of the Family of the Mantle, *erbabi tariki ali abai dervişan*. This description may not be proof that the dervishes of this *tekke* were Bektashis, but it is at least just the title that might be used if they were. At Pugrados, Evliya found what he called 'several *tekkes* of Abdal Dervishes,' *tekkei dervişan abdalan*,[42] again using the descriptive word 'Abdal' which is often used as synonymous with the word Bektashi.

On my visit to Albania in October, 1933, although I had no time for a thorough search, it became apparent that in the city of Kruje, Bektashiism certainly went back to the early seventeen hundreds. In front of the Zaviye of Mürteza Baba there was a tombstone bearing the Bektashi *tac* on the top and dated 1141 (1728). In the yard about the Zaviye of Haji Yahya Baba there were many tombstones bearing the Bektashi symbols. One of them, unfortunately with the top broken off, was dated 1130 (1717).

The Bektashi tradition, as described by a certain unusually intelligent and well-informed dervish named Haydar Baba, is that Bektashi *babas* came to Albania with the army of Murat and many of them settled there. A Bektashi named Kasim Baba[43] is believed to have come and settled in the time of Muhammad II (1451–1481). Beyazit II (1481–1512), whose conquests in Albania are so often mentioned by Evliya Çelebi, is said to have endowed many *tekkes*, and Haydar Baba assured me that the *vakfiye*'s deeding these properties should be on file at the Top Kapu Saray or the Hazinei Evrak. Although the writer's endeavours to find such have been unavailing it is to be earnestly hoped that under the enlightened policy of the present Turkish government the public archives will be more and more thrown open for the use of scholars, foreign as well as Turkish, until many an obscure page of History will have received new light.

The only event in the history of the Bektashi Order in Albania that seems quite certain is that Tepedelenli Ali Paşa, the Vizir of Epirus, who ruled Albania with a degree of complete independence from about 1790 to 1822, became himself a Bektashi and gave his support to the spread of the order. Certain missionaries of the Bektashi Way like Shemimi[44] were especially influential in winning adherents and in opening *tekkes*. It was from Shemimi that Ali Pasha is supposed to have received the *nasip* or initiation, and the great *tekke* in the plain below Kruje is named Şemimi Sultan Tekkesi after the one who built it in 1802 on the site of the tomb of one of the early traditional missionaries, Horasanli Ali Baba. In the anonymous Life of Ali Pasha, published in London in 1823, based largely on the diary of Theophilos Richards, there are two steel engravings of Ali Pasha, one showing him wearing the characteristic *tac* of the Bektashis, the other showing on his head a smaller cap but with the twelve sections symbolic in Bektashi lore and ritual of the twelve Imams. Although Ali Pasha apparently found it easy to be a 'pantheist with the Bektadgis' and to drink 'repeated bumpers to the health of the Blessed Virgin,'[45] with the Christians, these pictures set at rest any doubt as to the fact that Ali Pasha's having been a publicly recognized member of the Bektashi Order.

[Extract from: John Kingsley Birge, *The Bektashi Order of Dervishes* (London: Luzac 1937), pp. 70–73.]

1939
MARGARET HASLUCK
BABA TOMOR

Margaret Hasluck climbed to the top of Mount Tomorr, the sacred mountain, in 1931 and describes the atmosphere and beliefs she encountered.

In South Albania the peasantry, as they hear of the European upheaval, will more than ever be seeking omens from Baba Tomor. Every visitor to South Albania is fascinated by the striking mountain that overhangs the town of Berat. Twenty miles long and ten broad at its base, it sweeps up with fine, clean lines to a platform from which rise twin summits shaped like pyramids, one 7,933 and the other 7,861 feet above sea-level. On all but the short north side it is surrounded by low hills, which increase its apparent height and send it towering into the sky in splendid isolation. For nine months of the year its snowy cap glistens with unearthly beauty on a sunny morning, hides at midday behind a blue haze or a storm-laden cloud, and as the day declines again stands forth clear and beautiful.

To the older generation of South Albanians the mountain is as full of mystery as of majesty. These simple people, left without schools in their youth, are too uneducated to understand natural phenomena. They think it miraculous that while their lowland homes bake under the August sun the twin summits are sometimes assailed by hailstones and biting winds. They also do not understand why some of them, climbing the mountain unprepared, suffer physically from the altitude. With all solemnity they tell you that a dread Being called 'Baba (Father) Tomor,' or simply 'the Saint of Tomor,' lives on the top. He allows only the good to invade his solitude and makes the evil fall by the way or drives them off with hailstones, fierce winds, mountain sickness and strange bleedings at the nose. Many are even afraid to mention his name and talk of him anonymously and with averted glance as 'he' and 'that peak.' Hardened sinners may forswear themselves if put to the oath, according to their religion, on the Gospel or the Koran, but no one dares to make a false oath by 'Baba Tomor' or 'that peak.' A bird too sacred to be caught by human hands haunts the mountain and a sacred apple tree grows near the top. Only the pure in heart may climb up to pick the apples, and to this day no one has been found pure enough. The apples sometimes roll down to the path below as they ripen; unusually large and finely perfumed, they work miracles; a childless woman, for instance, has only to eat one to conceive. The tree is located by some in the black gully between the two summits and by others at the mouth of a cave above an inaccessible rock-face between the villages of Bargulas and Kapinova; these add that from both villages the tree may be discerned through field-glasses.

Every year more than a thousand South Albanians, little children as well as grown men and women, climb to the top of Tomor to pray and to sacrifice a ram. Their reasons are primitive enough. Some when ill had promised the saint to make the pilgrimage if he would cure them; others go to implore his help throughout the coming year for themselves and their families, their animals and crops. They bring offerings of money and candles as well as the ram. They dip pebbles from the mountain in the blood that spurts from the ram's throat in the moment of sacrifice and wear them afterwards as amulets against disease and other ills. They bring a handful of wheat to lay on the tomb at the topmost point, and they take away a few grains from the pile already there to mix with their seed-corn; these grains, sanctified by their contact with the holy tomb and spreading the sanctity to all the seed-corn, ensure that next year's harvest will be bountiful. To people so poor the assurance is vital.

At present the pilgrimage is managed by Bektashi dervishes, who say that the sacred spot on the top is the second grave of Abbas Ali, a Shia saint who is really buried at Kerbela, in Mesopotamia, and has been adopted, somewhat arbitrarily, by the Bektashis. It seems probably, however, that the cult had originally nothing to do with these dervishes. Their appearance on Tomor is frankly modern, and their organisation of the pilgrimage is still in process of development.

There is good evidence that the cult on Tomor is older than the Bektashis, who were not founded till the fourteenth century of our era. The vast majority of the pilgrims are adherents, if not members of the Bektashi Order, but sometimes Christians and Sunni Mohammedans make the pilgrimage and go through the same motions. The Bektashis raise no objections; most unorthodox of Mohammedans, they are almost free from religious fanaticism and everywhere make the followers of other creeds welcome at their shrines. The primitive beliefs, too, about the sanctity of the mountain are shared by all South Albanians, no matter whether Bektashis or not. Pilgrimage and beliefs seem to belong to a distant past to which all South Albanians, irrespective of religion, are heirs. They seem, in fact, to survive from a mountain cult similar to those practised in Biblical times on Horeb and Sinai and in classical times on Argaeus.

An experience of my own illustrates the method of transition from one religion to another. In 1931, the first foreigner to make the pilgrimage, I stood in glorious sunshine on the mountain top. Scores of pilgrims, Bektashis all, were busy with their sacrifices and devotions when a sudden squall struck the summit; a little more and the wind might have flung us over the precipice into the gulf between the two summits. 'HE is angry to-day,' muttered a pilgrim, suddenly pale with ageless fear. 'Who is HE?' I asked. 'The mountain,' said the pilgrim. 'Father Tomor,' said a bolder spirit. 'Abbas Ali,' reproved a dervish. Some clouds came scurrying by. The pilgrims glanced at them uneasily and chorused, 'HE is angry.' One more glance at the clouds and, mastered by their fears, they packs up their goods and went.

[Margaret Hasluck. 'Baba Tomor,' in: *The Manchester Guardian*, September 13, 1939.]

1953
THE MOKATTAM
TEKKE OF CAIRO

This informative article appeared in the summer of 1953 in the Egyptian magazine al-Idaa al-Misriyya. It gives a rare description of the Albanian Bektashi tekke in the Mokattam hills on the outskirts of Cairo a few years before it was closed down and abandoned.

Up in the hills from where Cairo looks as if it were in the palm of your hand, not to mention the Nile and the pyramids beyond it, lies the Bektashi *tekke*. Near it is the Mosque of Abdullah al-Maghawiri that was built behind the fortress of Mehmet Ali Pasha on the highest cliff of the Mokattam Hills.

It is a wondrous place indeed and is visited by Americans, Europeans, Arabs and many groups visiting Egypt from various countries. The grandeur of the *tekke* is apparent from the way it was constructed and from its surroundings. We must not forget to mention the dervishes who built it with great love and care. Mention must be made, first of all, of the naturally-formed cavern which arouses curiosity and amazement. Let us visit this broad cavern in the heart of the Mokattam. The first thing one notices are the Koranic verses on the gate, carved in beautiful Kufic script. On both sides of the entrance are the graves of dervishes. There is also a grave of an Egyptian woman there who died last March. We now proceed in the direction of the tomb of Abdullah al-Maghawiri. It was almost noon and the heat was unbearable as we approached the *tekke*. However, when we entered the building, everything changed. It was wonderfully refreshing.

We were accompanied by an assistant of Baba Sirri, the sheikh of the Bektashi, who explained everything to us. Now we were standing in front of the tomb of Abdullah al-Maghawiri and were much relieved after the oppressive heat outside. The metal doors opened and we could see a chamber which hundreds of women visit every day, hoping for a cure to their infertility. The women believe that they will be blessed if they stand at al-Maghawiri's grave, and they bring offerings with them, off which the dervishes live who tend to the grave and take care of the wonderful gardens. As to the tomb of al-Maghawiri, it is adorned with reddish marble and copper engravings in traditional style. On the far side of it is an intriguing fountain bubbling with cold water. There people can quench their thirst. The women love to drink the water, hoping that they will get pregnant. The assistant of Baba Sirri, an Albanian from Përmet, allowed us to enter the *tekke*, which consisted of an Oriental hall embellished with carpets, precious furniture and silks. On one of the walls was a photograph of Muhammed Naguib.[46] Before we could even sit down, a servant brought coffee in for us. Our hearts were gladdened and we were overcome by the atmosphere of it all, reminiscent of 1,001 Arabian nights.

From there, we moved on to the next room, and then to another where we noticed a photograph of Ahmet Zogu, the Albanian king. It is not widely known, but three of the dervishes running the *tekke* are Albanians. We then passed through a little doorway leading out into a garden full of trees. Grapevines shielded us from the sun. It was a virtual paradise.

We then accompanied the dervish up some stairs to a curious grave that Sheikh Ahmet Sirri, who now lives in Turkey, built for himself. Across from it was the grave of His Highness, Kamal al-Din Hussein, the son of Sultan Hussein Kamel, and a little lower down was another grave containing the remains of Princess Zeyneb, the daughter of Ismail Pasha, who was the grandson of Mehmet Ali Pasha. There was also a grave of one of the sisters of the Albanian king, Ahmet Zogu.

We remained for a while in that marvellous garden, the work of the Albanian dervishes. It was square-shaped and provided beautiful surroundings for visitors. The sunlight and the fresh air seemed to draw the moisture of the Nile and the beauty of Cairo right into it.

[Article from the Egyptian magazine *al-Idaa al-Misriyya*, 4 July 1953. Translated by Robert Elsie from the Albanian version published in: Emin Azemi and Shkëlzen Halimi (ed.), *Shqiptarët e Egjiptit* (Skopje 1993), pp. 74–76.]

1955
OSMAN MYDERRIZI
THE BEGINNINGS OF BEKTASHI LITERATURE IN ALBANIA

The Albanian scholar and orientalist Osman Myderrizi (1891-1973) was born in Tirana of a family of Muslim clerics. He attended a Turkish-language teaching school in Shkodra and studied in Constantinople. After his return to Albania in 1913, he opened an Albanian-language school in Ndroq. On 21 April 1921 Myderrizi became a member of the first Albanian parliament and also represented Tirana in the constitutional assembly in 1924, but with the rise of dictator Ahmet Zogu at the end of 1924, he fled abroad, as did many Albanian politicians and intellectuals. From 1947 to his retirement in 1966, he was active as a scholar at the Institute of Science and later at the Institute of History and Linguistics in Tirana. His name is linked primarily to his work on seventeenth-century Albanian literature written in Arabic script. In this field, he discovered and saved the manuscripts of many early Muslim poets, whom he transcribed, studied and made known.

The religious writing of the Bektashi plays an important role as part of Albanian literature in Arabic script. It is a recent literature that began in the early decades of the nineteenth century, and it was short-lived, for it subsided at the end of that century.

As far as we know, there are not many texts. Some of them we know of simply by their names, but we have never seen them. We do, however, have a number of large manuscripts, one of which contains 65,000 lines of verse.

Although this literature is religious in inspiration, it appeared in a particular literary genre, the epic, which was later cultivated and developed in the writing of the Albanian national awakening.

The Bektashi faith in our country is older. In the account of his journey through Albania in the second half of the seventeenth century, the well-known Turkish traveller, Evliya Çelebi, tells us that he discovered a Bektashi *tekke* with a lot of dervishes in Kanina. In addition to this, he encountered Bektashi dervishes at the mausoleum of Baba Sultan near the town of Vlora. As to the *tekke* of Kanina, Evliya Çelebi says that it was founded by Ghazi Sinan Pasha who, according to him, was buried in a mausoleum near the *tekke*. Ghazi Sinan Pasha, according to Evliya Çelebi, also built a fine mosque in Kanina.

In his Turkish-language encyclopaedia, Sami Frashëri notes that this Ghazi Sinan Pasha lived at the time of Sultan Mehmed II (1451-1481) and of Sultan Bayazid II (1481-1512). In view of this, we can assume that the *tekke* of Kanina was founded sometime between the end of the fifteenth and the beginning of the sixteenth century.

Aside from Kanina, Evliya Çelebi heard of no other Bektashi *tekkes* in Albania. In Gjirokastra, he notes, however, that there were many Alevites among the inhabitants and he came across the *tekkes* of three other *tarikats*, i.e. not Bektashi.

We have no written sources on the Bektashi in Albanian. The only Bektashi who left something in writing in Albanian was Dalip Frashëri. In the introduction to his *Hadikaja* [The Garden], the main work of Bektashi literature in Albania, he states that the first person to bring the Bektashi faith to Albania was Baba Shemimi who founded the *tekke* of Fushë Kruja sometime towards the end of the eighteenth century.

Pastaj edhe ndë Gegëri
hodhi sajei vilajet
dërgoi sulltanë Shemimi
sahibi ilm – y vilayet

U hapi sytë dynjasë
Shqipërinë e bëri abad,
ndë katar t'Ali Abasë
i kalli i bëri irshad.

Then in Ghegeria, too,
He cast his holy shadow,
He sent Master Shemimi,
The blessed, master of wisdom,

Who opened the world's eyes
And made Albania flourish,
In the wake of Abas Ali
He encouraged them and showed them the path of righteousness.

(*Hadikaja*, p. 2)

From what we know of Dalip Frashëri, it would seem that the Bektashi *tekke* in Kanina had been destroyed much earlier and he had no knowledge of it.

From research on the foundation of the *tekkes* still existing in Albania, it appears that Dalip Frashëri was right, that the oldest *tekke*, as far as he was concerned, was that of Baba Shemimi in Fushë Kruja. The *tekkes* of Elbasan, Frashër and Konitsa were founded later.

In view of what Evliya Çelebi and Dalip Frashëri tell us, there would seem to be two phases in the spread of the Bektashi: an older phase beginning with the Turkish occupation and ending perhaps at the beginning of the eighteenth century, and a younger phase beginning with the foundation of the *tekke* of Fushë Kruja and continuing up to the present day.

Baba Shemimi, the founder of the *tekke* of Fushë Kruja, was himself from Kruja, apparently of the family of Zenel Hoxhaj. Before he became a *baba*, he was a *müderriz-dersi-am* (teacher of theology) in Istanbul but then abandoned this position to become a Bektashi. He was made a *baba* at the *pir evi* (the home of Haji Bektash) in Anatolia. For a while, he lived at the *tekke* of Köprülü.[47] Baba Shemimi moved to Kruja with a companion called Baba Hajdar Hashimia with the written agreement of the people there. In Fushë Kruja at that time there was an old mausoleum called the Mausoleum of Baba Ali, and Baba Shemimi decided to construct his *tekke* nearby. The head of another *tarikat* who had a *tekke* in town opposed this, but, as Baba Shemimi had the support of the leaders of Kruja, he built his new *tekke* anyway and began his work there.

Those who subsequently founded other *tekkes* in Albania were his followers. In his epic poem *Hadikaja*, Dalip Frashëri notes that Baba Tahir Nesibiu, who founded the *tekke* of Frashëri, was his dervish.

Shumë botë pa haberë
ndë Shqipëri bëri ymran,
që u bënë dedelerë
gjenë nesibnë me zeman.

Bahysus edhe Nesibiu
nga ay shemi u bë iz-har,
ia bëri myjesser Aliu
hodhi mi të piri nazar.

Many ignorant people
In Albania became learned,
When they became *dedes*
they were initiated in time.

Especially Nesibiu
Glowed from him like a candle,
Aliu touched and moved him,
And cast a first glance at him.

(*Hadikaja*, p. 2)

Baba Shemimi was killed in 1807 and the *tekke* of Fushë Kruja was abandoned after his death. However, the Bektashi faith that had taken root in Kruja grew instead of declining.

Haxhi Et'hem of Tirana, a pupil of his, recorded the date of the death of Baba Shemimi, whose full name was Qemalyddin Shemimi Ibrahim Dede, in this chronogram:
Pencei Ali Abaden tarih oldi feiz-yab,
Pir-i shahi shehidan oldi Ibrahim Dede 1222 AH (= 1807 AD)
In view of the date of the death of Baba Shemimi, we can assume that the *tekke* of Fushë Kruja was founded about 1790.

In the first phase we do not know whether the *babas* were Albanians, but by the second phase up to 1912, it is generally acknowledged that they were all Albanians.

The Bektashi faith was a powerful force in Turkey from the fifteenth to the end of the eighteenth century. The Janissaries, who were an important military force in the Empire, were Bektashi. Supported by the Janissaries, the Bektashi *tekkes* grew tremendously in influence, even in the sultan's palace.

Sultan Selim III took power in 1799. By this time, the Janissaries had become an undisciplined bunch and were no longer in a position to defend the empire. Attempts to reorganise and discipline them failed, so the young sultan decided to replace his force with a new, well-trained and disciplined army. The newly created force had no attachment to the Bektashi *tekkes* but was linked to another *tarikat*, the Mevlevi. The Bektashi thus lost their privileged position and began to suffer persecution. When the Janissaries realised that the new army meant their downfall, they rose in revolt and deposed Sultan Selim. However, in 1826, Sultan Mahmud II gathered a new army and, with the support of the people of Istanbul, he wiped the Janissaries out. The Bektashi *tekkes* suffered, too. Many of the *babas* in Istanbul were slain and the *tekkes* were closed down.

At the time of Sultan Selim III, Ali Pasha of Tepelena invited the persecuted *babas* to take refuge in Albania. He is said to have become a Bektashi himself in order to use the Bektashi faith as a weapon against the sultan. I have the impression that it was he who promoted the founding of the first *tekkes* of the second phase. This seems confirmed by the account that the Toptani gave of the murder of Baba Shemimi. It was said that Baba Shemimi was slain by Man Bushi, at the instance of Kapllan Pasha Toptani.

At the time of Baba Shemimi, Kapllan Pasha was an opponent of Ali Pasha of Tepelena, whereas Baba Shemimi was a close friend of the latter and endeavoured to help and serve him in his political activities. As a friend of his foe, Kapllan Pasha could not put up with the dervish in his home region, and thus had him killed.

As far as we know, the religious literature of the Bektashi began with Baba Shemimi. The early Albanian *babas* and intellectuals wrote in Turkish, and the verse of Baba Shemimi, that we have, was written in that language.

As to writing in Albanian, Sami Frashëri notes in his Turkish-language encyclopaedia that Baba Tahir Nesibiu wrote poetry in Albanian, Persian and Turkish. He was said to be from Frashër and died in 1250 AH (= 1835 AD).

The *tekkes* were, of course, the main centres of Bektashi religious literature. From the material preserved in the Historical Archives of the Institute of Science and in the Library of the *Kryegjyshata*, it is apparent that, for Albanian-language works, the most active centres of this literature were the *tekkes* of Frashër, Konitsa and Gjirokastra.

The most precious works of Bektashi religious literature in Albanian are the *Hadikaja* of Dalip Frashëri and the *Myhtarnameja* of Shahin Frashëri.

Dalip Frashëri

Dalip Frashëri was born in Frashër and died in Konitsa. We have no written documents attesting to the life of this excellent Bektashi poet, and the old scholars in the *tekkes* have no memory of him now. Nor does he seem to have any descendants in Frashër.

In the introduction to his *Hadikaja*, Dalip Frashëri says of himself only that he became a Bektashi at the *tekke* of Frashër after 'taking the hand' of Baba Tahir Nesibiu, its founder.

Nesibiu, veqil'i pirit,
shumëvet u rrëfeu erqan
m'u bë kismet edhe fakirit
i bëra niaz ndë taban

Nesibiu, disciple of the master,
Taught many how to pray,
It was my luck, poor wretch that I am,
That I said my prayers on the soles of my feet.

(*Hadikaja*, p. 2)

Later, on instructions from Baba Nesibiu, Dalip left Frashër and moved to Konitsa, but was deeply shaken by the transfer that appears to have been against his will.

Gjene Nesibiu ne himmet
më s'më nxori nga nazari,
nga vatani më dha hixhret,
këtu Konicë më solli.

Nga shtëpija kur ika
u bëshë bihud e hajran,
thashë të më rënkej pika
q'u bëshë aleme destan.

I was in the service of Nesibiu,
He never took his eyes off me,
He sent me into exile, away from my homeland,
And brought me here to Konitsa.

When I left my home,
I was confused and lost,
I thought that I would die,
And be known around the world.

(*Hadikaja*, p. 3)

Dalip Frashëri does not say why Baba Nesibiu sent him to Konitsa, or what he did and how he lived there. Perhaps a conflict had broken out in Frashër, and Baba Nesibiu removed him and sent him to Konitsa to protect him. In Konitsa, at any rate, he was received by the sage Baba Ismail, who welcomed and comforted him.

Këtu gjeçë të vëllanë
e m'u bë derdervet deva,
sulltan Ismail Babanë,
Veqil'e prit me byrhan.

Kurdo veje iqete bir
ndër ajni xhem, ndë mejdan
lytfi i ti më bëri tesir,
m'u bëri plagëvet derman.

Here I found a brother
Who soothed me and consoled me,
Master Ismail Baba
Welcomed his disciple with indisputable argument.

Wherever I went, here and there,
To the prayer room or to a public square,
His kindness touched me greatly
And gave remedy to my wounds.

(*Hadikaja*, p. 3)

Despite the consolation of Baba Ismail, Dalip's exile from Frashëri left a deep wound in his heart. For this reason he bore the pseudonym Haxhreti 'the exiled.'

Dalip Frashëri also tells us something about his work, the *Hadikaja*, saying that it is not original but translated from the Turkic *Hadikat üs-Süedâ* of Fuzûlî that has been published and republished in Istanbul many times.

However, even the *Hadikat üs-Süedâ* of Fuzûlî is not original. It was taken from the Persian, from the *Ravzatü ş-Şühedâ* of Hüseyin Vâiz, and is written in prose and verse. Fuzûlî's work is 309 pages long in 13 × 20.5 format. The *Hadikaja* of Dalip Frashëri is, by contrast, entirely in verse form and is 732 pages long, thus being twice the length of the *Hadikat üs-Süedâ* of Fuzûlî. With its 65,000 lines of verse, it has taken on its original form, that of a great epic.

Fuzûlî wrote his *Hadikat üs-Süedâ* in 950 AH [= 1544 AD]. Turkish prose was still evolving into a literary language by that time. Although Fuzûlî was without doubt a great poet, his prose is a bit stilted. He admits this himself when he notes that writing history in Turkish was not an easy matter because words did not have a clear and unequivocal meaning and sentences did not flow. His *Hadikat üs-Süedâ* is nonetheless a work of great literary value.

The full title of the work, *Hadikat üs-Süedâ*, means 'The Garden of the Martyrs.' Dalip Frashëri retained this full form of the title, but this version is now popularly known simply as the *Hadikaja*.

In his introduction, Dalip complains about the Arabic script in which Albanian was written at the time.

Gjerçë shqipja është zahmet
edhe nuke këndonetë,
se harfet janë gallet,
mire nuke qëronetë.

For Albanian is a difficulty
And it cannot be read
Because the letters
Cannot be interpreted well.

Dalip Frashëri translated the *Hadikaja* into Albanian out of religious motives, as had Fuzûlî. We know that Fuzûlî's Turkish *Hadikat üs-Süedâ* was sung during *matem* at the *tekke* of Konitsa, although it was in old Turkish and could hardly have been understood. As Dalip tells us, he wrote a new Turkish *Hadikat üs-Süedâ* instead and his version was sung for a time. As most of the students of the *tekke* of Konitsa did not know Turkish, neither old nor modern, there was a practical need for an Albanian translation.

This need was felt at other *tekkes*, too. We know that parts of an Albanian *Hadikaja* were sung at *matem* in verse form in Albanian at the *tekke* of Asim Baba (*Teqeja e Zallit*) in Gjirokastra several decades before the *Hadikaja* of Dalip Frashëri.

The expanded Albanian-language *Hadikaja* of Dalip Frashëri was probably used for several years. At the end of the manuscript there is a date, which no doubt marks the end of the translation work. It is 21 *rebiul-ahir* [second month of spring] of the year 58, i.e. 1258 AH [= 6 June 1842 AD].

Bën shyqyr, o more zelil,
të zu er'e merhametit,
Hadikan' e bëre teqmil
me himmet t' Ali Hajderit

Ndë këtë mybareq sene,
q'është pesëdhjetë e tetë,
ndë rebiul ahirënde,
njëzet e një dit vërtetë.

Give thanks, oh despised one,
May compassion be upon you,
This *Hadika* was finished
With the help of Ali Hajderi

In this blessed year
Which is the fifty-eighth,
In the second month of spring,
Truly twenty-one days.

(*Hadikaja*, p. 731)

We have never discovered the original manuscript of this *Hadikaja*. The Historical Archives of the Institute of Science have a copy that was written in

Leskovik in 1316 AH [=1899 AD], and there is a better copy at the Library of the *Kryegjyshata*, transcribed in Korça sometime after 1900.

The copy in the Historical Archives has one failing. The copyist omitted lines and stanzas here and there. Nonetheless it is beautifully written with diacritic signs to facilitate it being sung rapidly. This is the copy from which I have taken the quotations here.

But what was the *Hadikaja* of Dalip Frashëri? Fuzûlî's *Hadikat üs-Süedâ* was an Alevite text. When he translated and expanded it, Dalip Frashëri turned it into a Bektashi text. Fuzûlî has ten chapters, whereas Dalip has twelve. Fuzûlî has an introduction and a concluding text, as does Dalip. In the Albanian version, the introduction is seven pages long and the concluding text is eleven and a half pages long.

Both *Hadikats* are focused on the tragedy of Kerbela [Karbala] and its protagonist Husayn, the grandson of Muhammed and the son of Ali. The first chapter is on Adam and Eve and their expulsion from the Garden of Eden for original sin, and on the sufferings of the main prophets up to the time of Muhammed. Chapter Two deals with the sufferings of Muhammed from his people of the Kuraysh tribe. Chapter Three is on the death of Muhammed. Chapter Four is on the death of Fatima, the daughter of Muhammed and the mother of Husayn. Chapter Five deals with the murder of Ali. Chapter Six is on the poisoning of Hasan, the elder brother of Husayn. Chapter Seven deals with the exile of Husayn from Medina to Mecca. Chapter Eight is on the execution of Muslim ibn Aqeel, Husayn's emissary in Kerbela. Chapter Nine is about the arrival of Husayn in Kerbela from Mecca. Chapter Ten focuses on the Battle of Kerbela. Chapter Eleven deals with the death of Husayn as a martyr. Chapter Twelve, finally, is about the enslavement of the family of Husayn and their return to Medina.

The longest chapters, which take up over half of the manuscript, are those concerning Husayn, but all the chapters are linked to him by a thin thread of pain and suffering, beginning with Adam and culminating in the great tragedy of Kerbela.

The portion of the *Hadikaja* that is sung in the *tekkes* at *matem* is the one dealing with the events of Kerbela. This portion is sung every day for the first ten days of Muharrem, which are days of fasting for the Bektashi. Dalip Frashëri gives extensive coverage to this part of the story and deviates substantially from the *Hadikat üs-Süedâ* of Fuzûlî. He often repeats the final stanza as a refrain, with minor differences in text, and adds additional lines.

Imam Hysejni një nishan
më qiell e mbë dhe,
i lëvduari në Kuran
qani me male!

Imam Hysejni me delil
mahbubi Hyda
i lëvduari nd'Inxhil,
qani o fukara!

Jetimi pa nënë pa at,
nuri hanedan,
i lëvduari ndë Tevrat,
qani dudaman!

Imam Husayn was the target
In heaven and on earth,
Praised in the Koran,
Weep ye with the mountains!

Imam Husayn was the proof,
The beloved of God,
Praised in the Gospel,
Weep, ye wretched people!

An orphan motherless, fatherless,
He was radiant and well-bred.
Praised in the Torah,
Weep, ye anguished people!

(*Hadikaja*, p. 559)

The *Hadikaja* of Dalip Frashëri has many beautiful and moving parts to it. Some of them were profoundly felt and were expressed with great force. It was as a convinced Bektashi that he composed this great work.

[Excerpt from: Osman Myderrizi, 'Letërsia fetare e Bektashive', *Buletin për Shkencat Shoqërore*, Tirana, 3 (1955), pp. 131–137. Translated from the Albanian by Robert Elsie.]

1957
KURT SELIGER
MEETING THE POPE OF THE BEKTASHI

The Austrian journalist Kurt Seliger (1921–1999) had always wanted to go to Albania. He was particularly interested in history and was fascinated by the exotic country, having read much about the scandals and corruption at the court of King Zog in the 1930s and of the Italian invasion just before the start of the Second World War. As such, he got on his motorcycle and set off for Albania after having, with some difficulty, persuaded his wife Fritzi to go with him. The couple left Vienna in July 1956 and made their way through Yugoslavia, until they got to the Albanian border post of Han i Hotit. There, they made quite a stir with their bike. Albania did not have any tourists at the time, and certainly none on a motorcycle. In April 1957, they returned to the country for a second time. In Tirana, they parked their motorcycle at the famous Hotel Dajti and stored it there until it was time to leave the country. The state tourist agency Albtourist insisted on providing them with an automobile and a driver. On this trip, Seliger and his wife spent three months touring the country and paid a visit to the Kryegjshata in Tirana, in the company of the Albanian historian Aleks Buda (1910–1993). Seliger's account provides a rare glimpse of the Bektashi community in the early years of the Stalinist regime in power.

I asked Aleks Buda, 'What do the Bektashi think of the new order in Albania?'

'The best would be to go and ask them,' he replied. A few hours later we drove through the gypsy quarter of Tirana out to a hill on the outskirts of town from where there was a splendid view of Mount Dajti nearby and of the whole charming city. In the distance we could see a building with a large dome on it and realised that this was the residence of the world leader of the Bektashi.

We entered a large vestibule and were met by several *babas* or 'fathers,' as the dignitaries of the Bektashi are called, and a good number of dervishes. The *babas* wore green turbans and green robes. The oldest among them were particularly impressive with their long beards stretching down to their chests. As visitors, we of course knew nothing about Bektashi hierarchy. Were rank and importance determined by age, by the height of one's turban or by the length of one's beard? Accordingly, we didn't know which of the *babas* was their chief. At first I thought it must be the one with the wonderfully long, white beard who seemed to be the oldest and was the first one to approach us, but as soon as the greetings were over, a heavy-set man came up to us. He was about 45 years old, had strong and friendly features and an imposing dark black beard. He shook our hands, kissed me on both cheeks and then led us to his office. He was obviously the chief.

He sat down at his desk and the other *babas* took their seats in armchairs along with wall. We sat across from them. The walls in the office were covered with allegorical scenes. Beside the desk of Ahmet Myftari Dede, as he was called, was an old pendulum clock with curious figures on it. Ahmet Myftari Dede welcomed us once again and inquired about our health. Some dervishes then came in with liqueur, sweets and mocha coffee.

By this time, Aleks Buda had told the 'grandfather superior,' as Ahmet Myftari Dede was known, what we wanted to know. With calm and simple dignity he began:

> One of our wise men once said, 'Do not be arrogant because you are nothing but dust'. Another wise man said, 'If you want to know how the great men of this earth ended up, ask the earth. It will tell you, sure enough!' A third wise man said, 'Should you be in the company of a man higher than you, it is appropriate to show him respect. Should you be in the company of a man lower than you, it is appropriate to show him respect, too, for he has not yet made all the mistakes that you have made. If you are in the company of a wise man, show him all the honour you can because wisdom is the source of life, whereas stupidity is the source of death. A wise man will know not to raise himself above the masses because they possess more wisdom that you have in your head'.

Great sayings, I thought to myself, and this fellow is very good at expressing them. 'Our beliefs are all-encompassing,' Ahmet Myftari Dede continued.

> We seek the union of God, man and nature. We want to overcome the differences – the differences between you and me, the differences between have and have not, and we want to rid ourselves of everything that causes human suffering. But none of this can be achieved by force. Success would then only be superficial and lead to a pseudo-faith. Our tenets tell us: 'All people are made of the *same* matter and they must therefore know one another, love one another and help one another'. We seek spiritual purity and respect for our fellow human beings. This was the basis of our teachings from the very start and it still is today.

Ahmet Myftari Dede spoke slowly as if he were considering every word carefully. Yet he had a roguish face and a merry, lively expression. I had heard that the Bektashi kept their teachings and rites secret and was surprised that he was speaking so openly about them. I came to the conclusion that the Bektashi had given up all the mystery-mongering of the past. As I had seen the whirling dervishes in Shkodra, I ventured to ask him directly about Bektashi ceremonies.

The chief's reaction surprised me. With a twinkle in his eye, he looked at me as if to say, 'So you think you can get things out of me that I don't want to tell you? You'll have to do better than that!' What he actually said was,

> Please do not ask me about our rites. We do not reveal our convictions. This is no criticism of other religions. No one should condemn others wholesale. Take the Catholics, for instance. Some of them collaborated with the Italians and with the Germans, but we must not forget the great role that the Catholics played in the evolution of Albanian literature.

This only awakened my interest for their secret ceremonies all the more. At a moment when we and the *babas* were busy with our liqueur and sweets, I asked Aleks

Buda about them, but he did not want to reveal the secrets of the Bektashi that he no doubt knew, and simply replied that they said their prayers in silence at the graves of their holy men. The Bektashi focussed on contemplation, as opposed to the Rufa'i who demonstrated their union with Allah openly. This was all I was able to learn.

I took a look at the curious pictures on the walls, thinking that might help me discover more about the Order. One of the paintings was of a holy man surrounded by various animals. I asked about this, and the 'grandfather superior' replied:

> The meaning of the painting is that whoever requites evil with evil is a beast. Whoever requites good with evil is a serpent. Whoever requites good with good is a good man, and whoever requites evil with good is a magnanimous man.

I was stymied once again, so I decided to turn to more down-to-earth subjects. 'How many Bektashi are there in Albania?' I asked.

With that same twinkle in his eye, Ahmet Myftari Dede replied, but seriously this time: 'We are interested in the conscience of man, not in numbers, but if you want to know, there are about 200,000 Bektashi in Albania. Anyone can become a Bektashi, man or woman. The only conditions are that you have to be over eighteen and to go through an initiation ceremony. Catholics and Orthodox can join our community, too.'

I asked more about the ceremony. Aleks Buda replied with an anecdote from his home town: 'Once the son of a rich merchant wanted to become a Bektashi. This was at a time when the people were very poor. For the poor, a sheep's stomach was considered a delicacy, but it was something that rich people would not eat. So if anyone ate a sheep's stomach it meant that he was poor. As part of the ceremony to join the Bektashi, the son of the rich man was to buy a sheep's stomach and carry it openly through the town. You can imagine the reaction. And this was the way the young man was initiated.'

The *babas* reacted with merriment at the tale of Aleks Buda, who talked to them in Albanian and then translated for us: 'The superior would like to know if you are interested in visiting the rest of the building.'

'You can see everything, even the private rooms,' said Ahmet Myftari Dede. 'We have nothing to hide.'

And so we set off over the thick carpets, as if on cotton wool. The rooms had a strange atmosphere to them, with pictures of deceased *babas* and superiors. We then entered the prayer room, the floor and walls of which were decked out in oriental style, but there was nothing particularly secretive about it.

'Have a look at this,' Ahmet Myftari Dede called to me, pointing to a painting. 'This is a former head of our Order. He lived in Ankara until the 1920s and then, because of persecution by the Turks, he returned to his homeland, Albania. The Italians later assassinated him secretly.'

I took a closer look at the things on the wall: decrees, photos of dervishes and *babas* in partisan uniforms, some of them wearing medals for their parts in the liberation struggle. Clerics among the partisans? When we got back to the office, I asked him about this and was told:

In line with our teachings, we want to be patriotic sons of our country. We have never forgotten that we are children of our people, just like the men of our Order in Belgrade, in Macedonia, Bulgaria, Hungary and Egypt – wherever there are Bektashi. The founder of our Order, Haxhi Bektash Veli, taught us to foster the customs of the country in which we live. And Muhammed said, 'Love must be the basis of all deeds!' We recognise four types of love – love of the unity of God and man, love of mankind, love of duality in one, i.e. for one's parents, and finally love of the origin of everything, i.e. one's people. When our country was attacked, it was a normal part of our faith to fight for our people. Yes, we took part in the fight of our people, but we would never commit any aggression because we respect the rights of other peoples as our own. You want to know something about our role in the liberation struggle? Well, 32 *babas* and dervishes and 3,000 other Bektashi gave their lives in this struggle. Even I, as head of the Order, took my place in the ranks of the people's army in the liberation struggle. Perhaps you saw the citations in my office for the medals that were awarded to me.

And what do you think about the people's democratic government and the new social order that has been created?

We are aware of the propaganda in various countries, including yours, Austria. I can assure you that we have complete freedom to think what we want and to do what we want. You can tell people in your country that religion cannot be beaten into or out of people. We have our laws and we abide by them. When we see that new laws are passed that are better and more just than the old ones, we are the last to complain about them. Anyone who is reasonable understands the importance of religion, justice and love. But now that we have gotten ourselves into discussing politics, I would like to add something else. One of our maxims is: 'Judge an individual by his deeds.' Normally we would expect Western politicians to be religious people, and that is how they always describe themselves, but when we look at their deeds, we have our doubts. When we see, for example, how they interfere in the internal matters of other countries …

He stopped here, probably realizing that there was no need to go any further.

'To change the subject,' I said, 'How do you finance yourselves?' This was the same question I had asked of the highest representative of the Catholic Church in Albania.

'We own land and get subsidies from the government, as do all other religious communities. But in contrast to the others, we work on our land and get no salary. The chief and the *babas* served in the people's army and refused to accept any wages. It was our duty to serve. The government helps all the religious communities, but,' he added with another twinkle in his eye, 'it cannot make people religious by force.'

Ahmet Myftari Dede then spoke about the holy sites and the graves of their fathers where the Bektashi said their prayers, and then he led us up to the roof of his residence. Aleks Buda wanted to take a group photo of us. Suddenly, Ahmet Myfteri Dede called out to my wife: 'Not you. Good God! What would people abroad think of me if they saw me photographed with a woman!'

The Bektashi, as Aleks Buda explained, are normally much more liberal and progressive than the other religious communities with regard to women, but a women in a photo was obviously too much!

When we said farewell, I was kissed once again on the left and right cheeks. Ahmet Myftari then said, 'I wish you good health and great success and I wish your people all the best in their activities for peace.'

[Excerpt from Kurt Seliger, *Albanien, Land der Adlersöhne* (Leipzig: Brockhaus 1960), pp. 129-135. Translated from the German by Robert Elsie.]

1962
HANS JOACHIM KISSLING
ON THE ORIGINS OF THE BEKTASHI IN ALBANIA

Hans-Joachim Kissling (1912-1985) was a German orientalist and Turkologist from Munich. He held the chair for the history and culture of the Middle East and Turkology at the University of Munich from 1959 to 1980. Kissling was particularly interested in Islamic saints and religious phenomena in the Ottoman Empire.

Albania has been a bastion of the Bektashi for over three hundred years. The adherents of this curious and rather heretical dervish order were so numerous that it is more appropriate to speak there of a Bektashi community than of an order or a simple fraternity. Despite the great impact that the Bektashi have had on religious, cultural and social life of Albania, we know very little about the origins of the movement in and around Albania.

We do know that the Bektashi were relatively late to spread to Albania, but we have no reliable information on the date of their arrival. Bektashi oral tradition is naturally more in the realm of legendry so there is no real proof for the claim that the first Bektashi arrived and settled in Albania with the troops of Sultan Murad II (1421-1451). J. K. Birge, whose book *The Bektashi Order of Dervishes*[48] is still the main work on the subject, informs us that his informant, the Bektashi dervish Haydar Baba, told him about many early Bektashi settlements. He claimed that a Qazim Baba, a Yemin Baba, a Piri Baba and a Huseyn Baba arrived and settled in different parts of Albania under the reign of Sultan Mehmed II (r. 1451-1481), and spread the faith from there. He also said that Sultan Bayezid II (r. 1481-1512) had founded a number of Bektashi monasteries in Albania. Haydar Baba assured J. K. Birge that there were many documents in Istanbul that could prove his assertion, but Birge was unable to find any of them. It is therefore safer to assume that it is more likely that these early Bektashi settlements stem from the imagination of the dervish, in particular because Birge, as an expert, did not attach any great importance to this information.

Secondly, we must check and verify the claim, widespread in Albania and seemingly taken seriously by Birge, that the Bektashi owe their presence in Albania to the famed Ali Pasha of Tepelena (1741-1822). This legend, which was accepted by F. W. Hasluck,[49] can be disproved by the text of the *Seyahatname*[50] of the Turkish traveller, Evliya Çelebi (1611-c. 1684), who is certainly more reliable in such matters. He mentions the existence of a Bektashi monastery in the little settlement of Kanina and adds that it was founded by a Ghazi Sinan Pasha. Franz Babinger notes that this is the only monastery in Albania that Evliya Çelebi refers to specifically as being Bektashi.[51] Babinger rightfully rejects the assertion of Ghazi Sinan Pasha being buried in Kanina with the five-time Ottoman grand vizier, Kodja Sinan Pasha, because the latter died on 3 April 1596 and was buried not in Kanina but in Istanbul. The only person who fits the description is the Albanian Göyegü Sinan Pasha who died in 1503 and was Beylerbeyi of Anatolia under Sultan Mehmed II and grand admiral (*kapudan pasha*) under Sultan Bayezid II.[52] The person of this mysterious Ghazi Sinan Pasha has also been dealt with by Sami bey Frashëri,[53] Johann Georg von Hahn[54] and Ekrem bey Vlora.[55] Vlora claims this Sinan Pasha as his family's ancestor, but none of them have provided any decisive new information on him. If we do not cast any doubt on the information given by Evliya Çelebi – and there is no reason to do so in view of his undeniable expertise in this subject and especially of his amicable sentiments towards the Bektashi – and if the founder of the monastery is the same Sinan Pasha as the aforementioned Göyegü Sinan Pasha, we would have, as Babinger stresses, an early document confirming the presence of the Bektashi in Albania. Babinger is, however, not completely convinced that Ghazi Sinan Pasha is actually Göyegü Sinan Pasha, and rightly so.

Indeed, the claim that Ghazi Sinan Pasha is the same as Göyegü Sinan Pasha is faulty, as we will show here. In his description of Elbasan,[56] Evliya Çelebi notes that the said Ghazi Sinan Pasha who founded the Bektashi monastery in Kanina built a Djelveti monastery in Elbasan. This definitively disproves the claim and deprives us of our early record for the presence of the Bektashi in Albania. The Djelveti Order that was founded by Sheikh Üftade (1494–1580) and flourished under his successor Mahmud Huda'i (1543–1628)[57] could not have existed prior to 1503, the date of the death of Göyegü Sinan Pasha, because its founder, Üftade, was still a child at the time. Göyegü Sinan Pasha can therefore not be the founder of the Djelveti monastery. In fact, the founder of the monastery must be a contemporary of Evliya Çelebi, but it is not easy to find anything out about him.

Another candidate would be Sinan Pasha, the Mir Liva of Dukagjin, who according to Mehmed Süreyya, distinguished himself in battle in 1599 and was, no doubt, then rewarded with the title of Mir Liva.[58] There is no doubt about the fact that he was an Albanian. Although we do not know the date of his death, the foundation of the monastery would seem to have taken place around the same time as the rise of the Djelveti Order since the Mir Liva would probably have founded the monastery at an advanced age.

With this information, we believe we have proven beyond any doubt that Evliya Çelebi is not referring to Göyegü Sinan Pasha. The rise of the Bektashi in Albania cannot therefore have happened before the end of the sixteenth/beginning of the seventh century.

But the *Seyahatname* of our Turkish traveller reveals more, though indirectly. He seems to disprove that the Bektashi dervishes were present in Albania under the reigns of Sultan Murad II, Mehmed II and Bayezid II. After all, it would seem very unlikely that the Bektashi had made no progress whatsoever and had only succeeded in founding one monastery in Kanina in the 160 years between their alleged first appearance in Albania and the time of Evliya Çelebi's visit. This would be hard to accept in view of the major impact the Bektashi had in Ottoman times, their influence upon the Janissaries, and the many monasteries they founded elsewhere. It would seem just as unlikely that after a long period of stagnation, the Bektashi would suddenly flourish, right after Evliya Çelebi's tour of the country.

We believe that there must be a reason behind the more or less sudden appearance of the Bektashi Order in Albania. We would like to suggest, and only suggest, that the appearance of the Bektashi dervishes in Albania, right before Evliya Çelebi's first visit to the country in 1662 has to do with the blow the Bektashi Order suffered in Adrianopolis [Edirne] in 1644. In his description of Adrianopolis, Evliya Çelebi himself provides insight into the events that took place at the nearby Bektashi monastery of Hizirlik (Hidirlik).[59]

The one-time Bektashi monastery situated outside the town of Adrianopolis was probably originally a sanctuary to Saint George, as F. W. Hasluck, relying on J. Covel, rightly supposes.[60] Although Evliya Çelebi seems to support a pre-Islamic origin, he derives the word Hizirlik from a Bektashi sheikh called Hizir Dede, who lived there with a certain Sefer Shah at the time of Haji Bektash. Here he may be referring to the second grand master of the order, Hizir Lale Sultan.[61] At Evliya Çelebi's time, at any rate, Hizirlik was a flourishing monastery until the day it was closed down by force. The site was popular with the upper class in Adrianopolis for excursions because of the healthy air and the beautiful view it offered. These people, however, suspected that the monastery was inhabited by questionable individuals and that immoral acts were being committed there.

For this reason, according to Evliya Çelebi, in 1051 AH [which began on 12 April 1641 AD] the citizens of Adrianopolis sent a delegation to the Grand Vizier, Kara Mustafa Pasha, to demand that the monastery be shut down. The date does not concord entirely with Evliya Çelebi's subsequent information that the monastery was shut down a week before the Grand Vizier met a violent death, because the request for its closure in 1641/1642 would then only have been fulfilled on 4 January 1644. This is the date Evliya Çelebi gives. At any rate, the Grand Vizier had his steward, Kirk-Ayak Sinan (Sinan of the Forty Feet – so-called because of his industriousness), tear down the monastery. The Grand Vizier used the hundreds of cartloads of lead roofing for the *türbe* (mausoleum) he was building for himself in Istanbul. He also took fourteen copper lanterns.

In Evliya Çelebi's words, the Bektashi dervishes cursed all those involved in the destruction of the monastery of Hizirlik with cries of '*Allah-Allah!*' Then they departed and scattered. Their curses had an effect. A week later, Sultan Ibrahim delivered the Grand Vizier to the henchman, and the people of Adrianopolis who had demanded the destruction of the monastery died wretched deaths. Although some parts of Evliya Çelebi's description, such as the age-old accusation of immorality and the curse of the exiled dervishes, sound like the standard fare of legends, his report would seem credible, in particular since the destruction of the monastery of Hizirlik is confirmed by reports from European travellers. If we accept that the Janissaries and their supporters were behind the death sentence given to the quite capable Grand Vizier, Kara Mustafa Pasha, the above description would seem quite logical.

What is more important here, however, is what happened to the Bektashi dervishes who were driven out of Hizirlik. Evliya Çelebi says that they departed and scattered. It is unlikely that all the dervishes simply went into retirement. They would most likely have sought a new activity less visible to their foes. They would probably not have gone to Istanbul or Anatolia where their reputation as having been ostracized for immorality and conspiracy would have been known. This would have put their brethren in Istanbul and Anatolia in danger.

In view of this, it is quite likely that the period between the closing of the monastery of Hizirlik (1644) and Evliya Çelebi's first visit to Albania (1662) could correspond well to the initial arrival of Bektashi dervishes in Albania. As we know, Albania was never colonised by the Turks and as such Islam never dominated as the only religious belief in the country. Crypto-Christianity was common in Albania right up to the nineteenth century and the beliefs of the Bektashi, with their many Christian elements and rites, would have promoted their influence there.

As such, although there is no definitive proof, Sinan Pasha, the Mir Liva of Dukagjin, would seem to be a figure of significance and it is quite possible that he as the one who received the Bektashi dervishes driven out of Hizirlik and gave them a new home in Kanina, far from the Bosphorus.

[Hans Joachim Kissling, 'Zur Frage der Anfänge des Bektašitums in Albanien', *Oriens, Journal of the International Society for Oriental Research*, Leiden, 15 (1962) pp. 281–286. Translated from the German by Robert Elsie.]

1962
DOROTHEA RUSSELL
THE BEKTASHI MONASTERY IN CAIRO

Lady Dorothea Russell Pasha (d. 1968), wife of Sir Thomas Wentworth Russell (1879–1954), Cairo's police chief from 1917 to 1946, was the author of an historical guidebook, entitled Medieval Cairo and the Monasteries of the Wadi Natrun, *that was published in 1962. It includes a description of the Albanian Bektashi tekke of Cairo shortly before it ceased to function.*

At the corner we turn up the hill, with the prison wall on our right, while on the left, beneath the towering Citadel walls, are rubbish, ruins and a 'flea market'. We continue to the Powder Magazine, a large low square building at the base of the cliff, and here we will stop at the foot of the stair which takes us up to the Bektashi Monastery.

This eyrie in the cliffs is one of the most charming spots in Cairo. It is only of recent years that it has become a tourist haunt; when first I knew it, no one except personal friends of the Abbot ever went there and it was a refuge from the noise and bustle of the town, where one sat peacefully chatting and drinking tea or tamarind syrup with the Abbot, in the kiosk overlooking the city. Here the hustle and bustle of the town seem far away and one talks of dreams and portents, of falling stars and distant wars.

These dervishes, whose headquarters are now at Lake Ochrida in Albania, came to their cave dwelling some six hundred years ago (uncertain date) from their still earlier *takiya* at Qasr el- 'Ayni. Here, ever since, they have lived and died, and been buried in the great cave in the hillside. Dervishes were suppressed in Turkey by Ataturk and this community is the last to remain in Egypt; there are now only about twenty of them, all Albanians (1954). They wear a high white felt head-dress and the traditional wool dress, in this case dark, of the Sufi; the Abbot's is white, and he has a crystal jewel depending from a buttonhole; the single ear-ring shows that they are celibate. Their language is Turkish.

Having climbed the steps and passed through the gate under the kiosk on the wall, we find ourselves in a shaded place with a fountain, beyond which is the door into the monastery. The rock face of the cliffs is honeycombed with the doors and windows of the monks' habitations. A passage leads between the little garden and the kitchen court to the great opening of the vast quarried burial cave; within, to left and right, are the tombs of the dervishes and at the far end the tomb of the founder of the Cairo *takiya*, enclosed within a railing; the walls have recently been lined with alabaster. At certain times there are many visitors to the tomb to which the usual superstitions are attached, and people are to be seen rolling or crawling from one end of the cave to the other. Return to the forecourt, putting a coin in the poor-box as you pass; the building behind the garden to the right is the Baba's (Abbot's) lodging and to the left (on the south) at the back of the little court is the great kitchen with its enormous cauldrons, used on the Day of Ashura, when large numbers of poor visit the monastery and are fed by the monks. After leaving the kitchen and the court, turn to the right by the fountain at the entrance and go through the garden to the terrace which overlooks the city. Behind this garden is another cave in the cliff, the burial place of Prince Kamal ed-Din, son of the late Sultan Husein.

You should have timed yourself to be here just before sunset. From the terrace there is a wonderful view over the city below; all Cairo is spread before your eyes and every building can be identified in the clear atmosphere and brilliant light. On the far side of the city is the gleaming line of the river with the Pyramids standing out clear beyond. To the right is the Citadel; the Fatimid city lies below, and to the north Shari' Muhammad 'Ali, just hidden from view by the projection of the fortress mass. In the foreground we can pick out Qal'at al-Kabsh and the minaret of the mosque of Ibn Tulun, the rubbish heaps of al-'Askar and Qatayi' (Tilul Zeinhom); farther south, nearer the river but hidden from us by the great mounds, is the site of Fustat. To the south the Qarafa shows clearly at the foot of the cliffs, bordering the populated area, and we can trace the line of the street by which for over a thousand years the dead have taken their last journey to Saiyida Nafisa and Imam Shafi'i. It is all incredibly beautiful at sunset, and just after it is almost more so. A thousand minarets stand out dark against the greenish sky and the magnificent outline of the velvety black mass of the Citadel steps down the night sky on the right to the hushed city below. Sit here and watch the city fading away into the afterglow until all finally vanishes into the soft night mist.

These Turkish Sufis are unorthodox Muslims of the Shi'a sect. It is estimated that some 60 per cent of the population of Turkey belonged to the dervish orders; so much for Sultan Selim's efforts to suppress them in the fifteenth century. This is a popular, as opposed to a systematized, religion. It was founded in a village of Anatolia by Hajji Bektash who died in 1337 and in whom the teachings of a long and broad line of Turcoman Babas from Asia bringing many pre-Islamic customs culminated. Their teaching is a pantheistic and mystic religion of the people based on Shi'a tenets, belief in the Twelve Imams, the Fourteen Pure Innocents, with a passionate, highly emotional veneration for 'Ali, who is rated higher than Muhammad and who, with God and Muhammad, makes a kind of Trinity in the eyes of these people. Fatima, the daughter of the Prophet (from whom Hajji Bektash was descended), takes a place which can be compared with that of the Virgin Mary in medieval Christianity and the resemblance of some of their hymns to the Nunc Demittis and to the Magnificat is striking. They evidently owe much to contact with Byzantine Christianity in Anatolia and to neo-Platonist doctrines and still further back to influences inherited from their remote Asiatic past, coloured by their Persian surroundings. Their teaching is mystical and comprises such esoteric systems as successive 'Gates' and a Teacher (the 'Murshid'). Heavenly love is pictured as the homesick longing of the reed flute for the bed from which the reed was torn, the mystic longing of the heart to return to its source.

The sect in its lower order or preliminary stage offered its members a social life centred in the monastery, where women were of an equal status with men and where they could meet in daily intercourse, the *takiya* thus becoming a village social centre; these were the non-initiates. This system was part of the secret of the sect's great popularity. The initiates were of two stages. The order in its upper hierarchy was celibate and the Baba was the teacher (the Murshid) of his *takiya*.

[Excerpt from: Dorothea Russell, *Medieval Cairo and the Monasteries of the Wadi Natrun. A Historical Guide* (London: Weidenfeld and Nicolson 1962), pp. 137–139.]

1963
JULES LEROY
A VISIT TO THE *TEKKE* OF THE BEKTASHIS IN CAIRO

The French Benedictine priest and scholar Jules Leroy (1903–1979) was born in Ablis near Rambouillet and studied from 1930 to 1933 at the Pontificio Istituto Biblico in Rome. He worked for many years as a research expert at the French National Centre for Scientific Research (CNSR) in Paris. As an art historian, he is remembered for his work on Christian iconography in the Middle East. In his exploration of Christian monuments on the Nile in the mid-1950s, Leroy had occasion to visit the Albanian tekke near Cairo, shortly before it was closed down.

The *tekke* is a delightful place. With all its palms, vines, flowers, terraces and arbours, it makes a pleasant change from the bare, arid Muqattam, the limestone hill which rises on the western bank of the Nile to a height of over six hundred feet. For Egypt, it qualifies as a mountain and at one time, about AD 1000, the Christian monastery of Der el Busair stood on its southern flank. Now the monastery has vanished, but thanks to the Bektashis, monastic life has not died out completely in Cairo.

Even from the outside their monastery looks attractive. Worn stone steps, with a wrought-iron handrail covered with bougainvilleas, lead up to the main entrance. Passing through the gate, you come straight into the middle of a network of courtyards, well-kept kitchen gardens, flower-beds with ditches of running water cutting through them, ponds that mirror the blue sky, Turkish-style summerhouses buried deep in foliage. Coming straight from the monasteries of the Wadi el Natrun to this brilliant oasis of colour, you cannot help feeling the sudden change of atmosphere. Everything is restful, orderly, and clean. The same air of peace envelops the *tekke* and the other monasteries we have visited, but here it is almost Franciscan, so earnestly do the Bektashis love nature, just as did the little friar of Assisi. This is the first thing that strikes you; you see it in the well-cared-for look of the trees and animals.

There are only about a dozen monks here now guarding the tomb of Sheik Abdullah el Maghaouri and the tombs of his followers who wished to be buried beside him. The little community lives under the benevolent rule of its leader, the Baba Ahmed Serri Dede; they spend their time gardening or looking after the farm animals – the hens, turkeys, tame gazelles, clean oxen, the large-uddered cows which although they belong to the monks still follow the Oriental custom and wear round their necks or over their foreheads a string of blue pearls to ward off the Evil Eye.

The Baba, who was elected some years ago, is a fine old man; his natural dignity is enhanced by his magnificent costume, a striped green-and-white robe with the white cloak of the Bektashis. Round his waist he has a broad brown cummerbund with the stone amulet called *teslim tash* attached to it, though it should normally be worn round the neck. He has also a staff with a small double-bladed axe on the top of it. His headdress is the white, usually twelve-sided bonnet which is the uniform of the order, and round it he has a green turban to indicate his rank of

Baba. His heavy silver ear-rings shaped like the crescent moon show that he has taken the vow of celibacy.

The Baba is a very easy man to talk to. When he is not taking a siesta he wanders about his fairy gardens and is very willing to talk about the history of the Bektashis. They were founded, so he says, seven hundred years ago, and follow the doctrine of Islam, though they lay more emphasis on prayer and meditation; their doctrines and principles of introspection are preserved in manuscripts which have never been published or translated, 'because foreigners would not understand what it was all about.' They number to-day about six million members.

All this information is most readily and graciously given, but with the particularly Eastern imprecision and indifference to reliable statistics and accurate historical data which must warn the unwary against taking it at its face-value. If one had only the Baba's information to go on one would still be very much in the dark about the Bektashis and the place they occupy in the Moslem world. Either through ignorance or a desire not to explain too fully the nature of a sect which is reputed to be heretical, the head of the *tekke* prefers to remain diplomatically silent and let the visitor try to find out for himself.

[Excerpt from: Jules Leroy, *Monks and Monasteries of the Near East* (London: George G. Harrap 1963), translated by Peter Colin, pp. 56–58.]

1971
GEORG STADTMÜLLER
THE BEKTASHI DERVISH ORDER IN ALBANIA

The German scholar and historian Georg Stadtmüller (1901–1985) studied classical philology and European history at the universities of Freiburg am Breisgau and Munich. Around 1935, he toured Albania on foot on his way to Constantinople, and in the following year finished his seminal habilitation thesis 'Forschungen zur albanischen Frühgeschichte' (Research in Early Albanian History), Budapest, 1942, for which he is best remembered. In 1958, Stadtmüller took over the chair of southeast European history at the University of Munich, where he assisted in the establishment of the Albania Institute (Albanien-Institut) in 1963. He is also remembered as the author of numerous articles on questions of Albanian history, religion and literature, among which is the following article on the Bektashi Order.

Like every other world religion, Islam has had contact with the deep-rooted religious beliefs of the various people it conquered. These old popular beliefs have marked the further development of Islam. Of course, official theology has remained untouched by them, but the pre-Islamic heritage has nonetheless had a strong impact on people's beliefs. This is most evident in the veneration of saints that did not originally exist in Islam, a veneration that was focused on old religious sites and the graves of holy men. Curiously enough, Christian and Muslim saints were often mixed together. Asia Minor and the Balkans are rich in Muslim holy graves which people visit on pilgrimages to find inspiration and consolation – sentiments that the strict provisions of official Islam cannot offer them. Christian saints and even pagan idols live on in the garb of these Muslim holy men. There are many 'ultraquist' saints who were revered by both Christians and Muslims on their pilgrimages. One such curious pilgrimage site, for instance, is the monastery of Saint Naum on Lake Ohrid which was often visited by members of the Bektashi Order who revered the saint as Sari Saltik. There were also Christians who visited Muslim saints and revered them as their own. In addition, people of both religions revered many holy springs and sources which were most certainly relics of pagan beliefs.

The Ottomans, both as a people and as a nation, promoted the orthodox form of Islam, so-called Sunni Islam. When the Albanians were converted, it was therefore this form of Islam that the great majority of them adopted. However, under the Sunni surface, there were always other forms of belief in the Ottoman Empire, many of which were forms of Persian Shia. It was from this Shia Islam that the various dervish orders arose. Among them, and particularly widespread were the Bektashi.

The Bektashi Order arose initially in Asia Minor. The patron of the order was Haji Bektash Veli who moved from Khorasan to Asia Minor in the thirteenth century. He settled in a village near Kırşehir which was later named after him – Hacı Bektaş Köy. Many miracles were attributed to him which led to his reputation as a saint (*veli*). He is said to have founded ten monasteries (*tekkes*) and appointed his disciples to run them as *babas*. The order first received its definitive form in the early sixteenth century under its grand master, Balim Sultan. The beliefs of the Bektashi stem from various sources and, in general, one could say that they were highly critical of Sunni theology. They ignored the basic religious duties of Muslims. Regular attendance at a mosque and ritual prayer were not regarded as absolutely necessary. Wine, which is strictly forbidden by Sunni Muslims, played a part in their rituals. The mystical philosophy of the Bektashi was not substantially different from that of the other dervish orders. They believed in the transmigration of the soul, that when a person died, his soul was taken up by an animal. They were very tolerant towards Christians, firstly, because both of them suffered from the intolerance of Muslim orthodoxy, and secondly because many Christian beliefs had come to form part of the theology of the Bektashi. They had a sort of communion with wine, bread and cheese, and confession with absolution. The Bektashi were much attacked and defamed by the Sunni hodjas. The fact that they held religious services behind closed door in which women took part led to the accusation by Muslim clerics that they were celebrating nightly orgies, an accusation that was made of other orders, too.

The significance of the Bektashi Order in Ottoman history derives from its close ties to the Janissaries. According to legend, Haji Bektash personally gave his blessing to the first Janissaries, although this is historically untrue. The prominent headpieces of the Janissaries with the cloth hanging down their backs is said to be in memory of the wide sleeves of Haji Bektash that fell behind them when he placed his arms around on their necks to bless them. The whole Janissary corps was seen as being under the protection of its patron Haji Bektash. For this reason, all the Janissaries wore the order's well-known slogan '*Ya Ali*' on their left arm. Instead of a Sunni military clergyman (*tabur imam*), the Janissary troops had a Bektashi dervish of their own called *tabur baba*.

It is not known when the Bektashi first reached Albania. According to tradition, the first members of the order arrived there with the troops of Murad II (1421–1451). This early date would, however, seem unlikely. In his work *Seyahatname*, the Ottoman traveller Evliya Çelebi (1611–c. 1683) mentions a Bektashi *tekke* in Kanina, founded by a certain Sinan Pasha. There was also a pilgrimage site of Baba Sultan in Vlora frequented by Bektashi dervishes. Franz Babinger is of the impression that this Sinan Pasha is the same as Göyegü Sinan Pasha, the son-in-law of Bayazid II (1481–1512). Hans Joachim Kissling rejects this. He believes that the Sinan Pasha referred to by Evliya Çelebi is the Mir Liva of Dukagjin who was also called Sinan Pasha and only received his position after 1599. He thinks it is conceivable that the arrival of the Bektashi Order in Albania had to do with the closing down of the Bektashi monastery of Hizirlik in Adrianopolis [Edirne] in 1644. The first appearance of the order would then be dated to the end of the sixteenth or the beginning of the seventeenth century at the earliest. At any rate, the order attained its greatest expansion under Ali Pasha of Janina (1741–1822) who bestowed his favour upon it and is said, himself, to have been a Bektashi.

With the destruction of the Janissary Corps under Sultan Mahmud II in 1826, Albania became the order's new home. At the end of the eighteenth or beginning of the nineteenth century, a certain Shemimi is said to have arrived in Kruja and founded a monastery there. He apparently won over many new members who are said to have been supporters of Ali Pasha of Janina. Kaplan Pasha Toptani reigned in Kruja at the time and demanded that the dervish give up his political activities or leave the town. Shemimi is then alleged to have persuaded one of his followers to murder Kaplan Pasha, but the assassination attempt failed and the dervish emissary was shot by the pasha. Shemimi soon suffered the same fate. He was shot in a cell of his monastery by two agas. This violent act caused great unrest among the people of Kruja who were almost all Bektashi or at least sympathised with the order. Kaplan Pasha thus decided to move to Tirana. One of his relatives, Ibrahim Bey of Kavaja, who was also a Bektashi, unwisely announced that he was going to avenge the murder of Shemimi. Kaplan Pasha invited him over and, in violation of the laws of hospitality, imprisoned him in the fortress of Kruja, taking some of his land. In 1816, Kaplan Pasha was then murdered by an agent of the daughter of Ibrahim Bey who poisoned his tobacco.

The monastery founded by Shemimi fell to ruins after his death and for forty years, the dervishes lived in a little wooden hut there. It was only in the second half of the nineteenth century that the famed Baba Huseyn from Dibra rebuilt the monastery.

Kruja has remained the centre of the Albanian Bektashi up to the present day. The reason for this is probably the fact that a Bektashi saint, Sari Saltik, is said to be buried in a cave under the peak of a mountain near the town. According to tradition, Sari Saltik was a companion of Haji Bektash and ended his long life of wandering in Albania. In Kruja they tell that he slew a dragon with a wooden sword and freed a captive princess. This legend would seem to have been influenced by the cult of a Christian saint, probably Saint George. On top of the mountain, above the cave of Sari Saltik, are the remainders of an old church.

Another famous Bektashi sanctuary is located on the southern peak of Mount Tomorr (2,410 m). According to legend, the bones of Abbas Ali, the stepbrother of the Huseyn who died in the Battle of Kerbela, are said to be buried there. Every year on 15 August (the Feast of the Assumption of the Blessed Virgin), the Bektashi and Christians go on pilgrimage to this site. It can be assumed that there was once a pre-Islamic and possible pre-Christian sanctuary there. There were many other places in Albania that were designated as holy, too.

It is difficult to say anything about the actual number of Bektashi in Albania. The census that was carried out in 1918 by the Austro-Hungarian Military authorities in the occupied territories of northern and central Albania paid particular attention to the spread of the Bektashi for political reasons. However, it did not provide any statistical data on the true number of Bektashi. The Bektashi only dared to declare themselves as a religious community in the areas where they lived in compact groups. According to the census results, there were 1,708 Bektashi in the district of Elbasan, 1,406 in the district of Shinapremtja, and 1,458 in the district of Mallakastra. There were no data for the other regions of lower [i.e. southern] Albania, and there were very few Bektashi in upper [i.e. northern] Albania. In the Korça region, there are said to have been about 1,500 Bektashi. However, all of these various statistics provide a very incomplete picture. There are only estimates as to the total number of Bektashi. The upper limit is around 200,000 (Birge 1933). L. M. J. Garrett and F. W. Hasluck give the Bektashi population as 80,000. F. W. Hasluck states that 90 per cent of the Muslim population of southern Albania was Bektashi, as were 10 per cent of the Muslim population of northern Albania. Most of these statistics also included adepts of the order who visited the monasteries but were not members of the organisation. The number of actual dervishes is much lower.

What is of significance about the Bektashi is that they were active in the Albanian independence movement in the nineteenth century. They assisted in the distribution of banned Albanian books and magazines, helped the leaders of Albanian rebel bands fighting the Turks, hiding them when necessary in their monasteries, and allowed Albanian rebels to use their monasteries for meetings and assemblies.

It is of no surprise therefore that the most passionate supporter of Albanian nationalism, Naim bey Frashëri (1846-1900), was a member of the Bektashi Order. His *Fletore e Bektashinjet* (Bektashi Notebook) served as the political agenda for the Albanian Bektashi. Frashëri put emphasis on the nation – Albania. He called upon the Albanians to be united irrespective of religious differences. He endeavoured to separate the Albanian Bektashi from the mother abbey (*pir evi*) and wanted to see Albanian used as the language of the Order. Frashëri also tried to purify the Albanian language of Turkish words. He even tried to replace the traditional terminology of the Order, words such as *dervish, baba, dede*, etc., with Albanian terms, but he largely failed in having them accepted.

It is difficult to say to what extent the Bektashi took part in Albanian uprisings at the beginning of the twentieth century. There is no proof for F. W. Hasluck's assertion that the dervishes wanted to create Albania as a Bektashi State during the Young Turk revolt of 1908. However, it would seem certain that there were close relations between the Bektashi and the Young Turks. Leading Young Turks such as Riza Tevfik and Talat Pasha, etc., were members of the order. There was an interesting development after the Second World War. In addition to the Sunni Muslims, the Orthodox Christians and the Catholic Christians, the Bektashi were recognised as an official religious community in the People's Republic of Albania. However, during the Cultural Revolution in Albania in 1967, 2,169 mosques and churches were closed down and the Albanian Government declared the country to be the first atheist State in Europe, thus putting an end to the official existence of the Bektashi Order.

[Georg Stadtmüller, 'Der Derwischorden der Bektaschi in Albanien', in *Serta Slavica in Memoriam Aloisii Schmaus*, ed. W. Gesemann et al. (Munich: Trofenik 1971), pp. 683-687. Translated from the German by Robert Elsie.]

1995
FRANCES TRIX
THE ASHURA LAMENT OF BABA REXHEB

The American anthropologist Frances Trix (b. 1948), emerita professor of linguistics and anthropology at Indiana University, spent many years in close friendship with the late Baba Rexheb at the Bektashi tekke in Detroit. This contact gave her unique insight into the thinking of the erudite baba. In this article, she presents the Ashura Lament that Baba Rexheb composed in 1954 shortly after his arrival in Michigan.

It is a custom in the Balkans to serve something sweet when commemorating the dead. It is also a custom there to lament for the dead. People say that the sweetness of the food and the chanting of laments help to draw out the poison and pain of the sadness in death.

The celebration of the Muslim holiday of *Ashura*, which commemorates the suffering and death of Husein at Kerbela, also includes both the serving of sweet food in the form of the *Ashura* pudding, as well as the chanting of laments or *mersiye*. At the *Ashura* ceremony of the Bektashi *tekke* in America, Baba Rexheb closes the benedictory prayer with the following in Albanian:

Shtoje dhe embëlsoje këtë ushqim përkujtimor e dhuroi gjithë botës dhantit e Tua, Amin!

Increase and sweeten this nourishment of remembrance and give Your blessings to all, Amen.

What has been blessed by this prayer, through numerous litanies, is the *Ashura* pudding. Thus, the phrase, 'this nourishment of remembrance,' refers literally to the specially prepared and blessed wheat-based *Ashura* pudding, replete with sugar, raisins, and nuts. But I also see the phrase, 'this nourishment of remembrance,' as referring to all the prayers and the lament that have preceded in the ceremony, as well as to the entire gathering.

In this paper I will focus on the lament chanted at the *Ashura* ceremony of the Bektashi *tekke* in America. In presenting this Albanian lament, I will first explore its context of recitation, then its immediate Ottoman and general Balkan antecedents, and finally its ceremonial context. By so doing I hope to show how the lament as part of the *Ashura* ceremony serves as a particular 'nourishment of remembrance,' helping bind together the immigrant Albanians who make up the Bektashi community in America.

This lament was composed in 1954 by Baba Rexheb, the now 85 year-old Albanian *baba* of the American *tekke*. It was composed for the first *Ashura* ceremony at the then newly opened Bektashi *tekke*. Since that first time, the lament has been chanted each year at the *Ashura* ceremony. Along with the *Ashura* pudding, it continues to be a focal point of the ceremony.

The context of recitation

We are fortunate in having what amounts to stage directions written by Baba Rexheb in 1954 for the reciting of the lament. These directions were printed with the text of the lament in a pamphlet put out by the *tekke* for potential adherents. My English translation of them reads:

> The *Merthiye* is chanted with a loud voice in a doleful melody in front of the caldron wherein the *Ashura* is cooked. It is chanted in chorus by all those present at this ceremony.[62]

But as so often happens, the actual chanting of the *mersiye* or lament in the ceremony went somewhat differently. This was necessitated in part by the sheer number and diversity of those who gathered for the first *Ashura*. Here I should note that the *Ashura* ceremony of which I speak is an innovation of Baba Rexheb in the sense that it is in addition to the usual fasting, recitings, and private ceremonies of the initiated Bektashis at the time of *Ashura*. It takes place after the private ceremonies, and is open to whomever wishes to attend: initiated *muhiban, aşiklar* or people attached to the *tekke* by love, respect, and service, but not yet initiated and friends of the above including non-Muslims. Baba designed this ceremony as an inclusive gathering at the time of the major annual religious holiday, so that the community could be known.

The ceremony is held at the *tekke*, a former farmhouse set on twenty acres of land on the outskirts of Detroit, Michigan. The first public *Ashura* ceremony, in 1954, was performed outside, as there was no room in the farmhouse for the two hundred some people who attended. The participants included, as have all following *Ashuras*, mostly Muslims, but also Albanian Orthodox Christians and Albanian Catholics. All were Albanian immigrants, a core group of whom had come to America as early as 1912, but the majority of whom had come after World War II. It is interesting that out of this crowd of two hundred, only five were initiated Bektashis.

With such a large and disparate crowd, they reportedly did not all chant, nor could they gather in front of the caldron. Rather, Baba instructed six people with strong voices in the chanting of the lament, and the others chanted the refrain. This custom of a solo or small group chanting has persisted today. As for the caldron, people remember seeing the smoke from its fire for miles away, for the fire had to be large to cook pudding for several hundred. But instead of gathering in front of the caldron as the written directions would have had it, the people gathered in front of Baba. This focus on Baba has persisted in the organization of seating at *Ashura* ceremonies held today in the 1980's, to which some five hundred people attend. This singular focus on Baba is in keeping with all the activities and ceremonies of the *tekke*.

The Ottoman antecedent

Baba Rexheb has always referred to the Albanian *Ashura* lament he composed as 'a translation,' and points to the famous *mersiye* in Ottoman Turkish by Sheikh

Safi.⁶³ Baba had grown up hearing the *Ashura* lament chanted in Turkish, for at the Bektashi *tekke* in Gjirokastër in southern Albania, where Baba was trained and served as a dervish for over twenty years, the *mersiye* was chanted in Turkish. In comparing the Albanian lament with its Ottoman precursor, I will look first at what has been preserved of the older lament in the matrix of the newer one, and then at how the laments differ.

A striking similarity of the Ottoman and Albanian laments is in the melodic contour. This is of course not apparent from written texts, and metric analyses only distract. The Albanian is in trochaic octosyllables, an accentual meter; where the Ottoman is analyzed as a quantitative sort of *remel*. But when Baba chants the Ottoman *mersiye*, and when he or the people he trained chant the Albanian one, the melodic contours are very similar. This is not particularly unusual as melodic structures are some of the most persistent of cultural structures, preserved beneath the conscious level of words.

Another similarity between the Ottoman and Albanian laments, and one apparent to both ears and eyes, is the refrain. Both have unvarying refrains that invoke Husein: 'Ya Huseyin' in the Turkish, and 'O Imam Hysejn' in the Albanian. These refrains, which are characteristic of laments in general, relate laments to incantations, and perhaps to earlier dialogues with the dead. The direct questions posed in the laments,

'Where is he, what has happened to our dearest, our beloved? O Husein' (Ottoman)
'Where is the beautiful prince? O Imam Husein' (Albanian),

coupled with the constant direct address of the refrain, reinforce the dialogic character. These invariant refrains also allow for participation of many people or people new to the ceremony. Like the five mysteries of Mary recited at Catholic commemorative services, by the third mystery, even non-Catholics have picked up on the 'Hail, Mary.'

Another obvious similarity of the Ottoman and Albanian laments are the first lines. The Ottoman:

Ey nur-i çeşme Ahmed-i Mukhtar Ya Huseyin,
Ey yadigar-i Hayderi Kerrar Ya Huseyin

is matched closely in meaning by the Albanian first couplet, which I have here translated into English:

Oh light of the eyes of Mukhtar	O Imam Husein,
Oh remembrance of Haidar	O Imam Husein

After the first couplets, however, the Ottoman and Albanian laments part. The Ottoman proceeds to laud the beauty of Husein in multiple couplets, whereas the Albanian strikes a more narrative note. This is a pervasive difference in the two laments. Where the Ottoman extolls, the Albanian recounts and instructs. For example the fifth couplet of the Ottoman begins:

To the dust on your mouth, O Shah,
Pearls of paradise and rubies of Bactria
are but fragments of stone   O Husein.

The Albanian by this point has set the time as the month of *Muharrem,* the month of mourning, and as for descriptions of Husein, they tend to be short epithets:

In this month of suffering	O Imam Husein,
The light-giving star was destroyed	O Imam Husein,
Dry-lipped one, unquenched	O Imam Husein.

Or later, other examples of epithets of Husein in narrative:

They said, Where is the beautiful prince	O Imam Husein,
Angel-like with fluttering wing	O Imam Husein,
We do not see him, where has he gone	O Imam Husein.

Here it is important to note that while the Albanian is more narrative, that is, it describes events in a chronological order, the narrative is not that of Husein's martyrdom, but rather that of the mourners' discovery of Husein's death, their mourning, praise of Husein, and finally requests for intercession.

The Ottoman too winds up with a request for intercession, but here it emphasizes the individual and with a particular clerical title:

I am a dervish, I have come to your threshold and bowed my face,
You are gracious, Oh Shah, be kind to me   O Husein.

The Albanian, in contrast, does not make reference to clerical titles among the mourners. But more importantly, the Albanian refers always to the plural body of mourners. There is no 'I' in the Albanian lament, only a 'we':

The month of *Muharrem* has come to us   O Imam Husein.

The emphasis on the mourners as a group is clear in the curse and oaths or self-curses:

We will never forget you	O Imam Husein,
We remember the martyrdom	O Imam Husein,
We curse Yezid	Oh Imam Husein.

This emphasis on the mourners as a group builds through the Albanian lament to the last stanza where a single clause contains multiple references to this group. A word for word translation of such a line being:

That you stay close to us   O Imam Husein.

General Balkan antecedents

As mentioned at the beginning of this paper, lamenting the dead is an age-old custom in the Balkans, currently performed by both Christians and Muslims, and attested to in classical Greek times. The metric structure of Baba's lament places it squarely in this Balkan tradition. The line in epic verse and dirges in Albanian folk poetry is an eight-syllable trochaic line with special emphasis on the penultimate syllable.[64] The lines in Baba's lament have this same structure:

'Drita jote na ndritoftë.'
'May your light shine upon us.'

Besides line structure, the imagery in Baba's lament is typical of Balkan laments. This is not to say that the Ottoman lament does not contain some of the same images. But the imagery in the Ottoman lament is much more varied, and it builds, hyperbole on hyperbole. In contrast the images in Baba's lament are restricted to those of light and water, and build in more narrative fashion with standard Balkan terms. For example, both Sheikh Safi's lament and Baba's include sections on the mourning of Nature for Husein.

The Ottoman begins this section of Nature's mourning with:

Even the dawn cried blood, O Shah,
in compassion for you

In this same section on Nature mourning, the Ottoman leads to:

Rain with great sadness fell like a flood   O Husein.

The Albanian also refers to dawn in the section on all Nature mourning:

| So too the morning from its bed | O Imam Husein, |
| Arose reddened as with blood | O Imam Husein. |

But the Albanian then leads to:

Black clouds amassed	O Imam Husein,
They covered the whole sky	O Imam Husein,
They poured down poison rain	O Imam Husein.

The image of poison rain, of tears as a sort of poison and of the dead as having poisoned the living by dying are very common in Balkan laments. An example of this is found in the following contemporary Greek lament:

I bid farewell to my kin, to all my relatives. I leave my mother three glasses of poison: The first to drink in the morning, the second
To drink at noon, and the third, the most poisonous,
To drink in the evening when she lies down to sleep.[65]

The other main image in Baba's lament, of light as source of life and the divine, is extremely pervasive. Husein is 'the light-giving star', 'the light of the Holy Family', 'a blessed star', 'a great light that will not go out', and a source whose light is requested to bring the mourners light. This recalls the way Telemachos is addressed in *The Odyssey* as 'sweet light.' A twelfth-century lament in the writings of Eustathios of Thessaloniki also has much in common with the light imagery in the twentieth-century Albanian lament:

> I had my child as the sun, and now that my child is obscured I, his mother, am without sun. My child was a bright star, but now he is hidden, and the gloom of night has enshrouded me, his mother. My child was light to me, but he is quenched, and now I walk in darkness.[66]

In contrast is one of the images of light in Sheikh Safi's Ottoman lament:

On your shining face
is the sura 'the Sun and the Morning'.
For your glory the verses
of the Qur'an came down   O Husein.

Certainly the sense of light as *'nur'* is in the Ottoman lament. But rather than translate what are Qur'anic references, Baba's Albanian lament for people with little religious training uses epithets and images common to Balkan laments, and known orally.

Besides the use of the images of light and water in Balkan fashion, Baba's lament contains an ethical dimension related to codes of honor and bravery in combat. These elements are especially characteristic not of Balkan laments in general, but of Albanian dirges and Albanian epics and songs. This ethical dimension is illustrated in Baba's lament in the following:

From the way of truth you did not turn back	O Imam Husein,
With blood You colored the land	O Imam Husein,
You gave to us a model, for all of us	O Imam Husein.

Or later, and here not only are the mourners a group, but Husein too has become part of a group of fighters:

How dared the nation without honor?	O Imam Husein,
How dared Shimir of Kufa	O Imam Husein,
Do away with you, son of Fatima?	O Imam Husein.
How were they assembled	O Imam Husein,
Yezidists with Marwan	O Imam Husein,
They surrounded you and killed you	O Imam Husein,
Together with your companions	O Imam Husein,
You laid value on our religion	O Imam Husein,
And so you are remembered forever	O Imam Husein.

By way of comparison is the following from an epic song of southern Albania:

On the Kolonjë road at lonely Mpsar,
Myftar Labi with his eighteen men lies in ambush.
He wants to rob our guest, he wants to kill him.
Lest people scorn us, let's fight to the last![67]

Nowhere in the Ottoman lament is this sense of militaristic group honor present.

The ceremonial context

While the first *Ashura* ceremony at the American *tekke* took place outside, those of the last twenty years have been held indoors in a large meeting hall in the basement of the *tekke*. At one end of this meeting hall, raised on a platform, is Head Table. In front of this table and at right angles to it are all the long tables where the people sit. Baba sits in the middle of Head Table with distinguished guests and members of the *Teqe* Commission to either side of him.

On the wall behind Baba, to the left is a large American flag, to the right an equally large Albanian flag – the double-headed eagle, and in the center behind Baba is a red banner. This banner is red for the blood of Husein, with passages in white letters from the *Qur'an* translated into Albanian. In the corners of the banner are the names: Allah, Muhammad, Ali, and Haxhi Bektash Veli. Here is the Albanian text, a translation of the *Qur'an* from *Sura II al-baqara, Sura* XLVIII *al-fath*, and the English translation:

Allah   Muhammed
Kur u-tha Zoti engjëjvet: u jam tuke krijuar një
zëvëndsin t'im në faqen e dheut; kjo ësht' vendosja
e vjetër e të lartit Zot të plot fuqishëm. Dhe ti
O Muhammed, do ndricosh botën në rrugën e drejtë.
Të gjith ata që kanë zënë dorën tënde njesoj
kanë zënë dorën e Zotit. Dora e Zotit ësht mbi fuqin
e duarvet të tyre. Kushdo që thyen këtë besë-
lidhje dëmton vetëm vehten e tij dhe kushdo
që mban besëlidhjen do të shpërblehet me së miri
Ali   Kurani   Haxhi Bektash Veli

Allah   Muhammed
When thy Lord said unto the angels: I have created a
representative of mine on the earth; this is an ancient
decision of the High and All-Powerful God. And thou,
O Muhammad, will illuminate the true way for the world.
All those who swear allegiance unto thee,

swear allegiance unto Allah. The Hand of Allah is
above their hands. Thus whoever breaks this oath
damages his own soul; while whoever
keeps his oath, on him will be bestowed immense reward.
Ali   the Qur'an   Haji Bektash Veli

 This banner is the only visual marking of the room as Islamic, and Bektashi. Of course the building itself is clearly Bektashi with a *meydan* upstairs and a large facsimile of a *tac,* the green and white headgear of Baba, on the roof of the *tekke.* The presence of Baba, in full garb of *hirka, kemer* and *tac* is however, by far, the most powerful symbol of the identity of the place.
 Turning to the public *Ashura* ceremony, it can be divided into three parts. The first part is made up of the opening prayer, and the prayer of benediction of the pudding, with the chanting of the lament sandwiched between these prayers. The second part of the ceremony includes a speech, often by a guest, followed by two listings: of those who have died that year, and of those who supported the *tekke* with amounts contributed. These listings are punctuated by *fatihas* in Arabic. The third part of the ceremony centers on food with the serving and eating of the *Ashura* pudding, followed by the serving and eating of a full lamb dinner.
 The antecedents of the ceremony, like those of the lament, include the particular private rituals of initiated Bektashis at the time of *Ashura,* as well as Balkan commemorative ceremonies for individual dead put on by their families. The prayer of benediction of the pudding, with all its litanies, is appropriate to individual commemorative ceremonies, and has been used at such occasion. The lament, however, is appropriate to a *tekke* setting. The sweet pudding followed by a lamb meal is appropriate to both.
 Concentrating then on the first part of the ceremony, the opening prayer and the benedictory prayer are both recited by Baba. Both are patriotic in the sense that they both include prayers for the people and government of America, and thanks for the freedom of religious conscience there. They also both include prayers for the Albanian people, with the obvious omission of the Albanian government. The criticism of the Communist regime is clearest in the benedictory prayer:

For the nation of our people, for its rescue from the misery and danger that surround it, for the prosperity and happiness of that land, bless this, O Lord.[68]

 These prayers also include much that is Islamic, and specifically Bektashi, but the patriotic element is worthy of note. I would relate this patriotic element in the prayers to the two flags on the wall behind Baba. The presence on the wall of these two flags symbolizes the common experience of the participants. This common experience is that of immigration, of being cut off from one's native land or land of one's families, and of newly starting out in America.
 In-between these flags is, however, the red banner with Qur'anic lines translated by Baba into Albanian. This I would relate to the lament in that it joins the religious tradition with the language of the land of the people. As such, it asserts

and strengthens their identity in another way. Recently though, there has been an addition to the wall decor. On the upper part of the banner, the framed picture of the architect's rendering of the completed *türbe* for Baba has been hung. In trying to deal with Baba's inevitable death, the community has already built his *türbe* or mausoleum on *tekke* grounds. I see this picture as another powerful symbol of what holds the Bektashi community together, and that is love for Baba.

In his bringing of ceremonies, and melding of traditions, in his translating of prayers, and remembering of melodies, epitomized so well in the *Ashura* lament, Baba has brought the immigrant Albanians a precious 'nourishment of remembrance.' In his passing and burial on *tekke* grounds, he will make a place in their new land holy.

The English and Albanian texts of the Ashura Lament

'This "Lament" is an elegy on the sacrifices and sufferings of Imam Husein who was killed on the Plain of Kerbela by the treacherous hand of the cursed Yezid. The Lament is sung out loud to a mournful melody in front of the caldron where Ashura is cooked. It is sung in a choir by all those who are present at the ceremony. Here is the text of the "Lament" translated into English.'

Oh, light in the eyes of Mukhtar,	O Imam Husein!
Oh, remembrance of Haidar,	O Imam Husein!
Ruler of the human heart,	O Imam Husein!
Jewel of the spiritual world,	O Imam Husein!
The month of Muharram has come to us	O Imam Husein!
Reminded us of your suffering,	O Imam Husein!
And wounded our hearts.	O Imam Husein!
In this month of suffering,	O Imam Husein!
The light-giving star was destroyed,	O Imam Husein!
Dry-lipped one, unquenched,	O Imam Husein!
Right on the Plain of Kerbela,	O Imam Husein!
You fell victim to the battle,	O Imam Husein!
Oh, light of Ali Abbas,	O Imam Husein!
You left not the path of righteousness,	O Imam Husein!
You bathed the world in your blood,	O Imam Husein!
You set an example to all of us,	O Imam Husein!
Throughout the whole world,	O Imam Husein!
Fires rages all around,	O Imam Husein!
When they sacrificed you,	O Imam Husein!
So, too, the morning from its bed	O Imam Husein!
Arose reddened as with blood,	O Imam Husein!
All was flame and mourning,	Oh Imam Husein!

They covered themselves in mourning,	O Imam Husein!
The earth, the sky – they lamented,	O Imam Husein!
For you they wept, they were poisoned,	O Imam Husein!
Black clouds amassed,	O Imam Husein!
They covered the whole sky,	O Imam Husein!
They poured down poison rain,	O Imam Husein!
All wept and mourned,	O Imam Husein!
They drenched you in their tears,	O Imam Husein!
Loud they shouted and sought you,	O Imam Husein!
Saying 'Where is the beautiful prince?	O Imam Husein!
Angel-like with fluttering wings,	O Imam Husein!
We do not see him, where has he gone?'	O Imam Husein!
When they saw you fallen,	O Imam Husein!
Your body pierced with arrows,	O Imam Husein!
They called out: 'Oh, blessed star!'	O Imam Husein!
How dared the nation without honor,	Oh Imam Husein!
How dared Shimir of Kufa,	Oh Imam Husein!
Do away with you, son of Fatima?	Oh Imam Husein!
How were they assembled,	Oh Imam Husein!
The Yezidists with Marvan,	Oh Imam Husein!
They surrounded you and killed you!	Oh Imam Husein!
Together with your companions,	O Imam Husein!
You laid value on our religion,	O Imam Husein!
And so you are remembered forever,	O Imam Husein!
We will never forget you,	O Imam Husein!
We remember the martyrdom,	O Imam Husein!
We curse Yezid, O Imam Husein!	
May you be glorified and blessed,	O Imam Husein!
For all your honored life,	O Imam Husein!
A great and unquenchable light,	O Imam Husein!
Oh, man of sweetness,	O Imam Husein!
Oh, great sea of goodness,	O Imam Husein!
Keep us away from evil.	O Imam Husein!
May your light shine upon us,	O Imam Husein!
May it never be far from us,	O Imam Husein!
May it flourish for us forever,	O Imam Husein!
That you stay close to us,	O Imam Husein!
Cleanse our hearts,	O Imam Husein!
We beseech you, never forget us!	O Imam Husein!

'Merthijeja' është vajtimi që bëhet për sakrificat dhe vuajtjet e pësuara prej Imam Hysejnit, i cili ra dëshmor në Fushën e Qerbelasë prej dorës trathtare të Jezidit të *mallëkuar. 'Merthijeja' këndohet me zë të lartë dhe me një melodi vajtuese përpara kazanit ku gatuhet 'Ashureja.' Këndohet në kor prej të gjithë njerëzve që ndodhen prezent në këtë ceremoni. Këtu më poshtë po ri-prodhojmë 'Merthijene' të përkthyer në gjuhën shqipe:*[69]

O, drit' e syvet të Muhtarit	... ja Imam Hysejn!
O, kujtimi i Hajdarit	... ja Imam Hysejn!
Mbret' i zëmërës njerzore	... ja Imam Hysejn!
Vleft' e botës shpirtërore	... ja Imam Hysejn!
Hëna Muharem përshkoi	... ja Imam Hysejn!
Zinë tënde na kujtoi	... ja Imam Hysejn!
Zëmërat na i lëndoi	... ja Imam Hysejn!
Në këtë' e Hënë të mërzitur	... ja Imam Hysejn!
U shove o yll' i ndritur	... ja Imam Hysejn!
Buzë that' i pa ujtur	... ja Imam Hysejn!
Mu në fush' të Qerbelasë	... ja Imam Hysejn!
Re viktima e belasë	... ja Imam Hysejn!
O, drit' e Ali Abasë	... ja Imam Hysejn!
Nga rrug' e drejtë s'u ktheve	... ja Imam Hysejn!
Me gjak tokën Ti e leve	... ja Imam Hysejn!
Shëmbëll na dhe gjithë neve	... ja Imam Hysejn!
Gjithë bota an' e mbanë	... ja Imam Hysejn!
U ndez flakë më çdo anë	... ja Imam Hysejn!
Kur Ty të bënë kurbane	... ja Imam Hysejn!
Dhe mëngjezi prej jataku	... ja Imam Hysejn!
U ngrit i kuq posi gjaku	... ja Imam Hysejn!
Gjithësisë zi i flaku	... ja Imam Hysejn!
Në të zeza u mbuluan	... ja Imam Hysejn!
Toka, qiejt – të vajtuan	... ja Imam Hysejn!
Për Ty qanë, u helmuan	... ja Imam Hysejn!
Ret' e zeza tok' u mblodhe	... ja Imam Hysejn!
Gjithë qiellin e pështolle	... ja Imam Hysejn!
Shin' e helmit poshtë e hodhe	... ja Imam Hysejn!
Që të gjithë të vajtuan	... ja Imam Hysejn!
Me lot vaji të mbuluan	... ja Imam Hysejn!
Britnë fort e të kërkuan	... ja Imam Hysejn!
Thanë ku 'shte Mbret' i bukur?	... ja Imam Hysejn!
Engjëllosh me krahë flutur	... ja Imam Hysejn!
Ne s'e shohim ku 'shtë futur?	... ja Imam Hysejn!
Kur të panë të rrëzuar	... ja Imam Hysejn!
Trupin me shigjeta shpuar	... ja Imam Hysejn!
Thirren: O yll' i bekuar!	... ja Imam Hysejn!

Qysh guxoj kombi i pa besë?	*... ja Imam Hysejn!*
Qysh guxoj shimri i Qofesë	*... ja Imam Hysejn!*
Të cduk' bir' e Fatimesë?	*... ja Imam Hysejn!*
Qysh u mblodhë an' e mbanë	*... ja Imam Hysejn!*
Jezitistët me Mervanë	*... ja Imam Hysejn!*
Të rrethuan e të vranë!	*... ja Imam Hysejn!*
Bashkë me shokë të tjerë	*... ja Imam Hysejn!*
Fesë t'onë i vute vlerë	*... ja Imam Hysejn!*
Prandaj kujtoni për herë	*... ja Imam Hysejn!*
Neve kurrë s'ju harrojmë	*... ja Imam Hysejn!*
Therrorine e kujtojmë	*... ja Imam Hysejn!*
Jezitin e mallëkojmë	*... ja Imam Hysejn!*
Qofshi lart e të bekuar	*... ja Imam Hysejn!*
Gjithë jetën të nderuar	*... ja Imam Hysejn!*
Drit' e madhe e pa shuar	*... ja Imam Hysejn!*
O burrim i ëmbëlsirës	*... ja Imam Hysejn!*
O det' i math i së mirës	*... ja Imam Hysejn!*
Na mërgo prej ligësirës	*... ja Imam Hysejn!*
Drita jote na ndritoftë	*... ja Imam Hysejn!*
Nga ju kurr' mos na largoftë	*... ja Imam Hysejn!*
Për herë na lulëzoftë	*... ja Imam Hysejn!*
Afër nesh të na qëndroni	*... ja Imam Hysejn!*
Zëmërat të na i pastroni	*... ja Imam Hysejn!*
Aman! kurr' mos na harroni	*... ja Imam Hysejn!*

[Adapted from Frances Trix, 'The Ashura Lament of Baba Rexheb and the Albanian Bektashi Community in America', in *Bektachiyya. Etudes sur l'ordre mystique des Bektachis et les groupes relevant de Hadji Bektach*, ed. Alexandre Popovic and Gilles Veinstein. *Revue des Etudes Islamiques*, 60 (1992). Numéro spécial (Paris: Paul Geuthner 1993 and Istanbul: Isis 1995), pp. 413–426.]

1995
NATHALIE CLAYER
BEKTASHISM AND ALBANIAN NATIONALISM

The French historian Nathalie Clayer (b. 1960), research fellow at the Centre national de la recherche scientifique (The National Centre for Scientific Research) in Paris, has been the leading figure in Albanian Bektashi studies for the last quarter of a century. Among her major publications are: 'L'Albanie, pays des derviches: les ordres mystiques musulmans en Albanie à l'époque postottomane, 1912–1967' (Albania, Land of Dervishes: the Mystic Orders of Islam in Albania in the Post-Ottoman Period, 1912–1967), Wiesbaden 1990; 'Les voies d'Allah: les ordres mystiques dans l'Islam des origines à aujourd'hui' (The Ways of Allah: the Mystic Orders in Islam from their Origins to the Present Day), Paris 1996; 'Religion et nation chez les Albanais: XIXe-XXe siècles' (Religion and Nation among the Albanians, 19th–20th Centuries), Istanbul 2003; and 'Aux origines du nationalisme albanais: la naissance d'une nation majoritairement musulmane en Europe' (The Origins of Albanian Nationalism: the Birth of a European Nation with a Muslim Majority), Paris 2007. In this paper, Clayer analyses the important link between the Albanian Bektashi and Albanian nationalism, which she rightly interprets as the key to their popularity and success.

Just before the declaration of Albanian independence, an Albanian member of the Bektashi dervish order began a *nefes* (poem, usually of religious inspiration) with the words '*Shqipëri për Shqipëtarë*' (Albania for the Albanians). How could a Muslim, and all the more an Albanian Muslim, adopt such a clear-cut attitude to the Turkish occupation when the cradle of his movement was situated in Anatolia? This paradoxical position, shared by the great majority of the Albanian Bektashi at the time, shows that their order was of a predominately local character. Indeed, this orientation took on such proportions that the order developed into a religious community of its own. In this paper, we would like to demonstrate that Albanian Bektashism in the nineteenth and twentieth centuries was closely linked to nationalism as a central element of its doctrine.

The phenomenon can probably be dated from 1826. As is widely known, Sultan Mahmud II suppressed the Janissary Corps in that year and closed down all the Bektashi *tekkes* in the Ottoman Empire. The more recent *tekkes* were destroyed and other convents were given over to various other *tarikats*.[70] Their assets were confiscated and many members of the order were sent into exile. The persecution also affected the territory of modern-day Albania where about one-third of the *tekkes* suffered damage. In the Korça region, the *tekkes* of Melçan, Qatrom and Kuç were burned down, as were the *tekke* of Baba Aliko in Berat and the *tekke* of Veliqot near Tepelena.[71]

This being said, the blow delivered to the Bektashi order was not fatal, neither in Albania nor in the rest of the Ottoman Empire where the order continued to exist underground. On Albanian territory, however, the crackdown marked a turning point that saw the rise of nationalism and anti-Ottoman sentiment among the Bektashi which do not seem to have existed before. This reaction was facilitated by the special situation of what would become Albania. The country was inhabited almost entirely by Albanians though they had converted substantially to Islam (in 1912, 70 per cent of the people of Albania were Muslims). Accordingly, there were very few Turks in the ranks of the Bektashi faithful in this region.[72] As a very homogenous group, the Albanian Bektashi were consequently inclined to rally around nationalist sentiment and to support patriotic activity.

Nationalist sentiment took root in the conscience of the Albanian Bektashi in the second half of the nineteenth century. It blossomed and has continued to grow to the present day. With this in mind, we must distinguish two phases: the first being a *nationalist Bektashism* struggling for the creation of Albania, and the second, a *national Bektashism* in post-Ottoman Albania.

Nationalist Bektashism and the struggle for Albania

The 'movement of national revival' as the movement for the creation of Albania was called, began to crystalize after the Treaty of San Stefano when about fifty Albanians gathered on 10 June 1878 in Prizren (Kosovo) to set up a group what was to be known as the League of Prizren. These Albanians had gathered to protest against the clauses of the Treaty of San Stefano that gave parts of territory inhabited by the Albanians to neighbouring countries. However, aside from general discontent, the northern Albanians were more concerned about not losing the privileges they had gained in the Ottoman Empire. The southern Albanians, for their part, were beginning to think about autonomy.[73]

Among the few representatives of southern Albania in the League was the well-known Abdyl (or Abdül) Frashëri (1839–1892) who headed the gathering. Originally from the village of Frashër southeast of Berat, as his surname indicates, he stemmed from a great Bektashi family. His uncle, Dalip Frashëri, had made an Albanian translation of one of the best known and most recited works of Bektashi literature, the *Hadiqatû's-Su'adâ* of the Turkish poet of Persian origin, Fuzûlî.[74] Abdyl Frashëri had two brothers who were equally famous: Sami (Şemseddin) bey Frashëri (1850–1904), a political figure, scholar and author of the famed Ottoman encyclopaedia *Qâmûs al-a'lâm*, and Naim Frashëri (1846–1900) considered as the 'poet of the Albanian nationalist movement.' The Frashëris of course attended the Bektashi *tekke* in their village and where they were *muhibs*. It was founded in 1835 and became one of the most prestigious convents of the order on Albanian territory.[75]

When he got back from Prizren, it was with Baba Alush of the *tekke* of Frashër that Abdyl Frashëri organised, at the *tekke,* a meeting of notables from all over Toskeria, i.e. the southern Albanian regions inhabited by Albanian Tosks.[76] The assembly was attended by another member of the Bektashi clergy, Baba Adem, who headed the Bektashi *tekke* of Melçan near Korça.[77]

The first national gathering in the south of the country in which the Bektashi order played a major role (it provided the venue and ensured spiritual leadership) gave rise to other meetings like the one that took place in Kusereci south of Berat in 1881. It was attended by dozens of Bektashi *babas* and dervishes.[78] Nationalist ideas were thus being spread by members of the Bektashi clergy who stemmed both from the peasantry and from the higher strata of society, including local notables. But the spiritual influence of the Bektashi *babas* also extended to the Orthodox Christian population in the southern regions. Through their activities, the members of the order gained a certain prestige, as can be seen in the following song composed in honour of Baba Alush. It was once sung in the regions of Frashër and Përmet.

Kush do Shqipërinë, kush?
I miri Baba Alush.
Nukë vdiq, në qiell rron.
Dhe së larti na vështron,
Na vështron dhe na thërret,
'Përpiqi për mëmëdhet'.[79]

"Who loves Albania, who?
None but the good Baba Alush,
He did not die, he lives in heaven,
And from the heavens he observes us,
He observes us, calls out to us:
Strive for your Motherland!"

Xhevat Kallajxhi provides another version of this song:

Kush do Shqipërinë, kush?
I miri Baba Alush.
Nukë vdiq, po shkoj dhe rron,
Dhe së largu na vështron,
Na vështron edhe na thrret:
'Punoni për Mëmëdhet.
Cili është bektashi
Të punoj' për Shqipëri,
Të këndoj' gjuhën e tija,
Të heq' dorë nga Mavija'.[80]

"Who loves Albania, who?
None but the good Baba Alush,
He did not die, he left, lived on,
And from a distance he observes us,
He observes us, calls out to us:
'Work for your Motherland!
Whoever is a Bektashi
Let him work for Albania,
Let him read his language,
And keep away from Muavija.'"[81]

By his time, Bektashism was closely linked to the nationalist movement that, after the blow of 1881 when its leaders were arrested, revived and thrived in southern Albania at the dawn of the twentieth century. It should also be noted that, with regard to autonomy, the Young Turk Revolution brought a small glimmer of hope that was soon quenched. The struggle was carried on until the declaration of Albanian independence in Vlora on 28 November 1912.

The struggle for Albania

In this thirty-year period, the Albanian Bektashi clergy did not simply give its blessing to the national movement, it also took a very active part in it. This active participation can be seen in particular in its efforts to teach the Albanian language and to distribute Albanian books. Enormous progress was made. It was only in 1887 that the first Albanian school opened. This happened in Korça, with both the Ottoman authorities and the Greek Orthodox Church doing all they could to discourage parents and pupils from attending. In 1902, Sultan Abdul Hamid ordered the closing of all the schools and banned the publication of books in Albanian. After the Young Turk Revolution, schools were opened once again for a few months but were shut down in October 1910. An affirmation of Albanian identity was thus intrinsically linked to the promotion of Albanian as the language of writing and administration and to the campaign to teach the population to read and write. Almost all Albanians were illiterate at the time.

The Bektashi *tekkes*, where the dervishes themselves had only basic education, very soon turned into a network of underground schools and served as a system for distributing spellers, newspapers and books.[82] This network set up by the Albanian Bektashi was supported from outside Albania proper, for instance by the *tekke* in Cairo, from where a dervish of Albanian origin, Baba Meleq Shëmbërdhenji, was sent back to Albania on a mission to distribute books throughout the country.[83]

There are three good accounts of the role of the Bektashi in encouraging people to learn Albanian and in distributing books, testimonies of people who lived at the time. Here are the first-hand accounts in full. The first one illustrates life at the Bektashi *tekke* of Bllaca in the Dibra region and its role at the time of the national awakening from 1878 to 1912:

> I was poor, had neither land nor livestock, and left my village of Gorica to make a living. I came to Bllaca and worked as a servant at the Bektashi *tekke* there. At the *tekke*, I became friends with Jashar Zeneli, an educated fellow who was older than I was. He could speak Turkish and knew how to read Albanian. The *tekke* of Bllaca was a well-known centre for the teaching of the Albanian alphabet. There I met Jashar Zeneli, Tush Meta, Demir Tasha, Hysen Tasha, Seit Tasha, Selman Jella, Ram Osmani and several other men I have forgotten now. These fine men were learning to read and write Albanian and when they learned the alphabet, they began to read the books that arrived from Monastir [Bitola]. My friend, Jashar, taught me the Albanian alphabet, too, and gave me a spelling-book that I still own and cherish.

The *baba* of the *tekke*, Isuf, was delighted when he learned that I knew how to read the Albanian alphabet. For this reason he allowed me to take part in meetings at the *tekke*. On such occasions, he even let me put off my chores until the next day.

The meetings were organised by Baba Isuf and sometimes by Jashar Zeneli. I was happy to take part because they talked about the liberation of Albania and the founding of a strong and modern Albanian State. We then read the writings of Naim Frashëri or the Albanian newspapers that had arrived from Monastir.

Before the meetings closed, tasks were given out to the participants: For example, Tush Meta was to distribute books in Sopot, Zërqan, Peladhia, Kovashica and Homesh. The *tekke* was also allied with Mersen Demë.

Jashar Zeneli won over the *kaymakam* of Dibra and invited him to the *tekke* in Bllaca one day and offered him a fine Dibran costume. The *kaymakam* was very happy with it and told Jashar that he might carry on teaching Albanian, but only as long as Istanbul did not find out.

When freedom was declared,[84] reading and writing Albanian were taught in the open. Seit Tasha was a prominent figure in teaching. But when the big army of Turgut Pasha marched through (in 1910), he banned the teaching of Albanian for a while. This only made us prouder of Albania and filled us with a longing for freedom.[85]

The second account concerns the three *tekkes* in the vicinity of Korça (Melçan, Turan and Qatrom) between 1907 and 1912:

I learned the Albanian alphabet at the *tekke* of Qatrom with the help of Dervish Myftar who had been there since 1907. The peasants who had spelling-books in their homes and knew how to read and write bragged about it and we were envious of them. The place in the house where the Albanian spelling-book was kept was considered blessed by God.

When I went down to Korça to buy some eggs at the 'Albanian Shop,' I met Gavrilka (Gavril Pepo), a friend of mine who was my age and who worked in the shop. We would talk about the Albanian language and the spelling-books. [...] Since I was his best friend, I got to sit at the table where the patriots Themistokli Gërmenji, Ohran Pojani and Dr Haki Mbroja were gathered, and I loved listening to them.

By the time I got to Korça, I became better at reading the spelling-book that Gavrilka had begun to teach me and could even explain it to the other peasants. One day, Baba Hysen from the *tekke* of Melçan visited our village. My father, who was one of his friends, invited him to have dinner at our house. As is custom, the other villagers came over to greet him and keep him company. Before the start of the meal, I took my glass of *raki* and raised it to Baba Hysen, saying: 'Baba Hysen, let us drink to the health of the alphabet. Long live the alphabet!' Baba Hysen was delighted at this and all the villagers joined in, shouting: 'Long live the alphabet!' [...]

The countryside needs the town and the town needs the countryside. This is why I often went to Korça with the other villagers to go to market and to take care of various administrative matters. After market, I went back to the 'Albanian Shop' where Themistokli Gërmenji and Dr. Haki Mbroja took me aside, asked me questions and told me what to do with the villagers in Vinçan (a village northwest of Korça) to help the national question (the liberation movement). From this time on, Gavrilka put packages of spelling-books into my satchel.

One day at the 'Albanian Shop,' Gavrilka had a bag of spelling-books that had just come in from Bucharest and told me to distribute them to the peasants, but on leaving Korça, I was stopped by a gendarme. He put one hand on my shoulder and the other on my satchel. 'Not so fast, peasant,' he said. 'What have you got in your bag? What are those books?' and he put me in the police car.

On the way, we met the patriot Memdu Zavalani who took a look at me and recognised me. He glanced at the satchel and knew what was going on, so he went up to the gendarme and said: 'Hey, gendarme, what infraction has this peasant committed and where are you taking him?' The gendarme looked Memdu in the eye and pointed to the bag of books I was clutching in my hand. Memdu scowled and shouted at me, and was just about to beat me up. At that moment he seized the satchel I was carrying over my shoulder and shoved me away. He then told the gendarme to be off and not to waste his time, that he would be happy to take me where I deserved to be put. The gendarme was convinced and went his way. Memdu dragged me off and locked me in his office. He told me to be very careful because the Turkish government was taking drastic steps against all those involved in teaching the Albanian alphabet. After this, I recovered my satchel and hastened off to the *tekke* of Turan. Passing through the main gate, I met the dervish who had taught me to read the alphabet. In a room in the *tekke*, the dervish and I opened the satchel and counted the spelling-books in it. I left some of them for distribution at the *tekke* and kept the rest for myself. We had lunch together and I then set off for Vinçan. There I met Nuri and Karaman, two fine patriots, and gave them some of the spelling-books.

I continued on to the *tekke* of Melçan. At the village there, I met two men who wanted to learn the alphabet and gave them an Albanian spelling-book. I then trod up the hill and went into the *meydan* where I came across Baba Hysen. Baba Hysen was a true patriot and an inseparable friend of the nationalists of Korça, whereas Baba Qazim of the *tekke* of Qatrom was different. He was afraid of the government.

I told Baba Hysen what had happened and gave him the remaining spelling-books that I had in my satchel. The *baba* took one of them, kissed it and placed it against his forehead. He told me that our country would prosper with the help of these spelling-books, would be free and we would have a government of our own like the other peoples in the Balkans. Then he kissed me on the forehead and exclaimed: 'Long live the alphabet!'[86]

In the third account we come across some of the figures from the second text:

I was a farmer in the village and took care of the vineyards and crops. I had been conscious of the nationalist struggle from an early age and played the role of a 'good Albanian,' as they said at the time.

The Bektashi *tekkes* were centres of patriotic activity. I went to the *tekke* of Qatrom where I became friends with Dervish Ramadan[87] who talked to me about Albania and, beginning in 1900, taught me to read the national alphabet. I often went to Korça and always visited the Albanian café where I met Gavrilka[88] who was a waiter there. Gavrilka gave me a spelling-book and some readers and introduced me to Themistokli Gërmenji, Dr. Haki Mborja, Qamil Panariti, Mihal Grameno and Goni Katundi, etc.

I first met Themistokli in the village of Vinçan. He enjoyed being among the villagers and discussed agriculture and herding with them, but most of the time he focused on the national issue. When freedom was proclaimed (with the Constitution of 1908), Themistokli visited our village, as well as Melçan, Goskova, Porodina and the villages on the plain. So as not to be recognised by government authorities, he would dress up as a hunter with a rifle under his arm, a sack and a hare. But the sack was full of treatises and books in Albanian. Once and a while, he came to our village and would usually spend the night at our house. The men of the village gathered at nightfall in his room till it was full of people. They all listened with great attention to what Themistokli had to say about Albania's ancient history, about Scanderbeg, Naim Frashëri and the other patriots of the national revival. He told the men of the village that the people of Albania ought to rise up, rifles in hand, to liberate the country from the Turkish yoke.

Before the villagers departed, Themistokli Gërmenji opened his sack and brought out the treatises, spelling-books and readers and read them out.

The next day, in the morning, I accompanied him to the end of the village. Sometimes he went straight to the *tekke* of Melçan to meet the dervishes and Baba Hysen.[89] On several occasions I went with him with my brother Karaman.[90]

Reading these accounts makes it evident that the *babas*, such as Baba Hysen of the *tekke* of Melçan, played a significant role in the national revival. Nonetheless, some *babas*, such as Baba Qazim of the *tekke* of Qatrom, were more reserved out of fear of the authorities.[91] As seen in the first account, it was often possible to come to an arrangement with the authorities, but it also happened that the Bektashi suffered painful consequences for their activities. Several *babas* were arrested and imprisoned for more or less long periods of time.

In 1893, for instance, the new *baba* of the *tekke* of Prishta, Baba Ahmet, who got into a conflict with the bey of Këlcyra, was arrested and sent into exile, and the assets of the *tekke* were confiscated. Baba Ahmet died in 1902 while attempting to escape from the prison of Sinope where he had been sent.[92]

In 1900, Baba Salih, who had set up a clandestine school in his native village of Matohasanaj near Tepelena, was arrested and held in prison for several years. During his detention, he translated the *Hadiqatû's-Su'ada* of Fuzûlî into Tosk dialect, as had Dalip Frashëri. In one of his poems, he notes:

I am nothing at all,
God! I weep and implore you,
Ali! My tongue calls out to you,
Ali, Ahmet Myhtar!
Huseyn! My heart is weeping,
Haxhi Bektash, Hunqar!
I recite this poem for my suffering.
Some accursed men came after me
Because I was working for my language,
I wanted to awaken the Albanians.
I was in Kudhës near Vlora in
Three hundred and eighteen, The year in Turkish style,
Muawiya appeared before me!
Spies gathered round me
And burned my projects!
Turkey also learned
That I was spreading Albanian.

A couple of horsemen arrived,
They took and threw me into prison,
Oh Salih! Do not remain idle.
Take and translate from Fuzûlî,
There is much in Arabic and Persian,
So let the people now read Albanian.[93]

Closely connected to the issue of language teaching was the 'alphabet question,' i.e. choosing the alphabet in which the Albanian language was to be written. This reflected not only the need for unification but also the desire for autonomy. Several congresses were held on the subject. The basic choice was of course between the Arabic alphabet which inspired continuity within the Ottoman Empire, and the Latin alphabet which fostered a rupture and a change of direction. The Congress of Monastir (14–18 November 1908) decided in favour of Latin letters, but a year later, in the summer of 1909, the Young Turks organised a new congress in Dibra (Debar) at which they tried in vain to convince the Albanian delegates to use the Arabic alphabet. Their venture provoked the departure of some of the delegates who then assembled at a parallel meeting in a Bektashi *tekke*.[94]

Although they were part of the Muslim community and had earlier contributed to the advancement of Albanian literature in Arabic script, the nationalist Bektashi took the side of the supporters of the Latin alphabet.

At this time, Albanian territory was the venue of numerous political meetings, some organised by the Young Turks and others by the Albanian nationalists. For both the Young Turks and the nationalists, the easiest way to convince the majority of the population of their respective causes was to win over the Bektashi clergy whose spiritual influence in the south was too important to ignore. Here is an account from the Korça region:

The Albanian patriots were very involved in the alphabet question. Until about 1909, the Young Turks behaved well and did not bother us in our patriotic demonstrations, but this did not last for long. The Young Turk government began to interfere in our national movement and placed obstacles in our way in various matters. One of these was the alphabet question. In this connection, the Turks organised a meeting in Korça in 1910.[95] The government wanted to impose the Arabic alphabet on the Albanian population. They constructed a podium on the main corn market, ordered all the drummers to beat their drums and told the criers to summon the population. Few townspeople attended, only about two hundred families. That was all. The meeting was a failure. Then the 'Albanian Knowledge' Club decided to act. It invited all the villages and the *babas* of the *tekkes* in the Korça region to attend a conference on the alphabet that was to be held from 14 to 27 February.

The members of the club went from village to village and explained the issue well to the villagers, to the *babas* of the *tekkes* and to the simple dervishes. Those who remained in Korça fulfilled this task on market day.[96]

The Young Turks, for their part, also endeavoured to win over the Bektashi by sending a member of the order from Istanbul to one of the three *tekkes* in Gjirokastra:[97]

The Young Turks did everything in their power to slow down and impede our national movement and when all their efforts failed, they tried to deceive the population with the help of some blind fanatics, mostly uneducated hodjas, who were alas Albanians. They endeavoured to convince the Muslims that the Albanian language ought to be written in Arabic letters and, in Istanbul, a fanatic[98] from Elbasan began editing a newspaper in this script. As they knew that virtually the whole population of Gjirokastra was Bektashi, they sent a dervish there to make propaganda for the Arabic alphabet. At that time, many Bektashi people gathered at the *tekke* and spent the night there discussing various issues. The Turkish dervish arrived, was given accommodation at the *tekke* of Baba Manes and began his work. No one paid much attention to him. However, the others soon began to make fun of this dervish missionary and did everything they could to get this Satan to depart as soon as possible.

Veisel Bejkua, a sage judge who was held in great esteem by the whole population, called for a gathering of notables in the town. The meeting took place in a large hall at the *Liria* (Liberty) School and was chaired by Veisel Efendi himself. He began by saying: 'Is there anyone among us who thinks that the Latin letters with which we write our language is contrary to the Muslim faith?' All responded unanimously: 'No!' Veisel Efendi Beikua then called me over as secretary of the club to draft a resolution in the spirit of the assembly. I drafted the resolution in a large register and everyone signed it. The Turkish dervish received the news at the *tekke* and fled the next day, leaving Gjirokastra in shame.[99]

The Young Turks thus lost the cause, and it turned to the advantage of the Albanian nationalists.

The Bektashi clergy was also active in the creation and operation of the 'clubs' and 'patriotic societies' that flourished semi-officially and, later, officially in all the towns of Albania in the early twentieth century. Their main function was to promote teaching in the mother tongue and to publish newspapers and books, etc.[100] Here, too, there were rivalries between the Young Turks and the nationalists, a good illustration of which were the events that took place in Elbasan. It should be mentioned that Elbasan is situated more or less in the centre of Albania, on the banks of the Shkumbin River which forms the natural boundary between the two ethnic groups in the country – the Ghegs in the north and the Tosks in the south. Elbasan was itself a town with a strong Bektashi element, but it was also a place where the Sunni Muslims who were dominant among the northern Ghegs, were present, too. The Bashkimi (Union) Club, whose members were primarily from the Bektashi and Orthodox Christian communities of the town and surrounding villages, was in competition with another club, the Fukara Club, created by the Young Turks to rally the Sunni Muslims to their cause.[101]

In southern Albania, the Bektashi offered active support to the *çetas* (armed bands) who had taken to the mountains to liberate the country. They were in a position to provide this active support because their *tekkes* were mostly situated in the countryside, far from the Turkish authorities, and often in isolated regions. Some of these Bektashi *tekkes*, that served as virtual headquarters of the Albanian nationalist movement, were used to conduct secret meetings and clandestine assemblies. They were also essential in spreading information on activities and actions to be undertaken and in providing links between the *çetas* and the supporting population groups.

Among the *babas* who supported the *çetas* was Baba Hysejn (Huseyn), head of the *tekke* of Melçan. He was one of the leading members of the nationalist movement.[102] Not only did he take part in the movement, but he also exerted a substantial influence upon it. It was at his *tekke* that the first nationalist *çeta* was founded in 1906. According to Selim Pojani, who was a student at the Turkish secondary school in Monastir (Bitola) at the time and a member of the Monastir Committee founded in 1905 by a small group of Albanian nationalists including Jorgji Qiriazi, Bajo Topulli, Colonel Halit Bërzezhda and Fehim Zavalani, this committee decided 'to set up the first armed *çeta* to foment revolt for the liberation of Albania among the peasant masses and to conduct an armed struggle against the Ottoman government.'[103] Soon after this decision was taken, the patriots gathered at the *tekke* of Melçan:

> That day, at the *meydan* of the *tekke*, there was a meeting in which everyone took part, including the nationalist-minded dervishes. The meeting was opened by Baba Hysejn who held an ardent speech about love for the fatherland. He was followed by Bajo (Topulli) who said that the Ottoman Empire was a vestige of the past and called on us to assemble and take to arms to fight for the freedom of our country.

The çeta had been created. The patriots of Korça, such as Orhan Pojani, Thimi Marku, Vani Cico Kosturi and Grigor Cilka etc. were also aware of the meeting but did not take part in it because the Turkish government had learned what was going on and had infested Korça with spies. We stayed at the *tekke* for about a week and then left for Kolonja (to the south of Korça).

The main task of our *çeta* was to spread information and agitate among the peasant masses. We also distributed the books and spellers sent to us by Grigor Cilka. The *çeta* agitated in the villages of Kolonja, Gora and the Plain of Korça.[104]

It was also Baba Hysejn who persuaded the *çetas* of Çerçiz Topulli and Mihal Grameno to join Niyazi Bey, the leader of the Young Turk Revolution in southern Albania.[105] The Albanian nationalists let themselves be convinced for the sake of liberation, but the alliance with the Young Turks did not last long after the 1908 revolution.

Mihal Grameno wrote: 'At Frashër we met the nationalists and the dervishes, among whom there was a rebel officer who was none other than Niyazi Bey of Resna. Niyazi had fled the army after having made an alliance with his friends [...];'[106] 'We had long discussions with Baba Hysejn on nationalist affairs and in particular about a meeting with Niyazi Bey whose intentions were unclear to us. Baba Hysejn told us that Niyazi had the same objectives as we did and that we ought to support him. [...] We kissed the hand of Baba Hysejn and departed [...]'[107]

Shemso Hajro noted in this connection: 'Baba Hysejn received us at Melçan with great affection and told us that many of the patriots of Korça would be coming around for a meeting. He had advised Çerçiz to meet Niyazi Bey of Resna who had left his job at that time and escaped, proclaiming that he was against Sultan Abdul Hamid and for a democratic constitution.'[108]

The *tekke* of Frashër that had played an important role after the League of Prizren, under the leadership of Baba Alush, remained a very active nationalist centre under the aegis of Baba Abidin who also inspired the Muslims and Christians. His dervishes, about forty of them in all, gave proof of their active participation by going from village to village to make the native population aware of the nationalist cause. The *tekke*, the cleanliness, good organisation and rules of duties and discipline of which were noted by Mihal Grameno, welcomed the nationalist *çetas* whose leaders got information and advice from Baba Abidin.[109] The *çeta* of Çerçiz Topulli stayed there regularly and with Baba Abidin's help, avoided the patrols of the Turkish authorities. He was warned in advance and gave robes out to the members of the *çeta* so that they could dress up and look like dervishes.[110]

Other Bektashi *tekkes* aided the *çetas* and the nationalist movement in southern Albania, too. Although we cannot generalise, it can at least be said that between 1878 and 1912 the majority of the Bektashi were on the side of the nationalists and were working for Albanian autonomy.

Nationalist Bektashism

The initial reflections of this stance and these actions did not take long to appear in the doctrine and the writings of the Albanian Bektashi.

The first example came not from a member of the Bektashi clergy (a baba[111] or dervish), but from a Bektashi faithful – none other than Naim Frashëri, the brother of Abdyl. Naim Frashëri was the author of a sixteen-page brochure (in 16) called *Fletore e Bektashinjet* (Bektashi Notebook). This little work was published for the first time in Bucharest in 1896, but several other editions followed (1908, 1910 and 1921).[112] In it Naim Frashëri explained the maxims and rules of the Bektashi, but he also stressed the nationalism of the doctrine of the order: 'Yet above all, they love their country and their countrymen. This is the finest of all virtues.' In his view, the role of the *babas* ought now to be guided by nationalism alone:

> May they strive day and night for that nation that calls them father and swears by them. May they work together with the notables and the elders for the salvation of Albania and the Albanians, for knowledge and culture for their people and their fatherland, for their language and for all progress and well-being, etc., etc. […] Together with the elders and notables, may they encourage love, brotherhood, unity and friendship among all Albanians, that they not be divided among one another, that Christians and Muslims be together as one. May they make all things prosper so that the Albanian, who was once reputed throughout the world, not be despised today.

The *baba* is no longer simply a spiritual guide leading the faithful to God. He is also a guide (as are notables and elders, and perhaps better placed than the latter two) for the unification of the Albanians irrespective of religion, someone who places great value on their language and on progress.

At any rate, the Bektashi clergy adopted the direction proposed by Naim Frashëri. On occasion, he set forth his stance and nationalist convictions on paper, too. At the end of the nineteenth century, nationalism became a subject of inspiration for the composition of Bektashi *nefes* poetry in Albanian. In his work, *Misticizma dhe Bektashizma* (Mysticism and Bektashism), Baba Rexheb gave three examples of patriotic verse, two of which were composed by Baba Meleq Shëmbërdhenji[113] with the third one stemming from Baba Ibrahim of the *tekke* of Qesaraka (southeast of Frashër).[114] In form, these poems are just like the other Bektashi *nefes* poetry, with the poet introducing himself in the first line of the penultimate couplet.

The first *nefes* of Baba Meleq describes how he was pursued by the spies of the secret police when he was sent to Albania to distribute books in the Albanian language:

The spies are pursuing me, – but I will not spare myself,
Even if they roast me in fire, – I will not forget my Motherland.

Bit by bit they tear me up, – but my soul is not in sorrow,
No shame affects me, – I will die for my Motherland.

If I die for my Motherland, – it will be a great honour for me,
The spies do not let up, – they strike me on the brow like a pig.

My death is no great matter, – you, my Albanian brothers,
Do not keep sleeping, – as much and as swiftly as you can,

Let us live a day of pleasure, – why do we need a long life?
Oh, let us save our Motherland, – or abandon it entirely.

Leave behind the crab's sting, – take up your sword and rifle,
Strike on all sides, – leave no foe alive.

Let us not lie here sleeping, – let us seize our freedom,
The affair is not over yet, – let us make Albania shine.

Oh, to die for the Motherland, – heroes do not fear it,
For our parents once lived here, – it is now all our country.

Then the evil spies, – faithless as they are,
Will hide in the bushes, – will find no place to flee.

Let us work day and night, – for our sacred freedom,
Let us save our Motherland, – from these cursed spies.

Meleq! How will you strike them, – with your sword and your rifle?
We will not fall into the trap this time, – without seeing our freedom alive.[115]

    The second *nefes* of Baba Meleq is equally inflammatory:

Albania for the Albanians, – they have nowhere else to go,
They've inherited it from their forefathers, – they will have it all their lives.

God gave it to them at the start, – why are these faithless men seeking
To take the land of the Albanians? – it is here that they'll be buried.

Our foes wince and cringe in envy, – to get their hands on Albania,
May fire be in their midst, – a fire that will pursue them wherever they are.

You have cut Albania down, – taken what you wanted,
You tore down our walls and borders, – may you destroy your own country!

Leave us alone, you devils! – why have you thrown yourselves upon us?
Much have we suffered, – you yoked us like oxen.

You have your own way of thinking, – now we understand it,
You are carrion to be fed on, – but remember, we will free ourselves.

You occupied us all around, – like ever-thirsting vampires,
You changed the Albanian language, – tried to bring it to an end.

God has not abandoned us, – for he created us Himself,
Albania will survive, – for as long as we are alive.

God was never pleased – that the Albanian language should disappear,
His greatness preserves it, – let these foes burst and wain.

Meleq! they deceived us, – the foes do not like the Albanian language,
But our language has come back to us, – May God smite the foes.[116]

As to the poem of Baba Ibrahim, it expresses the same criticism of the Ottomans. But here, the author uses more imaginative language. The empire is described as being like the winter and the sultan is a cold. Summer, i.e. the liberation of Albania, is soon to arrive:

Oh, winter, hapless winter! – why do you give us a cold?
Hastily, quietly, – you have taken all our blood.

With that frigid frost, – why did you cover and wither us?
And with those daunting storms, – why did you scatter us?

You blackened hills and plains, – nowhere grass or leaves.
With snow and sleet, – you have shut us in forever.

You cut off our roads, – we have no way to escape,
We have little hope to survive, – as if swallowed by the clouds.

Oh February, may your life be short! – when will you leave us alone?
For it is unjust, – you have seized and enslaved us enough.

Be off, if you respect God! – from these snowy mountains
Will come the months of spring, – and all will have their rifles in their hands.

Be off, for summer is on its way! – a blessed summer is at hand,
We will dress in our wide robes, – and with guns in our hands.

Be off, listen to my words! – may none of us perish anymore,
A summer of heroes is on its way, – and it will strike you down.

Be off, withdraw from our midst, – oh summer, fair summer,
Hasten, come to us, – because you bring honour with you.

Ibrahim! may the call come, – soaring like an eagle,
Let us put the cold and flu behind us, – where will it go and be off to?[117]

By integrating nationalism into their doctrine and by playing an active role in the country's liberation, the Albanian Bektashi expanded rapidly, much more so than any other Muslim brotherhood on Albanian soil. This expansion was restricted to the southern half of the country, where the nationalist movement and the desire for autonomy first grew. In this region, the number of *tekkes* more than doubled from 1878 to 1912, going from about twenty to about fifty. It is obvious that the increase in the number of *tekkes* also meant a substantial increase in the number of followers, both in the towns and in the countryside, people who began to support the nationalist ideas promoted by the *babas* and dervishes or who simply wanted to learn to read and write at the *tekkes*, and joined the order.

On the eve of the collapse of the Ottoman Empire, the Albanian Bektashi in the south of the country had become a large and politically influential group due to the prestige that their clergy enjoyed among the population. They gradually distanced themselves from the Turkish Bektashi on the one hand and from the Albanian Sunni Muslims on the other, who were both opposed to Albanian independence and gave their support mostly to the Young Turks.

With its growing strength and clear identity, the Bektashi order was thus ready to play the role of an independent religious community in the new Albania on the horizon.

National Bektashism in a free Albania

An independent Albania did not yet mean a free Albania. Shortly after independence was declared by Ismail Kemal in Vlora on 28 November 1912, the Second Balkan War broke out. It was followed by a general spread of the conflict and the First World War. Albanian territory was occupied by foreign troops from many lands and the unification of the country proved elusive. The attempt by the Great Powers to impose a foreign sovereign, Prince Wied, on Albania turned out to be a total disaster. To counter this move, the Young Turks encouraged many of their supporters to create an Ottoman Principality of Albania. Organising a functioning government for the new country proved to be impossible, indeed several governments arose, each with only local authority, in northern Albania, in central Albania and in southern Albania. An account of the troubled history of this period, which has yet to receive impartial scholarly treatment, is, however, beyond the scope of this work.

What became of the Bektashi in the midst of this confusion, this cacophony of events? Their voice that had been heard so clearly before 1912 was now muffled by the destruction of most of their *tekkes* and the flight of their clergy.[118] Most of the destruction was carried out during the Greek occupation of southern Albania beginning in 1913. Worst affected were the *tekkes* in the regions of Korça, Leskovik, Tepelena and Gjirokastra that were pillaged and burned down since the Bektashi dervishes were regarded by the occupiers as being in cahoots with other Muslims. Some *tekkes* were used as barracks and armouries because they were built on easily defendable sites. The *babas* and dervishes were forced to take flight and seek refuge in nearby towns, in the Vlora region, or even abroad, in particular at other *tekkes* belonging to the order.[119]

Albanian Bektashism went through a very sombre period for three years, from 1913 to 1916, during which it continued to struggle for the liberation of the country. Members of the clergy, such as Baba Selim Ruhi who had been forced by the Greek occupation to seek refuge at his sister's house in Gjirokastra, which then served as a small *tekke*, were more popular than ever in the eyes of the local population. Such men were even respected by the Orthodox Christians. Indeed, it was the Christians who intervened to save Baba Selim when the Greek authorities want to send him into exile.

In view of the massive support that the Bektashi enjoyed, things changed after 1916 when the tide of destruction subsided. Convents were rebuilt, the clergy returned and Albanian Bektashism came to flourish once again. There was much work to be done and it was certainly no easy job to reconstruct forty *tekkes* in the economic disaster zone that was Albania in the early decades of the twentieth century. This is perhaps why the Bektashi turned to the Albanians in North America for help. Indeed, some of their leaders crossed the Atlantic to seek support.[120]

New *babas* had to be appointed to replace the old ones who had vanished, to manage the construction work that would last for several years.[121]

Albanian territory was finally liberated at the end of the First World War, with the exception of the Vlora region that was held by Italian forces until 1920. The Albanian Bektashi movement now rose like a phoenix from the ashes.

Free Albania

Albania, now liberated, had a lot on its hands for it had to set up totally new political, administrative and economic structures, etc. These changes caused much pain and tribulation throughout the twentieth century, and stability was only attained after much bloodshed and after a totalitarian regime that took root in 1944.

In 1920, a Supreme Regency Council was created, at a time when the definitive form of the Albanian State had still not been found, i.e. whether it was to be a republic or a monarchy. The consequences of this decision, as we will see, were decisive for the history of Albanian Bektashism. The new Council was to reflect the religious diversity of the Albanian population. There was no longer to be one religion favoured above the others, as had been the case in the past.

At that time, the country had a Muslim majority, about 70 per cent of the population. The Orthodox Christian community, very strong in the southern regions along the Greek border, represented about 20 per cent of the people, and the Catholics, almost all of whom lived in the north, constituted about 10 per cent of the population. But about one-fifth of the 70 per cent Muslim majority belonged to the Bektashi order, i.e. about 15 per cent of the total population of the country. There were thus more Bektashi than Catholics in Albania.[122] Of course, the Albanian Bektashi were at this time a simple dervish order without any particular structure, and most of their members considered themselves to be part of the Albanian Muslim community.

Nonetheless, the Supreme Regency Council had not three but four members – one for each religious community in the country: Abdi bey Toptani for the Sunni Muslims, Mihal Turtulli for the Orthodox Christians, Luigj Bumçi for the Catholic Christians, and Aqif Biçaku (Aqif Pasha Elbasani) for the Bektashi.[123] The Bektashi thus had their own representative. This recognition surprised many of the Sunnis who did not understand why the Bektashi should have a man of their own. According to Baba Rexheb, the reason given was simple: the recognition was a token of gratitude for the loyal services provided by the Bektashi during the long years of the national revival.[124] It was this 'nationalist Bektashism' rather than Bektashism in itself that gave them recognition as a religious community.

National Bektashism

Although Albanian Bektashism was now recognised as one of the country's religions, it was still not a community with a national organisation. In 1920, the Albanian Bektashi were still linked to both the *dede baba* in Hacıbektaş in central Anatolia and to the Albanian Muslim community.

As to the links with the *pir evi* in Anatolia and with the Bektashi order as a whole, it must not be forgotten that even at the end of the nineteenth century, some Albanian Bektashi, inspired by nationalist sentiment, wanted to get rid of the ties to the 'mother house' in Anatolia. Prominent among them was Naim Frashëri, author of the above-mentioned 'Bektashi Notebook.' His nephew, Mid'hat Frashëri, wrote of him:

> He put great effort into convincing the Bektashi that we needed a *dede baba* who could appoint *babas* directly, without the interference of the *pir evi*, and that this *dede baba* should be recognised by all the *babas* of Albania as their leader.[125]

For these nationalists, Bektashism needed autonomy and structures at the national level. Although the problems that shook the Empire in the early years of the twentieth century impeded this national structure from becoming a concrete reality, the active participation of the Albanian Bektashi in the nationalist movement forged links between the Albanian *tekkes*, old and new, that created a viable network, as we have seen. It happened on occasion that dervishes and *babas* were not able to get to Hacıbektaş to take part in ceremonies marking the appointment or promotion of *müjerred babas* and *dedes*. The ceremonies therefore took place at home, in the major Albanian *tekkes*. But this practice was not universal. In 1910, we know, for instance, of the case of two southern Albanian *babas*, Baba Ahmet Turani (of the *tekke* of Turan near Tepelena) and Baba Sulejman (of the Hajdërije *tekke* in Gjirokastra) who journeyed to the *pir evi* to be appointed *dedes*.[126] In such matters, the *tarikat* was sufficiently supple in its structure to enable each *tekke* to enjoy substantial autonomy in its activities. The Albanian Bektashi do not seem to have made any excessive demands at this time, or to have endeavoured to transform their spiritual order into an autonomous organisation, even though they were now united in their rejection of Ottoman rule. It was only in the early 1930s that the Albanian Bektashi came to form a structured national community, when they were pushed into doing so by external factors.

The Bektashi community acquired an identity of its own when a member was appointed to represent it on the Supreme Regency Council, yet it still had no organisational structure. It was most likely this recognition at the national level that encouraged some of the members of the order to take action in this respect. In 1921, Albanian delegates gathered for a congress and set forth the first statutes of the 'Albanian Bektashi Community'.[127] They were not interested in autonomy from the head of the order in Hacıbektaş, but simply in clarifying existing structures and set up a council of seven *babas*, headed by the highest-ranking *baba* among them. According to Baba Rexheb, this congress and the statutes that were promulgated at it had little or no real effect on the life of the Albanian Bektashi community, nor did the second congress that took place at the Hajdërije *tekke* in Gjirokastra in July 1924, where new statutes were promulgated.[128] This congress took place following an Albanian Muslim congress during which the Bektashi delegates, not having obtained the autonomy they sought from the Sunni Muslims, left the meeting, 'slamming the door behind them'.[129]

The Albanian Bektashi only became an official national community at the end of 1929, in line with the wishes of the country's leader. Ahmet Zogu had proclaimed himself King of the Albanians in 1928 and suggested (i.e. ordered) that the various religious communities in the country organise themselves and draft statutes that the government could officially recognise.[130] The new organisational form was thus linked to the will of the State to supervise and control them.

In 1929, the Bektashi met at the *tekke* of Turan near Korça. They set up the following organisational structure: Albanian territory was to be divided into six zones called *gjyshërias*, each being administered by a *gjysh* (*dede* or *halife* in Turkish terminology). His *tekke* served as the *gjyshata* (headquarters) of the zone in question.[131] In addition to the Holy Council (composed of seven of the highest-ranking *babas*) that was created at the 1921 congress and that represented the high-ranking spiritual leaders, there was also a General Council composed not only of members of the clergy but also of the faithful. It was to deal with administrative issues. But the most significant measure taken to strengthen the national destiny of the Albanian Bektashi was no doubt the creation of the post of a *kryegjysh* (*dede baba*) as the supreme leader of the Albanian Bektashi community. It should not be forgotten that the position of *dede baba* had been held up to then by the head of all the Bektashi – Turks, Albanians and others. When the dervish orders were banned by Mustafa Kemal in Turkey in 1925, the last *dede baba*, Salih Nijazi, left the *tekke* of Hacıbektaş and his position in Turkey was abolished. It was not in the interests of continuity that the Albanian Bektashi invited him to come (he was of Albanian origin), but rather simply because none of the *babas* in Albania who were qualified to take over the position were willing to leave their *tekkes* for Tirana, where a new centre was to be built and which consequently did not have the prestige, the rich past and the local authority of convents like those of Frashër, Prishta, Korça and Gjirokastra.[132]

After the third congress, the statutes were approved by the government. The Bektashi community was thus recognised by the State[133] and entered the phase of National Bektashism that lasted until the end of the official existence of the community. In 1967 the Bektashi were banned by the Government of the People's Republic of Albania, as were the other religions. Two other congresses, in 1945 and 1950, were held before the ban and new statutes were promulgated that confirmed the national character of the Albanian Bektashi community that was now totally independent of the Sunni Muslim community, but obviously increasingly under the control of the State.

The 'eternally nationalist' Bektashi

With the independence of Albania, the Bektashi, strengthened by their patriotic endeavours in the past, continued to be nationalist.

Baba Rexheb recalled something that happened during the Greek occupation (between 1913 and 1916) and which well illustrated the nationalist attitude of the Bektashi clergy at the time:

> Two hodjas from the town of Gjirokastra were walking along the walls of the fortress on their way to prayer on Friday when some Greek soldiers occupying the town began throwing stones at them. The two hodjas turned around and went back, and since they were near the home of Baba Selim,[134] they decided to pay him a visit. They explained to the *baba* that their initial intention had not been to visit him but to attend Friday prayer. Baba Selim then responded: 'I have told you what the Prophet Muhammed said: *hub ul watan-i min al'iman*, love of one's country, i.e. supporting its independence, comes from religion. You must understand that we must all be united for our country, without any others'.[135]

The purpose of this anecdote was probably to show that the Bektashi alone were on the right path leading to Albania's independence. Bektashism was thus understood as being linked to patriotism.

Nationalism appeared much more officially in many of the articles of the statutes of the Albanian Bektashi community. In Articles 63 and 65 of the 1924 Statutes, for instance, patriotism plays a major part in Bektashi rituals:

> During religious ceremonies, a green flag with a white hand on it and the Albanian national flag are to be raised.
>
> During Bektashi ceremonies, prayers are to be conducted for the expansion of the country and for progress for the Albanian people.

Article 67 of these Statutes stresses the work of the community for the nation:

> The Bektashi community will never join forces with any anti-national group endeavouring to jeopardise peace in the country or compromising the existence of the nation.

Patriotism and fraternity are proclaimed jointly (Article 71) in line with the spirit of the 'Bektashi Notebook' of Naim Frashëri:

The most sacred duty of the Council of *Babas* is the fraternity of the Albanian Bektashi with other nations, and a patriotic attitude.

And of course in Article 64:

The official language of the Bektashi faith is Albanian.

Patriotism continued to be stressed after 1945, but it was now at the service of the new regime.

'In addition to promoting religious sentiments, the Bektashi clergy will also promote among the faithful, loyalty towards the government and the People's Republic of Albania as well as patriotism. For this reason, clergymen and officials of the Bektashi Community must be Albanian citizens who are honorable and loyal to their people and Fatherland and who enjoy all civil rights.'

In the same spirit, the new national flag is present at religious ceremonies:

The religious banner of the Bektashi Community carries Koranic verses and sayings on a red background, with a *teslim taxh* in the middle and a star on the right side. (Article 62 of the Statutes of 1950).

As at the end of the Ottoman period, we continue to find expressions of strong nationalist sentiment in the literature of the Albanian Bektashi. It is particularly evident in the writings of one of the most active Albanian *babas* of the twentieth century, Baba Ali Tomorri,[136] in particular in his 32-page brochure devoted to Bektashi literature.[137] It is dedicated 'with great respect to Mid'hat Frashëri,[138] the nephew of the torchbearers of the national revival and true patriot in the spirit of his fathers.' Baba Ali Tomorri included two Bektashi poems he wrote in nationalist spirit in honour of Ahmet Zogu, the president of Albania, and of Naim Frashëri. Under the poems was the following remark:

Important remark: I set the poem composed in honour of His Excellency, our beloved president, to music as a national anthem and a private hymn. But I would be delighted if an expert were able to set it to music better and if it joined the choir of national anthems.[139]

What was this hymn that an Albanian *baba* proposed for his country and that he had composed 'in honour of His Excellency, the President of Albania'?

Out of the azure sky comes the call to fight,
 Proud is the new generation of Albanians,
In the mountains and in the lowlands echoes the call:
Men, oh men, sons of the Pelasgians,

> Who have as their president
> The famed patriot,
> The brilliant Ahmet Zogu,
> An equal of Scanderbeg.

The voice of God comes to us,
Albania will no longer suffer,
Rejoice, oh Albanian land!
For we have founded a courageous republic,

> That has as its president
> The famed patriot,
> The brilliant Ahmet Zogu,
> An equal of Scanderbeg.

The sea and the earth quiver now
As they herald a prosperous world.
Mankind in its suffering is not lost
For it has inherited a shining weapon,

> And has as its president
> The famed patriot,
> The brilliant Ahmet Zogu,
> An equal of Scanderbeg.[140]

Bektashism and nationalism have been nourishing one another in Albania since the second half of the nineteenth century. The Bektashi were often at the forefront of nationalist leadership in Albania. Indeed, many Albanians joined them as religious affiliates simply to be part of the nationalist movement. Nationalism was part and parcel of the doctrine of the Albanian Bektashi. As they were later recognized as a religious community of their own by the highest levels of State authority, they were able to form structures and create a solid organisation at the national level.

But why the Bektashi and not the other *tarikats*? With regard to the Albanian dervish orders as a whole, it is clear that the Bektashi were different in at least three basic aspects that enabled them to gain influence over the general population and to take their place in the nation's history. These were things that the other orders did not achieve.

1. The Bektashi community was much better organised and maintained close links with both initiated and non-initiated members;
2. its leaders were appointed by merit and not because they were members of a family, such as was the case of the Halveti, the Rifa'i, the Sa'di and the Kadiri;
3. most importantly, the Bektashi had a heterodox character or, rather, they were able to imbibe and assimilate external elements which enabled them to integrate nationalism into their doctrine and thus flourish among the Albanians.

Even under the communist dictatorship, nationalism among the Albanians (of Albania) continued to derive a good part of its inspiration from the Bektashi, although many would have denied this! Naim Frashëri remained a hero in the minds of that 'eternally Stalinist' generation, even though Marx himself had stated that religion was the opium of the people. In those years, Albanians were forced to admit to their children that religions had played an important role in the life of the poor and that Naim Frashëri had been compelled to rely on Bektashism, this religion being 'somewhat better than the others.' Along these lines is the following extract from an article by Zija Xholi:

> What was it that pushed Naim Frashëri, a conscious patriot, towards Sufism and Bektashism? What was the reason that attracted him to the heresy of Bektashism, whose followers were often persecuted to the extreme? [...] What was it that forced Naim Frashëri to profess Bektashism and promote it actively? What was it that caused him to embrace Sufi ideas in his lyric work? The answer to all of these questions lies not in his Bektashi family background and milieu [...] but elsewhere. The reason for his inclination towards Sufism, pantheism and mysticism must be sought in the historic endeavours that Naim Frashëri undertook and fought for. [...] As a heresy, Sufism was a convenient ideological framework in which to express the opposition and protest of the people to feudalism, the opposition and protest of a subjected and oppressed people to Ottoman rule. [...] Finally, it must not be forgotten that since our people were educated for centuries in the spirit of religion, they understood the language of religion better than anything else. For this reason, it is no surprise that Naim Frashëri sought to touch the heart and soul of the Albanian people by clothing his ideas in the garb of religion. [...] Be this as it may, in his struggle for patriotic and democratic values, Naim Frashëri detached himself again and again from religion and theology to become a partisan of free and progressive thought. Religious activities and ideas are now a thing of the past, but the patriotic, illuminist and humanitarian ideas of Naim Frashëri are the key to our heritage, a heritage for future generations.[141]

Even today, the Albanian Bektashi (outside of Albania proper) define themselves in good part by their nationalism. The *tekke* at Taylor near Detroit that was founded by Baba Rexheb (a one-time dervish at the *tekke* of Asim Baba in Gjirokastra)[142] in 1954 is not a Bektashi *tekke* but an Albanian Bektashi *tekke*. Further proof of this is the black double-headed eagle on a red background that is to be seen in front of the building and in the *meydan* of the *tekke*, and the text found in the periodical published by the *tekke*:

> In America, the Albanians, like other peoples, found not only a country in which they could live in happiness and prosperity, but also a country in which they were able to carry on the struggle for the defence of their country of origin. [...]
> We Albanian Bektashi also freely celebrate the anniversary of the date of birth of the Great Ali. With all our hearts, we express the best wishes for the

good of the country that has taken us in with such generosity, and for the good of the country where we first saw the light of day.[143]

We have endeavoured in this paper to show, from the second half of the nineteenth century onwards, to what extent the history of Albanian Bektashism was linked to the history of Albanian nationalism. With the help of historical texts, the messages of which are clear and irrefutable, we believe that we have drawn an image of Albanian Bektashism in the nineteenth and twentieth centuries that is more precise and nearer to reality, and that is quite different from the descriptions usually given in publications from Albania, Turkey or elsewhere.

[Nathalie Clayer, 'Bektachisme et nationalisme albanais', in *Bektachiyya, études sur l'ordre mystique des Bektachis et les groupes relevant de Hadji Bektach*, ed. A. Popovic and G. Veinstein. *Revue des Etudes Islamiques* 60 (1992). Numéro spécial (Paris: Paul Geuthner 1993 and Istanbul: Isis 1995), pp. 277–308. Translated from the Albanian by Robert Elsie.]

1996
NATHALIE CLAYER
THE SACRED HAUNTS OF THE ALBANIAN BEKTASHI

In this text, the French scholar Nathalie Clayer casts light on the history and significance of the two major sites of Bektashi pilgrimage in Albania: the cave of Sari Saltik on Mount Kruja and the mausoleum of Abbas Ali on the peak of Mount Tomorr.

Mountains are ubiquitous in the Balkans. The mountain range that divides Bulgaria into two was the one that gave the peninsula its name, a peninsula that would often seem more turned towards the Orient and with its back to Europe. Mountains dominate and determine the lives and movements of the inhabitants of the region. It is therefore not surprising that we find some of the most sacred haunts of local Islam here. Are these sites not the symbols of the religion of the Ottoman conquerors that penetrated into the most isolated, inaccessible and reclusive reaches of the peninsula?

It was on the western side of the Balkan peninsula where the mountain ranges are the most rugged that the spread of Islam was the most thorough. During the five centuries of Ottoman rule, most of the Sons of the Eagle, as the Albanians are often called, converted to Islam. Initially only a few of them were attracted by the new faith, but from the eighteenth century onwards conversions became more widespread. By the time the Albanian State was created in 1912, about 70 per cent of the population was Muslim. This made Albania the only country in Europe with a Muslim majority.

The mystic orders of Islam seem to have played an important role in the consolidation of the recently converted Albanian population, if not of Islam in general. What is more, many of them set up solid networks in the west of the Balkan Peninsula. The Halveti order had up to two hundred centres, and the Bektashi a little over sixty. However, we should not attribute too much importance to these figures because it was the Bektashi, the dervish order born in central Anatolia with a heterodox and syncretic doctrine, that was to gain the largest number of adherents from the second half of the nineteenth century onwards. The Bektashi also played a major role in the Albanian national awakening and developed into a religious community of their own in independent Albania, side by side with the Sunni Muslims. In Albania before the Second World War, about one Muslim in five was a Bektashi.

These mystic orders infused Albanian Islam with a strong element of Sufism, especially in their most sacred haunts. These sites were all linked in one way or another. Sufi saints were venerated in most of the sacred sanctuaries attended by dervishes. In the northern half of the country, we know of the cave of Sari Saltik above the town of Kruja, the cave of Balim Sultan in the Martanesh region, and the sanctuary of Sari Saltik on the summit of Mount Pashtrik. In the southern half of the country, there is the grave of Abbas Ali on Mount Tomorr. All of these sites are located in isolated mountain regions. They were only accessible by a steep climb in the summer months and few foreign travellers seem to have reached them.

Pilgrimages, in groups or of individuals, ceased almost entirely between 1967 and 1990, during the period in which Albania was the only officially atheist State in the world. However, once the ban on religion was overturned, the sanctuaries revived, even faster than the mosques and *tekkes*. The faithful felt a great need for the intercession of saints and holy men, in particular in view of the difficult economic and social conditions that arose in the early modern period. The revival of the cults of local saints also helped to legitimise the role of the leaders of the Muslim communities at a time when the population had long had no contact with religion.

It was in this context that the two great annual pilgrimages, one to the cave of Sari Saltik and the other to Mount Tomorr, were re-established by the Bektashi community that had once been in charge of them.

A relatively large group, led by the few babas who were still alive, made its way recently to the top of Mount Tomorr to visit the grave of Abbas Ali and to carry out the traditional sacrifice of livestock there (it is said that about 150 animals were slaughtered). This was an opportunity for young Albanians to pay their respects for the first time, but also for the first time in their lives to enjoy copious portions of mutton roasted on a spit. These sacred sites, now symbols of the revival of the Bektashi after the fall of communism, were always of great importance for the spread of Islam and for the history of Muslim communities in the region.

* * *

The cult of Sari Saltik in Kruja has been known since the second half of the sixteenth century. Of the 81 Muslim families in the region at the time (the area was still largely Christian), ten were mentioned in the register of the Ottoman administration as being responsible for the upkeep of the path leading to the cave at the top of the cliffs, 600 metres above the town.

> On the mountain of Kruja is the tomb of Sari Saltik to which the people of the neighbouring districts come for pilgrimage. The road mentioned is very arduous and difficult and gives visitors much trouble. It has been recorded in the previous register that the ten persons mentioned, who are for the greater part the descendants of those who were of old in charge of repairs, have been charged with levelling the above-mentioned road and repairing it whenever it is in disrepair. After having fulfilled this duty and after having paid their tithes, they are discharged and liberated from the extraordinary tax for the Divan and the duties based on the Common Law.[144]

A century later, the famed mid-seventeenth-century Ottoman traveller, Evliya Çelebi, who had elsewhere devoted a passage of his work to the cult of Sari Saltik, made no mention of the saint's tomb above the town of Kruja. Taking his information from the dervishes of Kaliakra (now in Bulgaria), he listed several mythical shrines (in Crimea, Poland, Bohemia and Sweden) and other real shrines (in Babadag in the Romanian Dobrudja region, and in Kaliakra and Babeski near

Edirne). The sanctuary in Albania, that Evliya Çelebi does not seem to have visited, must have been of purely local significance as it had been a century earlier.

We must move on to the end of the nineteenth and the beginning of the twentieth centuries to find any more substantial reports about this sacred site bathed in legends. These reports were made by interested diplomats and Orientalists. What the foreign visitors of the period noted when they reached the town of Kruja (which was by now entirely Muslim) was the number of tombs of holy men throughout the town and in its surroundings, sites that gave the town an aura of sanctity. The Austro-Hungarian consul in Shkodra, Theodor Ippen, noted:

> We were captivated when we saw this unique settlement. Through the extensive growths of ancient olive trees, the light green hues of which were broken up effectively by copses of dark green cypress trees, emerged the vaulted domes of mausoleums, picturesque homes and the acropolis surrounded by high walls, with a massive clock tower and a slender minaret in striking contrast to one another.
>
> The rows of little stone shops in the bazaar at the foot of the mountain had nothing of particular interest to offer. Much more pleasant was a walk in the park among the olive trees with its various views and lookouts, and the gravestones. The number of *tyrbes* in Kruja is given as 366, most certainly an exaggeration on the part of local patriots. [...] All of these *tyrbes* make a vivid impression on the visitor. They transpire peace and tranquillity. [...] The appeal of the sacred surroundings is heightened all the more if a dervish or a *baba* is present to tend the grave. These men, who have withdrawn from the world, receive guests with extraordinary kindness and hospitality and offer philosophical thoughts free of any of the fanaticism that characterises and divides all of the Orient.[145]

Among the many shrines in the town and its surroundings, the best known and most venerated was undoubtedly that of Sari Saltik. This is perhaps because it was only reachable in good weather, being at the top of the mountain overlooking the town. To get there, one had to climb a twisty and rocky path, an ascent from the town that takes about two and a half hours. At the summit, there were three buildings – one for pilgrims of note and rank, one for the dervish guarding the site, and one for the masses of ordinary visitors. The Albanian Bektashi were all to make the pilgrimage once in their lives, and the inhabitants of Kruja were to visit the shrine once a year. The pilgrims usually stayed for twenty-four hours. They arrived in the afternoon, had a picnic and drank spirits. Then they spent the night at the top of the mountain, and at sunrise, they fired off their guns. Wednesday was reserved for the women. Most of the pilgrims, individuals and groups, visited the site from early May to the end of August, but there were two days in particular that attracted many people: Saint George's Day around 6 May and Saint Elijah's (Elias) Day around 2 August. The shrine is located in a cave with the entrance to the west, to the left of the buildings. There, the pilgrims took off their shoes and entered the cave, climbing down a stone staircase. In the shadows below is the *tyrbe* attributed to Sari Saltik, surrounded by other tombs where dervishes are buried. Two special attractions of the cave are a deep and narrow crevice behind the *tyrbe* and a roundish rock hanging from the ceiling, from which crystal-clear, frigid water drips.

Even today, the weather is a major factor in getting to the cave. If conditions are bad, the locals will advise you not to go up the mountain. You can now avoid the steep climb by taking a wider, unpaved road around the mountain, one that can be used by cars. The farther up you get, the more magnificent is the view of the town, the plains and the sea in the distance. From time to time, you pass by men going back down to Kruja with their donkeys laden with wood. On the plateau at the top there are barracks and a hut. At the edge of the mountain top, you have to climb down a few steps to reach a platform.

Across from the entrance to the sanctuary there was a portico with a sheepskin stretched over it. The drops of blood on the ground showed that the place had been used for sacrifices recently. The door to the cave was closed, with a sign on it explaining that the complex had been destroyed in 1967 when religion was banned, and had been rebuilt in 1991 by the people of Kruja. Inside the complex, after a few more steps down into the cavern, there was a polygonal construction built against the wall. In it was a wide and deep gap with pieces of burning cotton soaked in oil that had been left there by visitors. Climbing further down, you get to the tomb of Sari Saltik and three other graves under the rock at the left. Below it is a fountain with holy water flowing out of it. Just as a hundred year ago, you can also see the water dripping from the crevice above the tomb of Sari Saltik that is mentioned in the legend about the saint.

The local version of the legend that was told at the end of the nineteenth century to the French consul, Alexandre Degrand, is as follows:

> In Kruja, there was once a Christian prince who had a charming daughter. He would have been the happiest father and prince, had it not been for a dragon, a terrible and immense monster which housed in a cave on the top of the mountain, where it spent the nights. In the daytime, the dragon took up residence in the ruins of a church that it seemed to guard. In order to protect the country from the attacks of the monster that they failed to kill, the people were forced to offer it one inhabitant of the town per day, as food for the monster. The victims were chosen by lots. One day, a venerable old man turned up in Kruja. No one paid any attention to him as they were all upset at the fate of the prince's daughter who had been chosen for the next day. The next morning, the old man set off on the path up the mountain, and met up with the young girl who was in tears. Such was the heat that the maiden began complaining of thirst. Thereupon, the old man plunged his staff into the cliff and out gushed a spring of water. The dragon approached and attacked them three times. The dervish brandished his wooden sword and lopped the seven heads off the monster. The old man later settled in the cave. But the inhabitants of Kruja were afraid of his supernatural powers and decided to kill him. Warned in time, he managed to escape and reached Corfu in four huge strides. A *tyrbe* was constructed at the site of each step he took, one near Kruja at a place called Gjurma e shejtë (The Holy Footprint), one in Shijak and one in Durrës.[146]

The spring and the red-coloured water dripping from it are part and parcel of the local legend. The spring arose when Sari Saltik struck the rock with his staff. The red colour of the water stemmed from the watermelon he hurled into the air when he heard of the coming attempt to kill him. The fight with the seven-headed dragon is reminiscent of Saint George in the version told by Evliya Çelebi. He had claimed that Sari Saltik was sent to Europe by Haji Bektash, the founder of the Bektashi order, and settled at Kaliakra, where he killed a seven-headed dragon, saved a princess and was buried in seven tombs.

The legendary figure of Sari Saltik, a Muslim missionary in the land of the infidels who is often confused with Christian saints such as Saint Nicholas, Saint Spyridon (of Corfu), Saint George, Saint Elijah (Elias), Saint Simeon and Saint Naum (of Ohrid), is said to be based on a historical figure – a Turkmen religious leader. He and his tribe stemmed from the Sinope region on the coast of the Black Sea. They became the first Turkish colonists to settle in Dobrudja in the thirteenth century, a region which formed a buffer zone between the Byzantine Empire and the Tatars of the Golden Horde. The Byzantine sovereign, Michael VII Palaeologus, had called on the Muslim population to protect him from Tatar incursions.

Long after his death in about 1300, Sari Saltik became a symbol for the spread of Islam in the Balkan Peninsula, a movement that took place after the Ottoman conquest when the original Turkish colonists had returned to Anatolia or had converted to Christianity. In the *Saltukname*, a work written in the second half of the fifteenth century at the behest of Sultan Jem, the town of Baba Eski near Edirne is described as being the headquarters of Sari Saltik, from where he initiated his campaigns to convert the population and colonise the Balkans. The *Vilayetnâme* of Haji Bektash presents him as a contemporary of the holy founder of the Bektashi, sent to Europe by the latter. Indeed it was primarily the members of the Bektashi order who appropriated the figure of Sari Saltik. According to the Albanian Bektashi, Sari Saltik was the one who introduced the order to their country and was the first Bektashi missionary in Europe. He is said to have travelled through the Balkans dressed as a Christian monk. He journeyed through Romania, Thrace, Macedonia and Albania and ended his days on the island of Corfu where his main centre was situated. He is reputed to have founded seven sanctuaries on the peninsula, run by his disciples who, like their master, dressed as Orthodox monks. The most prominent of these establishments were Ohrid, Budapest and Kruja. At the death of Sari Saltik, his body was divided into seven parts, and seven coffins were transported to the seven sanctuaries tended by his disciples.

The Bektashi were not the only order on Albanian-speaking territory to have adopted Sari Saltik. The other orders also acted as guardians of the new shrines. The Rifa'i in Peja in Kosovo maintained a sanctuary located two kilometres from town where the tomb of the saint was venerated not only by Muslims but also by Christians (the latter celebrated him as Saint Vasiliye). A great pilgrimage took place on 2 August, which was known to the Muslims as Ali Day and to the Christians as the feast of Saint Elijah. A little to the south, the Sa'di of the Grand *Tekke* (*Teqja e madhe*) in Gjakova were in charge of another shrine of Sari Saltik, four hours from town on foot, on Mount Pashtrik along the Albanian border. Legend had it that the founder of this oldest Sa'di *tekke* in Gjakova, Ajize Baba, who introduced the Sa'di to the region, had a vision in which he was shown the site where his tomb was to be built. Before the Second World War, thousands of people from the towns and villages on both sides of the border (Peja, Gjakova, Prizren, Bicaj and even Dibra) went there on pilgrimages on Ali Day (2 August).

> There was a very particular and strictly followed ceremony on the pilgrimages to the tomb of Sari Saltik. At the head of five or six dervishes beating their *kudums* (type of drum) was the sheikh of the *tekke* of Ajize Baba, with a leather tambourine in his hand into which everyone threw coins as he approached the tomb solemnly, step by step. The festivities lasted for several days and every morning they beat their *kudums*.

* * *

The cult of Sari Saltik may also have spread to the south of Albania from the seventeenth century onwards. [...] However, southern Albania had a local Islamic shrine of its own of a later date – the tomb of Abbas Ali on the top of Mount Tomorr, south of the town of Berat. Some legends attribute to him a symbolic role in the spread of Islam in the region, although Abbas Ali himself – a purely legendary figure supposed to be the son of Ali (son-in-law of the Prophet Muhammed) and half-brother of Hasan and Huseyn – is in no way comparable to Sari Saltik. The legends enable us to date the shrine to the early seventeenth century. Evliya Çelebi, who travelled through the region in 1670, does not mention him. Concerning Mount Tomorr, he was informed that it was a 'very high mountain which can be seen five to six days' march away. There are all sorts of useful plants and herbs and grasses on this mountain. Every year, physicians come here from Western Europe and Latinistan,' and that the region was good for hiking and hunting.

The oldest text we know of that mentions the shrine is a short passage written in Albanian in Arabic script, dating from the second half of the eighteenth century at the earliest. It concerns the life of one of the early sheikhs of the Sa'di order in that region who was executed by the local authorities in 1630 in the little settlement of Tepelena (between Berat and Gjirokastra). Demir Han, as he was known, was made a sheikh of the Sa'di on his return from a pilgrimage to Mecca. He was appointed by the head of the *tekke* of Djiba (near Damascus), a leading centre of the order. The text reads as follows:

> Demir Han received a decree for Albania with instructions to go to Berat and, from there, to visit the *mekam* of Abbas Ali on Mount Tomorr. With a recommendation from Sheikh Hüseyin Tusiu of Djiba, he went to see Mustafa Tusiu in the little town of Vokopola and, with this person who was responsible for the holy site, he visited the *mekam* of Abbas Ali. There he received a sign telling him to go to the little town of Tepelena. He went there and founded a *zaviye*.

The tomb of Abbas Ali must thus have existed at the time of Demir Han's visit. Osman Myderrizi, an Albanian Orientalist who published the text in question, gives a local legend, according to which one of the first missionaries residing in Vokopola was responsible for the shrine:

> As proof of his capacity as a missionary, he brought with him a handwritten Koran, a sword and a sack containing soil from the place where Imam Huseyn, Abbas Ali and others were martyred in Kerbela. When he found out that the Albanians regarded Mount Tomorr as a holy mountain, he buried the soil from Kerbela on the summit and built the *mekam* of Abbas Ali.

According to information gathered by Osman Myderrizi, the building of the shrine did not make it a pilgrimage site immediately. This took place a hundred years later when Islam had spread and the tradition had really taken root. The existence of the shrine and the pilgrimage are only recorded with certainty at the end of the nineteenth century, when they had been taken over by the Bektashi.

It is to Ekrem bey Vlora, scion of a great Albanian family, that we owe the first description of a climb up Mount Tomorr and of the shrine of Abbas Ali, published in Sarajevo in 1911:

> Up on a high plateau at 1,600 metres in altitude, the mountain rises to gentle summits, ending in its highest peak. [...] Refreshed, we set off on our way to climb over the last ridge to the summit of Abbas Ali. We were surrounded by a sea of rocks in which there was very little vegetation. Thick fog prevented us from seeing very far. All we could see were the frightening gorges and ravines to the east. The whole peak of Tomorr is terribly jagged, both to the west on the Berat side and to the east towards the river of Tomorica. We left our pack animals in a hollow protected from the wind and then climbed up to the top of Tomorr, to an elevation of 2,396 m. according to the general map of the Institute for Military Geography of the Double Monarchy, which also indicates the presence of a building.
>
> This was a site of religious importance for the whole region, a place that we entered with mixed feelings. It was a circular construction of well-hewn stone blocks put together without mortar as a ring wall, and had a narrow entrance to the southeast. It is called a *mekam*, an Arabic word for a site, or more specifically a pilgrimage site. In its present form, the construction dates from the year 1880. Inside the walls there was nothing aside from a niche of rough stonework facing southwards, in which there were two candlesticks and tin plate. On the plate were a few coins donated as alms by the faithful. The *mekam* is a site that is holy both to Muslims and to Christians. Even the most unscrupulous of robbers never dare to steal these coins. Mount Tomorr would no doubt strike them dead with a bolt of lightning.
>
> On 15 August (old style), this desolate site comes to life for the feast of the Assumption of the Virgin Mary. It is mostly dervishes of the Bektashi order who come here on pilgrimages to pray, sacrifice and collect alms. Among my travelling

companions there were several Bektashi who only ventured to penetrate the ring wall on their knees. In the battle between Imam Hussein, the son of the fourth Caliph Ali, and Yazid, according to their beliefs, the son of Muawiyah, the stepbrother of the former, called Abbas Ali (a son of Ali by another wife), managed to flee the carnage of Kerbela and after long wanderings reached the peak of Mount Tomorr which he chose as his place to die. Historically speaking, this figure is unknown.[147]

In 1916, after the chaos of the Balkan Wars and the beginning of the First World War, a *tekke* was constructed below the peak, about three hours from the top, at the initiative of a Bektashi dervish from the region. The *baba* and the dervishes who lived there were responsible for maintaining the shrine and receiving and lodging the pilgrims. According to Joseph Swire, an English traveller, about eight to nine thousand people made the pilgrimage every year in the 1930s. He visited the site himself:

> The morning was wet; but later the sun broke through the greyness and the low storm-clouds, torn to tatters, drifted and eddied in confusion between our feet and the valley's bed, clinging to spurs and hiding in hollows till the sun thrust down its shafts and chivvied them away. So we climbed to Tomori's holy summit. An hour's stiff scrambling brought us to the ridge – which is broken on its eastern side by precipices and steep screes but falls away more gently to the west. There was snow in the hollows and 12-foot snow cornices above the eastern precipices; yet the grassy parts were thick with cowslips and forget-me-nots, crocuses and narcissi. Eddying clouds shut out our view, but we followed the ridge easily by a succession of crests to the southern of the two main summits and came to a new-built shrine encircled by a stone wall – the shrine of Abas Ali, mythical saint of the Bektashis.
>
> One August 25 long ago, goes the legend, Abas Ali came from Arabia to Berat; and mounting a great white horse (which has left hoof-marks upon the mountain) he fought the barbarians of the neighbourhood. When he had overcome them he rested for five days on Tomori, then went to dwell on Mount Olympus; but every year he returns on August 25 for five days, when there come Bektashis – and Christians too – sometimes eight or nine thousand people, to pay him homage. They bring their sheep for food, slaughter them on the summit, then take them down to their bivouacs by the *tekké*. So Tomori is a holy mountain and *për Baba Tomorit* a sacred oath. The shrine was built, so *Baba* Tyrabiu told me, on the site of an antique pagan shrine, so Abas Ali probably inherited his supernatural powers from the pagan god he displaced.[148]

The legend that the Bektashi associated with this sacred site of their religion was astoundingly similar to that of the Sa'di earlier. In a work written in the 1920s on the history of the Bektashi, the author, the *baba* of the *tekke* of Tomorr, noted:

> In 1600 AD, Hadji Baba from the *tekke* of Hacıbektaş arrived at the top of Mount Tomorr and on that peak venerated by the Albanians since ancient times, he set

a sign and told the people that the site would thereafter be visited in the name of Abbas Ali, the brother of Imam Husein and standard-bearer of Kerbela. After leaving this sign on Tomorr, Hadji Baba went to Përmet where he died. From there, his body was taken to Qesaraka in the Kolonja region where a *tekke* and a *tyrbe* were built in his honour that still exist in all their glory to the present day. For three hundred years, Baba Tomorr, a mountain of the pagans for two thousand years, has been a centre of veneration for the great martyr of Kerbela and a true site of pilgrimage, being visited by all the Bektashi of Albania every year on 12 August (old style).[149]

In 1957, the *mekam* was still being visited by people from throughout southern Albania. The faithful continued to come by the thousands despite the campaign against religion that was being waged by the political authorities. The pilgrimages began on 23 August and lasted for three days. Ten years later, the ban on religious organisations put an end to the practice for a quarter of a century.

* * *

The history of the two sacred haunts of the Albanian Bektashi, the cave of Sari Saltik above the town of Kruja and the tomb of Abbas Ali on the top of Mount Tomorr, is still rather unclear and their origins are veiled in legends. One wonders whether these impressive sites, made by Mother Nature, were once Christian or even pre-Christian sanctuaries. They are, at any rate, places that would seem predestined as religious sanctuaries. Their location in the mountains might suggest that we categorise them as sanctuaries linked to mountain cults. Nature has endowed them with mysterious, magical attributes: the spring in the cave of Sari Saltik, the water dripping from a crack, and the imposing surroundings of Mount Tomorr, as described by Ekrem bey Vlora:

> The high elevation is predestined for a shrine: the imposing mountain surroundings, the nearby forests of mighty oaks, and the dramatic weather conditions. Everyone in central Albania is convinced that before any event of great importance takes place, Mount Tomorr lets out a ball of fire that explodes in a deafening clap of thunder. Of the people in my entourage, over ten claimed that they could remember seeing and hearing such an occurrence just before the last Russo-Turkish War broke out.[150]

However, it is difficult to prove the continuity of religions, from pagan to Christian and from Christian to Muslim, from the earliest times. In the case of Kruja, there were still the remains of an old church on the mountain peak around 1900, though this does not necessarily prove that the cave was used by the Christians. As to the summit of Mount Tomorr that the Albanian Bektashi of the early twentieth century claimed to be the site of an ancient pagan temple, it certainly does seem to have been worshipped by the surrounding population who swore their oaths 'by Father Tomorr' (*për Baba Tomorr*) long before the shrine of Abbas Ali was associated with it. However, there is still no concrete evidence of any ancient, pre-Muslim shrine there.

Although we cannot solve the mystery as to whether these sites are of pre-Muslim origin, we do know that, once they became Islamic sanctuaries, they were closely associated with the spread of Islam among the local population. The figure of Sari Saltik is a fine example of this phenomenon, not only in Albania but throughout the Balkan Peninsula as we have seen. These sacred haunts were associated with certain orders of Islamic mysticism and the expansion thereof into these regions, an expansion that such figures made legitimate. The legends show them as intrinsically linked to early Muslim missionaries. In the case of Mount Tomorr, one is struck by the similarity between the two legends, the Sa'di one and the Bektashi one. In both cases, one of the early sheikhs of the order in question arrived in southern Albania, somewhere between Berat and Gjirokastra, and climbed Mount Tomorr where he received a sign to settle in the region and build a *tekke*. The British scholar, F. W. Hasluck, stressed that the Bektashi used the cult of Sari Saltik to their own ends, and by the second half of the nineteenth century, the Bektashi order was expanding rapidly throughout southern Albania. According to a history of the Bektashi written around 1850 by an Albanian Bektashi, there were originally very few Bektashi followers in the regions of Skrapar and Berat (to the south and west of Tomorr). It was then that Baba Tahir, who had been a dervish in Crete, then at the *tekke* of Hacıbektaş in Anatolia, and subsequently at the *tekke* of Melçan near Korça, was sent by the head of the latter convent to establish a *tekke* in Prishta where he won over a large part of the population, including the beys. A little later, in the early 1880s, when the order was still growing, the Bektashi movement took on a decisively nationalist character. It is said to have been at this time that the round edifice on the top of Mount Tomorr was built (or rebuilt), sometime after 1880 according to Ekrem bey Vlora. Does this mean that the Bektashi pilgrimage to the top of Mount Tomorr was dictated by political circumstances at the beginning of the Albanian national revival, when Albanian land was being threatened by the appetites of neighbouring countries? It is not unlikely. Naim Frashëri, the poet of the Albanian national revival, who was a Bektashi himself, commemorated Abbas Ali in a volume of poetry entitled *Lulet e verës* (Summer Flowers), published in 1890:

Abas Aliu zu' Tomorë,
Erdhi afër nesh,
Shqipëria s'mbet e gjorë,
Se Zoti e desh.

Abbas Ali took over Tomorr,
He came to live with us,
Albania was no longer afflicted
For God came to love it.

Collective pilgrimages served to activate local Muslim communities and could be taken advantage of politically and ideologically. They could take on wide significance, not only religious but political, too. For instance, the pilgrimage to the shrine of Abbas Ali was used to promote the expansion of the Bektashi in southern Albania, but could also serve to awaken national awareness among the Albanian population. As an extreme example of nationalist thinking, a young Albanian nationalist visiting Kruja in 1907 explained to the Albanian newspaper in Boston that the tomb of Sari Saltik that he had been shown was in fact none other than the tomb of Scanderbeg, the Albanian national hero. He added: 'Sari Saltik was a good saint in the eyes of God and for himself, but Scanderbeg was for all Albanians.'

The shrine in Kruja remained associated with Sari Saltik, but several years later, in independent Albania, we know that the Bektashi were endeavouring to paint another of their sanctuaries, the one on Mount Tomorr, in more national and nationalist colours. Baba Ali Tomorri who was head of the *tekke* situated under the mountain peak, wrote:

> Since the new establishment by Dervish Iljaz in 1916 near the holy shrine, Tomorr has become a site of great national and religious significance, not only for the Bektashi but for all Albanians.[151]

In the communist period, the new political authorities banned most of the pilgrimages that were considered mass demonstrations. However, some pilgrimages persisted in a clandestine form, even in communist Albania where all religious practices were banned in 1967. In Kruja, for example, some people – less than in earlier years of course – continued to visit the cave of Sari Saltik. Family picnics were organised up on the mountain. Three people would approach the edge of the cliff. Two kept watch and the third person would go down into the cave to pay his respects to the saint. One woman in town defied the ban and the presence of military personnel at the nearby barracks, and climbed up the twisty path every night to visit the tomb of Sari Saltik and to light candles.

It is clear throughout the Balkans that large pilgrimages to the sacred sites of local Islam have now resumed, after being banned for decades in the communist period. They have revived quickly and now serve the heads of the local Muslim communities to strengthen their cohesion. In Albania, the pilgrimages that take place in Kruja and on Mount Tomorr have certainly given strength to the Bektashi community, whose situation has been particularly difficult after years of void.

The sacred sites of Islam have also been rehabilitated in recent years in the neighbouring countries, and in a more political environment. At Ajvatovica, a shrine set in a natural environment near Prusac in Bosnia, the pilgrimage, banned in 1947, was revived in 1990 and 1991, just before the civil war broke out. The leading religious authorities in Bosnia and Herzegovina revived the tradition for largely political purposes, in a situation where tempers were running high. The pilgrimage served to mobilise the local Muslim community and strengthen its identity. [...] The same thing was true of Bulgaria in the summer of 1992 when

Ahmed Dogan, leader of the Movement for Rights and Freedoms, the party supported by virtually all voters of the Turkish minority, took part in a pilgrimage to the *tyrbe* of Demir Baba, the most famous shrine in the country.

Like many other sanctuaries, the sacred shrines of the Albanian Bektashi have an ambivalent character. On the one hand, they are natural sites that seem to have existed forever, unmoved up in the mountains, lost in the clouds, and rising high, far from the madding crowds. When they became symbols of Islam and Bektashism, they lost their immobile, eternal character, being transformed by men who wrapped them in new legends and gave them new meaning according to the situation and needs of the surrounding Muslim communities. But such changes were often ephemeral and soon forgotten. What is quintessential is the immobile, eternal nature of these sites. They stay where they are and give legitimacy to any new symbols added to them.

In the post-communist era, new legends about the cave in Kruja and the peak of Mount Tomorr are perhaps in the making to reaffirm the presence and the role of the Bektashi in Albania, among the Sons of the Eagle.

[Nathalie Clayer, 'Les hauts lieux du bektachisme albanais', in *Lieux de l'islam. Cultes et cultures de l'Afrique à Java*, ed. Mohammad Ali Amir-Moezzi (Paris: Editions Autrement 1996), pp. 168–183. Reprinted in: Nathalie Clayer, *Religion et nation chez les albanais, XIXe-XXe siècles* (Istanbul: Isis 2003), pp. 137–150. Translated from the French by Robert Elsie.]

2009
MACHIEL KIEL
DURBALI SULTAN RESURRECTED?

The Dutch scholar Machiel Kiel (b. 1938), former director of the Netherlands Institute in Turkey, was in the Balkans in the 1950s and 1960s to do research on Islamic architecture. The fruits of his research in Albania appeared in his seminal Ottoman Architecture in Albania, 1385–1912 *(Istanbul 1990). He has published several articles on the Bektashi in Albania and in the Balkans, including this information on the fate of the tekke of Durbalı Sultan in Thessaly.*

At the top of a wooded hill overlooking the little-used railway line from the inland town of Pharsala to the port of Volos in the Central Greek province of Thessaly lie the ruins of a vast complex of buildings that once used to be the great Bektashi *Tekke* of Durbalı Sultan. In the 18th and 19th century it was the largest Bektashi centre on Greek territory (not counting the *Tekke* of Kızıl Deli near Mikró Déreio/Küçük Derbend in Western Thrace, part of Greece since 1920).

The eastern half of Thessaly, with the largest plain of Greece, was part of the Ottoman Empire from 1387–1388 to 1881 (the western plain, with Trikkala from 1395 to 1881). Pharsala was the Ottoman Çatalca, a small town which was inhabited by Turks by two-thirds and possessed some remarkable Ottoman monuments. Except for the great bridge over the Alpheios River, built by Ratip Ahmed Pasha shortly before 1756, nothing Ottoman remains in Pharsala. Volos only became a place of importance in the 19th century, when it developed from a small 16th century Ottoman castle with a similarly small open suburb into the most important harbor of Central Greece. In Volos, too, all Ottoman structures are gone.

What we saw in 1967, 1972 and 1974 on the lonely hill above the village of Ireni were two domed mausolea, *türbes*, a large cemetery with many Bektashi gravestones, a guesthouse, other domestic buildings, and huge stores for the agricultural produce of the land and the vast herds the *tekke* must once have possessed. The name of the nearby village, Ireni, is not Greek but a Greek corruption of the Turkish name Örenli, or 'village with (or at) the ruins.' This name is an echo of the ruins of an 11th-12th century Byzantine monastery that stood on the site, with the remains of an ancient Greek temple near or below it. Spolia from both structures, studied by Giannopolos, are incorporated into the present structure, symbolizing the spiritual continuity of the site. In the Ottoman period more than half of all villages of the district of Pharsala had Turkish names and Muslim inhabitants. Many of the Muslims were descendants of Yürük settlers of the earliest part of the Ottoman period. We find them in the *tahrir defters* of Thessaly of 1466, 1506, 1521 and 1569/70 preserved in the Ottoman archives in Istanbul (B.O.A.). Many of these people had a heterodox background, where Bektashi preaching found a willing ear. This is known better than anybody else by Irène Melikoff, in whose honour we have written these lines.

The last occupant of the *Tekke* of Durbalı Sultan, Baba Seyyit, died in March 1973 and was buried in the passageway linking the two *türbes*. Decay set in because of a total lack of care. Some local inhabitants of the nearby villages appropriated part of the land belonging to the *tekke*. In the 1950s the Greek State had confiscated 13,000 *stremma* (10 *stremma* is about 1 hectare) of land belonging as *Vakf* to the *tekke* and distributed it to the villagers of the surrounding area. The *tekke* kept 2,960 *stremma* and 700 sheep and goats. The Greek State had sequestrated the property as 'enemy real estate' because Greece and Albania were officially still in a state of war. Within a few years after Baba Seyyit's death, the remaining carpets, lamps and calligraphed *levhas* were stolen.

Although the *tekke* had officially been declared a 'historical monument,' nothing was done for its maintenance for years. In the 1990s Greek nationalist fanatics desecrated the *türbes*, threw out the *sanduks* and other remaining objects, and broke and destroyed many old gravestones. Their work was finished off by local treasure hunters, who believed that all the dervishes were rich and had been buried with lots of money on them. They broke into the graves and scattered the bones of the deceased. This state of affairs was reported to us in November 1992 by Dimitris Stamoulis, son of the last official guardian and shepherd of the *tekke*, then living in Paris. These most recent developments induced me to publish the material collected at the spot in 1967–1974 and in the Ottoman archives in Istanbul. It appeared in 2005 in Ankara in the great volume edited by Yaşar Ocak on 'Sufism and Sufis in Ottoman Society.' For me it was the end of the old *tekke* whose 'history was destroyed before it was written.'

Some time ago, around the year 2000, the fate of the decaying *tekke* took a surprising new turn. Small groups of Muslim Albanians with a Bektashi background, living legally in Greece for years, heard about the *tekke*. They were mostly from the extreme south of Albania, from the little town of Leskovik, which in the past had been known as an important Bektashi centre. In the cemetery of the *tekke* still stands undamaged (2009) the beautifully decorated tomb of Kâni Pasha of Leskovik illustrating the link between the *tekke* of Durbalı Sultan and southern Albania. Kâni Pasha died in 1918.

The descendants of the Leskovik Bektashis knew by heart a number of songs and ballads about Durbalı Sultan and his *tekke*, transmitted to them by their mothers during the dark days of the communist dictatorship and its aggressive atheism. A piece of living oral history. As the ruins of the *tekke* appeared on no map and no indication was given of their existence, it took a bit of time for them to find the place. The group decided to stop the process of decay and on long weekends they worked to clean and restore the two historical *türbes*, to re-install *sanduks* over the graves of the holy men and to bring a bit of order to the half-destroyed and terribly neglected old cemetery. At irregular dates, the groups also held a religious ceremony which they called a '*kurban*.' Initially, the local police intervened and forbade the group from being active. A second group of Muslim Albanians, now living in Athens, then came into being. Greeks intellectuals also got interested and started to write about the *tekke* in various newspapers.

The Greek lawyer Kostis Tsitsilikis from Thessaloniki applied to the official Greek Ombudsman in Athens, explained the case and pleaded for the return of the property to the Muslim Community taking care of the *tekke*. The case is rather complicated and at the time of writing is still pending. Meanwhile a third group of Muslim Albanians was formed in Larissa, the capital of Thessaly. They were much closer to Durbalı Sultan than the groups based in Athens and Thessaloniki. The new group, being much 'closer to home,' cleaned up more of the cemetery and placed lamps at each of the graves. Inside the compound of ruins, they also built a room where they could spend the night and decorated it with inscriptions of Ali, etc. This building activity was clearly illegal but the Greek police of the area, knowing of the actions of the Ombudsman, left them undisturbed.

In 2009 an NGO group interested in the history and conservation of ancient and Byzantine monuments also took an interest in the *tekke*. This group of broad-minded people, with great technical expertise, wanted to make detailed architectural drawings of the entire complex, something that had never been done before. The group also wrote an official letter to the Ombudsman in support of the case still pending at court. What is lacking now is a legal body that could unite all the groups interested. As part of the process of making the *tekke* known to a larger public, a book of over 200 pages, written by K. G. Tsikoumis, was published in 2006, and in 2007 preparations were made for a film about the *tekke*, to be shown on Greek television. These preparations took me back again to the *tekke* after more than thirty years.

The least we may expect for the next few years is the resurrection of the old *tekke* as an official religious centre for the Muslim Albanians living in Greece and the further consolidation, or even restoration, of the remaining ruined buildings and the restitution of at least some of its old property to give this old spiritual centre a solid material base.

[Adapted from: Machiel Kiel, 'Durbali Sultan Revisited', *Türk Kültürü ve Hacı Bektaş Velî Araştırma Dergisi*, 52 (2009), pp. 53–58.]

3

THE *TEKKES* AND SHRINES OF THE ALBANIAN BEKTASHI

TEKKES AND SHRINES IN ALBANIA

Map of Albania showing cities and towns of *tekkes* and shrines.

Alipostivan, District of Përmet, Albania
Tekke of Baba Ali, *tekke* of Baba Abdullah
Location: About 10 km east of Këlcyra, northwest of the road to Frashër. 40°18' N, 20°18' E.

The *tekke* of Baba Ali is said to have been founded in the mountains around 1767. The site is probably older as there are said to be ancient ruins nearby. It was probably part of an old trade route from Skrapar to Përmet. The *tekke* was refounded in 1857 by the said Baba Ali, and around 1903 it was established again by Baba Abdullah from the *tekke* of Konitsa and contains his *tyrbe*. The Scottish anthropologist Margaret Hasluck (1885–1948) visited the site in 1923 and encountered a *baba* and three dervishes. Some say alternatively that the *tekke* was founded by a Baba Ali in 1860.

On 14–17 January 1921 the *tekke* of Alipostivan was represented by Baba Meleq at the First National Congress of the Bektashi, held at the *tekke* of Prishta in the Skrapar region. It functioned as a *tekke* until 1967 when it was torn down by the surrounding villagers in the communist campaign against religion. After the fall of the communist dictatorship the site was restored at its location on the mountainside, with a splendid view of the Përmet valley and the Dhëmbel mountains in the distance. Reconstruction began in 1997 and resulted in a rather oversized *tekke* building and several large *tyrbes*. It is currently administered by Baba Hekuran Nikollari (b. 1963). The name Alipostivan is said to derive from *Ali, post i vendit* 'Ali, sheepskin-sitter (i.e. *baba*) of the place'.

cf. F. W. Hasluck 1914–1916, p. 118, 1929, p. 438 (544); N. Clayer 1990, p. 247.

Aranitas, District of Mallakastra, Albania
Dervishia of Aranitas
Location: About 7 km east of Ballsh. 40°35' N, 19°48' E.

This *dervishia* was founded before 1923. There never seems to have been an actual *tekke* here and it is uncertain how long the *dervishia* existed.

Backa, District of Skrapar, Albania
Tekke of Baba Fetah, *tekke* of Backa
Location: About 30 km east of Çorovoda. 40°29' N, 20°24' E.

This *tekke* was founded in 1889 by a Baba Hamit from Melçan. It was administered by six *babas* up to the year 1923, including Baba Abedin who died in 1913. The most noted among them was Baba Fetah who taught people how to read and write Albanian. He is said to have run the *tekke* 'with intelligence, justice and love'. The rebel leader and writer Mihal Grameno (1871–1931) wrote of his visit in about 1905:

> We sang on our way until we got to Backa, where we went to the *dervishia* and were taken in by the dervishes. The *dervishia* is wonderfully situated, in a small field surrounded by hills and forests. Through the *dervishia* runs a brook, so it is a truly beautiful site. The reverend Baba Fetah chose it himself and added much to the natural beauty of the surroundings. He planted all sorts of trees,

grapevines, and other things, all in perfect order. As such, any traveller passing through Backa cannot help but admire his work and will say: 'Glory to your soul, Baba Fetah!'[152]

The *tekke* of Backa was destroyed by Greek forces during the Balkan Wars, but was rebuilt in 1923. It was represented by a Baba Mestan at the First National Congress of the Bektashi, held at the *tekke* of Prishta in the Skrapar region on 14–17 January 1921. In an Ottoman Turkish inscription at the *tekke* mention is made in 1921–1922 [1340 AH] of a Pirani Baba. From 1930 onwards it was under the administration of the *gjyshata* of Prishta.

In 1967 during the communist campaign against religion, the *tekke* of Backa was closed down but was not destroyed as it had been declared a monument of culture. It was used instead as a school during the communist period.
The faithful gathered here as pilgrims on the feast day of 20 June.
cf. F. W. Hasluck 1929, p. 440 (548); P. Pepo 1962, p. 43; Baba Rexheb 1970, p. 300, 383; N. Clayer 1990, pp. 250–251; M. Tütüncü 2017, pp. 246–247.

Bënça, District of Tepelena, Albania
Dervishia of Bënça
Location: Village of Bënça, *c.* 9 km southwest of Tepelena. 40°15' N, 20°00' E.

Little is known of the one-time *dervishia* in Bënça near Tepelena. Baba Rexheb mentions it briefly. This *dervshia* is referred to on the map made in Albania for the German scholar Franz Babinger in 1962, so it must still have been active in some form at that time.
cf. Baba Rexheb 1970; N. Clayer 1990, p. 253.

Berat, District of Berat, Albania
Tekke of Baba Ali
Location: In a small park under the fortress of Berat, about 20 m from the old Gorica Bridge over the Osum River. 40°42' N, 19°56' E.

There was once a large *tekke* here. It was quite old as it is said to have been burned down in July 1826 in the crackdown under Sultan Mahmud II (r. 1808–1839), 'when priceless books of mysticism and philosophy in Arabic and Persian were destroyed'.[153] It is unclear whether it was rebuilt, as there is some confusion in historical records with the nearby *tekke* of Velabisht. What remains in Berat is an unroofed *mekam* to the left of the main road into Berat which is dedicated to Baba Ali or Aliko. It is still visited by pilgrims who bring flowers and light candles.
cf. N. Clayer 1990, p. 254; H. Norris 1993, p. 125.

Bllaca, District of Dibra, Albania
Tekke of Baba Jusuf
Location: About 10 km west of the Bulqiza-Peshkopia road. 41°34' N, 20°21' E.

The *tekke* of Baba Jusuf was founded in about 1893 by a Baba Jusuf or Isuf, also known as Baba Sufa. It was destroyed, no doubt during the First World War, and was reconstructed in the early 1920s as a two-storey edifice by his successor, Baba

Rushit Tollja (b. 1878) of Strikçan. Rushit Tollja had been *baba* in Bllaca since the death of Jusuf Baba and in 1924 he was appointed to the *tekke* of Martanesh, too, thus serving both *tekkes* at the same time. However, he preferred to reside in Bllaca.

In the early years of the twentieth century, this *tekke* was a centre of clandestine learning in the Dibra region. Here are the words of a poor Albanian who went to the *tekke* in search of a job:

> I was poor, had neither land nor livestock, and left my village of Gorica to make a living. I came to Bllaca and worked as a servant at the Bektashi *tekke* there. At the *tekke*, I became friends with Jashar Zeneli, an educated fellow who was older than I was. He could speak Turkish and knew how to read Albanian. The *tekke* of Bllaca was a well-known centre for the teaching of the Albanian alphabet. There I met Jashar Zeneli, Tush Meta, Demir Tasha, Hysen Tasha, Seit Tasha, Selman Jella, Ram Osmani and several other men I have forgotten now. These fine men were learning to read and write Albanian and when they learned the alphabet, they began to read the books that arrived from Monastir [Bitola]. My friend, Jashar, taught me the Albanian alphabet, too, and gave me a spelling book that I still own and cherish.
>
> The *baba* of the *tekke*, Isuf, was delighted when he learned that I knew how to read the Albanian alphabet. For this reason he allowed me to take part in meetings at the *tekke*. On such occasions, he even let me put off my chores until the next day.
>
> The meetings were organized by Baba Isuf and sometimes by Jashar Zeneli. I was proud to take part because they talked about the liberation of Albania and the founding of a strong and modern Albanian State. We then read the writings of Naim Frashëri or the Albanian newspapers that had arrived from Monastir. Before the meetings closed, tasks were given out to the participants. Tush Meta, for example, was to distribute books in Sopot, Zërqan, Peladhia, Kovashica and Homesh. The *tekke* was also allied with Mersen Demë.
>
> Jashar Zeneli won over the *kaymakam* of Dibra and invited him to the *tekke* in Bllaca one day and offered him a fine Dibran costume. The *kaymakam* was very happy with it and told Jashar that he might carry on teaching Albanian, but only as long as Istanbul did not find out.
>
> When freedom was declared,[154] reading and writing Albanian were taught in the open. Seit Tasha was a prominent figure in teaching. But when the great army of Turgut Pasha marched through (in 1910), he banned the teaching of Albanian for a while. This only made us prouder of Albania and filled us with a longing for freedom.[155]

In the 1920s, the *tekke* was administered by a Sejdi Baba, who was appointed by Baba Ahmet of Turan. The *tekke* of Bllaca is currently under the administration of Baba Ismail Jangulli.

The feast day of this *tekke* is 10 June.

cf. F. W. Hasluck 1929, p. 443 (551); Baba Rexheb 1970, p. 358; N. Clayer 1990, pp. 255–256, 2003, pp. 108–109; S. Kaliçani 1990. pp. 123–132.

Borsh, District of Saranda, Albania
Tekke of Baba Xhafer
Location: On the coastal road, 35 km north of Saranda. 40°03' N, 19°51' E.

This *tekke* was destroyed by Greek forces in 1914. There was a *tyrbe* at the site from about 1920 to 1967 when it was destroyed by the local villagers in the communist campaign against religion. The *tyrbe* was reconstructed in the 1990s.

Brerima, District of Skrapar, Albania
Tekke of Baba Xhafer
Location: Near Gjerbës overlooking the Tomorrica River. 40°35' N, 20°15' E.

The *tekke* of Brerima or Gjerbës served as the winter quarters for the *baba* and dervishes of the *tekke* of Kulmak on Mount Tomorr. It was represented by a Baba Xhafer at the First National Congress of the Bektashi, held at the *tekke* of Prishta in the Skrapar region on 14–17 January 1921. The *tekke* was destroyed by the local villagers in the communist campaign against religion in the spring of 1967. It has since been restored with three or four *tyrbes* that are in the charge of a local custodian. Pilgrims still visit the site, though it is isolated and difficult to reach.

Bubës i Parë, District of Përmet, Albania
Tekke of Baba Jemin, *tekke* of Baba Dalip
Location: About 30 km north of Këlcyra. 40°30' N, 20°05' E.

The nineteenth-century *tekke* of Baba Jemin seems to have been constructed after the crackdown under Sultan Mahmud II in 1826. It was a large *tekke* with much land and survived until 1967 when it was torn down by the local villagers in the communist campaign against religion. A *tyrbe* was reconstructed here at Bubës i Parë (i.e. First Bubës) in the 1990s to which pilgrimages are held on 1 July.

Bubës i Sipërm, District of Përmet, Albania
Tekke of Bubës, *tekke* of Baba Ali
Location: About 30 km north of Këlcyra. 40°30' N, 20°05' E.

This *tekke* in Bubës i Sipërm (Upper Bubës), also known as Bubës i Dytë (Second Bubës) or Bubës Zaimllar, had much land. It was a *dervishia* in the nineteenth century and survived until 1967 when it was torn down by the local villagers in the communist campaign against religion. The site was reconstructed with a solid and attractive building in the 1990s by the Zaimllar family. It is difficult to reach as there is no road, but pilgrimages are, nonetheless, held to it on 15 June.

Bulqiza, District of Bulqiza, Albania
Tekke of Bulqiza
Location: Town of Bulqiza. 41°29' N, 20°12' E.

This *tekke* was founded by Baba Fejzë Bulqiza in the nineteenth century. Fejzë Bulqiza trained in Anatolia and returned to Albania in 1827 to spread the Bektashi faith. He was active primarily in the region of Dibra and Bulqiza and became a *baba* in 1832. He opened schools in the surrounding area and endeavoured to create a league of Bektashi *tekkes*. He is said to have been slain by Turkish forces in 1860 when the *tekke* was destroyed, but he has no known grave. A new *tekke* was raised in his honour around 1900. It was closed down in 1967 during the communist campaign against religion, but was reopened as a *tyrbe* after the dictatorship, in 1994.

Cakran, District of Fier, Albania
Tekke of Cakran
Location: In the mountains above the village of Cakran, about 15 km southeast of Fier. 40°36' N, 19°37' E.

This *tekke* survived until 1967 when it was torn down by the local villagers in the communist campaign against religion. A *tyrbe* was reconstructed here in the 1990s where services are occasionally held. Pilgrims visit the site on its feast day of 22 March.

Çerrica, District of Skrapar, Albania
Tekke of Çerrica
Location: On the right (east) side of the Tomorrica River, about 35 km north of Çorovoda. 40°40' N, 20°15' E.

This *tekke* had a *baba* until 1967 when it was torn down by the local villagers in the communist campaign against religion. A *tyrbe* was reconstructed here after the reintroduction of democracy in the 1990s.
cf. N. Clayer 1990, p. 258.

Çorrush, District of Mallakastra, Albania
Dervishia of Çorrush
Location: On a hillside above the village of Çorrush, north of the Vjosa river. 40°26' N, 19°48' E.

This *tekke* served as a gathering point for *muhibs* from the districts of Mallakastra, Vlora and Tepelena. Mention is made of a Baba Sherif, or Sherif of Çorrush, who was buried there. The *dervishia* survived until 1967 when it was torn down by the local villagers in the communist campaign against religion. There is now a *tyrbe* at the site.
cf. N. Clayer 1990, p. 260; Sh. Hysi 2004, p. 112.

Delvina, District of Delvina, Albania
Dervishia of Beqir Efendi
Location: About 15 km northeast of Saranda. 39°56' N, 20°05' E.

The *dervishia* of Beqir Efendi is said to date from 1770. It survived until 1967 when it was torn down by the local villagers in the communist campaign against religion. There is now a *tyrbe* at the site.
cf. N. Clayer 1990, p. 261.

Drisht, District of Shkodra, Albania
Tyrbe of Baba Kamber
Location: About 15 km northeast of Shkodra, on the road to Mount Cukali. 42°07' N, 19°36' E.

Bektashi influence has been rare in northern Albania, north of Kruja, since the early nineteenth century, when Mustafa Pasha Bushatlliu (1796–1860) of Shkodra

drove the Bektashi out of the region, suspecting them of being supporters of his southern Albanian rival, Ali Pasha Tepelena (1844–1822). However, there was a Bektashi *tyrbe* of Baba Kamber in the old mountain village of Drisht (Drivasto) that was a popular place of pilgrimage for the Muslims of Shkodra a century ago. It seems to have been constructed around 1908, but the original shrine may date from the sixteenth century. The keepers of the shrine were Bektashi. The *tyrbe* was closed down in 1967 during the communist campaign against religion and was reopened after the dictatorship in 1995. The faithful gathered here as pilgrims on the feast day of 3 May.
cf. T. Ippen 1908, p. 23; P. Bartl 1968, p. 105, 107, N. Clayer 1990, p. 263.

Drizar, District of Mallakastra, Albania
Tekke of Baba Xhelal
Location: Between the Vjosa River and the old Ballsh-Tepelena road. 40°29' N, 19°47' E.

This *tekke* was founded around 1900 by a Baba Xhelal. It was subordinate to the *tekke* of Koshtan, about 30 km to the southeast. The *tekke* of Drizar was represented by a Baba Rakip at the First National Congress of the Bektashi, held at the *tekke* of Prishta in the Skrapar region on 14–17 January 1921. It was reconstructed by Dede Baba Ahmet Myftari, who was interned in Drizar from 1958 to 1967 with his disciple Reshat Bardhi (later to become *kryegjysh*).

The *tyrbe* of the *tekke* was reconstructed and reopened in 1994.
cf. F. W. Hasluck 1929, p. 436 (543); N. Clayer 1990, p. 264.

Dukaj, District of Tepelena, Albania
Tekke of Dukaj
Location: About 10 km west of Tepelena on the old road to Vlora. 40°19' N, 19°56' E.

This was a large *tekke,* founded in 1900, with which many *babas* were associated. It was destroyed in 1967 by the surrounding villagers during the communist campaign against religion. There is now a *tyrbe* at the site.
cf. N. Clayer 1990, p. 264.

Dushk, District of Gramsh, Albania
Tekke of Baba Ahmet
Location: Village of Dushk near Grabova, about 25 km southeast of Gramsh. 40°47' N, 20°20' E.

The *tekke* of Dushk, situated near the village of Grabova, was founded in the 1880s by Baba Ahmet Nazereci or Nazereka (d. 1890) from Opar in the Korça region. He was made a *baba* in 1880 by Baba Adem of Melçan who sent him to the Gramsh region. It was in Dushk that Baba Ahmet found land to construct his three-room *tekke*. He was murdered in 1890 in a local conflict with the villagers of the region.

Baba Ahmet was followed by: Baba Arif Pervekushi or Devekushti (d. 1896) from Skapar who had been a dervish at the *tekke* of Backa; Baba Jonuz Zhepa or Xhepa (d. 1902) from Tomorrica; Baba Kameri (d. 1908) from Leshnja in the

Skrapar region who bought more land and gathered more followers around him; Baba Shaban (d. 1912) from Barmash in Kolonja; and Baba Rexheb (d. 1949) of Plevisht in the Korça region who increased the properties and constructed new buildings. Baba Rexheb headed the *tekke* for thirty-seven years, from 1912 to 1949.

The *tekke* was burned down in June 1914 by Sunni Muslim rebels supporting the central Albanian uprising of Haxhi Qamili (1876–1915) and its property was confiscated. Baba Rexheb returned to the *tekke* in 1920 and reconstructed it with a two-storey building and a *tyrbe* for its founder, Baba Ahmet Nazereci. Baba Rexheb is thus considered the second founder of the *tekke* of Dushk. He was followed in September 1951, after an interregnum, by the Baba Tahir Hyseni of Qesarat who had been *baba* at the *tekke* of Balim Sultan in Martanesh and was transferred to Tomorr in August 1959.

The relatively large *tekke* of Dushk survived until 1967, under Baba Pajo Hasa, when it was torn down by the surrounding villagers in the communist campaign against religion. The site was reconstructed in the 1996 and is tended to by a custodian.

We do know that the faithful were wont to gather here as pilgrims on the feast day of 30 July. The *tekke* of Dushk was subordinate to the *gjyshata* of Elbasan.
cf. F. W. Hasluck 1929, p. 438 (544); N. Clayer 1990, p. 266; Q. Dedej, *Fillimet* 1997, pp. 86–94.

Elbasan, District of Elbasan, Albania
Tekke of Ibrahim Xhefai Baba, *tekke* of Fakri Mustafai Baba, *tekke* of Krasta
Location: Krasta, to the east of Elbasan. 41°07' N, 20°06' E.

The *tekke* of Ibrahim Xhefai Baba, sometimes known as the *tekke* of Fakri Mustafai Baba, and more commonly simply as the 'big *tekke*' (*teqeja e madhe*), is located in Krasta, a few kilometres to the east of Elbasan near the road to Librazhd. It is said to have been founded in 1803 [1218 AH] by Fakri Mustafai (d. 1816),[156] no doubt under the aegis of Shemimi Baba of Fushë Kruja. Its first *baba* was the said Ibrahim Xhefai (d. 1829) after whom the *tekke* is usually named. The *tekke* was no doubt closed down with the banning of the Bektashi Order under Sultan Mahmud II in July 1826. Local legend has it that when the population was duefully tearing the edifice down, a great storm arose, with beating rain and hail. Fearful that they were committing a sin, the workers abandoned their activities, ran away and got lost in the storm.[157]

From 1850 to 1861 [1277 AH], the *tekke* was administered by Baba Daut Agjahi who originally belonged to the Sinani sect. He was followed by Baba Mustafa Qefshi (d. 1868),[158] also called Mustafa Baltëza, of Fushë Kruja who headed the *tekke* from 1862 [1278 AH] to 1868 [1284 AH]. The administration of Baba Mustafa was interrupted by a Baba Hysen Duhanxhiu (d. 1863)[159] from Gjirokastra, with the two *babas* vying for power for some time. Baba Mustafa went on a pilgrimage to the *pir evi* in Hacıbektaşköy and was decreed a *halife*.

After two years of interregnum under Mulla Ali Dedej, Mustafa Qefshi was succeeded in 1870 by Haxhi Hazbi Hyseni[160] who bought new land for the *tekke* and planted groves of olive trees (later called the Groves of Baba Hazbi). He also had new buildings constructed and did much charity work. Baba Hazbi Hyseni died in 1874 [1291 AH] and was buried in the *tyrbe* of Baba Daut. He was followed by Baba Ali Dedej[161] (1836–1897), the son of Ibrahim Peqini, who was appointed by Baba Ali Haqi of Gjirokastra and administered the *tekke* for twenty-three years, from 1874 [1291 AH] to 1897 [1314 AH]. He was also known as Hylki Ali Baba.

The next *baba* was Salih Dedej[162] (1842–1914), the younger brother of his predecessor, who administered the *tekke* of Ibrahim Xhefai Baba from 1897 [1314 AH] to 1914 [1332 AH]. He was originally the imam of the Agaj Mosque in Elbasan but joined the Bektashi in 1863, becoming a *muhib* of Baba Mustafa Qefshi. Like Baba Mustafa, he went on a pilgrimage to the *pir evi* in Hacıbektaşköy and was decreed a *halife*.

The French travel writer Gabriel Louis-Jaray (1880–1964) visited the *tekke* in 1909 and left the following impressions:

> The Bektashi, for their part, have their dervishes who, in solemn ceremonies, make vows and swear not to marry. They devote themselves to prayer and religious ceremonies, and to their work in the fields. It is their duty to care for the tombs which, in this case, was that of a great saint. His sepulchre was enclosed by a hexagonal stone construction a few metres above all the other buildings. The monks took me out to see it. On one side of the building there was a low open doorway and on the other sides there were narrow windows. I was invited into the interior where there was not really enough light to see. It contained a wooden grave in the ground covered in part by a green cloth. At the foot of the grave there were some pieces of embroidered linen and at the head there was a wooden stake planted obliquely, around which a gauze veil had been wrapped. That was all. There was nothing on the whitewashed walls, no inscriptions, not a word. The silence of the dead.
>
> Leaving the *tekke*, I asked my guide if the monks came here to mediate. He responded simply: 'They don't need to because they live here.' It was difficult to pursue the conversation and I tried to imagine the state of mind of the dervishes who were accompanying me and to figure out how they differed from Western hermits. [...]
>
> There is no element of torment or struggle in the life of Muslim monks, and the *tekke* is a place of refuge where the spirit is at rest. The sacred tomb does not cast its shadow over the existence of others, and the dervishes around me did not seem to know about anything but the beauty of the site chosen for them at the whims of the founder of the *tekke*.
>
> The nearest dervish invited me over to sit down under the trees that looked out upon the valley where the shadows were growing longer. A table was set up and covered in grapes rinsed in fresh water and tiny cups of aromatic coffee. The heat of the day had receded and the veil of night was extending up the valley dominated by the *tekke*. One of my companions, seized no doubt by memories of days gone by, broke into song, a proud and sad-sounding melody that the others took up – an Albanian song about Scanderbeg. [...]

When the melancholic song was over, silence and tranquillity enveloped the *tekke* all the more. The wind died down and not a branch quivered. The acacia and laurel trees filled the air with their fragrance as the last rays of the sun turned the nearby vineyards to gold. Twilight is short-lived here and we had to get back to Elbasan before nightfall, but before leaving with my companions, I opened the door of the tomb and, as Albanian custom prescribes, left some alms – a few copper coins that I placed in a collection box on the wall, and several pieces of silver on the tomb itself.

The monks expressed their best wishes for a long and happy life for the 'Frank' who had come from overseas to visit his friends in Albania. For my part, I wished them a second Scanderbeg who would revive all the aspirations, sentiments and ideals I saw in them during the short time I spent at the Bektashi *tekke*.[163]

The *tekke* was burned down in June 1914 by Sunni Muslim rebels supporting the central Albanian uprising of Haxhi Qamili, and Baba Salih Dedej was taken into custody and died in prison in Durrës on 20 December of that year.[164]

The *tekke* of Ibrahim Xhefai was revived in 1916 by Baba Ahmet Dedej[165] (1863–1926) who had been imprisoned in Durres in 1914 with Baba Salih, but was later released and escaped to Vlora. Initially residing in a nearby barn, he administered the *tekke* in Elbasan from 1914 [1332 AH] to 1926 [1344 AH].

The French parliamentarian Justin Godart was at the *tekke* in 1921 and recorded his visit as follows:

The *tekke* of Elbasan is situated on a hillside at the end of the gorge of the Shkumbin River. To get there from Elbasan, one crosses a large plain studded with tombstones. The *tekke* was burned down by Essadist rebels and was not rebuilt. The ruins standing on a number of terraces are slowly being overgrown in wild vines and fig trees. A long staircase led up to the tombs of the *babas*, encircled as they were by lofty cypress trees, the dark green of which made the surrounding olive trees look all the paler. The *baba* and his servants had found quarters in one of the farm buildings, for this *tekke* has quite a bit of farmland at its disposal. The tombs of the faithful lie under the olive trees on the hillside and it is here that are buried the members of the family of Aqif Pasha Elbasani, one of the members of the High Regency Council.[166]

Margaret Hasluck visited the *tekke* about two years later and described it as follows:

The *tekke* half an hour east of Elbassan was destroyed by the Ghegs and is temporarily housed in what was formerly the granary of the *tekke,* but fruit trees, flowers, and running water combine to make the site a paradise. The founder was Mustafa Baba, who is buried here. Lately there has been an improvement in the relations of Sunnis and Bektashis in North Albania, even in Elbassan, where there are said to be now about five hundred Bektashi families. The reason is mainly the emphasis laid by the Bektashis on patriotism as a virtue.[167]

The British travel writer Paul Edmonds was accompanied to the *tekke* by the noted political figure and scholar Lef Nosi (1877–1946) at about the same period and recorded:

> Excursions farther afield were made possible by the kindness of the prefect of Elbasan, Mr. Izet Dibra, who placed a Ford car at my disposal. One such excursion took me to a Becktashi, or dervish, monastery, and another to a Greek monastery, both visits proving of considerable interest. At the first we (for Mr. Nossi was with me) were received by a dignified old priest who was wearing the same kind of flowing white robes and tall white hat as the dervish I had met at Koritza. While we sat in a vine-covered arbour outside the entrance, smoking cigarettes and drinking coffee, he told us how the monastery had been attacked during the revolution of 1914 by adherents of the Suni sect. The revolution was that in which Prince William of Wied, the regent, was deposed; and the Sunis are a sect of Mohammedans who hate their fellow religionists, the Becktashis, with a hatred only possible to religious fanatics. Under cover of the revolution they not only burned down the monastery chapel, but also arrested the old '*baba*' (priest) who was entertaining us, and kept him in prison until the return of Essad Pasha to power some six months later.[168]

In late 1926, the *tekke* came under the administration of Baba Mustafa Haqi[169] (1875–1950), who was appointed by Baba Ahmet Turani and came to hold the rank of a *gjysh*. He ran the *tekke* for twenty-four years and was said to be a man of great culture.

Baba Mustafa Haqi was succeeded in May 1950 by his cousin Qazim Dedej[170] (1891–1962) who became a dervish in 1944 and administered the *tekke* from 1950 to 1962. After the ephemeral administration of a Baba Ibrahim Kukës (January to September 1963), the last head of the *tekke* of Ibrahim Xhefai before the ban on religion in Albania was Baba Sherif Canometaj (1908–1994) who ran it from 1963 to 1967. It is presently under the administration of the aged Baba Faik Selmani, as is the nearby *tekke* of Baba Xhemali. He is assisted by a resident dervish.

Administratively, the *tekke* of Ibrahim Xhefai was one of the most important *tekkes* in Albania, serving as one of the six *gjyshatas* of the Bektashi community from 1930 to 1967.

cf. G. Louis-Jaray 1914, pp. 96–109; J. Godart 1922, pp. 163–165; P. Edmonds 1927, pp. 237–238; F. W. Hasluck 1929, p. 441 (548–549); Baba Rexheb 1970, pp. 291, 383; N. Clayer 1990, pp. 272–273; Q. Dedej, *Fillimet* 1997.

Elbasan, District of Elbasan, Albania
Tekke of Baba Ali Horasani, *tekke* of Baba Xhemali
Location: Elbasan, south of train tracks near the Nazaresha Mosque. 41°06' N, 20°05' E.

The *tekke* of Baba Ali Horasani was founded in 1929 by Baba Selman Xhemali, who administered it until his death in September 1949. Xhemali, who was born and raised in Istanbul where he had served at the Şehidlik *tekke* at Rumelihisarı, moved to Albania in early 1926 when the *tekkes* in Turkey were closed down under Atatürk.

The *tekke* of Baba Xhemali, as it is usually known, was built at the site of the *tyrbe* of Baba Ali Horasani in Elbasan (who is also said to be buried in Fushë Kruja) and was several years in the making. Other edifices were constructed on the site in the 1930s. Baba Selman bought much of the surrounding land to be used for orchards and was the author of philosophical and mystic verse in Turkish. The American scholar John Birge (1888–1952), who met him and described him as his honoured friend, left the following description:

> In the new *tekke* which Cemali Baba is building (Oct. 1933), there is a certain large square pillar, on each of the four sides of which is a doorway, symbolizing the Four Gateways. The symbolism will be true to the doctrine only if one encircles the pillar returning through the four doors to the Reality from which one came.[171]

Baba Selman Xhemali was succeeded in November 1949 by a Baba Ali Rizaj from Porodina in the Korça region. He had served in Osmënzeza and ran the *tekke* of Baba Xhemali until September 1953, when he was made *gjysh* of the *gjyshata* of Kruja. Among the subsequent *babas* was a Baba Sherif Canometaj (1908–1994) of Zhapokika in the Tepelena region who headed this *tekke* and the nearby *tekke* of Ibrahim Xhefai Baba until the ban on religion in 1967.

With the return of democracy a quarter of a century later, it was Baba Sherif who re-opened the *tekke* of Baba Xhemali on 14 June 1993 and headed it until his death in February 1994. He was succeeded by Baba Sadik Ibro (b. 1972) from Luz i Madh in the Kavaja region.

The *tekke* is now a relatively large complex situated south of the train tracks in Elbasan, and not far from the Naziresha Mosque. It is currently headed by Baba Faik Selmani.

cf. J. Birge 1937, p. 107; Baba Rexheb 1970, pp. 365–367; N. Clayer 1990, pp. 267–268; Q. Dedej, *Fillimet* 1997, pp. 110–120.

Elbasan, District of Elbasan, Albania
Tekke of Baba Hamit, *tekke* of Baba Ali Riza, *tekke* of the Well That Washes Itself (*teqeja e pusit që lahet vetë*)
Location: Elbasan. 41°07' N, 20°04' E.

The third *tekke* of Elbasan is far less known than the other two. It was founded around 1920 by Baba Hamit (d. 1921) of Dibra who had served in Istanbul and at the Harabati *tekke* in Tetova, where he had been in conflict with other figures over the *tekke*'s assets. He moved to Elbasan after the Balkans Wars. In May 1920, he wrote to Baba Ahmet Dedej of the *tekke* of Ibrahim Xhefai Baba to seek permission to settle in the ruins of the *tekke* of Sheh Hysen Dylgjeri in the quarter of town of the same name. In the ruins he built a new *tekke* later to be known as the *tekke* of Baba Hamit, where he was buried. This *tekke* was situated near the 'Well That Washes Itself' (*Pusi që lahet vetë*). This well, constructed in 1467 to provide water for a new mosque, had healing powers and people came from far and wide to drink here. It is said that it overflowed in the night every New Moon. Thus the curious name.

Baba Hamit's successor was Ali Riza (1876-1944) of Kruja who had travelled to the holy sites in the Middle East before returning to Albania and had been a dervish in Martanesh. He was appointed as the *baba* of this *tekke* by Baba Ahmet Turani and administered it from November 1921 to December 1941.

At the death of Salih Nijazi Dede in November 1941, none of the *babas* in Albania wanted to replace him as *gjysh* in Tirana. Baba Ali Riza hesitantly accepted the position because he had been a friend of Salih Nijazi. He thus became *kryegjysh* or *dede baba* of the Bektashi Community from 1941 to his death in 1944. In actual fact, Ali Riza never really took up his new position in Tirana as he felt (or was considered) unqualified. He remained primarily at his post in Elbasan and was replaced in Tirana by Baba Kamber Ali (1869-1950).

Baba Ali Riza was succeeded at the *tekke* by a Baba Rystem Llacja of Gjirokastra who administered the *tekke* from June 1944 to March 1945. He had once been defrocked by Baba Selim Ruhi of the *tekke* of Asim Baba in Gjirokastra, and then served as a dervish in Elbasan. He functioned briefly as the *baba* of the *tekke* of Baba Hamit before being made the *gjysh* of the *gjyshata* of Korça in 1945. He was followed by a Baba Muharrem Mahmutaj of Lazarat near Gjirokastra who served until 1961. Further successors were Baba Adem Mahmutaj from 1961 to 1963 and a Baba Hajro from 1963.

cf. N. Clayer 1990, p. 269; Q. Dedej, *Fillimet* 1997, pp. 103-109.

Frashër, District of Përmet, Albania
Tekke of Baba Tahir Nasibi
Location: In the Dangëllia mountains between Këlcyra and Erseka. 40°21' N, 20°25' E.

The *tekke* in Frashër is named after the holy man and mystic poet Baba Tahir Nasibi of Frashër. He spent some time in the Middle East visiting the holy sites and founded the *tekke* upon his return in 1825. In 1835 after his death, a *tyrbe* was constructed in his honour which became an important pilgrimage site.

This large and well-endowed *tekke* played an important role in the Albanian nationalist movement of the late nineteenth century. Indeed, it was one of the richest and most celebrated *tekkes* in Albania, even though it was located in the 'back country' at a substantial distance from the main roads.

It was here in 1879, in the presence of Baba Alush (c. 1816-1896) and of Baba Adem of Melçan, that the nationalist leader Abdyl bey Frashëri (1839-1892) organized an important meeting of southern Albanian leaders to promote nationalist objectives at the time of the League of Prizren. The *tekke* later served as a centre for the illicit distribution of Albanian books and for spreading nationalist sentiment, in particular under Baba Alush. He was followed by a Baba Hysejn and a Baba Zejnel Abedin from Backa in the Skrapar region. Baba Zejnel Abedin (d. 1913) gave refuge to the ailing Albanian poet, nationalist figure and guerrilla fighter Mihal Grameno and, during a raid by Turkish forces, dressed him and his fighters up as novices of the dervish order to hide them (see Trix, July–October, 1995). Grameno praised the *tekke* in 1907 and added a poem:

> Frashër was a sacred site for Albania because it was from Frashër that the emissaries and preachers of the Albanian language set out to illuminate their people. Frashër will therefore forever remain a holy place for Albania. When we got up into the Kolonja mountains, above Frashër, I dedicated this verse to it.
>
> *Si ty o Vithlehem e Mek'e Arabisë*
> *Ku janë lindur Muhamet e Krisht i Krishtërisë,*
> *Për mua ësht Frashër, vënt i Perëndisë,*
> *Tek është lindur Naim Beu, zemr'e Shqipërisë.*
>
> 'For you, oh Bethlehem and Arabia's Mecca
> Where Muhammed and the Christ of the Christians were born,
> For me is it Frashër, the home of the Lord,
> Where Naim Bey, the heart of Albania, was born.[172]

Of his stay at the *tekke*, Grameno also noted:

> From Kurtes, we returned to Frashër and camped out above the *tekke* where Servet bey and Hysen bey, the dervishes, Hasan Effendi who was the hodja of Frashër, and many other nationalists came around. This was a veritable nest of patriots because there was the *tekke* there, the great school of the nation![173]

> We then returned to the *tekke* of Frashër. When we entered the building, we were amazed at the tranquillity, cleanliness and orderliness that reigned there. You would have thought you were in another world with all the dervishes and their incomparable organisation. Each of the dervishes had his own chores and no one infringed upon the orderliness, obligations and discipline.
>
> His Holiness, Baba Abedin, can rightly be called holy for he possesses the loftiest of virtues. He sacrifices himself to assist the poor and needy and to heal their wounds. With the benevolence and wisdom given to him by the Almighty, he has won over all of the people, both Muslims and Christians, such that they grow up in a spirit of humility and honour, and obey only the words of Baba Abedin.
>
> It must also be noted that the 15–16 dervishes who surround His Holiness, Baba Abedin, are just as he is. They are sage, well-educated and make ardent patriots. They are making invaluable contributions to the national movement with their endeavours as emissaries, wandering from village to village to spread national sentiment. I am greatly frustrated that I did not record the names of all the dervishes and ask for their forgiveness. The only names I can remember are Meço, Mustafa, Sheme and Murat.[174]

Before the First World War, the *tekke* had about twenty dervishes. In June 1914, however, both the *tekke* and the *tyrbe* of Tahir Baba were burned down by

Greek forces, but they were rebuilt around 1923 with the assistance of Albanians in America.

The *tekke* of Frashër was represented by Baba Mustafa at the First National Congress of the Bektashi, held at the *tekke* of Prishta in the Skrapar region on 14–17 January 1921. Margaret Hasluck, who visited it around 1923, described it as a pleasant *tekke* amid fantastic scenery.

Under the reforms of 1930, Frashër was made a *gjyshata*, one of the six new Bektashi administrative districts in Albania, initially under Gjysh Mustafa Qerezi (r. 1930–1933) and then under Gjysh Murat (r. 1934–1941). In 1945, Baba Mehmet Zykaj was arrested and imprisoned for fifteen years. He died in 1959. The *tekke* of Frashër became the seat of the prefecture of Vlora and the sub-prefecture of Berat, but it lost its *gjyshata* status around 1950. This *tekke* is referred to on the map made in Albania for the German scholar Franz Babinger in 1962, so it must still have been active in some form at that time. It was not razed to the ground in 1967 during the communist campaign against religion because it was associated with Abdyl bey Frashëri and his patriotic deeds at the time of the League of Prizren. The *tekke* was restored in 1995. Its feast day is 5 September.

cf. A. Tomorri 1929, p. 85, 89; F. W. Hasluck 1914–1916, p. 118, 1929, p. 440 (547–548); S. Skëndi 1967, pp. 41–42; Baba Rexheb 1970, pp. 300, 358, 383; O. Daniel 1985, pp. 21–34; N. Clayer 1990, pp. 275–278, 2003, pp. 106, 117–118; F. Trix, *The Resurfacing* 1995, p. 547; A. and N. Frashëri 2014.

Fratar, District of Mallakastra, Albania
Dervishia of Fratar
Location: About 20 km southeast of Ballsh on the old road to Tepelena. 40°31' N, 19°48' E.

This *dervishia*, possibly an earlier *tekke*, is said to have been founded around 1912. It is referred to on the map made in Albania for the German scholar Franz Babinger in 1962, so it must still have been active in some form at that time.
cf. N. Clayer 1990, p. 279.

Fushë Kruja, District of Kruja, Albania
Tekke of Shemimi Baba
Location: A few kilometres north of Fushë Kruja on the old road to Lezha. 41°29' N, 19°43' E.

The *tekke* of Shemimi Baba, also known simply as the *tekke* of Fushë Kruja, was established outside the town at the site of the *tyrbe* of Ali Baba Horasani, who died in 1562. Its foundation in 1799 is linked to Shemimi Baba, who was murdered soon thereafter, in 1803. With the death of Shemimi Baba, the *tekke* was abandoned, but several decades later there were *babas* living there in a wooden shack.

In 1852–1853 [1270 AH], Baba Hysen Kukeli of Dibra reconstructed the *tekke* and headed it for forty years, i.e. until about 1893 [1310 AH]. It was in the second half of the nineteenth century that the *tekke* grew in reputation and prosperity, in particular because of its well-administered lands. It was to become one of the fundamental centres of the Bektashi movement in Albania. Baba Hysen's successor was Baba Haxhi, who was born in Kruja.

The Austrian scholar and diplomat Theodor Ippen (1861–1935) visited the *tekke* in the early years of the twentieth century and described it as follows:

> The monastery of Tekke Fushë Kruja is situated not far from the postal road at the bottom of the hills, on the part of the plain belonging to Kruja, i.e. Fushë Kruja. Surrounded by lush green meadows, it offers an attractive though simple view. One would not guess what is to be found here, even when seeing the minaret. One has the impression of approaching the manor of some wealthy landowning family. The monastery consists of a complex of simple, unadorned buildings with irregular, badly whitewashed facades and numerous windows of various sizes. The interior also resembles a house. We were invited up a wobbly wooden staircase to a reception room simply furnished with carpets and divans. On the walls were pictures with religious sayings in calligraphy, but also with human figures. [...]
>
> After being offered refreshments, we were invited to have a look at the sacred parts of the monastery. Behind the buildings, on a meadow of blooming flowers, there was a very tall and picturesque cypress tree in the tall grass and two whitewashed mausoleums – that of the founder of the monastery, Baba Ali, and that of Baba Hussein who died in 1890. The latter is also venerated as a holy man. Even during his lifetime, his authority was far superior to that of the head of the *tekke* of Fushë Kruja, a highly respected man himself. All of the surrounding region beckoned to his call. Most of the room in the chapels is taken up by the sarcophaguses, five-sided in form, resting on the tiled floors. They are draped in cloth of silk and velvet, in which sayings and prayers have been embroidered and woven. Miracles can occur by touching the coffins. There is an alms box in every room. The dervishes who were with us told us that the huge cypress tree outside grew out of the boards with which Baba Ali had once made himself a cottage in the meadow. The legend arose as such from the particular shape of the branches of the tree. It is a Mediterranean cypress (*Cupressus horizontalis*). They are very large and so flat that they resemble boards and planks.[175]

The *tekke* of Shemimi Baba was destroyed in the summer of 1914 by Sunni Muslim peasants supporting the central Albanian uprising of Haxhi Qamili. The English historian Frederick Hasluck (1878–1920) describes it from his visit at the time (1913–1915):

> At the *tekke* in the plain ('Fusha Kruyes') the chief buried saint is Baba Ali, who is said to date from 150–200 years back and to be older than Sheikh Mimi. An abbot and three dervishes are living there, but the *tekke* was burnt by the Ghegs and is as yet only half rebuilt. In the precinct are two remarkable trees, one with flat, plank-like branches being said to have sprung from a plank stuck in the ground by Baba Ali of Khorasan, who was a contemporary of Skanderbeg.[176]

It was only about 1927 that the *tekke* was rebuilt by the dervishes living there. At this point it was under the direction of Baba Mehmet Çeno (1882–1934) who lived there with three or four dervishes. After 1934, the *tekke* was administered by Baba Ali Myrteza (1912–1947) who, when the communists took power, was tortured and committed suicide in 1947.

John Birge visited the *tekke* in October 1933, and noted 'In front of the *Zaviye* of Mürteza Baba there was a tombstone bearing the Bektashi *tac* on the top and dated 1141 (1728).'[177]

From the time of the reorganization of the Bektashi community in 1930 to 1967, the *tekke* of Fushë Kruja functioned as one of the six administrative *gjyshatas* in the country and was responsible for all the north of Albania – Shkodra, Durrës and after 1950 even Peshkopia. It had numerous dependencies, including Gjorm, Martanesh and Zërqan.

The famed *tekke* of Fushë Kruja was closed down and partly destroyed in 1967 in the communist campaign against religion. From that time, until the end of the 1980s it functioned as an agricultural co-operative. In 1989, there was still a large Ottoman inscription on one of the walls bearing silent witness to the past. It has since disappeared.

What has remained of the past at this evocative site is a large, old and (for Albania) rather ornate twelve-sided *tyrbe* with the grave of Ali Baba Horasani, and a huge old cypress tree. There are three other *tyrbes* among the olive trees on the property, one of which contains the grave of Shemimi Baba. A nice and very green two-storey *tekke* has been reconstructed and is now under the direction of Baba Halil Curri.

cf. T. Ippen 1907, pp. 77–79; F. W. Hasluck 1914–1916, pp. 121–122, 1929, p. 442 (549–551); R. Busch-Zantner 1934; J. Birge 1937, p. 71; Baba Rexheb 1970, pp. 248–252; N. Clayer 1990, pp. 325–332, 355.

Gjirokastra, District of Gjirokastra, Albania
Tekke of Asim Baba, known commonly as the Gravel *Tekke* (*Teqeja e Zallit*). Location: Gjirokastra, south of the town on the road to Greece. 40°03' N, 20°09' E.

The *tekke* of Asim Baba was founded by Seyyid Muhammed Asim Baba of Üsküdar (Istanbul) in 1780. It is also known as the Gravel *Tekke* (*Teqeja e Zallit*), or, more poetically, the *Tekke* of Pebbles because it is located at the side of a usually dry river bed. Asim Baba administered it for sixteen years until his death in 1796. He was succeeded by: Hasan Baba Turku from 1796 to 1798, Sulejman Baba of Gjirokastra from 1798 to 1806, Ali Baba Gega from 1806 to 1830, Haxhi Jahja Baba of Kruja from 1830 to 1836, Ibrahim Baba Turku from 1836 to 1846, Hysejn Baba Elbasani from 1845 to 1861, Ali Haqi Baba of Elbasan from 1861 to 1907 and Selim Ruhi Baba of Elbasan from 1907 to 1944. As many of the *babas* here were well-educated figures, the *tekke* grew in reputation and culture. It had a large library of books and manuscripts in Arabic, Persian and Turkish and later of books in Albanian. Greek forces were quartered in the *tekke* for three years during the Balkan Wars and the First World War, during which time the *baba* and dervishes fled. They were later able to return and the *tekke* was restored in 1916. Margaret Hasluck, who seems to have visited the *tekke* around 1923, noted:

Asim Baba's *tekke* on the other side of Argyrokastro was founded 'two hundred years' ago and is reckoned one of the oldest in Albania. The founder and his successor are buried on either side of the gateway so that they may pray for all who enter. There are now seven dervishes with the learned Selim Baba as abbot. The Rule of the *tekke* is unusually strict: no spirits are allowed and dervishes are forbidden to quit the *tekke* grounds. In addition, they wear a four-ridged *taj* outside the ordinary twelve-ridged Bektashi hat in souvenir of the disaster of 1826, when only by adopting some such disguise could Bektashi dervishes escape destruction.[178]

Dutch scholar Machiel Kiel (b. 1938) remarked after his visit to the *tekke* in 1983:

The buildings we see today are certainly 18th century and deserve closer examination. The *tekke* is built in a fortress-like manner around a closed courtyard and with a thick wall all around. The most remarkable feature of this building is the entrance, which is flanked on either side by a domed *türbes*. These *türbes* follow the usual plan and method of construction of Albanian-Epirot architectural work, with polygonal walls of broken or little worked stone, somewhat clumsy proportions and a dome calotte masked by a slated roof. The other parts of the *tekke* show the style of an Epirot manor house. After the Cultural Revolution in 1967 the *tekke* served as a home for mentally handicapped people.[179]

cf. F. W. Hasluck 1929, p. 435 (541); Baba Rexhebi 1970 pp. 289–291; H. Kaleshi 980, pp. 10–11; N. Clayer 1990, pp. 280–290; M. Kiel 1990, p. 143; Sh. Hysi 2004.

Gjirokastra, District of Gjirokastra, Albania
Hajdërije *tekke, tekke* of Shtuf, also known as the *tekke* of Baba Sulejman. Location: On a hill in the valley outside of Gjirokastra. 40°05' N, 20°08' E.

This *tekke* was founded in the mid-nineteenth century by a certain Baba Hajdër (or Hajdar), also known as Baba Hajdër Plaku (the Elder), and named after him, i.e. the Hajdërije *tekke*. Margaret Hasluck notes that it was delightfully situated on a small isolated eminence near the town, and that the earliest of the four *tyrbes* containing the graves of deceased *babas* there were dated from 1862 to 1863. This may provide an approximate indication of the date of foundation of the *tekke*. It was traditionally an important *tekke*, but second in rank to the *tekke* of Asim Baba (i.e. the Gravel *Tekke*) to the south of Gjirokastra.

Other *babas* associated with this *tekke*, following Baba Hajdër Plaku, were Baba Selim the Elder of Elbasan and Baba Hajdër of Kardhiq (d. 1904) who both 'took the hand' of Ali Haqi Baba of the *tekke* of Asim Baba in Gjirokastra in the late nineteenth century. Baba Hajdër of Kardhiq was active in the nationalist movement after the League of Prizren in 1878 and was imprisoned in Janina for several years for his activities. He was succeeded in 1904 by Baba Sulejman (d. 1934), known for short as Baba Manes, who was to be persecuted, too. At that time, i.e. in the last decade of Ottoman rule, the *tekke* was denounced as a refuge of Albanian-language books and as a centre of Albanian-language teaching. It was surrounded by troops, and Baba Sulejman and his dervishes, including Mehmet Çeno (1882–1934), later to become *baba* of the *tekke* of Fushë Kruja, were arrested and sent to prison in Janina. In the years before the Balkan Wars, the *tekke*, which was surrounded by high walls and tall cypress trees, was home to some twenty dervishes.

After the Young Turk Revolution, the new authorities in Istanbul sent a Turkish dervish to the Hajdërije *tekke* to promote use of the Arabic alphabet instead of the Latin alphabet that was favoured by most Albanian nationalists. The unpopular newcomer, whose activities at the *tekke* were deemed unacceptable by the other dervishes, was soon sent packing:

> As they knew that virtually the whole population of Gjirokastra was Bektashi, they sent a dervish there to make propaganda for the Arabic alphabet. At that time, many Bektashi people gathered at the *tekke* and spent the night there discussing various issues. The Turkish dervish arrived, was given accommodation at the *tekke* of Baba Manes and began his work. No one paid much attention to him. However, the others soon began to make fun of this dervish missionary and did everything they could to get this Satan to depart as soon as possible.
>
> Veisel Efendi Bejkua, a sage judge who was held in great esteem by the whole population, called for a gathering of notables in the town. The meeting took place in a large hall at the *Liria* (Liberty) School and was chaired by Veisel Efendi himself. He began by saying: 'Is there anyone among us who thinks that the Latin letters with which we write our language are contrary to the Muslim faith?' All responded unanimously: 'No!' Veisel Efendi then called me over as secretary of the club to draft a resolution in the spirit of the assembly. I drafted the resolution in a large register and everyone signed it. The Turkish dervish received the news at the *tekke* and fled the next day, leaving Gjirokastra in shame.[180]

In 1914, the *tekke* was looted and burned down by Greek forces. In the 1920s there were only about a dozen dervishes left, among whom were seven adepts, but the *tekke* held its own.

The French parliamentarian Justin Godart paid a visit to the Hajdërije *tekke* in 1921 and left the following description:

> The *tekke* of Gjirokastra was built not far from the town on a hill which it crowns with its walls, its tombs and its lofty dark cypress trees. We trudged up the terrible trail in the rain and were received under a canopy at the top of the steps by the dervishes in their white robes. Silently they led us in to see the *baba* [...]. Baba Sulejman and his dervishes accompanied us down to the bottom of the hill. Dressed in white, they took us through the dark cypress trees to the tombs of former *babas*, on which lamps had already been lit for the night. The oldest of the dervishes, in a gesture of kind affection, handed us a little bouquet of wild geraniums and rock flowers with their simple country fragrance. We were quite

moved as we departed, leaving these sage men behind us. They stood and watch us for a long time before they turned and went back to their tranquil asylum.[181]

In the period 1921-1924, the entire Bektashi community in Albania was administered by a council of seven *babas* presided over by Baba Sulejman.[182] In July 1924, under his aegis and that of Baba Ahmet of Turan, the Hajdërije *tekke* played host to the Second National Congress of the Bektashi Order in Albania. Bektashi *babas* gathered there from throughout the country and agreed on new statutes for the Albanian Bektashi community that had parted ways with the majority Sunni Muslim community the year before. They also agreed in Gjirokastra on an advisory board of elected *babas*.

After the Second World War, the communist authorities transformed the *tekke* into a hospital. The head of the *tekke* at the time, Baba Ibrahim, was transferred to head the nearby *tekke* of Asim Baba, following the execution of Baba Ali Tomorri in 1947. It ceased to function around 1952.

Machiel Kiel remarked after his visit to the *tekke* in the communist period:

When we visited it, in 1983, it was still largely preserved, including the four *türbes*. These *türbes* are plain structures built of broken stone on a hexagonal plan. They have small Ottoman inscriptions mentioning the year of the construction, all from the second half of the 19th century. Because of their modern function (they were being used as munition stores for the army), no detailed study was possible.[183]

After the dictatorship, the Hajdërije *tekke* and surrounding land was inhabited by Roma families for several years. The property was eventually returned to the Bektashi community and the current *tekke* is headed by Baba Skender Dervishi. cf. J. Godart 1922, pp. 163-165; F. W. Hasluck 1929, p. 435 (541); Baba Rexheb 1980, p. 384; N. Clayer 1990, pp. 291-294; M. Kiel 1990, pp. 143-144.

Gjirokastra, District of Gjirokastra, Albania
Tekke of Baba Zejnel, *tekke* of Zejnel Abedin Baba
Location: In the town of Gjirokastra 40°04' N, 20°08' E.

The *tekke* of Zejnel Abedin Baba, or *tekke* of Baba Zejnel, was the third *tekke* in Gjirokastra, after the *tekke* of Asim Baba and the Hajdërije *tekke*. It was situated on a hill between the town and the Hajdërije *tekke*, just above a cheese warehouse. There is now a nettle tree on the site, on the right side of the cobblestone road from Fusha e Vjetër to the polyclinic. The *tekke* of Baba Zejnel was founded in the last quarter of the nineteenth century when Baba Zejnel Abedin Gjoksi from the *tekke* of Frashër, who was staying in Gjirokastra at the *tekke* of Asim Baba, did not get along with the other dervishes. He therefore asked Ali Haqi Baba to find him a place where he could live on his own. Baba Zejnel received ten medjidijes in payment and settled at what would become the *tekke* of Zejnel Abedin. He did not conduct religious ceremonies at his small *tekke* as there was sufficient ceremony at the other two.

Baba Zejnel Abedin was active in the nationalist movement and was interned in Janina by the Ottoman authorities at the same time as the *babas* of the other two *tekkes* in Gjirokastra. The *tekke* was damaged during the Balkan Wars and was abandoned in 1953.
cf. F. W. Hasluck 1929, p. 435 (541); Baba Rexheb 1970, p. 300; N. Clayer 1990, pp. 295–296; Sh. Hysi 2004, pp. 104–105.

Gjonëm/Gjorm, District of Kurbin, Albania
Tekke of Hajdar Baba
Location: To the south of Laç, on a hill east of the old Laç-Mamurras road. 41°36' N, 19°43' E.

The *tekke* of Hajdar Baba, which Hasluck described as a 'big *tekke*', was founded around 1793 by Hajdar Hatemi Baba, a companion of Shemimi Baba of Fushë-Kruja. From 1930 onwards, it was subordinate to the *gjyshata* of Fushë-Kruja. The small settlement is called Gjonëm or Gjorm, and is not to be confused with the *tekke* of Gjorm in the district of Vlora. This *tekke* survived until 1967 when it was torn down by the local villagers in the communist campaign against religion. All that survived were one of the cypress trees (the largest one), some grating and a few handcarved stone inscriptions in the rubble. Two white rectangular and domed *tyrbes* in green trim were reconstructed on the site in the 1990s. One contains the grave of Hajdar Baba and another person said to be his brother. The second *tyrbe*, open and visible through the preserved grating, is newer. Sir Robert Graves (1858–1934), who was British Consul General for Macedonia in Salonica, paid a brief visit to the *tekke* in 1912 and noted:

> It would be hard to exaggerate the beauty of the country through which we rode next morning, a land of mountain, oak forest and crystal streams, halting at noon at Derven, where in the garden of the Bektashi Dervishes's *Tekké* we were shown a cedar tree the trunk of which five of us could barely span. There we were met by Essad's carriage, in which I drove with him and Hadji Adil to Tirana.[184]

The faithful gathered here as pilgrims on the feast day of 20 September.
cf. F. W. Hasluck 1929, p. 442 (551); Baba Rexheb 1970, p. 248; N. Clayer 1990, p. 298.

Gjorm, District of Vlora, Albania
Tekke of Gjorm
Location: On the left (west) bank of the Shushica River, about 16 km south of Drashovica. 40°18' N, 19°38' E.

This *tekke*, which is not to be confused with the one in Gjonëm/Gjorm in the district of Kurbin, was the residence of many *babas* over the years. It survived until 1967 when it was torn down by the local villagers in the communist campaign against religion.
cf. N. Clayer 1990, p. 299.

Gllava, District of Tepelena, Albania
Tekke of Ismail Baba
Location: On the mountain road between Këlcyra and Berat, about 35 km north of Këlcyra. 40°28' N, 19°58' E.

The *tekke* of Gllava or of Qafë Gllava (Gllava Pass) was founded in the 1880s, possibly 1883, by Ismail or Smail Baba who had 'taken the hand' of Ali Haqi Baba of the *tekke* of Asim Baba in Gjirokastra. It was not far from the *tekke* of Rabija and other Bektashi convents, but it possessed little land and was relatively poor. In 1912, it was administered by a Baba Myheddin or Medin who had his own *çeta* (band) of fighters. According to Baba Ali Tomorri, the *tekke* was attacked by Sunni extremists in 1914 during the central Albanian uprising of Haxhi Qamili. His men had destroyed virtually all the Bektashi *tekkes* down to Berat, but after fierce fighting they were eventually thrown back at Gllava. 'Baba Myheddin of Gllava, the deputy of the venerable Baba Ismail, put up heroic resistance with the men of the immortal Tafil Buza, before his *tekke* was burned down by the rebels. To escape from their merciless hands, he sought refuge in Bari, in Italy.'[185] In the Second World War, the reconstructed *tekke* of Gllava was administered by a Baba Qamil who was appointed in 1937 by the *kryegjysh* Salih Nijazi Dede. Sir Robert Graves (1858–1934), who was British Consul General for Macedonia in Salonica, spent a night there in 1912. The *tekke* of Gllava was represented by a Baba Murat at the First National Congress of the Bektashi, held at the *tekke* of Prishta in the Skrapar region on 14–17 January 1921. In the Second World War, the *tekke* was administered by Baba Qamil Gllava who took part in the resistance, and who was executed by the communists in Gjirokastra in 1946. There is also mention of a Baba Mehdi Gllava who died in Gjirokastra in December 1945, Baba Abedin Gllava in 1956 and Baba Qamil Kapllani of Vërzhezha until 1967. The *tekke* of Gllava survived until 1967 when it was torn down by the local villagers in the communist campaign against religion. A *tyrbe* was reconstructed there after the fall of the dictatorship. The feast day of this *tekke* is 30 April.
cf. F. W. Hasluck 1929, p. 437 (544); R. Graves 1933, p. 269; P. Pepo 1962, p. 463; N. Clayer 1990, pp. 300–301.

Golimbas, District of Vlora, Albania
Tekke of Haxhi Baba Mehmet Aliu
Location: Near Sevaster and Ploça on the old road from Vlora to Tepelena. 40°23' N, 19°44' E.

There is little concrete information about the early history of the *tekke* of Golimbas. It may date from the nineteenth century and was founded no doubt by the said Baba Mehmet Aliu. Mention is made subsequently of a Baba Zenel, Baba Sali Matohasani who was active there in the first decade of the twentieth century, Baba Bektashi and a Baba Bektash Aliaj around 1939. The *tekke* survived until 1967 when it was torn down by the local villagers in the communist campaign against religion. A *tyrbe* was reconstructed on the site after the fall of the dictatorship.
cf. N. Clayer 1990, p. 302.

Gorisht, District of Vlora, Albania
Tekke of Gorisht
Location: In the Selenica region about 15 km east of Vlora, near Kocul and Vllahina. 40°28' N, 19°39' E.

The *tekke* of Gorisht survived until 1967 when it was torn down by the local villagers in the communist campaign against religion. A *tyrbe* was reconstructed on the site in 1999.
cf. N. Clayer 1990, p. 303.

Greshica, District of Mallakastra, Albania
Tekke of Baba Husejn
Location: About 8 km southeast of Ballsh. 40°33' N, 19°46' E.

The *tekke* of Greshica was founded around 1860 by a certain Baba Husejn or Hysen. Little else is known of its activities. It was burned down in the Second World War, but seems to have been rebuilt.[186] The *tekke* of Greshica survived until 1967 when it was torn down by the local villagers in the communist campaign against religion. A twelve-sided *tyrbe* and adjacent *tekke* building have since then been reconstructed on the hilltop. The *tyrbe* contains the graves of Baba Hysejn, Baba Dino, Baba Sulo and Baba Fetah. The feast day of this *tekke* is 5 March.
cf. F. W. Hasluck 1929, p. 436 (543); N. Clayer 1990, p. 305.

Gumen, District of Përmet, Albania
Tekke of Baba Husejn
Location: Near Panarit and Këlcyra.

This small *tekke* was founded around 1908 by Baba Husejn. It was subordinate to the *tekke* of Prishta. The *tekke* of Gumen survived until 1967 when it was torn down by the local villagers in the communist campaign against religion. The little *tyrbe* or *dervishia* has been reconstructed at the site.
cf. F. W. Hasluck 1929, p. 437 (544); N. Clayer 1990, p. 306.

Hekal, District of Mallakastra, Albania
Tekke of Hekal
Location: About 6 km south of Ballsh. 40°33' N, 19°44' E.

The Austrian historian and archaeologist Carl Patsch (1865–1945) visited the region in May 1900 and came across a Bektashi cemetery, which he photographed, noting:

> On our archaeological investigation of the area, we came across a Muslim cemetery below Gradishta which was remarkable because of its orderly condition. On a free and open space surrounded by dry wall reinforced by thornbushes woven into it were the graves of three holy men of the very liberal Bektashi sect to which all the people in the Mallakastra region, including my host, belonged. The Hermes-like gravestones showed the heads of the deceased wearing turbans. One could see bits of arms and an iron earring through an ear. Around the gravestones were candles and lanterns in wooden boxes that had been lit in memory of the dead.[187]

On his visit through the region in 1914, F. W. Hasluck noted a *tyrbe* in Hekal, but no *tekke*. However, there was later a *tekke* here that survived here until 1967 when it was torn down by the local villagers in the communist campaign against religion. The *tekke* and *tyrbe* were reconstructed after the dictatorship and are presently cared for by a local custodian.
cf. C. Patsch 1904, pp. 117–118; F. W. Hasluck 1929, p. 436 (543); N. Clayer 1990, p. 307.

Kanina, District of Vlora, Albania
Tekke of Sinan Pasha, *tekke* of Kanina. 40°26' N, 19°31' E.
Location: (1) Outside the eastern wall of the fortress of Kanina; (2) in the village of Kanina, south of the fortress.

The original *tekke* of Kanina, called the *tekke* of Sinan Pasha, would seem to be one of the oldest Bektashi foundations in Albania. It was situated just outside the walls, on the eastern side of the fortress of Kanina, a mountain village some 7 kilometres southeast of Vlora. The fortress commands an excellent view of Vlora and the Ionian Sea and was of notable significance in the Ottoman period.

On his journey through southern Albania in November 1670, the Turkish traveller and writer Evliya Çelebi visited the fortress and noted:

> There is also a *tekke* of Hadji Bektash Veli here, which was also endowed by Sinan Pasha. This *tekke* is famous throughout Turkey, Arabia and Persia. Here one finds many devotees of the mystical sciences and the dervish life of poverty. Among them are lovely young boys. Visitors and pilgrims are fed copious meals from the kitchen and pantry of the *tekke* because all the surrounding mountains, vineyards and gardens belong to it. Near the *tekke*, the benefactor of the endowment, Ghazi Sinan Pasha, lies buried along with all his household and retainers in a mausoleum with a lofty dome – may God have mercy on their souls. In short, it is a rich and famous *tekke*, beyond my powers to describe.[188]

During or after the closing of all the Bektashi *tekkes* and the banning of the Bektashi Order under Sultan Mahmud II in July 1826, the *tekke* of Kanina seems to have been handed over to the dervishes of the Halveti Order. It was still an object of veneration during the visit of the German scholar Johann Georg von Hahn (1811–1869), in 1850, who reported:

> The fortress is now in ruins, but only seems to have been abandoned recently by its owners who spend the hot summer season here. These are the descendants of the first Turkish conqueror of the region, the famed Sinan Pasha of Konya, whose grave can be seen in a small *tekke* situated at the foot of the fortress. People come here from far and wide on pilgrimages because Sinan is considered holy by the Turks.[189]

The shrine was subsequently returned to the Bektashi, probably in the second half of the nineteenth century, although it does not seem to have functioned as a *tekke* for very long. In the early years of the twentieth century, it stood abandoned and we have little information about it after this time. The Albanian writer Ekrem bey Vlora (1885–1964) visited the site in 1908 and noted:

> It is curious that the two graves [in Berat] are simple mounds of earth without any enclosure or tombstone. The graves in the *tekke* of Sinan Pasha, the ancestral father of the Vlora family, in Kanina, look quite the same. In both places, the graves appear to have been desecrated either by thieves who have broken in to them or by the guardians of the *tekke* in hope of finding rich treasures.[190]

Machiel Kiel paid a visit to the site, probably in 1983. Although there was nothing much to be seen at that time, he paid tribute to its one-time grandeur:

> Gazi Sinan Pasha had also founded a very magnificent *tekke* for the Bektashi Order, which was the abode of a most pious sheikh and many faithful dervishes. It had a very hospitable 'Kitchen of Keyvakus'. The *vakf* of this *tekke* was very rich, and included all the garden land and orchards in the surroundings. Gazi Sinan Pasha was buried in a lofty *türbe* in this *tekke*, together with all his relative and servants.[191]

In April 2000, a decade after the end of the communist dictatorship, all that remained of the original *tekke* was a boulder covered in white candle wax.

Legend has it that this *tekke* was tended by two Bektashi missionaries, Baba Xhevher and Baba Ali Horasani, from Persia. These two men, who had trained in Anatolia, settled initially at the Harabati *tekke* in Tetova and moved then to the *tekke* of Kuzum Baba in Vlora. From there, they arrived in Kanina. Baba Xhevher died in the mid-sixteenth century and was followed by Baba Ali Horasani.

In addition to the now-enclosed site of the original *tekke* just under the walls of the fortress, a round shrine is currently being constructed farther down the hill, near the cemetery, in honour of Baba Xhevher and Baba Ali Horasani.

There is, however, a second *tekke* emplacement in Kanina. This *tekke* is situated on a square in the middle of the village of Kanina, to the south of the fortress. The site comprises two old buildings: a two-storey, currently roofless *tekke* building of old stone with vaulted windows and doorways, now mostly walled in; and a large, square *tyrbe* superimposed by an octagonal dome. There is a magnificent view of the Gulf of Vlora and the Island of Sazan to be had from the garden. It is here, in the garden of the *tekke*, that the father of Albanian independence, Ismail Qemal bey Vlora (1844–1919), was initially buried in early 1919,[192] although his remains were later transferred to the town of Vlora. Also buried here, more recently in a white marble tomb, is Ekrem bey Vlora, whose remains were transferred there from Vienna in March 2014.

The Austrian writer Friedrich Wallisch (1890–1969) visited the site around 1930, and noted the following:

Below the fortress is the large village of Kanina. At one of the most attractive spots in the village and on the hill is a simple brick building. It is a *tekke*, a little dervish convent. Under a lofty tree in front of this building there is a small rectangular plot of earth surrounded by a wire fence. This is the grave of the man who created the Albanian State, Ismail Kemal. A sallow wreathe of withered flowers hangs on the fence. There is no tombstone or inscription to mark the grave bearing the father of Albania. But from the site where he lies, there is a panoramic view of his homeland with the dark olive groves, the bright plains below and the blue velvet hues of the Gulf of Vlora.[193]

From 1930, to the extent that it was still active, the site was subordinate to the *gjyshata* of Koshtan, but here is no mention of any *baba*. This *tekke* is, nonetheless, referred to on the map made in Albania for the German scholar Franz Babinger in 1962, so it must still have been active in some form at that time.
cf. J. von Hahn 1854, p. 72, 2015, p. 34; E. Vlora 1911, p. 51, 1955, pp. 7–8; F. Babinger 1930, pp. 24–25; F. Wallisch 1931, p. 133; R. Busch-Zantner 1939, p. 198; H. Kaleshi 1980, pp. 9–10; N. Clayer 1990, pp. 308–310; R. Dankoff and R. Elsie 2000, pp. 132–133.

Kapaj, District of Mallakastra, Albania
Tekke of Baba Ismail
Location: About 10 km southeast of Ballsh. 40°32' N, 19°49' E.

This *tekke* was founded around 1901 by a Baba Ismail who died before 1923. It was subordinate to the *tekke* of Koshtan. The *tekke*, which was probably the site of an earlier shrine, survived until 1967 when it was torn down by the local villagers in the communist campaign against religion. The *tekke* and three *tyrbes* have now been reconstructed in a very attractive setting. The faithful gathered here as pilgrims on the feast days of 22–25 March.
cf. F. W. Hasluck 1929, p. 436 (543); N. Clayer 1990, p. 311.

Këlcyra, District of Përmet, Albania
Tekke of Hasan Dede
Location: At the end of the town of Këlcyra on the road to Përmet. 40°18' N, 20°11' E.

The *tekke* of Hasan Dede was probably founded in the early twentieth century, no doubt after 1912. Of the town of Këlcyra (Klissura), Margaret Hasluck noted that the *beys* were Bektashis, and men swore by Hasan Dede, a local saint who was the brother of a local chief, Jadikula. Healing powers were attributed to him. It was later a *dervishia* subordinate to the *gjyshata* of Prishta that survived until 1967 when it was torn down by the local villagers in the communist campaign against religion. There is now a modest *tyrbe* at the site.
cf. F. W. Hasluck 1929, p. 437 (544); N. Clayer 1990, p. 312.

Kiçok, District of Tepelena, Albania
Tekke of Baba Kamber

Location: On the road between Këlcyra and Berat, some 30 km north of Këlcyra. 40°25' N, 20°04' E.

This *tekke* seems to have been founded by a Baba Kamber around 1890. It was completely destroyed by Greek forces in the period 1913–1914 as were most of the *tekkes* in the region, and Baba Kamber and his dervishes fled. Kamber went to Bulgaria and founded another Bektashi *tekke*, that of Ruse (Rustchuk) on the Danube in about 1920. The dervishes of Kiçok for their part went to Maricaj, north of Tepelena, and helped construct a *tekke* there. The *tekke* of Kiçok was rebuilt about 1920 and was represented by a Baba Sulejman at the First National Congress of the Bektashi, held at the *tekke* of Prishta in the Skrapar region on 14–17 January 1921. It survived until 1967 when it was torn down by the local villagers in the communist campaign against religion. A *tyrbe* was reconstructed at the site in 1994 or thereafter. The faithful gathered here as pilgrims on the feast day of 7 July. cf. F. W. Hasluck 1929, p. 437 (544); N. Clayer 1990, p. 313.

Komar, District of Tepelena, Albania
Tekke of Baba Islam
Location: To the east of the Këlcyra-Berat mountain road, between Qafë Gllava and Selcka. 40°28' N, 19°59' E.

The little *tekke* in Komar was founded in the early years of the twentieth century, perhaps around 1903, by a Husejn Baba. It was no doubt destroyed by Greek forces in the period 1913–1914 but was rebuilt in about 1920. It was represented by a Baba Shaban at the First National Congress of the Bektashi, held at the *tekke* of Prishta in the Skrapar region on 14–17 January 1921. When Margaret Hasluck passed through the region in about 1923, there was no resident *baba*. It was later subordinate to the *gjyshata* of Gjirokastra. The *tekke*, which was actually quite well known in the region, survived until 1967 when it was torn down by the local villagers in the communist campaign against religion. There is now a modest *tyrbe* and a two-room *tekke* building for guests and the custodian at the site. cf. F. W. Hasluck 1929, p. 437 (544); N. Clayer 1990, p. 314.

Koshtan, District of Tepelena, Albania
Tekke of Baba Sadik
Location: Northwest of Memaliaj, between Qesarat and Zhabokika. 40°24' N, 19°52' E.

The *tekke* of Baba Sadik was founded in the nineteenth century, perhaps as early as 1807 in the ruins of two old *tyrbes*. Its founder, the said Baba Sadik, stemmed from the noted *tekke* of Durballi Sultan in Thessaly. If, as Baba Rexheb suggests, it was founded under the aegis of Baba Shemimi of Fushë Kruja, it would probably be somewhat older as Shemimi was murdered in 1803. Of the heads of this *tekke*, mention may be made of Baba Ismail whom Hasluck describes as the 'saint' of the *tekke*, and Baba Muharrem. Then came Baba Ahmet Resuli, who opened the first Albanian school in the Tepelena region at the *tekke* on 18 October 1908 and whose bust now stands in the courtyard. He fled to Egypt when the *tekke* was ravaged by Greek forces in 1913–1914, and died before 1920. Some time thereafter there was a Baba Kaso or Kasem who represented *tekke* of Koshtan at the First National Congress of the Bektashi, held at the *tekke* of Prishta in the Skrapar region on 14–17 January 1921. In 1942 we know of a Baba Shefqet Koshtani, also known as Shefqet Mahmuti or Baba Shefqet Gllava, who was tried and executed by the communists in January 1948 during the witch-hunts.

The venerable *tekke* of Koshtan was itself of some importance and had numerous offshoots. From 1930 onwards, it was subordinate to the *gjyshata* of Gjirokastra, but following the Second World War, probably after 1950, Koshtan became the *gjyshata* itself, i.e. one of the six administrative divisions of the Bektashi Order in Albania. It was closed down in 1967 during the communist campaign against religion, but was not destroyed because of its historical significance as a centre of early Albanian-language education.

The *tekke* building is still preserved (2017) on a promontory overlooking the valley of the Vjosa River and the mountains of Kurvelesh. People visit the *tekke* on the feast day of 18 October each year.

cf. F. W. Hasluck 1914–1916, p. 117, 1929, p. 436 (542); Baba Rexheb 1970, pp. 249, 367, 384; N. Clayer 1990, pp. 317–318; K. Boriçi and S. Xhelaj 2016.

Kosina, District of Përmet, Albania
Dervishia of Kosina
Location: On the north side of the road from Përmet to Këlcyra, half way between the two. 40°16' N, 20°18' E.

Little is known of this *dervishia* in Kosina. It is said to have burned down at the end of the nineteenth century. Margaret Hasluck notes that 'at Koshina [*sic*] there is now no *tekke*, but only lodging for travellers and attendant dervish'.[194] It seems to have been rebuilt in 1923, but there is little information on it after that time.

cf. F. W. Hasluck 1929, p. 438 (544); N. Clayer 1990, p. 316; Sh. Hysi 2004, p. 111.

Kostrec, District of Përmet, Albania
Tekke of Kostrec
Location: In the Dangëllia mountains about 20 km northeast of Përmet. 40°18' N, 20°24' E.

The *tekke* in Kostrec, also called Ogren-Kostrec, survived until 1967 when it was torn down by the local villagers in the communist campaign against religion. A *tyrbe* has been reconstructed at the site.

Krahës, District of Tepelena, Albania
Tekke of Baba Husejn, *tekke* of Harakop
Location: On the west side of the old Ballsh-Tepelena road, about 25 km northwest of Tepelena. 40°26' N, 19°50' E.

The *tekke* in Krahës, also known as the *tekke* of Harakop, was founded in the 1870s. Margaret Hasluck, who visited the region in about 1923, spoke of a succession of four *babas* here, of whom Baba Husejn was the first and was buried here. In 1912, the *tekke* of Krahës was administered by a Baba Sulo. It was represented by a Baba Hasan at the First National Congress of the Bektashi, held at

the *tekke* of Prishta in the Skrapar region on 14–17 January 1921. After the Second World War, it was subordinate to the *gjyshata* of Koshtan. It survived until 1967 when it was torn down by the local villagers in the communist campaign against religion. A *tyrbe* has been reconstructed at the site. It should be noted that there are two villages in this district called Krahës. On the mountainside above Krahës is the *tyrbe* of Baba Zoto. The feast day of this *tekke* is 17 September.
cf. F. W. Hasluck 1929, p. 436 (542–543); P. Pepo 1962, p. 463; N. Clayer 1990, p. 319.

Kremenar, District of Mallakastra, Albania
Tekke of Baba Hasan
Location: About 3 km to the west of the Ballsh-Tepelena road. 40°31' N, 19°47' E.

The *tekke* of Baba Hasan in Kremenar was founded in the early years of the twentieth century, around 1905, by one Baba Hasan. It was destroyed, no doubt by Greek forces, in the period 1913–1914. Baba Hasan fled to the village of Krahës but the *tekke* was later rebuilt, probably around 1920. It survived until 1967 when it was torn down by the local villagers in the communist campaign against religion. A *tyrbe* has been reconstructed at the site.
cf. F. W. Hasluck 1929, p. 436 (543); N. Clayer 1990, p. 320.

Kreshova, District of Kolonja, Albania
Tekke of Baba Hasan, *tekke* of Baba Selim
Location: Village of Kreshova, north of Starja, situated to the east of the main Erseka-Korça road, at the foot of the Mount Gramoz. 40°23' N, 20°43' E.

The *tekke* of Baba Hasan in Kreshova was founded by the said Baba Hasan at an unknown date. He had trained in Melçan and came to visit his brother in Kreshova. When he saw how beautiful the site was, he resolved to build a *tekke* there, probably around 1900, but he died shortly thereafter. The *tekke* of Kreshova was represented by a Baba Selim at the First National Congress of the Bektashi, held at the *tekke* of Prishta in the Skrapar region on 14–17 January 1921. Margaret Hasluck reports that in 1923 the *tekke* was enlarged by Baba Xhemal, who held the rank of a *halife*, and that there were three dervishes living with him there. Her impression was that it was richer than the *tekke* in Starja. The faithful gathered here as pilgrims on the feast day of 28 August.

In the 1940s, the *tekke* was headed by Baba Muharrem Agushi of Tepelena. He was arrested by the communists soon after they took power since the village of Kreshova had supported the anti-communist resistance group *Balli Kombëtar* (The National Front). He was charged with agitation and propaganda, the standard indictment for all opponents of the new regime, and was imprisoned for fifteen years of reclusion and hard labour. Baba Muharrem was followed by Baba Selim from Maslavica, now in Greece, Baba Xhemal, and Baba Avdulla who administered the *tekke* until it was destroyed in the Cultural Revolution of 1967–1968. At that time, the *tekke* was razed to the ground by the 'revolutionary' young people of the village and surrounding region, although it is said that many of the Bektashi villagers refused to take part in the action.

The site, just above the village of Kreshova, now has of a new *tekke* building, finished on 28 August 2010, and two *tyrbes*. The first *tyrbe* contains the graves of Baba Hasan, Baba Xhemal and Baba Selim, and the second one has the graves of Baba Muharrem, Baba Avdulla and three dervishes.
cf. F. W. Hasluck 1914–1916, p. 118, 1929, p. 439 (545); N. Clayer 1990, p. 321; F. Trix, *The Resurfacing* 1995, p. 547.

Kruja, District of Kruja, Albania
Tekke of Baba Hamza, *tekke* of Haxhi Hamza
Location: To the west of the fortress of Kruja, just west of the bazaar street. 41°30' N, 19°47 E.

The Austrian scholar and diplomat Theodor Ippen visited the *tekke* of Hamza Baba in 1904, situated to the west of the bazaar street in the town, and said it was surrounded by a graveyard with Bektashi tombstones. The saint had apparently died in 1533–1534 [940 AH]. Ippen learned that the *tyrbe* had been built at the end of the eighteenth century by order of Kapllan Pasha Toptani, as a memorial to his victory over the troops of his opponent, the vizier of Shkodra, Kara Mahmud Bushatlli. According to Hasluck, it was Shemimi Baba who urged Kapllan Pasha to build the *tyrbe* for Hamza Baba.[195]

The *tyrbe* of the *tekke* was still standing when Machiel Kiel visited Kruja in 1967. He described the site as follows:

> The *tekke* of Hadji Hamza was until the early seventies situated on a terrace immediately below the Albtourist Hotel. In 1967 only the *türbe* was preserved. [...] The *türbe* was a massive structure of about ten square metres. The low dome rose weakly above an octagonal tambour. The four corners of the cube, forming the shoulders of the building, sloped down a little in the manner of 16th-century Macedonian mosques. The whole was built of rough broken stone which was covered with a very thin coat of plaster. Style and proportions betray the very late date of the *türbe*. It looks as if it were built in the late 18th century, or even slightly later. [...] In 1967 I saw several dozen historical gravestones with Bektashi headgear in the walled garden of the *türbe*. They lay about scattered and broken, a sad reminder of the events of the spring of 1967. Unfortunately no detailed research was possible, nor could photographs be taken. The tomb of the saint, Hamza Baba, was removed in the spring of 1967. When I revisted Kruja, in 1978, the *türbe* was demolished and only its site was still recognisable. All epigraphical material had been removed and presumably destroyed.

When Kiel discussed the value of the epigraphical material in this graveyard with the Director of Antiquities of Kruja in the spring of 1967, the director observed: 'material not of importance for the national history of Albania will be destroyed.'[196]

Numerous *babas* are associated with this *tekke*, which was in good condition. It survived until 1967 when it was torn down by the people of Kruja in the communist

campaign against religion. A *tyrbe* and a modest one-room *tekke* building now function at the site.
cf. Th. Ippen 1904, p. 71; M. Kiel 1990, pp. 181-182, 1993, pp. 271-272.

Kruja, District of Kruja, Albania
Tekke of Haxhi Jahja Baba.
Location: Unknown.

According to Baba Rexheb, Haxhi Jahja Baba had served as *baba* of the *tekke* of Asim Baba in Gjirokastra from 1830 to 1836 and returned to Kruja to see his family. He never went back to Gjirokastra and founded instead a new *tekke* in Kruja, probably around 1836.

The American scholar John Birge came across the *tekke* of Haxhi Jahja Baba during his visit to Kruja in October 1933, and wrote: 'In the yard about the *Zaviye* of Haji Yahya Baba there were many tombstones bearing the Bektashi symbols. One of them, unfortunately with the top broken off, was dated 1130 (1717).'[197] The Birge dating of the tomb (1717 AD) would mean that Jahja Baba built his *tekke* over a century later beside the *tyrbe* of a new anonymous holy man. The *tekke* survived until 1967 when it was torn down by the people of Kruja in the communist campaign against religion. A *tyrbe* and a one-room *tekke* building have been reconstructed at the site.
cf. J. Birge 1937, p. 71; Baba Rexheb 1970, pp. 290-291; N. Clayer 1990, pp. 333-334.

Kruja, District of Kruja, Albania
Tyrbe of Mustafa Dollma
Location: In the southern corner of the fortress of Kruja. 41°30' N, 19°47' E.

The *tyrbe* of Mustafa Dollma stems from the late eighteenth century, 1779-1780 [1193 AH]. On a painted inscription in the interior we read 'This holy dome was built by Toptanzade ... in the year 1193', signifying that it was built by Adem Aga Toptani (d. 1784). In form, the building looks more like a mosque than a shrine and was probably used as a mosque since it has a *mihrab* (prayer niche). The interior contains the graves of the Dollma family, in particular the shrine of Baba Mustafa Dollma and the grave of a dervish Hysen Dollma. The walls are embellished with Arabic calligraphy and wall paintings, not as yet restored. The main inscription in the interior of the *tyrbe*, a twenty-line poem to Kaplan Pasha, transliterated recently by Mehmet Tütüncü,[198] dates from 1807 to 1808 [1222 AH].

The monument is commonly called the *tekke* of Dollma and it may have served as such at the time of Baba Mustafa Dollma, but what remains is simply a shrine. If there ever was a *tekke* here it must have been destroyed long ago. The faithful gathered at this site as pilgrims on the feast day of 11 August.

Machiel Kiel who visited Kruja in 1967 described the *tyrbe* as follows:

The *türbe* measures 7.20 square metres and is surmounted by a squat dome. Its façade is built of finely cut and dressed stone of a yellowish colour and is enlivened by windows and a door spanned by arches in the style of late Ottoman baroque. There is no inscription or date but among the interior decorations (ornamental wall paintings) the date of 1194 (1780) is clearly legible. Behind the *türbe* the tombstone of the alleged founder, Adem Aga Toptan, still stands (situation 1982); he died, according to the date there, in 1198 (1784–1785). Around the *türbe* a few Bektashi gravestones are preserved, some crowned with the usual twelve-sided *Hüseyni tac* and some of them with the very rare *Elifi tac* in the shape of a bishop's mitre. The latter bears the date 1277 (1860–1861) but its text is rather damaged. The others are the graves of a *türbedar*, Dervish Abulbaki, from 1239 (1823–1824) and his son, bearing the following text: 'He! Date of the demise of Ali, son of Dervish Abdullah, *türbedar* of Haci Mustafa Baba of the Path of Bektash. A prayer for his soul…' (date broken off). The group of stones is unique for Albania and very rare in the Balkans. In 1978 I pointed this out to the Albanian authorities in charge of the preservation of historical monuments, who reacted by restoring the little complex. In 1982 this restoration was completed.[199]

There are also Bektashi graves around the *tyrbe* on the outside, including the fine marble tomb of the said Adem Aga Toptani, dating from 1784 to 1779 [1198 AH]. It reads: 'Year 1198 / God the Merciful / Date of Passing / The one who has earned his place in paradise / Toptanzade Adem Aga, son of Ibrahim Aga / Son of Ali Beg from Akçihisar [Kruja].'[200]

In the communist period, up to the end of the 1980s, the *tyrbe* was locked up, with a chain on the door, but candles were still being lit on the doorstep despite the communist campaign against religion.

cf. T. Ippen 1907, p. 74; R. Busch-Zantner 1934; N. Clayer 1990, pp. 323–324; M. Kiel 1990, pp. 182–183, 1993, p. 272; M. Tütüncü 2017, pp. 120–126.

Kruja, District of Kruja, Albania
Tyrbe of Zemzi Baba
Location: In the town of Kruja, to the north of the fortress and bazaar. 41°30' N, 19°47' E.

This small roadside *tyrbe* is said to have been constructed in 1912.

Kruja, Mount, District of Kruja, Albania
Tyrbe of Sari Saltik
Location: Cave at the top of Mount Kruja. 41°31' N, 19°48' E.

The *tyrbe* of Sari Saltik in a cave at the top of Mount Kruja (Albanian: *Mali i Krujës*) was an important pilgrimage site since its foundation. It was dedicated to the legendary figure Sari Saltik (Albanian: *Sari Salltëk*, Turkish: *Sarı Saltuk,* from *Saır Saltıq*), who is said to have been either a dervish at the court of Sultan Orhan (1326–1360) or a direct disciple of Haji Bektash Veli, founder of the Bektashi Order. It is more likely, however, that he was a figure of early Balkan and not originally of Bektashi or Muslim legendry. The site had previously been used for a church dedicated to Saint Alexander. It is here, according to legend, at any rate that the miracle-working Sari Saltik appeared as a Bektashi dervish.

Machiel Kiel discovered an imperial Ottoman register from *c.* 1567 to 1568, which contains a note about repairs to the road leading up to the tomb of Sari

Saltik in Kruja. This document shows that the site had been a venue of widespread veneration in Albania much earlier than previously thought:

> On the mountain of Kruja is the tomb of Sari Saltik to which the people of the neighbouring districts come for pilgrimage. The road mentioned is very arduous and difficult and gives visitors much trouble. It has been recorded in the previous register that the ten persons mentioned, who are for the greater part the descendants of those who were of old in charge of repairs, have been charged with levelling the above-mentioned road and repairing it whenever it is in disrepair. After having fulfilled this duty and after having paid their tithes, they are discharged and liberated from the extraordinary tax for the Divan and the duties based on the Common Law.[201]

In the cave there is an inscription dating from the year 1692–1693 [1104 AH], and the masonry at the spring is dated 1776 [1190 AH]. The people of Kruja were wont to visit, despite the difficult two-hour climb, in particular on Sari Saltik's feast day of August 22, and drank holy water from the bottom of the cave. Indeed it was a religious obligation for the Bektashi of Kruja to visit the cave twice a year. The pilgrims brought offerings with them and usually stayed for twenty-four hours, i.e. spending the night at nearby accommodation. They drank *raki* in the evening and fired off their rifles at sunrise before departure. Wednesdays were reserved for the women.

Theodor Ippen visited the site in the early years of the twentieth century and described it as follows:

> The largest burial sanctuary of the town, however, is up on the ledge of the plateau of Mount Kruja, in a crevasse in the cliffs, up through which leads a difficult, winding path over the scree. It is dedicated to Sarisaldik [Sari Saltik], the 'blond apostle'. A few steps lead down to a grating at which one is obliged to remove one's shoes. One proceeds through an antechamber containing the sarcophagi of the disciples of the saint and enters a well-tended chapel with the grave of the holy man himself. Our guide said a prayer and visitors place donations in an alms box. All of these *tyrbes* make a vivid impression on the visitor. They transpire peace and tranquillity. The soul is filled with composure and contemplation until, with some difficulty, one comes to oneself. The appeal of the sacred surroundings is heightened all the more if a dervish or a *baba* is present to tend the grave. These men, who have withdrawn from the world, receive guests with extraordinary kindness and hospitality and offer philosophical thoughts free of any of the fanaticism that characterises and divides all of the Orient.[202]

Though it is often called a *tekke*, the cave of Sari Saltik was actually a *tyrbe* (mausoleum), or at best a *dervishia* (small dervish lodge) because there is no record of any *baba* here. Nearby there were three buildings: one for prominent guests, one for the dervishes looking after the site and one for ordinary guests.[203] The dervishes at the *tyrbe* were subordinate to the *tekke* of Fushë Kruja.

This site, like all the other Bektashi centres in Albania, was closed down during the campaign against religion in 1967. The *tekke* building on the mountain was destroyed by the communists, but the interior of the cave was not substantially damaged. Despite the ban, the *tyrbe* continued to be frequented by the people of Kruja, although it was traditionally abandoned in the winter months. It was rebuilt in 1992 after the fall of the dictatorship and welcomes visitors. A bronze bust of Sari Saltik was set up at the entrance to the cave in September 2009, and a paved road has recently been built enabling people to drive up to the site by car.

The faithful gathered here as pilgrims in particular from 14 August to 14 September. cf. J. A. Degrand 1901, pp. 236-243; T. Ippen 1907, pp. 69-79; F. W. Hasluck 1929, p. 442 (550-551); F. Babinger 1928, 1929, 1934; Rr. Zojzi 1944; R. Kriss and H. Kriss-Heinrich 1960, 1, pp. 335-336; H. Kaleshi 1967a, 1967b, 1969; N. Clayer 1990, pp. 336-339; M. Kiel 1993; H. Norris 1993, pp. 131-132, 146-157; N. Ibrahimi 1998, pp. 235-245; N. Malcolm 1998, pp. 131-132; J. Rexhepagiqi 2003.

Kuç, District of Devoll, Albania
Tekke of Baba Kasem
Location: Half an hour beyond Bilisht on the road to Florina. 40°34' N, 20°58' E.

The *tekke* of Kuç (not to be confused with the *tekke* in the village of Kuç in Skrapar) is one of the oldest in Albania and was founded, it is said, by Kasem (Kasëm or Qazim) Baba of Kastoria in the second half of the fifteenth century. It was burned down in July 1826 in the crackdown under Sultan Mahmud II, but was refounded in 1878 by one Ibrahim Baba of Lemnos. New buildings were constructed in 1906-1907 [1324 AH] by a Baba Hafiz, who was shot by Greek forces in 1914. According to Margaret Hasluck, it was small and insignificant in 1915 and 'tenanted only by an abbot, who was gone in 1921. Baba Hafiz's bloodstained *taj* was shown to visitors, as were the bloodstains on the floor which resisted all attempts at washing them away'.[204]

The *tekke* of Kuç was represented by a Baba Ahmet at the First National Congress of the Bektashi, held at the *tekke* of Prishta in the Skrapar region on 14-17 January 1921. In 1923, it was inhabited by one *baba*, no doubt Baba Ahmet, and three dervishes.[205] Machiel Kiel visited the *tyrbe* of Baba Kasem in 1959 and states that it thereafter disappeared. This *tekke* is, however, referred to on the map made in Albania for the German scholar Franz Babinger in 1962, so it must still have been active in some form at that time. It was reconstructed in the 1990s, after the destruction of the communist period.

The site, now under the administration of the elderly Baba Imir, currently consists of a *tekke* building and a pleasant garden and, at the end of a path leading up a hillside, a twelve-sided *tyrbe* containing the grave of Baba Kasem marked by an old pink marble gravestone. The original *tekke* seems to have been on a field beside the *tyrbe* until 1967 when it was torn down by the local villagers in the communist campaign against religion.

cf. A. Tomorri 1929, p. 89; F. W. Hasluck 1914-1916, p. 119, 1929, pp. 424 (525), 439-440 (543-548); Baba Rexheb 1970, p. 384; N. Clayer 1990, pp. 340-341; M. Kiel 1993, p. 271; R. Elsie, *Dictionary* 2001, pp. 213-214.

Kuç, District of Skrapar, Albania
Tekke of Kuç
Location: Village of Kuç about 20 km to the east of Mount Kulmak, above the right (east) bank of the Tomorrica River. 40°36' N, 20°17' E.

This small *tekke* of Kuç (not to be confused with the *tekke* near the village of Kuç in Devoll) was founded in 1880. It was subordinate to the *tekke* of Prishta. This *tekke* of Kuç was represented by a Baba Islam at the First National Congress of the Bektashi, held at the *tekke* of Prishta in the Skrapar region on 14–17 January 1921. It survived until 1967 when it was torn down by the local villagers in the communist campaign against religion. The *tekke* and two *tyrbes* were reconstructed at the site around 2009.
cf. N. Clayer 1990, p. 342.

Kulmak
cf. Tomorr, Mount.

Kuta, District of Mallakastra, Albania
Tekke of Baba Rifat
Location: East of the Vjosa River, about 10 km from the Ballsh-Tepelena road. 40°8' N, 19°46' E.

The *tekke* of Kuta was founded around 1923 by a Baba Rifat (Rifaat Baba, Baba Refat). It was initially located in his house. It was firstly an outpost of the *tekke* of Çorrush and was later subordinate to the *tekke* of Koshtan. It survived until 1967 when it was torn down by the local villagers in the communist campaign against religion. There is now a *tyrbe* at the site.
cf. F. W. Hasluck 1929, p. 436 (543); N. Clayer 1990, p. 343; Sh. Hysi 2004, p. 112.

Lavdar, District of Skrapar, Albania
Tekke of Lavdar
Location: About 10 km west of Çorovoda. 40°30' N, 20°06' E.

The *tekke* of Lavdar, across the Lavdar River from that of Bubës i Sipërm, was quite large. It is referred to on the map made in Albania for the German scholar Franz Babinger in 1962, so it must still have been active in some form at that time. It seems to have survived until 1967 when it was torn down by the local villagers in the communist campaign against religion. There is nothing but ruins there now.
cf. N. Clayer 1990, p. 344.

Leskovik, District of Përmet, Albania
Tekke of Baba Abedin
Location: On a hill above the road to the Greek border, about 7 km from town. 40°08' N, 20°36' E.

The *tekke* of Leskovik was founded by Baba Abedin Leskoviku, also known as Dede Abidin Akbaba,[206] who trained at the Bektashi *tekke* of Durballi Sultan in Thessaly under Baba Muharrem Mahzuni and was active at the Şah Kulu *tekke* of Merdivenköy in Istanbul. Baba Muharrem sent him back to Leskovik as a *baba* where he founded the *tekke* in 1887 [1293 AH]. We know that the fountain of the '*tekke* of Abedin Pasha' (*Abidin Paşa tekkesi*) was repaired in 1893-1894 [1310 AH] and that a kitchen was built for the *tekke* in 1904 [1322 AH].[207] The *tekke* was burned down and destroyed by Greek forces in the First World War. Margaret Hasluck noted that it was 'said to have been about thirty-five years old; it contained the grave of the founder Abiddin Baba, and housed seven or eight dervishes. The new *tekke* has been under construction since 1921, but there is only an abbot as yet in residence'.[208] Baba Abedin probably died shortly after Albanian independence in 1912. He seems to have been replaced by a Baba Seit (Seyid) who was appointed by Baba Ahmet Turani. Baba Seit served in Leskovik at least until 1942 and was replaced by one of his dervishes, Baba Riza. A Baba Islam Islamaj of Leskovik was later imprisoned by the communists and is now buried in Saranda.

The *tekke* survived until 1967 when it was torn down by the local villagers in the communist campaign against religion and replaced by an agricultural co-operative. Strangely enough, the beautiful old twelve-sided *tyrbe* overlooking the property near which the *tekke* would have stood survived the ravages, and has been left intact. It contains the graves of Baba Abedin, Baba Seit and a Baba Syrja, and some stone inscriptions in Ottoman script.

There is said to have been a second *tekke* in Leskovik, constructed in 1921, but little else is known of it.

cf. F. W. Hasluck 1914-1916, p. 118, 1929, p. 438 (545); N. Clayer 1990, pp. 346-347.

Lushnja, District of Lushnja, Albania
Tyrbe of Baba Skënder
Location: In the town of Lushnja. 40°56' N, 19°41' E.

The *tyrbe* of Baba Skënder survived until 1967 when it was torn down by the local villagers in the communist campaign against religion. It was reconstructed after the dictatorship.

Luz i madh, District of Kavaja, Albania
Tekke of Baba Sako
Location: About 5 km west of the main road from Kavaja to Rrogozhina. 41°06' N, 19°34' E.

The *tekke* of Baba Sako is the only one in the Kavaja region which is otherwise an eminently Sunni Muslim area. It survived until 1967 when it was torn down by the local villagers in the communist campaign against religion. After the dictatorship, a *tyrbe* was reconstructed at the site.

Maricaj, District of Tepelena, Albania
Tekke of Baba Musa
Location: About 15 km northeast of Memaliaj. 40°23' N, 20°02' E.

The little *tekke* of Maricaj (formerly Marican) was founded in the 1890s by a certain Baba Musa. He died during the Greek occupation of southern Albania, when the *tekke* was destroyed. After the First World War, no doubt in the early 1920s, the *tekke* was rebuilt with the help of dervishes who had fled from Kiçok. Of its later history, little is recorded. Fejzi Dede, the *dede baba* in Hacıbektaşköy in central Anatolia until about 1913, was from Maricaj. The *tekke* of Baba Musa survived until 1967 when it was torn down by the local villagers in the communist campaign against religion. A *tyrbe* has been rebuilt at the site.

The faithful gathered here as pilgrims on the feast day of 2 April.

cf. F. W. Hasluck 1929, p. 436 (542); N. Clayer 1990, p. 350.

Martanesh, District of Bulqiza, Albania
Tekke of Balim Sultan
Location: In the mountains near the village of Martanesh. 41°24' N, 20°12' E.

There were two *tekkes* in Martanesh. The first one, the *tekke* of Balim Sultan, was up in the mountains, whereas the second and subsequent one, the *tekke* of Haxhi Hysen Baba, was in the village itself. Both *tekkes* were usually administered by the same *baba*.

The *tekke* of Balim Sultan, also called Balim Sultan i epërm (Upper Balim Sultan), is said to stem from the late eighteenth century, from the time of Mahmud Pasha of Shkodra, no doubt from around 1770–1790. It was named after the second founder of the Bektashi Order, Balim Sultan, whose grave was said to be here. There was initially a simple *tyrbe* in a cave. According to legend, Mahmud Pasha, marching with his troops from Ohrid to Shkodra, spent the night at the cave. In his dreams he saw a dervish who told him: 'I am the only ruler here, so get up immediately and leave this place.'[209] Mahmud Pasha arose to find that his troops had departed and set off in terror to find them. Convinced of the sanctity of the site, he later ordered a *tyrbe* to be built there in the form of a 'vizier's tower' for which a dervish was appointed to light a lantern every night.

The *tekke* itself was first founded here, like most of the *tekkes* in Albania, in the second half of the nineteenth century, apparently around 1870 [1286 AH]. The first *baba* was Hysen Rama (d. 1877) of Martanesh,[210] also known as Hysen Martaneshi, from the nearby village of Lena. He was followed by Baba Jashar Krena[211] from Sopot near Zërqan who served there from 1877 [1294 AH] to his death in 1910–1911 [1328 AH]. Baba Jashar received land and donations and was a good friend of the influential Aqif Pasha of Elbasan (1861–1926). As such, he was able to begin work on a solid *tekke* building in 1898. He also played a major role in pacifying blood feuds in the Bulqiza and Dibra regions.

Baba Jashar was succeeded by the young Baba Hajdar Leskoveci[212] (1896–1923) from the Përmet region, who was appointed by Baba Ahmet Turani and served there until his death. The Albanian writer Thanas Floqi (1884–1945) of Korça, who was working for the new Albanian Ministry of Justice, met him in Martanesh in 1914:

> Martanesh has a large Bektashi *tekke* in the village and a smaller one in the mountains. The one in the mountains, which is inhabited by a dervish and two or three servants, is snowed in in the winter and they can hardly get a path open so that the men inside can breathe. Most of the people of the village are Bektashi, but even the Sunni people respect the *tekke* and the *baba*. Whenever there is a dispute among the inhabitants, the *baba* uses his spiritual influence

to pacify them. Baba Hajdar, the present *baba*, is from southern Albania and was a dervish at this *tekke* for several years. He became the *baba* after the death of Baba Jashar who is said to have been the actual founder of the *tekke*. He was very much respected by the people of the region for the good deeds he did. Baba Hajdar was terrified that Haxhi Qamili or 'Haxhi the Firebrand' as the men of Martanesh called him, would burn the *tekke* down. In fact, it would have been a great tragedy to see that wonderful building in the mountains destroyed. He appealed to a commission in Tirana, but no one came for fear of suffering the same fate as the other *babas*.[213]

In 1914, Sunni Muslim peasants were attacking and destroying Bektashi *tekkes* during the central Albanian uprising of Haxhi Qamili. The Bektashi in Martanesh feared for their lives, but 300 of the local men took up arms and defended the *tekke*, lying in wait there for a period of three months. The danger passed, but not long thereafter the *tekke* was destroyed by Serbian forces when they passed through the region in the First World War. F. W. Hasluck notes that, to add insult to injury, the Serbs shaved the *baba*'s beard off.

The Alsacian geologist Jacques Bourcart (1891–1965), who was in Albania with the French Armée de l'Orient from 1916 to 1920, got to the *tekke* in Martanesh around 1920 and photographed it, noting:

> This monastery, situated in the high mountain pastures at the edge of an impenetrable beech forest, was built of wood with a very steep board roof that reminds one of the curious houses in the Bosnian bocage.[214]

Baba Hajdar was succeeded by Baba Hajro of Turan in Tepelena who, however, proved unsatisfactory and divisive, and departed for Kruja six months later. He was replaced in November 1924 by Baba Rushit Tollja[215] (1878–1928) of Strikçan in Bulqiza. Baba Rushit had been *baba* in Bllaca, where he had constructed a two-storey *tekke*. He then served as *baba* of both *tekkes*, Bllaca and Martanesh, and the latter *tekke* was reconstructed. Baba Rushit was well respected and his word was law. Like his predecessors, he was able to resolve many of the endemic blood feuds in the region. He was replaced by Baba Xhafer from the Gjirokastra region. After the death of Baba Xhafer in 1928, the *tekke* was left for some time without a *baba* and was under the administration of the *gjyshata* of Elbasan.

The next head of the *tekke* was Baba Xhaferr Karriqi of Gjirokastra who served from 1928 to 1932. The British journalist and writer Joseph Swire (1903–1978) met him there in about 1930 and left the following description:

> We left this enchanted place sadly and went up the valley to *tekké* Balim Sultan where *Baba* Xhafer, white bearded and stately, came out to greet us. He had heard we were nearby and why had we not come to stay at the *tekké*? A *tekké* was first built here in 1870, and at the same time another in the valley near Martanesh; but in 1921 the Serbs burnt the one here, though they did not harm the lower one which was strongly defended by local people. The lower *tekké*

was threatened in 1914 by rebels from Tirana but was saved by some fighting. The new *tekké* here is strongly built of stone to the height of its single storey, surmounted by a very high roof with wide eaves, very steep to throw off snow, made of handsawn planks. It stands in a courtyard with a high arched entrance gate. Within was dark and cavernous. In the *Baba*'s room the floor was spread with white fleeces by the walls and two gaily embroidered saddlebags hung from pegs. We sat for coffee in the shade of the arched gate. In the two *tekkés* there were only eight dervishes and Baba Xhafer – who was *Baba* of both; but there were several probationers, one a well-educated young man from Korça who spoke French. He led us by a narrow path up the shady hillside to a little door in a white stone wall which hid the mouth of a cavern. We went in – it was like stepping into a refrigerator. Inside, close to the door, were several mugs and a petrol can holding holy water collected from the drippings in the cave (and having perhaps, medicinal value); this water is given to sick children whom it cures – but of what it cures them our friend did not say. Further in are two shrines, one that of the holy man Balim, a contemporary of Mahomet. Beyond the shrines a passage led into the mountain side, and this we followed for some paces. The air became, if possible, colder, till it rattled my teeth and the passage narrowed till it was hard to go on. Here our guide stopped, saying no one could go further – one *dervish* who tried was overcome. In the cold I felt unheroic and came out. The sun-heated air was like a blast from a furnace as we passed back into the open. *Baba* Xhafer explained the cave is sacred. The legend is that Mohamet himself made the passages which may not be defiled by man; and they lead underground, so he said with solemnity, to the top of Tomori and to the *tekké* on the crag above Kruja. *Baba* Xhafer wished us a good road, first giving us provision of bread and cheese. Now we headed direct for Tirana.[216]

The next *baba* was Mustafa Xhani[217] (1910–1947), who was elected in May 1934. He was subsequently known as Baba Faja Martaneshi. He did much to improve both *tekkes* in Martanesh. During the Second World War, he was an active and well-known figure in the pro-communist partisan movement. The *tekke* was burned down during the war, apparently by Italian forces, and was reconstructed in the period 1953–1958.

After the war, Baba Faja spent most of his time in Tirana, until he was spectacularly shot and killed there by the *kryegjysh* (*dede baba*) of Albania, Abaz Hilmi, on 18 March 1947. His position in Martanesh had been assumed by Baba Ali Rizaj from the Korça region from 1945 to 1948, followed by Baba Tahir Hyseni of Qesarat in the Tepelena region from 1948 to 1951. In February 1953 Selim Kaliçani of Peja was appointed by Ahmet Myftari Dede Baba as head of the *tekke* of Martanesh. Baba Selim laboured on the reconstruction of the *tekke* and seems to have held this position until all the *tekkes* were closed down in 1967.

cf. T. Ippen 1908, p. 61; F. W. Hasluck 1929, p. 442 (551); J. Bourcart 1921, p. 182; J. Swire 1937, pp. 279–280; N. Clayer 1990, pp. 354–356; D. Smiley 1984, p. 84: S. Kaliçani 1997. Q. Dedej, *Fillimet* 1997.

Martanesh, District of Bulqiza, Albania
Tekke of Haxhi Hysen Baba
Location: In the village of Martanesh. 41°25' N, 20°12' E.

The *tekke* of Haxhi Hysen Baba was located in the village of Martanesh. It was much more recent than the nearby *tekke* of Balim Sultan in the mountains. It was founded by Baba Haxhi Hysen Kukeli from the *tekke* of Fushë Kruja who died sometime between 1890 and 1893. Joseph Swire who visited the *tekke* in 1934 states that it was founded around 1870. In the early years of the twentieth century, it was run by a Baba Jashar Krena, who was a respected figure in the population. He died on 23 April 1911 and was replaced by a Baba Hajdar (1896–1923) who headed both *tekkes* in Martanesh. In 1914 the *tekke* was threatened by Sunni peasants at the time of the central Albanian uprising of Haxhi Qamili, but the local people defended it. It was subsequently attacked by Serbian forces when they passed through the region in the First World War, but not severely damaged. As F. W. Hasluck notes, 'their attack on the *tekke* in the town was foiled by the townspeople, though they are mainly Sunnis and fanatical at that.'[218]

In 1923 there were two dervishes and a *baba* at this *tekke*. Its subsequent history is similar to that of the nearby *tekke* of Balim Sultan, both administered by the same *baba*. Like the other *tekke*, it is said to have been burned and destroyed in fighting during the Second World War, apparently by Italian forces.

The *tekke* has been reconstructed and is currently under the administration of Baba Hysni Shehu, who is also responsible for the nearby *tekke* of Balim Sultan.
cf. F. W. Hasluck 1929, p. 442 (551); J. Swire 1937, pp. 279–280; N. Clayer 1990, pp. 351–353.

Matohasanaj, District of Tepelena, Albania
Tekke of Baba Salih
Location: About 25 km west of Tepelena, on the old Vlora-Tepelena road. 40°21' N, 19°49' E.

This *tekke* is linked to a Baba Salih, who was born in Matohasanaj in the second half of the nineteenth century and was a great promoter of Albanian education in the surrounding region. As of 1878, around the time of the League of Prizren, the *tekke* was used as a clandestine school for the teaching of Albanian. It is doubtful whether it was always an actual *tekke*, and certainly declined in significance after the death of Baba Salih. It probably ceased functioning entirely after the Second World War. The building survived until 1967 when it was torn down by the surrounding villagers in the communist campaign against religion, but a *tyrbe* now graces the site. Interesting is the fact that many of the houses in the village of Matohasanaj have a Bektashi symbol, the stonecarved *teslim*, on their gates.
cf. Baba Rexheb 1970, pp. 380–382; N. Clayer 1990, pp. 357–358.

Mazreka, District of Korça, Albania
Tekke of Mazreka
Location: At the source of the Mazreka river in the Opar region, about 20 km west of Voskopoja. 40°36' N, 20°25' E.

Little is known of this *tekke* in the isolated Opar region, founded probably around the time of the First World War. It survived until 1967 when it was torn down by the surrounding villagers in the communist campaign against religion. A *tyrbe* was constructed on the site after the dictatorship.
cf. N. Clayer 1990, p. 359.

Mbyet, District of Fier, Albania
Tekke of Baba Ali Horasani
Location: Near the cemetery of the town of Fier. 40°42' N, 19°33' E.

This was a relatively old *tekke*, dating perhaps from the sixteenth century. It was torn down in the spring of 1967 by the 'revolutionary youth' of Fier in the communist campaign against religion. A *tyrbe* was constructed at the site after the dictatorship.

Melan, District of Gjirokastra, Albania
Tekke of Baba Ali, *tekke* of Melan
Location: 2 km southeast of Nepravishta, near the present Greek border. 39°59' N, 20°16' E.

The *tekke* of Melan (not to be confused with Melçan near Korça) was founded by Ali Haqi Baba of Gjirokastra around 1870 as an offshoot of the *tekke* of Asim Baba in Gjirokastra. The *tekke* of Melan is one of the rare old Bektashi building of Albania. It was situated on a hill between Nepravishta and Peshkëpia, which is now very near the Greek border. The site is old because there are as yet undated archaeological remains from ancient times nearby. It was a large, imposing *tekke* surrounded by cypress trees. Indeed, its size is somewhat of a surprise in a region with a majority Orthodox population. There were only Bektashi in Nepravishta and Libohova. The *tekke* was administered initially by Baba Sejfullah Melani from Nepravishta who 'took the hand' of Ali Haqi Baba of Gjirokastra. When Greek forces occupied the region in the Second Balkan War (June–July 1913) they evicted the occupants of the *tekke*. The second head of this *tekke* was Baba Qamil Gjini of Vlora (b. 1870) who was appointed by Baba Selim Ruhi of Gjirokastra and who was alive at least until 1944 when the communists took power. In 1946 there was only one dervish left there. In the communist period, the *tyrbe* was destroyed but the *tekke* itself was left intact as it was used as an observation post for Albanian border troops. The observation post was later abandoned, but the building survived. The roof was made of timber brought in from Persia, and the cypress trees around the *tekke* were planted in such a way as to form the word 'Allah' in Arabic script. The trees were wilfully damaged during the campaign against religion in 1967, but were replanted in the 1990s. Unfortunately, these new trees were then destroyed in a forest fire in July 2001.[219] The *tekke*, reopened in 1996, is currently administered by a resident dervish. It is one of the most beautiful in Albania as much of its early decorative art has remained undestroyed.
cf. F. W. Hasluck 1929, p. 435 (542); Baba Rexheb 1970, p. 298, 300; H. Kaleshi 1980, p. 13; N. Clayer 1990, pp. 360–361; F. Trix, *The Resurfacing* 1995, p. 543; I. Gjipali et al. 2013, pp. 258–259.

Melçan, District of Korça, Albania
Tekke of Baba Hysen, *tekke* of Baba Abdullah Melçani
Location: On a hilltop on the west side of the road between Korça and Maliq, *c.* 5 km from Korça. 40°38' N, 20°43' E.

The prestigious *tekke* of Melçan (not to be confused with Melan near Gjirokastra), situated on a flat hilltop, the site of an earlier fortification, is said to have been founded by Shemimi Baba in the late eighteenth century. It was subsequently administered by Baba Abdullah of Melçan from northern Albania who was no doubt a dervish of Shemimi Baba. One of the two early *tyrbes* at the site bore the date 1806 [1221 AH]. We know that the *tekke* existed before the 'Auspicious Event' of July 1826 because it was burned down during the closing of all the *tekkes* under Sultan Mahmud II that year. A few years later, Baba Abdullah invited Baba Salih Elbasani to take his place in Melçan. Baba Salih Elbasani, who had fled from his *tekke* in Köprülü (Veles in Macedonia) because of persecution and, as a *gjysh*, was of a higher rank than Baba Abdullah, arrived in Melçan but soon departed and founded the nearby *tekke* of Turan. Baba Abdullah thus resumed his functions in Melçan.

Baba Abdullah played a major role in spreading Bektashism in southeastern Albania and helped to found the no less prestigious *tekke* of Prishta. He also wrote verse in Albanian. A *tyrbe* was constructed in his honour at his death in 1857 [1274 AH] and was visited by many a pilgrim.

His successor, Baba Adem, was active in the Albanian national movement at the time of the League of Prizren (1878) and took part in an important gathering of the notables of southern Albania at the *tekke* of Frashër.

The *tekke* of Melçan attained its greatest renown under its following leader, Baba Hysen (d. 1914) from Vërlen, a village in the Devoll region. Under Baba Hysen, it became a veritable centre of the Albanian national movement. It was here in March 1906, in the presence of seven or eight *babas*, that the nationalist figure Bajo Topulli (1868–1930) formed the first armed guerrilla band in the Korça region. The guerrillas made their headquarters at the *tekke* and the population came here to receive instructions during the revolt against the Turkish authorities.

A photo of the site taken in 1917 shows a whole ensemble of buildings said to include three *tekkes* in one: a *tekke* of Baba Abdullah, a *tekke* of Hysejn Ali Dede, and a *tekke* of Baba Hysen of Melçan, in addition to various auxiliary buildings.

There was much turbulence at this *tekke* at the time of the First World War. It was looted in 1914 by Greek forces, but was otherwise not substantially damaged. That same year, Baba Hysen, who had fled to a nearby *tekke*, died. He was replaced by his nephew, dervish Zylfo (d. 1943), who was made *baba* of Melçan in 1915 by Baba Sulejman of Gjirokastra. French troops occupied the Korça region in 1916 and the hilltop *tekke* of Melçan, a strategic site, was taken up by the armed rebels of Sali bey Butka (1857–1938). Perhaps as a result of this, Baba Zylfo was exiled by the French authorities to Mytilene on the Greek island of Lesbos and was replaced by Baba Qazim of Qatrom, who was invested with an *ixhazet* by Baba Xhemal of Kreshova. When Baba Zylfo returned to Korça in 1919, two decades of bitter conflict ensued between the two *babas*, Baba Zylfo and Baba Qazim, for rule over the *tekke* of Melçan, a conflict in which the whole Bektashi community and indeed the Albanian State were caught up. Baba Qazim had the support of the local population, but Baba Zylfo had the Council of *Babas* behind him. Baba Zylfo, who administered the nearby *tekke* of Turan, was supported by the short-lived government of Fan Noli in 1924, whereas the supporters of Ahmet Zogu, who took power at the end of that year, preferred Baba Qazim. The Albanian government was asked to solve the issue, but was rightly reluctant to get involved in an internal matter of the Bektashi Community. As such, the matter dragged on for ages, throughout the 1920s and 1930s, virtually until the death of Baba Zylfo in 1943.[220]

From the 1930s onwards, the *tekke* of Melçan functioned as the seat of the *gjyshata* of Korça, one of the six Bektashi administrative districts in Albania.

The next head of the *tekke* of Melçan was Dede Rustem Melçani, secretary of the Fourth National Congress of the Bektashi that was held under communist rule in May 1945. He was subsequently imprisoned by the communists. Mention is also made of a Baba Zeqir who was imprisoned by the communists. In about 1950, Melçan lost its position as seat of the *gjyshata* of Korça to Turan.

The *tekke* of Melçan survived until 1967 when it was torn down by the surrounding villagers in the communist campaign against religion. Many of the buildings, walkways and one *tyrbe* survived in ruins until after 2010, but were then bulldozed to make way for a new, oversized *tekke*, paved driveways, a parking lot and gardens.

cf. F. W. Hasluck 1914-1916, p. 119, 1929, pp. 439 (546-547, 525); F. Bitincka 1925; H. Norris 1993, p. 135, Baba Rexhebi 1970, p. 282; N. Clayer 1990, pp. 362-367, 2013; F. Trix, *The Resurfacing* 1995, p. 547.

Memaliaj, District of Tepelena, Albania
Tekke of Memaliaj, *tyrbe* of Baba Hasan
Location: Town of Memaliaj. 40°21' N, 19°58' E.

According to Margaret Hasluck, the 'rich *tekke*' of Memaliaj was founded in the 1840s and its 'chief saint' was a Baba Hasan or Husejn. This may or may not be the same figure as the Baba Husejn Axhemi who administered the *tekke* at the time of the League of Prizren, *c*. 1878. Baba Husejn Axhemi was followed by Baba Mustafa who 'took the hand' and was appointed by Ali Haqi Baba of the *tekke* of Asim Baba in Gjirokastra and died around 1920. Baba Mustafa was followed by a Baba Hasan who 'took the hand' of Baba Ahmet Turani. The *tekke* was razed by Greek forces in June 1914 but was rebuilt, only to be destroyed again by an earthquake in the region of Tepelena in the early 1920s. The *tekke* of Memaliaj was represented by Baba Hasan at the First National Congress of the Bektashi, held at the *tekke* of Prishta in the Skrapar region on 14-17 January 1921. Margaret Hasluck came across two resident dervishes there during her visit in 1923. The *tekke* survived until 1967 when it was torn down by the local villagers in the communist campaign against religion and was long in ruins. The *tyrbe* of Baba Hasan was reconstructed in the centre of Memaliaj in the 1990s. The faithful gathered here as pilgrims on the feast day of 15 May. The *tekke* of Memaliaj is currently headed by Baba Abdyl Shehu.

cf. F. W. Hasluck 1929, p. 436 (542); Baba Rexheb 1970, p. 300, 384; N. Clayer 1990, pp. 368–369.

Ngrançija, District of Mallakastra, Albania
Tekke of Ngrançija, *tekke* of Nuri Baba
Location: About 10 km north of Ballsh. 40°38' N, 19°43' E.

The *tekke* of Ngrançija in Mallakastra, founded perhaps in the early twentieth century by a Baba Nuri, was a large building. It was reconstructed in 1923 after the destruction of the First World War. It survived until 1967 when it was torn down by the local villagers in the communist campaign against religion. A *tyrbe* was reconstructed here in the 1990s. Pilgrimages are held on its feast day of 21 November. It is not far from the *tekke* of Lapulec.
cf. N. Clayer 1990, p. 304.

Osmënzeza, District of Berat, Albania
Tekke of Baba Iljaz
Location: West of the village of Plashnik. 40°33' N, 19°53' E.

The small *tekke* of Osmënzeza was founded around 1905 by a Baba Iljaz (Elias) who died sometime before 1923. It was represented by a Baba Ahmet at the First National Congress of the Bektashi, held at the *tekke* of Prishta in the Skrapar region on 14–17 January 1921. Publisher Teki Selenica (1882–1962) asserted that it was one of the main *tekkes* in the Berat region, ranking with those of Tomorr and nearby Plashnik, but this would seem somewhat exaggerated, and there is little further information about it. It was subordinate to the *tekke* of Prishta and may have been a simple *dervishia* after the death of its founder. Later associated with this *tekke* was Baba Barjam Mahmutaj (1907–1997) who was imprisoned by the communists for seventeen years and then sentenced to a further fifteen years of hard labour digging canals. The *tekke* of Baba Iljaz survived until 1967 when it was torn down by the local villagers in the communist campaign against religion. A *tyrbe* was reconstructed at the site after the dictatorship.
cf. T. Selenica 1928, p. 189; T. Selenica 1928, p. 189; F. W. Hasluck 1929, p. 436 (543); N. Clayer 1990, p. 370; F. Trix, *The Resurfacing* 1995, p. 547.

Pacomit, District of Përmet, Albania
Tekke of Pacomit
Location: To the northeast of the road between Këlcyra and Përmet, just north of the junction with the road to Frashër. 40°18' N, 20°16' E.

Përmet, District of Përmet, Albania
Tekke of Baba Bektash, *tekke* of Baba Xhafer
Location: On a hillside above the town. 40°13' N, 20°20' E.

This *tekke* was founded on the hillside above Përmet around 1890 by a certain Baba Bektash. Legendry links it to the early seventeenth-century Bektashi holy man, Haxhi Baba Horasani. Haxhi Baba is said to have died in Përmet and was originally buried in the town where a *tyrbe* was constructed in his honour. Baba Bektash was buried near the *tyrbe* of Haxhi Baba, as was his successor Ismail Baba.

The English traveller and writer Edith Durham (1863–1944) visited the *tekke* on 30 March 1904 and noted:

> We proceeded to explore things Moslem. In a little garden, hedged round by towering cypresses, lay the tomb of a holy Bektashite Dervish; here the good man had lived and died, and the spot is holy and works miracles. He was beheaded and died a martyr, but he picked up his head and carried it back to his garden. Of the respect in which he was held there was no doubt, for the grave was strewn with small coins, and a little wooden money-box was hung on the wall, and the spot was quite unprotected, save by the good man's spirit. Seeing that I was interested, the young officer, no doubt a Bektashite himself, at once offered, to my great surprise, to take me to a 'tekieh' (Bektashite monastery) that lay high on the hillside, above the town – a rich tekieh, so he said, owning wide lands and sunny vineyards. It was a small, solid, stone building with a courtyard in front. At the entrance we waited while the officer went in to interview the 'Baba' (Father). My Christian guide doubted that we should be let in. We were, however, requested to go round to the back-door, and soon told the Baba was ready. In we went, to a bright little room with a low divan round it, and texts in Arabic on the walls, and big glass windows that commanded a grand view of all the valley. The Baba entered almost at once, a very grave and reverend signor in a long white robe; under which he wore a shirt with narrow stripes of black, white, and yellow; on his head a high white felt cap, divided into segments like a melon, and bound round by a green turban; and round his waist a leathern thong fastened by a wondrous button of rock crystal, the size and shape of a large hen's egg, segmented like the cap and set at the big end with turquoises and a red stone. He was very dark, with piercing eyes, shaggy brows, gray hair, and a long beard. [...]
>
> After he had given us coffee he said that, as it was the first time I had ever visited a Bektashite tekieh, perhaps I should like to see all the building. There were two other small dwelling-rooms. A priest and a pupil lived with him; their life, as I could see, was very simple, he said. They had many men to till the fields and make the bread. Giving bread to the needy was one of the duties of the monastery. He led us to the kitchen, a fine room with a huge fire-place, arched over by a stone vault carried on four columns. Rows and rows of great loaves were laid out on benches, and more were being made. Lastly, he showed the chapel. Of this I had but a passing glimpse from the doorway, for he did not invite me to enter. It had a divan round three sides of it, and an altar with candlesticks at one end, and was quite unlike a mosque. When we left he showed us out at the front-door, shook my hand three times, said a long blessing over me, and hoped that I should be led that way again. I thanked him and he thanked me, and we parted. The young officer was greatly pleased with the success of the visit, and appeared to reverence the Baba greatly.[221]

Margaret Hasluck reports that 'in 1915 Greeks troops were quartered in the *tekke*, so the abbot and dervishes betook themselves to the town annexe, where they have since remained, the *tekke* proper being now used by the Albanians as a barracks'.[222]

In later years, the *tekke* was under the administration of Baba Xhafer Sadiku, who was appointed around 1920 by Baba Ahmet Turani. He was still in office in the Second World War when he took part in fighting at the head of a band of pro-communist fighters in the Dangëllia region. In February 1945, the new regime put him up as a candidate to replace the non-communist *kryegjysh* in Tirana, Abaz Hilmi, but Baba Xhafer died three months later.

The *tekke* was closed down and destroyed in 1967. The *tyrbe*, with the graves of Baba Bektash and Baba Xhemal, has been reconstructed amidst the pine trees and, below it, the old stone house of the one-time *tekke* lies abandoned and in ruins (2017).

cf. E. Durham 1905, pp. 270–273; F. W. Hasluck 1914–1916, p. 118, 1929, p. 438 (544–545); N. Clayer 1990, pp. 371–373.

Përmet
Tekke of Baba Ali
Location: At the entrance of town, coming from the north, before the bridge. 40°14' N, 20°20' E.

The *tekke* of Baba Ali is said to date from 1861. It survived until 1967 when it was torn down by the 'revolutionary youth' of Përmet in the communist campaign against religion.

Përmet
Tekke of Baba Zenel
Location: undetermined. 40°13' N, 20°21' E.

This little *tekke* survived as a *dervishia* until 1967 when it was torn down by the 'revolutionary youth' of Përmet in the communist campaign against religion.

Petran, District of Përmet, Albania
Tekke of Petran
Location: 7 km southeast of Përmet, on the road to Leskovik. 40°12' N, 20°25' E.

The *tekke* of Pétran was quite old, dating perhaps from the sixteenth century. The building survived until 1967 when it was torn down by the surrounding villagers in the communist campaign against religion.

Picar, District of Gjirokastra, Albania
Dervishia of Baba Hasan
Location: North of Mashkullore on the road from Tepelena to Gjirokastra. 40°10' N, 20°03' E.

There was a small *dervishia* in Picar (Koronë-Picar) that seems to have been founded in the post-Ottoman period, although it may date from as early as 1870. According to Baba Rexheb, it was a simple house, inhabited by the dervish Hasan Picari whom the faithful from the surrounding region visited for *muhabet*. Baba Rexheb, then himself a dervish in nearby Gjirokastra, records that he was asked by Baba Selim Ruhi to deal with a problem that had arisen in Picar. The said Dervish Hasan had gotten drunk and fallen asleep with a cigarette in his hand. As a result, the *dervishia* caught on fire, but the maize with which the house was roofed burst into popcorn and woke the dervish up so that he was able to call for help. The *gjyshata* later requested that Dervish Hasan not drink so much. He had no successor.

The *dervishia* of Baba Hasan, which was associated in the 1950s with a Baba Kasem, survived until 1967 when it was torn down by the surrounding villagers in the communist campaign against religion. It reopened in the 1990s and now consists of two *tyrbes*: the *tyrbe* of Baba Hasan and the *tyrbe* of Baba Kasem, in addition of a two-room *tekke* building for guests and the custodian at the site.
cf. Baba Rexheb 1970; N. Clayer 1990, p. 315.

Plasa, District of Korça, Albania
Tyrbe of Plasa
Location: 8 km northeast of the town of Korça. 40°41' N, 20°50' E.

The *tyrbe* of Plasa, constructed around 1912, survived until 1967 when it was torn down by the surrounding villagers in the communist campaign against religion. It was rebuilt after the dictatorship.
cf. N. Clayer 1990, p. 374.

Plashnik, District of Berat, Albania
Tekke of Baba Muharrem
Location: About 20 km south of Berat. 40°33' N, 19°57' E.

The Albanian publicist Teki Selenica describes the *tekke* of Baba Muharrem in Plashnik as one of the main *tekkes* in the prefecture of Berat. It may have been constructed around 1912. It was represented by Baba Muharrem at the First National Congress of the Bektashi, held at the *tekke* of Prishta in the Skrapar region on 14–17 January 1921. It survived until 1967 when it was torn down by the surrounding villagers in the communist campaign against religion. A *tyrbe* and a small one-room building for the custodian were built on the site after the dictatorship.
cf. F. W. Hasluck 1929, p. 436 (543); T. Selenica 1928, p. 189; N. Clayer 1990, p. 375.

Podgoran, District of Përmet, Albania
Tekke of Podgoran
Location: On the eastern flank of Mount Trebeshina, about 15 km northwest of Këlcyra. 40°22' N, 20°07' E.

The *tekke* of Podgoran survived until 1967 when it was torn down by the surrounding villagers in the communist campaign against religion. A new *tyrbe* now graces the site.

Polena, District of Korça, Albania
Tekke of Baba Ismail
Location: About 8 km southwest of the town of Korça. 40°35' N, 20°41' E.

The *tekke* of Baba Ismail in Polena was constructed around 1911. It survived until 1967 when it was torn down by the surrounding villagers in the communist campaign against religion. There is now a new *tyrbe* at the site.

Prishta, District of Skrapar, Albania
Tekke of Baba Tahir
Location: About 15 km south of Çorovoda. 40°25' N, 20°13' E.

The original *tekke* of Prishta is said to have been established in the late eighteenth century by Shemimi Baba and was refounded in 1860 or earlier by Baba Tahir of Crete. Baba Tahir had been sent by Baba Abdullah of Melçan to spread Bektashism in the Skrapar and Mallakastra regions and was buried in Prishta.

The *tekke* of Prishta was considered to be among the richest *tekkes* in Albania, owning Suka and three other *çifligs*. It was looted and destroyed by Greek forces on 18 January 1914, but was reconstructed in 1921. It was at the *tekke* of Prishta that the First National Congress of the Bektashi was held in January 1921. Prishta also served as one of the six *gjyshatas* of the Bektashi community from 1930 to 1967. The faithful gathered here as pilgrims on the feast day of 30 May.

The *tekke* was administered a number of noted *babas*, including Baba Xhafer who died in 1893. Baba Ahmet, head of the *tekke* from 1893 to 1898, was a colourful figure who spent most of his time in exile in Sinope on the Turkish Black Sea coast, where he died in 1902. Baba Shaban headed the *tekke* from around 1900 to the time of the Greek occupation in 1913–1914 when he fled to Egypt, where he died in 1918. He was buried at the *tekke* in Cairo. His successor in Prishta, Baba Husejn, died in 1921 and was replaced by Baba Kamber Ali who served as head of the *tekke* of Prishta until 1944 when he was elected *kryegjysh* in Tirana. Thereafter came a Baba Muço who was imprisoned in 1945 and died in Burrel prison in 1950, and a Baba Iljaz who was a *gjysh* in 1952.

Joseph Swire visited the *tekke* in about 1930 and left the following description:

> Going again, we followed a steep-rising valley where a stream flowed beneath big trees, then climbed heavily to the *tekké* of Prishtë. The approach to the *tekké* is worn across the face of a precipice of clay and shale so slippery that we took off our boots – though the ponies, shod with flat iron shoes, thought nothing of it.
>
> The *tekké* of Tahir Baba was built admirably by dervishes in 1921, of stone, with many neat windows. There are two square blocks with two storeys, joined by a single-storey central part which consists of storerooms and kitchen off a stone-flagged cloister. The kitchen is cavernous, with smoke-blackened rafters and a vast open fireplace beneath an immense chimney-piece on four pillars, its pewter dishes and crockery and table spotlessly clean. Apart from the *tekké* are the outhouses where vats and kettles for making *raki* are kept; and a fine stoned-up spring in a porch. Below the *tekké*, upon a knoll among dark cypresses, stands a shrine with a dome, where the dead of the *tekké* lie.
>
> A *tekké* was first built here about 1870 but was destroyed by Greek bands in 1914 – the Greeks destroyed about forty *tekkés* (apart from shrines) but now there are more than fifty in Albania. All the inhabitants of the district fled to

Vlona; but they returned when the Italians came and the dervishes were able to contine 'teaching the people to be honest and kind'. Prishtë has ten dervishes, who claim to convert about 500 Moslems annually in their neighbourhood. Their *tekké* stands beautifully upon a spur, below scrub-covered ridges and above slopes under vineyards, maize fields, orchards and vegetable plots. Far beyond the valley towers Mali Tomori and Abas Ali's shrine may just be seen.

Through my mind there rushed thoughts of Omar Khayyám, of Hadji Baba, of Druids even, as three dervishes came from this modern building to meet us. They wore white hats somewhat like turbans, heavy beards (one red and luxuriant) and full white robes with sleeves, girdled by scarlet sashes; and two had long black gowns like students'. Quietly they bade us welcome, regretting *Baba-i-madh* Kamber Ali had not returned; but they led us to the *Baba* in charge, a placid patriarchal man with flowing white beard and the gentleness of his creed upon his features. With him we drank coffee. Then two dervishes showed the way about and plucked sweet-scented roses for us and for themselves. There were cats everywhere – sleek cats, contented as the dervishes. Kamber Ali's room had a divan covered by bright cushions down three sides and a gay carpet on the floor – a colour scheme of cherry and mauve – and several cupboards with well-carved doors. Here the people come from nearby villages to pray and be taught. A gong calls the dervishes to meditation at dawn and sunset, and between times they work, or study in their rooms. Our room was large, with four windows; mattresses, quilts and gay cushions on the floor; shelves, table and chairs. With *meze* as much of Prishtë's famous *raki* as we dared drink, then supper. We slept thankfully like the cats. We were sad to leave, and the *Baba* would take nothing for his *tekké*'s hospitality – not even for the poor.[223]

For some reason, the *tekke* of Prishta was not torn down in the communist campaign against religion in 1967, but was simply closed and used instead as a barn and as storage rooms. It later fell to ruins by itself. After decades of abandonment, it was reconstructed in 2006.
cf. A. Tomorri 1929, p. 85; F. W. Hasluck 1929, p. 437 (544); J. Swire 1937, pp. 257–259; Baba Rexhebi 1970, p. 282; N. Clayer 1990, pp. 377–381.

Progonat, District of Tepelena, Albania
Tekke of Progonat
Location: About 20 km southwest of the town of Tepelena. 40°12' N, 19°56' E.

The *tekke* in the isolated region of Progonat is said to stem from 1912. It survived and indeed had a *baba* until 1967 when it was torn down by the surrounding villagers in the communist campaign against religion. A *tyrbe* was built at the site after the dictatorship.
cf. N. Clayer 1990, p. 382.

Pulaha, District of Korça, Albania
Tyrbe of Pulaha
Location: About 15 km southwest of the town of Korça, not far from the road to Vithkuq. 40°32' N, 20°41' E.

The *tyrbe* of Pulaha survived until 1967 when it was torn down by the surrounding villagers in the communist campaign against religion. It was reconstructed after the dictatorship.

Qatrom, District of Korça, Albania
Tekke of Beqir Efendi
Location: About 4 km southwest of Korça. 40°35' N, 20°44' E.

This *tekke* is said to have been built around 1770, and its founder, Beqir Efendi, was buried there. It was burned down during the closing of all the *tekkes* under Sultan Mahmud II in July 1826 and was restored only in 1883 by a Baba Qazim. The *tekke* of Qatrom served as a centre of the Albanian nationalist movement and Albanian was taught there secretly, in particular by a Dervish Myftar and a Dervish Ramadan. Baba Qazim, for his part, was too afraid of the Turkish authorities to take part in such illicit activity. Qazim was succeeded by Dervish Ramadan in 1918. Baba Ramadan (d. 1935) played an important role in political events in the Korça region from 1916 to 1921. He represented the *tekke* of Qatrom at the First National Congress of the Bektashi, held at the *tekke* of Prishta in the Skrapar region on 14–17 January 1921, and had three dervishes under his administration. This *tekke* is referred to on the map made in Albania for the German scholar Franz Babinger in 1962, so it must still have been active in some form at that time, but it was no doubt shut down in 1967 during the communist campaign against religion.

The *tekke* of Qatrom, situated in solitude and tranquillity on the Plain of Korça, is now virtually abandoned but can be visited. It consists of a spacious walled-in area with two or three old buildings and a few fruit trees. In one corner is an octagonal green-roofed *tyrbe* containing the well-tended graves of Baba Zenel, Baba Qazim Plaku, Baba Ramadan and Baba Efendi (no doubt its founder, Beqir Efendi).

cf. F. W. Hasluck 1914–1916, p. 119, 1929, p. 439 (546); P. Pepo 1962, pp. 68–69, 328; N. Clayer 1990, pp. 383–384, 2003, p. 111.

Qesaraka, District of Kolonja, Albania
Tekke of Haxhi Baba Horasani
Location: Village of Qesaraka, about 15 km west of Qafëzez on the Erseka-Korça road. 40°24' N, 20°32' E.

This *tekke* was built, probably in the nineteenth century, in honour of Haxhi Baba Horasani (i.e. of Khorasan in Central Asia), to whom many miracles were attributed. According to a Bektashi legend,

> In 1600 AD, Hadji Baba from the *tekke* of Hacıbektaş arrived at the top of Mount Tomorr and on that peak venerated by the Albanians since ancient times, he set a sign and told the people that the site would thereafter be visited in the name of Abbas Ali, the brother of Imam Husein and standard-bearer of Kerbela. After leaving this sign on Tomorr, Hadji Baba went to Përmet where he died. From there, his body was taken to Qesaraka in the Kolonja region where a *tekke* and a *tyrbe* were built in his honour that still exist in all their glory to the present day.[224]

The *tekke* of Haxhi Baba Horasani was one of the two *tekkes* in Albania that did not observe the rule of celibacy. The *babas* of this *tekke* were successively: Baba Jahja, Baba Selman, Baba Shukri, Baba Shaban Shkëmbi (d. c. 1910) and the poet, Baba Ibrahim Shkëmbi. The *tekke* of Haxhi Baba Horasani, which Baba Rexheb describes as 'beautiful and majestic', was burned down and destroyed by Greek forces around 1913. Frederick Hasluck describes it from his visit shortly after the events (1913-1915):

> Kesaraka, some hours north-west of Kolonia, is a *mutehhil* convent. Before the war there were five or six dervishes besides the abbot, now the abbot only is left; the *tekke* is not very popular, dervishes preferring the celibate system. The foundation was due to Haji Baba of Khorasan, who died, as related above, at Premet. He hides in a handsome *turbe*, which the Greeks looted but did not entirely destroy.[225]

It was here that the Albanian educator Petro Nini Luarasi (1865-1911) sought refuge in 1903 when an attempt was made on his life.

The *tekke* of Haxhi Baba Horasani was not destroyed in the communist campaign against religion in 1967 as it had been declared a monument of culture. It was used as a warehouse and was restored with German funds in the 1990s. The last head of this *tekke* was the poet Baba Xhemal Shkëmbi (d. c. 2015) and the *tekke* is now virtually abandoned.

The feast day of this *tekke* is 7 June.

cf. F. Hasluck 1914-1916, p. 119, 1929, p. 440 (547); Baba Rexheb 1970, p. 360; J. Faensen 1980, p. 126; N. Clayer 1990, pp. 385-387.

Qesarat, District of Tepelena, Albania
Tyrbe of Qesarat
Location: About 10 km northwest of Memaliaj on the main road. 40°23' N, 19°52' E.

The *tyrbe* of Qesarat (not to be confused with Qesaraka) survived until 1967 when it was torn down by the surrounding villagers in the communist campaign against religion. It was reconstructed after the dictatorship.

Rabija, District of Tepelena, Albania
Tekke of Baba Selman
Location: About 4 km west of the Gllava Pass. 40°28' N, 19°56' E.

Legend has it that the area of Rabija was initially visited by Baba Ali Horasani and two dervishes. A *tekke* was founded there around 1887 by a Baba Selman (1843-1909) of Martanesh who 'took the hand' of Ali Haqi Baba of the *tekke* of Asim Baba in Gjirokastra. The *tekke* included a *tyrbe* in honour of Baba Ali Horasani who was thought to be buried there. There is also mention of a Baba Abbas (Abaz) in the nineteenth century. The *tekke* no doubt suffered the same fate as the rest in the period 1913-1914 at the hands of Greek forces when the region of Tepelena and Mallakastra was devastated.

Mention is made of a Baba Husejn Gumaj around 1912 and of Baba Abaz Malaj from the nearby village of Allkomemaj, who represented the *tekke* of Rabija at the First National Congress of the Bektashi, held at the *tekke* of Prishta in the Skrapar region on 14–17 January 1921 and who died in the Second World War.[226]

The *tekke* was a large two-storey building with about twenty rooms and a courtyard, all surrounded by a stone wall. It owned much land as well as extensive herds of sheep and goats. Nearby was the *tyrbe* with the graves of Baba Ali Horasani and Baba Selman.

During the Second World War, the *tekke* of Rabija, under Baba Abaz Sherif Memushaj, supported the communist partisans of the 'national liberation movement'. In fighting around the *tekke* on 17 July 1943, Italian forces from Berat were pushed back towards Mallakastra and abandoned their arms and ammunition in the field. They returned in strength on 22 July and, when they discovered that their weapons had been collected by the *baba* and were being stored at the *tekke* for the partisans to pick up, they summarily shot the *baba* and four dervishes. The male villagers of Allkomemaj were lined up and shot at the *tekke* the following day. The *tekke* itself was burned down a year later, during fighting in June 1944, but it continued to function in some sense until 1967 when it was razed to the ground by the surrounding villagers in the communist campaign against religion.

A *tyrbe* was reconstructed on the site after the dictatorship. People gather here every year on 23 July in commemoration of the massacre.

cf. F. W. Hasluck 1929, p. 437 (544); Baba Rexheb 1970, p. 300; N. Clayer 1990, p. 388; Sh. Hysi 2004, p. 109.

Rodenj, District of Përmet, Albania
Tyrbe of Rodenj
Location: About 14 km north of Këlcyra, not far from Ballaban and Suka. 40°23' N, 20°08' E.

This *tyrbe*, belonging to the *gjyshata* of Përmet, was torn down in 1967 during the communist campaign against religion.

Rozeç, District of Tepelena, Albania
Dervishia of Rozeç.
Location: Undetermined.

A *dervishia*, perhaps initially a *tekke*, was built here in 1912. It is referred to on the map made in Albania for the German scholar Franz Babinger in 1962, so it must still have been active in some form at that time. The surviving *tyrbe* was torn down in 1967 during the communist campaign against religion.

cf. N. Clayer 1990, p. 389.

Sanjollas, District of Kolonja, Albania
Tekke of Baba Sulejman
Location: In the village of Sanjollas, west of Barmash, just off the road from Leskovik to Erseka. 40°15' N, 20°35' E.

The *tekke* of Sanjollas, a tiny settlement near Barmash on the road from Leskovik, was founded around 1883 by a Baba Sulejman from Tetova. Before 1912, it was under the administration of a certain Baba Hasan, who was buried there. The *tekke* was destroyed by Greek forces in 1914. Baba Ali Tomorri noted that Baba Sulejman of Barmash was 'caught in Berat in 1914 and martyred after endless tribulation'.[227] Margaret Hasluck remarked in 1923 that it still had one *baba* and one dervish.

There are currently (2017) three *tyrbes* with unmarked graves on the hillside in the village.

cf. F. W. Hasluck 1914–1916, p. 119, 1929, p. 438 (545); N. Clayer 1990, p. 252; Sh. Hysi 2004, p. 114.

Saranda, District of Saranda, Albania
Tekke of Dede Reshat Bardhi
Location: On the coast a few kilometres west of the town of Saranda. 39°52' N, 19°57' E.

This new *tekke* was built around 2013. It includes impressive, richly designed reception rooms, a small historical museum, a *tyrbe* and gardens overlooking the Ionian Sea. The *tekke* of Saranda is dedicated to the memory of Haxhi Dede Reshat Bardhi and is headed by Baba Sadik Ibrokodheli. In the *tyrbe* are the graves of a Baba Bilal Beqiri and a Baba Islam Leskoviku.

Shëmbërdhenj, District of Gramsh, Albania
Tekke of Baba Mustafa
Location: Near Skënderbegas, about 20 km southeast of Gramsh. 40°46' N, 20°14' E.

The *tekke* of Baba Mustafa was founded in 1868 in the village of Shëmbërdhenj, south of Gramsh, by Mustafa Braçi (d. 1877) who had been a dervish under Baba Abdullah at the *tekke* of Melçan near Korça before he returned to his native village. Here Baba Mustafa acquired a building and land, and headed the *tekke* until 1877. He was succeeded by Baba Hysen (d. 1885) of Skorovot in the mountains of the Kolonja region, and Baba Hasan Mollasi who administered it from 1885 to 1891. In 1887 the *tekke* caught fire and burned down, but it was rebuilt. Baba Hasan left the *tekke* in 1891 as the result of some conflict with the local population. He was followed by Baba Meleq Staravecka (1842–1918), also known as Baba Meleq Shëmbërdhenji, who had returned from Egypt after the League of Prizren (1878) to distribute books in the region. He headed it, initially as a dervish, from 1891 to 1918. It was in October 1910 that dervish Meleq was officially appointed *baba* of this *tekke*, which served as a centre for the illicit teaching of Albanian in the late Ottoman period. The *tekke* was burned down in 1914, after Albanian independence, by Sunni Muslim rebels supporting the central Albanian uprising of Haxhi Qamili and its property was confiscated. Baba Meleq fled abroad, but he later returned and rebuilt the *tekke*. He is thus regarded by many as the second founder of the *tekke* of Baba Mustafa.

Baba Meleq was followed by Baba Bektash Kodheli from Istanbul who ran it from 1918 to 1922. He is remembered for having built a *tyrbe* for Baba Meleq and a well near the *tekke*. Baba Bektash abandoned the *tekke* in 1922 and went to Kushova in the Kolonja region, being replaced by his nephew, Baba Hilmi Kurtezi of Kolonja, who had more or less pushed him out of the position. In 1944 the *tekke* was burned down, it is said, by the Germans, and in 1946 Baba Hilmi was arrested by the communists and sentenced to fifteen years in prison.

The once-famed *tekke* of Shëmbërdhenji does not seem to have been rebuilt in the communist period. In the second half of 1947, the *kryegjysh* in Tirana, Ahmet Myftari, appointed Veli Agushi from Skrapar to head what remained. He lived most of his time in a little hut, though he did his best to gather building material to begin the reconstruction of the *tekke* buildings. He was transferred to Kruja in August 1959. There then followed a Baba Abedin Hoxhaj from 1959 to 1961 and a Baba Zeqir from the Korça region from 1961 onwards. The current *tekke* is administered by a resident dervish.

The faithful gathered here as pilgrims on the feast day of 6 August.
cf. F. W. Hasluck 1929, p. 441 (548–549); Baba Rexheb 1970, pp. 345–355; N. Clayer 1990, pp. 390–391; Q. Dedej, *Fillimet* 1997, pp. 94–102.

Shkoza, District of Vlora, Albania
Tekke of Shkoza
Location: On the left bank of the Vjosa River, about 20 km east of the town of Vlora. 40°24' N, 19°46' E.

The *tekke* of Shkoza survived until 1967 when it was razed to the ground by the surrounding villagers in the communist campaign against religion. A *tyrbe* was reconstructed on the site after the dictatorship.
cf. N. Clayer 1990, p. 394.

Shullaz, District of Kurbin, Albania
Tekke of Baba Isak
Location: At a curve on the old road from Laç to Milot. 41°39' N, 19°42' E.

The *tekke* founded by Baba Isak, with its large green dome visible from a distance, is situated just above the road from Laç to Milot in Kurbin territory. It was closed down, but not overly damaged in the communist campaign against religion in 1967 and was used as a school. It has since been reconstructed and consists of two rooms: one for the custodian and guests, and the other serving as the *tyrbe* with the grave of the said Baba Isak. To the one side of the building are a pleasant terraced garden and a graveyard. The *tyrbe* is regularly visited by the faithful who light candles and pray for the intercession of the holy man.

Smokthina, District of Vlora, Albania
Tekke of Smokthina
Location: In the Kurvelesh mountains, about 25–30 km southeast of the town of Vlora. 40°16' N, 19°40' E.

The isolated *tekke* of Smokthina survived until 1967 when it was torn down by the surrounding villagers in the communist campaign against religion. A *tyrbe* was reconstructed on the site after the dictatorship.

Starja, District of Kolonja, Albania
Tekke of Baba Husejn, also known as the Baruç *tekke*.

Location: In the Baruç quarter of the village of Starja, 5 km northeast of Erseka. 40°21' N, 20°43' E.

This small *tekke* was founded at the end of the nineteenth century, probably around 1893, by a certain Baba Husejn who was later buried there. Margaret Hasluck visited it in 1923 and came upon only one dervish. She noted that sick people went to the *tekke* there to be healed. It survived until 1967 when it was torn down by the surrounding villagers in the communist campaign against religion. A *tekke* building and two *tyrbes* were rebuilt on the site after the dictatorship.
cf. F. W. Hasluck 1914–1916, p. 119, 1929, p. 438 (545); N. Clayer 1990, pp. 395–396.

Straficka, District of Skrapar, Albania
Tekke of Baba Meleq
Location: In the hills on the right side of the Tomorrica River to the east of Mount Tomorr, about 17 km northeast of Çorovoda. 40°37' N, 20°17' E.

This *tekke* is referred to on the map made in Albania for the German scholar Franz Babinger in 1962, so it must still have been active in some form at that time. It was torn down by the surrounding villagers in the communist campaign against religion in 1967. A *tyrbe* was rebuilt on the site after the dictatorship.
cf. N. Clayer 1990, p. 396.

Suka, District of Përmet, Albania
Tekke of Baba Tahir, *tekke* of Suka
Location: About 10 km north of Këlcyra. 40°22' N, 20°09' E.

The *tekke* of Suka was founded in 1810 by a Baba Tahir. It is said to have played an important role in the Albanian nationalist movement. The initial *tekke* was no doubt burned down by Greek forces in 1913–1914, like most of the other southern Albanian *tekkes* and the new one was built by the dervishes in 1920. It was an offshoot of the nearby *tekke* of Prishta, with which it shared a *baba*. The faithful gathered here as pilgrims on the feast day of 5 July.

In about 1930 the British journalist Joseph Swire visited the *tekke* that reminded him of a Yorkshire dales farmhouse and left the following description:

> We camped outside Leskovik and returned next day to Permeti. Then leaving Këlcyra on our left we went to the Bektash *tekké* of Suka in a narrow cultivated valley. The *tekké*, strongly built of stone by dervishes in 1920, is rectangular and somewhat like a Yorkshire dales farmhouse; it stands on a hillside, owning about fifty acres which are tilled by its ten dervishes. Passages and rooms were very clean but sparsely furnished. *Baba-i-madh* (Grandfather – or bishop) Kamber Ali who happened to be there, a portly jovial old man in flowing white robe and very ecclesiastical manner, has his seat at the *tekké* of Tahir Baba at Prishtë. He had been to America and spoke English. A dervish brought coffee and cigarettes and *lokoum*, and a rose each – for the rose is an emblem of Bektashism; but the *Baba-i-madh* would not let me photograph him because he had drunk no water for twelve days (a self-disciplinary practice) – though what that had to do with it he did not explain.[228]

The *tekke* of Suka was closed down but not destroyed in the communist campaign against religion in 1967. It subsequently functioned as a hospital.

The buildings of the *tekke* still stand in ruins on the hillside (2014). A pilgrimage is held here on 5 July.

cf. F. W. Hasluck 1929, p. 437 (543–544); J. Swire 1937, p. 240; N. Clayer 1990, pp. 397–398.

Tepelena, District of Tepelena, Albania
Tekke of Demir Han
Location: In the town of Tepelena. 40°17' N, 20°01' E.

The *tekke* of Demir Han in Tepelena survived until 1967 when it was torn down by the townspeople of Tepelena in the communist campaign against religion. All that remain are a few candles at the site from time to time.

Therepel, District of Skrapar, Albania
Tekke of Baba Behlul
Location: On a hillside about 12 km northwest of Çorodova. 40°31' N, 20°07' E.

This *tekke* was founded in 1887 (or 1873?) by Baba Behlul who, it is claimed, lived from 1801 to 1911. As a young man, Behlul went to Turkey to train as a dervish, but he failed his exams or was otherwise not accepted. According to legend, to prove his qualifications, Behlul scooped hot Ashura pudding out of a scorching cauldron with his bare hands and did not burn himself. Those around him were suitable impressed and accepted him as a spiritual leader. He later 'took the hand' of Ali Haqi Baba of the *tekke* of Asim Baba in Gjirokastra. Mention is made of him during the Albanian national awakening. Baba Behlul was followed in 1911 by Baba Halim from Nishova. The *tekke* of Therepel was represented by Baba Halim at the First National Congress of the Bektashi, held at the *tekke* of Prishta in the Skrapar region on 14–17 January 1921. He was imprisoned by the communists after the Second World War. Thereafter the *tekke* was run by a dervish Shahin from Gjana near Bubës i Sipërm in Përmet.

The *tekke* of Baba Behlul, situated on a terrace above the village of Therepel with a magnificent view of Mount Tomorr on the other side of the valley, consisted of a 12-metre-high *tyrbe* (a 6-metre-high dome superimposed on 6 metres of walls) and a two-storey, L-shaped main building with twenty-seven rooms including a large *meydan*, together with auxiliary edifices for farming equipment and the animals. These buildings surrounded a main courtyard of quince trees. It was a wealthy *tekke* with much property and farmland.

The *tekke* of Baba Behlul survived until 1967 when it was torn down by the surrounding villagers in the communist campaign against religion. Before the mob arrived to raze the *tekke* to the ground with pickaxes and shovels, to the accompaniment of a band playing revolutionary music, the grandson of Baba Behlul managed to remove his grandfather's remains from the *tyrbe* and hid them in his garden.

An octagonal *tyrbe* was reconstructed after the communist dictatorship, in 2006, and the remains of Baba Behlul were laid to rest once again. The *tyrbe* contains three graves: Baba Behlul, Baba Halim and dervish Shahin. There is also a new three-room *tekke* building for guests and the custodian, who is the great-grandson of Baba Behlul.

Pilgrims visit this *tekke* on the feast day of 7 July.

cf. F. W. Hasluck 1929, p. 437 (544); Baba Rexheb 1970, p. 300; N. Clayer 1990, p. 399.

Tirana, District of Tirana, Albania
Kryegjyshata
Location: In the eastern outskirts of Tirana. 41°19' N, 19°50' E.

The *Kryegjyshata* is the headquarters of the Bektashi Order and the seat and residence of the *kryegjysh*. The dervish orders were banned in Turkey under Mustafa Kemal Atatürk in 1925 and all the *tekkes* were closed down there. As a result, at their Third National Congress held in 1929 at the *tekke* of Turan near Korça, the Albanian Bektashis decided to create a *kryegjyshata* of their own in Tirana. As none of the *babas* was willing to leave his *tekke* and move to Tirana, they resolved to invite Salih Nijazi Dede from Turkey, the *dede baba* (*kryegjysh*) who was himself of Albanian origin. They bought a building on the outskirts of Tirana for this purpose and Salih Nijazi Dede arrived from Turkey at the end of 1930.

The Albanian *Kryegjyshata*, which calls itself the World Headquarters of the Bektashi Order, began functioning in 1931, although the new and more representative building, begun in the 1930s, was only completed in 1941 during the Italian occupation, with financial support being provided by the Albanian government under King Zog. Salih Nijazi Dede was assassinated on 28 November 1941 under circumstances that have remained largely obscure.

The Bektashi clergy met in Tirana in January 1942 to find a new *gjysh*, but once again, none of the *babas* would accept the position. Eventually Ali Riza of Elbasan agreed to take over, but he died shortly thereafter. He was replaced after new elections in April 1944 by Baba Kamber Ali of the *tekke* of Prishta who was later arrested by the new communist authorities and imprisoned for life. Kamberi Ali was replaced by Xhafer Sadiku of the *tekke* of Përmet who presided over the Fourth National Congress of the Bektashi in Tirana in May 1945 but he died on 2 August of that year, three months after his appointment. Xhafer Sadiku Dede was replaced on 6 September 1945 by Baba Abaz Hilmi of Frashër, who then committed suicide on 19 March 1947 after a spectacular incident in which he killed Baba Faja Martaneshi and Baba Fejzo Dervishi in a heated argument allegedly over religious matters.

Hard times then followed for the *Kryegjyshata* because of the communist takeover of Albania. With the ongoing Stalinist purges in the country, the communist authorities had complete control over the Bektashi Order and most of the *babas* were frightened into submission or at least into silence. The *Kryegjyshata* was assumed on 8 June 1947 by Baba Ahmet Myftari, who had no choice but to be a puppet of the regime. He was succeeded by Baba Fehmi of Tepelena.

New statutes were once again promulgated at the Fifth National Congress of the Bektashi that was held in Tirana on 16 April 1950. Little is known of the role of the *Kryegjyshata* in the period thereafter until the new Albanian Constitution of 1967 banned religion entirely. That year, it was closed down and later transformed into an old people's home. It remained as such until the fall of the regime in 1990.

After a quarter of a century of communist dictatorship, the *Kryegjyshata* was reopened on 22 March 1991 in the presence of *Kryegjysh* Reshat Bardhi and of Mother Teresa, and work was begun on rebuilding three *tyrbes* for the graves of the former heads of the Bektashi community (*tyrbet e dedelerëve*). In 2004, work began on a prestigious glass odeon to serve as a venue for festive gatherings. It was inaugurated, after much delay, on 7 September 2015. In the basement of the building, a Bektashi museum was opened, and offices were reserved for a library and archives.

cf. Baba Rexheb 1970, p. 356; A. Popovic, *Les ordres mystiques* 1986; N. Clayer 1990, pp. 400–405.

Tomorr, Mount, District of Berat, Albania
Tekke of Kulmak, *tekke* of Mount Tomorr, *tyrbe* of Abbas Ali
Location: On Mount Tomorr, 40°38' N, 20°09' E.

The Bektashi pilgrimage site on the southern peak of Mount Tomorr is one of the most famous in Albania. The *tyrbe* (*mekam*) of Abbas Ali, at an elevation of 2,410 m, was originally constructed in 1620 and was rebuilt in 1880, 1928 and 2001. It is venerated by pilgrims during a five-day festival that takes place on the mountain on 20–25 August every year. According to one legend, Abbas Ali is supposed to have spent five days on Mount Tomorr before departing to live on Mount Olympus. He returns to Tomorr every year for five days, hence the August pilgrimage.

The earliest historical reference to the sanctuary on Mount Tomorr dates from the second half of the eighteenth century and concerns a Sa'di holy man called Demir Han who was killed in Tepelena in 1630. While travelling in the Middle East:

> Demir Han received a decree for Albania with instructions to go to Berat and, from there, to visit the *mekam* of Abbas Ali on Mount Tomorr. With a recommendation from Sheikh Hüseyin Tusiu of Djiba [near Damascus], he went to see Mustafa Tusiu in the little town of Vokopola and, with this person who was responsible for the holy site, he visited the *mekam* of Abbas Ali. There he received a sign telling him to go to the little town of Tepelena. He went there and founded a *zaviye*.[229]

A shrine to Abbas Ali must thus have existed on the mountain at that time. The Albanian orientalist Osman Myderrizi (1891–1973) recounts another version of the legend of foundation by a missionary:

> As proof of his capacity as a missionary, he brought with him a handwritten Koran, a sword and a sack containing soil from the place where Imam Husejn,

Abbas Ali and others were martyred in Kerbela. When he found out that the Albanians regarded Mount Tomorr as a holy mountain, he buried the soil from Kerbela on the summit and built the *mekam* of Abbas Ali.[230]

The Albanian aristocrat Ekrem bey Vlora visited the site in 1907 and described it as follows:

> It was a circular construction of well-hewn stone blocks put together without mortar as a ring wall, and had a narrow entrance to the southeast. It is called a *mekam*, an Arabic word for a site, or more specifically a pilgrimage site. In its present form, the construction dates from the year 1880. Inside the walls stood nothing aside from a niche of rough stonework facing southwards, in which there were two candlesticks and tin plate. On the plate were a few coins donated as alms by the faithful. The *mekam* is a site that is holy both to Muslims and to Christians. Even the most unscrupulous of robbers would never dare to steal these coins. Mount Tomorr would no doubt strike them dead with a bolt of lightning.
>
> On 15 August (old style), this desolate site comes to life for the feast of the Assumption of the Virgin Mary. It is mostly dervishes of the Bektashi Order who come here on pilgrimages to pray, sacrifice and collect alms. Among my travelling companions there were several Bektashi who only ventured to penetrate the ring wall on their knees. According to their beliefs, in the battle between Imam Hussein, the son of the fourth Caliph Ali, and Yazid, the son of Muawiyah, the stepbrother of the former, called Abbas Ali (a son of Ali by another wife), managed to flee the carnage of Kerbela and after long wanderings reached the peak of Mount Tomorr which he chose as his place to die. Historically speaking, this figure is unknown.
>
> The Christians pray here to Saint Mary, the holy virgin. Both religious communities use the oath '*për Baba Tomor!*' (by Father Tomorr!). They also believe that there was a temple here in ancient times.[231]

A two-room stone *dervishia* was built on the mountain a few hundred metres below the *tyrbe* in 1908–1909 but it was burned down by Greek forces in the spring of 1914. In 1916 a new *tekke* of Kulmak was founded and constructed by Dervish Iljaz Vërzhezha (d. 1923) just below the old *dervishia*.

The first *baba* there seems to have been a Baba Haxhi who died in Përmet. From 1921 to 1925, the *tekke* was headed by Baba Ali Tomorri (1900–1948). Around 1930, there were about five dervishes living there.

The British journalist and writer Joseph Swire visited the *tekke* on Mount Tomorr in about 1930:

> At our level (6,000 feet) stretched a narrow shelf from which the upper heights of Tomori rose precipitously among gaunt pines, thrusting tusks of rock and cornices of snow into the wild cloud-wisps 2,000 feet above. On this shelf stands the *tekke* of Kulmak, a single storey stone-built house with

courtyard and outhouses. There used to be only a two-roomed place here where one dervish lived, but in 1914 Greek bands destroyed it. [...] Every winter the *tekke* is cut off by snow and wolves howl round its walls. Then a bare room with a great fireplace was put at our disposal, and though the fire vomited thick smoke we were most thankful for it and for the strong tea we brewed by it. [...]

The morning was wet; but later the sun broke through the greyness and the low storm-clouds, torn to tatters, drifted and eddied in confusion between our feet and the valley's bed, clinging to spurs and hiding in hollows till the sun thrust down its shafts and chivvied them away. So we climbed to Tomori's holy summit. An hour's stiff scrambling brought us to the ridge – which is broken on its eastern side by precipices and steep screes but falls away more gently to the west. There was snow in the hollows and 12-foot snow cornices above the eastern precipices; yet the grassy parts were thick with cowslips and forget-me-nots, crocuses and narcissi. Eddying clouds shut out our view, but we followed the ridge easily by a succession of crests to the southern of the two main summits and came to a new-built shrine encircled by a stone wall – the shrine of Abas Ali, mythical saint of the Bektashis.

One August 25 long ago, goes the legend, Abas Ali came from Arabia to Berat; and mounting a great white horse (which has left hoof-marks upon the mountain) he fought the barbarians of the neighbourhood. When he had overcome them he rested for five days on Tomori, then went to dwell on Mount Olympus; but every year he returns on August 25 for five days, when there come Bektashis – and Christians too – sometimes eight or nine thousand people, to pay him homage. They bring their sheep for food, slaughter them on the summit, then take them down to their bivouacs by the *tekké*. So Tomori is a holy mountain and *për Baba Tomorit* a sacred oath. The shrine was built, so Baba Tyrabiu told me, on the site of an antique pagan shrine, so Abas Ali probably inherited his supernatural powers from the pagan god he displaced.

Abas Ali was good to us, for as we came to his shrine the bitter wind drove the clouds away down the mountain-sides, unwrapping a land of congealed ink flecked with untidy wisps of cotton wool and streaked with curling silver ribbons stretching to a molten sea. There was the whole coastline with Durrës, black Saseno, and the dark Acroceraunian wall. Nearer, though far below, lay the white houses of Berat like a handful of tiny pearls dropped into a fold of a crumpled green velvet carpet: and the Osum river winding between little moss-green hills mottled by woods and meadows and the sun-splashes. North and south were the snow-patched heights of our range, but east of us the Tomorica valley still held a boiling sea of cloud.[232]

There is little information about the *tekke* in the communist period. A Baba Sami was arrested and died in internment. In 1957, pilgrims from throughout southern Albania were still flocking to the site in August and stayed there for three days. Ten years later, when the communist regime abolished religion, the practice more or less died out until the end of the dictatorship. In 1967 both the *tyrbe* and the *tekke* were destroyed on the pretext that the mountain peak was needed by the armed forces as a strategic military post.

The *tekke*, which was reconstructed in 1992, is presently headed by Baba Shaban, and the site is more active than ever during the annual pilgrimage on 20–25 August every year. The main ceremony takes place on 22 August when the *kryegjysh* from Tirana is present. People in their thousands now attend from around the world. The *tyrbe* of Abas Ali itself was reconstructed in 2008.

cf. E. Vlora 1911, pp. 106–107; T. Selenica 1928, p. 189; A. Tomorri 1929, p. 93; F. W. Hasluck 1929, p. 441 (548); J. Swire 1937, pp. 251–254; Baba Rexheb 1970, pp. 367–368; G. Stadtmüller 1971, pp. 686–687; N. Clayer 1990, pp. 406–411, 2003, pp. 143–146.

Turan, District of Korça, Albania
Tekke of Baba Salih Elbasani
Location: *c.* 3 km west of Korça. 40°37' N, 20°44' E.

This *tekke*, not to be confused with the *tekke* in another settlement called Turan near Tepelena, was built in the first half of the nineteenth century, possibly around 1812. There is no reference to it from the time of the closing of all the *tekkes* under Sultan Mahmud II in July 1826. It was founded by Baba Salih Elbasani, who had earlier been head of the Bektashi *tekke* of Köprülü (Veles in Macedonia). Baba Salih had had a dream and foreseen the persecution that would accompany the closing of the *tekkes*, so he fled with his dervishes to Korça and Elbasan. Sometime thereafter, Baba Abdullah Melçani invited him to replace him as *baba* of Melçan. Baba Salih, who as a *gjysh* was of a higher rank, arrived in Melçan, but soon thereafter continued on and founded the nearby *tekke* of Turan, where he was buried. The grave of one *baba* there dates from 1889 to 1890 [1307 AH].

In the early years of the twentieth century, the *tekke* of Turan, under Baba Hajdar (1857–1928) from Qëncka in the Gora region of Korça, played an important role in the Albanian national movement. Secret meetings of Albanian patriots were held there and Albanian books were distributed illicitly. During the First World War, the *baba* of Turan had to flee and was absent for a period of three years, but in 1923 there were four dervishes living there once again. In 1924 the *tekke* came under the administration of Baba Zylfo of Melçan. In 1929, Zylfo organized the Third National Congress of the Albanian Bektashi in Turan, so we can assume that the *tekke* was of national significance. As a *gjysh* in the 1930s, Baba Zylfo had about 200 *muhibs* and many non-initiated followers under his administration at the *tekke*. He took part in the Second World War on the side of the anticommunist *Balli Kombëtar* (National Front) and was killed at the *tekke* in 1943 by an unspecified *çeta* band. From 1950 to 1967, the *tekke* of Turan served as the *gjyshata* of the Korça region.

Machiel Kiel had occasion to visit the *tekke* in the 1960s, and noted:

> In 1967, I have an opportunity to visit the Turan *Tekke*, just after the Cultural Revolution had tried to destroy all outward signs of religion. The *tekke* is situated four and a half km west of Korça on the beautiful east Albanian plain, just outside

the village of Turan. The buildings preserved are not examples of great Ottoman art, but are highly representative of Bektashi buildings in Albania in the last century and shall therefore be described briefly. The domestic buildings lie on one side of the Voskopoja road. There is a large two-storey manor house built of wood, adobe bricks and plaster. Opposite the lodge, in a garden with different kinds of trees, is the architecturally most important part of the *tekke*, two *türbes*. The lesser *türbe* is a polygonal, nearly round structure with purple-red plastered brick walls, white pilasters and a lead-covered dome. Although not later than the end of the 19th century, this *türbe* still has some dignity and is certainly inspired by older Ottoman structures. The *türbe* is preceded by a domed portico on two slender columns. The older *türbe* is a much larger structure, a rectangle built of well-cut blocks of hard gray limestone. The rectangle is divided into two compartments which have separate vaults. The central vaulted section is covered by a dome, the lateral section by cross vaults. Next to the main room is another room, added at a later date. It is covered by a transversally placed barrel vault. The interior of both *türbes* is empty; the older one originally contained the tombs of at least three sheikhs, but these were removed just a few weeks before my visit. In the graveyard surrounding the *türbes*, the graves of the deceased brethren were opened, the bodies removed, and shoes and jackets of those recently buried lay about in several places, a horrifying vision of the day of resurrection. This may give an idea of the fury with which the Albanian Cultural Revolution struck religion and especially the cult of saints and miraculous graves. The buildings of the *tekke* and the two *türbes* were turned into a chicken farm.

Above the entrance of the older *türbe* is preserved a fine 19th-century inscription with a carved hand on it and two *teslim taşlar* of polished precious stone. Beside the inscription is another one in modern Albanian, concerning a recent repair of the *türbe*. This repair is possibly responsible for the excellent state of preservation of the buildings. The Albanian inscription runs as follows:

Tyrbe e ribërë prej Baba Sabriut,
Zotin e paçim ndihmë, 18.06.1957

The *türbe* was made new (repaired) by Baba Sabri
Through the help of the Lord, 18.06.1957

An older inscription is from 1293 AH (1876–1877).[233]

The older *tyrbe* inscription reveals the building to be the shrine of Baba Ali and Baba Salih, that was reconstructed in 1876–1877 [1293 AH] by Baba Adem of Backa. It reads:

Oh, Excellency, Haxhi Bektash, the Holy, I begin with 'In the name of God, the all-compassionate, the merciful'. The *tyrbe* of Ali Baba and Salih Baba has been renovated. May the glory of Adem Baba, its builder, increase. May those who visit it materially and spiritually be joyful, may the everlasting and all-auspicious

(Allah) be the helper of its builder in all respects. On the day of Friday, one thousand two hundred ninety-three, Muharrem and his name was Abid, the one who desires.[234]

Also preserved is the Ottoman inscription of a no-longer-existing fountain that was built by Baba Adem of Backa ten years earlier, in 1866–1867 [1283 AH].

The *tekke* was reconstructed in the 1990s, but the atmosphere of the original building has not been destroyed.

The faithful gathered here as pilgrims on the feast day of 25 March.
cf. F. W. Hasluck 1914–1916, p. 119, 1929, p. 439 (546); J. Birge 1937, p. 72, 163; Baba Rexheb 1970, p. 293; N. Clayer 1990, pp. 412–414; M. Kiel 1990, pp. 167–169; M. Tütüncü 2017, pp. 217–220.

Turan, District of Tepelena, Albania
Tekke of Baba Ali, *tekke* of Turan
Location: About 5 km northwest of Tepelena, on the old road to Vlora. 40°18' N, 19°58' E.

This *tekke* in the Tepelena region, not to be confused with the *tekke* in another settlement called Turan near Korça, was founded about 1900. It was first headed by Baba Ali Turani, who 'took the hand' of Ali Haqi Baba of the *tekke* of Asim Baba in Gjirokastra and died in 1908. He was followed by the better known Baba Ahmet Turani who was made a *gjysh* (*dede*) in 1910 at the *pir evi* at Hacıbektaşköy in central Anatolia. This position gave him and the *tekke* of Turan a certain renown. The *tekke* was burned down by Greek forces in June 1914, and Baba Ahmet and the whole population of the village and its surroundings fled to Vlora. In about 1920, he returned to Turan and rebuilt the *tekke* with the help of the local population and with financial support from Bektashi Albanians in America. Margaret Hasluck, who visited the region in 1923, noted that 'the *tekke* is rich and has now twelve dervishes'. The *tekke* of Turan was at its zenith in the 1920s, until the death of Baba Ahmet in 1928. It is referred to on the map made in Albania for the German scholar Franz Babinger in 1962, so it must still have been active in some form at that time. It seems to have been closed or destroyed in 1967 during the communist campaign against religion.

The *tekke*, together with the *tyrbe* containing the graves of Baba Ali Turani and Baba Ahmet Turani, is currently (2017) being rebuilt. It is now administered by a resident dervish.
cf. F. W. Hasluck 1914–1916, p. 117, 1929, p. 435 (542); J. Godart 1922, p. 166; Baba Rexheb 1970, p. 300; N. Clayer 1990, pp. 415–418.

Velabisht, District of Berat, Albania
Tekke of Baba Kamber
Location: On a hill about 2 km west of the village of Velabisht, itself situated on the left bank of the Osum River across from the town of Berat. 40°41' N, 19°56' E.

The *tekke* of Velabisht was built in 1870 by Baba Kamber Haskaj of Fratar (d. 1913). It was destroyed, like many other southern Albanian *tekkes,* around 1914.

F. W. Hasluck described it before the First World War as a 'handsome *tekke*'. It was subordinate to the *tekke* of Prishta. The *tekke* of Baba Kamber survived until 1967 when it was torn down by the local villagers in the communist campaign against religion. As in Therepel, the family tending the *tyrbe* managed to dig out the remains of the holy men and rebury them at home. These remains were returned when a new *tyrbe,* an attractive building on the hillside, was reconstructed in its original twelve-sided form in 2009. It contains the graves of Baba Kamber, Baba Iljaz and Baba Qazim of Aranitas (d. 1963) who headed the *tekke* from 1954. In the vicinity of the *tekke,* there was also a *tyrbe* of Dervish Rexhep.

The faithful gathered here as pilgrims on the feast day of 25 September.
cf. F. W. Hasluck 1929, p. 441 (549); N. Clayer 1990, p. 420.

Veliqot, District of Tepelena, Albania
Tekke of Baba Hysen, *tekke* of Veliqot
Location: A couple of kilometres to the west of Tepelena. 40°17' N, 20°00' E.

The *tekke* of Veliqot is reported to be very old. It was founded by a certain Baba Hysen or Husejn. The *tekke* was destroyed in July 1826 by emissaries of Sultan Mahmud II during the crackdown and closing of all the *tekkes* in the Ottoman Empire. A new *tekke* was built there only after the Ottoman period, perhaps around 1912. It survived until 1967 when it was razed to the ground by the surrounding villagers in the communist campaign against religion. A new *tyrbe* was built on the hill behind the village when democracy was restored.
cf. F. W. Hasluck 1929, p. 435 (542); N. Clayer 1990, p. 419.

Vloçisht, District of Korça, Albania
Tekke of Vloçisht
Location: Village of Vloçisht, later called Drithas, about 10 km northwest of Korça. 40°41' N, 20°43' E.

The *tekke* of Vloçisht, constructed around 1912, survived until 1967 when it was razed to the ground by the surrounding villagers in the communist campaign against religion. A *tyrbe* was reconstructed at the site after the introduction of democracy.

Vlora, District of Vlora, Albania
Tekke of Kusum Baba, *mekam* of Kusum Baba
Location: On the hill overlooking the town of Vlora. 40°28' N, 19°29' E.

This *tekke* of Vlora, set on the hill overlooking the town, was dedicated to the holy man Kusum Baba, also known as Kosum Baba, Kuzum Baba, Kus Baba, Kusmaba or Quzum Baba Sultan.

Kusum Baba was a dervish in the early years of Ottoman rule, who arrived in Vlora with several companions. According to a typical Bektashi legend, he was attacked by evil-doers who chopped off his head. The saint then stooped, picked up his head and continued his journey to a hill overlooking the town of Vlora, now called Kusum Baba after him. There he collapsed and expired, having first ordered his companions to dig a grave for him.

A *tyrbe* was built at the site, followed by a Bektashi *tekke*, which was subsequently supported by the aristocratic Vlora family.

The Turkish traveller Evliya Çelebi, who visited Vlora in the year 1670, noted the presence of the site in the following terms: 'To the east of the fortress and somewhat above it is a slope with olive trees. All the hills and fields in the area are covered in fruit trees, vineyards and olive orchards. On this high peak is situated the tomb of Kuzgun Baba Sultan with a few Bektashi dervishes.'[235]

The *tekke* seems to have prospered in early years but it was abandoned in the nineteenth century after the closing of all the *tekkes* under Sultan Mahmud II in July 1826.

The Austrian historian and archaeologist Carl Patsch visited the *tyrbe* of Kusum Baba in 1900.[236] Margaret Hasluck noted in this connection: 'He is sometimes called Kuzu Baba. It is said that permission to build a *tekke* by his grave was requested from the Turkish government but refused, Valona being fanatically Sunni. He is now called Shemsi Baba and is tended by a Sunni *khoja*.'[237]

The *tekke* was revived at some point, probably after 1920, since reference is made to the *tekke* of Quzum Baba Sultan in the statutes of the Bektashi community in 1950 when it was the seat of the *tekkes* of Vlora and Fier.

The *tyrbe* of Kusum Baba was reopened in April 1998 on the high cliff overlooking the town of Vlora and, now splendidly illuminated at night. It can be seen from all points of town. A large *tekke* was constructed soon thereafter on the land behind the *tyrbe*. It is currently administered by a resident dervish.

cf. C. Patsch 1904, p. 117; F. W. Hasluck 1929, p. 437 (543); E. Vlora 1955, p. 35; N. Clayer 1990, pp. 422–423; R. Dankoff and R. Elsie 2000, 361b, pp. 136–139; R. Elsie 2001, *Dictionary*, pp. 156–157.

Vokopola, District of Berat, Albania
Tekke of Baba Tahir
Location: A few kilometres west of Ura Vajgurore, northwest of Berat. 40°30' N, 20°04' E.

This was a relatively old *tekke*. There was also a *tyrbe* nearby. It survived until 1967 when it was razed to the ground by the surrounding villagers in the communist campaign against religion. A new *tyrbe* was built at the site when democracy was restored.

cf. N. Clayer 1990, p. 424.

Vrëpska, District of Korça, Albania
Tekke of Vrëpska
Location: Village of Vrëpska, now Gurkuq. It is situated in the hills south of Moglica on the road from Korça to Gramsh. 40°11' N, 20°36' E.

The *tekke* of Vrëpska was probably founded around 1912 and was represented by a Baba Bektash at the First National Congress of the Bektashi, held at the *tekke* of Prishta in the Skrapar region on 14–17 January 1921. In the period 1943–1944, the *baba* of the *tekke* of Vrëpska was slain by occupying German forces. The *tekke* survived until 1967 when it was razed to the ground by the surrounding villagers

in the communist campaign against religion. There is now a *tyrbe* and a custodian here.
cf. N. Clayer 1990, p. 425.

Zërqan, District of Bulqiza, Albania
Tyrbe of Baba Hysen
Location: On a hillside about 12 km east of Bulqiza on the road to Peshkopia. 41°30' N, 20°21' E.

The *tyrbe* of Baba Hysen of Martanesh, also called Baba Hysen Kukeli (1822-1893) or Baba Hysen Mali, stems from the eighteenth century and was reconstructed by the said Baba Hysen around 1877. Hysen Kukeli had trained and become a dervish under Baba Fejzë Bulqiza. In the mid-nineteenth century, Turkish forces under Avdi Pasha carried out a military campaign in the Dibra region and arrested both men. Baba Fejzë Bulqiza died in prison, but Hysen Kukeli, exiled to Monastir (Bitola), was eventually released and settled in Fushë Kruja. There he reconstructed the *tekke* of Fushë Kruja 1852-1853 [1270 AH] and was made a *baba*. He subsequently served at the *tekke* of Balim Sultan in Martanesh in 1870, before retiring to his native Zërqan, where he spent the rest of his life. A *tyrbe* was constructed in his honour there by Jasha Krena and has been maintained to the present day by the Hanku family, the present custodian being the elderly Dervish Xhafer Hanku.

The *tekke* was closed down in 1967 during the communist campaign against religion but was reopened in 1995. It is a simple shrine with an adjacent building, situated on a hill, called Kodra e Vakëfit, above the road and has a splendid view of the surroundings. Buried in the present shrine are: Baba Hysen, Baba Metin, Dervish Sulejman from Ohrid, and Baba Xhemal, who was the last *baba* here. Around the *tyrbe* are some beautiful gravestones from the Ottoman period.
cf. M. Hasluck 1954, p 118; N. Clayer 1990, p. 426.

Zhepova, District of Përmet, Albania
Tyrbe of Zhepova
Location: In the hills on the left (eastern) side of the upper Deshnica River, about 10 km north of Këlcyra. 40°23' N, 20°12' E.

This *tyrbe* survived until 1967 when it was razed to the ground by the surrounding villagers in the communist campaign against religion. A new *tyrbe* was constructed at the site after the introduction of democracy.

TEKKES AND SHRINES IN KOSOVO

Map of Kosovo showing cities of *tekkes* and shrines.

Gjakova, Kosovo (Turkish: Yakova, Serbian: Djakovica)
Tekke of Shemseddin Baba
Location: 46 Ferid Grezda St. in the old town of Gjakova. 42°22' N, 20°25' E.

The Bektashi are said to have made their initial appearance in Gjakova in 1790. Most of the dervish orders were present here by the nineteenth century. At their zenith, there were no less than fifteen *tekkes* in Gjakova, of which six belonged to the Sa'di Order. The Bektashi *tekke* itself was founded in the mid-nineteenth century by a Baba Shemseddin (Şemsettin Baba), also known as Baba Shemsi Plaku (the Elder), who originally belonged to the Sa'di Order.

The *tyrbe* contains the graves of Baba Shemseddin, Baba Abdylgani and Baba Haxhi Adem. Over the entrance to it, there was a Turkish inscription giving the following account of its history:

This *tekke* was founded by Shemseddin Baba who, when the time came, retired to a recess of solitude. Like other pious *muhibs*, he was guided by Haxhi Bektash Veli and found nearness to God. Shemseddin Baba died and was replaced as *post nişin* by Abdylgani Baba, scion of a most noble family, who remained the guide of the Path. This perfectly educated man passed away at the Gate of Bliss. Haxhi Adem Baba of Prizren then arrived. He had been a student at the *tekke* of *Hazret-i pîr*, and became a faultless celibate, detached from worldly things. This third *post nişin* to embellish the *tekke* unfolded the wings of grace and alighted on this abode. This *tekke* of the secret of God was extremely narrow and exiguous. Baba Adem, source of perfection, expanded it and raised it up. It was thanks to the zeal of the *pîr* that he refounded the *tekke*. He was the problem-solving guide in the town of Gjakova. The humble Vexh-hi gives the date of the refoundation of the *tekke*.[238]

Among the subsequent heads of the *tekke* were: the said Baba Abdylgani, also known as Baba Gani; Baba Haxhi Adem of Prizren (d. 1894), also known as Baba Haxhi Ademi Plaku (the Elder); Baba Mehmet Shemseddin from Gjakova (d. 1896), also called Baba Shemsi; Baba Abdurrahman (d. 1904); Baba Hafiz Ali (d. 1926) who served here around the time of the First World War and is remembered for his verse in Turkish and Persian; and Baba Adem Vexh-hi (1841–1927). The latter was the *baba* in Gjakova from 1921 to 1927 and was to play a significant role in public and political life in Kosovo. He was followed by Baba Hamza (1882–1952) who had been made the *baba* of the *tekke* of Shtip in Macedonia in 1912; and Baba Qazim Bakalli (1895–1981), 'an illustrious and greatly revered Baba with a long lifetime of service to the order'.[239]

Originally a teacher, Baba Qazim headed the *tekke* of Gjakova from 1947 until his death in February 1981. He was replaced by Baba Tajar Gashi from Gostivar who administered the *tekke* until his death in 1994. The current head of the *tekke* is Baba Mumin Lama who took over on 21 April 1996.

The *tekke* and *tyrbe* were burned down by Serbian forces in the 1998–1999 war, but, despite much irreparable loss, in particular to the *tekke* library, the buildings have been reconstructed.

cf. F. W. Hasluck 1929, p. 424 (525); H. Kaleshi 1980, pp. 14–15; N. Hafiz 1995, pp. 348–349; J. Norton 2001, pp. 188–189; J. Rexhepagiqi 2003, pp. 230–233.

Kaçanik, Kosovo
Tekke of Kaçanik
Location: Town of Kaçanik. 42°13' N, 21°15' E.

The Turkish traveller and writer Evliya Çelebi (1611–*c*. 1685) mentioned a Bektashi *tekke* on his journey through Kosovo in 1660. There is no further trace of it.

Mitrovica, Kosovo
Tekke of Mustafa Baba
Location: Mitrovica or Zveçan. 42°53' N, 21°51' E.

On his journey through Kosovo in 1660, the Turkish traveller and writer Evliya Çelebi (1611–c. 1685) referred to a shrine of Mustafa Baba at bowshot range from the fortress of Mitrovica. Beside the shrine was a *tekke* inhabited by Bektashi dervishes, where travellers could spend the night. He added that the *tekke* was near the town of Zveçan. There is now no trace of it.

Peja, Kosovo (Turkish: Ipek, Serbian: Peć)
Tekke of Peja
Location: Somewhere in the old town of Peja. 42°39' N, 20°17' E.

There was an early Bektashi *tekke* in Peja, but it was no longer active around the time of the First World War.
cf. F. W. Hasluck 1929, p. 424 (525); G. Louis-Jaray 1914, p. 99.

Prizren, Kosovo
Tekke of Baba Adem
Location: Near the Hasanbeg mill in the old town of Prizren. 42°12' N, 20°44' E.

The *tekke* of Prizren was situated on the right bank of the Lumbardh (Bistrica) River not far from the mill of Hasanbeg. It was founded by Haxhi Baba Adem from Gjakova around 1890. He was succeeded by Baba Adem Kovaçi from Gjakova, who wrote poetry in Turkish and Persian. The *tekke* is referred to by the British journalist Henry Brailsford (1873–1958) in 1906 and the French travel writer Gabriel Louis-Jaray in 1914. It was shut down after the Serbian invasion of Kosovo in 1912 and turned into a Serbian orphanage. The *tekke* closed definitively in 1924, but the building still stood as a private house in 1976.[240]
cf. H. Brailsford 1906, pp. 247–248; G. Louis-Jaray 1914, p. 99; F. W. Hasluck 1929, p. 424 (525); J. Rexhepagiqi 2003, pp. 227–228; N. Clayer 2007, pp. 476–477.

TEKKES AND SHRINES IN THE REPUBLIC OF MACEDONIA

Map of Macedonia showing cities with *tekkes* and shrines 37.

Kanatlar Municipality of Prilep, Macedonia
Tekke of Dikmen Baba, *tekke* of Mehmed Baba
Location: Between Prilep and Bitola/Monastir. 41°12' N, 21°30' E.

The *tekke* of Dikmen Baba is situated on a low hill above the Turkish-speaking village of Kanatlar (Albanian: Kanatllar, Macedonian: Kanatlarci) which is located on the plain of Pelagonia between Prilep and Bitola/Monastir. It is said to date from 1503 and seems to have been re-established in the early eighteenth century. The *tekke* was established with the help of a Mehmed Baba and thus also named after him.

The *tekke* of Dikmen Baba is a splendid site that still conveys the genuine atmosphere of an impoverished, though well-kept, Bektashi *tekke* in Ottoman times. It consists of several buildings behind the high walls, including five or six *tyrbes* and a spacious, colourful *meydan*, as well as a cemetery with many graves dating from the Ottoman period. The *tyrbes* are those of: 1. Dikmen Baba, 2. Ismail Baba, 3. Mustafa Baba, 4. Selman Baba and 5. Idriz Baba. The second *baba* of this *tekke*, Demir Baba, was buried elsewhere. For many years it was the only more or less functioning Bektashi *tekke* in Macedonia.

The current head of the *tekke* is Veli Baba (b. 1950) who has three dervishes, all of whom are Turkish. Though none of the *babas* here were Albanian and the *tekke* had and has stronger ties to Turkey than to Albania, it nonetheless had Albanian connections and, even today, it is still visited by pilgrims from Albania.

cf. F. W. Hasluck 1929, p. 423 (524); N. Clayer and A. Popovic 1992, pp. 44–46; L. Mašulović-Marsol 1995, pp. 352–353; J. Norton 2001, p. 188.

Kërçova, Municipality of Kërçova, Macedonia (Macedonian: Kičevo, Turkish: Kırcaova)
Tekke of Hidër Baba
Location: In the centre of the town of Kërçova (Kičevo). 41°30' N, 20°57' E.

A fine, large *tekke* had been demolished in Kërçova in Ottoman times.[241] In 1936, a Baba Muharrem (d. 1959) bought a house in Kërçova to found a new *tekke* there which he dedicated to Hidër (Khidr) Baba, whose *tekke* in Makedonski Brod had been burned down. Baba Muharrem had been invested as a *baba* by Salih Nijazi Dede of Tirana and died around 1950. He was succeeded in 1959 by Baba Musa of Gjakova who was invested by Baba Qazim Bakalli of Gjakova and stayed in Kërçova for two years. When Baba Musa was expelled by the Yugoslav authorities and sent back to Gjakova, he was succeeded in Kërçova by Baba Zija Pasholli of Kanatlar who served here from 1967 to 1992.[242]

In 1979, Baba Zija was ministering there to the faithful Bektashi community that continued to celebrate their traditional festivals, including picnics in the countryside at Hidrellez (6 May, regarded as the start of summer).[243] Meetings were regularly held on Thursday evenings with the participation of about thirty initiates (male and female) from among the approximately eighty Bektashi of the Kërçova region.[244] Nathalie Clayer, who visited the town in April 1990, noted that the Bektashi *tekke* was closed. All that remained was a sign on the door reading *Adar [= Hajdar] Baba Teke*.

Baba Zija is said to have been defrocked by the faithful in 1992 and returned to private life at his home in Kërçova, where he died around 2008. The origin of the conflict is unclear. He was replaced at any rate by the present Baba Ejup Rakipi (b. 1939) who had served as a *muhib* in Kërçova in 1993–1995 and had been inspired by the writings of Baba Rexheb. A large new *tekke* building was constructed on the site in 2004.

Though many of its *babas* have been Albanian to the present day, the *tekke* of Hidër Baba in Kërçova does not automatically recognize its supremacy of the *Kryegjyshata* in Tirana, and strives to maintain good relations with both Tirana and the Bektashi hierarchy in Turkey, represented by two heads, Haydar Ercan and Mustafa Eke.

In contrast to most *tekkes*, there is no *tyrbe* or shrine here, the grave of Hidër Baba being in Makedonski Brod.

cf. F. W. Hasluck 1929, p. 423 (524); Baba Rexheb 1970, pp. 261–264; T. Djordjević 1984, vol. 3, p. 386; N. Clayer and A. Popovic 1992, pp. 47–52; L. Mašulović-Marsol 1995, pp. 351–352; J. Norton 2001, p. 188.

Makedonski Brod, Municipality of Makedonski Brod, Macedonia
Tyrbe of Hidër Baba
Location: On a hillside in the town of Makedonski Brod. 41°30' N, 21°12' E.

A long stone staircase leads up to the *tyrbe* of Hidër Baba (also called Hëdër Baba, Hizir Baba or Khidr), which also serves as an Orthodox chapel dedicated to Saint Nicholas.

When the Turks arrived in the Kërçova (Kičevo) region, a dervish settled in what had once been an Orthodox monastery and converted it into the *tekke* of Hidër Baba, who is said to have been one of the forty dervishes of Durballi Sultan. An archival document in Istanbul, dated from 1544, confirms the precedence of the chapel: 'this is the *zaviye* of Khizir Baba, formerly called Nikola Baba.' The fame of Hidër Baba, who was reputed to perform many miracles, spread and people came from far and wide. It is said that the original large *tekke* was demolished here in Ottoman times, but a smaller *tekke* was later built to replace it. Before the First World War, it was attended by six or seven dervishes, but it was destroyed in 1918. Only the *tyrbe*/chapel remains.

Frederick Hasluck, who seems to confuse Makedonski Brod with Kërçova (Kičevo), 22 km to the west, noted: 'On the death of the last *baba*, the *tekke* was shut up and the Serbs arranged a church of Saint Nicolas in it, saying it had formerly been such.'[245]

The present, whitewashed edifice, on a terraced lawn on the hillside, is square-shaped and contains the grave of the holy man. Both Bektashi and Orthodox pilgrims come here and share the spot in harmony. One wall of the shrine is for the Orthodox, with an icon to Saint Nicholas and a metal container for candles, and the opposite wall is used by the Bektashi. Both groups bring their gifts to 'Saint Nicholas/Hidër Baba' and take holy water home with them. The town of Makedonski Brod is now entirely Macedonian Orthodox, with only a handful of Turkish families, so much of the old Bektashi atmosphere is gone, yet pilgrims still come from Albania to visit the grave of Hidër Baba.

cf. F. W. Hasluck 1929, p. 423 (524); A. Stojanovski 1979; L. Mašulović-Marsol 1995, pp. 362–363.[246]

Poroj, Municipality of Tetova, Macedonia
Tekke of Jarar Baba
Location: 3 km north of Tetova. 42°01' N, 20°59' E.

This was once a well-known *tekke* and is said to be as old as the Harabati *tekke* in Tetova. It is said to have had high, thick walls. It was initially Bektashi but was then taken over by the Nakshbandi Order, no doubt in 1826. It ceased to function in 1912. All that remained were a roadside wall and a *taxh* in the ground.

cf. N. Clayer and A. Popovic 1992, p. 59; L. Mašulović-Marsol 1995, p. 358.

Saint Naum, Municipality of Ohrid, Macedonia
Orthodox Monastery of Saint Naum
Location: Southern bank of Lake Ohrid. 40°54' N, 20°44' E.

According to legend, one of the many places where the Bektashi saint Sari Saltik is said to lie buried is the Monastery of Saint Naum on the southern bank of Lake Ohrid. Among Orthodox Christians, the site is identified with Saint Naum (Albanian: Shën Naum, Macedonian: Sveti Naum), one of the seven apostles of the Slavs. The Orthodox monastery and its land were formerly in Albania but were ceded to Yugoslavia by the Albanian dictator Ahmet Zogu (1895–1961) in June 1925.

Over a century ago, the Bektashi of the nearby Korça district went on pilgrimages to the monastery. In September 1863, the German scholar Johann Georg von Hahn came across a prayer-rug in the church:

> Next to the grave there was a Muslim prayer-rug and, when I asked what it was there for, they said that it was for the Muslims who venerated the saint here just as much as the Christians do. They came here and prayed at his grave. Muslim women were wont to visit the monastery, too, to have their ailing children anointed and to make solemn vows before the saint.[247]

Frederick Hasluck noted on his visit in 1914 that the Greek abbot told him 'he had received a visit from the *baba* of one of the Bektashi *tekkes* at Koritza [Korça], who told him, in turn, that Sari Saltik, on a visit to the monastery, had, with the Christian abbot, miraculously crossed the lake to Ochrida on a straw-mat'.[248]
cf. J. G. von Hahn 1867, p. 108; F. W. Hasluck 1913, pp. 111, 116–117.

Shipkovica, Municipality of Tetova, Macedonia
Tekke of Kojun Baba
Location: About 5 km up the valley of the Pena River from Tetova. 42°01' N, 20°54' E.

The German-Austrian geographer Ami Boué (1794–1881) referred to this *tekke* during his travels in the region in around 1836–1838. It was no doubt a dependency of the *tekke* in Tetova, and was destroyed and ceased to function in 1912. All that remained was a *tyrbe*, a long, low building containing the grave of Kojun Baba.

There are few people in Shipkovica nowadays, probably since the uprising of 2001, but those in the region have all heard of the *tekke* of Kojun Baba. What is left at the site on the hillside is a small, unkempt Bektashi cemetery with graves dating from Ottoman times, and abandoned farmhouses, one of which was no doubt the *tyrbe*.
cf. A. Boué 1840, vol. 2, p. 324; T. Djordjević 1984, vol. 3, p. 386; J. Trifunovski 1976, p. 350, 365; N. Clayer and A. Popovic 1992, p. 59; L. Mašulović-Marsol 1995, p. 358.

Skopje, Municipality of Skopje, Macedonia
Tekkes of Mustafa Baba, Sulejman Baba and Axhem Zade Hasan Efendi

Location: Old town of Skopje. 42°00' N, 21°26' E.

Before the First World War, there are said to have been three Bektashi *tekkes* in Skopje. The first one was at the *tyrbe* of Mustafa Baba that was destroyed by fire. After that, there was no *baba* there, only a married dervish. The second *tekke* was at the *tyrbe* of Sulejman Baba. It was a more recent establishment but was abandoned by 1923. The third *tekke*, that of Axhem Zade Hasan Efendi, was built in the late nineteenth century at the Xhemat of Kara Kapuxhi. It seems to have closed by 1940.

cf. F. W. Hasluck 1914–1916, p. 105; 1929, p. 423 (524); L. Mašulović-Marsol 1995, p. 364.

Tekija, Municipality of Ilinden, Macedonia
Tekke of Ahmet Karadja
Location: Beside the highway from Skopje to Kumanova, near the refinery, about 20 km northeast of Skopje. 42°00' N, 21°39' E.

There was once a small Bektashi *tekke* at Tekija (Turkish: Tekke Köy), a one-time Turkish Muslim settlement and now a small Macedonian Orthodox village. It contained the grave of Ahmet Karaja and was venerated by the Muslims of the region, but was also frequented by Christians on Saint George's Day in May.

The British archaeologist Sir Arthur Evans (1851–1941) visited the site in the late nineteenth century and reported on a two-roomed shrine in the charge of a dervish that was venerated by Muslims and Christians alike, especially on St. George's Day. Inside was the 2-metre-high stone pillar that, according to what he heard, was said to have flown there from Khorasan a thousand years ago:

> A sick Albanian was walking round the pillar when I first saw it, kissing and embracing it at every turn. The worshipper who would conform to the full ritual now fills a keg of water from a spring that rises near the shrine – another primitive touch, – and makes his way through a thorny grove up a neighbouring knoll, on which is a wooden enclosure surrounding a Mohammedan Saint's Grave or *Tekke*. Over the headstone of this grows a thorn-tree hung with rags of diverse colours, attached to it – according to a wide-spread primitive rite – by sick persons who had made a pilgrimage to the tomb. [...] In the centre of the grave was a hole, into which the water from the holy spring was poured, and mixed with the holy earth. Of this the votary drinks three times, and he must thrice anoint his forehead with it. This draught is the true Arabian *solwan*, or 'draught of consolation.' It was now necessary to walk three times round the grave, each time kissing and touching with the forehead the stone at the head and foot of it. A handful of the grave dust was next given to me, to be made up into a triangular amulet and worn round the neck. An augury of pebbles, which were shuffled about under the Dervish's palms over a hollowed stone, having turned out propitious, we now proceeded to the sacrifice. This took place outside the sepulchre enclosure, where the Priest of the Stone was presently ready with a young ram. My Albanian guide cut its throat, and I was now instructed to dip my right hand little finger in the blood and to touch my forehead with it. The

sacrifice completed, we made our way down again to the shrine, while peals of thunder rolled through the glen from the Black Mountain above. It was now necessary to divest one's self of an article of clothing for the Dervish to wrap round the sacred pillar, where it remained all night. Due offerings of candles were made, which, as evening drew on, were lit on the sunken hearth beside the stone. We were given three barley corns to eat, and a share of the slaughtered ram, of which the rest was taken by the priest and was set apart for our supper in the adjoining antechamber. Here beneath the same roof with the stone, and within sight of it through the open doorway, we were bidden to pass the night, so that the occult influences due to its spiritual possession might shape our dreams as in the days of the patriarchs.[249]

The *tekke* would have been frequented by Turks and Muslim Albanians who lived in nearby villages, until it was destroyed and abandoned in 1912, at the time of the Serbian invasion. Frederick Hasluck was told by a local Muslim in 1914 that 'the place was now formally claimed for St George by the erection of a cross, though the dervish in charge was not (as yet) evicted'.[250] Margaret Hasluck added that he was gone by 1923. The *tekke* was reconstructed by the guardian, Osman Jahja, but the last remains of the building were torn down in about 1960.

The French ethnographer Liliana Mašulović-Marsol, who visited the site in June 1987, and Nathalie Clayer, who was there in April 1990, encountered the remains – a fenced-in stone pillar and burned candles. The pillar in the centre of the village is still there (2017), and is still adorned with flowers and candles brought by the faithful who worship Saint George here.

On a hill on the other side of the highway, about 2 km southeast of the village, there is a Muslim cemetery, the oldest, upper part of which has some old Bektashi graves, with some gravestones dating from the Ottoman period. Many of them are crowned with a *taxh*. One of the plots is fenced in and is reputed to be the grave of Ahmet Karadja. People once came here and left colourful clothing in a nearby tree and a few coins as votive offerings. The graves, now abandoned and forgotten, are mostly overgrown with grass and thornbushes.

cf. A. Evans 1901, pp. 200–204; F. W. Hasluck 1913, pp. 110, 120–122, 1914–1916, p. 106, 1929, 1929, pp. 336–337 (403–405), 423 (525), 467 (582); M. Filipović 1932; N. Clayer and A. Popovic 1992, pp. 16–17; L. Mašulović-Marsol 1995, pp. 365–367.

Tetova, Municipality of Tetova, Macedonia (Macedonian: Tetovo, Turkish: Kalkandelen)
Tekke of Harabati Baba, *tekke* of Sersem Ali Baba
Location: Tetova 42°00' N, 20°95' E.

This *tekke*, one of the most beautiful in the southern Balkans, is said to have been founded by Sersem Ali Baba. According to legend, Sersem Ali Baba, a vizier under Sultan Suleyman (r. 1520–1566), saw Balim Sultan, the second *pir* (master, founder) of the Bektashi Order, in a dream and abandoned his post as a vizier to live the life of a simple dervish in the village of Hacıbektaşköy, where the Bektashi movement arose. Before his death in 1569, he ordered that all of his possessions be sold and the money be used to purchase land for a convent in Tetova.

The shrine was constructed accordingly by one Harabati Baba (d. c. 1779), after whom the *tekke* is named. Little else is known of this Harabati Baba aside from legends. In a *vakuf-name* from 1799, his successor, Rexhep Pasha of Tetova, declared the adjacent buildings of the *tekke*, built under his orders, to be *vakuf*, so they must have been built before that date.[251] Frederick Hasluck speaks of a Riza Pasha of Tetova (d. 1822) who, at the instance of Muharrebe Baba, discovered the tomb of Sersem Ali by revelation.[252]

At any rate, the *tekke* of Sersem Ali Baba is probably the oldest *tekke* on Albanian-speaking territory and has been administered since the early eighteenth century primarily by Albanian *babas*. It served as the *asitane* for all the Bektashi convents in present-day Macedonia and Kosovo, and was indeed the main *tekke* for all of Albania up until 1912. Among its heads in the eighteenth and nineteenth centuries were: Hysein Dede (d. 1784), Sadik Baba (d. 1789), Hasan Dede (d. 1793), another Hysein Dede (d. 1816), Ali Dede (d. 1833), Ali Baba (d. 1864), Haxhi Emin Baba (d. 1880), Haxhi Mehdi Baba (d. 1882) and Haxhi Ahmet Dede (d. 1901).[253]

Frederick Hasluck suggests that the *tekke* here may have been founded on a retrospective legend from the time of Ali Pasha Tepelena, who used the Bektashi to expand his realm and power:

> Sersem Ali is supposed to have died in the middle of the sixteenth century and has, beyond this reputed grave, no connection with Albania. Riza Pasha's tomb is dated 1238 AH (= 1822–1823 AD). It thus seems fairly clear that the tomb of Sersem Ali is not authentic, and that the dervish's vision was part of the Bektashi propaganda in Albania. To judge by the date of Riza Pasha's death (the same as that of Ali Pasha), the *tekke* may well belong to the series dating from the period of Ali's power.[254]

The *tekke* of Sersem Ali Baba was embellished and expanded at the end of the eighteenth and beginning of the nineteenth century by the reigning pashas in Tetova who were affiliated with or at least respected by the Bektashi Order, and was turned into one of the most beautiful *tekkes* in the Balkans. Christians identified the site with Saint Elias.

The French diplomat Max Choublier (1873–1933) from Saint Quentin in northern France, who was vice-consul in Monastir (Bitola) from about 1901 to 1911, visited the *tekke* on several occasions. He left the following impressions:

> It was in 1909 that I got to know Ali, the *baba* as they called him, or grandfather of the *tekke* of Kalkandelen. He was suffering from neurasthenia at the time as the result of an overly sedentary lifestyle and an over-indulgence in coffee. With this ritual drink of the Sufis, he was endeavouring to overcome the effects of too many large doses of *raki*. For some reason, he had confidence in the medical advice I gave him and was grateful to me, and showed me kind attention. His gratitude expressed itself in particular in regular gifts of the monastery's famous apples that were as translucent as wax and were traditionally reserved for the sultan's table.

One of my visits to the *tekke* in the autumn of 1905 lasted for five days. I had never actually experienced a Bektashi monastery in a state of deprivation, and the one in Kalkandelen was quite affluent. What is rarer and virtually unique for Macedonia and northern Albania, there was security.

Uskub [Skopje] is ten hours from Kalkandelen on horseback. After a long ride over the arid plain in the midday sun, on a dusty and desolate trail, the monastery, surrounded by withering yellow leaves, looked to me like the very abode of peace and tranquillity. It would not have been easy to enter it by force. The buildings and orchards were surrounded by high walls and over the only gateway was a balcony in the form of a terrace with parapets that gave onto a corridor between the two main buildings. The open door of the gatekeeper's room revealed five or six Martini-Henry rifles in a rack, in addition to a large old rampart gun no longer in use. Aside from this, there was nothing but peace and quiet, order and cleanliness.

To the left of the entrance, there was a pavilion over which rose a rectangular minaret. It served as a meeting place and was used for prayers. Straight ahead was a lawn and rose garden with ponds on both sides in which tamed herons stood unmoved. Around this central courtyard were the cells of the Bektashi fathers. In front of the largest of them, that of Ali Baba, there was a verandah above the ponds, and part of the wall below the verandah was covered in glazed, coloured tiles. In the evening to sunset, this was where the *baba* sat cross-legged on a white ritual lambskin.

From here he surveyed his little realm – some dervish fathers and just as many brothers with five or six initiates and about a dozen servants. The dervishes lived in separate cells, two or three of them in each, and seemed to spend most of their time in solitude in minor manual labour, this, I believe, being in conformity with the regulations of the Order.[255]

Frederick Hasluck noted around 1914 that the *tekke* 'doomed to extinction under the pressure of Serbian taxation, is quite likely to be replaced by a church of S Elias, with whom the Bektashi saint buried there (Sersem Ali) is identified by the local Christians'.[256]

He described it as follows:

The *tekke* stands within a rectangle of high walls, each pierced by a handsome gateway, just outside the town. The buildings include lodgings for the dervishes, two oratories (*meidan*), the tombs of Sersem Ali, Muharrebe Baba, Riza Pasha, and others, a large open *mesjid* standing on columns, guestrooms, kitchen, and farm buildings. All these seem to be of the date of the foundation; they are for the most part picturesque and rather elaborate wooden buildings with deep porticoes. Pleasant fruit and flower-gardens are included in the precinct.[257]

The Harabati *tekke* is one of the largest Bektashi *tekkes* in the Balkans, and is a complex of cultural and in particular architectural interest. It stopped being used as a *tekke* in the late Ottoman period as a result of a disputed inheritance and served as a motel and restaurant in socialist Yugoslavia. It has had a Bektashi presence since that time, in particular under Baba Qazim, Baba Musa and Baba Tahir Emini (1941–2009). The current representative is dervish Abdyl Beqiri (b. 1955) who has been at the *tekke* since 1994.

The *tekke* was occupied by Albanian militants in the uprising of 2001 and those imprisoned in the nearby youth detention centre were released or escaped to find refuge there. The *tekke* complex was then attacked on several occasions by Macedonian government forces and the hotel and restaurant burned down. The historical buildings do not seem to have suffered damage during the fighting.

In recent years there have been 'political' problems in connection with the Harabati *tekke*. A report, quoted here from Wikipedia, noted the following:

> In 2002, an armed group of members of the Islamic Community of Macedonia, the legally recognised organisation which claims to represent all Muslims in the Republic of Macedonia, invaded the Arabati Baba *Tekke* in an attempt to reclaim the *tekke* as a mosque, although the facility has never functioned as such. Subsequently, the Bektashi community of the Republic of Macedonia sued the Macedonian government for failing to restore the *tekke* to the Bektashi community, pursuant to a law passed in the early 1980s for returning properties previously nationalised under the Yugoslav government. The law, however, deals with restitution to private citizens, rather than religious communities. The ICM claim to the *tekke* is based upon their contention to represent all Muslims in the Republic of Macedonia, and indeed, they are one of the two Muslim organisations recognised by the government, both Sunni. The Bektashi community filed for recognition as a separate religious community with the Macedonian government in 1993 but the Macedonian government has refused to recognise them.

The political problems between the Bektashi community and the mufti of Tetova have not yet been resolved to mutual satisfaction, and a case of ownership may be brought before the European Court of Human Rights in Strasbourg. At the moment, the Bektashi are restricted to a small corner of the *tekke*, whereas the property as a whole seems to be under the control of the Islamic community who have cared for and restored the site, but also rebuilt a controversial mosque in the complex. They say they have no problem with the presence of the Bektashi as part of the Muslim community, but a certain tension nonetheless persists.

cf. F. W. Hasluck 1913, pp. 110, 117, 1914–1916, p. 106, 1929, pp. 423, 467 (524–525); G. Louis-Jaray 1914, pp. 175–178; M. Choublier 1927; G. Palikruševa and K. Tomovski 1965; E. Vlora 1968, pp. 247–248; A. Oy 1980; N. Clayer and A. Popovic 1992, pp. 58–59; H. Norris 1993, p. 134; L. Mašulović-Marsol 1995, pp. 354–357; A. Vishko 1997; J. Norton 2001, p. 188; J. Rexhepagiqi 2003, pp. 229–230.

Veles, Municipality of Veles, Macedonia (Turkish: Köprülü)
Tekke of Haxhi Baba, *tekke* of Köprülü
Location: Town of Veles. 41°42′ N, 21°46′ E.

This was one of the largest and oldest Bektashi *tekkes* in Macedonia. Although we know little about the early history of the *tekke*, we do know that from the middle of the eighteenth century, most of the *babas* and dervishes were Albanian. It was from here in the late eighteenth century that Baba Shemimi and Baba Hajdar Hatemi moved to the Kruja region to establish the Bektashi faith in Albania proper. At the time of the closing of the *tekkes* under Sultan Mahmud II in July 1826, the *tekke* of Köprülü was administered by Baba Salih Elbasani, who held the rank of a *halife*. It was destroyed at that time. According to legend, Baba Salih learned of the coming destruction of the *tekkes* in a dream. Baba Rexheb recounted this event as follows:

> In the time of Sultan Mahmud, when the *tekkes* were to be destroyed, there was a *tekke* in Köprülü in the Balkans, led by one by the name of Salih Baba. Salih Baba was originally from Elbasan, but was then serving as the *baba* at the Köprülü *tekke*. There were many dervishes at that *tekke*. When Salih Baba received a sign that the Bektashi *tekkes* would be destroyed, he called the dervishes to him, and said: 'Look here, my children. According to a sign from the *Pir*, the Founder of our order, our *tekkes* will be destroyed. It will be soon. There is nothing we can do. Until it happens, stay here in the *tekke*. When the time comes that they come here, you flee from here and go to Korça. Our *muhibs* are there in the nearby town of Plasa, among the notables there. As they are our *muhibs*, they will provide for you there. As for myself, I will take only Dervish Hasan with me and go to my relatives in Elbasan.'[258]

The *tekke* was later rebuilt and retained some importance for the dervish orders in the Ottoman and post-Ottoman periods. Nothing remains of it now.
cf. Baba Rexheb 1970, p. 248, 292; H. Kaleshi 1980, p. 12; N. Clayer and A. Popovic 1992, pp. 42–44; N. Hafiz 1995, p. 347; L. Mašulović-Marsol 1995, pp. 367–368; F. Trix 2009, pp. 28–29.

Vërtok, Municipality of Gostivar, Macedonia (Macedonian: Vrutok)
Tekke of Baba Xhafer
Location: Near the source of the Vardar River, *c.* 7 km southwest of Gostivar. 41°45' N, 20°50' E.

The *tekke* of Baba Xhafer was situated near the village of Vërtok, on a hill overlooking the source of the Vardar River. It is reputed to date from the time of the Turkish invasion of the Balkans. The Baba Xhafer in question stemmed from Anatolia and arrived in Macedonia with Ottoman forces, apparently before the foundation of the Harabati *tekke*. He was a celibate dervish and gathered around him a large number of supporters. Nothing is left of the *tekke* that was destroyed in a fire in 1913. What remains is a rectangular *tyrbe* superimposed by two green domes that contains the graves of Baba Xhafer and a Hëdër Baba. The *tyrbes* were once visited by the sick. The last *tyrbedar* to guard the shrine was a Baba Musa who died in 1953 and is buried nearby with the other guardians of the site. In the long grass of the overgrown garden are numerous Bektashi tombstones, some dating from the Ottoman period.
cf. L. Mašulović-Marsol 1995, pp. 359–360.

TEKKES AND SHRINES IN GREECE

Corfu, Island of Corfu, region of Epirus, Greece
Church of Saint Spyridon
Location: In the centre of the old town of Corfu. 39°37' N, 19°55' E.

The Orthodox church of Saint Spyridon in the old town of Corfu has a direct link to the Albanian Bektashi. It has to do with the legend of the Bektashi holy man, Sari Saltik of Kruja. Sari Saltik killed a dragon, but was betrayed by the people of Kruja. Forced to flee, he mounted a mule and vanished through a cliff. In the words of the French consul in Shkodra, Baron Alexandre Degrand (1844–1911), who recounted the legend as he heard it:

> When the dervish reached the top of the mountain, he got off the beast and, in four great strides, reached Corfu. The first step he took was to Kruja, the second was to Shijak, and the third was to Durrës. *Tekkes* were built in each of these places where the traces of his footsteps in stone are objects of great veneration. He is said to have died in Corfu.[259]

Sari Saltik, to whom many miracles are attributed, came to be identified in the Orthodox tradition with Saint Spyridon, Bishop of Trimythous in Cyprus, whose remains were brought to Corfu in 1489, after the fall of Constantinople. The church itself was built in the 1580s.

In the nineteenth century, many Albanian Bektashi went on pilgrimages to the Church of Saint Spyridon on Corfu to worship the patron saint of the island under his Islamic name. Frederick Hasluck noted:

> I am told by an English Corfiote of the older generation, Mr. Weale, that in his childhood many Albanian Moslems visited the cathedral at S. Spyridon's two festivals, and paid their respects to the saint's remains; they often brought with them offerings of candles and even of livestock.[260]

Interestingly enough, Hasluck suggests that a political ploy by Ali Pasha Tepelena (1844–1822) may have been behind the connection between Sari Saltik and Saint Spyridon.

> The adventures of the saint at Croia [Kruja] may well have been adapted from the original legend for local consumption by Ali's agent there, the missionary Sheikh Mimi [Shemimi Baba]. One of Ali's great political ambitions was to add the Ionian island to his dominions, and especially S. Mavra and Corfou, as being opposite respectively to Preveza and Sayada, and SS. Quaranta [Saranda], the ports of his capital Yannina. [...] Corfou had been prophetically promised him by a dervish named Sheikh Ali (d. 1817) in whom he implicitly believed. The alleged tomb of Sari Saltik would form in Corfou just such a religious bait to his followers as had been provided by the earlier version of the legend at certain points in Christian Europe.[261]

cf. J. A. Degrand 1901, pp. 236–240; F. W. Hasluck 1913, p. 117, 1929, p. 468 (584).

Didymóteichon (Dimetoka), region of Eastern Macedonia and Thrace, Greece
Tekke of Seyyid Ali Sultan
Location: Near the village of Mikro Derion (Turkish: Küçük Derbend) in the district of Didymóteichon (Turkish: Dimetoka, Bulgarian: Dimotika). 41°20' N, 26°29' E.

The *tekke* of the fourteenth-century Seyyid Ali Sultan, also known as the *tekke* of Kyzyl Deli Sultan, was the home of Balim Sultan, the second or actual founder of the Bektashi Order.

Seyyid Ali Sultan was instrumental in spreading Bektashism to Bulgaria, to Greece and even to Hungary. The *tekke*, with its famous library, was razed during the closing of all the *tekkes* under Sultan Mahmud II in July 1826. It was rebuilt but then burned down by Greek forces in the Balkan Wars.

cf. F. W. Halsuck 1913, p. 111, 1914–1916, p. 103, 1929, p. 421 (521–522); E. Zekini 1988; N. Hafiz 1995, p. 344; J. Norton 2001, p. 189.

Elassona, region of Thessaly, Greece
Tekke of Salih Baba
Location: On the northern outskirts of Elassona. 39°53' N, 22°11' E.

According to Frederick Hasluck, this small *tekke* was situated on the outskirts of Elassona, on the road in the direction of Kozani. In 1915 it was occupied solely by an Albanian *baba*. In 1922, during the visit of Margaret Hasluck, the *baba* was gone and the *tekke* was shut and deserted.

> The Greeks said this *tekke* was founded after the union of Thessaly with Greece (1882), but the occupants held that it was a good deal older. The chief saint was Salih Baba, who was buried in a simple *turbe* with the two successive *babas* of the *tekke*. [...] The *turbe* is dated 1834–1835 [1250 AH]. Salih baba was said to be a saint of a much earlier date who enjoyed a local vogue before the *turbe* was built at the instance of the first *baba*, Nejib Baba (Albanian: Nexhib Baba) and at the expense of certain local beys. [...] Nejib Baba probably established himself as guardian of the grave and received instructions in a vision from its saintly occupant as to the building of the *turbe*.[262]

cf. F. W. Hasluck 1914–1916, p. 110, 1929, pp. 427–428 (530–531).

Farsala, region of Thessaly, Greece
Tekke of Durballi Sultan
Location: Near Asprogeia between Farsala and Velestinc in Thessaly. 39°19' N, 22°38' E.

The *tekke* of Durballi Sultan is located west of Volos in Thessaly in central Greece. It is situated more specifically north of the road between Volos and Farsala (Turkish: Çatalca), near the village of Asprogeia, part of the community of Eretria. The site was known in Turkish as Rini, Irini or, more properly, Örenli, but the *tekke* is often simply referred to as the *tekke* of Farsala.

This *tekke* is one of the oldest Bektashi foundations in Europe. Legend has it that it was established in 1480 by a Bektashi missionary called Durballi Sultan, who was sent out by Seyyid Ali Sultan. Durballi Sultan is said to have served there for forty-two years until his death in 1522.

Machiel Kiel has pointed out, however, that since the *tekke* is not mentioned in any of the Ottoman land registers of the time, it is very likely that it was founded after 1570.

It seems, at any rate, to have been built in the ruins of an older Byzantine church or monastery, in particular because there are many Byzantine remains in the floor and walls of the *tyrbe*. Indeed it is assumed to be the site of a tenth-century monastery dedicated to Saint George.[263] Nearby are the remains of an ancient Greek temple.

In the early period, the large *tekke* of Durballi Sultan was one of the six *asitanes* (head monasteries) of the Bektashi Order in the Ottoman Empire, being the seat of a *halife*. Harry Norris (b. 1926) describes it as follows:

> This *tekke* was one of the most famous Bektashi establishments in the Balkans and from its well endowed and imposing portals went forth numerous missionaries, among them Ali Rismi Dede Khorasanli who founded the Bektashi *tekke* at Candia in Crete in 1650.[264]

Baba Rexheb has left us with an impressive list of the thirty-three *babas* of the *tekke* of Durballi Sultan, with their dates.[265] Aside from Durballi Sultan himself, there were two other *babas* buried in the *tyrbes* there: Xhafer Baba Halepi (of Aleppo) who served as the fourth *baba* from 1581 to 1596 and Mustafa Baba Lahori (of Lahore) who was the twelfth *baba* from 1655 to 1660.

Since about 1800, in particular since the time of Ali Pasha Tepelena (1844–1822), a promoter of the Bektashi, all of the *babas* have been Albanians and, even in the twentieth century, the site was known locally at the 'Albanian *tekke*'. Its fame is reflected in the southern Albanian folksong:

> Të keqen o Turballi
> me dervishët që nxjerr ti
> ç'i dërgon në Shqipëri
> bën shqiptarët bektashi[266]

> Glory to you, Durballi
> With the dervishes you produce,
> whom you send back to Albania
> to make the Albanians Bektashi.

The *tekke* flourished in the late nineteenth century, in particular under Baba Muharrem Mahzuni of Gjirokastra from 1845 to 1867 [1286 AH], who was a noted poet, and Baba Bajram Përmeti from 1869 to 1904. It had much property from which it derived its income and as late as 1888 there were fifty-four dervishes in residence there.[267] Mention may also be made of Baba Tahir Bubësi (d. 1956) who headed the *tekke* from 1905 to 1919 and then returned to the *tekke* of Merdivenköy in Istanbul, and Baba Qazim Berati from 1919 to 1942, who was succeeded, under Ali Riza Dede, by the last *baba* of the *tekke* of Durballi Sultan, Baba Seit Koka of Skrapar who died in March 1973 and was buried on site between the two historical *tyrbes* there. The faithful gathered here as pilgrims on the feast day of 1 May.

Machiel Kiel remarked that:

> In the interwar period, the *tekke* served as a spiritual centre of the minor groups of Albanians scattered over Thessaly and southern Macedonia, and was in lively contact with the main centres of Bektashism in Albania. This ended in 1944, when the communist administration sealed their country off from the outside world. Among the rural Greek population it was held in great veneration and money was offered regularly for its upkeep. The Christians came to visit the *tekke* on St. George's Day, and for this saint the dervishes, according to Zosimos, lighted a candle. The convent had some meadows and forests as *vakf* property which was recognised by the Greek state. Because it was not occupied by Turkish Bektashis, but exclusively by Albanians, the *tekke* was not included in the Lausanne Treaty but continued to function as an 'Albanian monastery'. It therefore escaped the destruction of the main other *tekkes* and monuments of Ottoman culture after 1923 and survived more than half a century longer, well into our time.[268]

Kiel visited the site in 1972 and described it as follows:

> A low wall surrounds the entire group of buildings, which included lodgings for the dervishes, stables, guest rooms (*mihmân evi*), bakery, kitchen and a common ceremonial hall (*meydan evi*). Most of the buildings, built in the vernacular style of the XVIIIth and XIXth century, have long been roofless and in ruins. The living quarters of the Baba, however, were inhabited and in good shape. Behind the living quarters, in a most lovely graveyard full of age-old Bektashi gravestones, crowned with the twelve-ribbed Bektashi cap, and shaded by a grove of fine old cypresses, stand two domed *turbes* linked together by a later structure which likewise serves as a sepulchre. [...] Inside, the *turbes* were furnished with carpets and adorned with candles, oil lamps, pictures of Bektashi saints and religious phrases calligraphed on board (*lawha*). From a religious historical and folklore point of view these untouched interiors were of great importance.[269]

After the death of the last *baba* in 1973, the Bektashi community in Detroit applied to the Greek authorities to have a new *baba* appointed, but the request was refused. With the passing away of Baba Seit in 1973, the *tekke* of Durballi Sultan was thus abandoned and fell into ruins. In 1956 and 1958, the Greek state confiscated 1,300 hectares of land as well as 700 sheep and goats belonging to the *tekke* and distributed them to the villagers of the surrounding area. The property was sequestered in 1959 as 'enemy property' because Greece was technically still at war with Albania.[270] In 1981, the *tekke* was declared an historical monument, but this did not impede its decay.

The Dutch scholar Fred De Jong (b. 1944) described the sad end of the *tekke* of Durballi Sultan as follows:

> Bektashiism came to an end in 1974 with the death of Baba Seit, the last head of the *Tekke* of Durbali Sultan near Farsala in Thessaly. The Greek authorities refused to admit a successor. Since the death of Baba Seit, the *tekke* has rapidly fallen into a state of dilapidation. Most liturgical objects have been stolen from the premises and the framed images and calligraphy hanging in the türbes are being destroyed by moisture and insects.[271]

Kiel noted later in this connection:

> After the death of Baba Seyyid [Seit] the situation of the *tekke* deteriorated rapidly. Manuscripts and Bektashi *lawhas* with interesting calligraphies were stolen, doors and windows smashed. In the 1990s Greek nationalist fanatics largely destroyed the existing buildings, smashed the calligraphed Bektashi grave stones, opened the tombs and graves, and scattered the bones of the dead, an act of vandalism unworthy of the descendants of the oldest civilised nation of Europe. Their work was finished off by local treasure hunters, who believed that all the dervishes were rich people and had been buried with lots of money on them. [...] The history of the great Bektashi *tekke* of Durbali Sultan was lost before it could be written.[272]

> Around 2000, a small group of Albanian Bektashi from Leskovik living in Greece found the *tekke* and on long weekends worked to clean and restore the two historical türbes, re-install *sanduks* over the graves of the holy men and to bring a bit of order to the half destroyed and terribly neglected old cemetery. Another group living in Larissa later cleaned more of the cemetery and placed lamps at each of the graves. They also built inside the ruined compound a room to sleep and decorated it with inscriptions of Ali, etc. The building activity was illegal, but the Greek police of the area, knowing of the actions of the [Greek] Ombudsman, left them undisturbed.[273]

In 2009 an NGO for the history and conservation of monuments took an interest in the *tekke*, so there is now some hope that it may be restored and perhaps returned to the Albanian Muslim community in Greece.

Pilgrims still gather at Durballi Sultan on the feast day of 1 May.

cf. F. W. Hasluck 1913, p. 110, 1914–1916, pp. 110–111, 1929, pp. 428, 467 (531–532); A. Tomorri 1929, pp. 65–66; N. Giannopoulos 1938; G. Thoma 1966; Baba Rexhebi 1970, p. 269; A. Karkavitsa 1973; F. De Jong 1989; H. Norris 1993, p. 135; L. Vairakliotis 1994; P. Tsiakoumis 2000; Sh. Hysi 2004, pp. 73–74; M. Kiel 2005, 2009; S. Choulia 2012; K. Nollas 2012; V. Noula-Karpeti, *Albanian Dervish Monastery c.* 2012; K. Tsitselikis 2012, pp. 359–362.

Heraklion (Candia), region of Crete, Greece
Tekke of Ali Dede Horasani, *tekke* of Candia, *tekke* of Rrisk Baba

Location: Three-quarters of an hour south of the town, near the site of Knossos and the village of Fortezza. 35°18' N, 25°08' E.

Although this *tekke* is relatively far from Albanian-speaking territory, there was much Albanian influence at it. Frederick Hasluck noted on this travels at the time of the First World War: 'Even in places as Crete and Lycia the majority of professed dervishes of the order seem to be Albanians.'[274]

According to Hasluck again:

> the *tekke* of Candia was founded before the fall of Candia (1669), in 1650, by a celebrated saint named Khorasanli Ali Dede (Ali Dede Horasani), who is buried there. The present venerable sheikh, who has the title of *khalife*, is an Albanian from Kolonja and a celibate. His predecessor was married and at his death it was thought more expedient for the convent that a celibate should succeed him. There are about a dozen dervishes, many of whom seem to be Albanian. The *tekke* has every appearance of prosperity and good management.[275]

Hasluck also noted that many Muslims emigrated from Crete in 1897. Before that time, according to estimates, there were about 5,000 Bektashi adherents in the Heraklion region and two decades later only about 500. In addition to the *tekke*, there was a *tyrbe* of the Bektashi holy man, Rrisk Baba, outside the New Gate of Candia (Heraklion).

Baba Rexheb tells us that the *tekke* was founded, or perhaps refounded in the nineteenth century by Ali Resmi Baba of Crete. He had trained at the Durballi Sultan *tekke* in Thessaly and returned to Crete to found the said *tekke*.

Baba Kamber Ali of Prishta (1869–1950) was in Candia during the First World War, up to 1916.

cf. F. W. Hasluck 1914–1916, p. 113, 1929, p. 431 (534–535); Baba Rexheb 1970, pp. 284–287.

Irini
cf. Farsala.

Juma (Djuma), region of West Macedonia, Greece
Tekke of Piri Baba
Location: About 15 km to the northeast of Kozani, to the east of the road to Ptolemaida (Turkish: Kayılar), near the village of Haragi (Χαραύγη). 40°19' N, 21°50' E.

Juma was one of three Bektashi *tekkes* in the Kozani region, known in Ottoman times as the district of Sarı Göl (the other two *tekkes* were Bujak and Baghej). Mention is made of a Piri Baba who is said to have settled there at the time of Sultan Mehmed II the Conqueror (r. 1451–1481). The *tyrbe* built there contained the graves of Piri Baba and Erbei Baba. The surrounding population was primarily Turkish and Bulgarian, but the *tekke* had some Albanian connections. Frederick Hasluck visited it around the time of the First World War and reported on it as follows:

Juma. The most important *tekke* of this group is built on a slight eminence just outside the village of the same name. It has every appearance of prosperity, and is occupied by an abbot and nine or ten dervishes. The saints buried in the adjoining *turbe* are Piri Baba and Erbei Baba. Their date is unknown, but the *turbe* was repaired, according to an inscription, by two dervishes (implying the existence of a foundation) in A.H. 1143 (1730–1731), while in the surrounding cemetery several graves are slightly older. Unlike most *tekkes* in this district, Juma seems to be a place of considerable religious importance. It is much frequented in May (especially Wednesdays and Saturdays) by Moslem women on account of the reputation of its sacred well for the cure of sterility. I was told by the abbot that Christian women made use of this well on Sundays, and, though this was denied by educated Greeks of Kozani, it may be true of the less advanced women of the adjacent Bulgarian villages. The *turbe* of the saints is used for incubation by lunatics, and contains a club and an axe, regarded as personal relics of the saints, which are used for the cure (by contact with the affected part) of various ailments. There is also a very simple oracle, consisting in an earthenware ball, suspended from the roof of the *turbe* by a string. The inquirer swings the ball away from him; if it strikes him on its return swing, the answer to his question is in the affirmative. [...]

The property of the *tekkes* at Juma and Bujak was confiscated in 1826 and acquired by a rich Greek of Kozani, who, however, never prospered after his sacrilegious purchase. The land was bought back 'about forty years ago' and the *tekkes* reopened. Vague traditions as to the Christian origins of these foundations are current in Kozani. Some say that all Christian church lands were seized at the Turkish conquest and that monasteries then became *tekkes;* there are equally certain that Ali Pasha was responsible. The dedications of the supplanted monasteries are similarly disputed.

Juma is variously said to occupy the site of a church of S. George or of S. Elias.[276]

Margaret Hasluck added that the oldest graves at the *tekke* dated from 1701 to 1702 [1113 AH],[277] but Machiel Kiel suggests that the centre is certainly older.[278] In the late nineteenth century, mention is made of a Baba Hysejni who 'took the hand' of and was thus appointed by Baba Ali Haqi of Gjirokastra. He was known as Xhumai Baba.

Machiel Kiel visited Juma in 1973 and could find no remains of the *tekke*, not even a single gravestone. The whole complex had been demolished at some point. All that was left was the site itself, a flattop hill with some very old cypress trees. cf. F. W. Hasluck 1914–1916, p. 108; 1929, pp. 426–427 (528); J. Birge 1937, p. 72; P. Bartl 1963, p. 103; Baba Rexheb 1970, p. 300; M. Kiel 1993, pp. 270–271; H. Norris 1993, p. 128.

Kastoria, region of West Macedonia, Greece
Tekke of Kasem Baba
Location: Entrance to the old town on the Florina road. 40°31' N, 21°15' E.

This *tekke* was founded by Kasem or Qazim Baba (Turkish: Kasım Baba), who is said to have lived at the time of Sultan Mehmed the Conqueror (r. 1451–1481) when he moved to the Balkans and settled in Kastoria (Albanian: Kosturi, Turkish: Kesrie), now in Greece. The *tekke* was situated on the outskirts of Kastoria, on the right side of the road to Florina. Kasem Baba enjoyed considerable fame as a miracle-worker. 'He is said during his lifetime to have converted many Christians by the somewhat crude method of hurling from the hill on the landward side of the isthmus of Kastoria a huge rock, which crashed into a church full of worshippers.'[279]

The *tekke* is mentioned in an Ottoman register dating from the last decade of the sixteenth century.[280] Evliya Çelebi saw the *tyrbe* of Kasem Baba when he visited Kastoria in the spring of 1661, noting: 'On the banks of Lake Kastoria is the *tekke* of Kasim Baba where there are some bushes.' Frederick Hasluck noted that it was 'small, insignificant, and in 1915 tenanted only by an abbot, who was gone in 1921'.[281]

There was also a Bektashi mausoleum, the *tyrbe* of Sancaktar Ali Baba, at Toplitza near Kastoria.

cf. F. W. Hasluck 1914–1916, pp. 106–107, 1929, p. 424 (525).

Katerini, region of Central Macedonia, Greece
Tekke of Abdullah Baba
Location: No. 3 '7is Merarchias' Street, Katerini (about 70 km southwest of Salonica). 40°16' N, 22°29' E.

It is not known when the *tekke* of Abdullah Baba was founded in Katerini. The British topographer and diplomat William Leake (1777–1860) noted that the local landowners of the region were Muslim in his day and that the *bey* of the village was connected by marriage with Ali Pasha Tepelena (1844–1822). Whether this connection is at the origin of a Bektashi *tekke* in a town that has long been ethnically Greek is uncertain.

Mention is made in the late nineteenth century of a Baba Abdullah who was appointed to the *tekke* of Katerini by Baba Ali Haqi of Gjirokastra. In the 1920s, the *tekke* was administered by a Baba Jafar (Xhafar) who made a pilgrimage to the *pir evi* in Hacıbektaşköy in 1910 and died around 1933. He was followed by a Baba Tahir. Ahmet Sirri Baba, a noted Albanian Bektashi cleric from the Mokattam *tekke* in Cairo, visited the *tekke* of Katerini and served as its head for two years (c. 1933–1935) before he returned to Egypt. In 1954, the *tekke* of Katerini was under the administration of Baba Veli Mustafa. In the late 1950s and 1960s, it was the only functioning Bektashi *tekke* in Europe outside the communist world, with the exception of the *tekke* of Durballi Sultan in Thessaly. The *tekke* of Katerini was later a private *vakuf* and belonged to the Bektash family. It remained the heart of the small Albanian community there. Those who were Albanian were close to the *tekke* and those who were close to the *tekke* were Albanian.[282] When the last *baba* passed away in the early 1970s, the *tekke* was closed and declared a historical monument. A little *tyrbe* and a water fountain are all that are left of this *tekke* in Katerini.

cf. W. Leake 1835, vol. 3, p. 415; F. W. Hasluck 1914–1916, p. 110, 1929, p. 428 (531); N. Clayer *Aux origines* 2007, pp. 492–493; K. Tsitselikis 2012, p. 359.

Konitsa (Konica), region of Epirus, Greece
Tekke of Hysejn Baba
Location: Old town of Konitsa. 40°02' N, 20°45' E.

According to Frederick Hasluck, there was a very old *tekke* in Konitsa. It contained the graves of Hysejn (Husain) Baba, the oldest *baba* buried there, and Turabi Baba beside him. At the time of his visit, the *tekke* was administered by a Baba Hajdar (d. 1941).

It was in 1842 [1258 AH], while he was in exile at the *tekke* of Konitsa, that the early nineteenth-century Albanian poet Dalip bey Frashëri, disciple of Baba Tahir Nasibi of Frashër, composed his 65,000-line poem *Hadikaja* (The Garden), based on the work of the Azerbaijani poet Fuzûlî (1494–1556).
cf. F. W. Hasluck 1914–1916, p. 118, 1929, p. 432 (536); N. Clayer 1993, p. 105; H. Norris 1993, p. 128.

Odra, region of Western Macedonia, Greece
Tekke of Emine Baba
Location: Near the village of Dislapo, later Dragasiá, in the Odra (Ontria) mountains, about 30 km southwest of Kastoria. 40°19' N, 21°08' E.

This small *tekke* was occupied in the early years of the twentieth century by a *baba* and two or three dervishes, all local but one, who was an Albanian. According to Frederick Hasluck, who visited the region before the First World War, 'the great attraction is a cave or chasm in the mountain said to have been formed miraculously by Emineh Baba, who smote the mountain with his sword.'[283] Local Greek tradition identified the Odra site with a former church of Saint Menas, to whom it attributed the miracle of the cave. The identification derives from the similarity between '*Emine*' and 'Αΐ Μηνᾶ'. The *tekke* was destroyed by Greek forces during the Balkans Wars.
cf. F. W. Hasluck 1914–1916, pp. 107–108, 1929, p. 426 (528); Sh. Hysi 2004, p. 72.

Vodhorina, region of Western Macedonia, Greece
Tekke of Emine Baba
Location: Greek Vouhorina, west of Neapoli and Tsotyli, about 45 km southwest of Kastoria. 40°13' N, 21°15' E.

The *tekke* of Emine Baba, situated high on the slopes of Mt Palaiomageiron in the Pindus range, consisted before the First World War of an ordinary house.

Of the said Emine Baba we know only that he is said to have been executed in Monastir (Bitola) in 1598–1599 [1007 AH] for professing unorthodox beliefs.

> He appeared to his sister on the night of his execution at her home in Lapsista. She was preparing a meal to which guests were invited. He helped his sister in her preparations and afterwards sat down to table. Some of the guests, noticing that he took nothing, pressed him to eat, which he refused to do, on the ground

that he was fasting. Finally, however, yielding to their importunity, he ate, with the words 'If you had not made me eat, I should have visited you every evening'. He then disappeared.[284]

The *tekke* suffered destruction during the closing of all the *tekkes* under Sultan Mahmud II in July 1826 but was rebuilt later in the nineteenth century, until it was destroyed again by Greek forces in the Balkan Wars. The main room had a commemorative cenotaph of Emine Baba, his habit and other relics, and was visited by those who hoped to be healed of their illnesses.

Margaret Hasluck recorded that at the beginning of the Balkan Wars, certain Greek Orthodox villages were 'preserved from destruction only by the personal intervention of the Bektashi abbot of Vodhorina'.[285]

cf. F. W. Hasluck 1914–1916, pp. 107–108, 1929, p. 425 (527); M. Hasluck 1925, p. 605; P. Bartl 1968, p. 1.

TEKKES AND SHRINES IN OTHER COUNTRIES

Hacıbektaşköy, central Anatolia, Turkey The *pir evi* of Hacı Bektaş Veli
Location: The town of Hacıbektaşköy half way between Kırşehir and Kayseri. 38°56' N, 34°33' E.

The *pir evi* of Hacıbektaşköy is the motherhouse or traditional headquarters of the Bektashi Order. It was the legendary Hacı Bektaş Veli (Albanian: Haxhi Bektash Veli) who is said to have founded the order. The *tekke* that arose in his memory was of prime importance to the movement. It contained the tomb of the legendary founder and of Balim Sultan, the second and actual founder. A mosque, something quite unusual for a Bektashi *tekke*, was added during the closing of all the *tekkes* under Sultan Mahmud II in July 1826 as a 'safety precaution' when the *tekke* was handed over to the Nakshbandi Order.

A century ago, the site was also visited by Christian pilgrims.

> This central *tekke* of the Bektashi Order is frequented by Christians, who claim that the site was once occupied by a Christian monastery of S. Charalambos. On entering the mausoleum (*türbe*) where Hadji Bektash lies buried, Christians make the sign of the cross. They are said to identify the tomb with that of S. Charalambos, who, however, has no connection with Cappadocia.[286]

The *tekke* was administered by the *dede baba* who resided there. According to Frederick Hasluck, there were eight other *babas* under him,

> each having had a separate 'residency' (*konak*). They presided over the various departments of work carried on in the *tekke*, directing the labour of the probationers under them. Their respective spheres were: the buttery (*kilerji baba*), the bakery (*ekmekji baba*), the kitchen (*asji baba*), the stables (*ataji baba*), the guest-house (*mehmandar baba*), the mausoleum of Balim Sultan (*Balum evi*), and the vineyards (*dede bagh, hanbagh*).[287]

The *tekke* originally had much land and lived off the revenues derived from 362 villages, the inhabitants of which were affiliated with the Bektashi Order. The number of these villages was gradually reduced by the government on various pretexts to 24.[288]

Although primarily attended by Turks and Kurds, there were also many Albanians who visited the site and quite a few Albanian dervishes who lived there. Indeed, an English professor, White, visiting the site in 1913 reported that 'even at the central *tekke* in Hadji Bektash in the heart of Asia Minor, the majority of the dervishes are Albanian'.[289]

When the dervish orders were banned in Turkey under Mustafa Kemal Atatürk in 1925 and all the *tekkes* were closed down, the *pir evi* was conveniently eventually transformed into a museum, a status that it retains to this very day despite all the pilgrims that visit it.

cf. F. W. Hasluck 1913, pp. 102–103, 1914–1916, pp. 86–89, 1929, pp. 406–407, 459 (502–503, 571–572).

Cairo, Egypt
Mokattam *tekke, tekke* of Abdullah Magauri
Location: Mokattam (Muqattam) near Cairo, Egypt. 30°00' N, 31°16' E.

The oldest Bektashi *tekke* in Cairo, that of Kaygusuz Sultan, was established in 1390 or thereafter in the Qasr al-'Ayn quarter by Kaygusuz Abdal, who was subsequently referred to by the Egyptians as Sidi Abdullah al-Maghawiri. He was the son of a governor of Anatolia and arrived in Egypt in 1388. At the time of his death, Kaygusuz Abdal asked to be buried in the Mokattam hills, now behind the fortress of Mehmet Ali Pasha, where the Bektashi traditionally buried their dead. In 1865, Baba Ali applied to the Khedive Abbas Pasha for permission to build a new *tekke* in the Mokattam hills. Permission was granted and the new *tekke*, commonly known as the Mokattam *Tekke* or the *Tekke* of Abdullah Magauri (= Sidi Abdullah al-Maghawiri), was constructed in the years 1867 to 1872 under the patronage of the khedivial family. From this period, the Albanians came to play a dominant role at the *tekke*. In 1899, the head of the *tekke*, Hajdar Mehmet Baba of Leskovik, secured the property rights and transformed the property into a *vakuf*, thus making it an official shrine.

In 1902–1903 [1320 AH] an explosion occurred at an ammunition depot that destroyed the *tekke* and its surroundings. The head of the *tekke* Mehmet Lutfi Baba (1849–1942) sought and received funds for its reconstruction, work that was carried out between 1903 and 1909.

With the closure of all the *tekkes* in Turkey in 1925, the Mokattam *tekke* in Egypt became the only functioning Bektashi *tekke* outside of southeastern Europe. In its best and most prosperous years (1901–1935) under Lutfi Baba, the *tekke* complex had extra rooms, catering facilities, drinking fountains and basins of water, bearing inscriptions and dedications in Arabic and Albanian.[290] It was a tranquil retreat in Cairo that attracted artists, poets and writers. Many of the visitors, including more and more Albanians who had taken up residence in Egypt between the two World Wars, brought donations with them, thus giving the *tekke* more financial stability.

An early guidebook for Egypt published the following description of the *tekke* in 1900:

> This is the retreat of the Bektâshî dervishes, and should by all means be visited. It is situated to the E. of the tombs of the Mamelukes; and just behind the modern buildings of the Military Arsenal behind the Citadel, and on the right hand of the road up the Mokattam Hills. The *tekiya* projects from the hill, and may be distinguished from afar by a bank of verdant foliage with which it is fronted. Ascending a long flight of steps and passing through a small garden, you enter the *tekiya* which has lately been rebuilt for the dervishes by the Khedive Ismail and some of the princesses. The hall for the devotions of the members, the rooms of the shêkh, and the sumptuous kitchen may be inspected. The shêkh of the order, and the other members of the fraternity, are most polite and hospitable. The small open court of the *tekiya* leads into an ancient quarry similar to those of Tûra and Masâra, and penetrating the rock for more than 20 ft. A pathway of

matting enclosed by a wooden railing leads to the innermost recess, where lies buried the Shêkh Abdullah el-Maghâwrî, i.e. of the Grotto or Cave (Maghâra). His original name was Kêghûsûz, and he was a native of Adalia. Sent as deputy shêkh to Egypt to propagate the doctrines of the fraternity, he settled there and took the name of Abdullah.[291]

The French art historian Gaston Migeon (1861–1930) passed through in the early years of the twentieth century and left the following description:

> On the slopes of the arid, rocky and fissured Mokattam hills that form a uniformly yellow wall for Cairo to the east, there is a tiny verdant oasis, a recess of refreshment in this otherwise desolate region. Through some spindly trees – pear trees and mimosas – there appears before us a pink-coloured lodge with three windows that open out onto the plain below. It looks pushed back, as if it were somehow fixed to the mountainside, with a façade painted in hues of light blue. This is the convent of the Persian Bektashi monks, and within it is the tomb of the founder of the sect, Bektash, who lived in the twelfth century. After wandering and preaching throughout the provinces of the Turkish Empire, he settled and died in Cairo.
>
> We have here one of the most perfect examples of such hermitages, sites that bring to mind the blithe hours of men uninterested in the vain pursuits of this world, hermits whose lives alternate between joy and religious fervour and who live in the serene contemplation of nature. Far from the madding crowds as they are in this safe retreat, the placid countryside offers to their indifferent but blissful eyes an ever-changing spectacle from season to season, from hour to hour – delicate mornings often enveloped in a fine mist, implacable noondays when the sun, reaching its summit in the azure sky, scorches the tawny land, the thin line of the distant Nile bathing the groves of verdant palm trees, and the wonderful nights when the silver-glowing moon smothers the countryside in silent mystery. Life as a hermit has, no doubt, more to offer here than within the walled convents of Europe. For souls desirous of calm and oblivion, solace is easily found in meditation and prayer, in the contemplation of nature and in the rapture of open spaces. Such souls are more inclined to prayer since nature offers them endless ineffable sources of poetic inspiration. But nowadays, the monks are living in a new age. They are no longer solitary, but receive visitors, and their order seeks support and contributions of its own accord. A stone staircase leads up from the foot of the mountain to the door of the convent. In a little courtyard refreshed by a fountain, we are greeted by a monk. He is clad in baggy trousers, a grey tunic and a high headpiece of white cloth. His beard has grown to a great length. A tamed gazelle wanders about in the courtyard in gracious, lively, yet apprehensive steps. A deep tunnel has been dug into the side of the mountain where the Bektash [sic] rests in a small sanctuary lit by a few candles. The floor of the cavern, dug into the hard sandstone, is covered in mats and carpets. On the walls hang weapons – lances and axes – and ridiculous-looking pictures.

We return gladly to the few square metres that these men have managed to transform into a verdant spot in this arid solitude. In the small gardens they have planted orange trees and cassia. The view from here is so enticing that the eye is never sated in the contemplation of it all.[292]

The *tekke* was maintained over the years primarily by *babas* and dervishes from Albania, in particular by Hajdar Mehmet Baba of Leskovik from 1885 to 1901, Mehmet Lufti Baba (1835–1942) of Gjirokastra from 1901 to 1935, and Ahmet Sirri Baba (1895–1963) of Glina near Leskovik from 1935 to 1957, and always had a strong Albanian connection. Ties were also close to the Egyptian royal family which was, itself, of Albanian origin. Prince Kemal ad-Din Hussein (1874–1932), the grandson of Khedive Ismail Pasha (r. 1863–1879), visited the *tekke* quite often and was a great friend of Baba Lutfi whom he took with him on his travels to Europe. After his death, his widow, Princess Nimet, continued to support the *tekke* financially with sixteen Egyptian liras a month. The remains of Princess Ruhije (1902–1948), the sister of King Zog of Albania, were interred there, and a special shrine was built for her in February 1950.

After attacks in the Egyptian press in the early 1950s, in particular an article published in the Cairo newspaper *al-Ahram* by the mufti of al-Azhar Mosque in October 1952, the Bektashi community on the Nile was put under increasing pressure to adapt to Sunni ways or to leave the country. Sirri Baba, who had been loyal to the Egyptian King Farouk, would have nothing to do with the rulers of the new Egyptian Republic and went to Turkey at the end of 1951 where he spent much of the following period. After the Suez crisis of 1956 and further defamation from Sunni Muslim circles, the Egyptian government took control of the *tekke* and closed it down in February 1957. The property was given over to the Egyptian military. The remaining dervishes were given a house in al-Ma'adi in compensation, where they continued their traditions until the death of Sirri Baba. Permission was given for Sirri Baba, who died on 4 January 1963, to be buried in a *tyrbe* on the hillside of the *tekke*. With his death, the Bektashi Order ceased to exist in Egypt.

Lady Dorothea Russell Pasha (d. 1968), wife of Sir Thomas Wentworth Russell (1879–1954), Cairo's police chief from 1917 to 1946, provides a short description of the *tekke* in its final years in her guidebook of mediaeval Cairo (1962):

This eyrie in the cliffs is one of the most charming spots in Cairo. It is only of recent years that it has become a tourist haunt; when first I knew it, no one except personal friends of the Abbot ever went there and it was a refuge from the noise and bustle of the town, where one sat peacefully chatting and drinking tea or tamarind syrup with the Abbot, in the kiosk overlooking the city. Here the hustle and bustle of the town seem far away and one talks of dreams and portents, of falling stars and distant wars.

These dervishes, whose headquarters are now at Lake Ochrida in Albania, came to their cave dwelling some six hundred years ago (uncertain date) from their still earlier *takiya* at Qasr el-'Ayni. Here, ever since, they have lived and died, and been buried in the great cave in the hillside. Dervishes were suppressed in Turkey by Ataturk and this community is the last to remain in Egypt; there are now only about twenty of them, all Albanians (1954). They wear a high white felt head-dress and the traditional wool dress, in this case dark, of the Sufi; the Abbot's is white, and he has a crystal jewel depending from a buttonhole; the single ear-ring shows that they are celibate. Their language is Turkish.

Having climbed the steps and passed through the gate under the kiosk on the wall, we find ourselves in a shaded place with a fountain, beyond which is the door into the monastery. The rock face of the cliffs is honeycombed with the doors and windows of the monks' habitations. A passage leads between the little garden and the kitchen court to the great opening of the vast quarried burial cave; within, to left and right, are the tombs of the dervishes and at the far end the tomb of the founder of the Cairo *takiya*, enclosed within a railing; the walls have recently been lined with alabaster. At certain times there are many visitors to the tomb to which the usual superstitions are attached, and people are to be seen rolling or crawling from one end of the cave to the other. Return to the forecourt, putting a coin in the poor-box as you pass; the building behind the garden to the right is the Baba's (Abbot's) lodging and to the left (on the south) at the back of the little court is the great kitchen with its enormous cauldrons, used on the Day of Ashura, when large numbers of poor visit the monastery and are fed by the monks. After leaving the kitchen and the court, turn to the right by the fountain at the entrance and go through the garden to the terrace which overlooks the city. Behind this garden is another cave in the cliff, the burial pace of Prince Kamal ed-Din, son of the late Sultan Husein.[293]

At about the same time, the French Benedictine priest and scholar Jules Leroy (1903–1979) visited the *tekke* in his exploration of Christian monuments in the Middle East and left the following impressions:

The *tekke* is a delightful place. With all its palms, vines, flowers, terraces, and arbours, it makes a pleasant change from the bare, arid Muqattam, the limestone hill which rises on western bank of the Nile to a height of over six hundred feet. For Egypt, it qualifies as a mountain and at one time, about A.D. 1000, the Christian monastery of Der el Busair stood on its southern flank. Now the monastery has vanished, but thanks to the Bektashis, monastic life has not died out completely in Cairo.

Even from the outside their monastery looks attractive. Worn stone steps, with a wrought-iron handrail covered with bougainvilleas, lead up to the main entrance. Passing through the gate, you come straight into the middle of a network of courtyards, well-kept kitchen gardens, flower-beds with ditches of running water cutting through them, ponds that mirror the blue sky, Turkish-style summerhouses buried deep in foliage. Coming straight from the monasteries of the Wadi el Natrun to this brilliant oasis of colour, you cannot help feeling the sudden change of atmosphere. Everything is restful, orderly, and clean. The same air of peace envelopes the *tekke* and the other monasteries we have visited, but here it is almost Franciscan, so earnestly do the Bektashis love nature, just as did the little friar of Assisi.[294]

cf. F. W. Hasluck 1914–1916, pp. 97–99; 1929, pp. 415–417 (514–516); E. Koliqi 1957; D. Russell 1962, pp. 137–139; J. Leroy 1963, pp. 56–59; Baba Rexheb 1970, pp. 183–198; F. De Jong 1981; E. Azemi and S. Halimi 1993, pp. 73–78; H. Norris 1993, pp. 211–227; F. Trix 2009.

Taylor (Detroit), Michigan, United States
The First Albanian Bektashi *Tekke* in America
Location: 21749 Northline Rd, Taylor, Michigan. 42°12' N, 83°14' W.

The Detroit *tekke* was founded in 1954 on the initiative of Baba Rexheb Beqiri (1901–1995) of Gjirokastra. Forced to flee Albania in 1944 and, having thereafter spent much time at the Mokattam *tekke* in Egypt, Dervish Rexheb emigrated to the United States in 1952 with the dream of founding a Bektashi *tekke* in America. In New York, he was advised that the best place would be Detroit which had a large Albanian and Bektashi community, where people were more traditional in their outlook. Moving there in 1953, he gathered around him a group of fifteen Albanians who agreed to raise funds to buy land for a *tekke*. They found a farm in Taylor with eighteen acres of land where, on 20 May 1954, the First Albanian *Teqe Bektashiane* in America was duly founded. Dervish Rexheb was made the *baba* of the *tekke* under a decree (*icazetname*) from the aging Ahmet Sirri Baba in Egypt. He presided over it as Baba Rexheb until his passing on 10 August 1995.[295]

Baba Rexheb was joined in Taylor by Dervish Arshi (1906–2015) of Vlora who had lived at the Durballi Sultan *tekke* in Thessaly, by Dervish Lutfi of Gjirokastra who had been at the Mokattam *tekke* in Egypt since 1929, Dervish Bajram (d. 1973) from Gjakova who arrived from Egypt in 1960 and Dervish Bektaş Karamartin from Turkey. They all worked on the farm and in its orchard to make themselves self-sufficient. In 1963 a major extension was added to the *tekke* farmhouse with a new two-storey building that made room for a *meydan*, a library, guest rooms, a meeting hall and a large kitchen. The building was painted in Bektashi colours (green and white) with a large metal *taxh* that made it recognizable from a distance. Although the number of dervishes diminished with time, the number of initiates actually increased: from seventeen in the 1950s to forty-three in the 1980.

The death of Baba Rexheb in 1995 left somewhat of a void among the Bektashi in America. He was succeeded by his long-term companion Baba Arshi Bazaj, who died in December 2015. Both Baba Rexheb and Baba Arshi are buried in a *tyrbe* on a *tekke* ground that has become a place of pilgrimage. It has been recently made more beautiful with tiles from Turkey by the current Dervish Eliton.

An earlier proposed successor, sent from Albania at the time of Baba Rexheb's passing, was Flamur Shkalla, who was, however, expelled by the tekke and defrocked by Baba Reshat Bardhi. Another *baba* from Germany was sent to Detroit temporarily but did not remain. Currently (2017) the *tekke* is administered by Dervish Eliton Pashaj, an Albanian dervish from Vlora who was educated in Turkey and who came when Baba Arshi was still with there.

cf. Xh. Kallajxhi 1964; C. Bayraktari 1985; F. Trix, *Ashura Lament* 1993, *Spiritual Discourse* 1993, 1994, 1995, *Sufi Journey of Baba Rexheb* 2009; oral testimony F. Trix 2018.

4

NOTED HISTORICAL AND LEGENDARY FIGURES OF THE ALBANIAN BEKTASHI

Abaz Hilmi, Dede Baba (1887–1947)

Bektashi religious figure Abaz Hilmi, of the *tekke* of Frashër, was born and raised in Mërtinj, a village of the Përmet region. He became a dervish around 1905 at the *tekke* of Prishta where he 'took the hand' of Baba Shaban. In January 1914, he and Baba Shaban were forced to flee when Greek forces occupied the region and pillaged and burned the *tekkes*, including that of Prishta. He spent four years in Egypt and returned to Albania in 1918.

Abaz Hilmi went back to the ruins of Prishta, and then served in Suka and Frashër, helping to reconstruct and overcome the widespread devastation. In 1920, he led a band of volunteers in Tepelena in the struggle against the Italian forces occupying the region, and was in close contact with Baba Ahmet Turani. That same year, he opened an elementary school in his native village. He also attended the first, second and third Bektashi congresses in 1921, 1924 and 1929, respectively. Abaz Hilmi was made a *baba* at the *tekke* of Frashër in 1942, where he served until 1945.

Soon thereafter he was made a *gjysh*. This was the chaotic period that covered the end of the Second World War and the communist takeover of Albania. The radical change of regime in the country caused discord and infighting between pro- and anti-communist factions within the Bektashi. All the while, the new communist authorities were slowly trying to take control of all religious communities, and Abaz Hilmi proved to be an impediment. In February 1945, they put up a candidate of their own, Xhafer Sadiku, to preside over the Fourth National Congress of the Bektashi in May of that year. In this delicate situation, on 6 September 1945, Abaz Hilmi was made *kryegjysh* (*dede baba*), the highest position in the Bektashi Order in Albania. However, he held the post for only a year and a half. It was at this time that the pro-communist Baba Faja Martaneshi, who had good contacts with dictator Enver Hoxha (1908–1985), was endeavouring to push through certain reforms, such as allowing clerics to marry, to shave their beards and to wear civilian clothes, reforms that Dede Baba Abaz Hilmi resisted. Baba Faja and Baba Fejzo Dervishi kept on pressuring him to accept these changes and made it known to him that he would be considered an enemy of the regime if he did not accept them. The conflict came to a head at the *kryegjyshata* on 18

March 1947, when Abaz Hilmi took out a gun and shot both of the renegades and then killed himself. It was the greatest scandal that the Bektashi community in Albania had ever experienced.

As Abaz Hilmi's successor, the communist authorities appointed Ahmet Myftari on 8 June 1947. The remains of Dede Baba Abaz Hilmi are now buried in a *tyrbe* at the *Kryegjyshata* in Tirana.

cf. F. De Jong 1981, pp. 248–249; N. Clayer 1990, p. 405; N. Vatin and Th. Zarcone 1991.

Abbas Ali

Bektashi and Muslim holy man. According to legend, Abbas Ali (Albanian: *Abaz Aliu*, Arabic: *'Alî Abbâs*) was the half-brother of Hasan and Husein and came from Arabia on a white horse to save the country from the barbarians. He is supposed to have spent five days on Mount Tomorr before departing to live on Mount Olympus. Popular belief has it that Abbas Ali returns to Tomorr every year for five days.

The Bektashi poet Naim bey Frashëri (1846–1900) mentions the saint in a poem:

Abas Aliu zu' Tomorë,
Erdhi afër nesh,
Shqipëria s'mbet e gjorë,
Se Zoti e desh.

Abbas Ali took over Tomorr,
He came to live with us,
Albania was no longer afflicted
For God came to love it. (*Luletë e verësë*, 1890)

Abbas Ali lies buried in a *mekam* (mausoleum) on the southern peak of Mount Tomorr and has been venerated by Bektashi pilgrims there for three centuries. This *mekam*, originally constructed in 1620, is located a few hundred metres above the Bektashi *tekke* on the mountain, which was built in 1916. The site is visited by the faithful every year from August 20 to 25 when animals are slaughtered in sacrifice.

Another Bektashi legend has it that Haji Bektash, seeing Christian pilgrims climb Mount Tomorr on August 15, the Assumption of the Virgin Mary, journeyed to Kerbela in Iraq to exhume an arm bone from the grave of Abbas Ali, and hurled it up to the peak of Mount Tomorr in order to consecrate the mountain as Abbas Ali's second grave. The name Abbas Ali, who is identified in the Christian tradition with Saint Elias, is still invoked by the local inhabitants in the expression, 'Baba Abaz!'

cf. F. W. Hasluck 1929, p. 441 (548); J. Swire 1937, pp. 251–253; M. Hasluck 1939; O. Myderrizi 1957, pp. 191–198; N. Clayer 1990, pp. 164, 409–411, 2003, p. 143; M. Tirta 1996.

Abdullah Baba of Melçan (1786-1857 (-1853?))

Bektashi religious figure, scholar and poet. Abdullah Melçani was from northern Albania, probably from the Kruja region and was no doubt a dervish of Shemimi Baba. He played a major role in spreading Bektashism in southeastern Albania and helped to found the prestigious *tekke* of Prishta. He also wrote much mystical verse in Albanian. 'Most of his verse is concerned with Sufism and in one of the poems that is best preserved he is laudatory towards Sari Saltik and other saintly personages of the Bektashiyya.'[296] A *tyrbe* was constructed in his honour at his death in 1857 [1274 AH] and was visited by many a pilgrim.

Margaret Hasluck recorded the following anecdote from her visit there in 1923:

> Abdullah Baba lies in a grave dated A.H. 1274. In relation to him an extraordinary story is now told. When the French army was at Koritza, a major dreamt that Abdullah Baba was beating him for having entered the *türbe* without taking off his boots. He was so much impressed that he put up a notice on the *türbe* forbidding any one to enter shod. Whatever the reason, the notice in French and Turkish was there in 1923, with the Frenchman's signature appended – unfortunately, not on Abdullah's *türbe* but the other.[297]

The hilltop *tekke* of Melçan is now usually named after him: the *tekke* of Baba Abdullah of Melçan. He was succeeded in Melçan by Baba Adem.
cf. F. W. Hasluck 1929, p. 439 (546); Baba Rexhebi 1970, pp. 281-283; N. Clayer 1990, pp. 365-366; H. Norris 1993, pp. 135-136.

Abedin Baba of Leskovik

Bektashi religious figure and poet. Abedin Leskoviku, as he was known, was born in Leskovik near the present Greek-Albanian border, and trained at the Bektashi *tekke* of Durballi Sultan in Thessaly under Baba Muharrem Mahzuni (d. 1867). Baba Muharrem sent him back to Leskovik as a *baba* where he founded a *tekke* there in 1887 [1293 AH]. Abedin Baba was a talented poet and wrote not only in Turkish but also in Albanian, including a hymn to Durballi Sultan. He probably died shortly after Albanian independence in 1912.
cf. Baba Rexheb 1970, pp. 318-321; N. Clayer 1990, p. 347.

Adem Baba of Prizren (d. 1894)

Bektashi religious figure. Baba Adem, also known as Baba Haxhi Adem Plaku (the Elder), was originally from Gjakova in Kosovo. His early travels took him through the Muslim world as far as India, and he studied in Bukhara, now in Uzbekistan in Central Asia. He visited Mecca, and was thus known as Baba Haxhi Adem. He was also in Rome, where he hoped to meet the pope, but he was not given an audience.

Baba Adem was active at the Bektashi *tekke* of Prizren in about 1890 and headed it until the Serbian invasion of Kosovo in 1912, when it was transformed into a Serbian orphanage. He survived the gruesome takeover in Prizren, which was referred to during the invasion as the 'Kingdom of Death',[298] and returned to live in Gjakova.

The British journalist Henry Brailsford met him in about 1903 and left the following impression:

> But to me the type of the good Bektashi is the sheikh of the Teké in Prizrend. Gentle, dignified, and courteous, he spends an innocent old age in a retired garden of red roses and old-fashioned stocks. To visit him was to step into an atmosphere of simplicity and peace. An active life lay behind him. He had spent long years wandering over the Moslem world. He had sojourned in India and studied in Bokhara, listening wherever some noted doctor had a thought to give or an influence to bestow. At the end of his pilgrimage, laden with the wisdom of the East, he even made his way to Rome, anxious to prove his tolerance by paying his respects to the Pope. He waited some months for an audience, and came away grieved at the rebuff with which his simple impulse of charity had been met. When his tale was finished, he turned to us with an earnest look in his thoughtful eyes, and tried through the unsympathetic medium of our Greek interpreter to convey his kindly mysticism to us. Something we caught about the community of souls, before the time came for us to leave him laden with his roses that seemed to carry with them the rarer fragrance of his gentleness and piety.[299]

Baba Adem lies buried in the *tyrbe* of the *tekke* of Gjakova.
cf. F. W. Hasluck 1929, p. 424 (525); H. Brailsford 1906, pp. 247–248; N. Hafiz 1995, p. 348.

Adem Vexh-hi Baba of Gjakova (1841–1927)

Bektashi religious figure and poet. Adem Vexh-hi was born in Gjakova in Kosovo, where he underwent Islamic training. He often visited the Bektashi *tekke* in Gjakova, was attracted to the order and, in 1860, 'took the hand' of his superior. He then went to the *tekke* of Melçan to serve under Baba Adem of Melçan and spent two years with him there. From Melçan he was sent on to Baba Alush in Frashër, where he became a dervish and functioned as the secretary of the *tekke*. In 1872, with his superior, Baba Alush, he had an opportunity to visit the *pir evi* in Hacıbektaşköy in central Anatolia. After his return to Frashër, he went on a long visit to the holy sites in the Middle East, to Mecca (thus taking on the title *haxhi*), Medina, Kerbela, Najaf, Palestine and India.

In 1877, Baba Alush sent him to Prizren, where he opened a new *tekke*. He was thus active there at the time of the Albanian League of Prizren (1878) and thereafter. In 1921 Adem Vexh-hi was made *baba* of the *tekke* of Gjakova, where

he remained until his death in 1927. Baba Adem Vexh-hi was the author of much mystic verse in Turkish.
cf. Baba Rexheb 1970, pp. 339-341; N. Hafiz 1995, p. 348.

Ahmet Baba of Prishta (d. 1902)

Bektashi religious figure. Baba Ahmet was a colourful and politically active figure. He was the *baba* of the *tekke* of Prishta from 1893 to 1898. After an open conflict with the Bey of Këlcyra, Baba Ahmet was arrested by the Ottoman authorities and taken away to Janina and Monastir (Bitola) where he was tried, sentenced, but then pardoned. He subsequently sued his persecutors in court and was arrested once again in 1898 and sent into exile to Tripoli in Libya. The Bey of Këlcyra took advantage of the moment to confiscate the property of the *tekke*. Baba Ahmet managed to escape from Tripoli but was caught in Istanbul and exiled to Sinope on the Black Sea, where he died in May 1902 while trying to escape once again.
cf. N. Clayer 1990, p. 380.

Ahmet Baba of Turan (1854-1928)

Bektashi religious figure and poet. Ahmet Turani, born in 1854 (or 1860), was from Turan near Tepelena (not to be confused with the Turan near Korça) and served for some time at the Hajdërije *tekke* in Gjirokastra. He was made a dervish by Baba Hajdër of Kardhiq, who was a noted figure in the Albanian nationalist movement. After several years there, Ahmet Turani travelled to the Middle East to see the holy sites and settled thereafter at the *tekke* of Turan under Baba Ali Turani. On the death of his superior there in 1908, he was made *baba* of Turan by Baba Ahmet Koshtani of Tepelena.

From 1909 Baba Ahmet was an active member of the Patriotic Club of Salonica. In 1910 he and Baba Sulejman of Gjirokastra travelled to the *pir evi* at Hacıbektaşköy in central Anatolia to be made each a *gjysh* (*dede*) by Fejzi Dede. Around 1913, his *tekke*, like many others, was burned down by Greek forces and he was forced to flee to Vlora, as did most of the terrified population of Kurvelesh. There he set up a soup kitchen in the olive groves outside the town for those who were in need. In 1920, he played an active role in the liberation of Vlora from Italian forces by gathering about 250 fighters in Tepelena for his Vlora Committee.[300] Baba Ahmet then returned to Turan and rebuilt the *tekke* with the help of the local population and with financial support from Bektashi Albanians in America. As the highest-ranking Bektashi cleric of the region, he appointed numerous new *babas* for the burned-out *tekkes* of the region. He is also said to have been a talented poet.
cf. Baba Rexheb 1970, pp. 357-359; N. Clayer 1990, pp. 416-417; F. Trix 2009, p. 60.

Ahmet Karadja

Bektashi holy man. Ahmet Karadja or Karadja Ahmet Sultan (Albanian: Ahmet Karaxha, Turkish: Ahmet Karaca) figures in Bektashi legends as a disciple of Haxhi Bektash and has several tombs in Anatolia. He is or was revered in the western Balkans at the formerly Muslim village of Tekija between Skopje and Kumanova in Macedonia. Ahmet Karadja is mentioned as a saint in the reign of Orhan (r. 1323–1362):

> The magnificent Carage Ahmed descended of the offspring of several kings of the Countrey of Persia. After he had made a journey to the city of Gezib, from thence he came to Greece and dwelt in a place nigh to Akhisar. His noble sepulchre is there well-known, and is a place of visit or pilgrimage. Among the common people of the Countrey of Greece it is famous for a place of hearing prayer, and the very earth is profitable for evil diseases.[301] [...] It would seem that the tomb of Karadja Achmet was occupied, like so many others, by the Bektashi in their prosperous period on the pretext that the saint was (spiritual) 'founder's kin'.

Presumably under Bektashi auspices the cult of Karadja Ahmet spread from its original home in Akhisar to Constantinople and to Tekke Köy near Skopje.[302] One typical Bektashi legend has it that he brought a stone pillar with him and placed it on the spot where his severed head fell to the ground.

On a hill on the other side of the highway, about 2 km southeast of the village of Tekija, there is a Muslim cemetery, the oldest, upper part of which has some old Bektashi graves. One of the plots is fenced in and is reputed to be the grave of Ahmet Karadja. People once came here and left colourful clothing in a nearby tree and a few coins as votive offerings.

cf. A. Evans 1901; F. W. Hasluck 1929, pp. 336–337 (403–405).

Ahmet Myftari, Dede Baba (1916–1980)

Bektashi religious figure. Ahmet Myftari, also known as Ahmet Myhtari or Ahmet Myftar Ahmataj, was born in Brataj, about 40 km southeast of Vlora. He attended school in Vlora in 1924–1929. In 1937, he was sent to the Dibra region to do military service and there, at the *tekke* of Bllaca, he became a dervish, 'taking the hand' of Baba Zenel. Myftari stayed in Bllaca until 1939 and was subsequently active in Elbasan and Turan near Tepelena. He returned to Vlora in 1942, and set to building a new *tekke* in his native village of Brataj. In view of the Second World War and incipient civil war in Albania, the project was, however, never completed. From 1942 to May 1944 he fought on the side of the communist partisans and was interned in Durrës. He was made a *baba* in Vlora in October 1945 and served from then to 1948 at the *tekke* of Kusum Baba there.

On 8 June 1948, Baba Ahmet Myftari was appointed by the communist authorities to head the whole Bektashi community as *kryegjysh* (*dede baba*) after

the suicide of Abaz Hilmi in March of that year. He had no choice but to be a puppet of the regime. In September 1953, for instance, he invited the Bektashi faithful to spend the Ashura feast in a spirit of 'hatred of the Anglo-American imperialists and of love for the people's power'. Nonetheless, he did what he could to keep the Bektashi community together at a very difficult time and was a respected figure. From about 1958 to 1967 he was interned in Drizar in Mallakastra with his disciple, dervish Reshat Bardhi, who would much later become *kryegjysh* himself. After the banning of the Bektashi Order in 1967, he lived in Kruja and Tirana, isolated from public life and ever watched by the secret police. He was succeeded by Baba Fehmi of Tepelena. He lies buried in a shrine at the *Kryegjyshata* in Tirana.
cf. A. Popovic, *Les ordres mystiques* 1986, p. 70; N. Clayer 1990, p. 405.

Ahmet Sirri Baba of Mokattam (1895–1963)

Bektashi religious figure. Ahmet Sirri Baba, also known as Sirri Çoçoli or Baba Serriu, was born in the one-time village of Glina near Leskovik in southern Albania in 1895–1896 [1313 AH]. His birth name was Ahmet Serri Glina. He joined the Bektashi Order in 1912 when he was seventeen years old and settled with Baba Sulejman in Leskovik. When Greek forces occupied the region, Ahmet Sirri escaped with Baba Sulejman to Janina and from there he fled on his own to the *tekke* of Baba Shaban in Prishta. It was there in 1913–1914 [1332 AH] that he became a dervish. When Prishta was occupied by the Greeks, Ahmet Sirri and Baba Shaban fled to Italy and found refuge for four months at Hotel Milano in Salsomaggiore Terme near Parma. From there they continued on to Cairo and were taken in by the Bektashi Mokattam *tekke* (also called the Magauri *tekke*) in the Mokattam hills.

After an initial period of stay, Lutfi Baba, the head of this *tekke*, sent Ahmet Sirri to serve at the *pir evi* in Haşıbektaşköy in central Anatolia, where he remained for two years. From there in 1922–1923 [1341 AH] he moved to the *tekke* of Tarsus where, upon the death of its leader, Sadiq Baba, he was appointed *baba*, with the seal of approval of Lutfi Baba in Cairo.

In 1924–1925 [1342 AH], Lutfi Baba sent for Sirri Baba to return to Cairo and designated him as his deputy and successor. In 1925–1926 [1343 AH], Sirri Baba spent six months in Albania for health reasons and subsequently went on a tour of the holy sites to Baghdad, Karbala and Najaf. As his health problems persisted, he sought relief in Salonica. Around 1933, he learned that Jafar Baba, the head of the Bektashi *tekke* of nearby Katerini, had died and he was invited by the men of the order there to serve as its head. Sirri Baba spent the following two years in Katerini, where his health finally recovered. In 1935, the aging Lutfi Baba requested once more that Sirri Baba return to Cairo and replace him as head of the Mokattam *tekke*.

With the violent death of Abaz Hilmi Dede Baba in Tirana in March 1947 and the communist takeover of the *Kryegjyshata*, the Bektashi community in Egypt met in January 1949 and resolved to promote Ahmet Sirri Baba to the office of *kryegjysh* (*dede baba*). He was recognized in this capacity by the heads of the only two functioning Bektashi *tekkes* in Europe outside the communist world: Farsala (the *tekke* of Durballi Sultan) and Katerini in Greece. However, his election as *kryegjysh* was more formal than real.

After attacks in the Egyptian press in the early 1950s, in particular an article published in the Cairo newspaper *al-Ahram* by the mufti of al-Azhar Mosque in October 1952, the Bektashi community on the Nile was under increasing pressure to adapt to Sunni ways or to leave the country. Ahmet Sirri Baba, who had been loyal to the Egyptian King Farouk, would have nothing to do with the rulers of the new Egyptian Republic and went to Turkey at the end of 1951, but was soon made to return to Egypt by the Turkish courts. After the Suez crisis of 1956 and further defamation from Sunni Muslim circles, the Egyptian government took control of the Mokattam *tekke* and closed it down in February 1957. The property was given over to the Egyptian military. Permission was, however, given for Ahmet Sirri Baba, who died on 4 January 1963, to be buried in a *tyrbe* on the hillside of the *tekke*. With his death, the Bektashi Order ceased to exist in Egypt.

The French Benedictine priest and scholar Jules Leroy (1903–1979) visited Ahmet Sirri Baba while on an expedition to investigate Christian monuments in the Middle East and commented as follows:

> There are only about a dozen monks here now guarding the tomb of Sheik Abdullah el Maghaouri and the tombs of his followers who wished to be buried beside him. The little community lives under the benevolent rule of its leader, the Baba Ahmet Serri Dede; they spend their time gardening or looking after the farm animals – the hens, turkeys, tame gazelles, clean oxen, the large-uddered cows which although they belong to the monks still follow the Oriental custom and wear round their necks or over their foreheads a string of blue pearls to ward off the Evil Eye. The Baba, who was elected some years ago, is a fine old man; his natural dignity is enhanced by his magnificent costume, a striped green-and-white robe with the white cloak of the Bektashis. Round his waist he has a broad brown cummerbund with the stone amulet called *teslim tash* attached to it, though it should normally be worn round the neck. He has also a staff with a small double-bladed axe on the top of it. His headdress is the white, usually twelve-sided bonnet which is the uniform of the order, and round it he has a green turban to indicate his rank of Baba. His heavy silver ear-rings shaped like the crescent moon show that he has taken the vow of celibacy. The Baba is a very easy man to talk to. When he is not taking a siesta he wanders about his fairy gardens and is very willing to talk about the history of the Bektashis.[303]

Ahmet Sirri Baba had been a close friend of the Egyptian poet Ahmad Rami (1892–1981), himself of Albanian origin, who translated the *Rubaiyat* of Omar Khayyam from Persian into Arabic and wrote lyrics for the famed Egyptian singer Umm Kalthoum (Um Kalsum, 1904–1975). The two men shared a taste for poetry and the *tekke* furnished a milieu where congenial company could be enjoyed, accompanied by recitation of verse and meditation.[304] Ahmad Rami wrote the following verse inscribed on the tombstone of Ahmet Sirri Baba:

> God have mercy upon His servant, Sirri Baba,
> And may He show regard to him, shepherding him with kind favour.
> May He give him a draught that is pure to perfection,
> And bestow on him the paradise garden of His bliss.
> He departed as one who emigrates from this fleeting world,
> And who spoke softly and in confidence with his Lord,
> And who enfolded himself within the truest faith.
>
> Sleep, cool and contentedly, betwixt the branch and foliage drawing nigh
> Below the shady mountain foot, beneath Mokattam,
> Within the hallowed spot of 'Abdullah, dweller in the caves,
> The Pole of true guidance, the treasure of desires.
> In truth, a bower, it is the soil whereof you watered,
> With a renewed acquaintance of its planting and with a kind affection.
>
> O resident of the fertile plot in Egypt,
> Between these sand dunes and those rich abodes,
> May God be satisfied with your accomplished deeds
> In this world, so that most fitting for you be
> The bliss of His Divine forgiveness.
> Therefore, abide safely, in the haven of Paradise, and receive
> The grace of My Lord, with praise and gratitude.[305]

Sirri Baba was the author of the small book *Al-Risāla al-Ahmadiyya fī tārīkh al-tarīqa al-'Aliyya al-Baktāshiyya bi-Misr al-Mahrūsa* (Cairo, 1939 [1358 AH]). cf. F. De Jong 1981, p. 249; H. Norris 1993, pp. 221–227; F. Trix, *Sufi Journey*, 2009.

Ali Baba of Berat

Bektashi religious figure. Baba Ali or Aliko was head of the Bektashi *tekke* of Berat that was burned down in 1826 under the reign of Sultan Mahmud II (r. 1808–1839), 'when priceless books of mysticism and philosophy in Arabic and Persian were destroyed'.[306] Baba Ali was said to have been a missionary who spread the Bektashi faith in the Berat region. He did not found the *tekke*, but died there and was buried in a *mekam*. There is now no trace of the *tekke* of Baba Ali and references to it may actually refer to the nearby *tekke* of Velabisht. The *mekam* of Baba Ali is now situated on the left side of the main road into Berat, about 20 m from the old Gorica Bridge.
cf. N. Clayer 1990, p. 254; H. Norris 1993, p. 125.

Ali Baba of Tomorr (1900–1948)

Bektashi religious figure and writer. Ali Tyrabiu or Turabiu, originally called Ali Abaz Skëndi, was born in 1900 or 1893 in Shalës near Tepelena. He was also known as Baba Ali Tomorri, or Baba Ali of Tomorr. After basic schooling in Berat, he studied in Kozani, now in Greece where he learned Turkish, Greek, a bit of Arabic and French. In 1913 he returned to Albania and was initiated as a *muhib* by Baba Shaban at the *tekke* of Prishta. There he took his vows and became a dervish. Under the Greek occupation in 1914 he followed Baba Shaban, Baba Ahmet Koshtani and other dervishes to Cairo in Egypt where they spent several years at the famed *tekke* there. On his return to Albania, Baba Ali Tomorri, who was known at the time as Varf Ali Prishta (i.e. dervish Ali of Prishta), began to play an active role in Albanian Bektashism. He was the person behind the periodical *Reforma* (Reform) that was issued from 1921 to 1923 and was one of the main organizers of the first three national congresses of the Albanian Bektashi community. In 1922, after the First National Congress, he was made a *baba* by Baba Ahmet Turani and was appointed to the small *tekke* of Kulmak on Mount Tomorr, thus the name Baba Ali Tomorri. This *tekke* was very soon to become one of the main centres of the Bektashi in the Berat region and, later, in all of Albania.

The British journalist and writer Joseph Swire (1903–1978) visited him on Mount Tomorr in about 1930:

> Two dervishes took us in to Baba Ali Tyrabiu – a tall man of charm and wit, young but bearded, who had taught himself good French. A white turban with green band (a mark of rank) and full white robe girded by a sash were his dress. But we shivered in this room. Every winter the *tekke* is cut off by snow and wolves howl round its walls. Then a bare room with a great fireplace was put at our disposal, and though the fire vomited thick smoke we were most thankful for it and for the strong tea we brewed by it.
>
> As the sun sank behind Tomori and the shadows crept down through the trees from the lonely heights, the Tomorica valley's depths lost their greens and browns for soft mauve shades; and the wild white clouds, brooding on the hills beyond, changed to pink, then mauve, then melted into the ink-blue night which flowed over the silent land. I watched this scene, then withdrew from the cold rapiers of wind to the smoky fire for *meze* and *raki* – and afterwards supper of mutton and *kos* and sweetened rice and talk with Baba Tyrabiu. […]
>
> That evening there was *meze* and supper with Baba Tyrabiu in his room where he lives and sleeps and prays with his dervishes. At one end stood a wooden erection like a broad step-ladder with three steps, on which burnt several candles. On the right of this affair was a low divan, covered with carpets, extending down the side of the room. On this sat the Baba in Turkish style, and on his right a servitor – a probationer not yet a dervish. Before the Baba was a *sofra*, and on the other side of it a low bench for us, covered with a carpet. On the walls hung pictures of men hallowed by the Bektashis (among them St. John the Baptist), a large pendulum clock with the hours in Turkish time, and a ball

of little yellow flowers with a musky smell, dried and wired tightly together – they are a common decoration hereabouts, and are said to grow only on one mountain near Këlcyra. For *meze* there were little pieces of liver and fat mutton which went down well with Prishtë's celebrated *raki*; then came soup, fried meat, maize bread, *kos* and coffee.

Dawn came grey and sullen. Baba Tyrabiu would take no payment until I begged him to accept a small present for poor wayfarers. With his last words he asked me to remember that Bektashism stood between all religions – and in Albania, for mediation and unity between all beliefs in the national interests.[307]

During the Second World War, Baba Ali Tomorri took part in the fight to liberate the country and in 1946, the communist government sent him to the *tekke* of Asim Baba in Gjirokastra to replace Baba Selim, who had died in 1944. But a year later, he was accused of espionage and collaboration with the British. A 'people's court' sentenced him to death and he was executed on 14 January 1948. This took place during the purges that the new regime carried out against its opponents and perceived opponents.

Baba Ali Tomorri was the author of six books of Bektashi inspiration, including poetry translations and original verse. They are: *Bektashinjt e Shqipëries* (The Bektashi of Albania), Korça 1921; *Thelbi i qëllimit* (The Core of the Purpose); *Literatyra e Bektashivet a vjersha të përkthyera prej shkrimtarëve bektashinj të vjetër* (Bektashi Literature or Verse Translated from Old Bektashi Writers), Tirana 1927; *Mercija, apo ceremonia e shënjtë e Bektashivet kur shënjtërohet Ashyrëja* (Mersiye, the Sacred Ceremony of the Bektashi When Ashura Is Observed), Tirana 1928; *Historija e Bektashinjvet* (History of the Bektashi), Tirana 1929; *Xhevher ose mendim edhe aforizma Bektashijsh të vjetër* (Jewels or Thoughts and Aphorisms of the Old Bektashi), Tirana 1934; and *Nefeze dhe gazele bektashiane* (Bektashi Nefes and Ghazels), Tirana 1934. He opposed all religious fanaticism in his writings and endeavoured to combine Christian and Bektashi elements. Baba Ali Tomorri was one of the rare Bektashi authors to abandon Arabic script and use the Latin alphabet for his publications, a change worthy of note. His articles in the Albanian press in the 1920s, 1930s and 1940s were widely read and made him well known. cf. Baba Rexheb 1970, pp. 367–372; H. Norris 1993, pp. 190–192; N. Clayer 1993, p. 304, 2003, p. 131.

Ali Baba Horasani of Fushë Kruja (d. 1562)

Bektashi religious figure, missionary and holy man. Ali Baba stemmed from Khorasan in Central Asia and was early to promote the Bektashi faith in Albania. He settled in Fushë Kruja and founded the *tekke* there. The French Consul Baron Alexandre Degrand records the following legend:

Four centuries ago, a poor dervish called Baba Ali arrived in Kruja. He was originally from Khorasan in Persia and settled in the lower part of the town where his *tekke* is currently located. He built himself a shack using four boards of cypress wood and lived off alms. He was loved by all because of the good deeds he did and the sage advice he gave to those who consulted him. One evening, he told the peasants who came to visit him: 'My children, I am going on a long journey.' When they went out to the fields the next day, they were surprised to see a magnificent cypress tree where the old man had built his shack. The four boards had transformed themselves overnight into a beautiful tree. Since the dervish had left his shack to go and die, they searched for his body and buried it nearby. On that spot they built a *tyrbe* to perpetuate his memory.[308]

Ali Baba Horasani was thus buried in a *tyrbe* at Fushë Kruja, where his remains are venerated, and it was near this *tyrbe* that the *tekke* of Fushë Kruja was founded.
cf. J. A. Degrand 1901, p. 243; F. W. Hasluck 1929, p. 442 (551); N. Clayer 1990, p. 330; H. Norris 1993, p. 125.

Ali Haqi Baba of Gjirokastra (1827–1907)

Bektashi religious figure, poet and writer. Ali Haqi Karaj was born and raised in Elbasan. He was introduced to the Bektashi Order by Baba Salih Elbasani from Köprülü and 'took the hand' of the *baba* of the *tekke* of Melçan near Korça. From 1854 he served for seven years at the *pir evi* at Hacıbektaşköy in central Anatolia. While in Turkey, he visited all the Shia pilgrimage sites, from Karbala in Iraq to Palestine.

Ali Haqi thereafter returned to Albania and settled in 1861 at the *tekke* of Asim Baba, also known as the Gravel *Tekke* (*Teqeja e Zallit*) in Gjirokastra. For this reason he was commonly known as Baba Ali Gjirokastra or Baba Ali Elbasani.

Baba Ali Haqi was an important figure in the revival of the Bektashi movement in Albania, half a century after the banning of the order and the destruction of the *tekkes* under Sultan Mahmud II in 1826. In Gjirokastra he replaced the old *tekke* with a new building. He also provided training for forty dervishes and appointed twelve other *babas*, thus enabling Bektashism to spread throughout southern Albania. He was, in addition, one of the rare *babas* to forbid the drinking of alcohol in his *tekke*. In all, Baba Ali Haqi served as *baba* of the Gravel *Tekke* in Gjirokastra for forty-six years, from 1861 to 1907, and, towards the end of this period, he enjoyed great renown throughout the south of the country.

Baba Ali Haqi was also the author of several books in Ottoman Turkish including an *Istilâhât-i Sûfîye* (a volume on mystical phraseology), a dictionary of Chagatay Turkish and *Siyâhatnâme* (an account of his pilgrimages), as well as poetry in Arabic and Persian. Their whereabouts is now unknown, but it can be assumed that they were destroyed in the great *tekke* library by the communists who took power in 1944. Baba Ali Haqi was the *murshid* and predecessor of Baba Selim Ruhi.
cf. Baba Rexhebi 1970, pp. 291–302; H. Kaleshi 1980, pp. 12–13; H. Norris 1993, p. 135; F. Trix 2009, pp. 35–42, 48; A. Bishqemi 2016, p. 10.

Ali Kamberi, Dede Baba

cf. Kamber Ali, Dede Baba.

Ali Myrteza Baba of Fushë Kruja

cf. Myrteza Baba of Fushë Kruja.

Ali Riza of Elbasan, Dede Baba (1876-1944)

Bektashi religious figure. Ali Riza was born in 1876 (or 1882) in Kruja, and is thus also known as Ali Riza of Kruja. He served at the *tekke* in Fushë Kruja for ten years and travelled around 1902 to the holy sites in the Middle East. On his return to Albania, he became a dervish in Martanesh. He was then appointed by Baba Ahmet Turani as the *baba* of the *tekke* of Baba Hamit in Elbasan and administered it from November 1921 to December 1941.

At the death of Salih Nijazi Dede Baba in November 1941, none of the *babas* in Albania was willing to replace him as *kryegjysh* in Tirana. Baba Ali Riza hesitantly accepted the position because he had been a friend of Salih Nijazi. He thus became *kryegjysh* or *dede baba* of the Bektashi community from 1941 to his death on 22 February 1944. In actual fact, Ali Riza never really took on his new position in Tirana as he felt (or was considered) unqualified. He apparently did not know enough about Bektashi rites and ceremonies. Ali Riza thus no doubt remained primarily at his post in Elbasan, though he did complete the main *Kryegjshata* building that Salih Nijazi Dede Baba had begun in Tirana. He was replaced as *kryegjysh* by Baba Kamber Ali (1869-1950).

Baba Ali Riza was succeeded at the *tekke* of Elbasan by a Baba Rystem Llacja of Gjirokastra, who administered it from June 1944 to March 1945.

Ali Tyrabiu

cf. Ali Baba of Tomorr.

Alush Baba of Frashër (c. 1816-1896)

Bektashi religious figure. Baba Alush was the son of the poet Dalip bey Frashëri. He was head of the *tekke* of Frasher in the second half of the nineteenth century from about 1846 onwards. In 1872, Alush had an opportunity to visit the *pir evi* in Hacıbektaşköy in central Anatolia and was active in the Albanian national movement, in particular at the time of the League of Prizren (1878). He was the teacher and spiritual master of the three Frashëri brothers, the so-called torchbearers of the national movement: Abdyl bey Frashëri (1839-1892), Naim bey Frashëri (1846-1900) and Sami bey Frashëri (1850-1904). In 1879, in the presence of Baba Alush, Abdyl bey organized an important meeting of southern

Albanian leaders to promote nationalist objectives. Baba Alush was succeeded in Frashër in 1896 by Baba Hysejn and then by Baba Abedin who died in early 1913.

The Albanian poet, nationalist figure and guerrilla fighter Mihal Grameno (1871-1931) composed a poem in the honour of Baba Alush that was once sung in the region of Frashër and Përmet:

Kush do Shqipërinë, kush?
I miri Baba Alush.
Nukë vdiq, po shkoj dhe rron,
Dhe së largu na vështron,
Na vështron edhe na thrret:
'Punoni për Mëmëdhet.
Cili është bektashi
Të punoj' për Shqipëri, Të këndoj' gjuhën e tija,
Të heq' dorë nga Mavija.'[309]

Who loves Albania, who?
None but the good Baba Alush,
He did not die, he left, lived on,
And from a distance he observes us,
He observes us, calls out to us:
'Work for your Motherland!
Whoever is a Bektashi
Let him work for Albania,
Let him read his language,
And keep away from Muavija'.

cf. A. Tomorri 1929, p. 85, 89; S. Skëndi 1967, pp. 41-42; N. Clayer 2003, pp. 106-107.

Arshi Baba of Durballi Sultan (1906-2015)

Bektashi religious figure. Arshi Bazaj was born in 1906 in Sevaster near Vlora. He was long active at the Durballi Sultan *tekke* in Thessaly; he joined Baba Rexheb in the United States in 1958 and served him faithfully for many decades. In 2005, he succeeded Baba Rexheb as head of the Bektashi *tekke* in Taylor near Detroit, Michigan, where he died in December 2015. He is buried to the side within the tyrbe of Baba Rexheb for whom he had served as *türbedar*.

Arshi Baba of Gjirokastra (d. 1621)

Bektashi religious figure. Arshi Baba was born in Diyarbakır in Anatolia in the late sixteenth century. When he grew up, he set off for Albania to spread the

Bektashi faith and settled in Gjirokastra where he founded a *tekke*, but he died soon thereafter. Arshi Baba was the author of Turkish-language verse, including poetry in praise of Gjirokastra. Most of it is now lost.
cf. H. Norris 1993, pp. 125, 134; Baba Rexheb 1970, pp. 213-214.

Asim Baba of Gjirokastra (d. 1796)

Bektashi holy man. Seyyid Muhammed Asim Baba was a holy man who is said to have stemmed from the house of the Prophet, thus the title Seyyid. He was born in the Üsküdar (Scutari) quarter of Istanbul and received his training as a Bektashi adept at the *pir evi* in Hacıbektaşköy in central Anatolia. In 1778, he was sent as a *baba* to Albania to spread the Bektashi faith. He faced stiff opposition from local Sunni Muslims who refused to shelter him. After living for two years in a tent, he founded a *tekke* in Gjirokastra in 1780 which was to become known as the Gravel *Tekke* (*Teqeja e Zallit*). He thus gave impetus to the Bektashi movement in southern Albania as there were no other functioning *tekkes* in the country at that time. Asim Baba headed the *tekke* for sixteen years and was buried in a *tyrbe* (mausoleum) near the *tekke* at his death in 1796 [1209 AH]. From his death to 1944, this *tekke* was administered by a total of eight *babas*, of whom one was a Turk and seven were Albanians. The *tekke* in Gjirokastra is said to have possessed a rich library, which was preserved until 1944 at least.
cf. Baba Rexhebi 1970, pp. 288-291; H. Kaleshi and H. J. Kissling 1980, pp. 10-11; N. Clayer 1990, p. 432; H. Norris 1993, p. 125.

Bakalli, Qazim
cf. Qazim Baba of Gjakova.

Balim Sultan of Dimetoka (1457-1517)

Bektashi religious figure and second founder of the Bektashi Order. Balim Sultan (Albanian: *Ballëm Sulltan*, Turkish: *Balım Sultan*) is regarded and venerated as the actual founder and *pir* (master) of the Bektashi. He was raised at the shrine of Seyyid Ali Sultan near Dimetoka (Greek: Didymoteichon), 22 km south of Edirne (Adrianople) in Thrace. His mother was a Bulgarian Christian. Balim Sultan set off for the shrine of Haji Bektash in Anatolia and became head of the Bektashi in 1501. He centralized the authority of the Bektashi there and is said to have codified hierarchical ranks, rites and practices of the movement, thus introducing a good deal of uniformity in the order for the first time.

He is referred to in an early document as follows:

Upon a sign that came from Seyyid Ali Sultan in a dream, he (Balim Sultan) first went to the palace in Istanbul, where he was shown respect and reverence by the sultan (Bayezid II). He headed for the convent of Hacı Bektaş with an imperial decree, and was the leader there until the year 922 AH (1516–1517 AD). The rituals and rules of the Bektashi Order, which are in agreement with justice and true religion, were prescribed by him. [...] Also the revenues allocated for the dervishes and the *çelebis* (that is, the descendants of Hacı Bektaş) residing in the convent were donated by the sultan in the time of Balim Sultan.[310]

In Albanian legendry, Balim Sultan is said to be buried in a cave in the mountains of Martanesh, in the district of Bulqiza. The isolated mountain venue is now the site of the *tekke* of Balim Sultan.

Bardhi, Reshat

cf. Reshat Bardhi, Dede Baba.

Bazaj, Arshi

cf. Arshi Baba of Durballi Sultan.

Beqiri, Rexheb

cf. Rexheb Baba.

Brahimaj, Edmond, Dede Baba

cf. Edmond Brahimaj, Dede Baba.

Braho Baba

cf. Ibrahim Baba of Qesaraka.

Çeno, Mehmet

cf. Mehmet Baba of Fushë Kruja.

Dedej, Qazim

cf. Qazim Baba of Elbasan.

Dylgjer Hysejni of Elbasan

Bektashi religious figure. Dylgjer or Dylgjar Hyseni was an early Bektashi missionary in Elbasan. A neighbourhood in Elbasan was named after him.
cf. H. Norris 1993, p. 125.

Edmond Brahimaj, Dede Baba (b. 1959)

Bektashi religious figure. Edmond Brahimaj, known popularly as Baba Mondi, is *kryegjysh* (*dede baba*), i.e. head of the Bektashi community in Albania. He was born in Tirana of parents from the village of Brataj near Vlora. He trained at the Scanderbeg military school and the military academy, and then studied law. From 1982 to 1990 he was an army officer. In 1990 he took part in the organizational council of the revived Bektashi community. In January 1992, he 'took the hands' of Baba Reshat Bardhi and Baba Barjam Mahmutaj and was consecrated as a dervish in May 1996, serving later as a *baba* at the *tekke* of Turan near Korça. He replaced Reshat Bardhi as *kryegjysh* in June 2011 and has since then led the Bektashi community in Albania and around the world.

Faja Martaneshi Baba (1910–1947)

Political and Bektashi religious figure of the Second World War period. Baba Faja Martaneshi, or Baba Faja of Martanesh, whose real name was Mustafa Xhani, was born in Luz i Madh in the district of Kavaja. He studied in the traditions of his Bektashi Muslim faith and in May 1934 became a *baba* at the *tekke* of Martanesh in the Bulqiza region, thus the new surname. Baba Faja joined the communist partisan movement during the Second World War and was chosen as a member of the national liberation council at the Conference of Peza in the summer of 1942. He took part in fighting in the central Albanian mountains and Elbasan, always stressing the anti-Islamic nature of the Italian occupation. In May 1944, he was made deputy chairman of the national liberation council, thus becoming a leading figure in the victorious communist movement. After the war, he represented Elbasan in the constitutional assembly and was deputy chairman of the presidium of the People's Assembly. As the leading Bektashi figure to collaborate with the communists, Baba Faja tried to introduce certain reforms, such as allowing clerics to marry, to cut their beards and to wear civilian clothes. He and Baba Fejzo Dervishi pressured the head of the community, Abaz Hilmi Dede Baba, to accept these demands or be considered an enemy of the regime, accusing him of being a reactionary. On 18 March 1947, seeing no way out, Abaz Hilmi shot both of the renegades and killed himself at the headquarters (*kryegjyshata*) of the Bektashi community in Tirana.

The British officer David Smiley (1916–2009), who was in Albania during the Second World War, noted of Baba Faja:

> His real name was Baba Mustafa, though he was always known as Baba Faja. A priest or *hoja* of the Bektashi sect. His monastery at Martenesh had been burnt down some time before by the Italians. He was a well-built and rather stout man, with a massive black beard. Apart from his priest's hat which he always wore, his usual dress was a loud check plus-four suit over which he slung his bandolier

and pistol. He was a likeable character, but a scoundrel, and he drank heavily (Bektashis are in fact permitted to drink alcohol, unlike other Moslem sects). He delighted in singing partisan songs in his deep bass voice, especially after consuming large quantities of raki. We did not take long to discover he was being used as a figurehead by the partisans, and always had a commissar at his elbow to keep an eye on him.[311]

Baba Faja is dead, killed by the Supreme Head of the Bektashi Sect, Dede Baba Abazi. It appears that a religious discussion between these two and another priest turned into a heated argument. Baba Abazi drew his pistol and shot both Baba Faja and the other priest, and then turned the pistol on himself and committed suicide.[312]

cf. newspaper *Bashkimi*, Tirana, No. 691, 19 March 1947, p. 1, No. 692, 20 March 1947, p. 1, 2, No. 693, 21 March 1947, p. 1, No. 5771, 23 April 1947, p. 1; D. Smiley 1984, pp. 84, 159–160.

Fetah Baba of Backa

Bektashi religious figure. Baba Fetah was born in Backa in the Skrapar region and lived in Prishta in the late nineteenth century. He headed the *tekke* or *dervishia* of Backa, where he taught people how to read and write Albanian. Baba Fetah is said to have run the *tekke* 'with intelligence, justice and love'. His influence in the local population was such that he was even able to reduce crime in the region. The rebel leader and writer Mihal Grameno wrote of him and his *dervishia*:

> We sang on our way until we got to Backa, where we went to the *dervishia* and were taken in by the dervishes. The *dervishia* is wonderfully situated, in a small field surrounded by hills and forests. Through the *dervishia* runs a river, so it is a truly beautiful site. The reverend Baba Fetah chose it himself and added much to its natural beauty. He planted all sorts of trees, grapevines, and other things, all in perfect order. As such, any traveller passing through Backa cannot help but admire his work and will say: 'Glory to your soul, Baba Fetah!'[313]

Gllava, Qamil Baba

cf. Qamil Baba of Gllava.

Hajdar Hatemi Baba of Gjonëm (early nineteenth century)

Hajdar Hatemi Baba served for several years at the *tekke* of Köprülü (Veles) in central Macedonia, where he lived with his friend and companion Shemimi Baba. After correspondence with and agreement from the elders of Kruja, the two men moved to Kruja in the last decade of the eighteenth century, where Hajdar

Hatemi Baba founded the *tekke* of Gjonëm near Laç around 1793 and Shemimi Baba founded the *tekke* of nearby Fushë Kruja in 1799. Hajdar Hatemi Baba, who composed verse in Turkish, died of poisoning.
cf. N. Clayer 1990, p. 298.

Hajdër Baba of Kardhiq (d. 1904)

Bektashi religious figure of Gjirokastra. Baba Hajdër (or Hajdar), who stemmed from Kardhiq north of Gjirokastra, 'took the hand' of Ali Haqi Baba of the *tekke* of Asim Baba in Gjirokastra in the late nineteenth century. He was active in the nationalist movement after the League of Prizren in 1878 and was imprisoned in Janina for several years for his activities. Baba Hajdër of Kardhiq was head of the Hajdërije *tekke* in Gjirokastra in the last decades of the nineteenth century. He was succeeded in 1904 by Baba Sulejman. Baba Hajdër of Kardhiq is not to be confused with the earlier founder of the Hajdërije *tekke*, Baba Hajdër Plaku (the Elder), after whom the *tekke* was named.
cf. Baba Rexheb 1980, p. 384; N. Clayer 1990, pp. 291-294.

Haji Bektash (1248-1337)

Bektashi religious figure and first founder of the Bektashi Order. Haji Bektash Veli (Albanian: *Haxhi Bektashi Veli*, Turkish: *Hacı Bektaş Veli*) was a Turkoman holy man from the Khorasan region of northeastern Iran who seems to have lived in the later thirteenth and early fourteenth centuries. There is little documentary evidence and much information about him stems from the realm of legendry. According to traditional lore, he was born in 1248 and left his homeland in 1281, at the behest of Ahmad Yasawi, to spread the faith in Anatolia. He settled in a little village in Cappadocia called Sulucakarahöyük, between Kırşehir and Nevşehir. This settlement was subsequently named after him, Hacıbektaşköy (Haji Bektash Village)

Haji Bektash is regarded as the initial founder and patron saint of the Bektashi. It was thus in the village of Hacıbektaşköy that the *pir evi* (master house or motherhouse) of the Bektashi Order arose and it was from here that the Bektashi movement spread. Haji Bektash is reputed to have wrought many miracles and healed the sick. He is said to have died in 1337.

Other legends link Haji Bektash to the founding of the Janissary corps in 1295, although this is historically unlikely. 'It is claimed that the Janissaries were founded by Haji Bektash or that he was at least present at their inauguration where he declared: 'Your name shall be *Yeniçeri* (New Force), may your hands be victorious, yours swords sharp and your spears ever ready to strike the foe!' As he said these words, he placed his hand on the head of one of these new soldiers. When he did so, the sleeve of his robe hung down over the young man's shoulders. In memory of that incident, Janissary headgear thereafter had a flap of material that hung down from its tall crown to the wearer's shoulders.'[314]

Hasan Dede of Përmet

Bektashi holy man. He was venerated in Përmet, and to a lesser extent in Tepelena and Berat. Hasan Dede was said to be 400–500 years old and was the brother of a local chief called Jadikula. Healing powers were attributed to him. Evliya Çelebi (1670) mentions the tomb of a Baba Hasan Dede Sultan as being among the foremost pilgrimage sites in Gjirokastra. Whether this is the same Hasan Dede is unclear.
cf. Evliya Çelebi, *Seyahatname*, VIII, 354b; F. W. Hasluck 1929, p. 432 (537), 437 (543); R. Dankoff and R. Elsie 2000, p. 79.

Hatemi, Hajdar Baba
cf. Hajdar Hatemi Baba of Gjonëm.

Haxhi Baba Horasani of Përmet (d. 1620)

Bektashi holy man from Khorasan (Horasan) in Central Asia. Many miracles were attributed to him. He was venerated in particular at a *tekke* situated above the town of Përmet. Haxhi Baba died in Përmet in 1620 and was originally buried there, but, according to a legend, on the day of his burial, the sun would not go down and his hand protruded from the grave to indicate that he wished to be buried in Qesaraka northwest of Kolonja. A *tekke* was, at any rate, built there in his honour.
cf. F. W. Hasluck 1929, p. 438 (545); Baba Rexheb 1970, pp. 360–362.

Haxhi Baba of Fushë Kruja

Bektashi religious figure. Baba Haxhi, born in Kruja, headed the *tekke* of Shemimi Baba at Fushë Kruja from 1893, when his predecessor, Baba Hysen Kukeli of Dibra, died. The French consul Baron Alexandre Degrand reports the following on him.

'During his travels, Baba Haxhi learned much and was no enemy of progress. He was the first *baba* to go to Trieste and buy farm machinery for his mill and land, but he was confronted with the superstition of the peasants and hatred from the proponents of the old regime who destroyed his new-fangled machinery on purpose. As he had no mechanic to repair the machines, they remained unused in a barn.'[315]
cf. J. A. Degrand 1891, pp. 245–246; N. Clayer 1990, p. 331.

Haxhi Bektash
cf. Haji Bektash.

Hidër Baba of Makedonski Brod

Bektashi religious figure. Hidër Baba (also called Hëdër Baba, Hizir Baba or Khidr) is venerated in particular by the Bektashi of Macedonia. His grave is said to be at the *tyrbe* of Hidër Baba/chapel of Saint Nicholas in Makedonski Brod, 22 km east of Këroçva (Kičevo). The Bektashi *tekke* in Kërçova is also named after him. According to local legendry, Hidër Baba was one of the forty dervish disciples of Durballi Sultan who travelled through Greece and Macedonia to spread the faith. He is associated with water.

Hidër Baba would seem to be a reflection of the mysterious Muslim saint Khidr (the Green Saint), who is identified as a companion of Moses, who discovered the Fountain of Life, and who was the patron saint of travellers. In the Christian tradition he is identified with Saint Elias and Saint George.[316] Khidr, or al-Khidr, was very popular and had an enormous reputation among Sufis in the Middle East. However, the exact evolution of Khidr to the Bektashi Hidër Baba is still unclear.

Hilmi, Abaz

cf. Abaz Hilmi, Dede Baba.

Horasani, Ali Baba

cf. Ali Baba Horasani of Fushë Kruja.

Horasani, Haxhi Baba

cf. Haxhi Baba Horasani of Përmet.

Hysen Baba of Melçan (d. 1914)

Bektashi religious figure. Baba Hysen (or Husejn) Melçani stemmed from Vërlen, a village in the Devoll region. He succeeded Baba Adem as head of the prestigious *tekke* of Melçan near Korça towards the end of the nineteenth century. Under Baba Hysen, the *tekke* became a veritable centre of the Albanian national movement, noted for the clandestine teaching of the Albanian alphabet. Here are the words of a villager from Qatrom on Baba Hysen and the struggle for the Albanian alphabet:

> One day, Baba Hysen from the *tekke* of Melçan visited our village. My father, who was one of his friends, invited him to have dinner at our house. As is custom, the other villagers came over to greet him and keep him company. Before the start of the meal, I took my glass of *raki* and raised it to Baba Hysen, saying: 'Baba Hysen, let us drink to the health of the alphabet. Long live the alphabet!' Baba Hysen was delighted at this and all the villagers joined in, shouting: 'Long live the alphabet!' [...]

I continued on to the *tekke* of Melçan. At the village there, I met two men who wanted to learn the alphabet and gave them an Albanian spelling-book. I then trod up the hill and went into the *meydan* where I came across Baba Hysen. Baba Hysen was a true patriot and an inseparable friend of the nationalists of Korça, whereas Baba Qazim of the *tekke* of Qatrom was different. He was afraid of the government...

I told Baba Hysen what had happened and gave him the remaining spelling-books that I had in my satchel. The *baba* took one of them, kissed it and placed it against his forehead. He told me that our country would prosper with the help of these spelling-books, would be free and we would have a government of our own like the other peoples in the Balkans. Then he kissed me on the forehead and exclaimed: 'Long live the alphabet!'[317]

It was at the *tekke* of Melçan in March 1906, in the presence of seven or eight *babas*, that the nationalist figure Bajo Topulli (1868–1930) formed the first armed guerrilla band in the Korça region. The guerrillas made their headquarters at the *tekke* and the population came here to receive instructions during the revolt against the Turkish authorities. Like many Albanian intellectuals, Baba Hysen initially supported the reforms of the Young Turks in 1908 and persuaded Albanian guerrilla fighters Çerçiz Topulli (1880–1915) and Mihal Grameno (1871–1931) to join forces with Niyazi Bey, the leader of the Young Turk Revolution in southern Albania, but he soon realized that the Turkish nationalism of the latter conflicted with his Albanian nationalism. Grameno wrote of his meeting with Baba Hysen in 1907:

When dinner was over, we departed and, proceeding slowly, arrived the next morning at dawn at the *tekke* of Melçan. We spent five days at the *tekke* where His Holiness, Baba Hysen, welcomed and received us hospitably. He assisted and blessed us. No words can describe the assistance His Holiness provided, for Baba Hysen is one of the great patriots and the backbone of the nationalist movement. Pages written in golden letters must be devoted to him in the annals of our history. A lot of nationalists arrived at Melçan, from Korça and the surrounding regions, to meet us. [...] The dervishes, who were true patriots, men inspired by national sentiment, did all they could to fulfil our every wish.[318]

Throughout the years, Baba Hysen had considerable influence over the nationalist movement, at least in the Korça region. He was replaced at his death by his nephew, Baba Zylfo (d. 1943).
cf. N. Clayer 2003, pp. 110–111, 116–117.

Hysen Kukeli Baba of Fushë Kruja (1822–1893)

Bektashi religious figure. Haxhi Hysen Kukeli Baba, originally of Dibra (probably Zërqan in the district of Bulqiza), reconstructed the *tekke* of Fushë Kruja in 1852–

1853 [1270 AH] and headed it for forty years. He was a good administrator and restored to the *tekke* some of its former glory. It also grew in prosperity under his rule. Haxhi Hysen also founded the *tekke* named after him in the village of Martanesh in Bulqiza. The title *haxhi* indicates that he made a pilgrimage to Mecca and saw the holy sites in the Middle East at some time. Around 1880 he gathered 300 men of Kruja to fight for the defence of Ulqin (Ulcinj) that was being taken over by Montenegro. He died in 1893 [1310 AH] and was succeeded by a Baba Haxhi. He lies buried at the *tekke* of Fushë Kruja, although he is also said to have been buried in Zërqan.
cf. M. Hasluck 1954, p 118; N. Clayer 1990, p. 426.

Ibrahim Baba of Qesaraka (d. 1930)

Bektashi religious figure and poet. Baba Ibrahim, also called Baba Braho, was from the *tekke* of Haxhi Baba Horasani in Qesaraka near Kolonja in southeastern Albania. He was appointed as a *baba* there by Baba Abedin of Frashër. Baba Ibrahim was active, like many other Bektashi leaders, in the Albanian nationalist movement and in the clandestine distribution of Albanian books and literature. He was particularly close to his teacher Petro Nini Luarasi (1865-1911) and gave refuge to him in 1903 when the latter was on the run. The rebel leader and writer Mihal Grameno met him in the mountains of southern Albania in 1905, noting: 'The next day, Ibrahim Effendi arrived, who is now the *baba* of the *tekke* of Qesaraka. This gentleman is one of the most distinguished patriots and best educated people we have, so I discussed Albania's situation with him at length.'[319] Baba Ibrahim also gave refuge in Qesaraka to the guerrilla fighter Bajo Topulli (1868-1930) and helped him to get to Gjirokastra, but he was arrested and imprisoned by Turkish military forces. When Greek forces occupied the region in 1913, Baba Ibrahim was arrested once again but he was subsequently freed by the rebel leader Sali bey Butka (1857-1938) and his guerrilla band. When the Greeks later returned to Kolonja, Baba Ibrahim was forced to flee. The *tekke* of Haxhi Baba Horasani was burned down and destroyed and Baba Ibrahim's mother, who had remained at the *tekke*, was slain.

Baba Ibrahim was also regarded as a talented poet; he compared the Albanian nation, ravaged by war and oppression under Ottoman rule, to the burden of a long hard winter.
cf. Baba Rexheb 1970, pp. 360-262.

Ibrahim Xhefai Baba of Elbasan (d. 1829)

Bektashi religious figure. Ibrahim Xhefai was a dervish of Shemimi Baba of Fushë Kruja and was called to Elbasan by Fakri Mustafai (d. 1816). When all the *tekkes* in the Ottoman Empire were closed down in July 1826 on the orders of Sultan Mahmud II (r. 1808-1839), Xhefai Baba fled to Luzi i Madh in the Kavaja region, where the population was mostly Halveti, but he was received well. He then spent three years in Frashër and returned to Elbasan in 1829 [1244 AH], where he died. cf. A. Tomorri 1929, p. 82; H. Norris 1993, p. 125; N. Clayer 1990, p. 272; Q. Dedej, *Fillimet* 1997.

Iljaz Vërzhezha, Dervish (d. 1923)

Dervish Iljaz Vërzhezha, also known as Iljaz Qafoku of Vërzhezha, was from the Skrapar region. When he was fifteen years old, he was sent to Istanbul to be with his brother. From there he visited the *pir evi* at Hacıbektaşköy in central Anatolia and the holy sites in the Middle East. On his return to Albania he visited many of the southern Albanian *tekkes* and settled in Prishta. Dervish Iljaz opened schools to promote the teaching of Albanian, led nationalist bands in the final years of Ottoman rule (1905-1908) and involved himself personally in public works: digging village wells, building bridges and making roads in the Skrapar, Përmet and Kolonja regions. Also known as *varf* Iljazi, he is remembered, in particular, for having founded the new *tekke* of Kulmak on Mount Tomorr, a few hundred metres below the existing *tyrbe* of Abbas Ali. For this memorable project, he solicited and collected funds, and oversaw the construction of the *tekke* in 1916.

The faithful gathered at a *tyrbe* in his honour in Cërrila in Mallakastra on 2 May, and do so now at a new *tyrbe* constructed in his honour in the village of Vërzhezha in Skapar.

Kaliçani, Selim

cf. Selim Kaliçani Baba of Martanesh.

Kamber Ali, Dede Baba (1869-1950)

Bektashi religious figure. Kamber Ali, also known as Ali Kamberi of Prishta or Kamber Ali Pagria, was born in 1869 or 1870 in the village of Pagria near Përmet. Raised in a Bektashi milieu, he 'took the hand' of Baba Abedin in Frashër and became a dervish, but he was also active in the nationalist movement and taught Albanian in the Skrapar, Përmet and Tomorrica regions. In 1910, he accompanied Ahmet Turani and Sulejman of Gjirokastra to the *pir evi* at Hacıbektaşköy in central Anatolia, where they were each made a *gjysh* by Fejzi Dede. He also had occasion to visit the holy sites in the Middle East, before returning to Albania in 1911. During the First World War, when most of the southern Albanian *tekkes* were burned down by Greek forces, he fled to the *tekke* of Candia (Heraklion) on Crete. From there in 1916 he continued on to the United States, where he endeavoured to raise funds for the *tekkes* among Albanian-Americans. He returned to Albania in 1919-1920 and was made *baba* of Prishta and of Suka the following year, after the death of Baba Hysen. He then began the arduous task of rebuilding some of the *tekkes* in the devastated region. He helped organize the First National Congress of the Bektashi at the *tekke* of Prishta in January 1921 and was elected there as a member of the Bektashi national council. He also presided over the Third National Congress of 1929 in Korça. He corresponded and was in close contact with Fan Noli (1882–1965). The British journalist and writer Joseph Swire (1903–1978) met him at the *tekke* of Suka around 1930 and described him as a 'portly jovial old man in flowing white robe and very ecclesiastical manner'.[320]

At the beginning of the Second World War, Kamber Ali was still serving at the *tekke* of Prishta which he had transformed into a modest oasis of refinement. In November 1942 he joined the anti-communist resistance movement *Balli Kombëtar*, and had close ties with one of its leaders, Ali bey Këlcyra (1891–1963). This later gave him a reputation among the Albanian communists of being pro-fascist.

On 12 April 1944, Baba Kamber Ali was elected *kryegjysh* or *dede* of the Bektashi community, to replace Ali Riza Dede Baba of Elbasan, but he did not hold this position for long. In December of that year, he was arrested by the communist partisans who had just taken power, and was sentenced (at the age of seventy-four) to life in prison. He died on 5 April 1950 in the Tirana prison hospital.

His remains are now buried in a *tyrbe* at the *Kryegjyshata* in Tirana.
cf. N. Clayer 1990, pp. 377–381.

Karaj, Ali Haqi

cf. Ali Haqi Baba of Gjirokastra.

Kasem Baba of Kastoria (late fifteenth century)

Bektashi religious figure. Kasem Baba, also known as Kasim or Qazim Baba, is said to have lived at the time of Mehmed the Conqueror (r. 1451–1481) when he moved to the Balkans and settled in Kastoria (Albanian: Kosturi, Turkish: Kesrie), now in Greece. His *tekke* was situated at the entrance to Kastoria on the Florina road. In his *Historija e përgjithshme e Bektashinjvet* (General History of the Bektashi), Baba Ali Tomorri states that Kasem Baba arrived in Kastoria in 1378. At any rate, he enjoyed considerable fame as a miracle-worker. 'He is said during his lifetime to have converted many Christians by the somewhat crude method of hurling from the hill on the landward side of the isthmus of Kastoria a huge rock, which crashed into a church full of worshippers.'[321]

Another legend has it that Kasem Baba went to Kuç, a village south of Bilisht in the Devoll region in southeastern Albania, and, at a pleasant spot where cypress trees now grow, he offered a meal to all the dervishes there. When the meal was over, he rose and returned to Kastoria.[322] Some say that the grave of Kasem Baba is actually in Kuç. In another legend, Kasem Baba is said to have left his hand in Elbasan.

The *tekke* of Kuç, which Kasem Baba is said to have founded personally, is at any rate among the oldest in Albania. The nearby tomb of Kasem Baba, probably in Kapshtica, was an object of special veneration by pilgrims, in particular on Mondays and Fridays. The *tekke* of Kuç was closed down in July 1826 on the orders of Sultan Mahmud II (r. 1808–1839), but was refounded in 1878 by one Ibrahim Baba. New buildings were constructed in 1906–1907 by a Baba Hafiz, who was shot in 1914 by the Greeks and whose bloodstained *taj* was shown to visitors. The *tekke* was still standing during Margaret Hasluck's visit in 1923, and was inhabited at the time by one *baba* and three dervishes.
cf. A. Tyrabiu (=A. Tomorri) 1928, p. 54; F. W. Hasluck 1929, pp. 424–425 (526), 439–440 (547); J. Birge 1937, p. 72; N. Clayer 1990, pp. 340–341; M. Kiel 1993, p. 265; R. Elsie, *Dictionary* 2001, pp. 213–214.

Koka, Seit
cf. Seit Baba of Durballi Sultan.

Kosum Baba
cf. Kusum Baba of Vlora.

Kukeli, Hysen Baba
cf. Hysen Kukeli Baba of Fushë Kruja.

Kus Baba
cf. Kusum Baba of Vlora.

Kusum Baba of Vlora

Bektashi holy man, also known as Kosum Baba, Kuzum Baba, Kuzgun Baba Sultan, Kus Baba, Kusmaba or Quzum Baba Sulltan. Kusum Baba lies buried at the Bektashi *tekke* in Vlora, where he is the object of veneration.

One version of the legend surrounding him has it that Kusum Baba (also said to be Seyyid Ali Sultan) was a Bektashi dervish in Anatolia in the fifteenth or sixteenth century, from where he was sent to Albania to spread the faith. After a short period at the *tekke* of Sari Saltik on Mount Kruja, he settled in the Budak neighbourhood of Vlora, where an original *tekke* was built. After eighteen years there, he paid a visit to Kruja. On his return, in the village of Babica, north of Vlora, he was stopped by some evil-minded men who begged for his assistance to cure an ailing child. Kuzum Baba agreed but first requested that he be able to do his ablutions (ritual washing). When he sat down to wash, they chopped off his head. To their amazement, Kuzum Baba then rose, picked up his head and continued his journey until he reached the site of his present *tyrbe* in Vlora, where he collapsed and died.

A mausoleum was built on the site, followed by a Bektashi *tekke*, which was subsequently supported by the aristocratic Vlora family. The Turkish traveller Evliya Çelebi, who visited Vlora in the year 1670, noted the presence of the site in the following terms: 'To the east of the fortress and somewhat above it is a slope with olive trees. All the hills and fields in the area are covered in fruit trees, vineyards and olive orchards. On this high peak is situated the tomb of Kuzgun Baba Sultan with a few Bektashi dervishes.'[323]

The *tyrbe* of Kusum Baba was reopened in April 1998 on the high cliff overlooking the city of Vlora and, now splendidly illuminated at night, can be seen from all points of town.

cf. C. Patsch 1904, p. 117; F. W. Hasluck 1929, p. 437 (543); H. Kaleshi and H. J. Kissling 1980, p. 10; R. Dankoff and R. Elsie 2000, pp. 136–139.

Kuzum Baba

cf. Kusum Baba of Vlora.

Leskoviku, Abedin Baba

cf. Abedin Baba of Leskovik.

Lutfi Baba of Mokattam (1849–1942)

Bektashi religious figure. Mehmet Lutfi Baba was born in the Dunavat quarter of Gjirokastra in 1849 [1265 AH]. In 1874 [1292 AH] he moved to Shkodra, where he worked as a merchant. It was there that he joined the Bektashi Order, having 'taken the hand' of his spiritual master, Hasib Baba. In 1882–1883 [1300 AH] he moved to Istanbul and joined the Shaquli Sultan *tekke* in Merdiven Köy on the Asian side of the city. In 1891–1892 [1309 AH] he visited the holy sites in Kerbela and 1892–1893 [1310 AH] he journeyed to the *pir evi* at Hacıbektaşköy in central Anatolia, where he took up residence for three years. Mehmet Lutfi returned to Istanbul in 1895–1896 [1313 AH] and then made a tour of the Bektashi *tekkes* in Rumelia. In 1899 he went on a pilgrimage to Mecca and lived for two years thereafter in Istanbul. In 1901–1902 [1319 AH] he was sent to Egypt and later succeeded Hajdar Mehmet Baba as head of the Mokattam *tekke* (also called the Magauri *tekke*) near Cairo. In 1902–1903 [1320 AH] an explosion occurred at an ammunition depot that destroyed the *tekke* and its surroundings. Lutfi Baba sought and received funds for the reconstruction of the *tekke*, work that was carried out between 1903 and 1909. He also built a fountain there, known as the 'Fountain of Lutfi Baba'. He was remembered as the 'father of the poor' for the gifts and financial assistance he

provided to those in need. Lutfi Baba was succeeded in 1935-1936 [1354 AH] by Ahmet Sirri Baba whom he had made his deputy in 1923-1924 [1342 AH]. Lutfi Baba died in 1942 [1360 AH].
cf. H. Norris 1993, pp. 218-221; F. Trix 2009, p. 100.

Mahzuni, Muharrem Baba

cf. Muharrem Mahzuni Baba of Durballi Sultan.

Manes Baba

cf. Sulejman Baba of Gjirokastra.

Mehmet Baba of Fushë Kruja (1882-1934)

Bektashi religious figure. Mehmet Çeno was a dervish at the Hajdërije *Tekke* in Gjirokastra. From the 1920s to his death in 1934, he served as the *baba* of the *tekke* of Fushë Kruja and played an important role in its reconstruction in about 1927. He lies buried in a *tyrbe* at the *tekke* there and was succeeded by Baba Ali Myrteza.
cf. N. Clayer 1990, pp. 331-332.

Mehmet Lutfi Baba

cf. Lutfi Baba of Mokattam.

Melçani, Abdullah Baba

cf. Abdullah Baba of Melçan.

Melçani, Hysen Baba

cf. Hysen Baba of Melçan.

Meleq Shëmbërdhenji Baba (1842-1918)

Bektashi religious figure and poet. Meleq Shëmbërdhenji, whose birth name was Meleq Muça or Meleq Staravecka, was from the village of Staravecka in the Skrapar region of southern Albania. His interest in the Bektashi faith was awakened under Baba Fetah at the *tekke* of Backa. He then trained at the Mokattam *tekke* near Cairo in Egypt, where he became a dervish under Baba Abaz. He returned to Albania and took part in the nationalist movement, in particular by illegally distributing books and spreading new ideas that were subversive for the Ottoman State. One of his followers reported many years later:

In Shtylla, people were being taught to read and write the Albanian language at the end of the nineteenth century. When I was little, I was taught by Baba Meleq Staravecka. This *baba* went around and visited the villages from time to time – Panarit, Staravecka and Shtylla. Wherever Baba Meleq went, he made popular the struggle of the Albanian people for freedom and national unity. He distributed Albanian books and, when he visited the villagers in their homes, he taught the young people to read and write. This patriotic *baba* visited our house in Shtylla, too, and taught me and the other young people to read and write our language. We are all grateful to him.[324]

Baba Meleq was associated with the *tekke* of Shëmbërdhenj, initially as a dervish, from 1891. He travelled to the holy sites in Anatolia in 1892, lived at the Şah Kulu *tekke* at Merdivenköy in Constantinople (around 1896), spent a couple of years in Monastir, Ohrid and Struga (around 1898), and lived in Romania (around 1904). He was officially appointed as the *baba* of the *tekke* of Shëmbërdhenj in October 1910. The *tekke* was burned down in June 1914, after Albanian independence, by Sunni Muslim rebels supporting the central Albanian uprising of Haxhi Qamili and its property was confiscated. Baba Meleq fled abroad, but he later returned and rebuilt the *tekke*. He is thus regarded by many as the second founder of the *tekke* of Baba Mustafa.

Baba Meleq Shëmbërdhenji was the author of both nationalist and religious verse in Albanian collected in a volume published in the 1920s. He is considered one of the best Bektashi poets of the period. Two volumes of his mystical lyrics were published posthumously under the titles *Muhamed Alinë dua* [I Love Muhammed Ali], Korça 1933, and *Besimi e atdheu* [Faith and Fatherland], Korça 1933. Baba Meleq was also a friend and admirer of Naim bey Frashëri whom he called, '*Zemra e Shqipërisë, gurra e urtësisë, pishtar i vegjëlisë, shejtor i njerëzisë*' (The heart of Albania, the fountain of wisdom, torch-bearer of the poor, saint of humanity).
cf. Baba Rexheb 1970, pp. 345–355; B. Ylli 1999; N. Clayer 2003, pp. 119–122; Q. Dedej, *Fillimet* 1997, pp. 98–99.

Mimi Baba

cf. Shemimi Baba of Fushë Kruja.

Mondi Baba

cf. Edmond Brahimaj, Dede Baba.

Muça, Meleq

cf. Meleq Shëmbërdhenji Baba.

Muhammed Asim Baba

cf. Asim Baba of Gjirokastra.

Muharrem Baba of Frashër (early nineteenth century)

Bektashi holy man said to have lived in the early nineteenth century. He was venerated at the southern Albanian *tekke* of Frashër. According to legend, when Muharrem Baba made a pilgrimage to the tomb of Haji Bektash in central Anatolia, the door of the *tekke* opened for him of its own accord. The abbot there, recognizing the miracle, said, 'It is thy fate (*nasib*),' thus giving him his subsequent name Nasib. This Nasib, whose mausoleum burned to the ground in 1914, is said to have foretold Ali Pasha Tepelena (1759–1822) his fate.
cf. F. W. Hasluck 1929, pp. 440 (547–548).

Muharrem Mahzuni Baba of Durballi Sultan (d. 1867)

Bektashi religious figure and poet. He was born in Gjirokastra and was the *baba* at the Bektashi *tekke* of Durballi Sultan near Farsala in Thessaly, one of the oldest in Europe, from 1845 to his death in 1867 [1286 AH]. His Albanian verse is permeated with Hurufi symbolism, i.e. the use of Arabic letters for numerical and mystical purposes. He was the twenty-seventh *baba* of the *tekke* of Durballi Sultan, and was buried in a *tyrbe* there.
cf. Baba Rexhebi 1970, pp. 269–270; R. Elsie 1986, p. 96; H. Norris 1993, p. 135; M. Kiel 2005, p. 428.

Myftari, Ahmet
cf. Ahmet Myftari, Dede Baba.

Myrteza Baba of Fushë Kruja (1912–1947)

Bektashi religious figure. Ali Myrteza Paja was the *baba* of the *tekke* of Fushë Kruja from 1934 to his death. He was a prominent figure in that period and was visited by many foreign dignitaries. Baba Myrteza was arrested by the communists, tortured and thrown out of a prison window. Seeing no hope, he committed suicide.

Nasib Tahir Baba
cf. Tahir Baba Nasibi of Frashër.

Nijazi, Salih
cf. Salih Nijazi, Dede Baba.

Pagria, Ali Kamber
cf. Kamber Ali, Dede Baba.

Prishta, Ahmet Baba
cf. Ahmet Baba of Prishta.

Prishta, Ali Kamber
cf. Kamber Ali, Dede Baba.

Prizreni, Adem Baba
cf. Adem Baba of Prizren.

Qafoku, Iljaz of Vërzhezha
cf. Iljaz Vërzhezha, Dervish.

Qazim Baba of Elbasan (1891-1962)

Bektashi religious figure. Baba Qazim, whose birth name was Musa Qazim Dedej, was born in Elbasan and finished his schooling in Salonica in 1910. He studied law there and in Istanbul, but was forced to interrupt his studies because of the Balkan Wars in 1912. On his return to Albania, he served in the first government of Ismail Qemal bey Vlora, as a judge in Fier and Skrapar and as a school teacher in Berat and Elbasan. He became a dervish in March 1944, having 'taken the hand' of Baba Mustafa Haqi, his cousin. In 1950 he was appointed as a *baba* to the Bektashi region of Elbasan, where he died in November 1962, a few years before the Bektashi faith was banned entirely. He was buried in the *tyrbe* of the great *tekke* of Elbasan. He was the author of two books on the history of the Albanian Bektashi, published posthumously.
cf. A. Bishqemi, 2016, p. 83; Q. Dedej, *Fillimet* 1997, pp. 66-68.

Qazim Baba of Gjakova (1895-1981)

Bektashi religious figure of the *tekke* of Gjakova. Qazim Bakalli was born in Gjakova and studied in Skopje to be a teacher. He taught school in Gjakova for a while and moved to Kruja in Albania in 1926, where he became a dervish in 1928 under Baba Mehmet Çeno. He also spent some of his Albanian years in Elbasan and on Mount Tomorr. In 1941, he moved to the Harabati *tekke* of Tetova and, having been made a *baba* in 1942 by Salih Nijazi Dede in Tirana, he headed the *tekke* in Tetova until it ceased to function on 19 November 1944.

In the politically tense period of 1944-1947, Baba Qazim was in Tirana and was made a *halife* by Xhafer Sadiku Dede Baba. He had been a supporter of the pre-communist Abaz Hilmi Dede Baba and, when the latter shot Baba Faja Martaneshi and committed suicide on 18 March 1947, Baba Qazim was seized by the communist authorities and escorted to the Yugoslav border. The Yugoslav communists held him in prison for two months in Skopje, but then released him as he was able to prove his innocence of any wrongdoing. In the summer of 1947, he was then able to return to Gjakova, where he exercised his functions as *baba* of the *tekke* there until his death on 15 February 1981. Baba Qazim, who was greatly revered by the Bektashi of Kosovo, was succeeded by Baba Tajar Gashi of Gostivar. cf. L. Mašulović-Marsol 1995, p. 357; N. Hafiz 1995, pp. 348–349; J. Norton 2001, pp. 188–189; J. Rexhepagiqi 2003, pp. 231–233.

Qamil Baba of Gllava (d. 1946)

Baba Qamil Gllava was from Kapinova in the Berat region. He was head of the *tekke* of Gllava in the Tepelena region during the Second World War, in which he took part. He was executed by the communists in Gjirokastra in 1945 or 1946. cf. Xh. Kallajxhi 1964, p. 31; N. Clayer 1990, pp. 300–301.

Qazim Baba of Kastoria

cf. Kasem Baba of Kastoria.

Reshat Bardhi, Dede Baba (1935–2011)

Bektashi religious figure who, as *kryegjysh,* was head of the Bektashi community in Albania for twenty years, from 1991 to 2011. Baba Reshat, whose birth name was Reshat Bardhi, was born in Lusna in the northeastern Luma region and moved with his family to Tirana in 1948. In 1950, after private religious training, he became a *muhib*, a spiritual member of the Bektashi community. In 1954 he became a dervish and in 1956 he attained the level of a *baba*. During the communist period, Baba Reshat was interned in the village of Drizar in Mallakastra from 1959 to 1967 with his mentor, *kryegjysh* Ahmet Myftari. He worked on a collective farm and in road construction, and kept a low profile after his release, these being the years when religion was banned in Albania (1967–1991).

On 22 March 1991, after the fall of the dictatorship, he reopened the *Kryegjyshata* in Tirana and was elected *kryegjysh* at the Sixth National Congress of the Bektashi in 1993. During his two decades as head of the Bektashi community and until his death, he oversaw the restoration of a dozen *tekkes* in southern Albania. He also travelled widely and represented the Albanian Bektashi community abroad. He died in Tirana on 2 April 2011.

Rexheb Baba of Gjirokastra (1901–1995)

Bektashi religious figure. Baba Rexheb, whose birth name was Rexheb Beqiri, was born in Gjirokastra. He was the nephew of Baba Selim Ruhi, who was his spiritual master for twenty years. At the age of sixteen, he entered the nearby Gravel *Tekke* (*Teqeja e Zallit*), where he completed his studies in Islamic theology, law and literature with private tutors, notably under Ragip Effendi of Delvina. Taking a vow of celibacy in 1922, the twenty-one-year-old Rexheb Beqiri became a dervish and served under his uncle, Baba Selim, until the Second World War. He used the pen-name Ferdi, 'the solitary one'. He received Fan Noli at the Gravel *Tekke* in December 1923 and served as secretary of the Second National Congress of the Bektashi at the nearby Hajdërije *tekke* in 1926.

Forced to flee from Albania in 1944 because of his public stance against communism and his ties to the anti-communist resistance movement *Balli Kombëtar*, he found refuge initially in camps for displaced persons in southern Italy. From there he continued on in January 1948 to the Mokattam *tekke* in the Mokattam hills near Cairo, in Egypt, and finally emigrated to the United States.

Dervish Rexheb arrived in New York as a dervish in 1952 with the dream of founding a Bektashi *tekke* in America. He soon moved on to Detroit, where, in 1953, he assembled a group of fifteen Albanians who agreed to collect funds to buy land for a Bektashi convent. On 20 May 1954, the First Albanian *Teqe Bektashiane* in America was duly founded in Taylor, Michigan. Dervish Rexheb was made a *baba* under a decree (*icazetname*) from the aging Ahmet Sirri Baba in Egypt and presided over the Michigan *tekke* as Baba Rexheb until his death on 10 August 1995.

Respected by Albanians of all faiths as a community leader and revered by the Bektashi as a spiritual master, Baba Rexheb was also the author of two books on Bektashism: *Misticizma Islame dhe Bektashizma* (New York 1970), partially translated into English by Bardhyl Pogoni as *The Mysticism of Islam and Bektashism* (Naples 1984); and *Kopshti i të përsosërvet* (Gjakova 1997), a translation of the *Hadîqatû's-su'adâ* (The Garden of the Blessed) by the great Azeri poet Fuzûlî (1494–1556). Baba Rexheb's biography has been published by Frances Trix as *The Sufi Journey of Baba Rexheb*, Philadelphia 2009.

cf. F. Trix, *Ashura Lament* 1993, *Spiritual Discourse* 1993, 1994, 1995, 2009, V. Dosti and E. Shehu 2001; S. Xhelaj 2001; H. Abiva 2008.

Ruhi, Selim

cf. Selim Ruhi Baba of Gjirokastra.

Salih Baba of Matohasanaj (nineteenth to twentieth centuries)

Bektashi religious figure and poet. Baba Salih was born in the southern Albanian village of Matohasanaj near Tepelena in the late nineteenth century. As a great promotor of education, he founded a school there with his own money, and used both the school and his *tekke* as venues for teaching Albanian, something that was illegal under Ottoman rule. In 1900, he was arrested for his activities at Kudhës near Vlora and exiled by the Turkish authorities to Tripoli in northern Africa.

Baba Salih was active there in the distribution of Albanian books that he would smuggle into the country with the help of Rexhep Pasha Mati, the governor of Tripoli. It was also during his exile that Salih Baba began translating the *Hadîqatû's-su'adâ* (The Garden of the Blessed) of the great Azeri poet Fuzûlî (1494–1556), as he tells us in a poem:

Unë s'jam vet asnjë thrrime,
Zot! Të lutem duke qarë;
Ali! thërret gjuha ime,
Alinë, Ahmed Myhtarë;
Hysejn, më qan zëmra shumë,
Haxhi Bektashë, Hunqarë,
Them kët vjersh' për brengën t'ime,
M'u qepn' ca të mallkuarë!
Pse punoj për gjuhën t'ime,
Dua të zgjuaj Shqiptarë.
Në Vlor' Kudhës tek po rija,
Treqind e tetëmbëdhjetë,
Viti turqishte ka qënë,
Sheshi kish dalë Mavija!
Spijunët bashkë u-bënë,
Më dogjnë planet e mia!
E mori vesh dhe Turqia,
Që përhapja shqipen unë,
Erdhi çifte suvarija,
Më muarr në burg më shpunë
O Salih! Mos rri pa punë
Merr shkruaj nga Fuzuliu,
Arabi, Farsi ka shumë
Shqip t'a marrij vesh njeriu.[325]

I am nothing at all,
God! I weep and implore you,
Ali! My tongue calls out to you,
Ali, Ahmet Myhtar!
Huseyn! My heart is weeping,
Haxhi Bektash, Hunqar!
I recite this poem for my suffering.
Some accursed men came after me
Because I was working for my language,
I wanted to awaken the Albanians.
I was in Kudhës near Vlora in
Three hundred and eighteen,
The year in Turkish style,
Muawiya appeared before me!

Spies gathered round me
And burned my projects!
Turkey also learned
That I was spreading Albanian.
A couple of horsemen arrived,
They took and threw me into jail,
Oh Salih! Do not remain idle.
There is much in Arabic and Persian,
So let the people now read Albanian.

The work of Fuzûlî had also inspired the nineteenth-century poet Dalip bey Frashëri. Dhimitër Shuteriqi notes that the manuscript of Baba Salih's translation was still at the *tekke* in 1950.
cf. Baba Rexheb 1970, pp. 380–382.

Salih Nijazi, Dede Baba (1876–1941)

Bektashi religious figure. Salih Nijazi or Njazi was born in Starja in the Kolonja region of southeastern Albania, but was raised in Constantinople, where his family emigrated when he was still at an early age. He received a Bektashi education at the *pir evi* in Hacıbektaşköy in central Anatolia. In 1897 he became a *muhib* of Fejzi Dede from Maricaj and in 1908 he was made a *baba* and was subsequently sent to Albania on a mission to solve a conflict between the *dede* and the rival Çelebi family, and to raise funds. On his return to the *pir evi*, he was made a *gjysh* (*dede*). In 1916, on the death of his predecessor Fejzi Dede, Salih Nijazi was appointed *dede baba* (*kryegjysh*) or head of the whole Bektashi Order. As such and as the spiritual leader of the *pir evi*, he enjoyed much prestige and authority in Bektashi communities from the Balkans to Iraq and Egypt. In 1925, the dervish orders were banned in Turkey under Mustafa Kemal Atatürk and their *tekkes* were all closed down.

> Salih Niyazi Dede, the head of all Bektashis from the *pir evi*, had gone to Mustafa Kemal to protest this new law, for he was his friend. Salih Dede reminded Mustafa Kemal of how the Bektashis had helped bring him to a position of high regard and of the assistance the Bektashis had afforded him and his forces. Salih Dede put it to him directly, 'And how is it now that you in your lifetime want to abolish us?' Atatürk responded, 'What can I do? I cannot make a special law for you. The entire Parliament resolved that the *tariqats* be abolished. For this reason, I can do nothing for you. It pains me, but I am unable to do anything.' Thus they closed down all the *tekkes* in Turkey.[326]

As a result, at the Third National Congress of the Albanian Bektashi, held in 1929 in Turan near Korça under Baba Zylfo of Melçan, the Bektashi in Albania decided to create a *kryegjyshata* in Tirana. As none of the *babas* was willing to leave his *tekke* and move to Tirana, they resolved to invite Salih Nijazi Dede from Turkey. Salih Nijazi Dede moved back to Albania at the end of 1929. Arriving in Saranda, he spent some time with Baba Selim Ruhi and then settled initially at the *tekke* of Melçan which became the first *de facto* headquarters of the Albanian Bektashi community. After a tour of the *tekkes* of southern Albania, he then established the world headquarters of the Bektashi movement in Tirana the following year.

Although a well-known figure in Turkey, Salih Nijazi Dede gave great impetus to the Bektashi movement in Albania. He introduced the important Bektashi ceremonies once held at the famed *tekkes* of Hacıbektaşköy in central Anatolia, Dimetoka (Didymoteicho) in Thrace, Kerbela in Iraq, and later in Merdivenköy near Istanbul, during which dervishes pronounced their vow of celibacy, but he did not have a wide following because he was much stricter than what the Albanian dervishes were used to. The new Bektashi headquarters, built on the outskirts of Tirana, was finished under the aegis of Salih Nijazi Dede in 1941, under the Italian occupation.

On 28 November 1941 Salih Nijazi Dede and his loyal Dervish Aziz fell victim to a plot and are said to have been murdered by Italian fascist circles. The exact details of the events leading to their deaths were never satisfactorily explained. It is claimed that they were murdered and the *tekke* was plundered as part of a campaign of terror and repression by the Italian occupiers aimed at crushing the liberation movement.[327] Italian sources claimed that they were murdered by brigands.[328]

cf. Baba Rexheb 1970, pp. 355–357; F. De Jong 1981, p. 248; N. Clayer 1990, p. 403.

Saltik, Sari

cf. Sari Saltik.

Sari Saltik

Bektashi holy man and legendary figure. Sari Saltik (Albanian: *Sari Salltëk*, Turkish: *Sarı Saltuk*, from *Saır Saltıq*) is said to have been either a dervish at the court of Sultan Orhan (1326–1360) or a direct disciple of Haji Bektash Veli, founder of the Bektashi Order. It is more likely, however, that he was a figure of early Balkan and not originally of Bektashi or Muslim legendry. The Bektashi simply took advantage of his popularity as a symbol of Islamic-Christian syncretism and religious tolerance in order to promote their own doctrines. The earliest legends associated with Sari Saltik were recorded by the Moroccan voyager and geographer Ibn Battuta (1304–1377). From documents dating from 1538, we know that such legends were very popular in the Balkans. According to one tale, Sari Saltik was a shepherd boy whose great intelligence was recognized early. Having been educated in Bektashi tradition, he was sent via Constantinople to Corfu, where the people were suffering under a terrible despot. There he put up a building, but in the form of an Orthodox church. From Corfu, he established seven centres in the Balkan Peninsula, headed by his disciples, simple Bektashi men who were, however, dressed as Orthodox monks. Among these foundations were Ohrid, Budapest and Kruja. At the end of his life, he asked his disciples to bring him seven coffins and to leave the room. When the disciples re-entered the room, they found seven bodies in the seven coffins which they took with them to their various centres.

As such no one knows where the original body of Sari Saltik is buried.[329]

According to another tale, the sultan sent Sari Saltik together with seventy disciples to Europe, where he travelled through Rumelia and the Crimea to Moscow and Poland. In Gdańsk (Danzig) he slew a Catholic holy man called Saint Nicholas and converted many people to Islam after putting on the saint's clothes. Sari Saltik is in fact often confused with Saint Nicholas, as well as with Saint George (see the legend of the slaying of the dragon) and Saint Simeon.

In Albania, Sari Saltik is particularly associated with the town of Kruja, where he is said to have appeared as a Bektashi dervish. The Dutch scholar Machiel Kiel discovered an imperial Ottoman register from *c*. 1567–1568, which contains a note about repairs to the road leading up to the grave of Sari Saltik in Kruja. This demonstrates that Sari Saltik was an object of widespread veneration in Albania much earlier than previously thought:

> On the mountain of Kruja is the tomb of Sari Saltik to which the people of the neighbouring districts come for pilgrimage. The road mentioned is very arduous and difficult and gives visitors much trouble. It has been recorded in the previous register that the ten persons mentioned, who are for the greater part the descendants of those who were of old in charge of repairs, have been charged with levelling the above-mentioned road and repairing it whenever it is in disrepair. After having fulfilled this duty and after having paid their tithes, they are discharged and liberated from the extraordinary tax for the Divan and the duties based on the Common Law.[330]

Sari Saltik, to whom many miracles are attributed, died on the Greek island of Corfu and is identified in the Orthodox tradition there with Saint Spyridon. In the nineteenth century, many Albanian Bektashi went on pilgrimage to the Church of Saint Spyridon on Corfu to worship the patron saint of the island under his Islamic name. F. W. Hasluck noted: 'I am told by an English Corfiote of the older generation, Mr. Weale, that in his childhood many Albanian Moslems visited the cathedral at S. Spyridon's two festivals, and paid their respects to the saint's remains; they often brought with them offerings of candles and even of livestock.'[331] According to other legends, Sari Saltik lies buried in the Church of Saint Naum on the south bank of Lake Ohrid, or on the top of Mount Pashtrik, which forms the border between the northern Albanian district of Has and the Gjakova region of neighbouring Kosovo. Before the Second World War, thousands of Albanians from Kosovo and northern Albania used to journey as pilgrims up Mount Pashtrik to the grave of Sari Saltik on August 22 or August 2, Ali Day.

Another important site of pilgrimage is the *tekke* in a cave at the top of Mount Kruja (Albanian: *Mali i Krujës*), which had an inscription dating it from the year 1692–1693 [1104 AH]. The site had previously been used for a church dedicated to Saint Alexander. This cave was closed but now destroyed in 1967 during the campaign against religion. It was reopened in 1991. The people of Kruja still go there despite the difficult climb, in particular on Sari Saltik's feast day of August 22, and drink holy water from the bottom of the cave.

All in all, Sari Saltik is said to have seven graves, the number seven often occurring in his legends, and each grave is said to contain a part of his body. The core of the Albanian version of the legend of Sari Saltik, which was recorded by the French consul in Shkodra, Baron Alexandre Degrand in 1901, is as follows:

> In Kruja, there was once a Christian prince with a fair daughter. He would have been happy, had it not been for a terrible Kulshedra which housed in a cave on the top of the mountain. Every day the dragon would bask in the sun in the ruins of a church, having demanded of the inhabitants of the town that they cast lots to be sacrificed and devoured, one man or woman every day. Many heroes had endeavoured to slay the beast, but to no avail. One day, an aged dervish with a white beard came to town, girded with a wooden sword and bearing the branch of a cypress tree in his hand. Having been informed of the terrible monster, he resolved to climb up to the cave. On his way up the mountainside the next day, he met the tearful daughter of the prince, who was on her way to the Kulshedra to be sacrificed. He said to her, 'Do not cry. We will go together and I will not abandon you for a moment.' On their way, the old man asked the maiden to scratch his head because his hair was full of lice. She agreed and the scratching brought the old man such relief that he fell asleep with his head in her lap, but was soon awakened by the maiden's tears. At sunset they reached the summit of the mountain, arid and parched as it was from the Kulshedra's fiery breath. There was such heat there that the maiden began complaining of thirst. Thereupon, the old man plunged his staff into the cliff and out gushed a spring of water. After they had quenched their thirst, they were attacked three times by the fiery Kulshedra, but the dragon could do them no harm.
>
> The dervish then pursued the monster into its cave and slew it with his wooden sword, cutting off its seven heads and sticking its seven tongues into his pocket. He then told the maiden to return home to her father.
>
> Overjoyed that his daughter had been saved from the Kulshedra, the prince resolved to offer her hand to the man who had saved her, still not knowing who had slain the beast. Many young men came forth pretending to have done the job, but none of them received the three apples the maiden held in her hands. When the dervish was called for, the townspeople began to mock him, not believing that such an old man could possibly have slain the dragon, but the maiden intervened and gave him the three apples, one by one. As proof of his deed, the dervish showed the prince the seven tongues of the Kulshedra, but declined to accept the hand of the maiden, saying, 'We dervishes do not marry women against their will. Keep your daughter and your treasures. Allow me

only to live in the dragon's cave, and have a bit of food brought up to me every day.' The prince agreed and so it was. After several years had passed, however, the inhabitants of Kruja grew envious of the powers of the dervish. They were convinced that he was going to slay them, too, and resolved to murder him first. But one of Sari Saltik's disciples, who brought him his food every day, warned the dervish in time, saying, 'Take this watermelon, eat it and flee, for the assassins are on their way.' The dervish, carving his watermelon, was infuriated at the unjust behaviour of the townspeople. Hurling the watermelon against the roof of the cave, he shouted, 'Here's their melon. They can have it back as a souvenir!' Ever since that time, there have been watermelon seeds and red juice in the cave, which the people of Kruja were wont to drink as a magic potent. Sari Saltik then rode up to the peak of the mountain on the back of a mule and, in four great strides, departed for Corfu, leaving his footprints in Kruja, Shijak and Durrës.

The first of these footprints, now in a mausoleum at the side of the main road leading from Fushë Kruja up to Kruja town, can still be seen today.

Among the many other sites in Albania traditionally associated with Sari Saltik are a grave in Shkëlzen in the northeastern Tropoja region, a cave near Mamurras (*Shpella e Sari Salltëkut*) in the Kurbin region north of Kruja, a pilgrimage site in nearby Laç, the footprint of Sari Saltik in Shijak near Durrës, the village of Rada near Durrës, the boulder of Sari Saltik in Dhëmblan in the Tepelena region, and a site on Mount Lazarat near Gjirokastra. In Kosovo he is also associated with the plain of Zejnel Aga near Peja and with the village of Zagatar in Opoja near Prizren. cf. J. Degrand 1901, pp. 236-243; F. W. Hasluck 1912-1913, 1929, p. 442 (550); F. Babinger 1928, 1929, 1934; Rr. Zojzi 1944; R. Kriss and H. Kriss-Heinrich, 1960, 1, pp. 335-336; H. Kaleshi 1967a, 1967b, 1969; P. Bartl 1963, p. 106; M. Kiel 1993; H. Norris 1993, pp. 131-132, 146-157; N. Ibrahimi 1998, S. 235-245; N. Malcolm 1998, pp. 131-132; G. Duijzings 2000, pp. 80-85; N. Clayer 2003, pp. 138-143; J. Rexhepagiqi 2003.

Seit Baba of Durballi Sultan (d. 1973)

Bektashi religious figure. Seit Baba, whose birth name was Seit Koka, was from Skrapar. He was the last *baba* of the famed *tekke* of Durballi Sultan in Thessaly (Greece). He died in March 1973 and was buried in the corridor between the two historical *tyrbes* there. With his death, the *tekke* of Durballi Sultan was abandoned and fell into ruins.

Selim Kaliçani Baba of Martanesh (1922-2001)

Bektashi religious figure. Selim Kaliçani was born in Peja in Kosovo and moved to Tirana with his brother in 1935. There he was given a job as a cowherd at the *Kryegjyshata*. He was a curious lad and wanted to know more of what was going on inside the *tekke*. Eventually he was allowed into the building and became increasingly intrigued and attracted by the goings-on. In 1938, he joined the Bektashi Order and applied to become a dervish. He was at the *Kryegjyshata* until 1941 and then fought in the Second World War on the side of the communist partisans. In February 1953 he was appointed *baba* of the *tekke* of Martanesh by Ahmet Myftari Dede Baba. After the communist dictatorship, Baba Selim served as the head of the *tekke* of Fushë Kruja until his death in 2001. He was the author of: *Histori e baballarëve të Teqesë së Martaneshit* (History of the *Babas* of the *Tekke* of Martanesh), Tirana 1997 and of an edition of Fuzuli's *Hadîqatû's- su'adâ,* entitled *Lulishte e Shenjtorëve* (Garden of the Blessed), Fushë Kruja 1997. He is buried in a *tyrbe* in the courtyard of the *tekke* of Fushë Kruja.

Selim Ruhi Baba of Gjirokastra (1869–1944)

Bektashi religious figure. Selim Ruhi was born in Elbasan. When he finished his religious training at the *medresa* there in 1885, his father took him to Gjirokastra to serve under Ali Haqi Baba at the Gravel *Tekke* (*Teqeja e Zallit*). He became a dervish officially in 1891. At the death of Ali Haqi Baba in 1907, Selim Ruhi took over as *baba* of the said *tekke*, a position he held until his death in 1944. He was considered the most cultured and enlightened cleric of his time. Baba Selim was forced to flee from the *tekke* and take shelter with his sister in town for a three-year period during and after the Balkan War when *tekke* was ravaged by Greek forces and one of the dervishes was murdered.

Baba Selim was the author of several books, including one known as *Mystic Guidance*, and three divans of poetry (one in Arabic, one in Persian and one in Turkish). Towards the end of his life, he also wrote in Albanian. The German scholar Franz Babinger (1891–1967), who visited Baba Selim at his *tekke*, described his verse as being exceptionally beautiful. Baba Selim was the *murshid* of Baba Rexheb who succeeded him as *baba* there. Baba Rexheb called him a 'sword that cuts from both sides', i.e. he had both outward and inward knowledge. When Salih Nijazi Dede was murdered in Tirana in 1941, the Bektashi clergy at the *Kryegjyshata* in Tirana urged Baba Selim to take over the order as *kryegjysh*, but he refused to leave Gjirokastra.

Baba Selim Ruhi played a prominent role in the nationalist, i.e. non-communist, resistance during the Italian occupation from 1939 to 1943 and opposed the Italian invasion of Greece. He thus remained unharmed when Greek forces occupied Gjirokastra in 1940. It was perhaps to his fortune that he died shortly before the communists took power in Albania on 16 October 1944.

Baba Rexheb gives a splendid account, recorded by Frances Trix, of the festivities of Ramadan before the Second World War, when Baba Selim Ruhi paid an annual ceremonial visit to the Mosque of Gjirokastra:

> Selim Ruhi Baba rode with several riders and servants in front. There were dervishes on each side as well, along with *muhibs* and *ashiks* (people drawn to

the Baba), maybe 100 people, all of whom went along. But Baba was in pure white. Even the horse he rode was white, a white horse from the Arabian line, and the dervishes, too, were in pure white, walking along to the mosque. The imam of the mosque was Bektashi, a *muhib* of Baba. They set the tables outside the mosque, as they do for holidays, so there was room for all the people, so it would not be restricted. Selim Baba sat there, as they laid out the entire meal. They thus celebrated the holiday. Then they brought out the *minbar*, from the steps of which the imam preached in the mosque, so each one could go up and kiss Baba's hand. This went on for half an hour. When this was done, they went back to the *tekke*, slowly by horse, as earlier. For a full fifteen minutes, or maybe twenty minutes, slowly by horse, with many people behind. They arrived back and stopped in the area in front of the main gate of the *tekke* compound. It was an open place, an outside courtyard. There, in front of the *tyrbes*, Baba descended from the horse and stood waiting. First of all the dervishes came, one by one, to kiss his hand, and to wish him '*id mubarak*' (a blessed holiday). Then the *muhibs*, the initiated members, came to kiss his hand, and after them, the *ashiks*, those drawn by their *ashk* or love of Baba, and then the children came, too, to kiss his hand. The Baba would go up to his room, a large room, fifteen meters long [...] and they filled the room. The dervishes came, together with the *muhibs* and there they performed prayer, Bektashi prayer, separately. [...] They brought in sherbet, red sherbet for the holiday. Then the children came in, too. They came in a line with their fathers. Holding on to their fathers' hands, they would fill up the rest of the room. Selim Ruhi Baba always ordered fifteen kilos of candied fruit for this day alone to give to the children. A dervish would take it and give it to them one by one, giving this much to one and to another in turn. Then they would stand in well-brought-up fashion and slowly, one by one, go to kiss the hand of Baba. Baba would greet them with, '*Rrofsh, mor bir!*' (May you live long, my son). Then each would return, not showing his back to Baba, but walking backwards, slowly and carefully. This is how they went. Thus it was.[332]

cf. Baba Rexhebi 1970, pp. 303–309; F. Trix, *Sufi Journey*, 2009, pp. 47, 51–52; A. Bishqemi, 2016, pp. 16–17.

Selman Xhemali Baba of Elbasan (d. 1949)

Bektashi religious figure and poet. Selman Xhemali was born in Istanbul in the late nineteenth century and was raised there. He is thus also known as Baba Xhemali Turku ('the Turk'). He served at the Şehidlik *tekke* at Rumeli Hisarı and 'took the hand' of Nafi Baba, promising to become a dervish. Later, he visited the *pir evi* at Hacıbektaşköy in central Anatolia and took a vow of celibacy there. In 1913, Nafi Baba made him a *baba* and sent him to Baghdad to head the Kazimije *tekke*. He remained there until the *tekke* was destroyed in the First World War. In early 1926, when the *tekkes* in Turkey had been closed down under Atatürk, he moved to Elbasan, where he founded and constructed the *tekke* of Elbasan that is named after him and where he lived until his death in September 1949.

The *tekke* of Baba Xhemali, as it is known, was built at the site of the *tyrbe* of Baba Ali Horasani in Elbasan and was several years in the making. Other edifices were constructed on the site in the 1930s. Baba Selman also bought much of the surrounding land to be used for orchards. Baba Selman was the author of philosophical and mystic verse in Turkish and, according to Baba Rexheb, was a man of culture and a talented poet. The American scholar John Birge (1888–1952), who met him and described him as his honoured friend, left the following description:

> In the new *tekke* which Cemali Baba is building (Oct. 1933), there is a certain large square pillar, on each of the four sides of which is a doorway, symbolizing the Four Gateways. The symbolism will be true to the doctrine only if one encircles the pillar returning through the four doors to the Reality from which one came.[333]

cf. Baba Rexheb 1980, pp. 365–367; N. Clayer 1990, p. 267; Q. Dedej, *Fillimet* 1997, pp. 110–113; N. Clayer and X. Bougarel 2013, p. 144.

Sersem Ali Baba of Tetova (d. 1569)

Bektashi religious figure. Sersem Ali Dede was born in Tetova (Kalkandelen) in Macedonia in the late fifteenth century and served as a vizier during the reign of Sultan Suleyman the Magnificent (r. 1520–1566). According to legend, he had a dream in which he saw the second founder of the Bektashi Order, Balim Sultan (1457–1517). He therefore abandoned his public office and departed for Hacıbektaşköy in central Anatolia to serve at the *tekke* there. He was made head of the *tekke* in 1550 and held the position until his death in 1569 AD [977 AH]. In his testament, he expressed the wish that all of his property and possessions be sold to build a *tekke* in his native Tetova. The result was the famed Harabati Baba *tekke*, also known as the *Tekke* of Sersem Ali Baba.

cf. Baba Rexhebi 1970, pp. 209–213; H. Norris 1993, p. 134.

Shëmbërdhenji, Meleq Baba

cf. Meleq Shëmbërdhenji Baba.

Shemimi Baba of Fushë Kruja (1748–1803)

Bektashi holy man and poet. Qemaluddin Shemimi Ibrahim, whose first name is also given variously as Kemaluddin, Shemseddin or Jelaladdin Ibrahim, was initially a teacher in Istanbul and became a *baba* at the *pir evi* at Hacıbektaşköy in central Anatolia. He then lived for several years at the *tekke* of Köprülü (Veles) in central Macedonia, where he served the Bektashi Order together with his friend and companion Hatemi Hajdar Baba. After correspondence with and agreement from the elders of Kruja, the two men moved to Kruja in the last decade of the eighteenth century, where Shemimi Baba, also known for short as Mimi Baba, founded the *tekke* of Fushë Kruja. This *tekke* was to become one of the fundamental centres of the Bektashi movement in Albania.

Ali Pasha Tepelena (1759–1822), the Lion of Janina, is said to have 'taken the hand' of Shemimi Baba, i.e. to have been received by him as a Bektashi follower, and it was no doubt with the support of Ali Pasha that Shemimi and others were able to spread the Bektashi movement throughout southern Albania. Ali Pasha himself made use of the Bektashi as a counterweight to the Sunni sultan in Istanbul.

With Ali Pasha's support, Shemimi Baba founded the *tekke* of Melçan near Korça, which was subsequently run by Abdullah Melçani Baba (d. 1857). Then followed the founding of the *tekke* of Prishta in Skrapar, which was taken over by Baba Tahir of Crete. Shemimi is also said to have founded the *tekkes* of Xhefai Ibrahim Baba in Elbasan and of Sadik Baba in Koshtan near Tepelena, both of which served as centres for further foundations in the south.

Shemimi Baba's alliance with Ali Pasha was not to the liking of the local potentate Kapllan Pasha Toptani and his ruling family who feared that, with the increasing number of Bektashi, Ali Pasha would take over Toptani land. The French consul in Shkodra, Baron Alexandre Degrand (1844–1911), records one version of events:

> He was soon involved in a struggle with Kapllan and the partisans of the Toptani family. His religious influence made him a dangerous adversary and, seeing that he was losing ground, Kapllan Pasha told him [Shemimi] to stop his activities or leave the town. The sheikh understood the danger he was now in and sent one of his dervishes to hand Kapllan over to the governor of Kruja.
>
> The dervish entered the Toptani manor. It was a hot and humid day and the aghas and servants were all asleep. Kapllan Pasha who was sleeping in the main hall woke up suddenly at the sound of the dervish and asked him what he wanted. Without saying a word, the dervish handed him a letter from the sheikh. While the pasha was busy reading it, the dervish drew his *teber* (a sort of double-bladed axe) from under his *hirka* and lunged to stab him. At that moment, Kapllan realized what was going on and shot and killed the dervish with his pistol. Awakened by the shot, two aghas rushed in and were shocked to see the dervish sprawled on the floor and their master with a smoking gun in his hand. 'Traitors!' he shouted at them, 'you let in this dog sent by the *baba* to murder me! If you do not want the same to happen to you, go and find his master, tell him to be off immediately and, if he refuses, kill him!'
>
> The two aghas, one of whom was called Bekir Ali, took three men with them, and snuck into the *tekke* at two o'clock in the morning. The sheikh's bedroom was open and he died there, struck by two bullets. The murderers' families still exist and live in utmost poverty.

The two murderers provoked such an outcry in the population of Kruja, that was almost entirely Bektashi, that Kapllan Pasha was compelled to move his residence to Tirana. On being informed that his son-in-law, Ibrahim Bey of Kavaja, who was a Bektashi, was going to kill him to avenge the death of Shemimi Baba, Kapllan Pasha invited him over and, disregarding their family ties and the laws of hospitality, had him imprisoned in the fortress of Kruja and confiscated his property.

After this, his daughter in Kavaja sent one of her stewards on the pretext of appealing for her husband's release. During their negotiations, the envoy took out a fine tobacco pouch with a double bottom, opened it up and took snuff. When the steward then gave a sigh of satisfaction, Kapllan Pasha, who was a great amateur of snuff himself, said: 'You seem to have some good tobacco there.' 'I don't think there is any better,' replied the steward. 'Would Your Excellency like to try it?' Turning the tobacco pouch over, he offered him poisoned tobacco from the secret compartment in it. Hardly had he left the manor when the pasha perished after suffering from vomiting and a terrible headache. This took place in the night in 1816.[334]

The great Baba Shemimi had thus been murdered in Kruja in 1803. He was laid to rest in a *tyrbe* constructed in his honour at the *tekke* of Fushë Kruja.
cf. J. A. Degrand 1901, pp. 210–211; A. Tomorri 1929, pp. 72–77; Baba Rexhebi 1970, pp. 248–252; H. Kaleshi and H. J. Kissling, *Baba Kâzim* 1980, p. 11; H. Norris 1993, pp. 133, 191, 239.

Sirri, Ahmet Baba

cf. Ahmet Sirri Baba of Mokattem.

Skënderasi, Tahir

cf. Tahir Baba Nasibi of Frashër.

Staravecka, Meleq

cf. Meleq Baba Shëmbërdhenji.

Sulejman Baba of Gjirokastra (d. 1934)

Bektashi religious figure of Gjirokastra. Baba Sulejman, known for short as Baba Manes, succeeded Baba Hajdër of Kardhiq as head of the Hajdërije *tekke* in Gjirokastra in 1904. He was interned by the Turks for three years in Janina. In 1910, he and Baba Ahmet Turani travelled to the *pir evi* at Hacıbektaşköy in central Anatolia, each to be made a *gjysh* by Fejzi Dede from Maricaj in the Tepelena region. In 1924, under Baba Sulejman, the Hajdërije *tekke,* commonly known at the time as the *tekke* of Haxhi Baba Sulejman, played host to the Second National Congress of the Bektashi Order in 1926, at which new statutes were agreed upon after the Bektashi had separated officially from the Sunni community in Albania.

The French parliamentarian Justin Godart paid Baba Sulejman a visit in 1921 and recorded the meeting as follows:

> The *tekke* of Gjirokastra is situated not far from the town on a hill which it crowns with its walls, its tombs and its lofty dark cypress trees. We trudged up the terrible trail in the rain and were received under a canopy at the top of the steps by the dervishes in their white robes. Silently they led us in to see the *baba*.
>
> Baba Sulejman was seated on a long-haired rug in the reception room. The floors were covered in carpets, some of which looked quite expensive. Over his white robe he was clad in a light green garment and wore the rigid cylindrical headpiece of the Bektashi. He received us warmly and had us seated on a small sofa. I had never felt as awkward as I did here on that ugly piece of modern furniture in the midst of such traditional surroundings, with our muddy boots set out on the Anatolian carpets rich in hues and design. A young dervish brought coffee in on a platter and every time he handed us a cup, his necklace of heavy cut glass banged against the metal tray. The conduct of the dervishes and of the *baba* was exemplary and left nothing to be desired.
>
> We started up a conversation. The *baba* was absorbed by the national cause. The Turks had interned him for three years in Janina when they discovered Albanian books at the *tekke*. In 1914, the Greeks pillaged and burned the *tekke* down, at a time when it had just been reopened. There were twelve dervishes in all, but seven of them were still at the candidate level and were being tested to see if they were fit to put on the robes. Dervishes can marry but if they do, they have to leave the *tekke* and live like everyone else. However, they lose nothing of their power and authority. Baba Sulejman wore an earring in his right ear that distinguished him as a dervish who had committed himself to celibacy. It was a triangular piece of silver which was symbolic of something or other only revealed to the initiated.
>
> What we learned from Baba Sulejman on the doctrine and role of the Bektashi can be summarized in the following few words: 'We strive for peace on earth and for the good of all mankind. We work to overcome fanaticism and are the friends of sincere believers of all religions.'
>
> Baba Sulejman and his dervishes accompanied us down to the bottom of the hill. Dressed in white, they led us through the dark cypress trees to the tombs of former *babas*, on which lamps had already been lit for the night. The oldest of the dervishes, in a gesture of kind affection, handed us a little bouquet of wild geraniums and rock flowers with a simple country fragrance. We were quite moved as we departed, leaving these sage men behind us. They stood and watch us for a long time before they turned and returned to their tranquil asylum.[335]

cf. J. Godart 1922, pp. 163-165.

Tahir Baba Nasibi of Frashër (d. 1835)

Bektashi holy man and mystic poet. Tahir Baba, whose birth name was Tahir Skënderasi, was born in the village of Frashër near Përmet. He travelled to the Middle East and is said to have studied in Iran. Tahir Baba became known as Nasibi 'the fortunate one', thus Tahir Baba Nasibi, after the doors of the *tekke* of Hacı Bektaş Veli in central Anatolia opened miraculously for him. On his return to Albania, he settled in his native village, where he founded a *tekke* in 1825. Tahir Baba headed this *tekke* until his death in 1835 and was buried in a nearby *tyrbe* which became a site of pilgrimage. It was burned down by Greek forces in 1914 but was subsequently reconstructed.

Tahir Baba was the author of much verse in Turkish and Persian and is said to have written poetry in Albanian. Sami bey Frashëri wrote of him in his Ottoman encyclopaedia, *Kamûs al- â'lâm*:

> Tahir Nasibi Baba is one of the Bektashi leaders. He was born in my village of Frashër and spent some time visiting the holy sites. After his return [to Albania], he founded a small *tekke* in Frashër which grew over time and is the biggest today. He died in 1835 and was buried in a *tyrbe* near his *tekke*, which is visited by many people nowadays. Nasibi wrote many poems in Albanian.
>
> Aside from these, he also wrote many ghazels in Turkish and Persian. Once, when he was returning to his home country after visiting the holy sites, he happened to stop at the town of Leskovik, where scholars of the time invited him in to test his religious education. Nasibi answered all their questions with a *qasida* [ode].[336]

cf. A. Tomorri 1929, pp. 79-82; Baba Rexhebi 1970, pp. 268-269.

Tahir Baba of Prishta (nineteenth century)

Bektashi religious figure. Baba Tahir, also known as Baba Tahir of Crete, was a dervish at the *tekke* of Candia (Heraklion) on Crete in the mid-nineteenth century. He travelled to the *tekke* of Melçan in Albania, from where Baba Abdullah of Melçan sent him to the region of Skrapar to spread the Bektashi faith. There he took over the *tekke* of Prishta which became a major centre of the Bektashi movement. Baba Tahir of Prishta was responsible for the spread of Bektashism in the Skrapar, Mallakastra and Tepelena regions in the second half of the nineteenth century, where there had earlier been few Bektashi.
cf. A. Tomorri 1929, pp. 80-82.

Tomorri, Ali Baba

cf. Ali Baba of Tomorr.

Turabiu, Ali
cf. Ali Baba of Tomorr.

Turani, Ahmet Baba
cf. Ahmet Baba of Turan.

Tyrabiu, Ali
cf. Ali Baba of Tomorr.

Vërzhezha, Iljaz
cf. Iljaz Vërzhezha, Dervish.

Vexh-hi, Adem Baba
cf. Adem Vexh-hi Baba of Gjakova.

Xhafer Sadiku, Dede Baba (1874–1945)

Bektashi religious figure. Baba Xhafer Sadiku was originally from Gjirokastra and served as a dervish under Baba Shemsi of the *tekke* of Izmir in Turkey. Around 1902 he visited the *pir evi* at Hacıbektaşköy in central Anatolia. After his return to Albania, he served at the *tekke* of Përmet, of which he was made head around 1920 by Baba Ahmet of Turan. He was still in office in the Second World War when he took part in fighting as the head of a band of pro-communist fighters in the Dangëllia region. Since the *kryegjysh* in Tirana, Abaz Hilmi, had become increasingly untenable for the new communist regime, it put up Xhafer Sadiku to preside over the Fourth Bektashi Congress that was held in Tirana in February 1945. Baba Xhafer died on 2 August 1945.
cf. N. Clayer 1990, p. 405.

Xhani, Mustafa
cf. Faja Martaneshi Baba.

Xhefai, Ibrahim Baba
cf. Ibrahim Xhefai Baba of Elbasan.

Xhemali, Selman Baba of Elbasan
cf. Selman Xhemali Baba of Elbasan.

GLOSSARY OF TERMS

Ashik. In the Bektashi hierarchy, an *ashik* is a non-initiated adherent of the order. He or she is an individual drawn to the Bektashi or to a *baba*, but who has not gone through initiation as a dervish. *Ashiks* make up most of the adherents of *tekkes*. The word stems from Turkish *aşık* 'lover, admirer'.

Ashura. Bektashi and Shi'ite feast marking the end of the ten-day fasting period of *matem*. Ashura, Albanian *ashuré*, def. *ashuréja*, or *hashuré*, def. *hashuréja*, is the high point of the Bektashi calendar, commemorating the suffering and death of Imam Husein, grandson of the Prophet Muhammed, at Kerbela in Iraq. Religious ceremonies are held in the *tekkes* with lamentations or *mersiye*, and then silent prayers. Visitors are traditionally treated to a bowl of Ashura pudding, made of cracked wheat, sugar, dried fruit, crushed nuts and cinnamon. This Ashura pudding is boiled in a large cauldron which is stirred by all the Bektashi present, in order of rank, and is then distributed to the faithful and guests. On this occasion the faithful are wont to invoke Imam Husein and to curse the Yazidi, i.e. the children of Muaviya, Albanian *Mavi,* who murdered Caliph Ali's two sons. Bektashi families then make the ashure pudding in their homes for the rest of the month of Muharrem and bring some to the tekke.
cf. N. Clayer 1990, p. 85; H. Norris 1993, pp. 171–173; F. Trix 1993a.

Asitane. A head monastery of the Bektashi Order, i.e. a *tekke* with a *baba* holding the superior rank of a *halife*.

Atë. Term signifying 'father'. This is the Albanian equivalent of the Turkish *baba*, although the Turkish term is still more commonly used in Albanian.

Baba. Turkish term signifying 'father' and referring to an individual with a certain rank in the Bektashi hierarchy. A *baba* is usually the head of a specific *tekke*, or dervish lodge, and has a number of dervishes under his responsibility. He can initiate others into the order, i.e. ordain dervishes, and give guidance. The term is sometimes translated as 'abbot'. When referring to a specific figure in Albanian, the word *baba* usually precedes the name, whereas in Turkish it usually follows the name, thus: Albanian: Baba Ahmet, and Turkish: Ahmet Baba. This distinction is not respected in this work, in which we use the word order interchangeably. The Albanian-language equivalent, *prind* (literally 'parent') is occasionally used, too.

Baba Tomorr cf. Tomorr, Mount.

Çiflig, also *çiflik*. A hereditary estate in Ottoman times.

Dede cf. Gjysh.

Dede Baba. Also *başdede*. Turkish term for the Albanian *kryegjysh*, head of the Bektashi community.

Dergâh cf. Tekke.

Dervish. In the Bektashi hierarchy, a dervish is an individual who has been fully initiated and has served some time in a *tekke*. He is the equivalent of a Christian monk and usually wears a specific costume.

Dervishia, also *dervishane*. A small dervish lodge or convent without a *baba*, as opposed to a *tekke* that normally has a *baba*. The word *dervishia* is the Albanian equivalent of Turkish *dervişhane* and means simply a 'dervish house'.
Ehli Beit. A term referring to the family of the Prophet Muhammed. It stems from the Arabic *ahl al-bait*, lit. 'people of the house'. It refers specifically to Muhammed, Imam Ali, Fatima, Hassan and Husein.
Gjysh. Albanian term signifying 'grandfather', equivalent to Turkish *dede*. A *gjysh* is responsible for a *gjyshata*, which is a specific administrative region.
Gjyshata. The term *gjyshata*, earlier *gjyshëria*, refers to an administrative region of the Bektashi community, and normally includes several *tekkes*. In Christian terms, it is the equivalent of a diocese. There were traditionally six *gjyshatas* in Albania. The headquarters of the *gjyshata* is usually a particularly important *tekke* under the administration of a *gjysh*, Turkish *dede*, 'grandfather'.
Halife, also *khalife*. Among the Bektashi a *halife* is a cleric above the rank of a *baba*, but below that of a *gjysh* (*dede*), i.e. someone responsible for all the *tekkes* of a certain region and who can appoint *babas*. The term derives from the Arabic word for a 'successor'.
Haxhi. Title of a dervish, *baba* or other Muslim who has visited the holy sites in Mecca, i.e. who has made the *hajj* pilgrimage, Albanian *haxh*.
Hirka. A long sleeveless vest worn by Bektashi clerics. Among the Bektashi, the *hirka* is usually white (except in North America where it is dark). The word stems from Turkish *hırka*.
Ixhazet. A diploma of investiture or authorisation to bear the title of *baba*. The word stems from Turkish *icazet* or *icazetname*.
Kaymakam. Turkish term for the governor of a provincial district.
Kemer. A belt or cummerbund worn by Bektashi clerics. The Albanian word *kemer* or *qemer* stems from Turkish *kemer*.
Khalife cf. Halife.
Kryegjysh. Albanian term meaning 'head grandfather'. It corresponds to the Turkish *dede baba*. He is the superior of all the *gjyshes* and is head of the Bektashi Order.
Kryegjyshata. The headquarters of the Bektashi Order that has been in Tirana since 1930. It is the seat of the *kryegjysh* 'head grandfather'.
Matem. Bektashi and Shi'ite period of fasting. *Matem*, from Persian *matem* 'death, mourning', falls on the first ten days of the month of Muharrem and commemorates the battle of Kerbela in present-day Iraq in 680 AD in which Imam Husein, the grandson of the Prophet Mohammed, was killed. It is a period of fasting or at least of abstinence from drink in memory of Husein and his troops who were encircled by the enemy and left without water before their much-lamented deaths. The Bektashi faithful are expected to show restraint and to avoid luxury during *matem*. As such, many of them do not drink water or eat meat or dairy products during this period. They also abstain from coffee for three days. Each of the ten nights of *matem* is dedicated to one of the Shi'ite imams, and extracts are recited from the *Hadîqatû's-su'adâ* (The Garden of the Blessed) by the Azeri poet Fuzûlî (1494–1556), dedicated to the martyrs of Kerbela. This period is followed by the feast of *Ashura*.
Medresa. A Muslim school or theological college.
Mekam. A mausoleum or shrine. In general usage, a *mekam* is the same as a *tyrbe*, but in stricter usage it often refers to a rectangular or square-shaped shrine, whereas a *tyrbe* is usually eight- or twelve-sided. The term is derived from an Arabic word meaning 'site', or more specifically a 'pilgrimage site'.

Meydan, also Albanian *mejdan*. The ceremonial room in a *tekke* where liturgical meetings called *muhabet* are held. The floor and walls are traditionally covered in rugs, and there are sheepskins on the floor for people to sit on.

Muhabet. Term normally meaning 'discussion, conversation'. In the Bektashi faith it can also refer more specifically to a ceremonial meeting and the special chanting of a spiritual poem in a *tekke*. The term stems from Turkish *muhabbet*.

Muhib, also Albanian *myhib, muhip*. In the Bektashi hierarchy, a *muhib* is a lay member of the Bektashi Order who has gone through an initiation ceremony at a *tekke* and has taken his first vow. He can take part in religious ceremonies. In the other dervish *tarikats*, a *muhib* is a non-initiated member. The term stems from an Arabic word meaning 'lover, friend'.

Murid. A novice or disciple of the dervish order. The term stems from Turkish *mürit*.

Murshid. A spiritual master or guide of the dervish order. The term stems from Turkish *mürşit*.

Myhetil, also *mutehhil*. A Bektashi clergyman who has married.

Myxherret, also *muxheret*. A Bektashi clergyman who has sworn a vow of celibacy. The term stems from Turkish *mücerred*.

Nefes. A spiritual poem that is often chanted at Bektashi ceremonies.

Nevruz. Bektashi feast. *Nevruz* or *Sulltan Nevruz* 'Sultan *Nevruz*' is the New Year's festival commemorated by the Bektashi and other Shi'ites on March 21–22. *Nevruz*, from Persian 'new day', was originally a feast of the spring equinox and was considered the first day of the Persian solar calendar. For the Bektashi and other Shi'ites, it also marks the birthday of Imam Ali, the son-in-law of the Prophet Muhammed.
cf. N. Clayer 1990, pp. 85–87.

Ofiqarë të shërbimit fetar. 'Officiants of religious services.' In the Bektashi hierarchy, these include all novices awaiting ordination as a dervish.

Pir. Turkish *pir* 'spiritual master, guide, saint'. It often refers to the founding saint of a dervish order. For the Bektashi, the first *pir* was Haci Bektaş Veli, Albanian Haxhi Bektash Veli, in Anatolia.

Pirevi. Turkish term for the original town or headquarters of the Bektashi. From Turkish *pir*, a spiritual master or guide and *ev*, a home or house.

Post-nişin. Turkish term used for a *baba* heading a *tekke*. The term means 'he who sits on the sheep skin'.

Prind cf. Baba.

Prindëria. Term used for the parish of a *tekke* run by a *prind*, i.e. a *baba*. In legal terms, it is the subdivision of a *gjyshata*.

Qemer cf. Kemer.

Raki. An unsweetened, occasionally anise-flavoured, alcoholic drink that is popular in Turkey, in Albania and elsewhere in the Balkans.

Take the hand. Ceremonial act by which spiritual power is transmitted. Thus a subordinate 'takes the hand' of his *baba*.

Talib. Also Albanian *talip*. A candidate for initiation into the Bektashi Order.

Tarikat, also *tariqat*. Mystical Sufi order of Islam, i.e. dervish order. The word is plural in the original Arabic, but is used as being in the singular in other languages.

Taxh. The *taxh* (pronounced 'tadj') is the cylindrical, white headpiece worn by Bektashi *babas*. The *Huseyn Tadj* (Albanian: *taxh hysejni*, Turkish: *tâc hüsejnî*) normally worn by the Bektashi has twelve folds. Much rarer is the *Elifi Tadj* (Turkish *Elifi tac*) that resembles a bishop's mitre. The word stems from Turkish *tac*.

Tekke. The *tekke* is the Turkish and international term for a Bektashi monastery or, more appropriately, a dervish lodge or convent. Albanian *teqe*, def. *teqeja* or *teqja*. Other terms used for a *tekke* are *dergâh* from Persian referring to a larger *tekke*, and *zaviye* referring to a smaller convent.

Teslim tash. A twelve-fluted stone worn around the neck, lit. 'the stone of surrender', from Turkish *teslim taşı*.

Tomorr, Mount. Holy mountain in central Albania. Tomorr, Albanian *Tomorr*, def. *Tomorri*, also spelled *Tomor*, def. *Tomori* ~ ancient Τόμαρος, is a mountain, or better a mountain range in the region of Berat and Skrapar which includes the highest peak in central Albania, at an altitude of 2416 m. The Bektashi honour Abbas Ali during an annual pilgrimage to the top of the mountain on August 20–25. The mountain is also sacred to Christians who used to climb it on August 15, Assumption Day, in honour of the Virgin Mary.

In central Albanian popular belief, Mount Tomorr was considered the home of the gods; indeed, it was personified as a god itself: *Baba Tomorr* 'Father Tomorr'. The peasants of the region swear by Father Tomorr, Albanian *për Baba Tomorr*, an oath considered stronger than any sworn on the Bible or the Koran. Many people in the region, out of respect or fear, referred to the mountain euphemistically simply as 'it' and swore *për atë çukë* 'by that peak'.

The legendary figure of Baba Tomorr is envisaged as an old man with a long white beard flowing down to his belt. Around him hover four long-beaked female eagles, which perch on his snowy slopes. The cult of Mount Tomorr is linked in particular to the romantic nationalism of the Rilindja age of national revival, especially in the Albanian literature of the period. Albanian writers such as Konstantin Kristoforidhi (1830–1895), Naim bey Frashëri (1846–1900), Anton Zako Çajupi (1866–1930), Asdreni (1872–1947), Hilë Mosi (1885–1933) and Ndre Mjeda (1866–1937) have devoted striking poetry and prose pieces to Father Tomorr.

Tyrbe. A mausoleum or shrine with the grave of a Bektashi holy man. It is usually octagonal or twelve-sided, and can contain one or more graves that are venerated and are often of great significance in the Bektashi faith. The term stems from Turkish *türbe*.

Vakuf. A pious, charitable foundation of the Islamic faith. It often refers to land, as a source of revenue, owned by a *tekke* or other Muslim religious institution. The term stems from Arabic *waqf* or *vakf*.

Varfë. Term signifying a 'poor dervish'. It is related to the Albanian word *i varfër* 'poor'.

Veli. Turkish term for a saint or holy man.

Zaviye cf. Tekke.

NOTES

Chapter 1

1. Naim bey Frashëri, *Fletore e Bektashinjet* (Bucharest 1896).
2. Ibid.
3. Z. Yürekli 2016, p. 33, taken from Ahmet Rif'at, *Mir'atü'l-Makasid* (Constantinople), p. 189.
4. J. Norton 2001, p. 183.
5. J. Birge, *The Bektashi Order of Dervishes* (London & Hartford 1937), p. 76.
6. Encyclopaedia of Islam, article on the Janissaries, as given in ibid., pp. 76–77.
7. Birge, *The Bektashi Order of Dervishes*, p. 77.
8. F. Trix, *Sufi Journey of Baba Rexheb* (Philadelphia: University of Pennsylvania Museum of Archaeology and Anthropology 2009), p. 333.
9. F. W. Hasluck 1913, pp. 113–117, *Christianity and Islam under the Sultans* II (Oxford 1929), pp. 470–473 (586–588); N. Clayer and A. Popović 2005, p. 272.
10. M. Hasluck 1925, p. 600.
11. A. Tomori 1929, p. 80; N. Clayer and A. Popovic 2005, p. 272.
12. N. Clayer and A. Popović 2005, p. 273.
13. M. Frashëri 1915, English translation at: http://www.albanianhistory.net/1915_Frasheri/index.html
14. J. Godart, *L'Albanie en 1921* (Paris: PUF 1922), p. 166.
15. A. Mousset, *L'Albanie devant l'Europe* (Paris: Delagrave 1930), p. 114.
16. Trix, *Sufi Journey*, p. 65.
17. Mousset, *L'Albanie devant l'Europe*, pp. 113–115.
18. H. Kaleshi 1980, p. 14.
19. S. Tchémalovitch 1934, p. 206.
20. F. Trix, 'The Resurfacing of Islam in Albania', *The East European Quarterly*, XXVIII, 4 (January 1995), pp. 533–549, p. 535.
21. Ibid., pp. 546–547.
22. A. Popovic et G. Veinstein, *Les ordres mystiques dans l'Islam* (Paris: Ed. de l'E.H.E.S.S., 1986), p. 70.
23. Ibid., p. 71.
24. Trix, 'The Resurfacing', p. 537.
25. Ibid., p. 535.
26. The Albanian Census of 2011 showed some surprising and controversial results: 57.12 per cent of the Albanian population declared themselves to be Muslims, 10.11 per cent Catholic and 6.8 per cent Orthodox. Only 2.11 per cent of the population declared themselves to be Bektashi, a figure that very much contradicted traditional assumptions. The main reason for the discrepancy is that the Census investigated real religious convictions rather than simple cultural affiliation.
27. Curiously, if you ask Bektashi people in Albania about their adherence to Islam, many believe they are Sunni. This is no doubt because they have little contact with other

Shi'ite communities, and the Sunni Muslims, being the vast majority in Albania, are the only Muslims they know.

Chapter 2

28 Reference is to the death of Sultan Murad I at the nearby Battle of Kosovo in June 1389.
29 The name of the village (= Village of the Tekke) in its Slavonic form is Tećino Selo. It lies in the hills a little north of the track from Skopje (Üsküb) to Istib, a short day's journey from the former place.
30 According to one account it was brought to its present position by a holy man from Bosnia.
31 Gen. xxvii, 18: xxxv, 14. See above, p. 132. Compare William Robertson Smith, *Lectures on Religion of the Semites: Fundamental Institutions* (London: Adam & Charles Black 1889), p. 232, who illustrates the late survival of the practice by the 'lapis pertusus' at Jerusalem described by the pilgrim from Bordeaux in the fourth century of our era. 'Ad quem veniunt Judaei singulis annis et ungunt eum.' Near Sidon the practice of anointing sacred stones with oil – in this case strangely enough Roman milestones – goes on to this day; Richard Pietschmann, *Geschichte der Phönizier* (Berlin: Grote 1889), p. 207. Theophrastus (16) makes the superstitious man anoint and worship smooth stones at the cross-ways. The practice itself is connected with the oriental custom of anointing living persons as a sign of honour (cf. Psalm xlv, 7) which still survives in the case of kings and ecclesiastical dignitaries.
32 Near it was a wooden coffer for money offerings.
33 It is permitted to drink it through a cloth or kerchief.
34 Smith, *Religion of the Semites*, p. 322. N. 3 remarks that this draught 'that makes the mourner forget his grief', consists of water with which is mingled dust from the grave (Wellhausen, p. 142), a form of communion precisely similar in principle to the Australian usage of eating a small piece of the corpse.
35 The hands were separated, still palms downwards, and the numbers of the pebbles under the right and left hand respectively were then counted.
36 Near him was a kind of low gallows from which was suspended a three-pointed flesh hook for hanging up the meat. This flesh-hook had to be touched three times with the tip of the right-hand little finger.
37 Evliya Çelebi, *Seyahatname*, vol. VIII (Constantinople 1670), p. 732.
38 Kamus ul Âlâm, II, 1078.
39 Çelebi, *Seyahatname*, VIII, 679.
40 *Boza*, according to Lane's '*Arabian Nights*' II No. 51, is a kind of beer, made usually from barley-bread. It is a drink used in the Near East even from the time of Herodotus.
41 Çelebi, *Seyahatname*, VIII, 680.
42 Çelebi, *Seyahatname*, VIII, 745.
43 Zylfo Baba of the Turan *tekke* near Korche also told me that Kasim Baba was one of the early Bektashi missionaries particularly in the district of Kastoria. Turabi Baba in his *Historija e Pergjitheshme e Bektashinjvet*, page 54, speaks of Kasim Baba who in 1378 came to Kosturi. In the same year Jemin Baba is said to have come to Vutrine of Naselich, Piri Baba to Djunia of Kayler and Hüsseyn Baba to Konitsa.

44 Not Sheikh Mimi as spelt in Hasluck's *Christianity and Islam under the Sultans*, 548 ff. More than once Bektashi friends in Albania sought to correct me on this point.
45 Anonymous, *The Life of Ali Pasha* (London: T. M'Lean 1823), p. 60.
46 The first prime minister of Egypt after King Farouk was deposed.
47 Now Veles, southeast of Skopje.
48 Birge, *The Bektashi Order of Dervishes*, p. 70.
49 Hasluck, *Christianity and Islam under the Sultans*, p. 537.
50 Çelebi, *Seyahatname*, VIII, p. 702.
51 Franz Babinger, *Rumelische Streifen* (Berlin 1938), p. 24, incl. footnote 3.
52 Babinger, *Rumelische Streifen*, p. 24, footnote 2.
53 *Qamus al-a'lam*, p. 2636.
54 Johann Georg von Hahn, *Albanesische Studien* (Jena 1854), vol. 1, p. 72.
55 Ekrem bey Vlora, *Aus Berat und vom Tomor* (Sarajevo 1911).
56 *Seyahatname* VIII, pp. 716–730.
57 See the doctoral dissertation of I. Beldeceanu-Steinherr, *Scheich Üftâde, der Begründer des Ğelvetijje-Ordens* (Munich 1961).
58 *Sicill-i 'Osmani III* (Istanbul 1311), p. 111.
59 *Seyahatname* III, p. 449 sq.
60 Hasluck, *Christianity and Islam under the Sultans*, p. 518 sq.
61 See Georg Jacob, *Beiträge zur Kenntnis des Derwischordens der Bektaschi* (Munich 1909), p. 23.
62 Baba Rexheb, *Zëri i Bektashizmës* (Detroit: by Teqe Komision 1954) II, 1, p. 21.
63 Sheikh Safi, 'Mersiye', in *Mir'at ut-Mekasid fi Def il-Mefasid*, ed. Ahmet Rifat Efendi (Istanbul: Ibrahim Efendi Matbaasi 1293 AH), pp. 202–204.
64 Arshi Pipa, 'Albanian Folklore: Structure and Genre', in *Albanische Forschungen* (Munich: Dr. Rudolf Trofenik 1978) 17, pp. 7, 92, 102.
65 Loring Danforth, *The Death Rituals of Rural Greece* (Princeton: Princeton University Press 1982), p. 108.
66 Margaret Alexiou, *The Ritual Lament in Greek Tradition* (Cambridge: Cambridge University Press 1974), p. 188.
67 Pipa, 'Albanian Folklore', p. 119.
68 Albanian text of this passage is as follows: 'Për kombin e popullin t'onë, për shpëtimin/e tij nga fatkeqësit dhe reziqet q'e rethoin,/për mbarësin e lumtërin e atij vendi/e beko, O zot!'
69 Albanian Merthiye, *Zeri i Bektashizmes* (Detroit: by Teqe Commission 1954).
70 Some of the Bektashi *tekkes* were taken over by the Nakshbandi sect. In Albania, where the Nakshbandi were not well represented, the Bektashi *tekke* of Kanina near Vlora was given to the Halveti. cf. H. Kaleshi 1980, p. 10, and E. Vlora 1955, p. 8, who notes that the *tekke* of Kanina, having fallen to ruins, was taken over by the Halveti in 1805.
71 cf. Xh. Kallajxhi 1964, p. 24; and Hasluck, *Christianity and Islam under the Sultans*, p. 435 (542), 439–440 (546–547). Hasluck notes that in the early twentieth century that the dervishes of one of the *tekkes* of Gjirokastra (that of Asim Baba) still wore 'a four-ridged *taj* instead of the ordinary twelve-ridged Bektashi hat in memory of 1826. Only by adopting some such disguise could Bektashi dervishes escape destruction'. (ibid., p. 534 (541)).
72 Bektashism was introduced to Albanian territory by Turkish missionaries and the first *babas* to administer the *tekkes* established there were often Turks. Later, the Albanians took over not only the administration of the local *tekkes* but also of *tekkes* located elsewhere in the Balkans and indeed in Anatolia. The last *dede baba* at Hacıbektaş,

Salih Nijazi Dede, was himself of Albanian origin. He was born in the village of Starja south of Korça. cf. Baba Rexheb, *Misticizma*, pp. 355–357.

73 cf. S. Skendi 1967, p. 88. According to G. Gawrych, the Porte was in favour of the League since the Albanians would thereby keep their territory within the Empire, cf. G. Gawrych 1985, p. 28. Albanian autonomy was even more in the interests of Austria-Hungary.

74 To entice the population, the Albanian Bektashi began not only to write in Albanian, but also to translate works from Turkish and Persian, in particular the well-known work of Fuzûlî (c. 1489–1556), entitled *Hadiqatû's-Su'adâ* (The Garden of the Blithe), dedicated to the martyrs of Kerbela. Extracts of this work are recited during *matem*, the first ten days of the month of Muharrem.

The *Hadika*, as it is known is Albanian, was translated in part or in full several times, including the adaptation made for instance by Dalip Frashëri (called Hixhreti), from Frashër. He composed his 60,000-line epic at the *tekke* of Konitsa (in Greek Epirus), where he had been exiled for reasons unknown. His translation dates from 1842 and contains many additional elements compared to the original. According to Osman Myderrizi, the passages recited at *matem* had been translated in Gjirokastra as early as 1811. After the *Hadika* of Dalip Frashëri, there came other translations since some people felt that Frashëri's version was not faithful enough to the original. In the early twentieth century, the *Hadika* was translated into the dialect of Labëria (in southern Albania, around Tepelena) by Baba Salih of the *tekke* of Matohasanaj. cf. O. Myderrizi, *Letërsia shqipe* … 1955, *Letërsia fetare* … 1955; Dh. Shuteriqi 1965, pp. 226–228. It may be noted, in addition, that at the request of Baba Qazim of Gjakova, who died several years ago, and of his followers who could not understand the dialect of Dalip Frashëri, Baba Bajram encouraged Baba Rexheb who made a new translation of the *Hadika* at their *tekke* in Detroit in the United States. This translation is to be published shortly.

75 This can be seen in the following quatrain composed to the glory of the *tekke* of Frashër:

Si ty o Vithlehem e Mek'e Arabisë
Ku janë lindur Muhamet e Krisht i Krishtërisë,
Për mua ësht Frashër, vënt i Perëndisë,
Tek është lindur Naim Beu, zemr'e Shqipërisë.

For you, oh Bethlehem and Arabia's Mecca
Where Muhammed and the Christ of the Christians were born,
For me is it Frashër, the home of the Lord,
Where Naim Bey, the heart of Albania, was born.

cf. M. Grameno in P. Pepo 1951, p. 121. On the history of the *tekke* of Frashër, see my book, N. Clayer 1990, pp. 275–278, with a list of the Bektashi convents and all references.

76 The Albanians are divided into Ghegs and Tosks. The two groups differ from one another in their physical characteristics, their dress and their dialects. The Ghegs live mainly north of the Shkumbin River that flows past Elbasan and divides Albania into two. The Tosks are to be found to the south of the river. The Ghegs continued to live in tribes and large extended families, whereas the Tosks underwent Greek influence and lived in villages. Christianity divided them all the more, with the Ghegs becoming Catholics and the Tosks adopting Orthodoxy. In the Ottoman period, the Ghegs who turned Muslim were often regarded as religious fanatics, something that was never said of the Muslim Tosks.

77 On this gathering, cf. Rifat Frashëri in P. Pepo 1962, pp. 88–89, M. Grameno in P. Pepo 1962, p. 120, and S. Skendi 1967, pp. 41–42.
78 S. Skendi 1967, pp. 78–79.
79 M. Grameno in P. Pepo 1951, p. 120.
80 cf. Xh. Kallajxhi 1964, p. 29.
81 Muavija who was responsible for the death of Huseyn, the grandson of the Prophet, of course represents the Ottoman Empire in the eyes of the Bektashi.
82 These publications were printed outside of Albania, in particular in Monastir (Bitola) and in towns where Albanian exiles had gathered, such as Bucharest, Sofia, Salonica and Cairo.
83 Baba Rexheb, *Misticizma*, p. 345.
84 i.e. the proclamation of the Second Constitution of the Young Turks in 1908.
85 'Teaching the Alphabet in Bllaca' by Osman Xheka, in P. Pepo 1962, p. 71.
86 'Long Live the Alphabet' by Isuf Azabella, in P. Pepo 1962, pp. 68–69, N. Clayer 2003, pp. 110–111.
87 Dervish Ramadan later became the baba of the *tekke* of Qatrom and played an important role in politics in the Korça region in the years 1916–1920 (note by P. Pepo).
88 Gavril Pepo later took to the hills to join the band of Themistokli Gërmenji and was head of the people's council of the town of Korça during the national liberation war (note by P. Pepo).
89 Baba Hysen of the *tekke* of Melçan was an eminent patriot who turned the *tekke* into a centre of nationalist activity. The villagers of the Gora and Rreza regions often came to the *tekke* to meet the patriots of the Korça Committee and to receive instructions from them for the coming struggle to liberate the country from the yoke of Istanbul (note by P. Pepo).
90 'Themistokli Gërmenji in the Village of Vinçan' by Nuri Dervishi, in P. Pepo 1962, p. 328.
91 Turkish sources give an indication of the attitude of Baba Qazim. In an article in the periodical *Muhibbân*, we read: 'In the past, in an interview with the sheikh of the *dergâh* of Qatrom near Korça, the sheikh stated sincerely that he was completely neutral as to any uprising in Albania and that he was profoundly opposed to subversive ideas and condemned the uprisings' ('*Arnâvûtluk ahvalı bektaşiler*', *Muhibbân*, 2, 7–8, 28 *recep* 1329/1911, p. 161, quotation taken from Th. Zarcone 1990, p. 80).
92 cf. *Kalendari Kombiar* (Sofia: Luarasi 1903), pp. 21–22.
93 Baba Rexheb, *Misticizma*, p. 381. Note that the year 318, i.e. 1318, corresponds to 1900 AD, and that Muawiya refers to the Ottomans.
94 S. Skendi 1967, pp. 378–380.
95 6 February 1910.
96 'The Alphabet Meeting' by Nepsi Kerenxhi, in P. Pepo 1962, p. 316.
97 Bektashi circles in Istanbul were in fact very much surprised at the stance of the Albanian Bektashi. Thierry Zarcone analysed how the managing editor of *Muhibbân*, a Sufi periodical in the early twentieth century, viewed the situation: 'The interpretation that Muhtar gave about the Albanian crisis of 1912 is quite surprising. He saw it as a 'Bektashi problem' and thought that it could be solved by talking to the Albanian members of the *tarikat* when they had been properly advised by the Istanbul Bektashi of the same branch, i.e. the celibate *babas*. Muhtar remarked that the Albanian Bektashi who were preparing for an uprising had been misled and deceived.' These strange comments can only be explained by the absolute

confidence that the managing editor of *Muhibbân* had in the *tarikat* and in the spirit of fraternity that was supposed to unite its members. It was difficult to imagine that the Bektashi would oppose Ottoman sovereignty and the spirit of the Constitution. For the Young Turk Bektashi like Ahmed Muhtar, the Constitution represented an emanation of Bektashi spirit (cf. T. Zarcone 1990, pp. 81-82).
98 Haxhi Ali (Hadji Ali).
99 'The Struggle for a National Alphabet' by Thomas Papagano, in P. Pepo 1962, p. 315.
100 For instance, Baba Selim of the *tekke* of Asim Baba helped found a club in Gjirokastra. cf. Baba Rexheb, *Misticizma*, p. 305. Baba Axhem of the *tekke* of Memaliaj was himself a member of the patriotic club of Tepelena. cf. Arshi Daut Shehu, *Klubi patriot i Tepelenës*, in P. Pepo 1962, p. 256.
101 Qamil Çeka, in P. Pepo 1962, p. 260.
102 His portrait can be seen among those of the heroes of the movement in a work that was published in Tirana in 1962, at a time when religion had fallen into disgrace. cf. *Rilindja kombëtare shqiptare*, Tirana 1962, p. 108.
103 'The First National Çeta' by Selim Pojani, in P. Pepo 1962, p. 111.
104 Ibid., pp. 112-113.
105 'Encounter with the Young Turks' by M. Grameno, in P. Pepo 1962, pp. 155-157.
106 Ibid., p. 155.
107 Ibid., p. 157.
108 'Meeting Bajo and Çerçiz in Gjirokastra,' by Shemso Hajro, in P. Pepo 1962, p. 160.
109 'The Çeta of Captain Çerçiz,' by M. Grameno, in P. Pepo 1962, pp. 120-121.
110 This is told by Baba Rexheb in an interview at the Bektashi *tekke* in Detroit (United States) in June 1989, and is also to be found in the work of Xh. Kallajxhi 1964, p. 29.
111 The term *baba* means 'father' in Turkish. The Albanians also use the word *atë* or *at*.
112 N. Frashëri, *Fletore e Bektashinjet*, 1st edition (Bucharest 1896), in 16, 32 pp.; second edition: Sofia: Mbrothësia, K. Luarasi 1908, in 16, 32 pp.; third edition, Salonica 1910; fourth edition, Korça, Shtyp. Dh. Koti, 1921, 32 pp. This manifesto in which Naim Frashëri set forth the beliefs, the ranks of hierarchy and the practices of the Bektashi order and stressed the role of Bektashism in civilisation and progress was translated into several languages: a partial translation (according to N. Jokl) into French by Faik Konitza, *Albania* (Brussels 1897), vol. A, pp. 174-176, 193, 212-213; a French translation by H. Bourgeois, 'Le Livre des Bektachi de Naïm Bey Frasheri', in *Revue du Monde musulman*, 49 (1922), pp. 105-120; a German translation by N. Jokl (the most detailed), 'Die Bektaschi von Naim Be Frashëri', in *Balkan-Archiv* (Leipzig 1926), pp. 226-256; and an English translation, 'Bektashi Pages' by Hasluck, *Christianity and Islam under the Sultans*, pp. 552-563.
113 Baba Meleq Shëmbërdhenji was born in Skrapar, a region southeast of Berat, probably in the village of Staravecka because he was also called Baba Meleq Staravecka. He took his vows to become a dervish at the Bektashi *tekke* in Cairo in Egypt. Sometime after 1878, the Albanians of Cairo sent him to Albania to distribute books to the population. He remained there travelling from village to village and inspiring the inhabitants with his nationalist ideas. Here is a statement given by a man from Shtylla who learned to read thanks to Baba Meleq: 'Wherever Baba Meleq went, he made popular the struggle of the Albanian people for freedom and national unity. He distributed Albanian books and, when he visited the villagers in their homes, he taught the young people to read and write. This patriotic *baba* visited our house in Shtylla, too, and taught me and the other young people to read and write our language. We are all grateful to him' (Rifat

Shtylla in P. Pepo 1962, p. 45). Because of his activities, Baba Meleq was under the constant observation of the secret police. Later, about 1900 perhaps, he was appointed to head the *tekke* of Shëmbërdhenj, where he remained until his death. After independence, the *tekke* was burned down by the Greeks and Baba Meleq was forced to flee abroad (possibly back to Egypt). It was in exile that he wrote numerous poems in Albanian, works of both patriotic and religious inspiration. See Baba Rexheb, *Misticizma*, pp. 346-355.

114 Baba Ibrahim is remembered for his support for the nationalist movement and turned his *tekke* into a lively centre of nationalist activity. He collaborated with the noted 'patriots' of the period (in particular with Petro Nini Luarasi who was his teacher and had taken refuge at the *tekke* in 1903 after having survived an assassination attempt, and with Sali Butka and Riza Velçisht who were rebel leaders). He also took part in the distribution of books in Albanian, but was caught in the act by Turkish troops and imprisoned. The Greeks arrested Baba Ibrahim in 1913, right after independence, but he was soon freed by Sali Butka and his men. Sometime thereafter, Baba Ibrahim and his dervishes were forced to take flight and their *tekke* was burned down by Greek forces who, according to Baba Rexheb, killed Baba Ibrahim's mother who had remained behind at the *tekke*. Her presence at the *tekke* stems from the fact that the *tekke* of Qesaraka was one of the two Albanian Bektashi *tekkes* belonging to the *müjerred* branch, i.e. of celibate dervishes. On this, see Margaret Hasluck, *The Unwritten Law in Albania* (Cambridge: Cambridge University Press 1954), p. 31, and on Baba Ibrahim, see Baba Rexheb, *Misticizma*, p. 360.

115 Baba Rexheb, Misticizma, pp. 347-348.
116 Ibid.
117 Ibid., p. 361.
118 About forty Bektashi *tekkes* were destroyed in this period.
119 Baba Shaban of the *tekke* of Prishta, for instance, found refuge at the *tekke* in Cairo, as did Baba Ahmet of the *tekke* of Koshtan and the future Baba Ali Tomorri (cf. Baba Rexheb, *Misticizma*, p. 367).
120 Dervish Kamber (later known as Baba Kamber of Prishta) of the *tekke* of Frashër, for instance. See Xh. Kallajxhi, (1964), p. 1 and *Kalendari i vatrës i motit* (Boston 1918), p. 180.
121 Some *tekkes* remained without a *postnişin* until at least 1925. Following the ban of the *tarikats* in Turkey, a group of eight *babas* arrived in Albania to fill the vacant posts (information from Baba Rexheb given during an interview conducted with him in June 1989 at the *tekke* of Detroit).
122 The religious divisions in the country remained more or less the same throughout the post-Ottoman period. A census in 1942 gave the following figures: 763,723 Muslims (68.9 per cent of the total population), consisting of 599,524 Sunnis (78.5 per cent of the Muslims) and 164,199 Bektashi (21.5 per cent of the Muslims) as well as 229,080 Orthodox (20.7 per cent of the population) and 113,897 Catholics (10.3 per cent of the population) (see *La Documentation française. Notes et études documentaires*, 1843, 2 March 1954).
123 Michael Schmidt-Neke, *Entstehung und Ausbau der Königsdiktatur in Albanien (1912-1939)* (Munich: Oldenbourg Verlag 1987), p. 54. In December 1921, Biçaku was replaced by Omer Pasha Vrioni (ibid., p. 96).
124 Information from Baba Rexheb.
125 Mid'hat Frashëri, *Jeta e Naim be Frashërit* (Sofia 1901), p. 36, as quoted by N. Jokl, (1926), p. 228. The same idea was expressed by Sami Frashëri in his little work

on Albania, its past, present and future, that was published in Bucharest at the end of the nineteenth century. In it, Sami Frashëri wrote: 'The Bektashi, who are quite widespread in southern Albania will have their own *kryebaba* (*dede baba*) somewhere in Albania who will appoint other *babas* and, with a council consisting of the *baba* and his dervishes, will administer and supervise the functioning of the *tekkes* of the *tarikat* (Sami Frashëri, 'Shqipëria, ç'ka qenë, ç'është e ç'do të bëhetë?' in *Vepra* (Prishtina: Rilindja, 2, 1978), published for the first time in Bucharest in 1899.
126 Baba Rexheb, *Misticizma*, p. 358.
127 This congress took place in January 1921 at the *tekke* of Prishta in Skrapar (southeast of Berat), cf. Justin Godart, *L'Albanie en 1921* (Paris: PUF 1922), p. 166.
128 *Statuti i Komunitetit Bektashian Shqiptar* (Vlora: Shtyp. Vlora 1924).
129 Albert Mousset, *L'Albanie devant l'Europe* (Paris: Delagrave 1930), p. 115. The Bektashi got full autonomy from the Sunni Muslim community only in 1945 (cf. *Area Handbook for Albania,* Washington, DC 1971, p. 97).
130 Information from Baba Rexheb.
131 In the old days, the Bektashi in the Ottoman Empire were divided into six zones under the administration of Haji Bektash (cf. Xh. Kallajxhi (1964) p. 16 and *Zëri i Bektashizmës, Organi i Elementit Bektashi, drejtohet e botohet prej komisionit të tekes* (Wyandotte, Michigan, s.d. [1955]), II, 2, p. 14.) Did the Albanian Bektashi want to reproduce this structure with six zones on Albanian territory? It is possible because in 1930 Albania was divided into six, not ten, districts.
132 Information from Baba Rexheb. The same problem occurred in 1942 on the death of Salih Nijazi Dede. None of the high-ranking *babas* was willing to take over the position of *kryegjysh*. The Bektashi community was administered for an interim period of several months by Baba Ali Riza, head of one of the three *tekkes* of Elbasan, though he did not move to Tirana. Devoted though he was, he did not have the proper competence to do so. Baba Kamber of Prishta eventually agreed to take over the position (information from Baba Rexheb).
133 Xh. Kallajxhi, (1964), p. 25, and H. Kaleshi, (1975), p. 14.
134 As the *tekke* of Asim Baba was occupied by the Greeks, Baba Selim went to live with his sister in town. Her home served as a little *tekke* for three and a half years. cf. Baba Rexheb, *Misticizma*, p. 305.
135 Information from Baba Rexheb.
136 Baba Ali Tomorri was born in the late nineteenth century in the little village of Shalës, half way between Tepelena and Mount Tomorr. After basic schooling, he went to Janina for secondary education, and learned Turkish, a bit of Arabic and French. Baba Ali Tomorri was initiated into Bektashism by Baba Shaban of the *tekke* of Prishta where he took his vows and became a dervish. Under the Greek occupation in 1913–1914 he followed Baba Shaban, Baba Ahmet Koshtani and other dervishes to Cairo in Egypt, where they spent several years at the famed *tekke* there. On his return to Albania, Baba Ali Tomorri, who was known at the time as Varf Ali Prishta (i.e. dervish Ali of Prishta), began to play an active role in Albanian Bektashism. He was the person behind the periodical *Reforma* (Reform) that was issued from 1921 to 1923 and was one of the main organisers of the first three national congresses of the Albanian Bektashi community. As of 1924, or perhaps earlier, he headed the little *tekke* of Tomorr which was very soon to become one of the main centres of the Bektashi in the Berat region and, later, in all of Albania. During the Second World War, Baba Ali Tomorri took part in the fight to liberate the country and in 1946, the communist government sent him to the *tekke* of Asim

Baba in Gjirokastra to replace Baba Selim who had died in 1944. But a year later, he was accused of espionage and collaboration with the British. A 'people's court' sentenced him to death and he was executed. This took place during the purges that the new regime carried out against its opponents. Baba Ali Tomorri was also known as a writer and poet. He published several works under the penname of Ali Tyrabi: *Bektashinjt e Shqipëris* (The Bektashi of Albania), Korça 1921; *Literatyra e Bektashivet a vjersha të përkthyera prej shkrimtarëve bektashinj të vjetër* (The Literature of the Bektashi or Verse Translated from Old Bektashi Writers), Tirana 1927; and *Historija e përgjithëshme e Béktashinjvet* (General History of the Bektashi), Tirana 1929 (I was unfortunately unable to access the first and last of these works). Baba Ali Tomorri is said to have opposed religious fanaticism and to have encouraged close relations between Christians and Bektashi. Cf. Baba Rexheb, *Misticizma*, pp. 367-372.

137 This was a little anthology entitled *Literatyra e Bektashivet* .... Baba Tomorri published it under his penname, At Ali Tyrabi (*At* means 'father' in Albanian and is the same as the word *baba*).

138 Mid'hat Frashëri (Janina 1880-New York 1949), son of Abdyl Frashëri and nephew of Naim and Sami, played a political role in the creation of Albania and, after retiring from political life for about fifteen years, he created the republican *Balli Kombëtar* (National Front) organisation in 1942. As he was an opponent of the communist regime, he was obliged to flee and sought exile in the United States.

139 At Ali Tyrabi, (1921), p. 5.

140 Ibid., p. 3.

141 Zija Xholi, 'A propos du panthéisme de Naim Frashëri', *Studia Albanica*, 1 (1965), pp. 131-152.

142 This *tekke* is now the only surviving reflection of Albanian Bektashism. See in particular the book published by Xh. Kallajxhi on the tenth anniversary of the opening of this centre (Xh. Kallajxhi, 1964); as well as Cemal Bayraktari, 'The First American Bektaşi Tekke', *The Turkish Studies Association Bulletin*, 9 (1 March 1985), pp. 21-24; and the thesis of Frances Trix, '*Tuning the Heart: Language Attunement of Master and Student in an Islamic Monastery*, a dissertation submitted in partial fulfilment of the requirement for the degree of Doctor of Philosophy (Linguistics) at the University of Michigan,' 1988, and the article 'The Ashura Lament of Baba Rexheb and the Albanian Bektashi Community in America', in: A. Popovic and G. Veinstein (ed.), *Bektachiyya, études sur l'ordre mystique des Bektachis et les groupes relevant de Hadji Bektach. Revue des Etudes Islamiques 60 (1992)*. Numéro spécial (Paris: Paul Geuthner 1993 and Isis: Istanbul 1995), pp. 405-418. On the periodical published by the *tekke* in 1954-1955, cf. N. Clayer, 'La Voix du Bektachisme, une revue bektachie albanaise publiée aus États-Unis (1954-1955)', *Anatolia Moderna/ Yeni Anadolu, II, Derviches et cimitières ottomans* (1991), pp. 227-235.

143 'Festimi në liri,' *Zëri i Bektashizmës*, II, 2, pp. 1-2.

144 M. Kiel 1993.

145 Th. Ippen 1907, p. 69.

146 paraphrased from A. Degrand 1901.

147 Vlora, *Aus Berat und vom Tomor*, pp. 105-106.

148 J. Swire 1937, pp. 252-253.

149 A. Tomorri 1929, p. 93.

150 Vlora, *Aus Berat und vom Tomor*, p. 107.

151 A. Tomorri 1929, p. 93.

Chapter 3

152 M. Grameno 1979, p. 136.
153 H. T. Norris, *Islam in the Balkans. Religion and Society between Europe and the Arab World* (London: Hurst & Co. 1993), p. 125.
154 i.e. the proclamation of the Second Constitution of the Young Turks in 1908.
155 Osman Xheka in P. Pepo 1962, p. 71; N. Clayer 2003, pp. 108–109.
156 Q. Dedej, *Fillimet e Bektashizmit në Shqipëri dhe në Elbasan* (Elbasan: Egnatia 1997), pp. 29, 34.
157 Ibid., p. 31.
158 Ibid., pp. 42–51.
159 Ibid., pp. 31, 47–49.
160 Ibid., pp. 52–54.
161 Ibid., pp. 54–56.
162 Ibid., pp. 57–59.
163 G. Louis-Jaray 1914, pp. 102–109.
164 Dedej, *Fillimet*, p. 32.
165 Ibid., pp. 60–62.
166 Godart, *L'Albanie en 1921*, p. 163.
167 Hasluck, *Christianity and Islam under the Sultans*, pp. 441 (548–549).
168 P. Edmonds 1927, pp. 237–238.
169 Dedej, *Fillimet*, pp. 63–65.
170 Ibid., pp. 66–68.
171 Birge, *The Bektashi Order of Dervishes*, p. 107.
172 M. Grameno 1979, p. 11.
173 Ibid., p. 136.
174 Ibid., p. 12.
175 T. Ippen 1907, pp. 77–79.
176 Hasluck, *Christianity and Islam under the Sultans*, p. 442 (550).
177 Birge, *The Bektashi Order of Dervishes*, p. 71.
178 Hasluck, *Christianity and Islam under the Sultans*, p. 435 (541).
179 M. Kiel 1990, p. 143.
180 Thomas Papagano in P. Pepo 1962, p. 315; N. Clayer 2003, p. 115.
181 Godart, *L'Albanie en 1921*, pp. 163–165.
182 *Annuaire du Monde Musulman* 1923, 1, p. 230, 2, p. 228, 3, p. 298, 4, p. 404.
183 M. Kiel 1990, pp. 143–144.
184 R. Graves 1933, p. 267.
185 A. Tomorri 1929, p. 91.
186 Dedej, *Fillimet*, p. 26.
187 C. Patsch 1904, pp. 117–118.
188 R. Dankoff and R. Elsie 2000, 361a, pp. 132–133.
189 von Hahn, *Albanesische Studien*, p. 72, 2015, p. 34.
190 Vlora, *Aus Berat und vom Tomor*, p. 51.
191 M. Kiel 1990, p. 150.
192 R. Busch-Zantner 1939, p. 198.
193 F. Wallisch 1931, p. 133.
194 Hasluck, *Christianity and Islam under the Sultans*, p. 438 (544).
195 M. Kiel 1990, p. 182.
196 Ibid., pp. 181–182, 190.

197 Birge, *The Bektashi Order of Dervishes*, p. 71.
198 M. Tütüncü 2017, pp. 122–124.
199 M. Kiel 1993, p. 272.
200 M. Tütüncü 2017, pp. 125–126.
201 M. Kiel 1993.
202 T. Ippen 1907, pp. 71–72.
203 P. Bartl 1968, p. 106.
204 Hasluck, *Christianity and Islam under the Sultans*, p. 440 (548).
205 Ibid., pp. 424 (525), 440 (547).
206 N. Vatin and Th. Zarcone 1991, p. 41.
207 Ibid., p. 41.
208 Hasluck, *Christianity and Islam under the Sultans*, p. 438 (545).
209 Dedej, *Fillimet*, p. 73.
210 Ibid., p. 75.
211 Ibid., pp. 76–77.
212 Ibid., pp. 78–79.
213 L. Nosi 2007, pp. 308–309.
214 J. Bourcart 1921, p. 182.
215 Dedej, *Fillimet*, p. 80.
216 J. Swire 1937, pp. 279–280.
217 Dedej, *Fillimet*, pp. 82–83.
218 Hasluck, *Christianity and Islam under the Sultans*, p. 442 (551).
219 Sh. Hysi 2004, p. 103.
220 N. Clayer 2013 provides a detailed account of the conflict.
221 E. Durham 1905, pp. 270–273.
222 Hasluck, *Christianity and Islam under the Sultans*, pp. 438 (544–545).
223 J. Swire 1937, pp. 257–259.
224 Ibid., pp. 252–253.
225 Hasluck, *Christianity and Islam under the Sultans*, p. 440 (547).
226 Dedej, *Fillimet*, p. 26.
227 A. Tomorri 1929, p. 91.
228 J. Swire 1937, p. 240.
229 N. Clayer 2003, p. 143.
230 Ibid., p. 144.
231 Vlora, *Aus Berat und vom Tomor*, pp. 106–107.
232 J. Swire 1937, pp. 251–254.
233 M. Kiel 1990, pp. 167–168.
234 M. Tütüncü 2017, pp. 219–220.
235 R. Dankoff and R. Elsie 2000, 361b, pp. 136–139.
236 C. Patsch 1904, p. 9.
237 Hasluck, *Christianity and Islam under the Sultans*, p. 437 (525).
238 N. Hafiz 1995, p. 349 (with Turkish text).
239 J. Norton 2001, pp. 188–189.
240 Ibid., p. 188.
241 Ibid.
242 L. Mašulović-Marsol 1995, pp. 351–352.
243 J. Norton 2001, p. 188.
244 L. Mašulović-Marsol 1995, p. 352.
245 Hasluck, *Christianity and Islam under the Sultans*, p. 423 (524).

246 Conserved in Istanbul, Başbakanlık Arşivi, tapu defteri No. 232, f. 210 r., as quoted by L. Mašulović-Marsol 1995, p. 363.
247 J. G. von Hahn 1867, p. 108.
248 F. W. Hasluck 1913, p. 111.
249 A. Evans 1901, pp. 203-204.
250 Hasluck, *Christianity and Islam under the Sultans*, vol. 1, p. 115, 467 (582).
251 G. Palikruševa and K. Tomovski 1965, p. 206.
252 Hasluck, *Christianity and Islam under the Sultans*, pp. 423 (524-525).
253 J. Rexhepagiqi 2003, p. 230.
254 F. W. Hasluck 1913, p. 117.
255 M. Choublier 1927, pp. 428-429.
256 Hasluck, *Christianity and Islam under the Sultans*, vol. 1, pp. 115-116.
257 Ibid., pp. 423 (524-525).
258 Trix, *Sufi Journey*, pp. 28-29.
259 J. A. Degrand 1901, p. 240.
260 Hasluck, *Christianity and Islam under the Sultans*, p. 468 (584).
261 F. W. Hasluck 1913, p. 117, *Christianity and Islam under the Sultans*, p. 474 (592).
262 Hasluck, *Christianity and Islam under the Sultans*, pp. 427-428 (530-531).
263 M. Kiel 2005, p. 426.
264 Norris, *Islam in the Balkans*, p. 135.
265 Baba Rexheb 1970, pp. 270-271.
266 A. Tomori 1929, p. 65.
267 Hasluck, *Christianity and Islam under the Sultans*, p. 429 (532).
268 M. Kiel 2005, p. 422.
269 Ibid., pp. 423-424, 426.
270 M. Kiel 2012.
271 F. De Jong 1989, p. 18, footnote 98.
272 M. Kiel 2005, p. 423, 2012.
273 M. Kiel 2009.
274 Hasluck, *Christianity and Islam under the Sultans*, p. 360 (438).
275 Ibid., p. 431 (535).
276 Ibid., pp. 426-427 (528).
277 Ibid., p. 426 (528).
278 M. Kiel 1993, p. 271.
279 Hasluck, *Christianity and Islam under the Sultans*, p. 424 (525).
280 M. Kiel 1993, p. 271.
281 Hasluck, *Christianity and Islam under the Sultans*, p. 424 (525).
282 N. Clayer *Aux origines* 2007, pp. 492-493.
283 F. W. Hasluck 1914-1916, p. 108.
284 Ibid., p. 107, *Christianity and Islam under the Sultans*, p. 425 (527).
285 M. Hasluck 1925, p. 605.
286 F. W. Hasluck 1913, p. 102.
287 F. W. Hasluck 1914-1916, p. 87, *Christianity and Islam under the Sultans*, p. 407 (504).
288 F. W. Hasluck, 1914-1918 (1929), p. 504.
289 White, *Contemporary Review* (1913), p. 694.
290 Norris, *Islam in the Balkans*, p. 224.
291 M. Brodrick 1900.
292 G. Migeon 1906, pp. 82-83.

293 D. Russell 1962, pp. 137–139.
294 J. Leroy 1963, pp. 56–57.
295 Trix, *Sufi Journey*, 191–199.

Chapter 4

296 Norris, *Islam in the Balkans*, pp. 135–136.
297 Hasluck, *Christianity and Islam under the Sultans*, p. 439 (546).
298 Lazzaro Miedia, Archivio della Sacra Congregazione di Propaganda Fide, Rome, APF, Nuova Serie, Rub. 109 (Vienna 1913), pp. 176–182.
299 H. Brailsford 1906, pp. 247–248.
300 S. Vllamasi 2012, pp. 218–219.
301 Seaman's *Orchan*, p. 120, as quoted by F. W. Hasluck 1913, p. 121.
302 F. W. Hasluck 1913, p. 121.
303 J. Leroy 1963, pp. 57–58.
304 Norris, *Islam in the Balkans*, pp. 224–225.
305 Translated by ibid., p. 226.
306 Norris, *Islam in the Balkans*, p. 125.
307 J. Swire 1937, pp. 252–254.
308 J. A. Degrand 1901, p. 243.
309 Xh. Kallajxhi 1964, p. 29.
310 Z. Yürekli 2016, p. 33, taken from Ahmet Rif'at, *Mir'atü'l-Makasid*, p. 189.
311 D. Smiley 1984, p. 84.
312 Ibid., pp. 159–160.
313 M. Grameno 1979, p. 136.
314 J. Norton 2001, p. 183.
315 J. A. Degrand 1891, pp. 245–246.
316 Hasluck, *Christianity and Islam under the Sultans*, vol. 1, pp. 266–276.
317 Isuf Azabella in P. Pepo 1962, pp. 68–69, N. Clayer 2003, pp. 110–111.
318 M. Grameno 1979, pp. 149–150.
319 Ibid., pp. 135–136.
320 J. Swire 1937, p. 240.
321 Hasluck, *Christianity and Islam under the Sultans*, p. 424 (536).
322 A. Tomori 1929, p. 54.
323 R. Dankoff and R. Elsie 2000, 361b, pp. 136–139.
324 Rifat Shtylla in P. Pepo 1962, p. 45; N. Clayer 2003, p. 119.
325 cf. Baba Rexheb 1970, p. 381.
326 Trix, *Sufi Journey*, p. 65.
327 cf. *Naval Intelligence Service* 1945, p. 230 sq.
328 cf. E. Rossi 1942.
329 A. Tomori 1929, pp. 49–50.
330 M. Kiel 1993.
331 Hasluck, *Christianity and Islam under the Sultans*, p. 468 (584).
332 Trix, *Sufi Journey*, p. 47.
333 Birge, *The Bektashi Order of Dervishes*, p. 107.
334 J. A. Degrand 1901, pp. 210–211.
335 Godart, *L'Albanie en 1921*, pp. 163–165.
336 Şemseddin Sami, *Kamûs al-â'lâm, dictionnaire universel d'histoire et de géographie*, vol. 6 (Constantinople 1889–1896), p. 4580.

BIBLIOGRAPHY

Abiva, Huseyin. *Reflections on Baba Rexheb, and the Bektashi Presence in North America* (Babagan Books, 2008).
Ahmataj, Kujtim. *Shërbestari i harkasë* (Tirana: MediaPrint, s.a. [c. 2016]) 110 pp.
Ahmataj, Kujtim & Martini, Ilir (ed.), *Komuniteti Bektashian. Kongresi 7 Botëror Bektashian. 23-24 shator 2000, Tiranë* (Tirana: Urtësia, 2001) 143 pp.
Ahmataj, Sokrat. *Bektashizmi nën smogun e një libri*. Biblioteka e Bektashizmit (Tirana: Urtësia, 1999) 184 pp.
Arnakis, George G. Futuwwa Traditions in the Ottoman Empire. Akhis, Bektashi Dervishes, and Craftsmen. in: *Journal of Near Eastern Studies*, 12, 4 (1953), pp. 232-247.
Arnold, T. W. *The Preaching of Islam. A History of the Propagation of the Muslim Faith* (London: Luzac, 1896, Reprint 1913, 1935, Lahore: Sh. Muhammad Ashraf, 1961, 1979).
Azemi, Emin & Halimi, Shkëlzen. *Shqiptarët e Egjiptit* (Skopje: Logos A, 1993) 144 pp.
Babinger, Franz. Im Lande der Skipetaren. in: *Deutsche Allgemeine Zeitung*, July 1928. 4 articles.
Babinger, Franz. Bei den Derwischen von Kruja. in: *Mitteilungen der Deutsch-Türkischen Vereinigung*, IX (1928), 8-9, pp. 148-149, 10, pp. 164-165; and in: *Münchner Neueste Nachrichten*, Munich, 7 January 1929, pp. 3-4.
Babinger, Franz. With the Dervishes of Krooya. in: *The Sphere*, CXVII, 1525 (13 April 1929), pp. 63-64.
Babinger, Franz. Ewlija Tschelebi's Reisewege in Albanien. in: *Mitteilungen des Seminars für Orientalische Sprachen*, Berlin 33 (1930), II. Abteilung, pp. 138-178; and in: *Rumelische Streifen* (Berlin 1938) pp. 1-40; and in: *Aufsätze und Abhandlungen zur Geschichte Südosteuropas und der Levante*, 2 (Munich 1966), pp. 51-89.
Babinger, Franz. Das Bektaschikloster Demir Baba. in: *Mitteilungen des Seminars für Orientalische Sprachen*, Berlin, 34 (1931); and in: *Aufsätze und Abhandlungen zur Geschichte Südosteuropas und der Levante*, 1 (Munich 1962), pp. 88-96.
Babinger, Franz. Sari Saltik Dede. in: *Enzyklopädie des Islam*, Bd. IV, S-Z (Leiden & Leipzig: Brill and Otto Harrassowitz, 1934).
Bartl, Peter. *Die albanischen Muslime zur Zeit des nationalen Unabhängigkeitsbewegung 1878-1912*. Albanische Forschungen 8 (Wiesbaden: Harrassowitz, 1968) 207 pp.
Bartl, Peter. Religionsgemeinschaften und Kirchen. in: Klaus Detlef Grothusen (ed.), *Albanien*. Südosteuropa-Handbuch, 7 (Göttingen: Vandenhoeck & Ruprecht, 1993), pp. 587-614.
Basha, Ali Musa. Muslim Communities under the Anti-religious Regime in Albania (1845-1990). in: *Religion und Kultur im albanischsprachigen Südosteuropa*. Herausgegeben von Oliver Jens Schmitt. Redaktion Andreas Rathberger. Schriftenreihe der Kommission für südosteuropäische Geschichte, Band 4 (Frankfurt am Main: Peter Lang, 2010), pp. 163-172.
Bayraktari, Cemal. The First American Bektaşi Tekke. in: *Turkish Studies Association Bulletin*, 9, 1 (March 1985), pp. 21-24.

Berisha, Anton Kolë. Islamization–Seed of Discord or the Only Way of Salvation for Albanians? in: *Religion in Eastern Europe*, 15, 6 (1995), pp. 1–7.
Bilici, Faruk, Clayer, Nathalie, Thombie, Jacques & Baque-Grammont, Jean Louis (ed.), *Derviches des Balkans, disparitions et renaissances*. Anatolia Moderna, 4 (Paris: Maisonneuve, 1992).
Birge, John Kingsley. *The Bektashi Order of Dervishes* (London: Luzac, 1937, Reprint 1965, 1982, 1994, 2015) 291 pp.
Birge, John Kingsley. *Bektaşilik tarihi*. Çeviri Reha Çamuroğlu (Istanbul: Ant Yayinlari, s. a, 1937) 339 pp.
Bishqem, Astrit. *Elbasani ndër vite për librin. Biobibliografi enciklopedike* (Tirana: Dy lindje dhe dy perëndime, 2016) 254 pp.
Bitincka, Dervish Feim Hamdi. *Histori e teqes së Melçanit*. Botim i 1re (Korça: Dhori Koti, 1925) 48 pp.
Boriçi, Kujtim & Xhelaj, Syrja. *Baba Shefqet Gllava, martir i demokracisë* (Tirana: Urtësia, 2016) 228 pp.
Boriçi, Kujtim & Xhelaj, Syrja. *Autorë të huaj për bektashizmin shqiptar* (Tirana: Urtësia bektashiane, 2017) 324 pp.
Boué, Ami. *La Turquie d'Europe ou observations sur la géographie, la géologie, l'histoire naturelle, la statistique, les moeurs, les coutumes, l'archéologie, l'agriculture, l'industrie, le commerce, les gouvernements divers, le clergé, l'histoire et l'état politique de cet empire*. 4 vols. (Paris: A. Bertrand, 1840) 526, 539, 590, 592 pp.
Bourcart, Jacques. *L'Albanie et les Albanais*, avec 19 photographies prises par l'auteur et une carte hors-texte (Paris: Bossard, 1921) 266 pp.
Bourgeois, Henri. Le Livre des Bektaschi de Naim Bey Frasheri. Traduit de l'albanais. in: *Revue du monde musulman*, Paris, 49 (1922), pp. 105–120.
Bousquet, G. H. Notes sur les reformes de l'Islam albanais. in: *Revue des Etudes Islamiques*, Paris, 9 (1935), IV. pp. 399–410.
Bousquet, G. H. Islam in the Balkans. in: *The Moslem World*, 27 (1937), pp. 65–71.
Brailsford, Henry N. *Macedonia: Its Races and their Future* (London: Methuen, 1906, Reprint New York: Arno, 1970) 340 pp.
Brodrick, Mary. *Handbook for Travellers in Lower and Upper Egypt*. Tenth edition, revised. (London: John Murray, 1900) 1,006 pp.
Bulo, Jorgo. Mali i shenjtë i Tomorrit. Nga kulti pagan te miti romantik. in: *Perla, revistë, shkencore-kulturore tremujore*, Tirana, 4 (1997), pp. 3–7.
Busch-Zantner, Richard. Die Sekte des Bektaschi in Albanien. in: *Petermanns Geographische Mitteilungen*, Gotha, 78 (1932), p. 245.
Busch-Zantner, Richard. Die Stadt der verbotenen Derwische. in: *Moslemische Revue*, Berlin, (January 1934), pp. 1–6.
Busch-Zantner, Richard. *Albanien, neues Land im Imperium* (Leipzig: Wilhelm Goldmann, 1939) 224 pp.
Cahen, Claude. Bab Ishaq, Baba Ilyas, Hadjdji Bektash et quelques autres. in: *Turcica*, 1 (1969), pp. 53–64.
Ćehajić, Džemal. Bektashis and Islam in Bosnia and Herzegovina. in: *Anali Gazi Husrevbegove biblioteke*, Sarajevo, V-VI (1978), pp. 83–90.
Ćehajić, Džemal. *Derviški redovi u jugoslovenskim zemljama. Sa posebnim osvrtom na Bosnu i Hercegovinu*. Orientalni Institut u Sarajevu. Posebna izdana XIV (Sarajevo: Orientalni Institut u Sarajevu, 1986).
Çela, Elira. Fea dhe kleri në gjykimin e popullit. in: *Kultura popullore*, Tirana, 1 (1989), pp. 121–136.

Çela, Elira. *Tradita afetare të popullit shqiptar* (Tirana: 8 Nëntori, 1991) 204 pp.
Çela, Elira. Soupçons de religion dans le système social albanais. in: *Conscience et liberté*, Berne, 46 (1993), pp. 83-103.
Çela, Elira. Albanian Muslims, Human Rights and Relations with the Islamic World. in: Gerd Nonneman, Tim Niblock, Bogdan Szajkowski (ed.), *Muslim Communities in the New Europe* (Reading, UK: Ithaca Press, 1996), pp. 139-152.
Çela, Elira & Lamani, Genc. Political Change and the Revival of Islamic Consciousness in Post-Communist Albania. in: Suha Taji-Farouk & Hugh Poulton (ed.), *Muslim Identity and the Balkan State* (London: Hurst, 1997).
Çetiner, Yilmaz. *Bilinmiyen Arnavutluk. Bir röportaj dizisi* (Istanbul: Istanbul Matbaasi, 1966) 126 pp.
Choublier, Max. Les Bektachis et la Roumélie. in: *Revue des Etudes Islamiques*, Paris, 1 (1927), pp. 427-453.
Choulia, Souzana [= ΧΟΥΛΙΑ, Σουζάνα]. The Tekke Durpali Sultan in Asprogeia, Region of Farsala. in: *Thorakion*, Athens, 2004, pp. 417-442.
Choulia, Souzana [= ΧΟΥΛΙΑ, Σουζάνα]. *Tekes Ntourmbalé Soultan. I Othomaniki architektoniki stin Hellada* (Athens: YPPO, 2012).
Clayer, Nathalie. *L'Albanie. Pays des derviches. Les ordres mystiques musulmans en Albanie à l'époque postottomane (1912-1967)*. Balkanologische Veröffentlichungen 17 (Berlin, Wiesbaden: In Kommission bei Otto Harrassowitz, 1990) 505 pp.
Clayer, Nathalie. La voix du Bektachisme; une revue bektachie albanaise publiée aux États-Unis. in: *Anatolia Moderna/Yeni Anadolu*, II, Derviches et cimetières ottomans, Michel Tuchscherer, Jean-Louis Bacque-Grammont, Edhem Eldem, Thierry Zarcone (ed.) (Paris: Editions Adrien Maisonneuve, Jean Maisonneuve, 1991), pp. 227-235.
Clayer, Nathalie. Bektachisme et nationalisme albanais. in: A. Popovic & G. Veinstein (ed.), *Bektachiyya, études sur l'ordre mystique des Bektachis et les groupes relevant de Hadji Bektach. Revue des Etudes Islamiques* 60 (1992). Numéro spécial (Paris: Paul Geuthner, 1993/Istanbul: Isis, 1995), pp. 271-300.
Clayer, Nathalie. *Mystiques, état et société. Les Halvetis dans l'aire balkanique de la fin du XVe siècle à nos jours* (Leiden: E. J. Brill, 1994) iii + 426 pp.
Clayer, Nathalie. Les hauts lieux du bektachisme albanais. in: Mohammad Ali Amir-Moezzi (ed.), *Lieux de l'islam. Cultes et cultures de l'Afrique à Java* (Paris: Editions Autrement, 1996), pp. 168-183. Reprinted in: Nathalie Clayer, *Religion et nation chez les albanais, XIXe-XXe siècles* (Istanbul: Isis, 2003), pp. 137-150.
Clayer, Nathalie. *Les voies d'Allah. Les ordres mystiques dans l'Islam des origines à aujourd'hui*. Sous la direction de Alexandre Popovic (Paris: Fayard, 1996) 711 pp.
Clayer, Nathalie. Islam, State and Society in Post-Communist Albania. in: *Muslim Identity and the Balkan State* (London: Hurst and Co., 1997), pp. 114-138.
Clayer, Nathalie. Miti i Ali Pashës dhe bektashinjtë. in: *Përpjekja, e përtremuajshme kulturore*, Tirana, 15-16 (1999), pp. 39-43.
Clayer, Nathalie. *Tasavvuf*, Music and Social Change in the Balkans since the Beginning of the Twentieth Century with Special Consideration of Albania. in: Anders Hammarlund, Tord Olsson, Elisabeth Özdalga (ed.), *Sufism, Music and Society in Turkey and the Middle East* (Istanbul: Swedish Research Institute in Istanbul, 2001), pp. 137-146. Reprinted in: Nathalie Clayer, *Religion et nation chez les albanais, XIXe-XXe siècles* (Istanbul: Isis, 2003), pp. 159-170.
Clayer, Nathalie. The Myth of Ali Pasha and the Bektashis. The Construction of an >Albanian Bektashi National History. in: Stephanie Schwander-Sievers & Bernd J. Fischer (ed.), *Albanian Identities. Myth and History* (London: C. Hurst, 2002),

pp. 127–133. Reprinted in: Nathalie Clayer, *Religion et nation chez les albanais, XIXe-XXe siècles* (Istanbul: Isis, 2003), pp. 151–158.

Clayer, Nathalie. *Religion et nation chez les Albanais: XIXe-XXe siècles* (Istanbul: Isis, 2003) 449 pp.

Clayer, Nathalie. *Le bektachisme en Albanie. Bektashizmi në Shqipëri* (Tirana: AlbPaper, 2004).

Clayer, Nathalie. Le bektachisme entre contruction nationale albanaise et vision européocentrée de l'islam. in: Josiane Boulad-Ayoub et Gian Mario Cazzaniga (ed.), *Traces de l'Autre. Mythes de l'antiquité et peoples du livre dans la construction des nations méditerranéennes* (Pisa & Paris: Edizioni ETS-J. Vrin, 2004), pp. 169–188.

Clayer, Nathalie. Saints and Sufis in Post-communist Albania. in: Kisaichi Masatoshi (ed.), *Popular Movements and Democratization in the Islamic World* (London and New York: Routledge, 2006), pp. 33–42.

Clayer, Nathalie. *Aux origines du nationalisme albanais. La naissance d=une nation majoritairement musulmane en Europe* (Paris: Karthala, 2007) 794 pp.

Clayer, Nathalie. Bektashizmi mes ndërtimit të kombit shqiptar dhe vizionit eurocentrist të Islamit. in: *Hylli i dritës*, Shkodër, 2007, 1, pp. 5–23.

Clayer, Nathalie. The Bektashi Institutions in Southeastern Europe: Alternative Muslim Official Structures and their Limits. in: *Die Welt des Islams*, 52 (2012), pp. 183–203.

Clayer, Nathalie. Autorité locale et autorité supra-locale chez les Bektashis d'Albanie dans l'entre-deux-guerres. in: Nathalie Clayer, Alexandre Papas et Benoît Fliche (ed.), *L'autorité religieuese et ses limites en terres d'islam: Approches historiques et anthropologiques* (Leiden and Boston: Brill, 2013), pp. 159–194.

Clayer, Nathalie. Sufi Printed Matter and Knowledge about the Bektashi Order in the Late Ottoman Period. in: Rachida Chih, Catherine Mayeur-Jaouen & Rüdiger Seesemann (ed.), *Sufism, Literary Production, and Printing in the Nineteenth Century* (Würzburg: Verlag, 2015), pp. 351–367.

Clayer, Nathalie & Bougarel, Xavier. *Les musulmans de l'Europe du Sud-Est. Des Empires aux États balkaniques* (Paris: Karthala & IISMM, 2013) 358 pp.

Clayer, Nathalie & Popović, Alexandre. Sur les traces des derviches de Macédoine yougoslave. in: Faruk Bilici, Nathalie Clayer, Jacques Thombie and Jean Louis Baque-Grammont (ed.), *Derviches des Balkans, disparitions et renaissances* (Paris: Maisonneuve, 1992), pp. 14–63.

Clayer, Nathalie & Popović, Alexandre. Les turuq dans les Balkans à l'époque ottoman. in: Ahmet Yasar Ocak (ed.), *Sufism and Sufis in Ottoman Society* (Ankara: Atatürk Kültür, 2005), pp. 257–278.

Cordignano, Fulvio. Condizioni religiose del popolo albanese. in: *Albania*, a cura dell'Istituto di Studi Adriatici, Venice, 1939, pp. 71–90.

Çuni, Nuri. *Tomor, o mal i bekuar* (Tirana: Urtësia, 1999) 58 pp.

Çuni, Nuri. *Tek Abaz Aliu* (Tirana: Urtësia bektashiane, 2014) 100 pp.

Çuni, Nuri & Qesja, Kastriot. *Kalendari 2014. 1435-1426 Hixhri* (Tirana: Kryegjyshata Botërore Bektashiane, 2014) 80 pp.

Daniel, Odile. La communauté musulmane dans le mouvement culturel albanais à la fin du XIXe siècle au début du XXe siècle. in: *Lettre d'information*, Paris, 1985, 4, La transmission du savoir dans le monde musulman périphérique, pp. 21–34.

Daniel, Odile. Historical Role of the Muslim Community in Albania. in: *Central Asian Survey*, London, 9, 3 (1990), pp. 1–28.

Daniel, Odile. Nationality and Religion in Albania. in: *Albanian Catholic Bulletin/Buletini Katolik Shqiptar*, San Francisco, 11 (1990), pp. 90–98.

Dankoff, Robert & Elsie, Robert. *Evliya Çelebi in Albania and Adjacent Regions (Kosovo, Montenegro, Ohrid). The Relevant Sections of the Seyahatname*. Edited with Translation, Commentary and Introduction by Robert Dankoff and Robert Elsie. Evliya Çelebi=s Book of Travels. Land and people of the Ottoman Empire in the seventeenth century. A corpus of partial editions, edited by Klaus Kreiser. Vol. 5 (Leiden, New York, Cologne: E. J. Brill, 2000) 307 pp.

Dauer, Alfons Michael. Filmdokumentationen zur Situation Islamischer Kulturen des Balkans, insbesondere des Derwischwesens, 1971-1975. Ein Erfahrungsbericht. in: *Münchner Zeitschrift für Balkankunde*, Munich, 1 (1978), pp. 81-110.

Dedej, Qazim. *Fillimet e Bektashizmit në Shqipëri dhe në Elbasan* (Elbasan: Egnatia, 1997) 120 pp.

Dedej, Qazim. *Historia e themelimit të institutit bektashian të Elbasanit, Gramshit e Martaneshit: Teqja Fakri e Xhefai Babajt, e thirrur prej popullit Teqja e Madhe* (Elbasan: Egnatia, 1997) 120 pp.

Degrand, Jules Alexandre Théodore. *Souvenirs de la Haute-Albanie* (Paris: Welter, 1901) 353 pp.

De Jong, Frederick. The *Takiya* of Abd Allah al-Maghawiri (Qayghusuz Sultan) in Cairo. A Historical Sketch and a Description of Arabic and Ottoman Turkish Materials Relative to the History of the Bektashi *Takiya* and Order Presented at Leiden University Library. in: *Turcica*, 13 (1981), pp. 242-260.

De Jong, Frederick. The Iconography of Bektashism. A Survey of Themes and Symbolism in Clerical Costumes, Liturgical Objects and Pictorial Art. in: *Manuscripts of the Middle East*, Leiden, 4 (1989).

De Jong, Frederick. Pictorial Art of the Bektashi Order. in: R. Lifchez (ed.), *The Dervish Lodge: Architecture, Art and Sufism in Ottoman Turkey* (Berkeley, Los Angeles, Oxford: University of California Press, 1992), pp. 228-241.

Dierl, Anton Josef. *Geschichte und Lehre des anatolischen Alevismus-Bektaşismus* (Frankfurt: Dagyeli, 1985) 289 pp.

Djersa. *E permuajshme morale kulturale e shoqnore. Organi i Komunitetit Bektashian Shqiptar* (Tirana: Shtypshkronja Luarasi, 1945-1946).

Djordjevic, Tihomir R. *Naš narodni život*. 10 vols. (Belgrade, 1930-1934), reprinted in 4 vols. (Belgrade: Prosveta, 1984).

Doja, Albert. Confraternal Religion: from Liberation Theology to Political Reverse. in: *History and Anthropology*, 14, 4 (2003), pp. 349-381.

Doja, Albert. A Political History of Bektashism in Albania. in: *Totalitarian Movements and Political Religions*, 7, 1 (2006), pp. 83-107.

Doja, Albert. Spiritual Surrender: from Companionship to Hierarchy in the History of Bektashism. in: *Numen: International Review for the History of Religions*, 53, 2 (2006), pp. 448-450.

Doja, Albert. *Bektashizmi në Shqipëri: Historia politike e një lëvizjeje fetare* (Tirana: Instituti Shqiptar për Studime Ndërkombëtare, 2008) 117 pp.

Doja, Albert. *Bektashism in Albania: History of a Religious Movement* (Tirana: Albanian Institute of International Studies, 2008) 104 pp.

Dosti, Victor & Shehu, Eugen (ed.). *Baba Rexhebi: ky shenjt* (Tirana: Lumo Skendo, 2001).

Duijzings, Gerlachus. *Religion and the Politics of Identity in Kosovo* (London: C. Hurst & Co., 2000) 238 pp.

Duijzings, Gerlachus. Religion and the Politics of Albanianism. Naim Frashëri=s Bektashi Writings. in: Stephanie Schwander-Sievers & Bernd J. Fischer (ed.), *Albanian Identities. Myth and History* (London: C. Hurst, 2002), pp. 60-69.

Durham, Mary Edith. *The Burden of the Balkans* (London: Edward Arnold, 1905) 331 pp.
Dylgjeri, Tahsin. *Dy trandafilat e bukur. Ngjarjet dëshpëruese të Qerbelas*. Përkëthye prej Tahsin Dylgjerit (Durrës: Stamles, 1939) 319 pp.
Edmonds, Paul. *To the Land of the Eagle: Travels in Montenegro and Albania* (London: George Routledge, 1927) 288 pp.
Elsie, Robert. *Dictionary of Albanian Literature* (New York & Westport, CT: Greenwood, 1986) 171 pp.
Elsie, Robert. Albanian Literature in the Moslem Tradition. Eighteenth and Early Nineteenth Century Albanian Writing in Arabic Script. in: *Oriens, Journal of the International Society for Oriental Research*, Leiden, 33 (1992), pp. 287–306.
Elsie, Robert. The Currents of Moslem and Bektashi Writing in Albania. in: *Albanian Catholic Bulletin/Buletini Katolik Shqiptar*, San Francisco, 15 (1994), pp. 172–177.
Elsie, Robert. *History of Albanian Literature*. East European Monographs 379. 2 vols. (Boulder: Social Science Monographs. Distributed by Columbia University Press, New York, 1995) xv + 1,054 pp.
Elsie, Robert. Islam and the Dervish Sects of Albania. An Introduction to their History, Development and Current Situation. in: *The Islamic Quarterly*, London, 42, 4 (1998), pp. 266–289.
Elsie, Robert. *A Dictionary of Albanian Religion, Mythology and Folk Culture* (London: Hurst & Company/New York: New York University Press, 2001) 357 pp.
Elsie, Robert. *Literatura shqipe në traditën islame. Gjuha shqipe me gërma arabe gjatë shekullit 18të dhe 19të*. Përshtatur në shqip nga Olsi. on: Dielli.net, Kuala Lumpur, 2001.
Elsie, Robert. *Handbuch zur albanischen Volkskultur. Mythologie, Religion, Volksglaube, Sitten, Gebräuche und kulturelle Besonderheiten*. Balkanologische Veröffentlichungen, Bd. 36. Fachbereich Philosophie und Geisteswissenschaften der Freien Universität Berlin (Wiesbaden: Harrassowitz, 2002, Reprint: London: Centre for Albanian Studies, 2015) xi + 308 pp.
Elsie, Robert. Der Islam und die Derwisch-Sekten Albaniens: Anmerkungen zu ihrer Geschichte, Verbreitung und zur derzeitigen Lage. on: *Kakanien Revisited*, Vienna, 27 May 2004, pp. 1–11.
Elsie, Robert. *Albanian Literature: a Short History* (London: I.B. Tauris in association with the Centre for Albanian Studies/New York: Palgrave Macmillan, 2005) vi + 291 pp.
Elsie, Robert. *Leksiku i kulturës popullore shqiptare: besime, mitologji, fe, doke, rite, festa dhe veçori kulturore*. Përktheu nga anglishtja Abdurrahim Myftiu (Tirana: Skanderbeg Books, 2005), 282 pp.
Elsie, Robert. *Evlija Çelebiu në Shqipëri dhe në viset fqinje: Kosovë, Mali i Zi, Ohër. Në bazë të dorëshkrimit autograf*. Përgatitur nga Robert Elsie. Përkthyer nga Abdurrahim Myftiu (Tirana: Shtëpia Botuese 55, 2008) 213 pp.
Elsie, Robert. *Historical Dictionary of Albania*. Second Edition. Historical Dictionaries of Europe, No. 75 (Lanham, Toronto and Plymouth: Scarecrow Press, 2010) lxxiii + 587 pp.
Elsie, Robert. Die Derwisch-Sekte der albanischen Bektaschi, Anmerkungen zu ihrer Geschichte, Verbreitung und zur derzeitigen Lage. in: Albert Ramaj (ed.), *Poeta nascitur, historicus fit: ad honorem Zef Mirdita* (St. Gallen & Zagreb: Albanisches Institut & Hrvatski Institut za Povijest, 2013), pp. 589–608.
Evans, Arthur. Mycenaean Tree and Pillar Cult and its Mediterranean Relations. in: *Journal of Hellenic Studies*, 21 (1901), pp. 99–204.
Faensen, Johannes. *Die albanische Nationalbewegung*. Osteuropa-Institut an der Freien Universität Berlin. Balkanologische Veröffentlichungen 4 (Wiesbaden: in Komm. Harrassowitz, 1980) 195 pp.

Faroqhi, Suraiya. *Der Bektaschi-Orden in Anatolien (vom späten fünfzehnten Jahrhundert bis 1826)*. *Wiener Zeitschrift für die Kunde des Morgenlandes*. Sonderband II (Vienna: Institut für Orientalistik der Universität Wien, 1981) 171 pp.
Filipović, Milenko S. Zanimljivi kultni predmeti i običaji u selu Tekiji u srezu žegligovačkom. in: *Južni Pregled*, Skopje, 1932.
Filipović, Milenko S. The Bektashis in the District of Strumica (Macedonia). in: *Man, A Monthly Record of Anthropological Science*, London, 54 (1954), pp. 10-13.
Frashëri, Alfred & Frashëri, Neki. *Frashëri në historinë e Shqipërisë* (Tirana: SHBLSH e re, 2014) 464 pp.
Frashëri, Mid'hat bey (= SKENDO, Lumo). Gjashtë javë në Shqipëri. in: *Lirija*, Salonica, No. 78 (6 March 1910), p. 3; No. 79 (13 March 1910), p. 3; No. 80 (20 March 1910), p. 3.
Frashëri, Mid'hat bey (= SKENDO, Lumo) *L'Affaire de l'Epire: le martyre d'un peuple* (Sofia: L'Indépendance Albanaise, 1915) 48 pp.
Frashëri, Naim Bey. *Fletore e Bektashinjet* (Bucharest: Shtypëshkronjët të Shqipëtarëvet, 1896, Reprint: Salonica: Mbrothësia, 1909) 32 pp.
Frashëri, Naim Bey. Le Livre des Bektachis. Traduit de l=albanais. in: *Albania*, Brussels, 10 (1897), pp. 174-176.
Frashëri, Naim Bey. *Qerbelaja* prej N.H.F. (Bucharest: Diturija, 1898) 352 pp.
Frashëri, Naim Bey. Notizie sui Bektasci. Il libro del Bektasci. Traduzione dell=albanese. in: *La Nazione albanese*, Rome, 8 (30 April 1908), pp. 5-7.
Frashëri, Naim Bey. Le Livre des Bektaschi de Naim Bey Frasheri. Traduit de l'albanais par Henri Bourgeois. in: *Revue du monde musulman*, Paris, 49 (1922), pp. 105-120.
Frashëri, Naim Bey. Die Bektaschis von Naim be Frashëri. Herausgegeben und übersetzt von Norbert Jokl. in: *Balkanarchiv*, Leipzig, 2 (1926), pp. 226-256.
Frashëri, Naim Bey. Bektashi Pages. in: Frederick William Hasluck (ed.), *Christianity and Islam under the Sultans*. Edited by Margaret Hasluck. Vol. 2 (Oxford: Clarendon, 1929), pp. 444-453.
Frashëri, Naim Bey. *The Bektashi Pages*. Edited by Muhammad Abdullah Al-Ahari (Chicago: Magribine Press, 1996) [unreliable translation].
Fuzuli. *Hadikai Suada, Lulishte e Shenjtorëve*, botuar nga Selim Kaliçani (Fushë Krujë, 1997) 368 pp.
Fuzuli. *Hadikaja ose kopshti i të përsosurvet*. Botim i parë. Përkthyer nga Baba Rexhebi (Gjakova: Teqja Bektashiane, 1997) 497 pp.
Gadžanov, D. Mohamedani pravoslavni i mohamedani sektanti v Makedonija. in: *Makedonski pregled*, Sofia, 1, 4 (1925), pp. 5-66.
Gawrych, George Walter. *Ottoman Administration and the Albanians, 1908-1913*. A dissertation submitted in partial fulfillment of the requirements for the degree of doctor of philosophy (history) in the University of Michigan, 1980 (Arbor & London: University Microfilms International, 1985) 816 pp.
Gawrych, George Walter. *The Crescent and the Eagle: Ottoman Rule, Islam and the Albanians, 1874 to 1913* (London: I.B. Tauris, 2006) 272 pp.
Giannopoulos, Nikolaos [= ΓΙΑΝΝΟΠΟΥΛΟΣ, Νικόλαος]. Megali Vizantini Moni en to tourkiko teke ton mbektasion. in: *Epetiris Etaireias Vizartinon Spoudon*, tomos 14 (1938).
Gjinaj, Maksim, Bezhani, Petrit, & Çuni, Nuri (ed.), *Bektashizmi në Shqipëri. Bibliografi* (Tirana: AlbPaper, 2004) 638 pp.
Gjipali, Ilir, Përzhita, Luan & Muka, Belisa. *Recent Archaeological Discoveries in Albania* (Tirana: Botimet Albanologjike, 2013) 284 pp.

Godart, Justin. *L'Albanie en 1921*. Préface de d'Estournelles de Constant (Paris: PUF, 1922) 374 pp.
Goodwin, Godfrey. *The Janissaries* (London: Saqi Books, 1999) 288 pp.
Grameno, Mihal. *Kryengritja shqiptare* (Vlora: G. Direttore, 1925), reprinted in Mihal Grameno, *Vepra*. Vol. 2 (Prishtina: Rilindja, 1979).
Graves, Robert Wyndham. *Storm Centres of the Near East. Personal Memories 1879-1929* (London: Hutchinson, 1933) 375 pp.
Guidetti, Vittoria Luisa. A colloquio con l'Islam albanese. Il Bektashismo. Vittoria L. Guidetti, Bajram Baba, Reshat Baba. in: *Religioni e società*, 12, 27 (1997), pp. 111-118.
Guidetti, Vittoria Luisa. Elementi dualistici e gnostici della religione bektashi in Albania fra il XVII e il XIX secolo. in: *Destino e salvezza tra culti pagani e gnosi cristiana*. A cura di Giulia Sfameni Gasparro. Collana di studi storico-religiosi, 2 (Cosenza: Lionello Giordano Editore, 1998), pp. 239-264.
Guidetti, Vittoria Luisa. *L=Islam vicino. I Bektashi*. Prefazione di Giulia Sfameni Gasparro (Cosenza: Edizioni Lionello Giordano, 2002) 187 pp.
Haas, Abdülkadir. *Die Bektaşi. Riten und Mysterien eines islamischen Ordens* (Berlin: Express Edition, 1987) 183 pp.
Haas, Abdülkadir. Arnavutluk'ta Bektaşilik. in: *Cem*, Istanbul, 12 May 1992, pp. 53-57.
Haas, Abdülkadir. Le développement du bektachisme en Yougoslavie. in: A. Popovic & G. Veinstein (ed.), *Bektachiyya, études sur l'ordre mystique des Bektachis et les groupes relevant de Hadji Bektach*. Revue des Etudes Islamiques 60 (1992). Numéro spécial (Paris: Paul Geuthner, 1993/Istanbul: Isis, 1995), pp. 327-338.
Hafiz, Nimetullah. Yugoslavya'da Bektaşi tekkeleri. in: *Çevren*, Prishtina, IV, 11 (1976), pp. 57-67; and in: *Haci Bektaş Veli, bildiriler, denemeler, açikoturum*, Ankara, 1977.
Hafiz, Nimetullah. Le développement du bektachisme en Yougoslavie. in: A. Popovic & G. Veinstein (ed.), *Bektachiyya, études sur l=ordre mystique des Bektachis et les groupes relevant de Hadji Bektach*. Revue des Etudes Islamiques 60 (1992). Numéro spécial (Paris: Paul Geuthner, 1993/Istanbul: Isis, 1995), pp. 327-338.
Hahn, Johann Georg von. *Albanesische Studien*. 3 vols. (Jena: Fr. Mauke, 1854, Reprint Athens: Karavias, 1981) 347, 169, 244 pp.
Hahn, Johann Georg von. *Reise durch die Gebiete des Drin und Wardar*. Im Auftrage der kaiserlichen Akademie der Wissenschaften unternommen im Jahre 1863. Denkschriften der Kaiserlichen Akademie der Wissenschaften in Wien. Phil-hist. Cl., Vienna, 15 (1867), pp. 1-188; 16 (1869), pp. 1-177.
Hahn, Johann Georg von. *The Discovery of Albania: Travel Writing and Anthropology in the Nineteenth-Century Balkans*. Translated and introduced by Robert Elsie (London: I.B. Tauris, 2015) 214 pp.
Halimi, Kadri. Derviški redovi i njihova kultna mjesta na Kosovu i Metohiji. in: *Glasnik Muzeja Kosova i Metohije*, Prishtina, 2 (1957), pp. 193-206.
Halimi, Kadri. *Trajtime dhe studime etnologjike* (Prishtina: Instituti Albanologjik, 2000) 323 pp.
Hasluck, Frederick William. Studies in Turkish History and Folk-Legend. The Story of Sari Saltik. in: *Annals of the British School in Athens*, Athens, 19 (1912-1913), pp. 203-208.
Hasluck, Frederick William. Ambiguous Sanctuaries and Bektashi Propaganda. in: *Annals of the British School in Athens*, Athens, 20 (1913), pp. 94-122.
Hasluck, Frederick William. Geographical Distribution of the Bektashi. in: *Annals of the British School in Athens*, Athens, 21 (1914-1916), pp. 84-124.
Hasluck, Frederick William. The Fourth Religion of Albania. in: *The New Europe*, London, 13 (6 November 1919), pp. 106-107.

Hasluck, Frederick William. *Christianity and Islam under the Sultans*. Edited by Margaret Hasluck. 2 vols. (Oxford: Clarendon, 1929, Reprint Istanbul: Isis Press, 2000) 770 pp. [Note that page numbers given in the text and footnotes refer to the 2000 edition, with the page numbers of the original edition of 1929 added in parentheses.]

Hasluck, Margaret Masson Hardie. The Nonconformist Moslems of Albania. in: *Contemporary Review*, London, 127 (1925), pp. 599–606. Reprinted in: *Moslem World* 15 (1925), pp. 388–398.

Hasluck, Margaret Masson Hardie. Një kult i malit në Shqipnin e jugës. in: *Shkolla kombëtare*, No. 23 (1939), pp. 39–43.

Hasluck, Margaret Masson Hardie. Kulti i malit të Tomorrit. in: *Bota Shqiptare*, Tirana (1943), pp. 82–84.

Hasluck, Margaret Masson Hardie. *The Unwritten Law in Albania*. Edited by J. H. Hutton (New York: Cambridge University Press, 1954), xv + 285 pp.

Hysi, Shyqyri. Bektashizmi dhe disa personalitete bektashiane në Gjyshatën e Gjirokastrës. in: *Gjurmime albanologjike, Seria e shkencave historike*, Prishtina, 31–32 (2001–2002), pp. 261–294.

Hysi, Shyqyri. Ngjarjet e marsit të vitit 1947 në Kryegjyshatën Botërore Bektashiane. in: *Studime historike*, Tirana, 3–4 (2003), pp. 131–142.

Hysi, Shyqyri. *Mision Bektashian. Teqeja e Zallit. Monografi* (Tirana: AlbPaper, 2004) 234 pp.

Hysi, Shyqyri. *Historia e komuniteteve fetare shqiptare* (Tirana: Universi E. Çabej, 2006) 256 pp.

Hysi, Shyqyri. *Muslimanizmi në Shqipëri në periudhën 1945–1950* (Tirana: Mësonjëtorja, 2006) 236 pp.

Ibrahimi, Nexhat. *Kontaktet e para të Islamit me popujt ballkanike në periudhën paraosmane* (Skopje: Logos-A, 1997) 100 pp.

Ibrahimi, Nexhat. *Islam në trojet iliro-shqiptare gjatë shekujve* (Skopje: Logos-A, 1998) 298 pp.

Inalcik, Halil. Arnawutluk. in: H.A.R. Gibb et al. (ed.), *Encyclopedia of Islam* (London: Luzac, 1960). Vol. 1, pp. 650–658.

Insabato, Enrico. Gli Albanesi musulmani e le loro congregazioni. in: *Bolletino della R. Società Geografica*, Rome, 3 (1916), pp. 238–239.

Ippen, Theodor A. Von Alessio über Kroja nach Tirana und Ismi. in *Zur Kunde der Balkanhalbinsel*. Herausgegeben von Carl Patsch (Vienna & Leipzig: A. Hartleben, 1904).

Ippen, Theodor A. *Skutari und die nordalbanische Küstenebene*. Zur Kunde der Balkanhalbinsel. Reisen und Beobachtungen 5 (Sarajevo: Daniel A. Kajon, 1907) 83 pp.

Ippen, Theodor A. *Die Gebirge des nordwestlichen Albaniens*. Abhandlungen der k.k. Geographischen Gesellschaft in Wien, 7 Heft 1 (Vienna, 1908) 75 pp.

Izeti, Metin. Tarikati bektashi dhe reflektimi i tij në viset tona. in: *Studime orientale, revistë shkencore*, Prishtina 1 (2001), pp. 57–86.

Izeti, Metin. *Tarikati bektashian* (Tetovo: s.e., 2001) 184 pp.

Jacob, Georg. *Beiträge zur Kenntnis des Derwischordens der Bektaschi*. Türkische Bibliothek Bd. 9 (Berlin: Mayer & Müller, 1908) 50 pp.

Jacob, Georg. Die Bektaschijje in ihrem Verhältnis zu verwandten Erscheinungen. in: *Abhandlungen der K. Bayer. Akademie der Wissenschaften*, Munich 1909, I. Kl. XXIV. Bd. III. Abt.

Jacques, Edwin E. Islam in Albania. in: *Moslem World*, 28 (1938), pp. 313–314.

Jacques, Edwin E. *The Albanians: An Ethnic History from Prehistoric Times to the Present* (Jefferson, NC: McFarland & Co., 1995) 768 pp.

Jokl, Norbert. Die Bektaschis von Naim Frashëri. Herausgegeben und übersetzt. in: *Balkanarchiv*, Leipzig, 2 (1926), pp. 226-256.

Kaleshi, Hasan. Arnavut söylentilerinde Sarì Saltuk. in: *Sesler*, Skopje, III, 13 February 1967, pp. 43-60.

Kaleshi, Hasan. Legjendat shqiptare për Sarì Salltikun. in: *Përparimi*, Prishtina, 1, 1967, pp. 86-103.

Kaleshi, Hasan. Albanische Legenden um Sari Saltuk. in: *Actes du Premier Congrès International des Etudes Balkaniques et Sud-Est Européennes*, Sofia, 26 août - 1 septembre 1966 (Sofia: Académie Bulgare des Sciences, 1969), 7, pp. 815-828.

Kaleshi, Hasan. Das türkische Vordringen auf dem Balkan und die Islamisierung. Faktoren für die Erhaltung der ethnischen und nationalen Existenz des albanischen Volkes. in: Peter Bartl & Horst Glassl (ed.), *Südosteuropa unter dem Halbmond. Prof. Georg Stadtmüller zum 65. Geburtstag gewidmet* (Munich, 1975), pp. 125-138.

Kaleshi, Hasan. Die Bektashiye unter den Albanern. in: Baba Kâzim, Oberhaupt der Bektâshî-Derwische in Djakovica. *Publikationen zu Wissenschaftlichen Filmen. Sektion Ethnologie*. Göttingen, 1980, Serie 10, Nr. 49, pp. 9-15.

Kaleshi, Hasan. *Kontributi i shqiptarëve në diturië islame* (Prizren, 1991. Reprint: Riyadh: International Islamic Publ., 1992) 112 pp.

Kaleshi, Hasan & Kissling, Hans Joachim. Islam, Jugoslawien, Kosovo. Baba Kâzim, Oberhaupt der Bektâshî-Derwische in Djakovica. in: *Publikationen zu Wissenschaftlichen Filmen. Sektion Ethnologie*. Göttingen, 1980, Serie 10, Nr. 49, Film E 1970.

Kaleshi, Hasan & Kissling, Hans Joachim. Islam, Jugoslawien, Kosovo. Besuch im Tekye der Chalvetî-Derwische in Prizren. in: *Publikationen zu Wissenschaftlichen Filmen. Sektion Ethnologie* (Göttingen, 1980), Serie 10, Nr. 46, Film E 1967.

Kaliçani, Selim Rexhep. *Histori e baballarëve të Teqesë së Martaneshit* (Tirana: s.e., 1997) 222 pp.

Kaliçani, Selim Rexhep. *Historia e bektashizmit si sekt mistik islam* (Tirana: Koha, 1999) 320 pp.

Kaliçani, Selim Rexhep. *Dede Ahmeti i gjallë mes nesh* (Fushë Krujë: s.e., 2000) 152 pp.

Kaliçani, Selim Rexhep. *Testamenti bektashian* (Fushë Krujë: s.e., 2000) 123 pp.

Kallajxhi, Xhevat. *Bektashizmi dhe teqeja shqiptare n'Amerikë*. Parathënie e Hirësisë së Tij Baba Rexhebit. E boton Teqeja me rastin e 10-vjetorit të themelimit të saj (Detroit: s.e., 1964) 75 pp.

Kallajxhi, Xhevat. *Tingëllimet e zemrës. Vjersha* (Augusta, GA: s.e., 1988) 60 pp.

Karkavitsas, Andreas [= ΚΑΡΚΑΒΊΤΣΑΣ, Ανδρέας]. *O tekes ton mbektasidon*, Apanta Karkavitsa (Athens, 1973).

Kiel, Machiel. Güney Romanya'da Sarı Saltık'in Çalışmaları ve Doğu Bulgaristan'da Erken Bektaşilik Üzerine Tarihsel Önem Taşıyan Notlar. in: *Hacı Bektaş Veli, Bildiriler, Denemeler, Açıkoturum* (Ankara, 1977), pp. 13-29.

Kiel, Machiel. Aspects of Ottoman-Turkish Architecture in Albania. in: *Fifth International Congress of Turkish Art* (Budapest, 1978), pp. 541-548.

Kiel, Machiel. *Ottoman Architecture in Albania, 1385-1912* (Istanbul: Research Centre for Islamic History, Art and Culture, 1990) 342 pp.

Kiel, Machiel. A Note on the Date of the Establishment of the Bektashi Order in Albania: the Cult of Sarı Saltık Dede in Kruja Attested in 1567-1568. in: A. Popovic & G. Veinstein (ed.), *Bektachiyya, études sur l'ordre mystique des Bektachis et les groupes relevant de Hadji Bektach. Revue des Etudes Islamiques* 60 (1992). Numéro spécial (Paris: Paul Geuthner, 1993/Istanbul: Isis, 1995), pp. 263-270.

Kiel, Machiel. The Bektashi Tekke of Durbali Sultan in Central Greece. in: Yaşar Ocak (ed.), *Sufism and Sufis in Ottoman Society, Sources, Doctrines, Rituals, Turuq. Architecture, Literature and Fine Arts* (Ankara: Atatürk Supreme Council for Culture, Language and History, 2005), pp. 421-442.

Kiel, Machiel. Durbali Sultan Resurrected? Some Remarks on Recent Developments around the Bektashi Tekke of Durbali Sultan near Pharsala-Thessaly. in: *Türk Kültürü ve Hacı Bektaş Veli Araştırma Dergisi*, 52 (2009), pp. 53-58, and at: http://hbvdergisi.gazi.edu.tr/index.php/TKHBVD/article/viewFile/1110/1099

Kissling, Hans-Joachim. Zur Geschichte des Derwischordens der Bektashi. in: *Südost-Forschungen*, Munich, 15 (1956), pp. 237-268.

Kissling, Hans-Joachim. Zur Frage der Anfänge des Bektašitums in Albanien. in: *Oriens, Journal of the International Society for Oriental Research*, Leiden, 15 (1962), pp. 281-286.

Kissling, Hans-Joachim. Über die Anfänge des Bektaschitums in Albanien. in: Günther Reichenkron & Alois Schmaus (ed.), *Die Kultur Südosteuropas: ihre Geschichte und ihre Ausdrucksformen. Vorträge der Balkanologen-Tagung, 7.-10.11.1962 in München.* Südosteuropa-Schriften 6 (Wiesbaden: Harrassowitz, 1964).

Kissling, Hans-Joachim. Aus dem Derwischwesen Südosteuropas. in: *Grazer und Münchener Balkanologische Studien*. Beiträge zur Kenntnis Südosteuropas und des Nahen Orients 2, (Munich: Trofenik, 1967), pp. 56-70.

Koliqi, Ernest. Teqja shqiptare e Misirit u mbyll. in: *Shêjzat*, Rome, No. 2-3 (September-October 1957), pp. 91-92.

Kollegger, Willibald. *Albaniens Wiedergeburt* (Vienna: Wiener Verlagsgesellschaft, 1942) 148 pp.

Konitza, Faik. Notice sur la metaphysique des Bektachis. Shënim për metafizikën e bektashinjve. in: *Albania*, Brussels, 8 (1897), pp. 142-143.

Konitza, Faik. Notice sur les Bektachis. Shënim mbi bektashinjtë. in: *Albania*, Brussels, 7 (1897), p. 111.

Kordha, Hysen. Bektashizmi në Shqipëri. in: *Perla, revistë shkencore-kulturore*, Tirana, no. 1-4 (2001), pp. 97-104.

Krasniqi, Mark. *Aspekte mitologjike, Besime e bestytni. Mythological Aspects, Beliefs and Superstitions* (Prishtina: Rilindja, 1997) 393 pp.

Kressing, Frank. The Specific Situation of Religion in Albania and the Albanian Bektashis, an Example for Crossing Religious and Political Boundaries. in: Papers read at the 6th EASA conference, Kraków, July 26-29, 2000. Crossing categorical boundaries: religion as politics, politics as religion.

Kressing, Frank. A Preliminary Account of Research regarding the Albanian Bektashis, Myths and Unsolved questions. in: Frank Kressing & Karl Kaser (ed.), *Albania, a Country in Transition. Aspects of Changing Identities in a South-east European Country*. Ulmer Kulturanthroplogische Schriften, Band 11 (Ulm: Nomos, 2002), pp. 97-146.

Kriss, Rudolf & Kriss-Heinrich, Hubert. *Volksglaube im Bereich des Islam*, 2 vols. (Wiesbaden: Harrassowitz, 1960, 1962) 259 & 245 pp.

Küçük, Hülya. *The Role of the Bektashi in Turkey's National Struggle* (Leiden: Brill Academic Publishers, 2002) x + 289 pp.

Kushi, Enver, Hoxha, Sotirulla, and Çuni, Nuri (ed.), *Dede Ahmeti* [Album] (Tirana: Kryegjyshata Botërore Bektashiane, 2016) ca. 140 pp.

Kushi, Enver, Hoxha, Sotirulla, and Çuni, Nuri (ed.), *Udhëtimi i shpirtit bektashian* [Album] (Tirana: Kryegjyshata Botërore Bektashiane, 2016) ca. 170 pp.

Lakshman-Lepain, Rajwantee. The Bektashis, the Halvetis and the Baba'is. in: *Human Rights without Frontiers, European Magazine of Human Rights*, 2-3 (1996), pp. 19-20.

Leake, William Martin. *Travels in Northern Greece*. By William Martin Leake, late lieutenant- colonel of the Royal Artillery, Hon. D.C.L. in the University of Oxford, F.R.S., one of the vice- presidents of the Royal Society of Literature, and of the Royal Geographical Society, member of the Royal Academy of Sciences in Berlin, and corresponding member of the Royal Institute of Paris. 4 vols. (London: J. Rodwell, 1835, Reprint Amsterdam: Adolf M. Hakkert, 1967) 527, 643, 578, 588 pp.

Lederer, Gyorgy. Islam in Albania. in: *Central Asian Survey*, London, 13, 3 (1994), pp. 331-359.

Leroy, Jules. *Monks and Monasteries of the Near East*. Translated by Peter Collin (London: George G. Harrap, 1963) 208 pp.

Louis-Jaray, Gabriel. *L'Albanie inconnue*. Ouvrage illustré de 60 gravures tirées hors texte et d=une carte en noir. Préface de M. G. Hanotaux (Paris: Librairie Hachette, 1913) 239 pp.

Louis-Jaray, Gabriel. *Au jeune royaume d'Albanie. Ce qu'il a été, ce qu'il est* (Paris: Librairie Hachette, 1914) 251 pp.

Luxner, Larry. Albania's Islamic Rebirth. in: *Aramco World*, 43, 4 (July-August 1992), pp. 38-47.

Malcolm, Noel. *Kosovo, a Short History* (London: Macmillan, 1998) 491 pp.

Malcolm, Noel. Crypto-Christianity and Religious Amphibianism in the Ottoman Balkans: the Case of Kosovo. in: Celia Hawkesworth, Muriel Heppel & Harry T. Norris (ed.), *Religious Quest and National Identity in the Balkans*. School of Slavonic and East European Studies, University College London (New York: Palgrave, 2001), pp. 91-109.

Markgraf, Friedrich. *In Albaniens Bergen* (Stuttgart: Strecker & Schröder, 1930) 244 pp.

Massani, Giuseppe. *Albania*. Testo e foto di Giuseppe Massani (Rome: Il Rubicone, 1940) 196 pp.

Mašulović-Marsol, Liliana. Les Bektachis dans la République de Macédoine. Notes et matériaux d'une enquête sur le terrain (1986-1987). in: A. Popovic & G. Veinstein (ed.), *Bektachiyya, études sur l'ordre mystique des Bektachis et les groupes relevant de Hadji Bektach. Revue des Etudes Islamiques* 60 (1992). Numéro spécial (Paris: Paul Geuthner, 1993/Istanbul: Isis, 1995), pp. 351-379.

Mélikoff, Irène. Un ordre de derviches colonisateurs: les Bektachis, leur rôle social et leur rapports avec les premiers sultans ottomans. in: *Mémorial Ömer Lûtfi Barkan* (Paris, 1980), pp. 149-157.

Mélikoff, Irène. L'Ordre des Bektaşi après 1826. in: *Turcica*, XV (1983), pp. 155-178.

Mélikoff, Irène. Hasluck's Study of the Bektashis and its Contemporary Significance. in: David Shankland (ed.), *Archaeology, Anthropology and Heritage in the Balkans and Anatolia. The Life and Times of F. W. Hasluck, 1878-1920* (Istanbul: Isis Press, 2004), vol. 1, pp. 297-308.

Migeon, Gaston. *Le Caire, le Nil et Memphis* (Paris: H. Laurens, 1906) 160 pp.

Morozzo Della Rocca, Roberto. *Nazione e religione in Albania, 1920-1944* (Bologna: Il Mulino, 1990) 253 pp.

Mousset, Albert. *L'Albanie devant l'Europe 1912-1929*. Ouvrage couronné par l'Académie des Sciences morales et politiques en 1931 (Paris: Delagrave, 1930) 128 pp.

Mufaku, Muhamed. Al-Baktashiyya. in: *al-=Arabi*, 220 (1977), pp. 64-68.

Myderrizi, Osman. Letërsia fetare e Bektashive. in: *Buletin për shkencat shoqërore*, Tirana, 3 (1955), pp. 131-142.

Myderrizi, Osman. Letërsia shqipe me alfabetin arab. in: *Buletin për Shkencat Shoqërore*, Tirana, 2 (1955), pp. 148-155.

Myderrizi, Osman. Një dorëshkrim shqip i panjohur i Gjirokastrës. in: *Buletin i Universitetit Shtetëror të Tiranës, Seria Shkencat Shoqërore*, Tirana, 1 (1957), pp. 177-200.
Naval Intelligence Division. *Albania*. Geographical Handbook Series. B.R. 542 (Restricted). For official use only. August 1945 (Oxford: University of Oxford Press, 1945) xiii + 416 pp.
Nollas, Kamilo. A Balkan Tale. A Cross Media Project by the Goethe Institut Athen and Anemon Productions, 2012. at: https://www.behance.net/gallery/3139694/A-Balkan-Tale.2012
Norris, Harry Thirlwall. *Islam in the Balkans. Religion and Society between Europe and the Arab World* (London: Hurst & Co., 1993) 304 pp.
Norris, Harry Thirlwall. Bektaşi Life on the Border between Albania and Greece. in: David Shankland (ed.), *Archaeology, Anthropology and Heritage in the Balkans and Anatolia. The Life and Times of F. W. Hasluck, 1878-1920* (Istanbul: Isis Press, 2004), vol. 1, pp. 309-328.
Norton, John. The Bektashi in the Balkans. in: Celia Hawkesworth, Muriel Heppel & Harry T. Norris (ed.), *Religious Quest and National Identity in the Balkans*. School of Slavonic and East European Studies, University College London (New York: Palgrave, 2001), pp. 168-200.
Nosi, Lef. *Dokumenta historike për t'i shërbye historiës tone kombëtare*. Botim i dytë (Tirana: Instituti i Historisë, 2007) 351 pp.
Noula-Karpeti, Vasso. *Albanian Dervish Monastery in Asprogeia Farsala - Tekke (den) Ntourbali Sultan*. at: http://www.farsala.gr/en/culture/landmarks-monuments/item/81-albanian-dervish-monastery-in-asprogeia-farsalon-teke-den-ntourbali-sultan
Noyan, Bedri. *Bektaşilik, Alevilik: Nedir?* (Ankara: Doğuş, 1985) 373 pp.
Noyan, Bedri. *Bütün yönleriyle Bektaşilik ve Alevilik*, 9 vols. (Ankara: Ardıç, 2011).
Onuzi, Afërdita. Bektashizmi dhje përhapja e tij në Shqipëri. in: *Kultura popullore*, Tirana, 1-2 (1993), pp. 83-88.
Osmani, Edlira. God in the Eagle's Country: The Bektashi Order. in: *Quaderns de la Mediterrània*, 17 (2012), pp. 107-116.
Oy, Aydin. Kalkandelen'de Harabati Baba Tekkesi. in: *Çevren*, Prishtina, VII, 4 (1980), pp. 23-24.
Palikruševa, Galaba & Tomovski, Krum. Les Tekkés en Macédoine aux XVIIIe et XIXe siècles. in: *Atti del Secondo Congresso Internazionale de Arte Turca*, Naples, 1965, pp. 203-211.
Patsch, Carl. *Der Sandschak Berat in Albanien*. Schriften der Balkankommission. Antiquarische Abteilung III (Vienna: A. Hölder, 1904, reprint 1976) 200 pp.
Pepo, Petraq. *Kujtime nga lëvizja për çlirimin kombëtar (1878-1912)* (Tirana: Universiteti Shtetëtor i Tiranës, 1962) 517 pp.
Popovic, Alexandre. Les musulmans du sud-est européen dans la période post-ottomane. Problèmes d'approche. in: *Journal asiatique*, Paris, 263 (1975), pp. 317-360.
Popovic, Alexandre. *L'Islam balkanique. Les musulmans du sud-est européen dans la période post-ottomane*. Balkanologische Veröffentlichungen Nr 11 (Wiesbaden, Berlin: in Kommission Harrassowitz, 1986) 478 pp.
Popovic, Alexandre. Les ordres mystiques musulmans du Sud-Est européen dans la période post-ottomane. in: A. Popovic & G. Veinstein (ed.), *Les ordres mystiques dans L'Islam. Cheminements et situation actuelle* (Paris: Editions de l'Ecole des Hautes Etudes en Sciences Sociales, 1986), pp. 63-99.

Popovic, Alexandre. A propos des statuts des Bektachis d'Albanie. in: A. Popovic & G. Veinstein (ed.), *Bektachiyya, études sur l'ordre mystique des Bektachis et les groupes relevant de Hadji Bektach. Revue des Etudes Islamiques 60 (1992). Numéro spécial* (Paris: Paul Geuthner, 1993/Istanbul: Isis, 1995), pp. 301-326.

Popovic, Alexandre. *Les derviches balkaniques hier et aujourd'hui* (Istanbul: Isis, 1994) xi + 372 pp.

Popovic, Alexandre & Daniel, Odile. Les statuts de la communauté musulmane albanaise (Sunnites et Bektachis) de 1945. in: *Journal Asiatique*, 265, 3-4 (1977), pp. 273-306.

Popovic, Alexandre & Veinstein, Gilles (ed.). *Les ordres mystiques dans L'Islam. Cheminements et situation actuelle* (Paris: Editions de l'Ecole des Hautes Etudes en Sciences Sociales, 1986) 324 pp.

Popovic, Alexandre & Veinstein, Gilles (ed.). *Bektachiyya. Etudes sur l'ordre mystique des Bektachis et les groupes relevant de Hadji Bektach. Revue des Etudes Islamiques*, 60 (1992). Numéro spécial (Paris: Paul Geuthner, 1993/Istanbul: Isis, 1995) xii + 598 pp.

Popovic, Alexandre & Veinstein, Gilles (ed.). *Les voies d'Allah. Les ordres mystiques dans l'Islam des origines à aujourd'hui.* Sous la direction de Alexandre Popovic (Paris: Fayard, 1996) 711 pp.

Prishta, Varf Ali. *Bektashinjt e Shqipërisë* (Korça: Korça, 1921) 40 pp.

Putra, Sh. M. Islam in Albania. in: *Light*, Lahore, 5 (1935), pp. 1-2.

Raçi, Fatime. *Jeta dhe aktiviteti i Sheh Ahmet Shkodrës* (Tirana, 1994).

Ramsaur, Ernest. The Bektashi Dervishes and the Young Turks. in: *The Moslem World*, 1942, pp. 7-14.

Reforma, Gjirokastër. Fortnightly religious, political and literary periodical of the clergy of the Bektash order. 2-4 pp. Issued from 27 October 1921 to 1923. Leiter und Editor: Varf Ali Prishta.

Rémérand, Gabriel. *Ali de Tébélen, pacha de Janina (1744-1822)* (Paris: Paul Geuthner, 1928) 290 pp.

Rexhebi, Baba. *Misticizma Islame dhe Bektashizma* (New York: Waldon Press, 1970) 389 pp.

Rexhebi, Baba. *The Mysticism of Islam and Bektashism* (Naples: Dragotti, 1984) 173 pp.

Rexhebi, Baba. *Islamic Mysticism and the Bektashi Path* (Lulu.com) 502 pp.

Rexhebi, Baba. *The Mysticism of Islam and Bektashism.* Introduction by Peter R. Prifti. English translation from Albanian with a glossary and bibliography by Bardhyl Pogoni (Tirana: Urtësia bektashiane, 2015) 154 pp.

Rexhepagiqi, Jashar. *Dervishët dhe teqetë në Kosovë, në Sanxhak dhe në rajonet tjera përreth.* Përktheu nga boshnjakishtja Shefqet Riza (Peja: Dukagjini, 2003) 302 pp.

Riedl, Richard. Die tanzenden Derwische von Tirana. in: *Österreichische Rundschau*, Vienna, 11 (1907), pp. 230-231.

Ringgren, Helmer. The initiation Ceremony of the Bektashis. in: *Initiation, Contributions to the Theme of the Study. Conference of the International Association for the History of Religions held at Strassbourg*, September 17-22, 1964. Edited by C. J. Blecker (Leiden, 1965), pp. 202-208.

Robinson, [Vivian Dering] Vandeleur. *Albania's Road to Freedom* (London: George Allen & Unwin, 1941) 135 pp.

Rossi, Ettore. Credenze ed usi dei Bektasci. in: *Studi e materiali di storia delle religioni*, Rome, 18, 1-4 (1942), pp. 60-80.

Rossi, Ettore. Saggio sul dominio turco e l'introduzione dell'Islam in Albania. in: *Rivista di Albania*, Milan, 3 (1942), pp. 200-213.

RREGULLORE e Bektashijve shqiptarë (Korça: Shtypëshkronja e Gazetës së Korçës, 1929) 18 pp.

RREGULLORE e Bektashinjvet Shqiptarë. in: *Fletorja Zyrtare* 15, 25 February 1930 (Tirana Shtyp. Nikaj 1930) 21 pp.
RREGULLORE e përgjithshme e administrimit të mbrëndshëm të Komunitetit Bektashian Shqiptar (Elbasan 1951) 25 pp.
Russell, Dorothea (Lady Russell Pasha), *Medieval Cairo and the Monasteries of the Wadi Natrun. A Historical Guide* (London: Weidenfeld and Nicolson, 1962) 368 pp. + 32 illus.
Salihu, Hajdar. *Poezia e bejtexhinjve* (Prishtina: Rilindja, 1987) 511 pp.
Schwander-Sievers, Stephanie & Fischer, Bernd J. (ed.). *Albanian Identities. Myth and History* (London: C. Hurst, 2002) xvii + 238 pp.
Selenica, Teki. *Shqipria e ilustruar. L'Albanie illustrée. Albumi i 'Shqipris më 1927'. Album de l'Albanie en 1927* (Tirana: Tirana, 1928) xviii + 400 pp.
Seliger, Kurt. *Albanien. Land der Adlersöhne. Ein Reisebuch in Wort und Bild* (Leipzig: Brockhaus, 1960) 259 pp.
Shankland, David (ed.). *Archaeology, Anthropology and Heritage in the Balkans and Anatolia. The Life and Times of F. W. Hasluck, 1878–1920*. 2 vols. (Istanbul: Isis Press, 2004) 401 & 495 pp.
Shehu, Novruz. *Tomorriada. Baba Aliu. Bektashinjtë* (Tirana: Baça, 2002) 175 pp.
Shuteriqi, Dhimitër. *Shkrimet shqipe në vitet 1332–1850* (Tirana: Akademia e Shkencave, 1976) 315 pp.
Siçeca, Shpresa. Vende kulti të ritet islam në Prizren. Tyrbet e varret e shenjta. in: *Gjurmime albanologjike, Seria folklor dhe etnologji*, Prishtina, 25 (1995), pp. 179–191.
Sinani, Shaban. *Letërsi bektashiane në arkivat e Shqipërisë*. Manuscript. Mbajtur në sesionin shkencor Gjurmë bektashiane, Gjirokastër, nëntor 2001.
Sirri, Ahmad, Baba. *Al-Risāla al-Ahmadiyya fī tārīkh al-tarīqa al-'Aliyya al-Baktāshiyya bi-Misr al-Mahrūsa* (Cairo, 1939 [1358 A.H.], Reprint 1959) 64 pp.
Skëndi, Stavro. *The Albanian National Awakening, 1878–1912* (Princeton, NJ: Princeton University Press, 1967) 498 pp.
Skëndi, Stavro. Religion in Albania during the Ottoman Rule. in: *Südost-Forschungen*, Munich, 15 (1956), pp. 311–327. Reprinted in: Balkan Cultural Studies (New York, 1980) pp. 151–166.
Smiley, David. *Albanian Assignment*. Foreword by Partick Fermor (London: Sphere Books, 1984) 176 pp.
Soyyer, Yılmaz. *19. Yüzyılda Bektaşilik* (Izmir: Akademi Kitabevi Yayınları, 2005) 326 pp.
Stadtmüller, Georg. Die Islamisierung bei den Albanern. in: *Jahrbücher für Geschichte Osteuropas* N.F. 3 (1955), pp. 404–429.
Stadtmüller, Georg. Der Derwischorden der Bektaschi in Albanien. in: W. Gesemann et al. (ed.), *Serta slavica in memoriam Aloisii Schmaus* (Munich: Trofenik, 1971), pp. 683–687.
STATUTI i Komunitetit Bektashian Shqiptar (Vlora: Vlora, 1924) 20 pp.
STATUTI i Komunitetit Bektashian të Shqipnis. in: *Gazeta Zyrtare*, Tirana, 60, 10 October 1945.
STATUTI i Komunitetit Bektashian Shqiptar. in: *Gazeta Zyrtare*, Tirana, 43, 14 July 1950 (Durrës, 1950), 29 pp. & (Shkodra, 1950) 30 pp.
STATUTI i Komunitetit Bektashian, shqip & anglisht (Tirana: Ilar, 2000) 68 pp.
Stojanovski, Aleksandar. Edno potvrdeno predanie. in: *Muzejski Glasnik na Istoriskiot Muzej na Makedonija*, Skopje, 4 (1979), pp. 53–57.
Sunar, M. S. *Melâmîlik ve Bektaşilik* (Ankara: Ankara University Basimevi, 1975).
Swire, Joseph. *King Zog's Albania* (London: Robert Hale, 1937) 302 pp.

Tchemalovitch, Smail Aga. Les musulmans en Albanie. in: *Europe de l'Est et du Sud-Est*, Paris, 3, 5-6 (1934), pp. 203-209.

Thoma, G. *Teke Dourbali Soultan: to arvanitiko monastiri Farsalon. Ena istoriko ktisma tis Thessalias* (Volos, 1966).

Tirta, Mark. Kulti i Tomorrit, Bektashizmi, Abaz Aliu. in: *Urtësia*, botim i Komunitetit Bektashian Shqiptar, Tirana, 8 (1996), pp. 8-12.

Tirta, Mark. Kulti i Tomorrit e bektashizmi. in: *Perla, revistë shkencore-kulturore*, Tirana, 2002, No. 3, pp. 54-57.

Tomorri, Baba Ali (= TOMORI, Baba Ali; TYRABIU, Ali). *Bektashinjt e Shqipëries* (Korça: Korça, 1921) 40 pp.

Tomorri, Baba Ali (= TOMORI, Baba Ali; TYRABIU, Ali). *Thelbi i qëllimit, udha e shpëtimit prej Atë Ali Tomorri* (Korça: Dhori Koti, 1924) 47 pp.

Tomorri, Baba Ali (= TOMORI, Baba Ali; TYRABIU, Ali). *Literatyra e Bektashivet a vjersha të përkthyera prej shkrimtarëve bektashinj të vjetër* (Tirana: Mbrothësija, 1927) 32 pp.

Tomorri, Baba Ali (= TOMORI, Baba Ali; TYRABIU, Ali). *Mersija, apo ceremonia e shënjtë e Bektashivet kur shënjtërohet ashyréja. Përkëthim i mbaruar prej Atë Ali Tyrabiut, p.N. i teqes së Tomorit* (Tirana: Mbrothësija, 1928) 11 pp.

Tomorri, Baba Ali (= TOMORI, Baba Ali; TYRABIU, Ali). *Historija e Bektashinjvet. Periudhat para lindjes së Bektashizmës* [Historija i përgjithëshme e bektashinjvet prej Atë Ali Tyrabiut P.N. i teqes' së Tomorit. Shkruar në pjesa spirituale dhe dokumentale] (Tirana: Mbrothësia, 1929) 95 pp.

Tomorri, Baba Ali (= TOMORI, Baba Ali; TYRABIU, Ali). *Nefeze dhe gazele bektashiane*. Të marruna nga libri i posaçmë i Baba Ali Tomorit. Botuar prej Asqeri F. Lumani (Tirana: Luarasi, 1934) 50 pp.

Tomorri, Baba Ali (= TOMORI, Baba Ali; TYRABIU, Ali). *Xhevher ose mendime dhe aforizma Bektashijsh të vjetër*. Përmbledhje dhe përkëthime prej Baba Ali Tomori (Tirana: Mbrothësija, 1934) 18 pp.

Trifunovski, Jovan F., *Polog, antropogeografska proučavanja* (Belgrade: Srpska Akademija Nauka i Umetnosti, 1976) 565 pp.

Trimingham, J. Spencer. *The Sufi Orders of Islam*. With a new foreword by John O. Voll (New York & Oxford: Oxford University Press, 1971, Reprint 1998) 333 pp.

Trix, Frances. *Tuning the Heart: Language Attunement of Master and Student in an Islamic Monastery*. Thesis (Ann Arbor: University of Michigan, 1988).

Trix, Frances. The Ashura Lament of Baba Rexheb and the Albanian Bektashi Community in America. in: A. Popovic & G. Veinstein (ed.), *Bektachiyya, études sur l'ordre mystique des Bektachis et les groupes relevant de Hadji Bektach. Revue des Etudes Islamiques 60(1992)*. Numéro spécial (Paris: Paul Geuthner, 1993/Istanbul: Isis, 1995), pp. 405-418.

Trix, Frances. *Spiritual Discourse. Learning with an Islamic Master* (Philadelphia: University of Pennsylvania Press, 1993) 189 pp.

Trix, Frances. Bektashi Tekke and the Sunni Mosque of Albanian Muslims in Albania. in: Yvonne Yazbeck Haddad & Jane Idleman Smith (ed.), *Muslim Communities in North America* (Albany: State University of New York Press, 1994), pp. 359-380.

Trix, Frances. Bektashiyah. in: John L. Esposito (ed.), *Oxford Encyclopedia of the Islamic World*. Vol. 1 (New York & Oxford: Oxford University Press, 1995), pp. 213-215.

Trix, Frances. The Resurfacing of Islam in Albania. in: *East European Quarterly*, Boulder, 28, 4 (1995), pp. 533-549.

Trix, Frances.When Christians Became Dervishes. Affirming Albanian Muslim-Christan Unity through Discourse. in: *The Muslim World*, Hartford, 85, 3-4 (July-October 1995), pp. 280-294.

Trix, Frances. Alphabet Conflict in the Balkans: Albanian and the Congress of Monastir. in *The International Journal of the Sociology of Language*, 128 (1997), pp. 1-24.

Trix, Frances.The Stamboul Alphabet of Shemsettin Sami Bey: Precursor to Turkish Script Reform. in: *International Journal of Middle East Studies*, 31, 2 (May 1999), pp. 255-272.

Trix, Frances. Person in Epitaphs of a Line of Sufi Babas: Continuity and Change. in *Language Sciences*, special issue on "The Notion of Person," 21, 2 (July 1999), pp. 283-302.

Trix, Frances. Oral Muslim Saint Tales of Rumeli: A Socio-Structural Analysis of Narrative. in: Walter Andrews (ed.), *Intersections in Turkish Literature: Essays in Honor of James Stewart-Robinson, Distinguished Professor of Turkish* (Ann Arbor: University of Michigan Press, 2001), pp. 51-81.

Trix, Frances. *The Sufi Journey of Baba Rexheb* (Philadelphia: University of Pennsylvania Museum of Archaeology and Anthropology, 2009) 226 pp.

Trix, Frances. The Honor of Loving Service: Caring for our Muslim Baba. in: Lucinda M. Carspecken (ed.), *Love in the Time of Ethnography: Essays on Connection as a Focus and Basis for Research* (Lanham, MD: Rowman and Littlefield, 2017), pp. 127-144.

Tschudi, R. Bektashiyya. Article in *Encyclopedia of Islam* (Leiden: Brill Academic Publishers, 1960).

Tsiakoumis, Panagiotis [= ΤΣΙΑΚΟΥΜΗΣ, Παναγιώτης]. *O tekes ton mbektasidon sto Ireni Farsalon* (Athens, 2006) 207 pp.

Tsitselikis, Konstantinos. *Old and New Islam in Greece. From Historical Minorities to Immigrant Newcomers*. Studies in International Minority and Group Rights (Leiden: Brill-Nijhoff, 2012) 622 pp.

Tütüncü, Mehmet. *Corpus of Ottoman Inscriptions from Albania and Montenegro* (Haarlem: Sota, Research Centre for Turkish and Arabic World, 2017) 311 pp.

Uçi, Alfred, Bashota, Sali, Selmani, Ahmet, Ramadani, Ferit, Emërllahu, and Shaip (ed.), *Naim Frashëri. Bektashizmi dhe kombëtarizmi*. Sesioni shkencor i mbajtur më datën 20 tetor 2000, në kuadër të MLN ADitët e Naimit 2000," në Tetovë (Tetovo: MLN Ditët e Naimit, 2002) 125 pp.

Ulusoy, A. Celâlettin. *Hünkâr Hacı Bektaş Velî ve Alevî-Bektaş yolu* (Hacıbektaşköy, 1986).

Vairakliotis, Lakis [= ΒΑΙΡΑΚΛΙΩΤΗΣ, Λάκης]. Oi tekedes ton mbektasidon sta Farsala. in: *Thessaliko Imerologio*, tomos 25 (1994).

Vatin, Nicolas & Zarcone, Thierry. Le tekke bektaşi de Merdivenköy. in: *Anatolia Moderna*, 2 (1991), pp. 29-136.

Vishko, Ali. *Harabati Teqe e Tetovës dhe veprimtaria në të në periudhen e kaluar* (Tetova: Arbëria Design, 1997) 110 pp.

Vllamasi, Sejfi. *Ballafaqime politike në Shqipëri (1897-1942). Kujtime dhe vlerësime historike*. Botim i dytë i plotësuar me foto. Përgatitja për botim dhe ilustrimi fotografik Prof Assoc. Dr. Marenglen Verli (Tirana: Vllamasi, 2012) 554 pp.

Vlora, Ekrem bey. *Aus Berat und vom Tomor. Tagebuchblätter. Zur Kunde der Balkanhalbinsel I*. Reisen und Beobachtungen 13 (Sarajevo: D. A. Kajon, 1911) 168 pp.

Vlora, Ekrem bey. Aperçu sur l'histoire des ordres réligieux et en particulier du Bektachisme en Albanie. in: *Shpirti shqiptar (L'Anima Albanese)*, Turin, 3 (1955) pp. 30-36; 4 (1955), pp. 7-16.

Vlora, Ekrem bey. *Lebenserinnerungen*. 2 vols. (Munich: R. Oldenbourg, 1968, 1973) 275 & 301 pp.

Xhelaj, Syrja. *Baba Rexhebi, ky shenjt* (Tirana: Lumo Skendo, 2001) 192 pp.

Xhelaj, Syrja. *Rrugëtimi i shpirtit, ose dialog në vite me kryeshenjt Bardhin* (Tirana: Urtësia Bektashiane, 2012) 341 pp.

Xhelaj, Syrja. *Baba Rexhebi: qiell urtësie* (Tirana: Urtësia Bektashiane, 2013) 271 pp.
Ylli, Bardhyl. *Dashuria e të vërtetës* (Tirana, 1999) 120 pp.
Yürekli, Zeynep. *Architecture and Hagiography in the Ottoman Empire. The Politics of Bektashi Shrines in the Classical Age*. Birmingham Byzantine and Ottoman Studies (London: Routledge, 2016) 199 pp.
Zamputi, Injac. Një dorëshkrim bektashian i gjysmës së shekullit të XIX (1850–1860). in: *Buletin për Shkencat Shoqërore*, Tirana, 4 (1955), pp. 203–210.
Zarcone, Thierry. *Rizâ Tevfik ou le soufisme 'éclairé:' mécanismes de pensée et réception des idées occidentales dans le mysticisme turc sous le deuxième régime constitutionnel ottoman (1908-1923)*. Thèse de doctorat inedite, présentée sous la direction de Madame le Professeur Irène Mélikoff, Faculté des Sciences Humaines de l'Université de Strasbourg, 1990.
Zekini, Efstratiu Ch. *O Bektasismos sti D. Thraki. Simvoli stin istoria tis diadoseos tu musulmanismu ston elladiko choro* (Thessalonika: Institute for Balkan Studies, 1988) 313 pp.
ZËRI I Bektashizmës, Wyandotte, Michigan, 1954–1955 (periodical).
Zojzi, Rrok. Mali i Krujës. in: *Drini*, Tirana, 2 (1944), pp. 16–18.

Websites of interest

www.teqeusa.org
The website of the Bektashi Community of America.
www.bektashiorder.com
Website dedicated to the sacred memory of Baba Rexheb.
teqejasarande.com (in Albanian)
Dedicated to the *tekke* of Saranda and the history of Bektashism.

INDEX

Note: Locators with letter 'n' refer to notes.

Abas Ali shrine 168, 225, 236
Abaz Hilmi Dede Baba 12, 215, 222, 233, 273, 274, 279, 289, 303
Abbas Ali (Imam Ali's son) 49, 68, 81–3, 96, 124, 161, 162, 166–71, 226, 234, 235, 274, 296
    grave of 83, 96, 124, 161, 162, 166–9, 170, 274
    shrine 82, 167, 170, 171, 234–5
    tyrbe 234, 237, 296
Abbas Ali Tyrbe 234
Abdal Tekkes 93, 267
Abdullah al-Maghawiri Mosque 97
Abdullah Baba Tekke 263–4
Abdullah Magauri Tekke (Sidi Abdullah al-Maghawiri) 267–71
Abdylgani Baba 243, 244
Abedin Pasha Tekke 211–12
Abiddin Baba 212
Adam and Eve 106
Adrianopolis 115, 123
Ahmet Karadja (Karadja Ahmet Sultan) 250, 251, 278
Ahmet Karadja Tekke 250–1
Ahmet Myftari Dede 12, 108–12, 183, 215, 230, 233, 274, 278–9, 302, 304, 312
Ahmet Sirri Baba of Mokattam (Ahmet Sirri Baba of Glina) 97, 98, 263, 269, 271, 279–81, 300, 305, 316
Ajize Baba 166
Albania/Albanian
    admission to the League of Nations 58
    ban on religion 13, 14, 162, 169, 187, 188
    civil war 12, 171, 278
    Congress of Elbasan 53, 54
    Constitution 13, 57, 77, 144, 148, 156–7, 234
    flag 132, 133, 156, 157
    independence 2, 8, 9, 29, 57, 60, 63, 64, 77, 78, 81, 86, 87, 94, 201, 212, 229, 275, 301, 330 nn.113–14
    independence struggle 138–60
    nationalism 29, 60–1, 138–60
    religious harmony 14, 153–4
    Supreme Regency Council 153, 154, 155
    Venetian rule in 45
'Albanian Knowledge' Club 146
Albanian language 8, 73
    propagation of teaching/learning 8, 77, 141–8, 180, 193, 195, 204, 216, 229, 293–4, 296, 305–7
Albanian National Bank 8
alcohol 2, 27, 65, 66, 67, 84, 108, 123, 163, 223, 284
Alevi Islam 1
Ali, Imam 1–3, 30, 33, 50, 65, 67, 70, 94, 106, 118, 132, 159, 235
Ali Baba 51, 52, 70, 238, 252
Ali Baba Gega 193
Ali Baba Horasani of Fushë Kruja 283–4
Ali Baba Horasani Trybe 188, 191, 193, 284, 314
Ali Baba of Berat 281
Ali Baba Tyrbe 70, 191, 193, 238, 263, 284
Ali Day (2 August) 165, 166, 309
Ali Dede 252
Ali Dede Horasani Tekke 260–1
Ali Haqi Baba of Gjirokastra 2, 185, 193, 194, 196, 198, 217, 219, 227, 232, 239, 262, 263, 284, 291, 312
Ali Kamberi of Prishta 233, 296–7
Ali Pasha Tepelena and Yannina 6–7, 20, 56–7, 63, 85, 94, 98, 102, 113, 183, 256, 258, 262, 263, 302, 315
Alipostivan Tekke 15, 178

Ali Resmi Baba of Crete 261
Ali Riza Dede Baba 188, 189, 233, 259, 285
Ali Riza Dede Baba of Elbasan, 285, 297
Allah 22, 27, 52, 110, 115, 132, 133, 138, 217, 239
alms box 44, 47, 49, 54, 55, 117, 167, 186, 192, 209, 235, 284
altar 42, 65, 83, 221
America, Bektashi Albanians in 14, 126, 127, 137, 153, 239, 271, 277
   support to Albanians 153
amulet 40, 96, 120, 250, 280
Aqif Pasha Elbasani 59, 186, 213
Arabic script 8, 9, 41, 77, 89, 99, 104–5, 145, 166, 217, 283
Aranitas Dervishia 178
Arshi Baba of Durballi Sultan 286
Arshi Baba of Gjirokastra 286–7
ashik (lover) 3, 127, 312, 313
ashura feast (tenth day of Muharrem) 2, 12, 117
Ashura Lament (Baba Rexheb) 126–37
   Balkan antecedents 130–2
   ceremonial context 132–4
   English and Albanian texts 134–7
   Ottoman antecedent 127–9
Asim Baba of Gjirokastra 6, 11, 15, 105, 159, 189, 194, 196, 198, 207, 217, 219, 227, 232, 239, 283, 287, 291
Asim Baba Tekke (Gravel Tekke) 6, 11, 15, 79, 159, 189, 193–4, 196, 198, 207, 217, 219, 227, 232, 239, 284, 291
Askeri, Hasan 3, 30
Assumption of the Virgin Mary, feast of 49, 124, 167, 235
Atatürk, Mustafa Kemal 1, 11, 117, 188, 233, 266, 270, 307, 313
'Auspicious Event' of 1826 5, 7, 44, 63, 218
autonomy 2, 8, 29, 78, 86, 139, 141, 145, 148, 152, 154, 155
Avdi Pasha 242
Axhem Zade Hasan Efendi Tekke 249–50

babas/dervishes (leader/monks)
   appointment of 60
   cleanliness and orderliness 50, 51, 148, 190, 253
   exiled/imprisoned/refugees 6, 13, 75, 76–7, 79–80, 102–4, 115, 138, 144, 153, 191, 194, 218, 219, 220, 224, 232, 233, 242, 264, 277, 305–6, 327 n.74, 328 n.82, 330 n.113, 332 n.138
   hierarchical structure 3–4
   kindness and hospitality 44, 67, 70, 74, 82–3, 86, 108, 117, 168, 195–6, 201, 221, 225, 317
   married 31, 46, 51, 59, 64, 65, 250, 261
   obedience 45, 48
   pastimes 52
   services and duties 33
   support to *çetas* (armed bands) 147–8
   unmarried/celibate 4, 27, 31, 32, 46, 51, 55, 58, 59, 64–5, 67, 91, 112, 119, 121, 227, 244, 255, 261, 270, 280, 305, 308, 313, 317, 328 n.97, 330 n.114
   used as spies 6–7, 56
   wartime impact on 9–10, 76–80
Baba Abaz Hilmi of Frashër 233
Baba Abaz Malaj 228
Baba Abdullah 178, 218
Baba Abdullah of Melçan 224, 229, 237, 275, 300, 318
Baba Abdullah Tekke 178, 218, 229, 263, 275
Baba Abdurrahman 244
Baba Abdylgani 244
Baba Abdylgani grave 243
Baba Abdyl Shehu 219
Baba Abedin Gllava 198
Baba Abedin Hoxhaj 230
Baba Abedin Leskoviku 211–12, 229, 275, 299
Baba Abedin of Backa 76
Baba Abedin of Frashër 77–9, 148, 295
Baba Abedin Tekke 211–12
Baba Adem 139, 218, 244
Baba Adem Mahmutaj 189
Baba Adem of Backa 238, 239
Baba Adem of Melçan 75, 183, 189, 275, 293
Baba Adem Tekke 139, 245, 276, 293
Baba Adem Vexh-hi of Gjakova 244, 276, 319
Baba Ahmed Serri Dede 120–1, 280
Baba Ahmet 210, 224, 277
Baba Ahmet Dedej 186, 188

Baba Ahmet Koshtani 77, 80, 282
Baba Ahmet Nazereci/Nazereka 183, 184
Baba Ahmet of Koshtan 77, 80
Baba Ahmet of Prishta 144, 220, 277, 303
Baba Ahmet Resuli 203–4
Baba Ahmet Tekke (Dushk/Gramsh) 144, 183, 210, 220, 224, 277
Baba Ahmet Turani 10, 11, 79, 81, 154, 180, 187, 189, 196, 212, 213, 219, 222, 239, 273, 277, 282, 316, 319
Baba Ali 47, 100, 178
Baba Ali Dedej 185
Baba Ali Horasani 201, 227, 228, 314
Baba Ali Horasani of Persia 201
Baba Ali Horasani Tekke 187–8, 217
Baba Aliko Tekke 138
Baba Ali Myrteza of Fushë Kruja 12, 302
Baba Ali of Gjirokastra 75
Baba Ali Rizaj of Korça 188, 215
Baba Ali shrine 238
Baba Ali Tekke 7, 47, 178, 217, 222, 227, 239, 267, 284, 300
Baba Ali Tekke (Alipostivan) 178
Baba Ali Tekke (Berat) 179
Baba Ali Tomori (Ali Tyrabiu/Turabiu) 7, 12, 75–81, 85, 95–6, 157, 171, 198, 229, 235, 282–3, 297, 318–19
Baba Alush of Frashër 75–6, 139, 148, 189, 276, 285–6
Baba Arif Pervekushi/Devekushti 183
Baba Arshi Bazaj 271, 286
Baba Avdulla 205, 206
Baba Barjam Mahmutaj 220, 289
Baba Behlul 232
Baba Behlul of Therepel 78
Baba Behlul Tekke 232–3
Baba Bektash Aliaj 198
Baba Bektashi of Vlora 198
Baba Bektash Kodheli 229
Baba Braho. *See* Ibrahim Baba of Qesaraka
Baba Dalip Tekke 181
Baba Daut Agjahi 184
Baba Daut Tyrbe 185
Baba Dino grave 199
Baba Ejup Rakipi 247
Baba Eski 165
Baba Faik Selmani 187, 188
Baba Faja Martaneshi 12, 215, 233, 273, 289–90, 303

Baba Fehmi of Tepelena 233, 279
Baba Fejzë Bulqiza 181–2, 242
Baba Fejzo Dervishi 12, 233, 273, 289
Baba Fetah 178–9, 290, 300
Baba Fetah Tekke/grave 178–9, 199
Baba Gani 244
Baba Hafiz 210, 298
Baba Hafiz Ali 244
Baba Hafiz of Kuç 79
Baba Hajdar 216, 237, 264
Baba Hajdar Hashimia 100
Baba Hajdar Hatemi 255, 290–1
Baba Hajdar Leskoveci 213, 214
Baba Hajdër of Kardhiq 77, 194, 277, 291, 316
Baba Hajdër Plaku 194
Baba Hajro 189
Baba Hajro of Turan 214
Baba Halil Curri 193
Baba Halim of Nishova 232
Baba Hamit (of Dibra) Tekke 188–9, 285
Baba Hamit of Melçan 178
Baba Hamza 244
Baba Hamza Tekke 206
Baba Hasan 204, 205, 206
Baba Hasan Dede Sultan 292
Baba Hasan Tekke (Kremenar) 205
Baba Hasan Tekke (Kreshova) 205
Baba Hasan Tyrbe 219–20, 223
Baba Haxhi 235
Baba Haxhi Adem grave 243
Baba Haxhi Adem of Prizren 244, 275–6, 303
Baba Hekuran Nikollari 178
Baba Hilmi 229, 230
Baba Husejn 224
Baba Husejn Axhemi 219
Baba Husejn Gumaj 228
Baba Husejn Tekke/Baruç Tekke 230–1
Baba Husejn Tekke (Greshica) 199
Baba Husejn Tekke (Gumen) 199
Baba Hussein Tekke 47, 192
Baba Hysejn grave 199
Baba Hysejn of Backa 189
Baba Hysen Duhanxhiu 184
Baba Hysen Kukeli 191, 242, 294–5, 292, 298
Baba Hysen of Kruja 75, 76
Baba Hysen of Martanesh Tyrbe 242

Baba Hysen of Melçan 77, 78, 142, 144, 147–8, 218, 293–4, 300
Baba Hysen of Melçan Tekke 142, 144, 218, 293
Baba Hysen of Skorovot 229
Baba Hysen of Skrapar 81
Baba Hysen of Vërlen 77, 218
Baba Hysen Rama of Martanesh (Hysen Martaneshi) 213
Baba Hysen Tekke 218–19, 240
Baba Hysni Shehu 216
Baba Ibrahim 149, 151, 196, 295
Baba Ibrahim Kukës 187
Baba Ibrahim Shkëmbi 227
Baba Iljaz 224, 240
Baba Iljaz (Elias) 220
Baba Iljaz Tekke 220
Baba-i-madh Kamber Ali 84, 225, 231
Baba Isak Tekke 230
Baba Islam 203, 211
Baba Islam Islamaj 212
Baba Ismail 80, 103–4, 198
Baba Ismail Jangulli 180
Baba Ismail of Gllava 78
Baba Ismail Tekke 202, 223–4
Baba Isuf 142, 180
Baba Jahja 227
Baba Jashar Krena 213, 214, 216
Baba Jemin Tekke 181
Baba Jonuz Zhepa/Xhepa 183
Baba Jusuf Tekke 179–80
Baba Kamber 203
Baba Kamber Ali 189, 224, 233, 261, 285, 297, 302
Baba Kamber of Berat 80
Baba Kamber Tekke 202, 239–40
Baba Kamber Tyrbe 182–3
Baba Kameri 183–4
Baba Kasem Tekke 210
Baba Kasem Tyrbe 210, 223
Baba Kaso (Kasem) 204
Baba Manes 146, 194, 195, 316
Baba Meço 190
Baba Mehmed Ali of Merdivenköy 75
Baba Mehmet Aliu 198
Baba Mehmet of Fushë Kruja 195, 288, 300
Baba Mehmet Shemseddin of Gjakova 244
Baba Mehmet Zykaj 191

Baba Meleq 178, 229
Baba Meleq Shëmbërdhenji (Baba Meleq Staravecka) 76, 141, 149–51, 229, 300–1
Baba Meleq Shëmbërdhenji (Baba Meleq Staravecka) Tekke 231
Baba Meleq Shëmbërdhenji (Baba Meleq Staravecka) Tyrbe 229
Baba Meleq Staravecka. *See* Baba Meleq Shëmbërdhenji
Baba Mestan 179
Baba Muço 224
Baba Muharrem 203, 206, 223, 247
Baba Muharrem Agushi of Tepelena 205
Baba Muharrem Mahmutaj of Lazarat 189
Baba Muharrem Mahzuni 211, 275
Baba Muharrem Mahzuni of Durballi Sultan 300, 302
Baba Muharrem Mahzuni of Gjirokastra 258
Baba Muharrem of Koshtan 75
Baba Muharrem Tekke 223
Baba Mumin Lama 244
Baba Murat 190, 198
Baba Musa 254, 255
Baba Musa of Gjakova 247
Baba Musa Tekke 212–13
Baba Mustafa 184, 190, 191, 219, 289
Baba Mustafa Dollma Tyrbe 90
Baba Mustafa Dolma 45, 207, 219
Baba Mustafa of Frashër 81
Baba Mustafa Qefshi (Mustafa Baltëza of Fushë Kruja) 184, 185
Baba Mustafa Tekke 229–30, 301
Baba Mustafa Xhani (Baba Faja Martaneshi) 215
Baba Myheddin of Gllava 80, 198
Baba of Kastoria 210
Baba Pajo Hasa 184
Baba Qamil Gjini of Vlora 217
Baba Qamil Gllava of Tepelena 12, 304
Baba Qamil Kapllani of Vërzhezha 198
Baba Qazim 113, 143, 219, 226, 254, 288
Baba Qazim Bakalli of Gjakova 13, 244, 247, 303–4
Baba Qazim Berati 259
Baba Qazim (Kasem) Tekke 262–3
Baba Qazim of Aranitas 240
Baba Qazim of Elbasan 303

Baba Qazim of Qatrom 143, 144, 218–19, 226, 294
Baba Qazim Plaku grave 226
Baba Rakip 183
Baba Ramadan grave 226
Baba Ramadan of Qatrom 81
Baba Rexheb of Gjirokastra 13, 304–5, 312–13, 314
Baba Rexheb of Plevisht 184
Baba Rifat (Rifaat Baba, Baba Refat) 211
Baba Rifat Tekke 211
Baba Rushit Tollja 179–80, 214
Baba Rystem Llacja of Gjirokastra 189, 285
Baba Sadik Ibro 188
Baba Sadik Tekke 203–4
Baba Sako Tekke 212
Baba Salih Elbasani 218, 255, 284
Baba Salih Elbasani Tekke 237–9
Baba Salih of Elbasan 77, 79, 218
Baba Salih of Matohasanaj 144, 216, 305–7
Baba Salih shrine 238
Baba Salih Tekke 216
Baba Sali Matohasani 198
Baba Seit Koka of Skrapar 259
Baba Seit (Seyid) 212
Baba Sejfullah Melani 217
Baba Selim of Gjirokastra 79, 81, 217, 283
Baba Selim of Maslavica 205
Baba Selim Ruhi 153, 189, 193, 217, 223, 284, 304–5, 308, 312–13
Baba Selim the Elder of Elbasan 194
Baba Selman of Martanesh 227
Baba Selman Tekke (Tepelena) 227–8
Baba Seyyit 174
Baba Shaban 184, 203, 237, 273
Baba Shaban of Prishta 77, 78, 80, 279, 282
Baba Shaban Shkëmbi 227
Baba Shefket Koshtani of Tepelena 12, 277
Baba Shefqet Koshtani (Shefqet Mahmuti/Baba Shefqet Gllava) 204
Baba Sheme 190
Baba Shemimi 102, 255
Baba Shemimi of Fushë Kruja 100–1, 316
Baba Shëmin of Kruja 85
Baba Shemja of Frashër 79
Baba Shemseddin (Baba Shemsi Plaku) 243–4
Baba Sherif Canometaj 187, 188
Baba Sherif of Çorrush 182
Baba Shukri 227
Baba Skënder Tyrbe 212
Baba Sulejman 10, 59, 79, 81, 194, 195, 249
Baba Sulejman of Barmash 229
Baba Sulejman of Gjirokastra 154, 218, 277, 300, 316–17
Baba Sulejman of Leskovik 279
Baba Sulejman Tekke 228–9
Baba Sulo 204
Baba Sulo grave 199
Baba Tahir 170, 263, 315
Baba Tahir Bubësi 258–9
Baba Tahir Emini 254
Baba Tahir Hyseni of Qesarat 184, 215
Baba Tahir Nasibi of Frashër 264, 302, 316, 318
Baba Tahir Nasibi Tekke 189–91
Baba Tahir Nesibiu 101, 102–3
Baba Tahir of Crete 7, 170, 224, 315, 318
Baba Tahir Tekke/Tyrbe 84, 190–1, 224–5, 231, 241
Baba Tajar Gashi 244
Baba Tajar Gashi of Gostivar 304
Baba Tekke 20, 254, 314
Baba Xhafer 181, 214, 224
Baba Xhafer of Prishta 75
Baba Xhaferr Karriqi of Gjirokastra 214
Baba Xhafer Sadiku 12, 222, 233, 273, 319
Baba Xhafer Tekke 181, 220, 255
Baba Xhafer Tekke (Borsh) 181
Baba Xhafer Tekke (Brerima) 181
Baba Xhelal Tekke 183
Baba Xhemal (Baba Selman Xhemali of Elbasan) 205, 206, 242, 313–14, 319
Baba Xhemali Tekke 187–8, 314
Baba Xhemal of Përmet 77, 81
Baba Xhemal Shkëmbi 227
Baba Xhevher of Persia 201
Baba Zejnel Abedin of Backa 189, 190
Baba Zejnel of Gjirokastra Tekke 196–7
Baba Zejnel of Kruja 80
Baba Zenel 198, 278
Baba Zenel grave 226
Baba Zenel Tekke 222
Baba Zeqir 219
Baba Zeqir of Korça 230
Baba Zija 247

Baba Zija Pasholli of Kanatlar 247
Baba Zoto Tyrbe 205
Baba Zylfo 218–19, 237, 294
Baba Zylfo of Melçan 11, 307
Babinger, Franz 69–72, 113, 123, 179, 191, 202, 210, 211, 226, 228, 231, 239, 312
bacılar 2
Backa Tekke 178–9, 183, 300
Baghdad 2, 45, 46, 279, 313
Bairam Aga 20–1
Bajo Topulli 77, 147, 218, 294, 295
Bakir, Muhammed 3, 30
Balaban Bey 72
Baldacci, Antonio 27–9
Balim Sultan 4, 123, 287–8
Balim Sultan Tyrbe/Tekke 43, 213, 214, 216, 242, 251, 257, 266, 314
Balkan region
   spread of Bektashi in 6–7
Balkan Wars 8–9, 64, 67, 152, 168, 193, 195, 197, 257, 265, 303
Balli Baba Tekke 20
Balli Kombëtar (The National Front) (anti-communist resistance group) 205, 237, 297, 305
Bardhi, Reshat. *See* Dede Baba Reshat Bardhi
Bashkimi (Union) Club 147
Battle of Kerbela 106, 124
Battuta, Ibn 308
Bayezid II 4, 113, 114, 288
Bazaj, Arshi. *See* Arshi Baba of Durballi Sultan
beard 24, 36, 41, 63, 70, 74, 82, 108, 214, 221, 225, 268, 289, 310
Bejkua, Veisel Efendi 146, 195
Bektash Cakrani 78
Bektashi of Albania
   age, eligibility for initiation 110
   Alevi communities 14
   arrival and expansion in Albania 6–12, 63–4, 85, 93–4, 101, 113–16, 123–5, 154–6, 161–72
   banning and abolition of 5–6, 7, 12–13, 90, 125, 155, 169, 188, 200, 210, 284
   communist rule, impact of 12–13, 133, 159, 162, 171, 174, 178, 179, 181, 182, 183, 184, 191, 193, 196, 197, 198, 199, 200, 201, 202, 203, 204, 205, 206–7, 208, 210, 211, 212, 213, 215, 216, 217, 219, 220, 222, 223, 224, 225, 226, 227, 228, 230, 231, 232, 233, 234, 236, 237, 239, 240, 241, 242, 259, 263, 273, 274, 278, 279, 280, 283, 284, 289, 297, 302, 303, 304, 305, 312, 319, 331 n.136, 332 n.138
   conversion to Bektashism 8, 56, 57, 85, 161, 225, 263, 297
   core beliefs and features 1–4, 5, 8, 30–4, 48, 58, 62–3, 65–6, 84–5, 87, 91–2, 109, 118, 121, 123, 317
   decline of 15–16
   faith 3, 30–1, 101
   funding and subsidies 111
   Haji Bektash as founder of the order (*See* Haji Bektash Veli)
   hierarchical structure/ranks 3–4, 31–2, 46, 48, 54, 56, 58, 60, 64–5, 82, 91, 108, 118–19, 120–1, 122–3
   history and culture 1–16
   liberality of 2, 20, 28, 45, 48, 58, 60, 62, 70, 80, 82, 83, 84, 112, 199
   national spirit 29, 59, 60, 63–4, 75–81, 86, 110–11, 125, 138–60, 189, 215, 222, 282–3, 284, 286, 287, 301, 312
   origins (in Turkey) 1, 4–6, 56, 62–3, 70, 85, 87, 90, 113, 122–3, 161–72
   orthodox Muslims (differences/accusations/controversies) 44–5, 48, 54–5, 57, 58, 60, 65, 66, 67–8, 84, 86, 87, 92, 93, 110, 118, 121, 122–3, 196
   political perspective 2–3
   population and propagation in Albania 56
   post-1990 revival of 13–16
   recognised as an official religious community 10, 11, 87, 125, 153–6
   recovery of 13–14
   relations with Orthodox Christians 8, 27, 44, 54, 57, 60–1, 62, 64, 66–8, 71–2, 86, 89, 90, 109, 116, 118, 122, 123, 124, 153, 165
   reports and scholarly articles 17–175
   secrets/mysteries of Bektashism 84–5, 86, 109–10, 119, 123

statistics 14, 87, 110, 121, 124–5, 153–4
wartime impact 9–10
women 2, 31, 32, 37, 65, 66, 75, 84, 85, 95, 97, 112, 118–19, 123, 163, 209, 249, 262, 310–11
Bektashi Notebook *(Fletore e Bektashinjet)* 2, 3, 125, 149
Bektashi Order of Dervishes, The (Birge) 93, 113
Bektashism 1, 4, 8, 15, 56, 57, 64, 67, 68, 84, 85, 154, 158, 275, 284, 326 n.72, 329 n.112, 331 n.136
Bënça Dervishia 179
Beqir Efendi Dervishia 182
Beqir Efendi Tekke 226
Beqiri, Abdyl 254
Beqiri, Rexheb. *See* Baba Rexheb of Gjirokastra
Berat 7, 27, 48, 73, 79, 166, 170, 179, 292
Berat Tekke 48, 79, 220, 281
Bërzezhda, Colonel Halit 147
Bethel 39
betrothal 33
Beyazit I 93
Biçaku, Aqif (Aqif Pasha Elbasani) 154
Biçaku, Aqif Pasha 10
Birge, John Kingsley 93–4, 113, 188, 193, 207, 314
Bishop of Trimythous 256
Bismarck, Otto von 63
Bllaca Tekke 80, 141, 142, 179–80, 278
border disputes, Albanian-Greek 9–10
Borsh Tekke 181
Bosnia, Bektashi diaspora in 44
Bosnia and Herzegovina 92, 171
Boué, Ami 249
Bourcart, Jacques 214
boza (millet beer) 51, 93, 325 n.40
Braçi, Mustafa 229
Brailsford, Henry 245, 276
Brataj Tekke 278
bread 27, 42, 74, 83, 215, 221, 283
Brerima Tekke 181
brotherhood, Bektashi 27–8, 30, 66, 152
Bubës i Parë (First Bubës) Tekke 181
Bubës i Sipërm (Upper Bubës) Tekke 181
Buda, Aleks 108–10, 111–12
Buddhism 84
Bujak Tekke 261, 262

Bulqiza Tekke 181–2
Bumçi, Luigj (Bishop of Lezha) 10, 60, 154
burial 33, 44, 117, 270
Busch-Zantner, Richard 87–92
Butka, Sali bey 218, 295, 330 n.114
Buza, Tafil 80, 198

cabbalism 1, 52
Cairo Tekke 97–8, 117–19, 120–1, 141, 224, 267, 329 n.113, 330 n.119
Cakran Tekke 182
calligraphy 24, 46, 192, 207, 260
Candia Tekke 260–1, 296, 318
candles 23, 40, 65, 74, 95, 199, 248, 251, 309
Caritas 14
cat, as holy animal 90
Catholics, in Albania 14, 127, 153
Çelebi, Evliya 6, 17–18, 19, 75, 93, 94, 99, 100, 113–15, 123, 162, 163, 165, 166, 200, 241, 244–5, 263, 292, 299
celibacy 4, 27, 32, 46, 55, 58, 59, 64–5, 67, 117, 121, 227, 305, 308, 313
Çeno, Mehmet. *See* Baba Mehmet of Fushë Kruja
Çerrica Tekke 182
chapel 42, 44, 46, 47, 70, 83, 248, 293
cheese 27, 73, 123, 196
Chinese Revolution 13
Choublier, Max 50–2, 252
Christians and Bektashis, relations between 8, 13–14, 122, 332 n.136
churches
  destruction of 13
  revival of 14
Church of St. Demetrius 20
cigarettes 52, 84, 223, 231
Cilka, Grigor 148
Clayer, Nathalie 7, 138–72, 247, 251
coffee 50, 51, 55, 70, 71, 84, 108, 231, 283
communist dictatorship 12–13, 159, 174, 178, 201, 232, 234, 312
  recovery of 13–14
Conference of London 79
confession 27, 123
Congress of Berlin 7
Congress of Monastir 145

Constantinople 10, 28, 54, 57, 63, 87, 91, 256, 278, 301, 307
Convention on the Exchange of Greek and Turkish Population 9–10
copper 24, 25, 52, 55, 97
Corfu Tekke 38
Çorrush Tekke 182, 211
Covel, J. 115
Crete, Bektashi in 5, 7, 318
cudgels 23, 25, 26
Cultural Revolution, in Albania 13, 125, 238

Dede Baba Abaz Hilmi 273–4
Dede Baba Edmond Brahimaj 288, 289, 301
Dede Baba Reshat Bardhi 13, 183, 234, 272, 288, 304
Dede Baba Reshat Bardhi Tekke 229
Dede Rustem Melçani 219
Degrand, Baron Jules Alexandre 36–8, 164, 256, 283–4, 292, 310, 315
De Jong, Fred 260
Delvina, Sulejman bey 10, 29
Demir Han 166–7, 234
Demir Han Tekke 232, 270
Der el Busair monastery 120
Dervish Abulbaki 208
Dervish Arshi of Vlora 271
Dervish Aziz 308
Dervish Bajram of Gjakova 271
Dervish Bektas Karamartin of Turkey 271
Dervish Eliton Pashaj 271, 272
Dervish Hasan Picari 222–3
Dervish Iljaz 81, 171, 235, 296
Dervish Iljaz Vërzhezha 80, 235, 296, 303, 319
Dervish Lutfi of Gjirokastra 271
Dervish Myftar 142, 226
Dervish Ramadan 144, 226, 328 n.87
Dervish Rexhep Tyrbe 240
Dervish Shahin 233
Dervish Xhafer Hanku 242
Detroit Tekke. *See* Taylor (Detroit) Tekke
devshirme (child levy) system 6
Diakovo Tekke 54
Didymóteichon (Dimetoka) Tekke 257
Dikmen Baba Tekke 246–7
Dimetoka (Didymoteicho) Tekke 308

Djelveti Order 114
Djelveti Tekke 114
Djiba Tekke 166
donations 44, 45, 49, 213, 267. *See also* offerings
dream interpreters 52
dress. *See* robes and clothing
Drizar Tekke 183
Droja River 43
drums 26, 146
Dukaj Tekke 183
Dumbabists 9
Durballi Sultan 23, 248, 257–8, 293
Durballi Sultan Tekke 20, 22–6, 173–5, 203, 211, 248, 257–61, 263, 271, 275, 280, 286, 302, 311
Durham, Mary Edith 41–2, 221
Durrës 9, 15, 79, 186, 193, 278, 311
Durrës Tekke 38
Durri Najaf (precious stone) 46
Dushk Tekke 183–4
Dylgjer Hysejni of Elbasan 288

earring 4, 21, 59, 70, 82, 117, 121, 317
Eastern Orthodoxy 1
Edmonds, Paul 187
Egypt 9, 80, 82, 87, 111, 120, 267, 270, 271, 279, 299, 305, 307
Eke, Mustafa 247
Ekrem bey Vlora 48–9, 114, 167, 169, 170, 201
Elbasan 6, 10, 11, 53, 54, 58, 59, 77–9, 88, 93, 114, 146, 147, 184, 187, 188, 237, 278, 284, 289, 303
Elbasan Tekke 53–5, 59, 79, 100, 186, 187–9, 285, 303, 314
Emine Baba 264
Emine Baba Tekke 264–5
Erbei Baba 261
Ercan, Haydar 247
Essad Pasha of Tirana 57, 64
Essad Pasha Toptani 80
European Court of Human Rights 254
Eustathios of Thessaloniki 131
Evans, Sir Arthur 39–40, 250

Fadil Pasha Toptani 77
Fadlullah 62
Fakri Mustafai Baba 184, 295

Fakri Mustafai Baba Tekke 184–5
Farouk, King 269, 280
fasting 2, 32, 45, 82, 91, 127
fate 41, 66, 68, 174
fatihas 133
Fatima (Imam Ali's wife) 1, 3, 65, 106
feeding/helping the poor 42, 80, 221, 299–300
Fejzi Dede 76, 212, 277, 307, 316
Ferid Pasha Vlora 48
Fier Tekke 241
First World War 8, 9, 152, 153, 168, 179, 190, 193, 212, 214, 216, 218, 237, 244, 261, 296
Floqi, Thanas 213
folksong 77, 258
food 18, 27, 40, 51, 84, 126, 133
fortune-telling 52
Fourteen Pure Innocents 118
Frashëri, Abdul bey 63–4, 76, 139, 149, 189, 191, 285–6
Frashëri, Dalip 99–100, 102–7, 139, 144, 264, 285, 327 n.74
Frashëri, Mid'hat bey 9, 60, 154, 157, 330 n.125, 332 n.138
Frashëri, Naim bey 2–3, 30–5, 49, 63, 64, 76, 125, 139, 144, 149, 154, 157, 159, 170, 274, 285, 301, 329 n.112
Frashëri, Sami bey 63, 99, 102, 113–14, 139, 285, 318, 330–1 n.125
Frashër Tekke 76, 78, 79, 102–3, 139, 140, 148, 189–91, 196, 218, 273, 285, 302
Fratar Dervishia 191
Friday prayers 1, 156
Fukara Club 147
Fushë Kruja Tekke 15, 46, 47, 69–72, 100–1, 191–3, 195, 209, 216, 242, 284, 285, 294, 295, 312, 315, 316
Fuzûlî 104–5, 106, 139, 144, 305, 307, 327 n.74

Garden of Eden 106
Garrett, L. M. J. 125
Gavrilka (Gavril Pepo) 142, 144
Gazi Evrenos 46, 72, 93
Gërmenji, Themistokli 142, 143, 144, 328 n.88, 328 n.90
Ghazi Sinan Pasha 18, 99, 113–14
gifts 14, 24, 25, 54

Gjakova Tekke 13, 155–6, 243–4, 276–7, 303
Gjirokastra 6, 12, 60, 79, 88, 102, 105, 146, 152, 153, 155. 170, 214, 217, 227, 269, 271, 284, 292, 295
Gjirokastra Tekke 58, 60, 77, 80, 128, 146, 155, 193–4, 277, 284, 287
Gjonëm 6, 197
Gjorm/Gjonëm Tekke (Kurbin) 197
Gjorm Tekke (Vlora) 197
gjysh (grandfather/*dede*), hierarchical structure 4, 31
Gjysh Mustafa Qerezi 191
Gllava Tekke 198, 304
Gnosticism 1
Godart, Justin 10, 58–61, 186, 195, 317
Golimbas Tekke 198
Gorisht Tekke 199
Göyegü Sinan Pasha 113, 114, 123
Grameno, Mihal 144, 148, 178, 189–90, 286, 290, 294, 295
Graves, Sir Robert 197, 198
graves/graveyard 24–5, 40, 43, 45, 46, 53–4, 111, 122, 194, 207, 222, 234, 240, 251, 260, 261, 262
Greece
 Bektashi in 5, 9–10, 174, 257, 297
 foreign aid to Albania 14
 struggle with Albania 9–10, 79, 86
 tekkes and shrines 256–65
Greek Orthodox Church 14, 141
Greek–Turkish war 9–10
green, colour's significance in Islam 82
Gulf States 14

habit. *See* robes
Hacıbektaş(köy) Tekke 81, 155, 170, 266, 308
Haci Mustafa Baba 208
Hadikaja [The Garden] (Dalip Frashëri) 99–100, 102–7, 264
Hadiqatû's-Su'adâ (Fuzûlî) 104–7, 139, 144–5, 305, 306
Hadji Baba of Hacibektas 81
Hadji Hasan Dede of Salonica 75
Hadji Mehmed Dede of Malatya 76
hair 24
Hajdar Baba Tekke 6, 197
Hajdar Mehmet Baba 269, 299

Hajdar Mehmet Baba of Leskovik 267, 269
Hajdër Baba of Kardhiq 291
Hajdërije Tekke 58, 77, 155, 194–6, 277, 291, 300, 305, 316–17
Haji Bektash Veli (founder and patron) 1, 2, 4, 24, 30, 44, 48, 62–3, 70, 75, 84, 87, 111, 115, 118, 122, 123, 132, 165, 208, 238, 278, 291, 308
  feast 51
  Tekke/shrine 4, 18, 68, 200, 287
Haji Hamsa Baba Tyrbe 43
Haji Hamsa (Five Hajis) Mausoleum 89
Haji Huseyn Baba Tyrbe 71
Haji Mustafa Užicanin 44
Haji Yahya Baba 94, 207
Hajro, Shemso 148
Hakk (the Truth) 1, 5
al-Hallaj 2
Halveti Order 7, 161, 200
Halveti Tekke 18
Hamid, Abdul 28, 54, 57, 76, 148
Harabati Baba Tekke 50, 251–4, 314
Harabati Tekke 50, 188–9, 201, 248, 253, 254, 255, 303
Harakop Tekke 204–5
hares, as forbidden 2
harvest 95–6
Hasan Dede 252
Hasan Dede of Përmet 292
Hasan Dede Tekke 202
Hasan (Imam Ali's son) 1, 3, 30, 45, 46, 106
Hasib Baba 299
Hasluck, Frederick William 6, 56–7, 113, 115, 125, 170, 192, 200, 214, 216, 240, 248, 251–3, 256, 261, 263, 264, 266, 309
Hasluck, Margaret 6–7, 62–8, 95–6, 178, 186, 191, 193–4, 202, 203, 204, 205, 210, 212, 219, 221–2, 229, 231, 239, 241, 251, 262, 265, 275
Haxhi Ahmet Dede 252
Haxhi Baba Adem of Gjakova 245, 276–7
Haxhi Baba Horasani of Përmet 292, 293
Haxhi Baba Horasani Tekke 226–7, 295
Haxhi Baba Mehmet Aliu Tekke 198
Haxhi Baba of Fushë Kruja 78, 292
Haxhi Baba Tekke 254–5
Haxhi Baba Tyrbe 221

Haxhi Bektash. *See* Haji Bektash Veli (founder and patron)
Haxhi Emin Baba 252
Haxhi Et'hem of Tirana 101
Haxhi Hamza Tekke 206
Haxhi Hazbi Hyseni 184–5
Haxhi Hysen Baba Tekke 216
Haxhi Jahja Baba of Kruja 193
Haxhi Jahja Baba Tekke 207
Haxhi Mehdi Baba 252
Haydar Baba 94, 113
headpiece/headdress *(taj)* 3, 21, 23, 27, 41, 70, 74, 94, 117, 120–1, 123, 291
headstones 25, 40
Hekal Tekke 199–200
Helena 19
heterodoxy 1
Hidër Baba of Makedonski Brod 247, 293
Hidër Baba Tekke 247, 248, 293
Hidër Baba Tyrbe 248, 293
High Regency Council 10, 59
Hilmi, Abaz 215, 222, 273, 279, 289, 319
Hilmi Dede 76
Hima of Struga 78
Historical Archives of the Institute of Science 102, 105–6
Hizir Dede 115
Hizir Lale Sultan 115
Hizirlik (Hidirlik) Tekke 115–16, 123
holidays, national 2
holy water 209, 215, 248
Horasanli Ali Baba 94
Horeb 96
Hoxha, Enver 273
Hoxhi, Koto 77
Hurufism 1, 62
Husein (Imam Ali's son) 1, 3, 30, 33, 49, 106, 124, 168, 274
  lament for 126–37
Husejn Baba Tekke (Krahës) 204–5
Husejn Baba Tekke (Melçan) 6
Huseyn Baba 113
hymns 118
Hysein Dede 252
Hysejn Ali Dede Tekke 218
Hysejn Baba Elbasani 193
Hysejn Baba Tekke (Konitsa/Konica) 264
Hysen Kukeli Baba of Fushë Kruja. *See* Baba Hysen Kukeli

Ibn Tulun mosque 118
Ibrahim Baba 210, 298, 315
Ibrahim Baba of Qesaraka 288, 295
Ibrahim Baba Turku 193
Ibrahim Xhefai Baba of Elbasan 15, 184, 295–6
Ibrahim Xhefai Baba Tekke 6, 53–5, 58, 184, 187, 188
initiation 3, 31, 66, 94
Insabato, Enrico 27
International Control Commission 9
Ipek Tekke 54
Ippen, Theodor 43–7, 91, 163, 192, 206, 209
Iran 14, 318
Ismail Baba 221, 247
Ismail Baba Tekke (Gllava/Qafë Gllava Tekke) 198
Ismail Pasha 98, 269
Ismail Qemal bey Vlora 77, 201, 303
Istanbul 6, 29, 75, 76, 102, 113, 115, 146, 173, 174, 187, 188, 195, 229, 259, 299, 303, 328 n.97
Italy/Italian occupation 9, 233, 289, 308, 312
Izet Zavalani 78

Jacob 39
Jafar Baba 279
Jahja, Osman 251
Jahja Baba 193, 207, 227
Janissary Corps 5–6, 20, 85, 123, 138, 291
Jarar Baba Tekke 248
Jelaladdin Ibrahim Shemimi Baba Tyrbe 70, 314
Jella, Selman 141, 180
Jesus 3, 30, 65, 85
    Apostles of 27
Juma (Djuma) Tekke 261–2

Kabashi, Rustem 52
Kaçanik 6, 17, 78
Kaçanik Tekke 244
Kalendari Enciklopedik 12
Kalenderi (Qalandari) 1
Kalkandelen (Tetova) Tekke 6, 50–2, 54, 251, 252, 314
Kallajxhi, Xhevat 140
Kalthoum, Umm (Um Kalsum) 280
Kamal al-Din Hussein 98

Kamal ed-Din, Prince 118, 270
Kanina Tekke 6, 7, 17–18, 19, 99, 100, 113, 114, 116, 123, 200–2, 326 n.70
Kâni Pasha 174
Kaplan Pasha Toptani 43, 102, 124, 206, 316
Karadja, Ahmet 250, 251, 278
Kara Mahmud Pasha Bushati 43, 85, 115, 206
Karaman 143, 144
Karkavitsas, Andreas 22–6
Kasem Baba of Kastoria 262–3, 297–8, 304
Kastoria Tekke 262–3
Katerini Tekke 263–4, 279–80
Katundi, Goni 144
Kavaja 8–9, 15, 124, 188, 212, 289, 295, 316
Kaygusuz Sultan 267
Kaygusuz Sultan Tekke 80
Kemal, Ismail 152, 202
Kemal, Mustafa 1, 11, 155, 233, 266, 307
Kemal ad-Din Hussein, Prince 269
Këròova Tekke 247–8, 293
Khayyam, Omar 225, 280
Khedive Abbas Pasha 267
Khedive Ismail Pasha 267, 269
Khizir Baba/Nikola Baba 248
Kiazim, Musa 3, 30
Kiel, Machiel 173–5, 194, 196, 201, 206–10, 237, 258–60, 262, 309
Kirk-Ayak Sinan 115
Kissling, Hans-Joachim 113–16, 123
knives 23
Kodja Sinan Pasha 113
Kojun Baba Tekke 249
Kolonja region 11, 79, 81, 169, 226, 229, 296, 307
Konitsa Tekke 100, 102, 103–4, 105, 178, 264, 327 n.74
Köprülü Tekke 100, 218, 237, 254–5, 290, 315
Koran 24, 25, 65, 68, 95, 131, 167, 234
Korça 6, 7, 11, 12, 15, 27, 29, 44, 60, 77–9, 86, 88, 92, 106, 124, 138, 141–6, 148, 152, 155, 183, 184, 188, 189, 213, 218–19, 226, 230, 237, 249, 255, 283, 294, 297, 301, 328 nn.87–9, 328 n.91

Koshtan Tekke 77, 183, 202, 203–4, 211, 282, 330 n.119, 331 n.136
Kosina Dervishia 204
Kosovo 6, 12, 13, 17, 165, 252, 275, 276, 304, 309, 311
  tekkes and shrines 243–5
  uprisings 78–9
Kostrec Tekke 204
Kosturi, Vani Cico 148
Kotta, Kostaq 86
Krahës Tekke 204–5
Kremenar Tekke 205
Krena, Jasha 213, 216, 242
Kruja 6, 12, 36, 38, 43–7, 69–72, 163, 207–10
Kruja Tekke 38, 43, 79, 206–10, 256
kryegjysh (head grandfather/*dede baba*) 4, 155, 189, 215, 233, 273, 278–80, 285, 289, 297, 307
Kryegjyshata 11–13, 15, 102, 106, 233–4, 247, 273–4, 279, 289, 297, 304, 307, 311, 312
Kuç Tekke 7, 79, 138, 210–11, 298
Kufic script 97
Kulakli Baba Tekke 20
Kulmak Tekke 181, 211, 234, 235, 282, 296
Kupekli Tekke 20
Kus Baba/Kuzum Baba. *See* Kusum Baba of Vlora
Kusum Baba of Vlora 18, 298–9
Kusum Baba Tekke/Mekam/Tyrbe 15, 201, 240–1, 278, 298–9
Kuta Tekke 211
Kyzyl Deli Sultan Tekke 257

L'Affaire de l'Epire: le martyre d'un peuple (The Epirus Question – the Martyrdom of a People) 9
lamenting/commemorating the dead 126–37
Lavdar Tekke 211
League of Prizren 76, 139, 148, 189, 191, 194, 216, 218, 219, 229, 276, 285, 291
Leake, William, Colonel 63, 263
Leroy, Jules 120–1, 270, 280
Leskovik Tekke 211–12, 231, 267, 275
literature, Albanian Bektashi 2, 99–107, 145, 157
  banned 125, 156

Louis-Jaray, Gabriel 53–5, 185, 245
love, gospel of 67, 111, 118, 134
Luarasi, Petro Nini 227, 295, 330 n.114
Lulet e verës (Summer Flowers) (Naim Frashëri) 170
Lushnja Tyrbe 212
Lutfi Baba of Mokattam Tekke 267, 269, 279, 299–300
Luz i Madh Tekke 188, 212, 289

Macedonia 6, 12, 16, 39, 50, 67, 77, 78, 111, 165, 197, 198, 244, 259, 278, 290, 293, 314, 315
  tekkes and shrines 246–55, 261, 263, 264
Magnificat 118
Mahmud Huda'i 114
Mahmud Pasha of Shkodra 43, 213
Mallakastra 15, 16, 44, 48, 78, 79, 88, 92, 124, 178, 182, 183, 191, 199, 202, 205, 211, 220, 224, 227, 228, 279, 296, 304, 318
Man Bushi 102
Manes Baba. *See* Baba Sulejman of Gjirokastra
Manfred, King 19
Marco Kraal 19
Maricaj (Marican) Tekke 212–13
Markgraf, Friedrich 82–3
Marku, Thimi 148
marriage 33, 37, 59, 67, 263
Martanesh Tekke 65, 80, 180, 189, 213–17, 289, 312
Mary 3, 30, 33, 49, 65, 118, 128, 167, 235, 274
Mašulovic-Marsol, Liliana 251
matem 2, 105, 106
Matohasanaj Tekke 216, 327 n.74
Mazreka Tekke 216–17
Mbroja, Dr Haki 142, 143, 144
Mbyet Tekke 217
meals 74, 82, 83, 142, 297
  prayer, before and after 33, 133
  ritual 18, 27
meat 40, 51, 74, 283, 325 n.36
Mecca 24, 84, 89, 106, 166, 190, 275, 295, 299
Medina 24, 75, 106, 276
meditation 22, 84, 121, 225, 268, 281
Mehdi, Muhammed 3, 30
Mehmed Baba Tekke 246–7

Mehmed the Conqueror 263, 297
Mehmet Ali Pasha 97, 98, 267
Mehmet Ali Pasha Vrioni 77
Mehmet Lutfi Baba. *See* Lutfi Baba of Mokattam
mekam (holy site) 49, 83, 166–7, 169, 179, 234, 235, 240, 274, 281
Melametism 1, 27–8
Melan Tekke 217
Melçan Tekke 6, 7, 15, 77, 85, 138, 139, 142–4, 147, 170, 217–19, 229, 275, 276, 284, 293, 294, 308, 315, 318, 328 n.89
Melikoff, Irène 173
Memaliaj Tekke 79, 219–20, 329 n.100
Merdivenköy Tekke 76, 211, 258, 301
Mersen Demë 142, 180
Meta, Tush 141–2, 180
metempsychosis 66, 68, 85, 123
Mevlevi Order 48, 102
meydan (private prayer room) 1–2, 133, 143, 147, 159, 232, 246, 271, 294
Michael, Despot of Epirus 19
Michael VII Palaeologus 165
Michigan Tekke. *See* Taylor (Detroit) Tekke
Middle Ages 19
Middle East 1, 8, 14, 189, 234, 270, 276, 277, 280, 285, 293, 295, 296, 318
Migeon, Gaston 268
Mimi Baba. *See* Shemimi Baba of Fushë Kruja
Misticizma dhe Bektashizma (Mysticism and Bektashism) (Baba Rexheb) 149
Mitrovica 6, 17, 244–5
Mitrovica Tekke 6, 17, 244–5
modernisation 1
Mokattam Tekke/Magauri Tekke 97–8, 263, 267–71, 279, 280, 300, 305
Mondi Baba. *See* Dede Baba Edmond Brahimaj
mortification 45
Moses 3, 30, 33, 65, 293
mosques
  communist impact on 13, 178, 179, 181–4, 191, 193, 197–200, 202–5, 207–13, 216–20, 222–8, 230–2, 239–42, 310

revival of 12, 14, 159, 174, 178, 201, 232, 234, 312
Mother Teresa 13, 234
Mount Tomorr Tekke 48–9, 73–4, 80–1, 124, 162, 166–72, 226, 231, 232, 234, 235, 274, 282, 296, 303
Mousset, Albert 11
moustache 24, 29
Muaviye 93
Muça, Meleq. *See* Baba Meleq Shëmbërdhenji
Muhammed, prophet 1, 5, 27, 67, 85, 106, 118, 132, 156, 215
Muhammed Ali 1, 3, 30, 31, 33, 34, 301
Muhammed Asim Baba. *See* Asim Baba of Gjirokastra
Muharrebe Baba 252, 253
Muharrem 2, 32, 34, 91, 106, 129
Muharrem Baba of Frashër 302
Muharrem Kocka 78
muhib (lover/sympathiser) 3, 139, 182, 185, 239, 244, 247, 282, 304, 307, 314
Mulla Ali Dedej 184
Murad Bey 71
Murat II 93
Musa Demi 78
Mustafa Baba Lahori 258
Mustafa Baba Tekke 17, 20, 244–5, 249–50
Mustafa Dollma Tyrbe 207–8
Mustafa Hexhri Baba of Ankara 78
Mustafa Pasha Bushatlliu 7, 182–3
Mustafa Usicanovic 92
Myderrizi, Osman 99–107, 167, 234–5
Myftari, Ahmet. *See* Ahmet Myftari Dede
Myhtarnameja (Shahin Frashëri) 102
mysticism 1, 149, 159, 170, 276
myxher (celibate). *See* celibacy

Nakshbandi Order 6, 248, 266
namaz (prayer) 23
Namik Selimi of Delvina 78
Nasib Tahir Baba. *See* Baba Tahir Nasibi of Frashër
National Congresses of Bektashi
  Eighth and Ninth 14
  Fifth 13, 234
  First 10, 178, 179, 181, 183, 191, 198, 203, 204, 219, 224, 228, 282, 297

Fourth 12, 219, 233, 273, 319
Second 11, 196, 305, 317
Seventh 13–14
Sixth 13–14, 304
Third 11, 156, 233, 237, 307
Naziresha Mosque 188
Near East 66, 68
nefes (spiritual chants) 138, 149–51
Neki, Ali 3, 30
Nevruz (Bektashi holiday) 2, 13, 34
Ngrançija Tekke 220
Nijazi, Salih. *See* Salih Nijazi Dede
Nimet, Princess 269
niyas (prayer) 33
Niyazi Bey of Resna 148, 294
Noli, Bishop Fan 60, 219, 297, 305
Norris, Harry 258
Norton, John 5
Nosi, Lef 187
novices 21, 46, 190
Nunc Demittis 118
Nuri 143
Nuri Baba Tekke 220

Oakley-Hill, Dayrell 73–4
Ocak, Yasar 174
offerings 23, 24, 25, 39, 40, 55, 70, 71, 89, 95, 97, 209, 251, 256, 278, 309
omens 95
open-mindedness 8
original sin 106
Osmani, Ram 180
Osmënzeza Tekke 188, 220
Ottoman Empire 5, 7, 9, 77, 122, 138, 139, 145, 147, 152, 173, 240, 258, 295
Ottoman flag 9
Ottoman Turkish (national language) 9, 127, 179, 284

Pacomit Tekke 220
paintings 24, 90, 110, 207
Panariti, Qamil 144
pantheism 3, 159
paradise 25, 30, 97, 129, 186, 208
Pasha of Scutari 56
patriotism, Albanian 7–8, 28, 34–5, 66, 68, 79
Patsch, Carl 199, 241
Pearl of Najaf 46

Pebbles Tekke 193
Peja Tekke 245
Peqini, Ibrahim 185
Percy, Sir Jocelyn 73
Përmet Tekke 28, 29, 41–2, 77, 78, 79, 81, 84, 97, 140, 169, 178, 213, 220–2, 226, 233, 235, 258, 292, 319
persecution 6, 12, 28, 44, 57, 76, 79, 84, 85, 102, 110, 138, 218, 229, 237, 295, 308
Petran Tekke 222
Philip IV 75
Picar Dervishia 222–3
pilgrimage 19, 39, 40, 45, 46, 49, 54, 81, 85, 95, 96, 122–4, 161–3, 165–72, 181, 183–5, 189, 208, 220, 232, 235, 237, 249, 250, 256, 263, 271, 276, 310, 311, 318
Pillar cult 39–40
pipes 22, 24
Pirani Baba 179
Piri Baba 113, 261–2
Piri Baba Tekke 261–2
Plasa Trybe 223
Plashnik Tekke 223
Podgoran Tekke 223
poetry 2, 3, 49, 149
Pogoni, Bardhyl 305
Pojani, Ohran 142, 148
Polena Tekke 223–4
Pope 12, 65, 108–12
pork, as forbidden 2
prayer beads 22, 23, 82
prayers 1–2, 121
    before and after meals 33
    benedictory 126, 133
    at betrothals 33
    chanting 126, 127, 133
    at feasts/ceremonies 33, 34, 84, 133
    at funerals 33
    patriotic element in 133–4
    sunrise and sundown 2, 65, 84
    at weddings 33
Prince Kamal ed-Din 118, 270
Prince Wied 10, 152
Prishta Tekke 6, 7, 75, 144, 170, 181, 183, 203, 204, 218, 219, 224–5, 228, 233
Prizren Tekke 54, 219, 245, 275–6
Progonat Tekke 225

pudding, *Ashura* 126, 133, 232
Pulaha Tekke 225–6
purges, Stalinist 12, 233
Pyramids 95, 97, 118

Qafoku, Iljaz of Vërzhezha. *See* Dervish Iljaz Vërzhezha
Qamili, Haxhi 9, 184, 186, 192, 198, 214, 216, 229, 301
Qâmûs al-a'lâm (Sami bey Frashëri) 139
Qasr el- 'Ayni Tekke 117
QatromTekke 7, 138, 142, 144, 226, 294
Qemali, Ismail 78
Qerbela 76
Qesaraka Tekke 149, 226–7
Qesarat Tekke 227
Qiriazi, Jorgji 147
Quzum Baba Sultan Tekke 240, 241

Rabija Tekke 198, 227–8
Ragip Effendi of Delvina 305
raki (ritual drink) 48, 50, 74, 142, 209, 293
ram 40, 95–6, 180, 250
Ramadan 33, 45, 312
Rami, Ahmad 280–1
Ramsay, Sir William 62
Ratip Ahmed Pasha 173
Red Cross, Albania 60
Reforma (Reform; periodical) 282
reincarnation 58, 66
relics 122, 262
Rexhep Pasha Mati 77, 306
Rexhep Pasha of Tetova 252
Richards, Theophilos 94
Rifa'i 165
Riza, Ali 3, 30, 189, 233, 285
Riza Pasha 253
Riza Pasha of Tetova 252
robes and clothing 3, 21, 23, 31, 41, 46, 51, 64–5, 70, 74, 82, 108, 117, 120, 195, 317
    belt 41
    caps 21, 51
    coat 23, 82
    teslim tash 46, 59, 70, 82, 120
Rodenj Tyrbe 228
Roman Catholicism 1, 85
rose, as emblem of Bektashism 84, 231

Rozeç Dervishia 228
Rrisk Baba 261
Rrisk Baba Tekke 260–1
Rubaiyat (Omar Khayyam) 280
Rufa'i 22, 110
Ruhi, Selim. *See* Baba Selim Ruhi
Ruhije, Princess 269
Russell, Dorothea 117–19, 269
Russell, Sir Thomas Wentworth 117, 269

sabres 26
sacred emblems 89
sacrifice 39, 40, 49, 83, 95–6, 134, 162, 164, 167, 190, 235, 250, 251, 274, 310
Sa'di (Grand) Tekke 165–6
Sadik, Jafer 1, 3, 5, 30
Sadik Baba 252, 315
Sa'di Order 166, 243
Sah Kulu Tekke 211, 301
Saint Alexander 208, 310
Saint Charalambos 68, 266
Saint Charalambos monastery 68, 266
Saint Elias of Mount Tomor 68, 252, 274, 293
Saint Elijah (Elias) 165, 253, 262, 274
Saint Elijah's (Elias) Day 163
Saint George 20, 21, 115, 124, 163, 165, 250, 251, 258, 262, 293, 309
Saint George's Day 39, 163, 250, 259
Saint Khidr (the Green Saint) 293
Saint Menas Church 264
Saint Naum 68, 85, 122, 165, 249, 309
Saint Nicholas 165, 248, 293, 309
Saint Quentin 50, 252
saints, veneration of 8, 20, 25, 65, 122
Saint Simeon 165, 309
Saint Spyridon of Corfu 68, 165, 256
Saiyida Nafisa 118
Salih Baba Tekke 238, 255, 257, 306
Salih Nijazi Dede 11, 155, 189, 198, 233, 247, 285, 302, 307–8
Salonica Tekke 27, 51, 75, 78, 197, 198, 277, 279, 303
Saltik, Sari 6, 36–8, 43–6, 68, 70, 71, 85, 89, 93, 122, 124, 161–6, 169–71, 208–10, 249, 256, 275, 298, 308–11
Sancaktar Ali Baba Tyrbe 263
Sanjollas Tekke 228–9
Sarajevo 44, 92, 167

Saranda Tekke 15, 229
Sari Saltik 36–8, 68, 70, 85, 122, 308–11
   footprint 38, 46, 164, 311
   tyrbe 89–90, 161, 163–6, 169, 170, 171, 208–10
sashes 23, 225
Scanderbeg 45, 55, 56, 69, 76, 78, 81, 85, 90, 144, 171, 185, 186, 289
Second World War 12, 62, 108, 125, 127, 161, 166, 196, 198, 199, 204, 205, 215, 216, 222, 228, 232, 237, 273, 278, 283, 289, 297, 304, 305, 309, 312, 319
secret ceremonies 2, 109
secret intelligence 56
secret signs 64, 84
Sefer Shah 115
Şehidlik Tekke 187–8, 313
Seit Baba of Durballi Sultan 298, 311
Sejdi Baba 180
Selenica, Teki 11–12, 220, 223
self-discipline 84
Seliger, Kurt 108–12
Selim Kaliçani Baba of Martanesh 296, 311–12
Selim Kaliçani of Peja 215, 245
Semimi Sultan Tekkesi 94
Sersem Ali 252
Sersem Ali Baba of Tetova 314
Sersem Ali Baba Tekke 6, 251–4, 314
Seyahatname (Çelebi) 113, 114, 123
Seyyid Ali Sultan 4–5, 257, 258, 287, 288
Seyyid Ali Sultan Tekke 257
Seyyid Muhammed Asim Baba 193, 287
Shafi'i, Imam 118
Shahin Baba Tekke 20
Shahin bey Kolonja 77
shaving, of head 65
sheaths 23–4
Sheh Hysen Dylgjeri Tekke 188
Sheik Abdullah el Maghaouri 120, 280
Sheikh Hüseyin Tusiu of Djiba 166, 234
Sheikh Mimi (Shemimi Baba) 192, 256
Sheikh Safi 127–8, 130, 131
Sheikh Üftade 114
Shëmbërdhenj Tekke 229–30, 300–1
Shemimi Baba 94, 206, 218, 224, 275, 290
Shemimi Baba, grave of 193

Shemimi Baba of Fushë Kruja 184, 197, 295, 314–16
Shemimi Baba Tekke 6, 191, 192, 291, 292
Shemseddin Baba Tekke 243–4
Shenusi Baba Tyrbe 89
Shi'ites 1, 5, 14, 87
   vs. Sunnis 56, 62
Shijak Tekke 38
Shkalla, Flamur 271–2
Shkoza Tekke 230
Shtip Tekke 244
Shtuf Tekke 194–6
silence 12, 13, 37, 45, 52, 55, 58, 82, 110, 121, 185, 186, 233
Sinai 96
Sinani 184
Sinan Pasha, Mir Liva of Dukagjin 114, 116
Sinan Pasha mosque 18
Sinan Pasha of Konya 19, 200
Sinan Pasha Tekke 200–2
Sirri, Ahmet Baba. *See* Ahmet Sirri Baba of Mokattam (Ahmet Sirri Baba of Glina)
Skënderasi, Tahir. *See* Baba Tahir Nasibi of Frashër
Skopje Tekke 249–50
Skrapar 7, 16
Skrapar Tekke 6, 10, 48
Smokthina Tekke 230
solidarity 48, 58
souvenirs 24
Stadtmüller, Georg 122–5
Stalinism 12
stallion 25–6
Stamoulis, Dimitris 174
Staravecka, Meleq. *See* Baba Meleq Shëmbërdhenji (Baba Meleq Staravecka)
Starja Tekke 205
stones, venerated as sacred object 38, 39–40
Straficka Tekke 231
Suez crisis 269, 280
Sufism 1–2, 159, 161, 174, 275
Suka Tekke 84, 231–2, 297
Sulejman Baba of Gjirokastra (Baba Manes) 193, 194–6, 316
Sulejman Baba Tekke 249–50

Sultan Abdul Hamid 76, 141, 148
Sultan Baba Tyrbe 89, 174, 259
Sultan Bayezid II 113, 114
Sultan Husein 118, 270
Sultan Ibrahim 115
Sultan Jem 165
Sultan Mahmud II 5, 7, 20, 63, 77, 113,
    114, 138, 179, 210, 261, 266, 281
Sultan Murad II 113, 114
Sultan Orhan 62, 208, 278, 308
Sultan Selim III 102, 118
Sultan Suleyman 251, 314
Sunni Islam 1, 2, 8, 14, 87, 122
    intolerance 67, 123
Sunni Muslim uprising 1914 8-9
Sunni Sublime Porte 92
superstitions 51, 84, 85, 117, 270, 292
Süreyya, Mehmed 114
Swire, Joseph 84-6, 168, 214-15, 224-5,
    235-6, 282-3
symbols, Bektashi 94, 133-4, 207, 216

Tafil Buza 80, 198
Talaat Pasha (Talat Pasha) 78, 125
Tasha, Demir 141, 180
Tasha, Hysen 141, 180
Tasha, Seit 141, 142, 180
Tatars of the Golden Horde 165
Tatar Tekke 20, 165
Taylor (Detroit) Tekke 13, 159, 271-2,
    286, 305
Teki, Muhammed 3, 30
Tekija Tekke 39-40, 250-1
tekkes (monasteries)
    as centres of patriotic activity 143-4
    cleanliness and good organisation of 148
    damage and destruction of 8-10, 13,
        15, 20, 59, 70, 79-80, 85, 91, 102,
        115, 138, 153, 174, 179, 181, 183,
        197, 198, 199, 203, 204, 205, 210,
        215, 216, 217, 219, 220, 223, 226,
        228, 229-30, 231, 232, 236, 237,
        241-2, 249, 255, 257, 260, 273, 281,
        295, 307, 313-14, 317
    meals served at (*see* meals)
    occupied by criminals 20
    re-establishment of 11-12, 15, 70,
        80-1, 153, 178, 179-80, 183, 188,
        193, 198, 199, 200, 204, 205, 206,

215, 217, 219, 220, 223, 225, 230,
231, 232-3, 234, 237, 238, 239, 241,
242, 261, 273
    wartime impact on 76-80
Tekke Köy 278
Tepelena 16, 138
teslim tash. See robes and clothing
Tetova Tekke 6, 50, 188, 201, 248, 249,
    251-4, 303
Tevfik, Riza 125
Thessaly 10, 20-1, 22
Timurlane, invasion of 93
Timur the Tartar 62
Tirana 11, 233-4
tolerance 8, 56, 60, 67, 68, 85, 86, 123, 276,
    308
tombs/tombstones 24-5, 51, 53, 55, 58, 59,
    63, 70, 94, 117, 120, 163, 165, 185,
    186, 193, 195, 201, 202, 206, 207,
    208, 238, 253, 255, 260, 267, 270,
    278, 280, 281, 317
Toptani, Abdi bey 10, 154
Toptani, Adem Aga 207, 208
Toptani family 45, 87, 90, 92, 315
Topulli, Bajo 77, 147, 218, 294, 295
Topulli, Çerçiz 77, 148, 294
Tourtoulis, Michael 10
Treaty of San Stefano 139
trinity 27, 118
Trix, Frances 12, 126-37, 305, 312
Tsikoumis, K. G. 175
Tsitsilikis, Kostis 175
Turani, Ahmet Baba. *See* Baba Ahmet Turani
Turan Tekke (Korça) 237-9
Turan Tekke (Tepelena) 11, 15, 142, 218,
    219, 233, 239
Turbali Sultan Tekke 20
turban 25, 26, 40, 41, 51, 70, 74, 91, 108,
    120, 199, 221, 225, 280, 282. *See
    also* headpiece
Turgut Pasha 142, 180
Turkey, Bektashi in 1, 4, 10-11, 76
    and Alevi communities 14
    and Constitution 57, 77
    origins 1, 4-6, 165
    relations with *Kryegjyshata* 11, 15-16
    Turkish revolt for freedom 77-8, 218,
        294
    wartime impact 10-11

Turtulli, Mihal 154
Tütüncü, Mehmet 207
Twelve Imams 1, 3, 5, 30, 33, 48, 65, 94, 118
tyrbes (mausoleums). *See individually listed tyrbes*

ulema (religious commission) 28
unity 2, 29, 33, 34, 56, 57, 61, 111, 149, 283, 301
universality 3

Vâiz, Hüseyin 104
Vatican 14
veiling, of women 65, 84
Velabisht Tekke 179, 239–40
Veles Tekke 254–5
Veli Agushi of Skrapar 230
Veli Baba 247
Veliqot Tekke 7, 138, 240
veneration, of saints 8, 20, 25, 70–1, 122
Vërtok Tekke 255
Vërzhezha, Iljaz. *See* Dervish Iljaz Vërzhezha
Vexh-hi, Adem Baba. *See* Baba Adem Vexh-hi of Gjakova
virtues 3, 24, 30, 31, 32, 66, 149, 190
Vloçisht Tekke 240
Vlora 8, 9, 18
Vlora, Ekrem bey 48, 114, 167, 169, 170, 201, 235
Vlora, Ismail Qemal bey 77, 201, 303
Vlora Tekke 6, 17, 18, 240–1
Vodhorina Tekke 264–5
Vokopola Tekke 167, 241
von Hahn, Johann Georg 19, 114, 200, 249
vows 31, 51, 55, 66, 82, 185, 249, 282
Vrëpska Tekke 241–2

Wallisch, Friedrich 201–2
water, abstention from 32, 84

Way of the Family of the Mantle 93
weekly meetings 27, 51
Wied, Prince Wilhelm zu 9, 10, 86, 152
women, equality of 2, 85, 118–19
World Headquarters, Bektashi 15, 73, 233, 308
  administrative districts 11, 15, 191, 219

Xhafer Baba Halepi Tyrbe 258
Xhani, Mustafa. *See* Baba Faja Martaneshi
Xhefai, Ibrahim Baba. *See* Ibrahim Xhefai Baba of Elbasan
Xhemali, Selman Baba of Elbasan. *See* Baba Xhemal (Baba Selman Xhemali of Elbasan)
Xholi, Zija 159

'*Ya Ali*' slogan 1, 123
Yakub Efendi Tekke 18
Yannina 7, 56
Yazid 49, 168, 235
Yemin Baba 113
Yezit 93
Young Turk Revolution 48, 64, 125, 141, 145–7, 148, 195, 294

Zaimllar family 181
Zavalani, Fehim 147
Zavalani, Memdu 143
Zaviye of Mürteza Baba 94, 193
Zein-el-Abidin 3, 30
Zemzi Baba Tyrbe 208
Zenel Hoxhaj 100
Zeneli, Jashar 141, 142, 180
Zeyneb, princess 98
Zhepova Tyrbe 242
Zog, King 11, 62, 87, 97, 155, 219, 269
Zoroastrianism 84
Zosimas of Mount Athos 20–1, 259

www.ingramcontent.com/pod-product-compliance
Lightning Source LLC
Chambersburg PA
CBHW070009010526
44117CB00011B/1475